POLITICAL SCIENCE

AN INTRODUCTION

J. ROLAND PENNOCK & DAVID G. SMITH

Department of Political Science, Swarthmore College, Pennsylvania

The Macmillan Company, New York

Political Science

AN INTRODUCTION

Collier-Macmillan Limited, London

To Helen and Carlota

Preface

 llllllllllllllllllllllllllllllllllllllll

Kipling tells us

> There are nine and sixty ways
> Of constructing tribal lays,
> And every single one of them is right.

Perhaps it is the same with introducing students to the complex and varied subject of politics and government. So one might judge from the many ways in which it is done. Many introductory courses proceed on the theory that it is best to start with a single government and, in the course of analyzing it, introduce the student to many of the major concepts of the subject. Others proceed on the assumption that a comparative study of several governments provides a broader base for the same idea. We have attempted—perhaps incautiously—to present political science systematically, emphasizing the unity of the discipline as a whole; for in all its variety, we believe it has unity; and in all its particularity, we believe it has principles. This position we seek to substantiate by elaborating numerous explanatory theoretical propositions, together with the presentation of enough factual material to give them both content and support. The purpose of this book is neither to develop or expound a science of politics nor to solve problems. Rather, it is to provide both factual and theoretical background that will provide useful starting point for both kinds of endeavor.

In the chapters that follow we deal principally with the following topics: (1) the most important concepts and theoretical tools used by the political scientists; (2) the foundations of politics, the psychological, socio-logical, and economic environment within which they operate, and the rela-tions between these aspects of the environment and distinctly political forces; (3) the ends of the state and the relation of political organization to basic human needs and purposes; (4) the development of political and legal institutions; (5) democracy, the operation of democratic institutions, and the relation of various organizational means to the ends previously discussed; (6) consideration of nondemocratic and semidemocratic forms of government in the light of principles previously developed; and finally (7), the problem of the relations among states and of various means for attempting to submit them to order.

Colleagues here and elsewhere have been generous with their assistance. In our own department we are especially indebted to Charles E. Gilbert for a careful critique of Chapters 12-17, and to Kenneth N. Waltz for a similar service with respect especially to Chapters 20 and 21. Solomon E. Asch, Professor of Psychology at Swarthmore College, by reading and commenting on Chapters 2 and 3, helped us immensely. Professor John W. Chapman, of the University of Pittsburgh, read the whole manuscript, except for Part V, and gave us many valuable suggestions. Paul Bohannan, Professor of Anthropology at Northwestern University, was good enough to read Chapter 7 and save us from at least some of the errors we would otherwise have committed. Chapters 7 and 8 also benefited from helpful suggestions given us by Ward H. Goodenough, Professor of Anthropology at the University of Pennsylvania, and George L. Haskins, Professor of Law at the same institution. Thomas I. Cook, Professor of Political Science and Chairman of that department at The Johns Hopkins University, read a number of the chapters at different times and stages and offered numerous critical and helpful comments. Finally, Carlota Smith gave clarity and compactness to many a vague and sprawling sentence. To all we express our thanks.

J. ROLAND PENNOCK
DAVID G. SMITH

Swarthmore College
Swarthmore, Pennsylvania

Contents

[ix]

POLITICAL SCIENCE

AN INTRODUCTION

Part

POLITICAL

FUNDAMENTALS

One

Part I of this book deals with a number of concepts that are basic to political science and, in particular, also deals with the relations of political science as a discipline and with politics as an activity to other academic disciplines and practical activities.

The treatment of "fundamentals" in the pages that follow is controlled by a particular view of political science that pervades the whole of the book, but is especially central to this Part. What this view entails we have outlined below in a set of propositions.

1. That political science should direct its attention *both* to the explanation and prediction of behavior *and* to making explicit and valid judgments about choices between policies and the reconciliation of competing goods or "ends."

    a. That these two activities can be separated only in part;

    b. That in considerable measure they go together and complement each other.

2. That the political scientist has, in particular, two kinds of aids to calculation and rational choice: a) laws, generalizations, and models of the behavior of man or

society; and *b*) knowledge of the functioning of formal institutions.

3. That the relation between political science and other disciplines is therefore vitally important—especially to psychology and sociology, *and* to law, economics, and administration.

4. Because the state and political activity are the instruments through which men order inclusively their public activities, political science is peculiarly concerned with questions of jurisdiction and "boundaries": it is, as Aristotle said, an "architectonic" science. Consequently, not only marginal choices, but also more fundamental questions of rights, of ends, and of the boundaries between the public and the private (or state and society), are especially the province of political science and of political philosophy.

The four propositions above have been set down in summary and abstract form. They are crucial to the understanding and application of the materials which follow in the next six chapters. As stated, however, these propositions convey little. Some examples may serve to make our meaning clearer and more explicit.

The traditional focus of the political scientist's interest has been the formal institutions of government; for instance, the Congress or legislature, the executive and administration, the courts and the judiciary. At an early stage in its evolution, the discipline of political science was largely concerned *only* with these subjects. Yet institutions are not readily understandable solely in their own terms. The Congress has its standing rules and its explicit or formal organization, the Interstate Commerce Commission its statutory organization and authority. But we learn relatively little about them from the documents or books of procedure alone without knowing both the informal organization and behavior that supplements the formal structure and the political forces that impinge upon it. If we were, for instance, interested in the reorganization of Congress (or a local zoning board of appeals), both the formal structure and the informal behavior and political influences that play on these formal institutions would be relevant. The latter are known in part through experience—by being around Congress or City Hall. But they are partly a matter of "laws" in the scientific sense and of "political behavior." The informal structure will change: new Congressmen will be elected and new political expressions will develop in time. Hence the need to relate the formal and the particular with more general knowledge about political behavior.

Another example will illustrate a second point. In the contemporary period of more positive and more extended governmental activities, the concern of lawyer, of economist, and of political scientist has turned increasingly to the substantive policies of government: what the various branches of government do by way of authorizing and implementing particular programs. The problem may be, for instance, how to administer foreign aid or what is the best way to coordinate transportation or transportation policy. In the latter instance, economics will be especially relevant for discovering the interests at stake, and also deciding what can be reasonably done without

2

prohibitive economic consequences will depend in large measure upon what the expertise of the economist can contribute. Note, however, that the political scientist should be able to say a considerable amount about the capacity of the political system to make or support particular kinds of decisions. Again, both in the case of transportation policy or the administration of foreign aid many questions will arise that go to basic political values; for instance, how much reliance should be placed upon private initiative and how much upon governmental action; or the merits in either case of political decision versus an administrative decision. One person might argue, for example, that the government should stimulate foreign investment rather than engaging in direct aid. With respect to transportation policy, people will differ about the value of central coordination and planning versus local decisions that may be more immediately answerable to the particular community's needs. They will also argue about the value of such approaches as more effective regulation through the Interstate Commerce Commission as contrasted with more informal collaboration of transport authorities and the industries concerned. The issues in either case are likely to involve not only law and economics as important related disciplines, but also to touch upon matters of basic political theory.

Finally, the decision by the United States Supreme Court that the schools must be desegregated illustrates the question of "boundaries." Here, we encounter not only rather broad questions of basic political theory and of human behavior, but also issues of politics that move into hitherto uncharted regions. New "boundaries" also emerge in the form of a rapidly changing political environment: the hydrogen bomb, the new states of Asia and Africa in the spheres of foreign policy and international relations, or the population explosion and automation on the domestic scene. Factors such as these raise questions of fundamental political philosophy; for example, of a new relation between man and the state. They also point to another way in which political institutions become important: namely, by helping us to make decisions that afford us a substantial measure of protection despite the fact that we are groping in the dark. A knowledge of human behavior helps in such situations to know in some measure what *people* are likely to do, but tells us relatively little about what *governments* are likely to do. Political history and a knowledge of the operation of political institutions and the experience of other governments is an aid. But also we need to choose for the future what we *ought* to do, and here we require especially an understanding of what we value and why we do so. Also, we need some sense of what values last, or "stand up" under severe tests. Inquiry into this kind of problem is certainly not the exclusive premise of the political scientist. Indeed, he does well, especially in such realms, to avail himself of the contributions other disciplines can offer. Our point is that political science is concerned with many issues that lie beyond the regular boundaries of government at any given time.

The treatment we shall give to the "fundamentals of political science"

3

reflects, then, the kind of view of political science we have outlined. We are not trying to suggest, as Oliver Wendell Holmes once said of the law, that political science is a "seamless web." It is, however, our view that the subject is best understood if the relations of different parts of the discipline and the relation of political science to other disciplines are kept continuously in mind. (See Figure 1 for a graphic representation of some of these relations.)

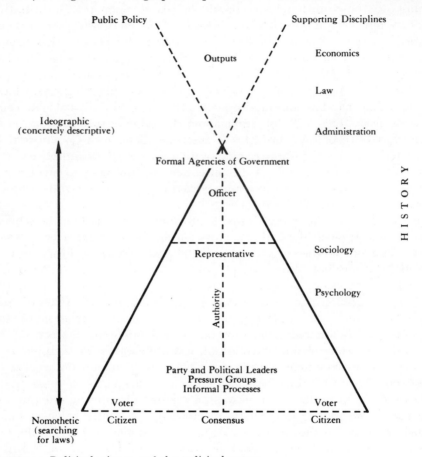

FIGURE 1   *Political science and the political system*

4

CHAPTER 1

What Is Political Science?

Political science, like economics, psychology, and sociology, is one of the social sciences. Since, unlike the latter two, it does not hide its claim to be a science in a Greek suffix, it is more often called upon to defend its right to the title. This chapter will consider the boundaries of "political science," the nature of its subject matter, and the question of the sense, if any, in which it is properly called a science.

WHAT IS POLITICS?

Since "political" means pertaining to politics, the start of our inquiry is the attempt to define "politics." Although many definitions of politics have been formulated, they are mostly of one or the other of two general types: one emphasizing the state and the other power as the focus of inquiry. As we shall see, these two types point to two aspects of a common phenomenon rather than being sharply opposing concepts. "Power" is the central organizing idea of our subject, while "state" or, better, "polity" is its key conceptual unit.

Politics Defined in Terms of the State

Derivations, although they do not establish present-day meanings, are at least useful starting points. "Politics" comes from *polis,* the Greek word for state.[1] "Politics" and the "state" are closely related; and the words "political" and "politics" are quite generally defined as having to do with the state, more specifically with the government of the state. The state itself may be tenta-

[1] It is frequently translated "city-state," for that is the form of organization to which the Greeks applied the term. The application of the English derivatives is not confined to any particular form of state.

tively identified as the social organization having final authority over all persons residing within a specified territory, and having for its primary purpose the solution of common problems and provision of common goods, with the maintenance of order as primary. Specifically then, "politics," in this type of definition, refers to the forces that constitute and shape the government of the state and its policies and actions.

Politics as Power

The second major type of definition fixes on the nature of the forces operating the state and defines politics as "power" or "power and influence." "Political science as an empirical inquiry," Lasswell and Kaplan declare, "is the study of the shaping and sharing of power."[2] These definitions emphasize the dynamic nature of politics, and they also call attention to the fact that the forces controlling the form and behavior of the state are similar to those that operate in other institutions. Churches, corporations, trade unions, colleges, and all kinds of associations have to provide for their internal government, and these governments operate in response to forces that it seems natural to call political.

Undoubtedly these forces *are* political in the sense that they are similar to the forces of politics proper. A scientific study of politics will not overlook these quasi-political relations as sources of insights into the political process and even as data that may be relevant to generalizations about political behavior.

For this and other reasons the emphasis on power serves a useful purpose in leading to a realistic analysis of the political process. It acts as a corrective to the formalism suggested by the definition of politics as the science of the state, and to the mistaken view that the state is the sole unit for the attainment of human welfare.

Yet the notions of power and influence alone are inadequate. They comprise too much. Power relations, for instance, prevail in the family, especially in the relations of parents and children. But to treat all the techniques of pressure and influence that characterize family life as the stuff of politics would do violence to ordinary linguistic usage and would give a distorted view of the family institution, ignoring its generally nonpolitical nature and purposes. At the opposite extreme, war is an attempt on the part of one political entity to exert power over another, if not to subjugate it completely. But to include it as a part of politics would be going too far, although it is a means often resorted to by political entities for political purposes.

[2] Harold D. Lasswell and Abraham Kaplan, *Power and Society, a Framework for Political Inquiry* (New Haven: Yale U. P., 1950), p. xiv.

An important omission from the second type of definition thus far is some such concept as that of "legitimacy," or "acceptance," or "authority." Of course we speak of politics within a highly autocratic or even tyrannical state. Nonetheless, relations of power and influence are called "political" only where they are in some degree organized (the result of which we call "government"), and where the acts of the organization are considered as having a kind of legitimacy, a claim to the obedience and respect of the people.[3] The political process typically leads to decisions that are accepted or recognized, by the bulk of those to whom they apply, as binding. Sometimes the word "authority" is inserted in the definition to convey this essential element. One author writes that "political life concerns all those varieties of activity that influence significantly the kind of authoritative policy adopted for a society and the way it is put into practice."[4] The study of politics then becomes the discipline concerned with "the authoritative allocation of values for a society."[5] In shifting the focus from power to authority an improvement has been made. The term suggests legitimated power, that is to say power that is generally accepted as binding in some sense. It might be added that political authority is also normally thought of as conclusive in the sense that it may be backed up by physical force if necessary.

The authority is not only conclusive, it is inclusive as well; it extends to all members of the society. This definition rightly suggests that the needs, the wants, the values of members of a society come into conflict. It is impossible for everyone to have all he desires. Consequently, someone or some institution, in Harold Lasswell's words, has to decide "who gets what, when, how."[6] The making of this kind of decision is among the central purposes of government. Lasswell's statement, though, carries with it too much the implication that government is merely a matter of dividing up the spoils, a difficulty that Easton's formulation avoids.

As these lines are being written, agencies of both state and national government are trying to reach an agreement on the location of a super highway within an area not far removed from the homes of the authors. Everyone wants the highway, but no one wants it to pass too close to his house or church or to divide his property. The decision will be made by agencies of government and it will be, in the best and proper sense of that word, a "political" decision. Moreover, the whole interplay of forces that actuates the governmental institutions and without which they would be lifeless and inactive is "politics." Of course, some people say, "Isn't it too bad that politics can't be kept out of this." This is a special, and sometimes confusing, use of the word.

[3] A fuller discussion of this point is given in Ch. 3.
[4] David Easton, *The Political System* (New York: Knopf, 1953), p. 128.
[5] *Ibid.*, p. 129.
[6] The reference is to a volume by Harold D. Lasswell, entitled *Politics: Who Gets What, When, How* (New York: McGraw-Hill, 1936).

If a decision were to be made—either for this particular case or for all such cases—to let the outcome be governed entirely by considerations of cost and the recommendations of traffic engineers, that decision would be a political one and it would be a feature of the politics of the society. Once the major determination is made some agency of government will be charged with administering it, with building the road or seeing to it that it is built, that it meets certain standards, and so on and so forth. This process, too, in the broad sense in which we are now using the word, is part of politics, and students of politics or political science are concerned with such matters, with the best organization and the best techniques for effectuating decisions about the "authoritative allocation of values" after they have been made.

We should note, too, that not all politics consists of settling disputes among conflicting groups or of determining that one "value" shall be given priority over another. Not all roads are controversial. By virtue of the power accruing from organization, from conjoint activity, people are able to do things that are of value to all, such as the provision of security against attack, building roads through trackless wastes, providing postal facilities, and in many other ways providing for the general welfare. Government not only allocates things of value among contending parties, it *creates* them; it satisfies common needs.[7]

A Definition

With the insights gained from these examples, let us return to the problem of definition. It is apparent that the two types of definition discussed essentially relate to the same matter. One focuses attention upon organization and system; the other emphasizes process and result. A state-type definition may exclude the politics of societies still too primitive to be called states. It also tends to emphasize form and legalism, detracting attention from power and influence, sometimes called the "stuff of politics." On the other hand, an exclusive emphasis upon power or process overlooks the concept of authority or legitimacy. Also, a definition solely in terms of process or power does not specify the group to which it applies, and would include all sorts of organized groups, such as the family, the church, and the trade union, most of whose activities are nonpolitical.

Any study of politics must be centrally, even though not exclusively, concerned with the state, its form and organization as well as its operation, because the former affects the latter. Formality secured through law is one of the state's most important characteristics. Procedures, the legally determined ways by which interests get themselves expressed and converted into public policy (whether it is a matter of the organization and procedure of

---

[7] See William C. Mitchell, "Politics as the Allocation of Values—a Critique," *Ethics*, 71 (1961), p. 79-89.

the legislature, the powers of the executive, or the operation of the courts), condition and shape the "outputs" of government. They may be fully as important as the needs, the demands, and the ideals of the people, and especially of the "influentials," which together make up the "inputs" of the political system. Further, the more fully developed the political system, the more valid the proposition that its own form and substance will shape the flow of power and influence.

Equally, the student of politics must be concerned with what makes things tick. Definitions of politics and of the study of politics that use the word "state" can encourage giving primary emphasis to the static—to the structure of government. Stress should rightly be placed upon the dynamic elements, the operation of government and its environment, the forces and conditioning circumstances that largely determine the behavior of government even while at the same time they are molded by it.

The dynamic and the static elements, the organizing idea and the conceptual unit, can be readily combined. The essence of the conceptual unit is that it is the most inclusive organization in any society that is recognized as having final authority over its members for the primary purpose of maintaining order. The essence of the organizing idea is that it relates to the means used by individuals to mold the product of that authority. *Politics, then, refers to all that has to do with the forces, institutions, and organizational forms in any society that are recognized as having the most inclusive and final authority existing in that society for the establishment and maintenance of order, the effectuation of other conjoint purposes of its members, and the reconciliation of their differences.* "Political" is the corresponding adjective.

THE "SCIENCE" COMPONENT OF POLITICAL SCIENCE

Having described and illustrated the meaning of "political" with sufficient accuracy for our purposes, we turn to the word "science" in the present context of "political science." An elementary misunderstanding must be warded off at the outset. When one speaks of "political science" one does not mean that the practice of government is conducted by scientists or that it is conducted in accordance with a body of scientific knowledge. Politicians, governors, make their decisions on the basis of opinion rather than certain knowledge; politics, as is often said, is an art. Decisions are reached by employing judgment, hunches, even intuition, rather than by means of mathematical formulas and calculations.

More specifically, in speaking of the actions of politicians and governors, we are dealing with three different things. First, there is the politician seeking to be elected or re-elected. Increasingly, he makes use of the science of opinion polling to guide his actions, but seldom is he completely guided by the findings of the practitioners of this relatively undeveloped science. Then there is the policy-forming official, whether an elected representative or not, who is trying to decide what needs are greatest, relative to their costs, and how to order the priorities of various claims on government. (For purposes of this analysis, we put aside his consideration of electoral advantage.) To put it in a word, "judgment" rather than "science" must be his guide. Finally, this same official, having determined what he wishes to accomplish, must seek the best means to the ends he has selected. Here, in varying degrees according to the subject matter, one science or another may be useful to him. To take an extreme case, if he has decided to build a hydrogen bomb, physical science will have a great deal to say that is relevant and governors will, of course, make use of it. If he has determined to reduce unemployment to a stated level, the science of economics will have something to say; but it is likely not to speak with a single voice. If he has decided to reform the constitution so as to achieve greater governmental stability without losing representativeness, political scientists could be of some assistance; but their contribution would be a modest one. (Perhaps they could speak with as great assurance as physicists in the spring of 1962 regarding the probable effects of a high nuclear explosion on the Van Allen belt!)

When we speak of political science, however, we refer to the study rather than to the practice of government. Almost any subject can be studied scientifically, although with varying degrees of success. Even the study of art (in the sense of the "fine arts") may be made the subject of scientific inquiry. It by no means follows that the person who has the fullest understanding of the principles of esthetics will be the best artist. It is plausible, however, that an artist who studies the principles of esthetics might well become a more successful artist than he was before.

Elements of Scientific Method

Science is most fully developed in the area of the physical sciences, for they have proved most responsive to its method. In a broad sense, however, all sciences form part of a single body of ordered knowledge: science. In fact, they all rely on the same generic method, but with such important differences, as we shall see, that it makes sense to speak of different scientific methods. We may safely assume that readers of this volume will have some familiarity with scientific method. Its fundamental components as they are traditionally stated comprise (1) observation and collection of data; (2) classification of these data into significant categories; (3) formulation and (4) verification of generalizations stated as laws, trends, or tendencies, according to what is justified by the analysis of the information available. (The first three may be vitally influenced by the scientist's hypotheses, of which more later.)

Further, sciences aim, wherever possible, to deduce from their generalizations relations of cause and effect that admit variously of prediction or control. The accent may be more on one or the other, depending on the nature of the subject of study. In astronomy, for instance, men have learned to predict eclipses with remarkable accuracy, but not to control them. The botanist and the zoologist, on the other hand, obtain rewarding results in the development of plants and animals better fitted to human purposes than were the originals.

Finally, there is still another and highly important aspect of science, both a component of scientific method and its ultimate objective: the development of a body of theory that relates all of the laws in one integral structure. A theoretical construct of this kind need not await the discovery of a large number of laws; it may be advanced as a tentative hypothesis from which *probable* testable laws may be deduced. Used in this fashion it is an aspect of scientific method and a powerful guide to research and to understanding.

Each of the steps mentioned above conceals a host of difficulties. Most of the data of science are not directly observed but are inferred from other evidence, as the roundness of the earth was originally inferred from the shape of the shadow it casts upon the moon. The classification of data into significant categories implies that we know in advance what categories will prove to be significant. In the early development of a particular science we usually do not. Doubtless for a long time men thought of whales as fish because they inhabited the sea. Later zoologists discovered that it was more useful for understanding the development of animal life to put in a single class all animals that feed their young from milk-secreting glands, regardless of their habitat; and discovered as well that whales and certain other denizens of the sea belonged in this category.

For the discovery of laws, much more than the observation of recurrences is required. Millions of men had noticed that objects tend to fall toward the earth before that famous (and legendary) day when Sir Isaac Newton was hit on the head by a falling apple; but no one had previously thought of a common principle or formula that would give a precise explanation of all such cases. Here enters the vitally important step of the hypothesis. It occurred to Newton—who had been wrestling with this problem for a long time—that gravitation might not be a peculiar quality of earth, but that it was possibly a general characteristic of all objects, bearing some fixed relation to their mass. This idea enabled him to work out laws that would account for all falling objects, including celestial bodies whose movement turned out to be of the same kind.

The role played in science by the creative hypothesis can hardly be exaggerated. Without a good hypothesis no amount of empirical work is likely to be scientifically fruitful. Here, imagination and knowledge must work hand in hand. At this point the qualifications of artist and scientist merge. The successful scientist must have a good imagination disciplined by thorough familiarity with the relevant or potentially relevant subject matter, and by a full understanding of the methods of science.

One further important point: the steps enumerated above need not be taken in the order mentioned. The hypothesis that directs observation and suggests categories may be the tentative conclusion. That is to say, it may be in the form of a suggested law or tendency. It may also be something much broader than this—something the researcher can hardly hope to verify as a whole. For example, a political scientist might construct a "model" of a political system based on the hypothesis that individuals behave rationally and that governments and political parties seek to maximize their political support. From the model (or elaborated body of theory) thus derived, various deductions may be made, such as that voters will not find it worth their while to educate themselves about political issues if their experience indicates that a change of government has little effect on their welfare. Only at this point does the scientific process move to empirical research and induction.[8]

The final step is that of verification. Sometimes this checking may be done by accurately observing natural events (like the movements of the planets), and comparing the results of these observations with the predictions that may be deduced from the theory in question. Under other circumstances, it is possible to conduct experiments so that the scientist may control the events he is going to observe and measure. He may for instance measure out a liter of gas, ascertain its temperature, increase the temperature by a given amount and then measure its volume again to determine whether or not it has expanded in the exact amount called for by Boyle's law. Or he may hold the volume constant and measure the change in pressure.

Application to the Study of Politics

In part, the social sciences in general, and political science in particular, attempt to apply the scientific method as just described to the study of society. Also, in part, as will appear, they vary the method as is appropriate to their special subject matter. In principle, all that has been said in the preceding paragraphs applies to social sciences as well as to natural sciences. But society presents the scientific student with much more refractory material than does the physical world. Compared to the accomplishments of physical science, the social sciences have discovered very few "laws." The economist has the laws of supply and demand, the law of diminishing returns, and a few others. But even these laws seldom precisely fit the real world; they are laws about what would hold true under certain "pure"

[8] For a vigorous argument to the effect that the pattern just discussed is much more typical of creative scientific work, whether in the physical or social sciences, than that which begins with the assembling and classification of data, see Thomas Landon Thorson, *The Logic of Democracy* (New York: Holt, Rinehart and Winston, 1962).

conditions, at best only approximated in real life. The political scientist is even more impoverished. Gaetano Mosca, an Italian political scientist who flourished during the latter part of the nineteenth and the early twentieth century, asserted that in every society there is a ruling class and that the larger the society the smaller, in proportion, is the ruling class. A Swiss, Roberto Michels, elaborated this theme and developed an "iron law of oligarchy." For a limited period and within certain types of societies, Mosca's proportion may have been true; and there is undoubtedly an element of truth in Michels' "law." Few contemporary political scientists, if any, would claim the status of a law for either of these propositions. Today we are generally content if we can discover trends, tendencies, and insights into cause-and-effect relations that enable us to make some limited and rough predictions and exercise some measure of deliberate control.

DIFFICULTIES

For a number of reasons, the social sciences generally, political science in particular, have not made rapid or great progress toward scientific accomplishments. Especially is this true with respect to that high point of scientific achievement, the discovery of scientific laws, and perhaps even truer of the ultimate aim of science: the construction of an all-encompassing body of theory that relates the laws to each other and provides the basis for explaining all operations, data, and relations within the field of the science in question. It will be worth while to give some consideration to these reasons.

Problems of Measurement. One of the most fundamental factors in the development of the natural sciences has been the discovery of increasingly accurate techniques of measurement. The discovery of the planet Neptune, for instance, came as a direct result of the observation of relatively minute deviations in the movements of Uranus from the theoretically established trajectory of that planet. This feat represents a nicety of measurement, of theorizing, and of calculation to which the social sciences can not aspire. We can count votes, measure costs in terms of dollars or other units of value, count convictions for violations of law (but not the violations themselves), and make many other measurements that are basic to social science; but such vital quantities as "wellbeing," "satisfaction," or "liberty" have thus far eluded all attempts at measurement. Suppose, for example, we wish to test the validity of the hypothesis that liberty of speech tends to encourage the development of original ideas. Suppose further that for this purpose we decide to compare two societies in one of which the law places a ban upon "dangerous thoughts," while in the other the law allows complete freedom in this regard. Almost certainly we shall discover other relevant differences. Perhaps in the first society the law is only spasmodically enforced; and in the second the *social* compulsion toward uniformity may be much stronger than in the first society. How can we tell in which society thought is more free? (We can not of course use the actual development of original ideas—assuming we could measure that—as an index, for this would be to assume the validity of the original proposition we set out to test.) Any number of further examples might be adduced to illustrate this type of difficulty.

Bias. Another obstacle appears in the form of prejudice and partiality. The fact that human beings are at once the observers and the subject matter of the observations makes effective disinterested observation difficult, and makes the temptation to confuse fact with moral judgment very great. That men may know themselves with an immediate and scientific intimacy, which is impossible when they are dealing with sticks and stones, or with other animal species, is no doubt true and not without significance; but it does not remove the difficulty under discussion. The man who is trying to discover the objective effects of freedom of expression is more than likely to have certain preconceived ideas on the subject—quite probably more the product of sentiment than of reason—that will make it hard for him to come to a purely objective conclusion on the matter. This likelihood of bias in the results is greatly enhanced by the lack of precise measuring rods discussed above. Where a vague sort of judgment must be substituted for scientific accuracy, it is much easier to conceal, even from oneself, the fact of irrationality.

The phrase "even from oneself," suggests a deeper dimension to the problem of bias. It is not just preconceived ideas that get in the way of scientific impartiality; it is fundamental attitudes, of which we are often completely unconscious. Attitudes are likely to be hard to change because of emotional involvement. If we are unaware of them, we do not even attempt to correct for them. It is like a person who is color blind and does not know it. Biases that are personal in the sense that they are not widely shared by others are fairly easily spotted, so the conscientious scholar can see and strive to correct for them, even when they are his own. But predispositions that are shared by a whole society or a large segment of it are far more difficult to recognize. One of Karl Marx's great contribution to social science was to point out, with abundant illustration, how a man's social class and economic status tend to warp his attitudes, to determine his assumptions, and to distort his judgments without his being aware of it. Doubtless Marx exaggerated. Especially, he himself distorted the truth by selecting a single type of conditioning factor, the economic, as all-important. But the essential idea has great force, particularly when it is broadened to include other than economic conditioning factors. A German sociologist, Karl Mannheim, has developed this idea at length. He denominated the study of how men's ideas are influenced by their backgrounds as the "sociology of knowledge."[9] While he believed that by constantly working at it a conscientious scholar could attain some approximation of objectivity, complete achievement of that goal is impossible. With this conclusion probably very few social scientists today

[9] See Karl Mannheim, *Ideology and Utopia*, translated by Louis Werth and Edward Shils (New York: Harvest Books, 1936).

would disagree. It may be added, however, that if we view social science as a body of ordered information, understanding, and laws, constantly being criticized as well as added to, it is plausible to assume that the doctrine and findings of fact which stand up over a considerable period and receive wide acceptance by scholars from various societies will more nearly approximate scientific validity than the contributions of any one man.

Complexity. The complexity of social life is also an unfavorable factor. Any society is constantly being played upon by both internal and external forces, by memories of the past and prospects of the future, by the material needs of its members, and also by their desires for nonmaterial satisfactions. The reciprocal interaction between physical events and ideas presents us with an added level of discourse, an element of complexity without parallel in the physical world. When we are dealing with things, only their behavior concerns us, but in the case of men we care also about their feelings and satisfactions.

Inability to Experiment. One of the most serious of all the methodological difficulties hampering the social scientist is the extremely limited extent to which he can conduct experiments; that is, compare different situations in which, in turn, all variables but one are held constant while the experimenter observes the consequences of varying that one factor. Not all social scientists are equally handicapped. The social psychologist, for instance, may compare the behavior of two groups of workers under differing types of leadership, where other elements of the situation have been made nearly enough identical for practical purposes. An economist might suggest to the leadership of a firm that they change their price lines to achieve greater volume of sales and then evaluate the results. To a certain extent the political scientist may make similar experiments; for example, with different ways of handling or organizing committees. For the most part, however, he is concerned with operations that are on too large a scale to admit such treatment. We may try to compare the cabinet form of government with the presidential form, but if we compare two different countries there are inevitably many other significant differences besides the differing governmental forms. If, on the other hand, we compare the two forms in the same country at different times, other changes will have taken place that will in some measure vitiate any conclusions that might be drawn. In other words, not only experimentation but also the observation of recurrences is in large measure denied to the would-be scientist of society. To be sure some social situations do repeat themselves in a general way. There is some continuity in our ways of doing things as well as in the values we hold. Were this not so, meaningful statements in this field would be impossible. Nevertheless, the situations in society do not repeat themselves in anything like the identical fashion with which many physical situations recur. This fact renders the problem of the social scientist very different from that of his colleague in the natural sciences.

"Self-fulfilling" and *"Self-defeating"* *Prophecies.* Another problem and a serious one for the social scientist, arises from the fact that the discovery and enunciation of laws or tendencies may itself influence social behavior. Thus the warning that a business recession is imminent may, in fact, bring it about by influencing the decisions of businessmen, regardless of the objective basis for the original prediction. This phenomenon is known as the "self-fulfilling prophecy." Prophecies may also be self-defeating. For instance, Karl Marx's prediction of social revolution in capitalist countries, made on the basis of what he believed were scientific laws of social evolution, may have had something to do with influencing the course of events in such a way as to nullify the revolutionary trends he detected.

ACCOMPLISHMENTS

Generalizations. In the light of all we have said about the difficulties confronting social science in general, and political science in particular, it may come as a surprise that anything can be accomplished at all. But some things clearly have been accomplished (partly by the use of procedures other than those discussed above), and we are entitled to anticipate further discoveries in the future. One true proposition is that, other things being equal, indirect elections are more easily controlled by a political "machine" than are direct elections. This generalization has emerged from a mere observation of recurrences. Others may be derived from certain constant tendencies in human nature, or at least in its manifestations within a given culture. Long experience of human societies suggests that there are long-lived consistencies in human motivations and reactions, on the basis of which it is possible to establish general rules of considerable predictive value. Montesquieu's assumption that those who possess unchecked political power will tend to abuse it draws support from both types of reasoning. So also does his further reasoning to the effect that a governmental system which requires the concurrence of mutually independent authorities or branches of government provides some assurance against tyranny.[10]

[10] A large number of more sophisticated and sometimes more precise propositions has been set forth and discussed in Harold D. Lasswell and Abraham Kaplan, *Power and Society: a Framework for Political Inquiry* (New Haven: Yale U. P., 1950). Lasswell and Kaplan make no claim to have established any "laws" of political science. They even hold that the search for such laws "in the grand style" is fruitless. What they have done, however, is to elaborate a large number of integrally related propositions to be considered as hypotheses for testing and as constituting, taken together, a framework for inquiry. Two of their propositions, even though taken out of context, may provide some notion of the nature of their work. "Propaganda in accord with predispositions strengthens them," they declare; "propaganda counter to predispositions weakens them only if supported by factors other than propaganda." Again, discussing the balance of power concept so familiar to students of international relations, they suggest that it can succeed in preventing violence only if "(1) variations in power are measurable and visible in early stages; (2) they are distributable among the participants in the balancing process; (3) the estimating process can be sentimentalized." *Op. cit.,* p. 133 and pp. 259-260.

Control. A further and even more significant point needs to be made. What is lost from the point of view of being able to establish laws on a grand scale may turn out to be a gain from the point of view of another objective of science: control. The very fact that a prediction may be self-defeating is an instance of control or of a process than can be used for conscious social control. If social processes are in any degree lawful, the only way in which man can escape the tyranny of these laws and exert any directing force over the ways of society is through understanding them. If, for instance, the formulation of certain laws about revolutions lead political leaders to anticipate and avoid a predicted revolution, this experience can hardly be called a failure of science, but rather the contrary.[11]

Model-building. The fact of the matter is, as the last paragraph implies, that there is more than one scientific method. An understanding of what can be accomplished in the field of political science will be furthered by a consideration of these various approaches. Among physicists, for instance, some prefer to experiment and to accumulate empirical data, while others devote their time to the elaboration of hypotheses for testing or to making deductions (reasoning, calculating) from a limited number of established generalizations. An excellent example in politics of this abstract deductive method is provided by the work of Thomas Hobbes, an English political philosopher of the seventeenth-century civil-war period, whose *Leviathan* is one of the great classics of political philosophy. Hobbes, fully conscious of the disorders of his time, and a keen observer of his fellowmen, began with certain assumptions about human nature, especially as it manifested itself in politics. He assumed that above all else men seek safety, gain, and glory. He then proceeded to evolve a theory of the nature and extent of political obligation, of men's duty toward government; a theory of rights, of men's claims on and against the political order; and a theory of the most desirable form of government. All of these theories apparently followed as logical deductions from his initial propositions about human nature.

While today it is generally recognized that Hobbes tried to deduce too much from an oversimplified view of the nature of man, a somewhat similar type of undertaking, with less ambitious pretensions, is gaining in popularity and is producing promising results. We refer to model-building, often combined with applications of game theory.[12] A model, in this context, means a theory or group of related theories used by scholars to aid in the under-

---

[11] What such an experience would signify would be that the believed "law" regarding revolutions was valid only when the relevant political leaders were ignorant of this law or for some other reason did not take advantage of it to avoid the revolutionary outcome. The real social or political law has not been destroyed; it has been put to use. The point discussed above is well put in Solomon E. Asch, *Social Psychology* (Englewood Cliffs, N.J.: Prentice-Hall, 1952), p. 268.

[12] For examples, see Anthony Downs, *An Economic Theory of Democracy* (New York: Harper & Row, 1957), and Herbert A. Simon, *Models of Man: Social and Rational* (New York: Wiley, 1957).

standing of the operation of an institution or set of institutions. A fairly simple version of this kind of endeavor may be seen in the work of Anthony Downs. Having described a simple form of democratic government, he makes a series of assumptions, such as that political parties are primarily concerned to achieve power and maintain it and that voters seek rationally to maximize their satisfaction. From his system as a whole, he derives a series of testable propositions, of which the following example is typical: "Among citizens who decide how to vote on the basis of issues, the records of each party (especially the incumbents) during the election period just ending are more important to their decisions than party promises about the future."[13] An interesting and much briefer experiment with a similar technique may be found in Buchanan and Tullock's application of game theory and model-building to the analysis of certain problems of majority voting, in which, incidentally, they conclude that majority voting is not necessarily the most efficient means for a democracy to maximize satisfaction.[14]

Empirical Studies. While the Downses and the Tullocks are evolving testable propositions, more empirically oriented political scientists are busy testing such propositions and also elaborating similar propositions of their own on the basis of empirical data they have accumulated and classified. Studies of political behavior, especially of voting, are much the fashion at the present time. In addition to actual election statistics and opinion polls, extended and repeated interviews with carefully selected panels of voters provide data for these studies. By these and similar devices much has been learned about voters' motivations, about the relative influence upon them of this or that issue, or of all issues put together versus matters of personality or of tradition, and so on.[15]

Empirical data may be obtained from the study of history as well as by means of current research in the field. In the natural division of labor among political scientists, some rely upon this method almost to the exclusion of all others. The work of an historian, Professor Crane Brinton, may be cited in this connection. He made a study of three "great revolutions," found certain uniformities in their course, and concluded that there was an initial presumption that the pattern discovered could be more generally applied to any major political revolution.[16] It would then be possible, in a revolu-

---

[13] Anthony Downs, *op. cit.*, p. 298.

[14] See James M. Buchanan and Gordon Tullock, *The Calculus of Consent: Logical Foundations of Constitutional Democracy* (Ann Arbor: Univ. of Michigan Press, 1962), Ch. 10.

[15] See, for instance, Bernard Berelson, *et al., Voting* (Chicago: Univ. of Chicago Press, 1954); and also Angus Campbell, *et al., The American Voter* (Ann Arbor: Mich.: Survey Research Center, 1960). For a critique of this whole approach and of these examples of it in particular, see Walter Berns, "Voting Studies," Chapter I in Herbert J. Storing (ed.), *Essays on the Scientific Study of Politics* (New York: Holt, Rinehart & Winston, 1962).

[16] Crane Brinton, *The Anatomy of Revolution* (New York: Norton, 1938).

tionary situation of the kind studied, to predict in general terms the course the revolution would follow.

Problem Solving. However, a great deal of work in political science, and in other sciences as well, starts with the attempt to solve problems. Often it is closer to "applied" than to "pure" science: It may or may not start from scientific propositions, but its objective is to solve a problem rather than to arrive at valid generalizations. Work of this kind often produces results far beyond the scope of the original problem. In other words, practical endeavor may lead to scientific advance. A political scientist, noting that democratic governments often fail when they are instituted among people in newly independent, relatively poor countries, may tackle a series of specific problems. He may seek to discover what kind of institutions would be acceptable to such people, would preserve values that he considers of primary importance, and yet avoid the worst difficulties that traditional democratic institutions have encountered in such situations. He may start by thinking out various possible solutions to the problem, using his own imagination and general knowledge of principles of political science and of conditions in the countries in question, supplemented perhaps by discussion with other experts or decision-makers. He will then give thought to the kinds of facts that would be needed to throw light on the plausibility of the various solutions he may have conjured up. Next comes the question of how these facts can be collected in the most helpful form and then the actual collection of these facts and others that may seem relevant as he proceeds. Finally, drawing appropriate inferences from the facts assembled, he will seek to determine which, if any, of his original ideas (or of others that may have since suggested themselves), appears most likely to work. He, or others later, may discover that in the process of solving the problem, he has discovered a general proposition of considerable scientific value. In using the problem-solving approach, the political scientist combines the empirical, the historical, and the deductive methods. He will tend to be guided in selection of methods not by an abstract preference for one method or another, but by their relative effectiveness in casting light upon the problem.[17]

Institutional Description and Analysis—Theory Building. The attempt to formulate and test hypotheses of predictive value, and the more pragmatic and instrumental approach described as problem solving, together do not exhaust the relatively scientific activities of political scientists. In fact, they

---

[17] In a critical review of Barbara Wootton's *Testament for Social Science*, L. J. Russell suggests that the following steps are generally typical of scientific method as used in the social sciences: (1) being presented with a problem; (2) thinking out possible answers; (3) thinking out what kinds of facts will throw light on the problem and how these facts can best be collected in helpful form; (4) collecting these facts and others that seem relevant as one proceeds; (5) framing a hypothetical answer to the problem as it was originally conceived, or to the problem as modified by the whole process up to this point in such a way that it can be tested by others, as well as by oneself; and (6) testing the answer thus arrived at. *The British Journal of Sociology,* **2** (1951), p. 79.

are neither the way in which most of the effort of a political scientist is likely to be employed nor the way in which the most characteristic contributions of the discipline are usually made. What political scientists mostly do can be termed institutional description and analysis.

This field of endeavor is neither wholly scientific nor wholly unscientific. One way of describing the activity would be to say that it is aimed at discovering the significant or important elements of institutions and how they work. How, for example, does a bureau, a public corporation, Congress, or the party system work? What are the key variables and properties of their organization? But to leave the account at this point is really to evade the problem of trying to say what sort of activity is involved.

One aspect of institutional description and analysis would probably qualify as "scientific" even by fairly strict canons of classification. Here we refer to the attempt to formulate general propositions about organizational behavior and to relate these propositions in such a way that they would be useful in understanding, for example, bureaucratic behavior in general or within a governmental department.[18] Much of the study of public administration has emphasized this kind of endeavor.

Institutional analysis also involves the formulation and testing of a good many "middle-range" hypotheses; or to put the matter in another way, the attempt to develop laws or principles of limited generality and applicability. Such hypotheses or laws are "middle-range" in two senses. For one thing they are of limited generality, applying only to a small class of cases. For example, it can be fairly well established that in American cities of a certain size since the Roosevelt era of the 1930's the political "machine" has played a diminishing role. Such regularities can also be middle-range in another sense—in relating part of a system to the system as a whole. Thus, we say that in the United States Congress seniority will generally determine the committee chairmanships. If, instead of stating a "law" or an observed regularity, the task is put in another way, "How would you make the committee system of the House of Representatives more responsive to party leadership?" the relation between the study of institutions and problem-solving becomes obvious.

Middle-range hypotheses and laws, however, have value only when related to a context within which they hold or a functioning system for which they have relevance. Therefore, a large part of institutional analysis is devoted to understanding how institutional systems as a whole work and how they are related to the polity within which they function.

Inquiry into the functioning of systems of organizations and even into the general principles relevant to an entire polity can be a relatively scientific endeavor. Many contemporary political scientists are, for example, trying to develop principles of considerable generality that would hold for

---

[18] Cf., Herbert A. Simon, *Administrative Behavior*, 2nd ed. (New York: Macmillan, 1957).

"underdeveloped" and "transitional" polities.[19] The same kind of activity can also be undertaken in a less inclusive manner in the study of institutions and practices that are similar or perform similar or closely related functions in many or most countries, as in the comparison of legal systems, or political parties, or interest-group behavior in the countries of Western Europe.

It is important to recognize, however, that much of institutional description and analysis, while it may be fairly dispassionate, is not wholly scientific and little pretense is made that it is. One of the major reasons why this is so is that objectives conflict, particularly the objectives of providing information that might be of some use now as opposed to building up a body of science that might or might not be useful and reliable at some time in the future. Also, the scientific propositions developed with respect to functioning institutions are, as yet, often not very powerful or novel, nor are they particularly reliable when compared with the insight and lore that has already been assembled. The study of institutions can be a disciplined endeavor, but it is in large measure dependent upon collected insight, lore and "understanding" that has yet to be reduced to scientific propositions. The value of the study to society depends partly upon a possible but by not means established relation to science as a whole. Even more, its value is a matter of some contribution (the amount of the contribution being a matter for dispute), to questions of "How do we achieve this?" and "What might we be forgetting in this endeavor that would lead to undesired results?"

BEYOND SCIENCE

The field of political science according to current usage, however, is not confined to description and the application of scientific method to the study of politics—not even when scientific method is interpreted broadly to include problem-solving or institutional description and analysis. Political science is generally understood to include the field of political philosophy. In doing so it enters the field of value judgments. The scientists, per se, may deal with value judgments; indeed, in the field of politics he can hardly avoid doing so. If he discovers, for example, that the people in a given country place a high value upon liberty of speech, this fact will be a relevant datum in his judgment as to whether or not detailed national economic planning is likely to endanger liberties essential to democracy. The political scientist will find that information of this sort plays an important role in his work. For this reason the study of political ideas, especially the ideas of the common man—the climate of opinion or the communal psychology of various times and places—will constitute an important part of his prepara-

[19] See, for example, Gabriel A. Almon and James S. Coleman (eds.), *The Politics of the Developing Areas* (Princeton, N.J.: Princeton U.P., 1960); also George McT. Kahin, Guy J. Pauker, and Lucien W. Pye, "Comparative Politics of Non-Western Countries," *The American Political Science Review*, **49** (1955), pp. 1022-1041.

tion. But this use of knowledge about what values people hold, who values what, is quite different from *making* value judgments. To engage in the latter activity takes the political scientist beyond the realm of science as that is generally understood. As scientist, to be sure, he is perfectly justified in making what may be called *intermediate* value judgments, as when he might assert that decentralization is a good thing, other things being equal, because it is favorable to liberty. But this judgment is made on the assumption that liberty is good, a proposition that can not be scientifically demonstrated—or only in terms of some more ultimate good that would have to be accepted without proof.

One of the differences between the study of economics and that of political science is that economists assume a set of values (*e.g.*, the value of material wellbeing), while political scientists often feel free to go beyond this point and *debate* the relative merits of various political values (such as liberty and order). In doing so, they are philosophizing rather than practicing science. As a matter of fact, for this very reason, there is much to be said for denominating our field of study as "Government" or "Politics" rather than by the more restrictive term, "Political Science." As it is, we must recognize that we have scientific political scientists and philosophical political scientists. There is an important place in the profession for those who leave questions of political ethics to others and who strive for the greatest possible detachment in judging trends and seeking to determine cause and effect in political matters. In other words, some division of labor is desirable between those who consider what goals should be pursued and those who concentrate on discovering the best ways of attaining particular goals, or who merely try to chart the course we are following and predict whither we are bound.

Political Science Broadly Defined

Early in this chapter we suggested that political science could be defined in terms of its two components, "politics" and "science." We are prepared now to propose a broader definition, at least as it applies to a conventional field of study. For this purpose we may define political science as the systematic study of government and of the political process, from the point of view of what is, of what ought to be, and of how to achieve the greatest coincidence between the two. With this statement in mind, we may proceed to explore it.

The study of "what is" seeks to understand the nature of the state, and more broadly, of political systems. The analysis of political systems is dual: sociological and legal. The former is concerned with the nature of the political process, of political power and of law, and of the relation of the polity to other institutions of society. The latter aims to discover the general relations that give form, definition and binding force to those aspects of society that we denominate as governmental. Progress toward these ambitious objectives largely depends upon description and analysis of political institutions, including particular governments, types of government, informal political institutions such as political parties and pressure groups, and political processes such as opinion formation, legislation, administration, and adjudication, and the relations between independent political units. Then comes the attempt to discover uniformities, laws, trends, tendencies, and causal relations. Here consideration is given to various determining factors in political stability and change, such as climate, geography, technological developments, class stratification, nationality, the spread and depth of consensus, the degree of tension between welfare level and welfare aspirations, the functional or disfunctional quality of the prevailing political myth, and of political institutions of all kinds. At this level the political scientist attempts to discover sound principles of public administration, of effective leadership, and of statesmanship, internal and international, including principles of effective organization, representation, and integration of interests. He also seeks an at best quasiscientific understanding of the nature and operation of political forces and institutions.

In studying the realm of political ethics, the sphere of "what ought to be," the political scientist is concerned to evaluate the purposes and ends of the state. His fundamental topics are the ethical foundations of authority; the nature and limits of political obligation; the rights and liberties of individuals, groups, and nations; and indeed the whole value and limitation of the governmental organization of society from the point of view of the ultimate ends of man himself. The approach may be analytical or speculative, or as in the case of Plato, a combination of the two.

Finally, the political scientist attempts to devise means for the attainment of ends judged valuable or, with the evaluation of existing devices and methods, from the point of view of their suitability for the attainment of those ends. According to the categories discussed earlier, much of this activity falls under problem-solving. Much of the work of the political scientist, as critic of the current scene or of particular policies, is of this kind; so also is his functioning as an expert when he is called upon to make recommendations for the reorganization of Congress, for the improvement of administrative efficiency, or to draw up a charter for a city or a constitution for a state.[20]

The ends-means dichotomy that we have been following involves an oversimplification. It tends to obscure an important aspect of the study and evaluation of public policy. The relation of means to ends is often not one of a given end for which the problem is to devise means; rather it is one in

---

[20] It should be noted that the discovery of principles of administration, leadership, and the like, as discussed above under the category of studying "what is," often occurs as a by product of the attempt to devise means for the attainment of ends judged valuable.

which both means and ends can vary within limits and the objective is to suggest or to implement the most desirable combination.[21] Much of the work of the political scientist as critic of the current scene or of particular policies is of this kind; so also is his sometime functioning as an expert in making recommendations for the improvement of local government, the reform of party finance, or the administration of social security.

Seldom, however, can the actual preoccupations of the political scientist be neatly categorized. In empirical studies he usually makes quasi-ethical or philosophical judgments. In philosophizing he is like to unearth new facts or look at old facts in new ways. And politics is so variously related to other human endeavors that the political scientist often must turn for assistance to the sociologist, the historian, the economist, or the psychologist.

SELECTED READINGS

CATLIN, GEORGE E. GORDON. *Systematic Politics*. Toronto: Univ. of Toronto Press, 1962. A general treatise, concerned especially with distinguishing between and at the same time relating political science (strictly defined) and political philosophy. The author also interprets the scope of political science broadly as dealing with the phenomenon of power.

BRECHT, ARNOLD. *Political Theory: The Foundations of Twentieth Century Political Thought*. Princeton, N.J.: Princeton U. P., 1959. The first three chapters of this imposing treatise are devoted to the theory of scientific method and of its applicability to the realm of values.

CRICK, BERNARD. *The American Science of Politics, Its Origins and Conditions*. Berkeley and Los Angeles: University Press, 1959. A history and critique of American political science.

DAHL, ROBERT A. "The Behavioral Approach," *American Political Science Review*, 55 (1961), pp. 763-772. An historical account and evaluation of the behavioral approach, arguing that it now generally suffuses the body of political science, or well on the way to doing so, and that it remains today primarily a "mood": "a mood of sympathy toward 'scientific' modes of investigation and analysis, a mood of optimism about the possibilities of improving the study of politics." (See p. 766.)

DIESING, PAUL. *Reason in Society, Five Types of Decisions and Their Social Conditions*. Urbana, Ill.: Univ. of Illinois Press, 1962. Chapter V discusses political science as "the study of decision-making structures."

EASTON, DAVID. *The Political System*. New York: Knopf, 1953. Although this book is largely argumentative and exploratory rather than expository, it supplies a most helpful inquiry into what the political scientist is, or ought to be about. See especially Chs. III-VIII.

DE JOUVENEL, BERTRAND. *Sovereignty*. Cambridge, Eng.: Cambridge U. P., 1957. Chapter I, the "Essence of Politics," of this original and stimulating book contains valuable insights.

[21] On the scientific status of this type of enterprise, see Charles E. Lindblom, "The Science of 'Muddling Through,'" *Public Administration Review*, 19 (1950), p. 79.

LERNER, DANIEL, and LASSWELL, HAROLD D. (eds.). *The Policy Sciences: Recent Developments in Scope and Method*. Palo Alto, Calif.: Stanford U. P., 1951. A symposium on scope and method emphasizing the study of policy and policy formation as of central importance. In spite of the passage of time, many of these essays have continuing merit. The volume is especially useful in relating political science to other "policy sciences."

Research Frontiers in Politics and Government (Brookings Lectures, 1955). Washington, D.C.: The Brookings Institution, 1955. See especially David B. Truman's lecture, "The Impact on Political Science of the Revolution in the Behavioral Sciences," pp. 202-231. A careful and thoughtful study of the "institutionalist" and "political behavior" tendencies in political science today and of the contributions especially to research technique made by the latter, and its limitations.

RIKER, WILLIAM H. *The Theory of Political Coalitions*. New Haven and London: Yale U.P., 1962. A rigorous theory of political coalitions based upon the theory of *n*-person games. Chapter 1 is especially pertinent to the discussion in the preceding pages.

STORING, HERBERT J. *Essays on the Scientific Study of Politics*. New York: Holt, Rinehart & Winston, 1952. Essays in criticism of "behavioral" political science.

VAN DYKE, VERNON. *Political Science: a Philosophical Analysis*. Palo Alto, Calif.: Stanford U. P., 1960. The author presents and supports his belief that the study of politics should be pursued with the objectives of natural science and discusses the methods appropriate to this enterprise.

WOOTTON, BARBARA. *Testament for Social Science, an Essay in the Application of Scientific Method to Human Problems*. New York: W. W. Norton, 1950. Not a technical work on methodology but a reasoned presentation of the position that the inherent limitations on what can be accomplished by the application of scientific method to human affairs are less serious than is commonly believed.

YOUNG, ROLAND (ed.), *Approaches to the Study of Politics*. Evanston, Ill.: Northwestern U. P., 1958. A collection of essays by leading political scientists, dealing with the nature of politics and the methodology of its study.

CHAPTER 2

Psychology and Politics

INTRODUCTION

Of all the social sciences, Psychology might well be thought *the* foundation or basis for political science. Psychology deals (among other things) with the most universal aspects of human cognitive behavior. If our study is political behavior, then psychology ought to be fundamental. Apparently, a good many students of politics in the past have thought so, for a number of them, from Thomas Hobbes through Jeremy Bentham, and even down to the present day,[1] have attempted to develop a whole science of politics based upon psychology—in fact, often based upon one or two psychological propositions such as "men prefer more power to less," or "people act always in their self-interest." In other words, they endeavored to develop a deductive science of politics.

Often for such people as Hobbes, the social philosophers of the French Enlightenment, or the later English Utilitarians, the model of physics or the methods of economic thought suggested like possibilities for a "science of politics." Obviously, in social behavior, man is the central object for study. If one could "measure" man scientifically, or failing this, could by introspection reduce human behavior to one or the few most basic principles, the conclusion would seem to follow that the foundations for a mature science of politics existed. Since part of our objective is to try to relate the two disciplines of psychology and political science, it will be useful at the start of our inquiry to examine some of the pitfalls that border the paths of political psychologists.

[1] See, for example, G. E. G. Catlin, *The Science and Method of Politics* (London: Kegan Paul, Trench, Trubner & Co., 1927); Also, Harold D. Lasswell, *Psychopathology and Politics* (Chicago: Univ. of Chicago Press, 1930).

Human Psychology Too Complex
for Deductive Political Theory

Early deductive theories of politics tended to be based upon simplistic notions of psychology. We have already alluded to Hobbes and his use of psychology in a theory of politics. Jeremy Bentham and his Utilitarian followers, men of great influence in nineteenth-century England, developed an elaborate and rigorous theory of political behavior based on the fundamental proposition that men act always and only in pursuit of their self-interest. What is often overlooked about such formulations is their emptiness. It does us no good to know that men act in pursuit of their self-interest unless they all have the same interests, or at least unless we have some way of knowing what their interests are. Macaulay long ago made this point in criticism of James Mill, in words difficult to improve:

> This truism that men act from self-interest only . . . means only that men, if they can, will do as they choose. When we see the actions of a man we know with certainty what he thinks his interest to be. But it is impossible to reason with certainty from what we take to be his interest to his actions. One man cuts his father's throat to get possession of his old clothes; another hazards his own life to save that of an enemy. One man volunteers on a forlorn hope; another is drummed out of a regiment for cowardice. Each of these men has, no doubt, acted from self-interest. But we gain nothing from knowing this, except the pleasure, if it be one, of multiplying useless words.[2]

In other words, the vague term "interest" covers many different kinds of motivation. Moreover, men frequently act contrary to what they consider to be their self-interest. Let the reader think how frequently he acts contrary to what he wishes to do, impelled by conscience or sense of duty. Most of us have also had the significant experience of deciding that our true interest lies in one course of action, and then impulsively or rebelliously do the contrary, against our better judgment, as we say.

Although modern psychology has greatly improved on the simple motivational theories of the Utilitarians, the complexity of human motivation as it is now understood would, *ipso facto,* pose an insuperable practical difficulty for such a deductive science of political psychology. The man in the street acts politically in a context of wants, loyalties, and identifications that are not present to him as a clear and neatly tagged set of known personal interests. The degree of his involvement in or knowledge of these interests is not self-evident. Even to guess how he *might* respond, an investigator would have to know what these interests meant to him; and this difficulty would immediately convert the task of predicting his political behavior from a deductive exercise into an extensive empirical inquiry.

[2] Thomas Babington Macaulay, *Critical and Historical Essays,* 3 Vols. (New York: Houghton Mifflin, 1899-1900), I, pp. 416-417.

Importance of Social Psychology for Political Science— and Its Limitations

Early psychological theories of politics were highly individualistic. Just as early economic theory often began with "two men higgling in the market," or with Robinson Crusoe alone on his island with his companion Friday, similarly, psychological theories of politics began with the individual and attempted to build a theory of society and politics from the basic elements of isolated individual behavior. The theories took little account of the way in which individual behavior is modified by group-centered activities or by the leader-led relation. Yet these are two of the most important concepts of politics, as they are of ordinary day-to-day behavior.

Modern psychologists study men in groups as well as individual behavior. This study of social psychology, as it is called, often has more direct relevance for the political scientist than does individual psychology, and we shall make use of some of its findings in this and later chapters. Social psychologists have much to say that is helpful in the study of politics, for example in understanding voting behavior, and in the study of group behavior within large organizations such as an administrative bureaucracy. Yet social psychologists would be the first to admit that they have by no means provided a body of scientific propositions that would support a general theory of politics.[3] Also, social psychology has as yet little to say about the behavior of groups in a situation where many groups act simultaneously and are affected by the activities of each other and of the system as a whole; for politics this situation is typical. Nor has social psychology gone very far in explaining the differences between peculiarly political or official behavior and most other kinds of group activity.[4] But this is also one of the things that politics is primarily about. Political behavior is mediated by institutions, especially political institutions. Their specific character plays a major part in determining political outcomes.[5]

[3] See, for example, Angus Campbell, Philip E. Converse, Warren E. Miller, and Donald E. Stokes, *The American Voter* (New York: Wiley, 1960). This study, a product of the University of Michigan's Survey Research Center, contains many examples of the kind of contributions that social psychology can make to the study of voting behavior. The authors concede that psychological laws must be supplemented by distinctly political factors to explain voting behavior.

[4] For a good summary of these applications of social psychology, see Sidney Verba, *Small Groups and Political Behavior—A Study of Leadership* (Princeton, N.J.: Princeton U. P., 1961). A succinct criticism is provided by Sam Krislov "Groping in Group Theory," *Public Administration Review,* 21 (1961), pp. 157-165. As a way of understanding some of the problems in this area, consider what happens to the group when the chairman says, "The meeting of the board will now come to order."

[5] For example, consider the role of institutions in "political socialization." Not only does the individual everywhere undergo a process of "political socialization," but the nature and effects of this process are significantly affected by the specific political institutions that characterize his political environment. Take the matter of political parties.

Two Kinds of Contributions of Psychology to Political Science

Although psychology can not provide the foundation for a complete political science, certain simple and elementary psychological propositions can improve an *understanding* of politics by contributing a knowledge of the broad contours of human nature. Much of this knowledge is almost at a common-sense level—though perhaps it is better to say that it is corrected and organized common sense. The "knowledge" is imprecise and the theories that relate this knowledge are "weak theories." On the other hand, it may be that the most significant contributions of psychology to political science have been made in this fashion. These contributions and the kinds of insights into politics to which they lead to are discussed in this chapter under the rubric "Human Nature and Politics."

Political science also makes considerable use of more rigorously formulated propositions that are essentially psychological, as some of the examples already cited would indicate. In this instance we are dealing with facts and theory that are more "powerful" but that also have more limited applicability. Such propositions can be used to develop an elegant body of related theories that are of some use. These theories, however, relate to much of politics only in a distant and indirect fashion. This subject of "strong theory" in political psychology and its relation to politics is discussed in the following section.

USES OF PSYCHOLOGY FOR POLITICAL SCIENCE

As a way of showing some of the uses (as well as the limitations) of more rigorous inquiries into political psychology, we have presented below a small number of central propositions that have been carefully investigated in various studies of political psychology, together with some of the corollaries that can be drawn from these propositions and some of their more distant implications. To avoid losing the forest for the trees, these propositions are presented in summary fashion without explication or discussion.

Studies show that the individual's reaction to particular issues cannot be predicated from knowledge of his personality, his interests, and his early ideological training and orientation. If as an adult he becomes affiliated with a political party and develops loyalty to it, it becomes an organizing principle for the issues that are presented to him and tends to determine his attitudes toward them. The same may be true of his citizenship in a particular state, his membership of a particular legislative body or administrative organization, and less directly political institutions such as the trade union, etc. See Herbert H. Hyman, *Political Socialization: A Study in the Psychology of Political Behavior* (Glencoe, Ill.: Free Press, 1959), pp. 46-47. The book as a whole is a useful summary of investigations in this field. This fact, it may be noted, places serious limitations on the development of a universalized political theory, confining much of the significant work of the political scientist to work within a particular institutional context.

The point to be noted here is the way in which theory can be built up[6] from a few simple propositions and the value that it has for a whole discipline.

A System of Theories

I. *Political Attitudes Among the Populace*

    A. Extremist attitudes in politics correlate strongly with ignorance, psychic deprivation, and social and physical isolation.

    B. Moderate attitudes toward politics correlate strongly with education, role security, and role satisfaction, and the fact or expectation of upward social mobility.

    Subsidiary Propositions

    1. Educated elites are favorable to civil liberties

    2. The "alienation" of farmer and worker diminish markedly with urbanization, the development of communications, and the change from extractive industries and basic processes to more modern industrial and productive techniques.

II. *Populace and Electoral Choice*

    A. Political symbols are relatively stable; often it is easier to establish an identification with a political symbol than to change the underlying attachment to that symbol.

    B. Political attitudes tend to cluster; they are tied up with other identifications such as "socioeconomic status" and with particular political symbols.

    C. People avoid direct discussion of politics, religion, class distinctions; in political discussions they often do not talk *to* each other, but *past* each other; they may avoid discussion of politics entirely.

    D. Communications to the populace via the "opinion leaders" of the groups in which people are members is an important way in which people get their information.

    E. Moderation of political attitudes comes both from the "mediators" and "communicators" of political opinion and from membership in a variety of groups.

    Subsidiary Propositions

    1. Politics without a basis of multiple group memberships or a stratum of moderate leaders connected with these groups is likely to be immoderate or extreme.

    2. Groups and opinion leaders are important in introducing a moderate and rational tone into politics.

[6] For an exceptionally good example of this process of theory building see Arnold Rose, "Theory of Social Organization and Disorganization," in his book, *Theory and Method in the Social Sciences* (Minneapolis: Univ. of Minnesota Press, 1954).

III. *Political Leaders*

    A. Politicians tend more than most leaders to be ambitious men and "power oriented."

    B. Politicians are often people that can sustain "cynical" and manipulative" relations with many groups at once.

    Subsidiary Propositions

    1. An important contribution of the politician is "brokerage"; that is, facilitating the kind of "amoral" trading necessary to the accumulation of large aggregations of power.

    2. Politicians should be watched and subjected to many institutional checks.

One of the most impressive things about such a system of theories is how much can be organized about a few propositions of high generality. Strictly speaking, these propositions are not related in a deductive fashion. Many of them are, however, formulated with an objective of employing similar methods of investigation and similar concepts or terminology; thus, findings about one such proposition will, in principle, contribute to the understanding of others. Such a body of theory can result in the identification of particularly important or crucial propositions. Once some of these propositions are identified, they can be studied intensively and sometimes with increasing exactness and theoretical sophistication. The efforts of many people are then cumulative.

The fact that such propositions are not simply an unassorted body of separate laws also contributes to their importance in another way. If they are related together as a body, then systematic organization itself aids greatly in understanding how to apply particular principles or specific propositions in other contexts, not immediately the subject that the original investigator had in mind. Thus, a proposition about the voters of Erie County or the political leaders of Chicago is relevant to those situations primarily; but it can also be applied to new circumstances with the benefit of some powerful theory to suggest what things to look for and what kinds of factors may be important in accounting for the novelty. A theory of leadership that holds for a small group situation, for instance, is often applicable to political leadership as well, or to the exercise of influence upon an official within a bureaucracy. Political parties and bureaucracies are, of course, different from the work group or the group of volunteers for a social psychologist's experiment. Yet they are also, in some situations, instances of behavior common to all groups. To know the elements of similarity and the elements of difference is a good way of finding out some of the specific properties of bureaucracy or of political leadership.

Political psychology and methods of investigation closely related to psychological theories of personality or the social psychology of groups have been important—of decisive importance—in the development of the study of voting behavior. Social psychology has also been useful in exploring the relations of informal to formal organization, especially in the study of administration and bureaucratic organizations. Many areas of politics and political behavior can be understood more comprehensively and in greater depth by the study of political psychology and the application of methods related to it.

Psychology and political psychology are also useful in another way. As the example of our system of theories would indicate, a few relatively precise and reliable laws can be of enormous help because they function as "parameters"[7] in interpreting a particular situation. The electoral process is itself an example. In elections voters and candidates are only part of the process: interest groups, parties, leaders from private life, and many officials (elected and otherwise) are active in varying degree. Making sense out of a dynamic and evolving "process" is difficult. A few simple and fairly reliable propositions about electoral behavior and the dispositions of voters help, particularly in setting some guides and limits for interpretation and prediction. For instance, it is known that people in the United States generally vote the way they say they are going to, and that few will in fact change from a disposition already present early in the election campaign. Consequently, it makes sense for parties and campaign groups to devote at least as much if not more attention to mobilizing the vote rather than attempting to persuade people to change their minds. Parties and interest groups during the campaign pursue a strategy that agrees closely with this proposition: they try to hit repeatedly issues with voter appeal; they try to register the voter and get out the vote on election day; they attempt to beat the other side largely if not primarily by marshalling more stalwarts and more sympathizers; but they waste little time on the opposition voters.

HUMAN NATURE AND POLITICS

Both the limitations and the potentialities of a scientific study of political psychology are great. One of the most important of these limitations is that political psychology, as a rigorous discipline, seldom says much about either specific political context, on the one hand, or broad historical perspective on the other. Also, it says little about the values people hold and the priorities they give them. These subjects relate more to what people have generally meant when they talked or wrote about "human nature and politics." Most of the more astute observers of politics have been political psychologists in this sense.

Knowledge of human nature helps also to explain some of the regu-

---

[7] *Parameter* is a mathematical term meaning a constant that restricts the other terms of an equation.

larities among political institutions and some of the trends in their development. As we turn to a discussion of these simple propositions and broad outlines, two points should be made clear. First, we do not pretend to offer a finished or complete theory of personality. Second, we have tried to discuss human needs and desires as they express themselves socially and politically.

The Desire for Self-Preservation: Security and Enjoyment

At its simplest, the desire for self-preservation is as fundamental as any drive in the human being and appears to be virtually universal. Under normal circumstances—exceptions will be discussed later—human beings desire to preserve their lives; and, again normally, they will take almost any means that seems to them necessary for the accomplishment of that purpose. So fundamental has this fact appeared to observers throughout the ages that it has commonly been asserted to be the first law of nature. Moral theorists like Hobbes, who have sought to ground their theories of morals and politics on a solid foundation of reality, have reached this conclusion, and even religious philosophers like the great Catholic, Thomas Aquinas, who have looked for a transcendental basis for morality, nevertheless recognized the basic claim of man's instinctive desire to preserve himself.

"Self-preservation" is by no means so simple as it might at first thought appear. Modern psychologists recognize no motive for self-preservation in itself. Rather it appears that we are characterized by a number of "adaptive" motives, the net result of which is that we tend to act in ways that preserve and further our lives. We seek food, we try to avoid danger, we follow pleasurable activities, and so on. Moreover, the desire to protect one's own life, whether it be a direct or derived desire, is only the beginning of self-preservation, even though it may be fundamental to it. We seek to preserve not only our lives but all else that we value, including the lives of our families and friends, and also our property; everything indeed that is essential to our life and to our enjoyment.

We stand here face to face with one of the peculiar characteristics of man: whatever may be true of his most elemental drives, his needs, psychological as well as physical, are not a fixed quantity. Practice, knowledge, custom, and association with other persons shape our needs, particularize and enlarge them. We develop new goals, become committed to new values; and all of these things we identify with ourselves. We then seek to protect and preserve and guard the security of this enlarged self with all the vigor once reserved for "self-preservation" in the more restricted sense. In the most extreme cases, the desire to protect that extended "self" with which we come to identify our personalities may lead to self-sacrifice or even to self-destruction.

Another aspect of this complex of traits poses serious problems. Today's luxuries become tomorrow's necessities. We seek the preservation not only of the bare essentials and what is instrumental to them, but also of whatever goes to make up our accepted standard of living, and the latter, as we all know, is strongly influenced by the society in which we live. The worker, the farmer, all of us, will fight to retain things that only a little while ago we never dreamed of having. The struggle for security on the economic level is unending because each increase in prosperity means that there is that much more to be preserved.

Still another facet of the drive for security, and one that appears at an early date, is the desire for predictability, and so for order.[8] The *threats* of unemployment or poverty, of immediate devastating war can be almost as terrible and as destructive of security as these eventualities themselves. Men need to be able to plan their lives and to count on a reasonably assured future for themselves and those close to them. They require security against other individuals and against external forces, physical or social, beyond their control. Equally, they desire also to be safe against the government —its power, its clumsiness, its myopia. Here we find potent support for the rule of law and, under certain circumstances, for some measure of national economic planning.

Man characteristically strives for the *assurance* of security, for freedom from fear and anxiety. Sometimes he can obtain it by establishing institutions that effectively minimize the likelihood of the things he fears. But the degree of real security that can be obtained is limited. Beyond this point man creates myths to give him assurance, to assuage his fears and his psychological insecurities. Myths help rob the future and the unknown of their terrors. The resort to myths in primitive societies illustrates their role, for in these societies the life of the individual is poorly protected against either the ravages of nature or the threats of feuds and intertribal strife. Note also the history of German National Socialism, a movement that was successful largely because of insecurities the previous regime had failed to eliminate and that achieved success in no small measure by providing an effective father figure and by developing anxiety-relieving myths. Finally, contemporary revolutionary movements, creating all manner of insecurities by their very nature, find the highly rationalized myth of Marxism exceedingly well adapted to their purposes. We shall have more to say about myths in the following chapter.

The role of myths suggests another aspect of security—man's need to feel secure in his interpretation of his relation to the external world—physical and especially moral. This is one of the deepest of human needs, and its frustration can produce some of the most explosive political or social consequences. A person who has been socially uprooted or one who suffers deep

---

[8] Men appear also to develop an *intellectual* desire for order and clarity that is independent of the need for security.

conflict over his various roles in groups or society becomes psychologically insecure. More concretely, the country youth who leaves his Asiatic or African village for the complexities of the city sometimes suffers extensive demoralization when his conceptions of his place and goals in society are rudely shattered. Many young Puerto Ricans in New York or Chicago fall into behavior patterns that were virtually unknown in their native society. The business executive or political leader who is subjected to too many conflicting loyalties to persons, groups, and ideals may break under the strain or protect himself from the burden of decision by retreating to cynicism. Modern society is increasingly diverse and often increasingly variable; part of the price paid by the men who live within it is a vast amount of agonizing over their roles.

The Desire for Self-Expansion:
New Experience, Adventure, Creativity, Power

Ambivalent Man. Man's search for security of his life, his property, his standard of living, and also of his *amour propre* is a powerful motive force and one that goes far to explain his behavior in society. Nevertheless, it is by no means his only important drive; nor, as we have seen, can we assume that he never acts contrary to it. Human beings are complex and paradoxical. Human nature is in many respects ambivalent so that man finds himself drawn in opposite directions. He seeks to preserve his life; yet he often glories in risking it. Both Nietzsche and Freud expressed a reaction to a cotton-wool world of security and assured status. The revolutionist, Trotsky, to cite another instance, also realized acutely the importance for men of new horizons. In his travels through the Balkans prior to the First World War, he observed to his amazement that workers, peasants, and plain people—those who above all should have abhorred the approach of war—in fact welcomed it. The daily round of their lives was drab and tasteless. A portentous future, adventure, even the terrors of war seemed preferable. The typically aggressive politics of totalitarian regimes may owe something to the fact that the internal life of these societies concentrates so heavily on security that little scope is given for man's desire for adventure.

The craving in men—at least some men—for adventure does not negate what we have said about their need and demand for security. The latter remains dominant for most people most of the time. Moreover, even the adventurer normally takes all feasible precautions. He may delight not just in adventure, but in the actual risk involved, for he is a gambler and, like all gamblers, he hopes to win. If the stakes are high in terms of prestige, perhaps he may accept long odds; but most people are not tempted by such opportunities, even if presented with them. The difference between risks taken for the sake of glory, on the one hand, and behavior of a kind that carries an overwhelming likelihood of death with little chance of great reward, is amply illustrated by the attitude of most of the civilized world today toward war. Since the advent of nuclear weapons and the general recognition of what their use would entail, there is little evidence of the popularity of policies that threaten the outbreak of general warfare.

THE NEED FOR NEW EXPERIENCE—EXPANSION OF THE SELF

The need for new experience is most primitively expressed in boredom with things as they are. Human desire is indefinitely expansible and tends always to exceed present satisfactions. Any particular desire, upon fulfillment, is replaced by another. It is the nature of man to have desires, to set value upon things, experiences, and conditions. As one value is realized others emerge. We not only seek the achievement of our goals but we also crave to be constantly setting and achieving new goals, expanding our "selves." Thomas Hobbes, who, for all his failure as a system builder, was a sagacious observer of human nature, clearly perceived this fundamental truth and expressed it well. He wrote:

> The felicity of this life consisteth not in the repose of a mind satisfied. For there is no such *finis ultimus*, utmost aim, nor *summum bonum,* greatest good, as is spoken of in the books of the old moral philosophers. Nor can a man any more live, whose desires are at an end, than he whose senses and imagination are at a stand. *Felicity is a continual progress of the desire, from one object to another. . . .*[9]

The form that the need for new experience takes, however, varies greatly with circumstances. Change and adventure are not synonymous; in many traditional societies neither much change nor adventure was experienced by the average man. But adventure and adventurous souls appear to be present in all societies, past and present. On the other hand, progress, as a secular goal, is relatively new; it has developed along with the era of rapid technological change ushered in by the Industrial Revolution. Hegel had this contrast in mind when he sneered at liberal democracy and the industrial economy as substituting modest enrichment and economic progress for the "ennobling" military adventure and fear of violent death of aristocratic societies.

The need for new experience may be a powerful, even a dangerous political force. The modern state as it emerged in France and England, especially in the era of mercantilism, was built upon the allegiance of devel-

---

[9] Thomas Hobbes, *Leviathan*, edited by Michael Oakeshott (Oxford: Basil Blackwell, 1946), Ch. 11, p. 63. (Emphasis added.) It may be argued that what has been asserted above involves exaggeration, that what is declared to be a characteristic of human nature is rather confined to certain (though numerous) humans in civilized societies. We need not argue the point. While the authors are inclined to agree with Hobbes on this matter, the more limited statement is sufficient for present purposes. Obviously, even in a dynamic society, many individuals—possibly with aspirations stunted by unfavorable circumstances —are quite content to vegetate.

oping classes of burghers, merchants, and soldiers who found new risks and new occupations profoundly challenging and stimulating as well as lucrative. Increasingly, twentieth-century men share in this "revolution of rising expectations," anticipating a better and richer future, engaged in a "career," and determined to get on in life. Security, man must have; but novelty and adventure he must have as well. Western civilization affords change and progress. Whether it affords enough adventure doubtless depends upon time and place. It seems to be especially in demand at certain times. Then it is the task of statesmanship to provide it, as Franklin Roosevelt in the United States did for many men who entered the government service during the 1930's. By a strange coincidence they found their adventure in experimenting with new devices for providing increased security for their fellow citizens. The challenge to the modern statesman is not to eliminate all insecurity for everyone, it is to provide institutions that permit each man to find for himself the equilibrium point between his various and conflicting urges. One of the great accomplishments of the dynamic industrial order of modern times, especially when it is supported by the political institutions of constitutional democracy, is that it permits change, diversity, and risk-taking, while providing safety and security for the society as a whole.[10] It is an important function of the modern state to provide socially harmless (and preferably useful) outlets for men's desire for adventure.

Like other human traits, the desire for new experience is not without limit. It is checked by its counterpart—inertia and the love of old habits and established ways of doing things. That astute observer of human nature, Niccolò Machiavelli, long ago observed that "men almost always walk in the paths trodden by others."[11] Whether or not Machiavelli exaggerates, it is true that the desire for new experience is not normally a desire for a sharp break from the past but only for variety and adventure within a general environment whose familiarity provides a sense of security. We all contain within us the elements of both conservatism and liberalism, and it is likely to be the accidents of early experience or environment that determines which will be dominant.[12]

THE DESIRE FOR POWER

Politically more significant than any other aspect of man's drive for self-expansion, as it was the genius of Hobbes to stress, is man's desire for power.

[10] We speak here of the internal accomplishments of the modern state. That it has not achieved like success in regulating its relations with other states is obvious.

[11] Niccolò Machiavelli, *The Prince and the Discourses*, Modern Library ed. (New York: Random House, 1940), *The Prince*, Ch. 6, p. 19.

[12] We do not mean to imply that conservatives necessarily oppose change. Many conservatives would argue that they, as well as liberals, desire a dynamic society, but they insist that this goal can and should be accomplished compatibly with maintaining stability, continuity of development, and the preservation of institutions embodying cherished values.

Hobbes's words are difficult to improve. "I put for a general inclination of all mankind," he wrote, "a perpetual and restless desire for power after power, that ceaseth only in death."[13] He seeks power partly as a means to other ends and partly for its own sake: to exercise it or to contemplate it. Sometimes, too, men seek power as a way of displaying superiority over others, for man is a prideful animal. He enjoys self-esteem and generally finds that his ego feeds on the esteem of others. An important way of achieving popular esteem is by the successful exercise of political leadership, the attainment of political power.

The manner in which the desire for self-expansion manifests itself varies from culture to culture, but nearly every society includes those who aspire to political leadership and the exercise of political power. As Hobbes pointed out, men seek power to protect and preserve what they already have and also to enable them to obtain more of the good things of life. Men also seek power over other men in order, like Napoleon, to forge a new and better regime so that the lives of all may be improved and the state be more glorious.[14] Few things, however, are more exciting than power itself, the opportunity to manipulate or to dominate and to be superior. Nothing more readily becomes an end in itself, nor is more subtly transmuted from its constructive and socially approved form into its exploitive and destructive one. A perennial threat of all societies has been that worship of power would become legitimate in some palatably disguised but nonetheless dangerous form. Forms of government, types of political and administrative control, private organizations—trade unions, corporations—are either well designed to minimize the corrupting influence of power or they are not. To understand what such institutions incite people to do and what sorts of arrangements can temper the drive for power and channel it to useful ends is one of the major concerns of the political scientist, and always has been. It was Aristotle, sometimes called "the father of political science," who declared

> He who bids the law rule may be deemed to bid God and Reason alone rule, but he who bids man rule adds an element of the beast; for desire is a wild beast, and passion perverts the minds of rulers, even when they are the best of men.[15]

Doubtless the pursuit of power for its own sake is a perversion just as much as the miserly love of money for its own sake, and one that may have far more serious consequences. But we must not overlook the fact that in politics as in economics it is the results not the motives that count. The best of motives often lead to disastrous results and the converse is also true. Fortunately one of the most effective and lasting ways of winning power is by

---

[13] Hobbes, *op. cit.*, p. 64.
[14] It is not implied that Napoleon did not have other, less noble motives.
[15] *Aristotle's Politics,* translated by Benjamin Jowett (Oxford: Clarendon Press, 1923), 1287a.

actions that contribute to the welfare of a whole society. Therefore, while the pursuit of power for its own sake should always be suspect, the fact is that by a principle of indirection often observed the power-seeker frequently serves his fellowman. Machiavelli had this truth in mind when he observed that bad men often made the best princes.[16]

The Desire for Freedom and Self-Expansion

Of the various meanings of freedom we shall have something to say at a later point. Here we need not put too fine a point upon it; we use the term in its most elementary sense, the absence of restraints. We shall treat also of the desire to use one's powers, which is little more than the obverse of the absence of restraints. Psychologists tell us that one of the very few of the apparently innate characteristics of babies is dislike of resistance to moving their arms and legs about. Hold their arms still for long and they will cry. Nor is it accidental that interference with freedom of movement—imprisonment—long ago became a major device for punishment, a grown-up extension of sending a misbehaving child to his room. Whether or not these methods for dealing with wrong conduct are sound, clearly the intention was to punish violators of the code by depriving them of something they prized most highly, their liberty.

This primitive desire for freedom, for the opportunity to move about as we will, and to exercise and develop our natural abilities, seems closely related to the desire for self-preservation. We desire not only to preserve our lives but also to exploit our potentialities. We desire not only to live, but to live well, by developing and using our physical and mental powers. The powers we exercise include those over, or in relation to, persons and things —leadership and domination, wit and suasion, craftsmanship and ingenuity, the mastery of sciences and manipulation of forces and organization—those human talents that contribute alike to growth, reliance, mastery, and pride. Much of earlier, secular ethics was grounded almost exclusively on this one psychological value. The good for man was an active, striving use and development of his powers. Thus happiness, to Aristotle, was an "activity." Spinoza linked it with *conatus,* or striving. Christians, to be sure, condemned this conception of happiness as pagan pride in individual talents, and admiration of self rather than God. In doing so, however, they were deliberately seeking to curb, or to transcend, man's nature; they were not denying the validity of the psychology we are discussing.

Some early writers naively assumed that, since freedom is the absence of restraints and government imposes restraints, the most complete freedom would be found in a "state of nature"; that is, in the absence of all government. The fallacy of this view is evident. One of the paradoxes of freedom

---

[16] The point is well argued by Thomas Hill Green in his *Lectures on the Principles of Political Obligation* (London: Longmans, Green, 1957), pars. 128-131.

is that it requires restraints, including the restraints of law. The point need not be labored. In congested areas removing the restraints of traffic regulations would not add liberty but would seriously curtail it. Each of us has to be kept from interfering, willfully or inadvertently, with the liberty of others. Only in a society where governments exist and perform this function can there be any liberty worthy of the name.

The relation of freedom to security involves another paradox; for while the two appear to spring from the same root they frequently conflict. Few people are as secure as the prisoner in his cell. The fullest opportunities for freedom, self-expression, and self-development are incompatible with maximum security. In this respect the desire for freedom is closely related to the desire for new experience. Both may conflict with the desire for security. Freedom also is often a necessary condition for various new experiences.

Freedom and the exercise of one's powers are widely thought to be necessary conditions for the development of individual responsibility and maturity. The validity of this belief and its implications for political institutions constitute one of the continuing concerns of political theorists. John Stuart Mill, philosopher of English liberalism, held that the central task of the state was just this—to produce a better man and citizen by allowing and encouraging him to use his powers creatively.

> The worth of the state in the long run [he declared] is the worth of individuals composing it, and a state which postpones the interests of their mental expansion and elevation, to a little more of administrative skill, a state which dwarfs its men, in order that they may be more docile instruments in its hands even for beneficial purposes—will find that with small men no great thing can really be accomplished.[17]

This view of the state, as justified by its role in enabling men to become better, more mature and responsible persons, was dominant in much of modern Western political history. The same view, in a diluted fashion, prevails widely today, for example in the common American attitude that free enterprise is in part desirable because it make a tougher, more self-reliant individual, or in the view of the United States Supreme Court that segregation in education must be condemned because it stunts the development of individual powers.[18]

Man's Social Side

The drives we have discussed so far have been essentially of an individualistic nature, relating to the preservation, expression, or expansion of the ego, although we have noted that their development has been socially conditioned. If only because many of man's desires can not be satisfied by

[17] John Stuart Mill, *On Liberty* (London: Longmans, Green, 1913), p. 68.
[18] *Brown v. Board of Education,* 347 U.S. 483 (1954).

individual action, they often lead to cooperative activity. Even Hobbes, asserting that men were almost completely self-centered and prideful, believed that they were led by a rational appreciation of the self-defeating nature of undisciplined egoism to establish governments for the enforcement of rules for social living. It may be doubted, however, whether a satisfactory society ever would have developed if man was as Hobbes described him, or if he possessed only the individualistic drives we have thus far discussed. Human nature also has its social side: drives toward life, gain, and glory by no means exhaust man's traits. He has impulses to unity as well, as it was one of the great merits of Rousseau to point out.

We may list the more directly social impulses as sociability, the desire to engage in cooperative activity, sympathy, and altruism. In a most fundamental and primary way, man is a social animal. Men, in general, like to associate with other human beings; they enjoy company and are unhappy if they are too much alone. The peasant crowd, with its exchange of news and witticisms and cheerful bickering, indicates that association meets needs for novelty and fresh excitement. Likewise the street corner gang. Moreover, many of the powers in which we most delight are those of social adeptness and management of human relations. *Sociability* may be a derived need, accounted for by the fact that it heightens other enjoyments; but as a specific desire it seems to be both definite and separate. In terms of its strength and generality it deserves to be counted as a fundamental human trait.

People not only like each other's company they derive a particular happiness from working together with other men, sharing their purposes and combining their efforts—in short, from *cooperation*. Tasks that are onerous and distasteful when performed singly become even enjoyable when done in cooperation with others. It is not simply that "misery loves company." Company, and the thrill of conjoint activity, may convert what was miserable into something joyous. Barn-raisings were festive affairs, as satisfying as they were useful. Community projects enlist enthusiastic voluntary participation in tasks which the individuals concerned would never have performed singly, even for pay. The desire to undertake some good task in common is a political force not to be neglected or taken lightly. Many of the successes of the Chinese Communists in their rise to power can be attributed to the skill and persistence with which they evoked this impulse to joint enterprise and cooperation.

Here as elsewhere we must remind ourselves that in speaking of fundamental traits we are not saying that they manifest themselves all the time. Man's sociability is balanced with a liking for privacy. His joy in working with others likewise has its limits. We are speaking of a tendency that can be capitalized upon for the good of society. When, under what conditions, and for how long this source of energy can be tapped for social and specifically political purposes is a problem for political scientists and practicing politicians.

Finally, we lump together for present purposes *sympathy and altruism,* although they are not the same thing. We meet here attitudes that involve relatedness to others in a particular and an interesting sense. Sexuality, sociability, and cooperative endeavor, it may be argued, serve egoism, especially in the sense that they often heighten or supplement the individual's direct gratifications. Sympathy or altruism, however, may lead persons to sacrifice their own interests to the dictates of fellow-feeling. At bottom, sympathy is literally what the derivation implies—a suffering or a feeling with others of their immediate reactions or emotions. It implies a basic recognition of likeness between one's self and others, and an immediate response to and sharing in their feelings. Sympathy provides the emotional foundation for a rational understanding of one's fellows and for a sharing in their interests. It also provides some of the emotional impulse to back up and strengthen the dictates of reasonable obligation. It is thus one of the fundamental motivations toward morality. A rational morality, or a reasonable morality with nonrational sanctions may cause men to conform to outward rules or even to develop some inner sense of duty toward others apart from outward compulsion. Without sympathy, however, to aid in the growth of morality and to support it, it is doubtful whether human society would be possible. At the very least, it would have to be bound together and disciplined by the most powerful bonds of autocratic rule, even as Hobbes, who grossly underrated human sympathy, declared. With sympathy and altruism, as Rousseau saw, not only society and government but also democratic government become possible.

It should be added that the effects of sympathy are not always good. For instance, sympathy in elemental form may provide the basis for irrational suggestibility. If so, it plays a major role in mass behavior, in mob psychology, and becomes an active political force, for example, in irredentist causes or lynch mobs. Moreover, sympathy for individuals may lead to an insufficient appreciation of the proper rights and demands of corporations or of the state itself. Thus jury determinations of damage cases against corporations notoriously tend to favor the injured party, if he is an individual rather than another corporation. Sympathy, unguided by reason, may go in any direction. But where reason points to social action, sympathy provides emotional and motivational support.

Imitativeness and *suggestibility* are two other human characteristics having great significance for man's social and political life. Gabriel Tarde, a French psychologist of the nineteenth century, held that the tendency to imitate was the dominant characteristic of the mass of men, and attempted to explain social development and behavior almost entirely by what he called "the laws of imitation." No such generalization is acceptable today and modern social psychologists regard Tarde's views as grossly oversimplified. Nonetheless, the importance of this tendency to imitate may be too readily ignored.

Probably two different factors, both with unifying effect, are at work in this propensity for imitation. One is the tendency most people have to emulate the leaders in the society, those who enjoy exceptional prestige, and members of the dominant group generally. The most popular members of any clique of school children tend to set the styles for the group. The shade of lipstick used by a beauty or brand of whiskey favored by a ballplayer are also subjects for emulation. We imitate that which we admire. Equally, however, there is the inclination most people have to conform to the manners, standards, and behavior of their particular society and subsociety. High-school adolescents dread being guilty of the slightest idiosyncracy of dress. But all societies, mature and adolescent, exhibit high degrees of conformity. Apparently such imitative conformity is one facet of the general craving for security. For however much men in society long to expand their individualities and exercise their powers, they must do so within a setting of security. They get this security in part from the feeling that they start from the mass of their fellowmen, and can always return to it.[19]

Suggestibility, for our purposes at least, is a closely allied trait. Most people tend rather easily, and often subconsciously, to accept the suggestions of others. To be sure there are contrary souls among us who are "counter-suggestible," but such conduct provides the exception rather than the rule. We are most likely to resist a suggestion when it is recognized as a deliberate attempt to influence our conduct. Otherwise, we will probably accept it, especially, and this point is extremely important if the suggestion comes from a person whose previous conduct has led us to have confidence in his recommendations or, more generally, in a situation of a kind that, on the basis of past experience, elicits our trust.[20] Thus understood, suggestibility, it will be seen, is conducive not only to social behavior in the limited sense of tending to lead people to accept common standards of behavior, but also that it is rational in the sense that it operates most forcefully where what is being suggested is in some sense rational.

Approbativeness, the desire to elicit approval, and avoid disapproval, probably comes almost as close as any human characteristic to being universal. It springs directly from the ego, but by definition it can be satisfied only by conduct that is pleasing to others. Security and self-esteem are never firm until they are met by the echoing reaffirmation of some community of persons that we recognize in turn. Without the sustaining recognition and approval of such a community all but the hero or the saint are helpless. This

[19] Although it seems clear that, on balance, emulation has a socializing and unifying effect, as is argued above, it must be pointed out that under certain circumstances it may work in precisely the opposite direction. The adolescent who wants to achieve distinction by emulating a distinguished person may find his path blocked by incapacity or lack of opportunity. Under such circumstances he may turn to antisocial activities in order to achieve a kind of comparable status.

[20] See Solomon Asch, *Social Psychology* (Englewood Cliffs, N.J.: Prentice-Hall, 1952), pp. 415-416.

fact is recognized and utilized by modern totalitarian governments. It is sometimes forgotten by Americans, as Tocqueville observed.[21]

The desire for approval supports conformity to the codes and rules of a society or group; but it may also be a basic cause of conflict of obligation and of maladjustment. It is a fundamental motivation in the search for leadership or for specialized distinction. It is also one of the major bases for restraining power-wielders and office-holders as well as for the selection and formation of like-minded leadership groups. While it may encourage considerate and just behavior, it can also lead to rationalization and self-justification—a common pattern, for example, in the career of a demagogue. Where an individual is surrounded by an approval-giving group that immunizes him from contact with the rest of society, it may also fortify a sense of rightness in pursuing a course that is either unethical or that flaunts the general mores of society—problems in aristocracies or revolutionary conspiracies. In brief, the desire for approval, possibly more than any other human trait, offers purchase for leverage and for the exercise of power or its abuse that is both great in quantity and subtle in quality. For the average person, however, its impact is clearly in support of social rather than anti-social behavior.

Finally, and of immense importance, man is an incorrigible norm-creating animal. Wherever men are found they have ideas of what is right and what is wrong, of how things ought to be done, ideas of justice. Within a given society a broad consensus on such matters usually prevails. And even among separate societies norms of conduct and of what constitutes justice tend to differ more on specifics than with regard to underlying principles. Moreover, with the development of civilized society the agreements on principles increase in number while the disagreements diminish. Of course men frequently quarrel over their respective "rights," but only a moment's reflection will make it clear that on the whole this tendency of man to create norms is a uniting rather than a divisive factor. Without it, it may well be doubted whether all of the other "impulses to unity" we have discussed would be enough to prevent the more egoistic and antisocial aspects of human nature from prevailing and making organized society on any large scale impossible.

In concluding this section, we should remark that man is a "social animal" not only in the sense of having basic impulses and sentiments that tend on balance to make for unity rather than separateness, for polity rather than anarchy, but also in the sense of being a product of society. Human characteristics as we know them are in important measure the product of social interaction, shaping and channelling basic impulses. Men react to other people reacting to them, and so on, *ad infinitum*. Each person's mind contains some

[21] For an excellent discussion of this subject, see Arthur O. Lovejoy, *Reflections on Human Nature* (Baltimore: Johns Hopkins Press, 1961), pp. 87-99.

sort of reflection of the minds of others, and thus, in an indirect and attenuated fashion, of the whole society. Discussions that begin by setting individual and society in opposition are likely to be misleading and generally betray a lack of understanding of the fact that the constant interaction between the two is one of the major factors in determining the nature of each.[22] Throughout this chapter, we have been speaking of basic human traits, those we observe in society. To what extent they would emerge if men lived solitary lives, and to what extent they are responses to the "requirednesses" experienced by men in social situations, we need not inquire.[23]

HUMAN NATURE: PLASTICITY AND RATIONALITY

Certain central issues that arise from any discussion of the psychological foundations of politics have thus far been largely avoided in this chapter. The first involves the constancy or malleability, the rigidity or plasticity of human nature. Are men in all ages and all places essentially the same? The second issue presents a challenge to a central assumption of liberal democracy: is man a rational animal? Do men behave in ways calculated to attain their goals? And are their goals such that they can be made to fit together into some sort of reasonably harmonious pattern? Or are their natures such that only the strong arm of a benevolent despot or a wise aristocracy or other governing elite can impose a rational pattern of social life?

Meaning of "Human Nature"

Much misunderstanding might be avoided if the question regarding the constancy of man's nature were restated. It seems safe to assume that man's most basic drives—hunger and sex, for instance—are here to stay. On the other hand, such features as the value men place on individual liberty of action vary from culture to culture and age to age. The important questions relate to what human characteristics are fixed and what are not, how readily the malleable features can be transformed, what means are most effective for this purpose, and whether certain powerful tendencies are always present or always appear under certain circumstances. Within this framework the question of the constancy of human nature is of immediate political significance. It greatly affects the validity of many practical proposals for the revision of political institutions. For example, the Reconstruction controversy following the American Civil War broached issues regarding the nature

---

[22] Some psychologists may go so far as to claim that the individual is plastic without limit. Although the authors believe that there are certain fundamental traits, some discussed above, of which this cannot be said, and that these traits tend to produce the kind of man we have been describing, our thesis would remain valid at least for all civilizations now existing on earth, regardless of whether or not this position is sound.

[23] Asch, *op. cit.*, Ch. 1.

of man. To one group, men could not change and it was harmful to try to change them. To another, the South could be changed, but only education and an awakening of conscience could do the job. Force would be of no avail. Yet another group believed that force could at least change behavior and that time and education would bring a revolution in attitudes. Much the same contentions and the same issues are involved in today's controversies over civil-rights legislation.

We cannot in this volume hope to resolve controversies of this kind. Perhaps we can, however, clear away some of the misunderstandings that have attended them. For instance, the person who asserts that human nature can be changed may have in mind the human tendency to respond to financial incentives. His opponent may argue to the contrary that when human conduct is changed, it is not the "nature" of man that has been changed, but only the manifestation of that nature under a certain set of circumstances. Indeed, he might continue, this same tendency to respond to financial incentives upon which they both agree is the evidence of a constant human nature. Similarly, one person may assert that man's competitive drive, far from being an instinct, is in fact the product of social conditioning and can by proper measures be transformed into cooperativeness. On the other hand, the adherent to the theory of fixed human nature may still be willing to admit that, under proper circumstances, the competitive spirit may lead to group cooperation (as a means to competition with other groups), or that competition for honor may be substituted for competition for financial gain. In other words, what is needed is to study what conditions produce cooperative behavior and what conditions lead to competitive behavior. Just *because* human nature is constant—just because there are laws of human psychology—behavior must change whenever the conditioning factors change.

Differing Views of the Nature of Man

Even when men agree on the constancy of human nature they often disagree on some feature of it. In such instances, when it is impossible to settle the matter on the level of abstract argument, agreement may often eventually be achieved by more pragmatic means. The United Nations has for many years sought assent to a universal declaration of human rights. Although the discussions revealed wide concurrence that men were everywhere the same in certain fundamentals—a fact of great significance in itself—yet there was profound disagreement, especially between industrial West and agrarian East, as to what particular rights could be derived from this common nature. Perhaps only when more members of each type of society have had practical, living experience with the situation confronted by the other, will agreement be likely.

On questions like the one just discussed something approaching universal agreement would be exceedingly useful to achieve; but this end will probably never be accomplished by means of abstract argument. Most likely, only a broader basis of common or like experience can measurably enhance the existing degree of consensus. But on the question of whether in fact men everywhere feel and express needs for security, for absence of restraint, for opportunity to express themselves, for human company, and for the approval of their fellows, there is little dispute except in matters of degree.[24] Possibly, the rulers of totalitarian regimes, Russian, Chinese, or other, may prove with experiments in Pavlovian psychology and calculated manipulation of masses of people that human nature can be changed more fundamentally and permanently than now seems possible. Thus far the evidence suggests that their success has been rather on the level of finding new ways to satisfy certain needs than of changing the needs themselves.[25]

In short, cultural differences are often less fundamental than they seem. Willingness to do without important liberties in order to "catch up" with other countries in terms of the material necessities and luxuries of life does not prove that dislike of restraints is not a fundamental, underlying trait of the people in question—especially not when they have had little experience of a free society and its advantages.

Finally, is man a rational animal? Or were the fascists right in building on the opposite assumption? Much of the political theory in the modern period has been based upon the belief that man is highly rational. Writers like Helvétius and many other French eighteenth-century rationalists believed that man was a highly calculating animal, suiting his behavior deliberately and thoughtfully to his ends, and that his ends themselves fitted together in a rational pattern of individual and social harmony. Some believed that this harmony of ends was achieved without conscious effort or direction, as by an "unseen hand," the phrase applied by Adam Smith to the operations of the market place. Mandeville, in his "Fable of the Bees," expressed the idea in verse in the following lines:

> Thus every part was full of Vice;
> Yet the whole Mass a Paradise; . . .
> This, as in Musick Harmony,
> Made Jarrings in the main agree;
> Parties directly opposite,
> Assist each other, as 'twere from Spight.[26]

[24] We must not overlook the fact that the great variety of cultures, traditions, and situations, may produce great variations in the ways in which each of these needs makes itself felt in various cultures.

[25] See Robert J. Lifton, "Thought Reform of Chinese Intellectuals," *The Journal of Asian Studies*, 16 (1956), pp. 75-88.

[26] Bernard de Mandeville, "The Fable of the Bees, or Private Vices, Public Benefits," ed. F. B. Kaye (Oxford, Eng.: Clarendon, 1924), Vol. I, p. 24.

Others, like Jeremy Bentham, felt the need to rely on the strong arm of the state that could manipulate rewards and penalties in such a way as to *create* a harmony of interests. Yet he and his Utilitarian followers never doubted that this could be accomplished and that a democratic state would tend to operate in this fashion from common recognition of mutual interest on the part of citizens.

These sanguine views of human nature never went unchallenged. Edmund Burke took mild exception to them when he declared:

> We are afraid to put men to live and trade each on his own private stock of reason; because we suspect that this stock in each man is small, and that the individuals would do better to avail themselves of the general bank and capital of nations and of ages.[27]

More radical attacks came from men like Nietzsche and from the great psychologist, Sigmund Freud. Nietzsche asserted that the will to power, not reason, is supreme. Freud's study of the unconscious led him to the belief that not harmony but disharmony and conflict characterize human motivation. Although the superego may sometimes enable us to repress our most irrational drives, according to Freud they will merely appear in different, often socially less desirable forms. The crux of the matter is that man's nature is bound to bring him into conflict both with himself and with others. He cannot find peace and contentment in society, nor yet out of society. He craves authority, yet rebels against it. He desires to be loved even while behaving in an aggressive fashion that repels love. "The tendency to aggression," he wrote, "is an innate, independent, instinctual disposition in man. . . ."[28] Apart from the question of whether or not man's most basic drives are radically at war with each other, twentieth-century psychologists, Freudian and otherwise, have emphasized the extent to which men act impulsively or on the basis of emotion rather than as a consequence of a deliberate weighing of values and a rational calculation of the most effective means for achieving maximum satisfaction.

IMPLICATIONS FOR POLITICS

Today, however, it is widely recognized that just as the eighteenth-century rationalists presented an oversimplified and unrealistic picture of human motivation and behavior, so likewise the reaction to these writers has gone to the opposite extreme. Man need not be a cold calculating machine in order for political institutions, even democratic institutions, to work with

---

[27] Edmund Burke, *Reflections on the French Revolution and Other Essays* (London: Dent, 1925), p. 84.

[28] Sigmund Freud, *Civilization and Its Discontents*, trans. Joan Riviere, 3rd ed. (New York: Jonathan Cape & Harrison Smith, 1930), p. 102. Much of the paragraph above is taken, without benefit of quotation marks, from J. Roland Pennock, *Liberal Democracy: Its Merits and Prospects* (New York: Holt, Rinehart & Winston, 1950), pp. 27-28.

a reasonable degree of success. Irrational behavior tends to fly off in all directions, resulting in mutual cancellation. Since not all behavior is irrational—a proposition no thinking person will deny—there remains at least a residuum of rationality to give direction and some measure of harmony to the whole. Furthermore, emotional reaction is not the opposite of rational behavior. Our emotions tend to be related to our goals and so to aid us in attaining these goals. Of course they by no means always do so, but they have this tendency. It would not be far wrong to say that our emotions have a logic of their own that relates them to our organized purposes.[29]

The importance of institutions must be stressed again in this connection. The statement that "institutions are only men" is false. Institutions are men acting under a particular discipline. Legislatures are carefully contrived devices for focusing opinion in a manner conducive to a full and instructive consideration of issues. Courts are scrupulously insulated from certain types of opinion and emotional appeals in the interests of an impartial weighing of the relevant evidence. In short, constitutional government is a technique for meeting some of the problems posed by the imperfections of man's reason and his lapses from rationality. Aristotle's observation that "whereas law is passionless, passion must ever sway the hearts of man," reminds us that laws are potent checks on irrational behavior. Both psychological research and ordinary observation suggest that men under stress are likely to behave irrationally. Correspondingly, among the necessary tasks of government is the endeavor to maintain sufficient stability and social harmony within a particular polity not to prejudice too extensively the conditions requisite for rational collective consideration of issues and decisions upon them. Obviously too, mobs and crowds are less inclined to sober reflection and rational judgment than an audience, a discussion panel, or a committee. Again, constitutional government may be viewed in part as a technique for allocating each decision to a body appropriately fashioned for deciding the kind of problem it involves and for insuring that a particular constituency is asked to conclude only such questions as it understands and has some basis for judging. The man in the street, that mythical average voter, is called upon in the United States to choose between two men for the presidency or between two political parties, but he is neither asked nor permitted to have a direct share in the decision as to what to do about the Cuban sugar quota, when or whether to have a summit conference, or the proper level for minimum wages.

The final proof of the pudding is in the eating. The behavior of much of mankind during two world wars and of those who controlled the totalitarian regimes that followed in their wakes has done more than all the theorizing of Sigmund Freud to alter, indeed to reverse, the basically optimistic picture of human nature so prevalent in the nineteenth century

[29] See Asch, *op. cit.*, Ch. 3.

and to spread the conviction that man's drives are basically irrational. These horrors should not blind us to the more commonplace evidences of humanity and rationality. The great achievements, scientific, intellectual, and social, that man has to his credit could never have been accomplished unless there were a strong thread of rationality running through human behavior. Yet what else have these achievements represented if not techniques and insights enabling men rationally to harmonize their interests, discover means for their accomplishment, or work with others for the realization of common purposes? To Burke's statement the response should be that the wisdom stored in the nation and its institutions ought to be understood as a supplement and guide to individual reason, not a substitute for it.

To view the matter more positively, people do, in rough and crude terms, behave with considerable rationality. In fact, the usual behavior of most people markedly parallels their interests as they perceive them and as we perceive them. For instance, in the political realm, where it is often said that the rational element is at a minimum, the policies and the programs of the great political parties in the United States (or in England) reflect in a general sort of way their major sources of support. The Republican party has been the party of businessmen and has advocated policies generally believed to be in business's interests. A much larger proportion of the nation's businessmen are Republicans than Democrats. The same relation holds between organized labor and the Democratic party. Furthermore, studies have shown that during periods of economic adversity switches in party adherence predominantly reflect a movement toward the party whose policies most nearly accord with the economic interests of the voters who shift. Yet American major parties—and the same can be said of Great Britain—are not widely separated in their policies. On the contrary they both tend toward the middle ground. This phenomenon is at least compatible with an even more fundamental rationality than that to which reference has just been made—to an underlying unity, or at least harmony, of human interests and to a substantial awareness of this harmony.

IN CONCLUSION

In sum, the stock of human rationality is not so mean a quantity. Furthermore, the histories of democratic nations indicate that the democratic virtues wear well and that men are in remarkable agreement upon their value, if not in all situations at least under a wide range of circumstances. To try to discover whether all men are one in nature and aim, or to attempt to prove them fully rational beings, masters of themselves and of the intricacies and the finesse of social living, misses the point. For self-government the mass of men need only a crude understanding of their interests.

The unity needed for government, too, is less than might be supposed. Men must rally together for crisis, they must consent to conduct political competition within broad limits of temperateness, and they must fulfill a rather restricted number of duties of citizenship. But cleavage within the modern community is a condition of progress; and diversity a requisite for cultural richness. If men were both completely rational and fully socialized they would not require coercive government. Understanding the needs for government and sharing the interests of *their* fellows, *they* would willingly submit to the necessary regulations. On the other hand, if Hobbes were right in supposing man to be natively bad (antisocial), the best that could be achieved in the way of a society would be a totalitarian or dictatorial regime, where the few imposed order upon the many. The doctrine of the mixed nature of man, of human nature as ambivalent, partly rational and partly irrational, and combining both social and antisocial tendencies, is at the basis of the belief in constitutional democracy. According to this belief, no man is good enough to be trusted with absolute power, but all men have sufficient potentiality for good to be trusted with a share in government. Both the science of psychology and practical experience lend support to this belief.

SELECTED READINGS

ASCH, SOLOMON E. *Social Psychology*. Englewood Cliffs, N.J.: Prentice-Hall, 1952. A careful and discerning treatise.

EYSENK, H. J. *The Psychology of Politics*. New York: Praeger, 1954. A summary and attempted integration of much of the work that has been done in the fields of attitude studies and of personality as they apply to political science.

FROMM, ERICH. *Escape from Freedom*. New York: Rinehart, 1945. A study in the psychology of man's quest for freedom and his fear of it.

———. *Man for Himself, an Inquiry into the Psychology of Ethics*. New York: Rinehart, 1947. A psychoanalyst delves into the nature of man.

HOBBES, THOMAS. *Leviathan* (Oxford: Blackwell, 1946). Part I, "Of Man," of this classic of political theory is replete with insights. Hobbes makes man's search for security fundamental.

HYMAN, HERBERT H. *Political Socialization: A Study in the Psychology of Political Behavior*. Glencoe, Ill.: Free Press, 1959. A summary of the literature in this rapidly growing field.

LANE, ROBERT E. *Political Life, Why People Get Involved in Politics*. Glencoe, Ill.: Free Press, 1959. A thorough and well-documented study by a leading student of political behavior.

LASSWELL, HAROLD D. *Power and Personality*. New York: Norton, 1948. Personality theory applied to politics and especially to problems of democratic leadership.

LOVEJOY, ARTHUR O. *Reflections on Human Nature*. Baltimore: Johns Hopkins Press, 1961. A study of political psychology, based on the works of the seventeenth- and eighteenth-century political philosophers.

MERRIAM, CHARLES EDWARD. *Political Power*. New York & London: McGraw-Hill, 1934. One of the most successful attempts to deal systematically and at length with this amorphous subject.

WALLAS, GRAHAM. *Human Nature in Politics*. 3rd ed. New York: Knopf, 1921. A study of the role of the irrational in politics and of how to cope with it. A modern classic.

CHAPTER 3

Sociological Foundations of Politics

PART I. BASIC CONCEPTS

The preceding chapter dealt with those elements of human nature most significant for the study of politics and government. Here we are concerned with the social and cultural matrix of politics. Some politically relevant patterns of behavior are imposed on man by the conditions of social life itself and certain psychological traits are brought out by society which in turn partly determine the social milieu. Beyond these considerations lies the additional fact that modern politics is increasingly one of the "Great Society"—a politics of multigroup bargaining, maneuver, strategy, and power in which group cohesion, channels of communication, access to influence or the influential, prestige and propaganda are counters in the political game.

Government is largely a mediated rather than a direct relation of state and citizen. Associations, the institutions and mores of society, are limiting channels for the satisfaction of individual needs, and they are the indispensable means. Society, in the form of a trade union or a blacklist can deny or assure a livelihood. Political influence for many a businessman, farmer, or sectarian is a matter of influence within or through his trade association, county agent, or church. And much of the impact of government is upon, or in relation to, social groups and their roles—the ground rules set and the powers sanctioned for these "subgovernments." What is true for democracy in this respect is only in degree less true for nondemocratic, even totalitarian governments. Studies of the Soviet Union reveal that the Kremlin too must make use of all kinds of organized groups, including trade unions, for the government of the state. These organizations are not simply instruments of government. They represent powerful social forces whose needs and desires must be taken into account. The vastness of the modern state, combined with the fact that increasingly the interests of the common man have everywhere achieved a recognition hitherto unheard of, accounts partially for the fact that organized and unorganized groups play such a vital role in the determination of policy. Also, the specialization of functions characteristic of an industrial society in which the division of labor has been pushed to great extremes, often makes the interest group a more significant political force than the town or district.

The definitions and descriptions offered below not only indicate how we shall use the terms in question, but also, by suggesting certain significant ideas and the relations of what they stand for to the political process, may help to avoid many common errors in thinking about politics. It is all too common to think of politics in terms of the state versus the individual, overlooking the rich and significant context of the individual's group memberships.

SOCIETY AND GROUPS; CLASS AND STATUS

We may define a "society" as a sizable group of people associated together more or less permanently, characterized by ordered relations mutually recognized by its members, and constituting norms of conduct for them. We also speak of "society" in the abstract, not referring to any particular group of people nor to humanity as a whole, but rather to the general fact of man's life in some society. It is the web of relations that is important, in any case, rather than the boundaries. Although states are sometimes spoken of as territorial societies, this manner of speaking might suggest an all-inclusiveness of social purpose that does not properly characterize the political institution.

The human social order is normally complex, involving many groups, associations and communities. By a *group* we mean any aggregation of people held together by mutual recognition of one or more common interests or common purposes. When such a group provides itself with an organization for the achievement of its purpose it becomes an *association*. While, as we shall see, the state is in certain respects unique, it corresponds very closely to the idea of an association. Finally, a *community* comprises all the people in a given area bound together by the ties arising out of neighborhood. It suggests strong ties of recognized common interest, but no organization.

Let us begin with the *group*—not the primary group, the family—but other groups of varying degrees of permanence and intensity. For our purposes the most significant property of the group is that of functional interdependence among the persons composing it. The group exists because of shared interests, evaluations, and purposes, which in turn imply the mutual dependence of its members upon each other for the realization of joint or shared objectives. The more stable and definite the purposes of the group, the greater is the tendency within it to evolve and to define a set of relations to which a member is expected to conform if he is to retain group membership. The individual member's behavior is controlled by allotting to him and securing his adherence to a *role:* a set of powers, rights, and duties that pertain to his position within the group—what is expected of him and what he has a right to expect of others.

Because a group does comprise a set of roles, group *norms* develop that reinforce and adjust these roles and the relations they entail, discriminating between legitimate and illegitimate aspects of particular roles from the standpoint both of behavior inappropriate for *any* member of that group and of behavior improper for a particular member. Thus, within some street-corner gangs no member of the group could retain his membership in the gang if he used the local police force as a makeweight in intragroup disputes. Moreover, if one or several members of the group attempted to displace the group leadership, it might be done only by disrupting the group itself.

Informal groups within formal organizations may be highly significant. Friendship groups within the United States Senate may have considerable influence on voting patterns. By the same token the Senate as a whole, because of its "clubbiness," may respond to powerful group norms not included in its official rules of procedure and of a nature different from, and even at odds with, what might be called the official theory of its role. Thus the institution of "senatorial courtesy"[1] frequently proves more powerful than party loyalty. Within formal organizations such as an administrative hierarchy informal group norms have a similar importance.

Social organization, even the informal kind, implies *status*—the ranking of an individual or a group according to an accepted hierarchy. Status does not imply immobility. A person's status may change as a result of his own merits and accomplishments; for instance, when he is promoted to a higher position. In a democratic society, this would be the normal experience. In some measure status is a necessary and beneficial adjunct to organization and the accomplishment of collective purposes. Within a work group or street-corner society, status facilitates communication and group action by creating a set of expectations that tend to direct the processes and techniques of consultation and decision-making. Status stabilizes the group by establishing a relatively fixed and coherent set of role-expectations.

The meaning of status may be further clarified and defined by means of another concept—*prestige*. Prestige signifies high reputation. It may go hand in hand with a particular status, but not necessarily. A workman who is especially skillful may enjoy great prestige among his fellow workmen and others for that reason. In the Soviet Union he might be singled out and given special status as a Stakhanovite. Then he would have a different status from that of his fellows and this recognition might further enhance his

---

[1] The custom or convention according to which senators refuse to vote to confirm a presidential nomination if the nominee is opposed by the senators of the president's party from the state of the nominee's residence.

prestige. As this example illustrates, both prestige and status may serve as rewards and therefore as incentives. A man's accomplishments may automatically give him prestige. The effect may be heightened if as a consequence he is given, or is recognized as having, a new and higher status. Prestige, a matter of reputation and the power that flows from reputation, is more personal than status. Both status and prestige attach to individuals. But prestige denotes a repute that derives from the personal achievements or abilities of an individual; status denotes position in the social hierarchy, however acquired and maintained. Thus, a doctor's wife may or may not have prestige in her own right, but is likely to enjoy high status as the spouse of a doctor—an esteemed profession.

Within the primitive tribe, status differentials and marks of special prestige serve as one of the primary means for stimulating competition among various clans in the fulfillment of public service. Similarly, in a bureaucracy or a private corporation, rank and status is symbolized in various traditional ways—by a private office, or an "outer office" for receiving visitors, and the like. Distinctions in status are an important part of income, often more valued even than money, for they entail unequivocal group recognition of the worth of personal expenditure of effort.

Status *tends* to order and divide society into entrenched and exclusive groups. Prestige accorded to distinction or merit is status only if it carries with it the notion of ranking according to an established hierarchy—as many a *nouveau riche* knows to his acute discomfort. The distinction was neatly made by Tocqueville when he noted that Americans anxiously and aggressively competed for prestige, but did not enjoy the security of status. As Max Weber observed, social status frequently involves a closing off of groups from society at large, devices for recruitment and expulsion from membership, whether by design or not, and often even a formal or informal group discipline to preserve the integrity of status codes.[2] The value of social status lies in its tendency to stabilize relations and to make particular expectations secure; its most common evils are these results carried to undesirable extremes.

Between a completely equalitarian society and a caste society there is a world of difference with an infinite number of gradations between the two extremes. These gradations are marked by differences in degrees or in fluidity of status. Even in such a well-established political democracy as Great Britain, for instance, social status still exercises great influence, although far less than in a semifeudal and socially stratified society like Spain. In the United States, on the other hand, status levels are much more fluid, ranks more easily attained or lost, although status has by no means disappeared.

[2] Max Weber: *Essays in Sociology*, trans. and ed. H. H. Gerth and C. Wright Mills (New York: Oxford U. P., 1946), pp. 187-191.

Generally, as status groups tend to cluster about certain broad public and private functions, they have been regarded as *classes*. The concept of "social class" is much wider than that of income group or occupational category. We shall use the term "class," to mean a stratum or wide aggregate of status groups primarily differentiated from other similar classes by occupation and mode of life. Thus, ancient and medieval society recognized a variety of servile classes, a clerical or a priestly class, a citizenry and a governing class, and several military classes. In primitive societies, mechanisms for creating status differentials may exist without identifiable classes; for example, when clans or subclans provide the primary foundation for group and status competition. Increasing division of labor and the inheritance of property and privilege tend to change this situation. Conversely, where styles of living or occupational divisions do not vary greatly or according to clearly discernible major patterns, for instance, in the United States, a society is sometimes spoken of as "classless."

COMMAND, POWER, AUTHORITY, LEGITIMACY

To understand the dynamics of social organization, we need also the concepts of command, power, and authority. Both within groups and in society at large, organization requires *the capacity to command*. Theoretically, command might not exist in a very small organization. All decisions might be made jointly, and group pressure ensure that they be carried out. But in any sizable organization, this mode of procedure soon becomes impossible. The press of time, the necessity for unity of purpose, the need for known procedure, and for reliable mechanisms to settle disputes, all work to create within any organization a hierarchy of command, more or less formal in character, extending from the top, often through numerous subordinate layers of authority and power down to the rank and file. All societies abound with such hierarchies of command. In society as a whole, size, complexity, and mutual dependence tend to increase the proportion of decisions that fall to command. One of the overriding problems of the contemporary political scene has become that of how to assemble the power and authority needed for this purpose, while keeping the aggregations of power and the dynamics of authority under control.

These concepts, power and authority, are slippery and require careful definition if they are to be useful and reliable for purposes of analysis. *Power,* here meaning "social power," we define as the capacity to influence or control others.[3] Influence and control are not easily distinguished, but

---

[3] Looked at from the point of view of the collectivity, power has been defined as "the capacity of a social system to mobilize resources to attain collective goods." Talcott Parsons, " 'Voting' and the Equilibrium of the American Political System," in Eugene Burdick and Arthur J. Brodbeck, *American Voting Behavior* (Glencoe, Ill.: Free Press, 1959), p. 81.

control generally implies more of the elements of constraint and sanctions than does influence. Some would distinguish between power and influence, confining the former to potential or actual control, where control is exerted by means of severe deprivation.[4] Others would confine power even more narrowly to the actual exercise of control or, more accurately, to participation in the making of decisions that control the activities.[5] Power, following David Easton's analysis, is called *manipulation* if the persons being influenced are unaware of it. The power of "hidden persuaders" falls in this category.[6] If power relies on rational arguments or winning consent, we speak of it as *persuasion;* finally, in an intermediate category, resides "authority." If one man accepts the command of another without questioning it or examining its justification, and yet not from pure fear or other external sanction, he is responding to authority. Generally, especially in the case of commands by public officials, he acts at least partly because he believes that it is right to obey commands from this source, this "authority" because they are "legitimate."[7]

It is self-evident that all governments must use power, must rely on it at every term, that it is of their essence. All governments too must place some reliance upon force. From the point of view of democratic values in particular, however, the distinction between power based on willing consent and power that operates by imposition is of the greatest importance.[8] Moreover, within the category of power by imposition, manipulation is from one point of view worse than bare force simply because it is so insidious.

Many other distinctions could be made among types and modes of power and authority, but the most significant for political science are those of formal or informal, with respect to authority, and concentrated or diffused, with respect to power. The authority that the doctor exercises may be almost entirely informal, dependent upon a neighbor's confidence in him and the deference that his manner inspires. In large-scale organizations, such as an army, titles and symbols of office are substituted for the informal and spontaneous social processes of ranking and ascription of authority. Power within an informal group is likely to be fairly well diffused, as evidenced by the process of group-wide bargaining and consultation that goes on when decisions are made. Power can also be both concentrated and diffused within

[4] Max Weber, for example. *The Theory of Social and Economic Organization,* edited by Talcott Parsons (New York: Oxford U. P., 1947), p. 152.

[5] Lasswell and Kaplan, *Power and Society, A Framework for Political Inquiry* (New Haven, Conn.: Yale U. P., 1950), pp. 74 ff. See also Carl J. Friedrich, *Constitutional Government and Democracy,* rev. ed. (Boston: Ginn, 1950), pp. 22 ff.

[6] Vance Packard, *The Hidden Persuaders* (New York: D. McKay, 1957).

[7] See David Easton, "The Perception of Authority and Political Change," in Carl J. Friedrich (ed.), *Authority* (Cambridge, Mass.: Harvard U. P., 1958), pp. 178 ff. The concept of legitimacy is discussed below, p. 58.

[8] The distinction made here is not identical with that between force and authority. While authority implies consent of a kind, it is compatible with a greater admixture of force, exerted or latent, than is the concept of "willing consent."

the same organization: for example, diffused among the divisions of a corporation, but concentrated within these divisions. In a democratic society, power is widely diffused; in an army command it is highly concentrated.

To the concepts already introduced, we must add that of *legitimacy*. This concomitant of political authority is an immensely significant factor in politics. Governments whose power is not considered "legitimate," which do not have at least this degree of acceptance by the bulk of the population, have little chance of surviving. Sometimes, when new governments are established by revolution, the governments of other states seek to undermine their authority by refusing to "recognize" them, implicitly implying that their power is not legitimate. Nowadays, however, the power of nationalist sentiment is so strong that action of this kind is likely to arouse widespread resentment against this "intervention," tending to defeat the purposes underlying nonrecognition. In July 1962, the United States refused to recognize a military regime that had seized power by *coup d'etat* from the constitutional government. Under such circumstances the action might have some effect of the kind intended. While legitimacy is fundamentally based upon moral considerations, upon people's belief in the "rightness" of a regime, these beliefs are affected by much more than the manner by which power was obtained. If the preceding regime was widely disapproved, had lost legitimacy, the resort to extralegal means to overthrow it, in the absence of effective democratic means, is not likely to stand in the way of popular acceptance of the new regime. The sheer effectiveness of a government, its ability to maintain order and security from foreign attack, to maintain public services, and to sustain some reasonable correspondence between expectations and reality in the economic realm, is likely to be of greatest significance in the long run. In the early stages, however, the other aspect of this reciprocal relation is likely to be most to the fore: a government cannot become effective without at least a measure of legitimacy; it cannot retain its legitimacy unless it becomes effective.

INSTITUTIONS

Closely related to both of the groups of concepts discussed above is that of an institution. By an "institution" we mean an established and recognized pattern of behavior characteristic of a group of people or a whole society, the violation or nonobservance of which causes some disturbance or discomfort in the group because it threatens widely held values. (Institutional practices have acquired legitimacy.) This definition includes institutions that are quite simple, like the practice of tipping, as well as exceedingly complicated ones, like the institution of private property. Institutions are often, but not necessarily, important social controls; and, as in the case of the institutions of property and of marriage, they are frequently given the support of law. In fact, the word *institution* sometimes is used broadly to cover whole complexes of institutions and institutional controls such as the state itself or the church.

These two institutions, state and church, together with the family, are among the most pervasive in human society. They are, in one form or another, almost coterminous with society. Together with economic institutions of various kinds, they provide much of the substance and also the form of any society.

The institutions in modern society constantly interact, especially those basic institutions that make competing claims upon the time and loyalty of almost all individuals. In some societies, as in that of ancient China, the family is the dominant institution and takes over most of the functions elsewhere performed by church and state. At other times and places, notably in Europe in the Middle Ages, the Church has been similarly dominant, whereas in the last century economic institutions were most fundamental. Today, in general, the political institution is primary.

Assuming a relatively free society, when some particular institution does become ascendant over others, its powers over them is limited because the drives and needs they express always create a certain degree of resistance to absorption. Rivalry among institutions, like that among groups, it may be observed, is characteristic of a healthy society, while a society in which one institution dominates all others—especially where it attempts by force or compulsive pressure to destroy them—cannot possibly do justice to the variety of human interests. It leads inevitably to stagnation or to revolution, or to each in turn. We are not suggesting that institutions should be mainly competitive in their mutual relations. In large measure they are rightly cooperative and are, moreover, functionally differentiated. But it is well that there should be rivalry at the margins among the great institutions of church, state, and family, if a proper balance of loyalties is to be maintained.[9]

ASSOCIATIONS

An "association" is a group with specified purposes and a more or less formal organization for their accomplishment. *"The* church" is an institution, but any particular church is an association. As contrasted with informal groups, associations are characterized by a separation between members and leaders, specialized interests of organized leadership, delegation of authority, and settled procedures for determining policy.

Associations, like societies, many groups, particular institutions, and the state itself, have the capacity of living beyond the lifetime of any particular member or set of members. From this point of view they might be more appropriately defined as a system of norms or rules governing their members with respect to their association membership. In accordance with these rules,

---

[9] See Frank Tannenbaum, "The Balance of Power in Society," *Political Science Quarterly,* **61** (1946), pp. 481-504.

officials are selected and empowered to act on behalf of the association, within stated limits, in accordance with prescribed procedures, and perhaps for stated purposes. Whether we think of individuals acting in accordance with a set of rules or of a set of rules governing the behavior of certain individuals is simply a matter of which side of the coin we are observing.[10]

The Multigroup Society and Democracy

As human capacities and interests vary greatly from individual to individual, men can assure their most satisfactory life and development only where there is a great number of different types of associations and less formal groups with which they may or may not affiliate themselves as they see fit. A healthy society will be one in which the individual has an abundance of opportunities for pursuing his own particular interests in collaboration with others. In general, the greater the number and variety of associations the better will be his opportunities.

Freedom to associate with like-minded individuals provides the indispensable basis for a stand against the overwhelming authority of society. A group or organization of eccentrics, for instance, frees the odd and peculiar by allowing them to find a sustaining and protective identification. Association, too, adds to the possibility of being heard or regarded with more than casual or contemptuous notice. With a voice in the court of public opinion, the dissident's efforts (for example with respect to suffrage or child labor) seem neither so futile nor so wrong-headed.

It is worth noting too that loyalty to the state is often derived rather than direct. Many citizens seldom think of the state as such, but they are loyal to a whole series of interlocking associations and institutions, some of them political and some not. This loose pattern of loyalties constitutes for them the real meaning of the society and the ground for their attachment to their nation as a whole.

Individuals may have interests and duties that conflict with those of the group or the association. Trade unions or business corporations may dominate the lives of their members to a degree incompatible with the interests of individuality. Sometimes the only remedy for such a situation is governmental intervention to protect the individual. But by far the most important means, in a modern democratic state, for insuring a healthy balance between individual and associational interests is to protect freedom of association and encourage competition among various groups and associations. In a pluralistic society many organizations compete with each other for loyalty and membership. The corporation that offers incentive plans, that provides facilities for recreation, that shoulders community burdens, is competing

---

[10] With respect to associations generally, and especially regarding the feature just discussed, see S. I. Benn and R. S. Peters, *Social Principles and the Democratic State* (London: Allen & Unwin, 1959), Ch. 11.

with other associations for membership and loyalty. Also, it is playing a role that might be assumed by a municipality, a trade union, or a church. In the competition for loyalty to their purposes, groups and associations offer services, answer needs. Government stimulates, regulates, and supplements, as well as participating in this competition. The whole process improves and equalizes the options among which the individual must choose, and the competition imposes on the group the condition that it respond to needs and desires if it is to acquire loyalties.

To suggest the importance of associations as *schools of government* is merely to point to the obvious fact that various associations such as the army, schools and universities, and occupational associations have an important part to play in the political socialization of the individual citizen.

As *subgovernments,* associations and institutions have another significance. They may become in practice an important device for allowing functions otherwise public or governmental to be cared for at the societal level through private, less formal, or more particular agencies. Thus trusts, equity, divorce, and wardship were once the province of ecclesiastical courts, exercising powers that would today be thought of as governmental and that even then were ultimately backed by the sanction of the state's authority. In a later age, private enterprise and free-market mechanisms in effect regulated a whole sphere of human activity. Now law and administrative regulation exercise extensive control in this sphere, but it is important to realize that government more generally cooperates with, corrects, and complements private activity than displaces it and that various methods of combining public and private endeavor are among the most important techniques by which a democratic government acts.

For the political scientist, probably the most important role of groups is a representative one, the articulation of interests. Here, we allude to what is sometimes termed the "group basis of politics."[11] Groups—more properly, associations—represent and speak for their members by appearing before legislative bodies, participating in the administrative process, and taking part in elections. In fact, their role in government is indispensable. They are sources of information, channels for communication, and centers for the development of collective political will that supplement the role of parties and the formal processes of government.

LAW

One of the prime features of society is a set of ordered relations and a matrix of institutions both reflecting and helping to create or sustain this order. All societies have rules or norms. By means of them the institutions of the society condition behavior. Some rules are vague and others are specific;

[11] Earl Latham, "The Group Basis of Politics: Notes for a Theory," *The American Political Science Review,* 46 (1952), pp. 376-397. The classic treatment of this subject is David B. Truman, *The Governmental Process* (New York: Knopf, 1951).

some are strictly enforced, while others are honored as much in the breach as in the observance. For, despite the traditional picture of custom and taboo-ridden cultures, nonconformity and violation of society's rules are problems everywhere.

Law constitutes the rules of a political society. Postponing a precise definition of law until later, we may note here two or three guides that will help mark it off from other social rules.[12] All societies have customs that no one would think of calling law. It may be the custom to have the main meal of the day at sundown, but no one would think it wrong for a family to do otherwise. Rules for worshipping the gods or performing magic may be considered religious rather than properly legal, although the line here may be vague. But rules that are socially useful, or thought to be, soon assume "rightness" in a unique sense. This peculiar quality we call "legal." Customs of this kind we speak of as "legal custom" or "customary law."

All law, customary or otherwise, has some method of enforcement, but the methods vary greatly in kind and degree. Enforcement may be left entirely to the injured individual, to members of his family, or it may be carried out by agents of the organized community. The means vary from mere expression of disapproval to the death penalty, and may include withholding of benefits, refusal to cooperate, ridicule, physical punishment, and banishment. When a society provides courts for the interpretation and application of law and organized force for its enforcement, we recognize that it has a system of law in the fullest sense of the word. Then, too, we have a state.

The Social Functions of Law

One of the most useful functions performed by law in any complex society is *to give definite statement to rights and duties* and to a minimally acceptable code of social behavior. Custom and informal devices may permit too much chicanery or evasion. Often in primitive society or in periods of social change, authority is shifting and obscure, and custom is surrounded by a penumbra of doubt. The certainty provided by a regime of law is sorely missed.

Both because of certainty of meaning and assurance of enforcement, law adds to the *predictability* of human behavior. Law enables men to make contracts with confidence that the other party will be compelled, if necessary, to carry out his undertaking. The effective freedom of the businessman to conduct his affairs would be disastrously circumscribed if he could not rely on the law to compel payment of debts. Custom may or may not be sufficient to provide the web of structured expectations that a given situation and set of social functions requires. Pedestrians on crowded sidewalks, partly by

---

[12] See pp. 127-130.

following customary patterns and partly by on-the-spot adjustments, achieve their objectives more fully and freely than they would if subjected to a legally defined and imposed traffic pattern. Yet without traffic laws, as a result of which drivers know what to expect of each other, the movement of automobiles, buses, and trucks on city streets would be chaotic, if not impossible. The art of government lies in separating the two cases, one in which custom is sufficient or even superior to law, the other in which custom requires the corrective of explicitly enjoined and generally enforced actions.

A further service performed by law is that of substituting *peaceful settlement of disputes* for brute force. This role of law is most obvious in primitive society. Among certain Eskimo tribes, for instance, the blood feud is the normal mode of resolving disputes. These feuds smolder on, embroil more and more families, with the result that numerous tribes have been actually exterminated as a consequence of their astoundingly bloody ways of enforcing "justice." Vigilantes, lynch law, and labor violence serve as reminders that this role of law remains vital even in contemporary societies. Despite its reliance upon force as a last resort, law is the great economizer of force and violence.

Lastly, law is important as *a technique of adaptation*, particularly in adapting old forms and procedures to changed conditions, in accordance with the society's sense of justice. If, for example, a norm of behavior requires universal conformity to be effective, law and not the spontaneous activities of society is needed to enforce it. Bad business practices may drive out the good; and if, for instance, the bad practice is competition through the use of sweated labor, a few malefactors may make good practice ruinous to those who try to adhere to them. Law is clearly demanded.

MYTHS, BELIEFS, AND IDEOLOGIES

Definition

Society is a network of ordered relations in which men are organized in many different ways and have their behavior, attitudes, and character determined by numerous established patterns in the form of institutions, customs, and law. It should be clear by now that men's attitudes are as important as their behavior, that their attitudes largely determine their behavior. "Attitude," however, is not broad enough to cover all the factors we have in mind. Every society is rife with formulas coupling together its valuations and beliefs, explaining or justifying its customs, institutions, and laws. These formulas, or myths, fulfill a vital function in providing psychological security. Their nature is neatly defined by a leading sociologist as "value-impregnated beliefs."[13] In this usage, it should be noted, the term is broader

---

[13] R. M. MacIver, *The Web of Government* (New York: Macmillan, 1947), p. 4.

than its common meaning as a story used to explain or justify a strongly held belief or a valued institution. Myths, in the sense here adopted, may include propositions that are true as well as those that are false, or that are partly true and partly false. They may also include assertions of the kind that cannot be said to be either true or false. The proposition that no man ought to be punished without a fair trial is, in the view of the authors, completely valid; but at the same time, especially when cast in terms of "the right to a fair trial," or "the right of every individual not to be deprived of his life, liberty, or property without due process of law," it becomes a part of the American myth, and of the myth of liberal democracy in general. In other words, it is not only accepted unquestioningly as valid, but it is one of the important elements of the democratic credo.

Complicated and Simple Myths

Myths may be either logically related systems of ideas (in which case they are often called "ideologies") or they may be single and unsubstantiated propositions. The taboos of primitive societies often rest upon the latter type of myths; for instance, the belief that the chief is descended from the gods, and that to raise a hand against him would be to incur divine wrath. Ideologies are generally complex rationalizations of a highly articulated set of beliefs, institutions, or patterns of organization. The liberal democratic myth, or belief system, including its specifically American version, lies somewhere between these extremes. It is worth noting that belief systems need not be internally consistent. In fact, they frequently embody contradictory propositions, reflecting the ambivalence of human nature. Finally, myths may be the deliberate creation of a particular leader or group of leaders, as in the case of the Nazi myth of "Aryan" superiority or the Communist myth of Marxism-Leninism; or, like folklore, their origins may be shrouded in antiquity, as is the case with the traditional "liberties of Englishmen."

Functions of Political Myths

Political myths provide a sense of security to the individual; they also add to society's security and stability. They give legitimacy to the government, the constitution, and the whole social order. Without this no regime can endure. The myths of individual rights, of equality, of "the American way of life" are stabilizing factors in American society.[14] Especially when values are in sharp conflict, as in the case of church-state controversies over

[14] Tensions between myth and reality operate also to stimulate conflict and progress. On the dynamic aspects of belief systems, see Gunnar Myrdal, *et. al., An American Dilemma —The Negro Problem and Modern Democracy* (New York: Harper & Row, 1944), Vol. II, pp. 1027-1070, methodological appendices by Arnold M. Rose.

aid to education or the great conflict of our time over racial integration, our political myths save us from disaster.

So important is a belief system to a society that it cannot function effectively without one, or at cross purposes to the one it has.[15] It is for this reason that great revolutions are always preceded by a period of intellectual ferment, when the intellectuals question and criticize the old reigning ideas, gradually undermining the popular adherence to them, and develop a new belief system to which loyalty to a new regime may attach. But it has not remained for modern anthropologists to recognize the importance of belief systems. Plato insisted in his *Republic* that the state should monopolize education and make great use of literature and mythology suitably revised or devised to give maximum support to the polity. The capstone of the system was the famous "myth of the metals" (or "convenient fiction," as Cornford calls it), designed to explain and give support to the Republic's class system.[16]

Throughout history religious beliefs have served not only to unite (as well as, on frequent occasions, to divide) peoples; they have also given specific support to the state and to a particular form of government and line of rulers. The most obvious example in our own tradition is furnished by the doctrine of the Divine Right of Kings. Among secular political theorists in previous ages who have been especially aware of the important political role of belief systems, Machiavelli, Montesquieu, and Rousseau are outstanding. Montesquieu in particular, like Aristotle centuries earlier, pointed out that each type and style of polity had its own distinctive system of beliefs and customs and that any attempt to legislate or organize the state that was not compatible with the existing belief system was likely to fail.[17] While Montesquieu stressed the importance of fitting the laws to the beliefs, Rousseau, at least when he wrote *The Social Contract,* was more optimistic about the possibility of creating the kind of state that was desirable and then creating an appropriate belief system for its support.[18] A now classic modern statement is contained in Gaetano Mosca's discussion of the "political formula." He writes: "According to the level of civilization in the peoples among whom they are current, the various political formulas may be based either upon supernatural beliefs or upon concepts which, if they do not correspond to positive realities, at least appear to be rational.

---

[15] Anthropologists tell of societies of head-hunters who, when forbidden by intruding Westerners from practicing their beliefs, refused to propagate and died out. For significant study of the operation of belief systems under difficult circumstances, see Alexander Leighton, *The Governing of Men* (Princeton, N.J.: Princeton U. P., 1945).

[16] See *The Republic of Plato,* translated with introduction and notes by Francis MacDonald Cornford (New York and London: Oxford U. P., 1955), Ch. X (412B-421C).

[17] See *The Spirit of the Laws,* by Baron de Montesquieu, trans. by Thomas Nugent, Introduction by Franz Neumann (New York: Hafner, 1949), Bks. III-VIII, XIX, XXIV.

[18] See Jean Jacques Rousseau, *The Social Contract and Discourses* (New York: Dutton, 1913), Bk. IV, Ch. VIII.

We shall not say that they correspond in either case to scientific truths. A conscientious observer would be obliged to confess that, if no one has ever seen the authentic document by which the Lord empowered certain privileged persons or families to rule His people on His behalf, neither can it be maintained that a popular election, however liberal the suffrage may be, is ordinarily the expression of the will of a people, or even of the will of a majority of a people.

"And yet that does not mean that political formulas are mere quackeries aptly invented to trick the masses into obedience. . . . The truth is that they answer a real need in man's social nature; and this need, so universally felt, of governing and knowing that one is governed not on the basis of mere material or intellectual force, but on the basis of a moral principle, has beyond any doubt a practical and a real importance."[19]

Revolutionary Myths

As the last statement implies, myths do not necessarily support existing authority. Some myths almost by their very nature are revolutionary. Myths that depict Utopia as attainable are bound to be revolutionary until Utopia is attained. Soviet Communism is based on the myth that once capitalism and the capitalist class is abolished, the state will wither away. One consequence of this fact is that today Soviet theoreticians have to expend great efforts to explain why the withering process has not yet begun, or to argue that it is in fact under way. The Christian belief in the equality of man has potential revolutionary implications in almost any society. Especially was this significant before the democratic era. Although for much of this period those implications were successfully hidden or disguised, often by the leaders of Christianity themselves, nonetheless their existence doubtless helped the Church play the role of effective counterweight to the claims of secular authority. At a later period the myth of equality and individual right did more than support one authority against another; it became actively anti-authoritarian.

Myths and Rational Criticism

Although myths by definition comprise beliefs that are held unquestioningly, they differ among themselves as to the ease with which they may be successfully subjected to rational criticism; and this for two reasons. In the first place, there may be little or much to criticize. Their assumptions may be true or they may be false; their implicit reasoning may be valid or fallacious. Second, their assumptions may be subject, in greater or less degree, to em-

---

[19] Gaetano Mosca, *The Ruling Class*, trans. Hannah D. Kahn, ed., rev., with introduction by Arthur Livingston (New York: McGraw-Hill, 1939), p. 71.

pirical verification, or they may be completely beyond that realm. Religious myths by their very nature are likely to fall in the latter category. Yet even these, when they are given political application, as in the extreme version of the doctrine of the Divine Right of Kings, are likely to become vulnerable to rational criticism. When divine sanction is claimed for every public act of patently evil rulers, and when the selection of reigning families obviously owes much to chance or even to knavery, not all the ingenuity of a Robert Filmer can long sustain the doctrine. On the other hand, the potentially democratic myth of the social contract is from the outset more easily subject to rational attack. Its initial assumption is not based on revelation. Rather it alleges certain factual foundations. "Men did agree. . . ." Where alleged facts and rational deductions from them are relied upon there is an open invitation to attack the myth on its own terms. To be sure it is the nature of myth to discourage all questioning, but the discouragement is weaker where the initial proposition is rationalistic.

To stop the analysis here, however, would be to miss what is perhaps the most important point of all. The strength of a myth does not rely simply upon its power to discourage criticism, but even more upon its power to withstand criticism. As long as the Divine Right doctrine was able to hold its critics at arms length it remained unscathed; but once rational attack secured an entering wedge, the structure collapsed like a house of cards. On the other hand, the idea of a social contract, weak as it is in detail, retains a remarkable degree of vitality in any society where in fact the idea of popular consent to the form of government is not too remote from the facts.

Myths as Organizing Ideas

The myth-based character of society adds an important dimension to politics: the notion of belief as not merely true or false, but as an organizing force of a special kind. To realize that most political disagreement derives from different beliefs and from different perceptions of reality is to make a major step in the understanding of the democratic process. The fact that the primary myths of a society are among its most important organizing formulae helps to account for, if not to explain entirely, the appeals of communism and nationalism in politics in which a great traditional myth has been irrevocably shattered. For example, several students of Chinese politics and history have commented that Communism to China was not only a dream for the future: it was at least as important to them simply because it gave them a coherent set of operative ideals upon which to unite, i.e., one creed rather than many.

Why, it is often asked, does it so frequently happen that newly emerging states or states that are experiencing or have recently experienced a great social revolution succumb to Communist ideology rather than attaching themselves to liberalism? Why is "their" myth more attractive, more powerful than "ours"? The search for an answer to this question must follow the path suggested by a distinction we have already made. Myths, we said, may be deliberately created by a Marx or a Hitler and a few of their followers, or, like Topsy, they may just grow. Usually, where social change is gradual, myths develop more or less automatically, without central direction. From time to time, a John Locke, a Thomas Jefferson, or an Abraham Lincoln will systematize a body of beliefs that have been slowly taking shape or will give them expression in words of such grace, elevation, and emotional compulsiveness that, like the Gettysburg Address, they become part of the national treasury of political sentiments. But no one of these formulations comprises the whole of the nation's political myth. The articulation of that whole is lost in its intricacy, in the fact of its diverse origins, and in the shadows of history. What is lost in terms of evident rationality is more than regained in the sentiment that attaches to things that are clothed with age and the smell of success. Also, a myth that has grown in response to felt needs over a long period of time is likely to fit those needs more accurately than one that is quickly devised. If at certain points the myth has not kept pace with the evolving life of society—as is almost sure to be the case—the flaw will not be serious, so long as the society is operating to the general satisfaction of its members. Where political, economic, and social organization keeps insecurity at a minimum, the need for myth is minimized.

The kind of myth that countries like the United States or Great Britain are likely to have, and that will best suit their needs, is not the kind that would have initial appeal in societies where social revolution is in process. Where change comes with revolutionary suddenness, tremendous insecurities are created by the breaking up of established ways of living and the reorganization of society based on new principles that run counter to the old belief-system. To assuage these insecurities, a new social myth has to be created and given wide currency within a short period of time. A country could no more adopt the myth of "the American way of life" overnight than it could adopt American folklore. To be sure the "right to revolution" is imbedded in our mythology, but by now it is overgrown by ideas more relevant to our present condition. Marxism, on the other hand, is literally made to order for a revolutionary society. It is a well-articulated whole, providing answers to every question, explaining both the necessity for current suffering and supporting faith in an ultimate Utopia—a Utopia, incidentally, that will embrace the democratic values of liberty and equality.

Seen in this perspective what needs explaining is not so much why Communism has found so many converts among newly emerging people as it is why it has not been far more successful. Fortunately, even ignorant, inexperienced, and excited people can sometimes see the vast chasm between Communist myth and Communist reality. This weakness is the Achilles' heel of the Communist ideological threat.

RULING CLASSES AND THE RULED

Although the concepts discussed thus far are all relevant to government and important for an understanding of politics, they do not deal exclusively with the governmental process. Some, like "law," "power," and "authority," come nearer being specifically political terms than others. The notion of a ruling class clearly falls in the category of the specifically political. It carries with it various ideas that are the subject of considerable difference of opinion among political scientists and the usefulness of the concept itself, as applied to a modern democratic society, is open to question. This latter attitude, shared by the authors, will be discussed in due course. For the moment we shall concentrate on the central concepts and the uses that have been made of them.

Theory of the Ruling Class

Many students of politics have argued that the multiplicity of power centers suggested by the foregoing discussion of groups, associations, institutions, and the like are of secondary importance. According to their view, politics is best understood simply in terms of rulers and ruled, or elites and masses. That rulership may actually be exercised through means other than law or by institutions and associations other than the state, they do not deny. The important point, they assert, is that a fairly determinate class of people effectively determine the goals and allocate the values in a given society. They operate through government, the military, churches, business, labor organizations, and in many other ways. This fact, rather than the complexities of social structure and behavior, is what counts. Whether the rulers are called "the nobility," "the Establishment," "the ruling class," or whether they are completely overlooked, is of little importance, according to this view. The fact is they are there, they exercise controlling power and determine the course of society. Their methods may be crude or subtle, they may rely heavily upon coercion or they may secure assent to their actions by a variety of manipulative devices, but their will is done.

A classic statement of this position was elaborated by the famous Italian political scientist, Gaetano Mosca. He declared that "the dominion of an organized minority, obeying a single impulse, over the unorganized majority is inevitable."[20] He further contended that "the larger the political community, the smaller will the proportion of the governing minority to the

[20] Gaetano Mosca, *The Ruling Class*, *op. cit.*, p. 53. See also James H. Meisel, *The Myth of the Ruling Class: Mosca and the Elite* (Ann Arbor: Univ. of Mich. Press, 1958). Theories in many ways similar to Mosca's were developed at about the same time by another Italian, Vilfredo Pareto. See his *The Mind and Society*, trans. Andrew Bongiorno and Arthur Livingston, 4 vols. (New York: Harcourt, 1935). A contemporary version of the ruling class theory is set forth by C. Wright Mills in *The Power Elite* (New York: Oxford U. P., 1956).

governing majority be."[21] In supporting the proposition that a minority class always rules, Mosca was stating a position that would have been widely accepted. When Plato described his ideal state, he divided the inhabitants into three classes, the uppermost being the ruling class. In this respect his ideal was in accord with contemporary practice. In all the Greek city-states of his day, the population was divided into distinct classes of landowners, artisans, merchants, slaves, and so forth; normally, certain classes were excluded entirely from participating in government, while political power was frequently the monopoly of a single class. Aristotle and subsequent students of politics down to modern times likewise assumed that the people of any state could be classified into rulers and ruled.

Nor was it generally assumed that the effective rulers were confined to those who held the principal posts of state. In most states in stable times, so the argument ran, the actual rulers were selected from, and governed in the interests of, an identifiable class of persons. Wealth, race, birth, military achievements, education—these and other factors, singly or in varying combinations—served to mark off the rulers from the ruled. In Machiavelli's terms, sometimes lions and sometimes foxes have been in the ascendant. In times of disorder and political expansion, military skills tend to be at a premium and determine the composition of the ruling class. In more stable periods in the past, economic power derived from the ownership of land was a more potent factor. Herein lay the foundation for Marx's oversimplified generalization that owners of the instruments of production are the ruling class.

Comment

Before going further with the discussion of the notion that rulers are selected from a particular class, we must note and consider one of Mosca's further assertions about the ruling class; namely, that it obeys "a single impulse." Here we are dealing with a very dubious proposition. Those who have defended Mosca's thesis have not bothered to examine whether the putative ruling class always or even generally acted as a unit. Even a cursory glance at history shows countless instances in which ruling classes were sharply divided over matters of policy. In a modern democracy, as we shall see, these divisions among the powerful become so extensive as to cast doubt on the validity of the whole theory. The burden of proof is upon those who would show that in American society, for instance, the leaders of big business, the military elite, the technologists, and scientific professionals act in unity. No convincing evidence to this effect has been adduced.

Returning to the concept of the ruling class itself, reference above to times of stability and times of disorder suggests that the history of ruling classes has been by no means smooth. Sooner or later ruling classes have lost their power. Some have been much more successful than others in retaining

21 *Ibid.*

their position. The more adaptable a class proves itself to be in the face of changing conditions the more likely it is to hold on to its power in the long run. A class that refuses to make concessions may maintain its position for a considerable period, but the ultimate outcome of such a policy is certain to be violent revolution. A corollary of the adaptability proposition is that a ruling class must avoid degeneration into a closed group or caste if it is to be enduring. It must be an open class, providing an opportunity for the most able and ambitious members of other classes to gain entrance, and also must have the means to rid itself of its own least qualified members. In short, to borrow from Pareto, there must be ample opportunity for "the circulation of the elite." The existence of such opportunity, increases the likelihood that the minority will not act with "a single impulse."

A ruling class that fails to keep itself open for recruitment of new blood may lose power suddenly and completely; for example, through a successful revolution. Frequently, however, what happens is that another class gains concessions. For instance, it may gain the right to vote or it may compel an alteration in the law governing the tenure of land, as is happening frequently today in underdeveloped countries in which old elites are being subjected to pressure from below. The dynamics of situations of this kind operate in two ways, both tending to qualify if not to nullify the ruling class thesis. Differences within the ruling class tend to be enlarged by the tendency for one group to appeal to outside groups for support. Moreover, where that appeal takes the form of extending the suffrage—as happened at successive stages in England during the nineteenth and early twentieth centuries—the result is to spread the power of ruling over more and more groups in the society. Thus the ruling class is at once weakened by internal division and by the accession to positions of power of new groups. In an expanding commercial and industrial society, these new groups tend to comprise a large and rather heterogeneous middle class, which tends to moderate the struggle for power between rich and poor, and casts doubt on the whole concept of a ruling class as applied to such a society.

Although the last few paragraphs have referred specifically to democratic Britain and the United States, much the same could be said, in varying degrees, of other industrial societies. In this era of the "common man" even a totalitarian regime such as the Soviet Union is far less monolithic than is generally supposed. The rulers must listen to the ruled, and many people belong to groups whose power or influence is of a middle rank, so that it would be hard to say whether or not they belonged to the "ruling class."[22]

[22] To be sure the official Communist line denies that any such thing as a social class exists in the Soviet Union. In large part this is a matter of semantics: the Russians would probably not deny that in their society some possess more political power than others; but they would contend that the opportunity to become a power-wielder was equally open to all, with no advantage accruing by virtue of birth or other adventitious circumstance. But even this modified statement is refuted by the evidence. See, for instance, Milovan Djilas, *The New Class* (New York: Praeger, 1957).

Classes, Rulership, and Contemporary Politics

The last remark suggests a final point with which we shall conclude this discussion. We have shown how ruling classes tend to disappear in modern states and how power becomes dispersed. One who would understand the dynamics of the modern state must deal not only with power, but also with influence. Where one shades off into the other is difficult to say; it is a matter of degree. But the concept of "the influential" is of more value to the modern political scientist than that of "the rulers."

This state of affairs is about what has come to pass in modern America and, to some extent, in certain other countries, such as Great Britain. America is not a "classless society"; but our classes are numerous, amorphous, and ill-defined. Polls show that most people consider themselves members of the "middle class," whatever that means. Countless factors—from movies and TV to the ubiquitous automobile and the increasing generality of higher education—serve to breach the lines of class and blur the distinctions. No longer does dress provide a clear indication of rank. Styles in clothing, slang, and other matters tend to permeate the whole of society, often originating near the bottom of the socioeconomic pyramid and spreading upward.

Moreover, class alignments are rivalled by others for political purposes. When it is a matter of bargaining for wage rates, employer and employee will generally line up as called for by the principles of a class-conscious society. But the issue of whether or not the tariff on watches is to be raised is pretty certain to bring about a united front between worker and "capitalist" that defies class distinctions.

In saying that in contemporary America—or Britain—no class rules, we are not only saying something about what has happened to classes, we are also saying that the very nature of "ruling" has changed. The word implies the existence of a ruler. It was easy to transfer the idea from a single individual to a class, but when classes give way to multiform societies "ruling" gets lost in the shuffle. Doubtless many a frustrated businessman or reformer, wishing to get something done quickly and finding himself thwarted at every turn wishes there were a ruler whose word was law. Unfortunately for him, or perhaps fortunately in the long run, it is not so simple. Even if he finds an official or a body having the authority to do what he wants, he will discover they are by no means free agents. Their effective power is limited by the necessity for considering the interests and demands of so many different groups that a good question is just who is ruling who. At least the question may *seem* good until one realizes that "ruling" is no longer an appropriate concept for understanding the workings of American government.

Power in America, even political power, is hopelessly dispersed. It may converge again at appropriate times and places, but it doesn't stay that way. It was centralized enough when President Truman dismissed General MacArthur as army commander in Korea. He took the action and stood by it.

But when he seized the steel mills to prevent a strike the Supreme Court intervened and re-established the *status quo ante*. Absolute power is nowhere to be found. Almost everyone possesses at least a microscopic amount of political influence. Most of us fall somewhere along a continuum between possessing absolute power and having none at all. Influence, of a group if not of a person, gradually merges into predominance. But no identifiable group is predominant in all matters. Seldom does one get its own way even on any practical question of much importance.

Even the word "compromise" does less than justice to the complexity of most political situations. Generally, many forces are at work and the final outcome is more analogous to what physicists call a "resultant" than to a compromise. Much of the fascination of politics derives from watching maneuvers that precede a showdown. Often a more or less prolonged period of testing, of feeling out of positions, goes on. Frequently, political power and economic power are involved in the same struggle.

In short, the concepts of ruler and ruled, of ruling class and subjects have given way to one of dynamic equilibrium. Not one, but many organized minorities contend with one another for power; none hopes to rule. At most they hope to have more power than others in the particular area or areas of their concern. Different minorities are active on different issues. Eastern consumers of Texas oil and natural gas battle over the regulation of the natural gas industry; coal interests are also involved, but the American Farm Bureau Federation is quite willing to sit this one out. Moreover, the same individual may find himself giving his support to the American Legion on one issue and opposing it on another. In a modern democracy the kaleidoscope has replaced the ruler and the political resultant is no more the product of a single human will, or even a united group of human wills, than is the weather.[23]

"Elites"

We have dealt up to this point primarily with the concepts of ruling classes and the ruled, rather than with the more modern terms, "elite" and "masses," for the simple reason that the former terms are somewhat less vague than the latter. Recent academic discussion, however, has largely been

[23] The thesis advanced above is not uncontested, as reference C. Wright Mills, *op. cit.*, p. 324. He writes: "The top of American Society is increasingly unified, and often seems wilfully coordinated: at the top there has emerged an elite of power. The middle levels are a drifting set of stale-mated, balancing forces: the middle does not link the bottom with the top. The bottom of this society is politically fragmented, and even as a passive fact, increasingly powerless: at the bottom there is emerging a mass society." Mills asserts far more than he proves. Evidence of regularly unified action on the part of the military, economic, and political elites has not been presented. For a critique of the Mills thesis, see Daniel Bell, *The End of Ideology* (Glencoe, Ill.: Free Press, 1960), pp. 43-67. Robert Dahl calls the American pluralistic system, as he found it in a detailed study of New Haven, Conn., one of "dispersed inequalities." Robert A. Dahl, *Who Governs? Democracy and Power in an American City* (New Haven: Yale U. P., 1961), p. 85.

cast in the latter terms. The term "elite," in particular, has the advantage of greater flexibility, which is precisely what makes it so difficult to discuss in general terms. When employed by C. Wright Mills, for example, it means substantially the same as Mosca's "ruling class." The political scientist, Harold Lasswell, however, defines the term as "those with most power in a group," noting the existence also of a "mid-elite" and a "mass."[24] That such a group exists in every political society is plainly evident, if not axiomatic. Its size, he remarks, is usually small compared with that of the mass.[25] But the flexibility, not to say the elusiveness of this concept, is indicated by another passage from the works of the same author. "The political elite," he declares, "comprises the power holders of a body politic. The power holders include the leadership and the social formations from which leaders typically come, and to which accountability is maintained during a given generation." In the same passage an "open elite," in which "a very considerable number of the members of a body politic are included" is distinguished from a "closed elite," which embraces only a few.[26] The remarks above about the nebulousness of the elite in a society like our own—a decidedly "open society" with a corresponding "open elite"—is not to deny the utility of the concept for the political analysis of less fluid and less pluralistic societies.

For all societies, but especially one like our own, political leadership is of immense, often critical importance. By definition, leaders influence more than they are influenced. Typically, they are characterized by a high degree of political empathy, enabling them to enter vicariously into the experiences and feelings of their followers, to express their needs and wants and, in a wide variety of ways, generate the requisite political support to achieve their satisfaction. Political leaders may hold positions of authority, such as the President of the United States, or they may be as informal and unofficial and parochial as a village storekeeper talking politics with his customers who tend to accept his opinions. They may be administrators, legislators, professional politicians, journalists, officers of pressure groups, distinguished citizens—almost anything. The more diverse and complicated a society is, the greater its demands upon political leadership, and the more leadership must be suffused throughout the body politic as well as exerted by persons in the positions of highest authority. The omnipresence of *Agitprop* (a branch of the Communist Party mechanism devoted to the task of political education and represented throughout the Soviet Union in even the smallest work units), testifies to the fact that the Soviet political elite is as aware as anyone of the importance of this function for the modern state.[27]

[24] Harold D. Lasswell and Abraham Kaplan, *Power and Society*, *op. cit.*, p. 201.

[25] *Ibid.*, p. 202.

[26] Harold D. Lasswell, *et al.*, *The Comparative Study of Elites* (Palo Alto, Calif.: Stanford U. P., 1952), p. 13.

[27] The literature on the subject is extensive. The student is referred particularly to

PART II. TRENDS AND TENDENCIES

We have discussed some aspects of society most relevant for political science. While we have referred to change, including revolutionary change, a description of separate elements (especially such building blocks of society as groups, classes, institutions, and associations), tends to give a static picture. Civilized society is dynamic and constantly changing. Thus, government is less a matter of "governing" in the more traditional sense than it is one of responding to change, anticipating it, controlling it, and even stimulating change in many ways.

We do not propose to discuss the many kinds of social change that may have some significance for political science, for most social trends are only incidentally relevant to politics or political science. (The student may find Table I suggestive of relations between the study of sociology and political science.) All governments rest upon a political system. *Ipso facto*, the relations of social impulse and political response are indirect, that is, mediated by the mechanisms of government and politics. Sociological factors and trends in social change have to be translated into the currency of politics. Also, the boundaries between the state and society are partially set by constitutional prohibitions and by the "political formula" or accepted elements of political style within a particular country. Governments usually can and do adjust polity to society or the society to the polity in the rather flat-footed fashion of limited diagnosis and marginal adjustment that Karl Popper has called "piecemeal social engineering,"[28] though occasionally social trends cumulate to give one "movement" (e.g., "integration"; "modernization") a distinctive urgency or thrust.

Some of the propositions advanced in earlier philosophies of history and comprehensive theories of society and its patterns of change do in fact reflect broad social tendencies in a way that aids in understanding the more specific developments of any particular time and place. System-builders like Hegel and Marx in the nineteenth century and Spengler and Toynbee in the twentieth have attempted to explain, in all-inclusive terms, the "meaning" of history and destiny of man. Today, most people are skeptical of such grandiose systems, despite the promise they hold of getting "on the side of

---

Alvin W. Gouldner (ed.), *Studies in Leadership* (New York: Harper, 1950), and Lester G. Seligman, "The Study of Political Leadership," *American Political Science Review*, 44 (1950), pp. 904-915. For a discussion of leadership in the context of democratic theory, see J. Roland Pennock, "Democracy and Leadership," in William N. Chambers and Robert H. Salisbury (eds.), *Democracy in Mid-Twentieth Century* (St. Louis, Mo.: Washington U. P., 1960), pp. 95-125.

[28] Karl Popper, *The Poverty of Historicism* (London: Routledge & Kegan Paul, 1957) pp. 51-59; 64-70. See also Charles Lindblom, "The Science of Muddling Through," *Public Administration Review*, 19 (1950), pp. 79-88.

history." We suggest, however, that such studies rightly point to social tendencies outside the political system (perhaps in the nature of man) that work themselves out, often despite anything that governments—even totalitarian governments—can do.

TABLE I

FORMS OF SOCIAL CHANGE

1. Cultural unification. For example, adoption of common modes of speech, dress, and behavior. More broadly, the development of a set of British mores, or an American "sense of national community."

2. Secularization of culture. In earlier history, such tendencies as "humanism"; more recently, changing attitudes toward such things as alcohol and temperance, marriage and divorce.

3. "Enlightenment" or cultural "improvement." The diffusion, for example, of more "rational" or more "humane" standards of behavior in relation to work, business practices, care for the aged, or the treatment of juvenile delinquency.

4. Changes in sanctions and incentives. Breaking down of family control; or a growing responsiveness to "professionalism" and its attendant sanctions and incentives—for example, the professional movement in business management, or administration.

5. Social mobility (horizontal and vertical). People "follow the job"; families in different social strata intermarry.

6. Increasing pluralism. A tendency for groups to form freely in response to needs for concerted action, and for membership in groups to be fairly open.

7. Changes in the structure of groups. The separation of ownership and management in the corporation; the growth of multi-employer collective bargaining; the federation of cooperatives.

8. Demographic changes. Aging populations; the population "explosion."

9. Urbanization.

10. Education.

11. Alteration in tastes. For example, the desire for more leisure as opposed to more disposable income; a better house rather than a better car (or two cars).

12. Improved communication. Alterations in the pattern of communication between groups, such as techniques which implement collective bargaining; also, the technology of rapid transit and television.

13. Changes in the forms of production and distribution. For example, the decentralization of many branches of industry, the centralization of others.

14. Technological changes.

In the pages that follow, we have singled out as especially important the tendencies toward freedom, toward justice, and toward ethnocentrism. We do not suggest that these tendencies work in a simple or unilinear fashion—for indeed they often oppose or qualify each other—and extrinsic factors, such as technological developments, rapid growth of populations, or the state of international relations condition their relative force at any given time. Our contention is only, as Engels once said of economic factors, that they "finally assert themselves."

THE TENDENCY TOWARD FREEDOM

It appears, as Hegel maintained, that over the course of history societies have tended to develop forms and institutions that provide for greater individual freedom. True, the technological complexity of the modern world has subjected man to distant forces beyond his control, has greatly increased his dependence upon other people, and accordingly has forced him to accept restraints that run counter to his immediate interests and desires. But in most cases his acceptance of these restraints is ultimately won because he recognizes that his effective liberty is thereby increased. Also, men's competences grow, and as they grow their claim to use their new powers is pressed more urgently. Men who read soon demand the right to judge for themselves the issues they study.

An increasingly complex world places limits upon certain freedoms, it also enables and even requires expansion of freedom in other respects. Generally, the more complex the technical organization of a society, the more necessary is the willing collaboration of subordinate and superior, the more valuable is consultation, and the greater the scope that must be afforded independent judgment and self-reliant conduct. Also, wealth and material surplus, which have certainly grown over the centuries, work for freedom. Material riches lessen the necessity to subjugate populations to the purely instrumental task of winning the bare surplus of goods needed for government, defense, and leisure of the few. Also, wealth, especially liquid wealth, enhancing the opportunities that freedom affords, makes it more precious In short, we are saying two things: first, that man's proclivity to seek opportunities for developing and exercising his powers exerts a constant pressure toward enlarging the area of individual freedom; and second, that technological developments, while they often occasion new restraints, bring new opportunities and demands for freedom.

The general liberating trend is intimately related to the increase in the use of reason. Freedom from tradition and authority permits man to make greater use of his reason. At the same time, reason is itself a liberating factor. The man who uses his reason to calculate the probable consequences of a number of alternative lines of action, then concludes which would contribute most to his ultimate purposes, is more effectively free than one who only follows the strongest impulse at any given moment, for impulsive actions may be mutually self-defeating and are likely to conflict with settled purposes. It is the nature of reason to bring conflicting elements into a harmonious pattern, to create order out of disorder, with all the liberating effects that that entails.

The results of the tendency towards rational calculation may be observed in various ways. For example, contrast the primitive societies with our own. In the former (even when allowance is made for the fact that earlier accounts of primitive conformism were exaggerated) , taboos, superstitions, and customary law leave small scope for spontaneity. All are brought up in the same beliefs, trained and compelled to practice the same religious rites. All are hemmed in by the same irrational fears. Choice of mates is rigidly circumscribed by elaborate rules. Men's and women's occupations and daily routines of activities are subject to the narrowest possible range of choice. The history of civilization has been marked by many ups and downs in human freedom, but the net result provides persuasive evidence of a tendency in human affairs toward the removal of barriers to freedom. In modern society, technological advance (itself a product of the free use of human reason) , relative freedom from superstition and other irrational restraints, and a general attitude that is favorable to variations in beliefs and behavior, assure most people a degree of freedom, and a range of varied satisfactions for their diverse personalities that are undreamed of in tribal societies.[29]

Something of the same contrast exists between different periods in the development of civilized society. The most familiar example is the Renaissance. That period was characterized by revolt against the authority of the Church and the restrictive laws and customs of feudal society. The general trend of development in succeeding centuries has been aptly described by Sir Henry Maine, the great English legal historian, as a movement from status to contract; from a situation where a man's ways of life was determined by the group, class, and calling he inherited, to one where he was largely able to master his fate and determine his rank by the free bargains he made as an individual. Even though in certain respects, this trend has been modified of late, most modern limitations on free contract are designed to create equalities between contracting parties, and so to expand man's overall liberty. In fact, in many areas the system of free contract is maintained and increased. For instance, each decade finds women free to engage in occupations previously barred to them. Negroes also have been making steady gains of the same kind. The trend has been one of gradual erosion of arbitrary distinctions and servitudes, and their replacement by a system of rights and obligations possessing a rational basis.

Many writers would take a less optimistic view of the long-term trend toward liberty than we have been suggesting. Professor Sorokin, for example, argues that liberty on the whole has not increased at all through the ages.[30] Others who might not be willing to subscribe to Sorokin's sweeping statement would nevertheless hold that limitations inherent in a mass society at least prevent any increase in liberty. It is true that liberty manifests itself in so many ways that it is difficult to measure it "on the whole." While certain

---

[29] It must be remembered, however, that modern society imposes its own restraints and attendant frustrations.

[30] Pitirim Sorokin, *Society, Culture, and Personality* (New York: Harper & Row, 1947), p. 474.

gains are being noted, counterbalancing losses may escape the eye. (But the reverse of this proposition is equally true.) The essential point here relates to a tendency rather than a trend. It is true that new conditions have sometimes brought about great losses of liberty for extended periods.

But the Roman Empire, and still more, republican Rome, had known far more freedom than the centuries that followed the collapse of Roman power, while the liberty of classical Athens, short-lived though it was, is proverbial. In general, however, the reversions from freedom in human history have accompanied some great crisis in affairs brought about by enlargements of the area subject to common government (Greece), the amalgamation of civilized with previously uncivilized peoples (Middle Ages), or the adjustment to economic transformations largely caused by developments in technology (the present).[31] Human reason and the will to freedom may prove unable to cope with the problem of organizing a free society under the conditions brought about by modern science. It may, but the historical record does not support such a presumption. Thus far, regardless of periodic reversions, the long-term trend has been toward that increase in the scope of effective and significant individual choice that is the heart of freedom. Today, however, the explosive pace of population growth and the threat of nuclear war pose hazards whose ultimate impact no one can foretell.

THE DEMAND FOR JUSTICE

Like "liberty," "justice" has meant different things to different people and at different times.[32] Yet throughout the ages there has been a common core of agreement. Where men might not agree on the precise dictates of

---

[31] Chapter 20 is devoted to a discussion of totalitarianism.

We have been viewing liberty largely from the angle of that freedom over which the state has some control. Many believe that the coming of mass society, with mass media, mass culture, and of course mass production, is imposing upon society a cult of conformism. People accept the same standards, do not wish to deviate, except marginally, and are intolerant of anyone who does not conform. They seek "adjustment" rather than freedom. Of all this, according to this widely held theory, McCarthyism was just one especially blatant outcropping in the political sphere. See especially David Riesman, *The Lonely Crowd* (New Haven: Yale U. P., 1950). To attempt to evaluate this thesis would take us beyond the purview of this book. Suffice it to say that the evidence offered by most writers of this cast of thought deals with a short period of time and the data are not available for comparing social conformism today with what has prevailed at various past periods. We stated earlier that conformism is a marked characteristic of primitive societies. In the mid-nineteenth century, generally thought of as an individualistic age, John Stuart Mill was greatly exercised about the prospects for liberty. "The disposition of mankind," he wrote, in his essay "On Liberty," "whether as rulers or as fellow citizens, to impose their own opinions and inclinations as a rule of conduct on others, is so energetically supported by some of the best and by some of the worst feelings incident to human nature, that it is hardly ever kept under restraint by anything but want of power . . ." John Stuart Mill, *Utilitarianism, Liberty and Representative Government* (New York: Dutton, 1910), p. 77.

[32] The meanings of these terms are discussed in Chapter 6.

justice, they nonetheless were in broad agreement as to what was unjust and therefore what common abuses were to be fought against. To punish a man for another's act, unless he were in some way responsible for that person, has probably universally been thought unjust, as well as to punish him for an act he did not and could not have known was wrong. Likewise, to treat unequally people who were in all relevant respects equally situated, has uniformly been conceded to be almost the prototype of injustice. Men often disagree as to what is relevant under given circumstances; but here, too, diversity of judgment is not without limit, and it is generally agreed that justice demands that departure from the rule of equal treatment be somehow justified, whether in terms of need, effort, contribution to society, or other generally accepted principle. It is with this equalitarian aspect of justice, rather than with retributive justice, that we shall be concerned here. The demand for justice in this sense has always provided a powerful force in politics. For centuries men might accept an inferior status and think it right, but let them once gain the idea they were in a significant sense equal to those who enjoyed power or privilege and their sense of outrage knows no bounds.

Here, as in the case of liberty, the course of history has not been regular nor its direction unswerving. Primitive societies provide less contrast with the present than in the case of liberty. In such societies, the standard of living is generally so low as to admit only limited economic differences; caste is not a common phenomenon, and government is likely to be so rudimentary that, regardless of the location of political power, differences in its distribution seem, to the outsider at least, to be of small import (although it is possible they assume great significance in the eyes of the participants). Moreover, the early development of civilized society, with its great capacity for producing wealth and great organization of power, supplied both the opportunity and the need for the concentration of wealth and power in the hands of a few. The inevitable accompaniment of this evolution, in Egypt, in China, in early Greece and Rome, was the growth of social classes and the establishment of systems of privilege.

The history of Greece and Rome discloses a series of alternations between the power of the privileged and wealthy few and that of the masses, with at least some parallel shifts in the distribution of wealth. Not until the Commercial and Industrial Revolutions can it be said that these periodic swings of the pendulum gave way to a secular trend. As soon as the power of landed property began to decline in favor of other forms of wealth that were more fluid and that depended on skill and brains for their acquisition and retention, the situation was fundamentally altered. Since then the power of privileged classes has been vulnerable to attacks of the masses, at least those of the talented masses. Income from skill or the "rent of brains" as the Fabian Socialists termed it, could compete with other forms of rent. The base of power has been broadened by the same technological progression.

The cheap firearms of the serf could penetrate the expensive armor of a lord. The printing presses and literacy broke the monopoly of writing skills and made possible a popular bureaucracy. Diversities of economic interest, in common with advancing technology, have led first one privileged class, then another, to seek the favor of the masses in order to conquer their rivals, whether by force of arms or, at a later stage, through the ballot box. Sensible of these same trends, over a century ago Alexis de Tocqueville wrote:

> The gradual development of the principle of equality is . . . a providential fact. It has all the chief characteristics of such a fact: it is universal, it is lasting, it constantly eludes all human interference, and all events as well as all men contribute to its progress. (Alexis de Tocqueville, *Democracy in America*, Reeve trans., ed. Phillips Bradley, [New York: Knopf, 1945] Vol. I, p. 6.)

Technological and economic change here provided both condition and incentive for the evolution toward equality. Mass production has made mass consumption, even of yesterday's luxuries, not only a possibility, but also a virtual necessity. The continued health and expansion of the economy demands it. And one of the first consequences is the sharp diminution of class and caste styles and modes of living.

Equally important, however, is the tendency for any society to develop ideals of social justice embodying equalitarian concepts. These ideals and the legal systems that, in large measure, embody their demand for equal treatment for those who are similarly situated can be powerful engines working for equality. The diffusion of culture and a rising cultural level also promote equality by blurring the lines of division between patron and client, citizen and immigrant, and putting arbitrary inequalities on an awkward footing. Both trends reflect a powerful human compulsion to insist that all differences in treatment or condition be related to a recognized difference in merit.

Although the development of equality may be a providential fact, it generates its own opposing forces, which often check the trend toward equality and even reverse it for substantial periods of time. We all desire unity with our fellow man, and this powerfully supports equality. But we also desire to use our creative energies and feel our powers grow through work and challenge. We love approbation and deference, and so seek distinction. The able as well as the privileged tend to be enemies of equality. The consequence is, as Aristotle long since observed, that two ideals of justice— absolute equality and relative equality—are constantly at war with each other. Equality of opportunity itself tends to be self-defeating, at least in the second generation. A man whose abilities enable him to get ahead of others financially is able to provide for his children benefits of schooling, connections, and "background," that give them a head start against their less fortunate fellows. Further, there is a persistent tension between the principles of absolute equality and of functional inequality. Hard and dangerous work merits special incentives. According to an old proverb, "Eat well or sleep well." The deserts of the man who takes the cares of his job home with him are greater. His needs are greater. Few and rare are the men who can sustain extra effort and not wonder "whether it is all worth it," without tangible proofs that their effort is valued. The conflict has to do with whether effort should be rewarded, and, if so, how much. In the political sphere we find men disputing as to whether all men should have equal power or whether it should vary in accordance with intelligence or knowledge of political affairs.

What is significant, today, however, is how few would argue that "the masses" should be denied all political power, or that any group should have power because of their birth rather than because of their contribution to society.[33] Our modern civilization has narrowed the distance between the pinnacle of society and its base, and has also broadened the base. Functionless privilege yields to the more rational perquisites of the talented and the energetic. Modern communications, transportation, and industrial processes have made both government and market decisions sensitive to the masses. The power of governors becomes more dependent upon numerous aids, the support of many different elites, representing diverse specializations, and the morale of the whole population. Possibly, an elite of skill, such as the Soviet Communist Party could entrench itself in privilege, defend its power, and hold power indefinitely. But it could do so only by continuing to be responsive to these tendencies. It must inevitably share and broaden its rule.

ETHNOCENTRISM

Man is not only a social animal: he also forms more or less permanent and specific social groups, bound together by strong ties of sentiment. This characteristic we call ethnocentrism. Possibly it is an aspect of his search for security—psychological as much as physical. Its most obvious form today goes under the name of "nationalism"; but national attachment is only a particular form of the broader phenomenon. Among primitive peoples the

---

[33] In a challenging article based upon limited field research, Robert E. Lane has argued that neither the commercial classes nor the working classes have much affection for the ideal of equality. It is probably true, as he argues, that most people most of the time have rationalized their particular status. They hold that it is right and are rather fearful than desirous of any great change in their position. Yet, on Lane's own showing, while most people do not care much about *equality* of opportunity they do want an opportunity to be somewhat better off than they now are. This of course is a demand for a move *toward* equality. Here is something, too, for a political leader to play upon. And that is all that is needed. Changes, movements, are not initiated by the masses; they are initiated by leaders who see more clearly than their followers—and before them—what the latter can be roused to demand. For Professor Lane's findings and analysis, see Robert E. Lane, "The Fear of Equality," *The American Political Science Review*, 53 (1959), pp. 35-51.

tribe is the center of dominant corporate sentiments. Ancient Greece had its tribal sentiments, its sentiments toward particular city-states, and finally the sentiment that in some measure united all Greeks as opposed to barbarians. Similarly, in the Middle Ages, men possessed a variety of corporate attachments. They gave loyalty to a guild, a locality, a feudal lord, and a kingdom, to mention some of the most important. In the modern world men also form strong sentimental attachments to numerous groups. Today the modern state is a political unit decisively superior to all subordinate political units. It is likewise relatively independent of outside political entities. Often, too, the area of political independence is co-extensive with an area of common language and literature. Further, modern wars have contributed greatly to solidifying sentiment along these lines. As a consequence, nationalism has become by all odds the strongest of corporate sentiments in the Western world. Only recently have modern technology, economic interest, humanitarian sentiments, and fundamental clashes of ideologies tended in some areas of the world to undermine its force and appeal. There are some indications that this is happening in Western Europe today. A new ethnocentric sentiment that transcends the barriers of language and the old nationalisms may be in process of formation.

Political organization is of course vitally affected by this universal tendency toward group attachments. Here we shall simply make two points that suggest something of the nature and extent of that effect. First, the more complicated the society and the more it is dependent upon the cooperation of its members, the greater appears to be the need of a powerful common sentiment to preserve unity. Otherwise conflict bred either of other forms of irrationalism or of short-sighted rationalism tends to occur. (The Western European trend referred to above suggests no qualification of this statement; only a possible shift from nationalism to a different and more inclusive form of ethnocentrism.) Second, in the past, a powerful force in the development of specific national sentiments has been rivalry and war between national groups. This combination of factors—the need for something akin to nationalism and the close relationship between nationalism and war—poses a dilemma. A worldwide sentimental tie among all humans might provide the basis for political unity, if it could be developed. The crucial question is whether the rivalry of independent political entities we are seeking to escape is itself a condition of the development of the required sentiments.[34] Possibly a solution may be found in the intensification of sentiments in areas smaller than the great nation-states combined with weaker sentimental ties on supranational levels.

Turning from practical to theoretical implications of ethnocentrism, we note here as elsewhere interactions between it and other basic tendencies of political sociology growing out of the nature of man. Hegel saw nationalism

[34] This subject is discussed further in Chapters 20, 21.

as one of the great progressive and liberating forces of the modern world. And so it has been. Not only has it helped peoples free themselves from foreign domination, it has also aroused them to effective demands for internal political liberty. But nationalism carried to the extreme, sometimes called "integral nationalism," becomes a powerful repressive force. In the present century fascist movements, drawing heavily on nationalistic sentiments, but also growing out of a frustrated need for security, have shown how far repression can go. Equality, too, bears an ambivalent relation to nationalism. As a powerfully uniting community sentiment, nationalism tends to break down the sense of class and its attendant privileges. Perhaps this aspect can best be seen in the new nationalism that characterized France under Napoleon. Even German nationalism under Hitler, while abolishing political equality, did much to enhance the fact and feeling of social equality among "Aryan" Germans. Yet, as in the case of political liberty in the last example, it may work the other way—one national group may subject another to its dominion.

THE TIDELIKE CHARACTER OF SOCIAL CHANGE

Apart from the threat of nuclear war, the average man in the industrialized countries of the world today is probably more secure, certainly more healthy, and enjoys a longer life expectancy than ever before. It also seems fair to say that he enjoys greater liberty and equality of opportunity. These improvements in areas of greatest importance have largely been made possible by the advances of science and technology, and given direction in their application by the human developmental tendencies we have described.

As one views the course of history, however, he is struck more by the appearance of tides and cycles than by unilinear evolution. Civilizations rise and fall. A given society at a particular stage of its development concentrates on attacking a particular evil, such as insecurity or special privilege, or on advancing a particular value, such as liberty or equality, at the expense of other objectives. Sooner or later a new imbalance is created and new counteracting tendencies assert themselves. Sometimes these tendencies amount to powerful, far-reaching, and long-lived reversions from liberal ideas and institutions. We have seen this happen to Greek democracy and to Roman republicanism. And even since the advent of modern science and technology we have seen the temporary but dreadful reversion to barbaric tendencies in modern Germany.

Many attempts have been made to develop philosophies of history in terms of cycles, a "law of the pendulum," or dialectical movements. Social and cultural development through time has been described as a series of cycles or as a spiral. The pattern of history is less rhythmical than many have believed. Sometimes the ebbs and flows that are referred to occur within a given civilization, while at other times they are applied to the rise and fall of civilizations themselves. Sometimes they apply to nearly all aspects of a society at once, at other times what appears as a progressive movement in the history of liberty, for instance, may accompany a retrogression in some other aspect. It is fairly clear, however, that at least with respect to particular phases, the direction of social development, is subject to periodic changes and even reversals. It is to this phenomenon that the remarks in this section are directed. Whether broader generalizations can be sustained and whether there is an overall direction of movement that converts cycles into spirals —these questions we shall not attempt to answer.

Insofar as history does reveal ebbs and flows, recurrences, and cycles or spirals, it is plausible to suppose that at least part of the reason is to be found in man's ambivalent nature. It is man's unhappy faculty to crave at one and the same time mutually incompatible things, as in the case of security and adventure. More broadly, there are marked tensions among various of man's wants and within the structure of tendencies in society. Pursuit of the ideal of liberty for everyone always runs the risk of meaning liberty for anyone who is able to enslave whomever he can. In similar fashion liberty and equality are sometimes at cross-purposes.

On a different level, economic changes constantly exert disturbing pressures upon society. They may originate in environmental changes (climatic changes, for instance) , from the discovery of new resources or the exhaustion of old ones, or, most frequently, from scientific advances and technological developments that alter the way in which men use their resources, or add to their longevity. It is obvious, for example, that the development of rapid and inexpensive means of transportation and communication calls forth radical changes in social organization. It is equally obvious that the growth of an industrial society in place of one based on agriculture calls for new and more complicated governmental regulations, and thus profoundly affects the problem of maximizing liberty. Such developments are likely to bring about changes that offset some of the gains that have been made. In fact, rapid changes of many kinds—especially enlargements of the polity, mixing of civilized and uncivilized populations, economic transformations—are likely to cause striking reversions with respect to the progress that has been made with order, liberty, or justice.

Man is a creature of sentiment as well as of reason. While these two forces need not be opposed to each other, sometimes they are. In particular, men tend to form strong sentimental attachments to things as they are, but the law of life is change. A rational consideration of changing conditions may point to the need for change, while powerful sentiments resist it.

So it is that a tidelike movement in human affairs seems inevitable as long as man is only partly rational, as long as he tends to seek a degree of equality that defeats some of his other interests and has sentiments and deep-set attitudes; that is, as long as he is man as we know him.

If we know something of the tendencies at work in promoting social and political change and giving it direction, we shall know where we can direct our own efforts most constructively—a datum of considerable practical significance in our dealings with the underdeveloped areas of the world, for instance. If we are aware of the tensions caused by contradictory demands in any society, especially where change is rapid, we can do something to anticipate the explosions these tensions may cause and possibly even ward them off. Communists may be wrong in much of their reading of history, but they have a good understanding of revolutionary forces and they put it to good use in furthering their own ends. Similar understanding—one hopes an even better understanding—can be put to use equally well in furthering security, liberty, and justice by processes of peaceful change.[35]

SELECTED READINGS

BENN, S. I. and R. S. PETERS. *Social Principles and the Democratic State.* London: Allen & Unwin, 1959. An excellent treatise on social philosophy. See especially Chs. I and II in connection with the topics covered in this chapter.

CASSIRER, ERNST. *The Myth of the State.* New Haven: Yale U. P., 1946. A profound study of the history and role of political myths.

DAHL, ROBERT A. *Who Governs? Democracy and Power in an American City.* New Haven: Yale U. P., 1961. A major work relating the findings of an extensive empirical study of a community influence structure to the theory of democracy.

DE JOUVENEL, BERTRAND. *Sovereignty—An Inquiry into the Political Good.* Cambridge: Cambridge U. P., 1957, Chs. 2-4. The author's study of authority, leadership, and groups is not an empirical study, but it is a carefully thought out philosophical treatment.

DIESING, PAUL. *Reason in Society: Five Types of Decisions and Their Social Conditions.* Urbana, Ill.: U. of Ill. Press, 1962. Ch. III of this thought-provoking book is particularly relevant to the subject matter of this chapter.

LANE, ROBERT E. *Political Life: Why People Get Involved in Politics.* Glencoe, Ill.: Free Press, 1959. A thorough and thoughtful organization and analysis of the extensive body of literature on this topic.

LEIGHTON, ALEXANDER. *The Governing of Men.* Princeton, N. J.: Princeton U. P., 1945. The psychological foundations of politics studied from the experience of a camp for displaced Japanese during the Second World War.

LIPSET, SEYMOUR MARTIN. *Political Man, the Social Bases of Politics.* Garden City, N. Y.: Doubleday, 1960. All of the author's studies collected in this volume enrich our understanding of political sociology. For this chapter, note especially Ch. I.

---

[35] In connection with the argument of this section, the student will find much of interest in Paul Diesing's *Reason in Society* (Urbana, Ill.: Univ. of Illinois Press, 1962). "Rational trends," he writes, "can be checked for a time by some persistent opposing factors. Even such a widespread rational trend as technological progress is dormant in large areas of some cultures for long periods of time. In fact . . . the various forms of rationality are partly opposed to one another . . . ." (p. 7). Consequently, he continues, all forms of rationality can not occur at the same time.

MacIver, R. M. *The Web of Government*. New York: Macmillan, 1947. This study in political sociology is less "scientific" in its approach than many more recent studies but the author's wisdom and breadth of view make it still valuable.

Myrdal, Gunnar. *An American Dilemma: The Negro Problem and Modern Democracy*. New York: Harper & Row, 1944. This classic work exhibits many of the basic concepts and techniques of social science being put to work.

CHAPTER 4

Economics and Politics

The relations between economics and politics have been a center of controversy in political thought for many centuries and will undoubtedly continue to be so. This controversy is related closely to many central issues of political science, such as the limits of political change, the forces that influence institutions and decisions, and the rationality of particular choices. We have attempted in this chapter to lay the foundations that would support an inquiry into such issues. In particular, we have dealt with three aspects of the relation between economics and politics that seem most important to political science. We discuss, first, economic forces and interests as determinants of political processes and of political behavior. Next, two schematic models of economic systems and their relations to government are examined in some detail, partly by way of illustrating some of the variations of cause and condition in the relations of politics and the economy, but also—and primarily—to suggest the importance of economic organization and activity for government. Lastly, we discuss the ways in which the concerns of politics and of the political scientist diverge from those of economics.

ECONOMICS AS A DETERMINING INFLUENCE IN POLITICS

Some students of society and politics have argued that economics determines politics; many more that economic factors, from basic resources to prevalent techniques of production and distribution, shape political institutions and set the bounds within which the statesman must operate. The opposing position, that political forms or political power shape and determine the use and significance of resources and the functioning of the market also has its defenders. We take a median position: politics and economics alike are always with us; they are always interdependent, never independent, but their relative importance, and the specific working of their reciprocal interaction, are matters for empirical observation and are reducible to only a very rough system.

Some Classical Theories

Many of the leading figures in the history of political philosophy have taken a stand on the role of economic factors in shaping political institutions and determining political decisions. Karl Marx is notable for the pre-eminence he attributed to economic factors and particularly to the mode of production. All depended upon the latter in the final analysis, he argued. Government, law, politics, not to mention art, philosophy, and the whole realm of ideas, comprised but the superstructure, built upon and determined by the economic base. That base, the mode of production, contained within it the elements of the class struggle which, together with changes in the mode of production, provided the dynamics of history. As the mode of production changes—as the windmill gives way to the steam engine, to cite one of Marx's examples—so change all other aspects of society, including the political superstructure. The latter changes, however, would not be immediate or direct. Here the "relations of production" enter. This phrase refers to the relations, both actual and legal, between those who control the instruments of production and those who labor. Any given mode of production has a corresponding system of relations of production that lend themselves best to its operation. Also, in any such system, one class of people owns the instruments of production and are able, by virtue of this fact, to extract wealth and privileges for themselves at the expense of the workers. Since changes in the method of "exploitation" would involve the displacement of the owning class, they are resisted. The "forces of production" change, as technology develops, but the "relations of production" tend to become ossified. Consequently, as any particular economic system "matures" it generates "contradictions," or disharmonies between the "forces of production" and the "relations of production." This process continues, according to Marx, until the tension becomes so great that a revolution occurs and the ruling class is overthrown, shorn of its power and privileges, both political and economic. Finally, with the overthrow of the capitalist system, private ownership of the instruments of production is completely abolished and classes are no more. With the subsequent establishment of a classless society, a communist commonwealth, the need for coercive government will vanish and men will live in complete freedom and equality.[1]

---

[1] Marx's ideas are spread throughout many volumes, but his classic statement of the determinative character of the mode of production is to be found in a single paragraph in his Preface to "The Critique of Political Economy." See Karl Marx and Frederick Engels, *Selected Works*, 2 vols. (Moscow: Foreign Languages Publishing House, 1955), Vol. I. pp. 362-364. A discussion of the role of class struggle may be found in the "Com-

Niccolò Machiavelli, one of the shrewdest political observers of all time, held to a sharply different view. By no means neglecting the importance of economic considerations, he nevertheless cast them in a subordinate (perhaps we should say supporting) role. Political leadership, he insisted, piling example upon example, often makes the difference between the success and failure of a regime. Moreover, he held that the successful political leader, although he might sometimes be perfidious and cruel, generally must rely on winning active support of his people. No sentimentalist he, yet he stressed the power of sentiment. A people's love of their ancient traditions and their ancient liberties, he said, constituted a most powerful force; and patriotism, far more than pay, makes an effective army; indeed, a prince's best fortress is the love of his people.[2]

Before turning to direct analysis of the problem, we would do well to note the position of the "father of political science," Aristotle. In classifying states, he declared, the key fact is whether the state is ruled by the rich or the poor. Moreover, the way the bulk of the people earn their living, whether they are farmers, herdsmen, mechanics, shopkeepers, or day-laborers will have much to do with determining the nature of the state and its government. His discussion of revolution, too, is based on the proposition that the struggle for power between rich and poor is the underlying cause of most revolutions. (The establishment and maintenance of a large middle class, he held, was the key to political stability.) Yet Aristotle was not an economic determinist. He felt that men were in some measure master of their fate; that by the distribution of property and their constitutional arrangements, they could make a state better or worse. Like Machiavelli he stressed the role of leadership. Further, he argued, it was not economic factors themselves but men's thoughts and feelings about them that determined human conduct; and these, while they represented reactions to facts of equality and inequality, were not invariant.[3]

Analysis

The doctrine that economic factors are dominant in politics is at once seductive and elusive. It is seductive because of the obviousness of certain economic necessities and because of the intellectually attractive character of

---

munist Manifesto." *Ibid.*, pp. 34-69. Key portions of the works of Marx and Engels are available in many briefer and more readily available sources than the one cited above. Perhaps the most useful, for present purposes, is Marx and Engels, *Basic Writings on Politics and Philosophy*, edited by Lewis S. Feuer, Anchor Books (Garden City, N.Y.: Doubleday, 1959). See especially Sec. I, III.

[2] *The Prince and the Discourses by Niccolò Machiavelli*, introduction by Max Lerner, Modern Library (New York: Random House, 1940). See especially "The Prince," Chs. 17, 24, and "The Discourses," Bk. I, Ch. 55; Bk. II, Ch. 10.

[3] See *The Politics of Aristotle*, translated with an introduction, notes and appendixes by Ernest Barker (Oxford: Clarendon, 1946). The *Politics* is shot through with references to and discussions of the role of economics, but Books III and V will be found especially fruitful in this respect.

any theory that reduces a difficult and complex problem to a simple formula. It is elusive because its proponents are often far from clear as to precisely what they are asserting. Examination discloses at least five distinct ideas that may be held either singly or in various combinations by economic determinists. First one encounters the notion of the determining role of natural resources—of oil, water, minerals, climate, or soil fertility. From another point of view, attention may be directed to human motivation, stressing man's demand for food, clothing, shelter, and creature comforts —in a word, his "materialism." Again, economic power, especially the power of ownership, may be held up as the great determinant. Or group or class (economic) interest may be held to be the determining factor. Finally, emphasis may be placed on technology and "know-how," on the state of the arts and sciences as they relate to the exploitation of resources. We shall deal with each in turn. (Of these the second, third, and last are crucial for Marx's position. Unless at least one of them is sound, his theory fails.)

NATURAL RESOURCES

The natural resources of a country, including its climate, undeniably exert a great influence on the course of its development. Among political philosophers, Montesquieu was greatly enamoured of the theory that stresses this element—especially climate. But he also pointed out a number of non-economic factors. In particular, he emphasized the role of human resources —the ideas men have and their traditions and beliefs—as of equal importance.[4] A modern writer might observe also, with respect to climate, that man is learning to make his own climate. Portions of the tropics once thought useless for human purposes are being cleared of jungle and, partly with the aid of air conditioning, being made to produce minerals and contribute to the wealth of nations. Even though we concede that, in a given state of the arts and sciences, a nation's natural resources will have a great deal to do with determining its political power *vis-à-vis* other nations, this is only one aspect of the field of politics. Knowledge of a country's natural resources gives little clue to the form of government and whether its people enjoy liberty or are subjected to tyranny. For that matter, national strength, largely depends upon the nature of political alignments. An alliance of two or three weak states may be able to overpower one state that is considerably stronger than any one of the allies. And in the determination of alliances it is fairly obvious that many more factors than resources, or than any matters of economics, may be influential and even crucial.

ECONOMICS AND MOTIVES

According to the motivation theory, the need for food, clothing and shelter, and the desire for comforts and luxuries primarily determines human conduct in the mass. Within small and intimate groups like the family,

---

[4] Baron de Montesquieu, *The Spirit of the Laws*, trans. Thomas Nugent (New York: Hafner, 1949), Bks. II-VIII; XV-XIX.

other motives may prevail, but in the large arena of politics, economic motivation, the desire for material goods and services, determine the main outlines of conduct. Among the many things that could be said about this point
of view, only two broad points need be made here. In the first place, even
if the theory were true as stated, the fact that economic considerations dominated would tell us little. We could not predict political developments, even
in the large. The trouble with the theory is that so much can come under the
heading of economic motivation. Of course, man cannot live without food
and the other material necessities of life. In this sense those things are basic.
But societies may organize themselves for producing and distributing these
necessities in many ways. Since most societies, especially among the industrialized states of the world, produce more than is required to meet the bare
necessities of life, there is room for great variations in what is produced, how
it is distributed, and who makes the decisions regarding these important
questions. Here one may run the gamut between democracy and autocracy
and between freedom and regimentation.

The second criticism of this type of theory cuts even deeper. People, as
Machiavelli pointed out, have other important concerns that cannot be
brought within the broad ambit of "economic," as defined above. They may
act even in defiance of the dictates of material considerations, from love of
liberty, or love of country, or love of glory. Only a few decades ago, Fascism
in Italy and, still more, National Socialism in Germany, demonstrated to
the world the power of such noneconomic motivations as the desire for a
place in the sun, or for belonging to a mighty nation that was able to make
others nations tremble, to mobilize political support where other means had
failed. And in democratic England, Churchill's appeal for "blood, sweat, and
tears" did not owe its success to hope for material gain or even to the desire
to preserve existing economic benefits. While the determination to assert,
and assert successfully the dominance of the political over the economic is
uniformly a popular plank of fascist platforms, surprisingly enough the same
phenomenon may frequently be observed in Communist countries where the
Marxist version of economic determinism presumably prevails. The Soviet
Union started off on such a tack when Lenin convinced his followers that,
although Russia was not yet ripe for a Communist revolution according to
orthodox Marxist theory, a determined revolutionary party could speed up
the process of change, telescoping into a few short years developments that
might otherwise have been expected to take many generations.

ECONOMIC AND POLITICAL POWER

According to the third version of economic determinism, it is the holders
of economic power who call the tune. Marx, with his theory of class struggle,
relied heavily upon this theory. Politics, the so-called science of who gets
what, when, how?, only reflects or responds to the shifts and balances of
economic power. Most of the proponents of this theory (but not Marx),

fully recognized that political means might be used to shift the base of power itself, that is, the ownership of property. Aristotle and Harrington (a mid-seventeenth-century political theorist) tended to think of this kind of major shift in the distribution of property and therefore of economic power as feats that could be accomplished only in great constitution-making epochs. In modern democracies, however, the voters constantly possess and frequently exercise the power to make substantial alterations in the distribution of property. In Great Britain, to take a striking example, estate taxes accomplish drastic redistributions of wealth whenever a wealthy man (or woman) dies. And in most industrialized countries progressive taxation is a powerful force for the redistribution of economic power.

Yet property is a great source of power. While it has a political foundation, as Hobbes pointed out, and while that foundation can be changed by the political power of the electorate in a democracy, nonetheless the general laws of property and even of taxation are normally fairly stable. Accordingly the owners of property at any given time have power that is relatively independent of politics. The two kinds of power are clearly apparent in the case of the politician who may need to raise funds for campaign expenses from wealthy contributors and at the same time win the electoral support of a majority of voters in his constituency. In this practical situation, many a politician has doubtless wished it were possible to say that either economic power or political power was fundamental, so fundamental that he could afford to disregard the other. Unfortunately, from his point of view, he often can make no such judgment and his personal success may depend upon obtaining a substantial amount of both political and economic support.[5] The latter by no means always produces the former, for if it did the Republican Party would virtually monopolize political power in the United States.[6]

ECONOMICS AND POLITICAL ALIGNMENTS

The fourth version of economic determinism might be treated as a variant of the motivation theory. It stresses the proposition that "interests" or "interest groups," meaning groups (or classes) having a common eco-

---

[5] Some wag has said that the art of the politician is that of getting money from the rich and votes from the poor on the pretext that he is protecting each from the other.

[6] A point that has no relevance to the question of whether or not economic power is prior to political power but which does relate to the validity of the Marxist version of the economic power argument should that reason be mentioned. We have spoken of economic power almost as though it were identical with property. In the past this assumption had considerable validity. Today, however, the fact of organized labor has radically changed this situation. As anyone knows who has observed the course of a strike, the steel strike of 1959 for instance, the power of organized labor—economic power, clearly—is very great indeed. Frequently it can fight on better than equal terms with the opposing powers of the owners of capital. In this situation it becomes clear that to speak of economic power as though it were a unity, as Marxists tend to do, is highly unrealistic. The question that then becomes important is not, Is economic power dominant? but rather it is, Whose economic power is dominant?

nomic interest, are the primary units of influence within the state. If the groups are confined to classes and if the theory purports to explain all political behavior, it becomes the Marxist theory. In more moderate form James Madison in the *Federalist* papers espoused this doctrine. "The various and unequal distribution of property," he declared, "is the most common and durable source of factions."[7] Madison's view, however, was far short of complete determinism. He recognized that so long as men had different faculties, were creatures of passion and fallible reason, there would be differences of interest, regardless of particular economic arrangements. It was, moreover, to political means—a large state and representative government —that he turned to ameliorate the ills of faction. The limited Madisonian view that economics divides people into factions and sets many of the issues of politics has perhaps much to commend it, at least upon superficial inspection. The political divisions into a mercantile interest, a landed interest, the mechanics and the debtors, are notable in the past history of the United States, as are their historic successors today. Yet even on this score, the influence of economics upon politics is less than might seem intuitively to be the case. For one thing, as Madison himself recognized, other divisions and alignments—religious, ethnic, sectional, and traditional—may be politically as important or more important than the economic divisions and alignments. Intuitively, for instance, it would seem that sectionalism must decline as the economy becomes more national in scope and character. Yet the evidences of decline indicate that if such a tendency exists it is a slow process at best; and the data are by no means subject to an unambiguous interpretation.[8] Sectionalism often acquires a different base, that is, sectionalism once based upon cotton or immigrant attitudes comes to rest upon the production of textiles or upon attitudes toward government intervention in the economy. But older political alignments persist despite the new content. The fact that older forms persist is important. If it is possible to say that political culture and political forms in large measure set the conditions under which differences must be fought out—that they determine the kind of men that get to power, the tools they will use when in power, and the way in which issues must be presented in order to win the largest following—then politics is to a significant degree autonomous.

TECHNOLOGY AND POLITICS

Finally, we have the view that technology, or more broadly the state of men's knowledge of arts and sciences as they affect production, determines both political institutions and political and social change. Marx's view, as we have indicated, was clearly overdrawn. However, it is one thing to see in

[7] Alexander Hamilton, J. Jay, and J. Madison, *The Federalist* (New York: Dutton, 1926), p. 43 (No. 10).
[8] V. O. Key, Jr., *American State Politics: An Introduction* (New York: Knopf, 1956), pp. 26-28. *Note:* V. O. Key, Jr., died while this book was in press.

technological change the key to all else (a view which not even Marx held) and another to stress the importance of technology and "know-how." The philosopher, John Dewey, and his contemporary, Thorstein Veblen, were also impressed with the key importance of technology.[9] Dewey, for instance, held that *the* great division of attitude separating the modern from the ancient mind results primarily from the creation of a technology capable not only of extorting a meager sustenance from nature, but of assuring ever-increasing abundance. If the total income of society is fixed, then mobility in status or a sharing out of material goods is, for practical purposes, impossible: they only poison the society with hatred and destroy the meager economic surplus that goes to compensate the governing classes and those who conserve and advance social and cultural values. Therefore, government, before the modern era, sought to preserve the status quo while religion and moral instruction counselled resignation to the plight of human existence.

The mark of modern society is its capacity through science and technology to transform nature. Certainly, no other single change in recorded history had a more revolutionary impact in enlarging the horizon of the average man than the industrial revolution. As man's powers for controlling nature and his physical welfare grew, quietism gave way to activism, often in political form.

Probably the real point of dispute about technological causes and politics is not whether technology has been of vast importance, but how to interpret its role. On this score, two questions seem relevant, namely: 1) in what way, primarily, is technology an influence; and 2) what are we talking about when we speak of technology as a cause?

The journalist, Lincoln Steffens, once said that Adam's fall from the Paradise of Eden ought to be attributed not to the serpent but to the apple. Men are ruined not by the knowledge of good and evil, but by the creation or appearance of new wealth. Steffens' observation suggests at least one important truth about economics and politics: wealth and material power stimulate men's appetites and arouse their acquisitiveness, unleashing powerful forces and leading to disputes as to the ways and means of distributing the spoils. The culture of the tractor is bound to be different from that of the hoe. The introduction of gunpowder and of the printing press worked revolutionary changes throughout Western society. Technological changes make tremendous changes in the limits of what is possible—democratic government of a vast domain would be unthinkable without the printing press and modern means of communication. Clearly technology—or more broadly the state of the arts and sciences with respect to production—is a powerful conditioning and motive force in the dynamics of history.

[9] John Dewey, *Liberalism and Social Action* (New York: G. P. Putnam's Sons, 1935), pp. 6-7; Thorstein Veblen, *The Place of Science in Modern Civilization and Other Essays* (New York: Huebsch, 1919), especially title essay.

But, for all its importance, technology must take its proper place among other causal factors. No technological or even economic explanation would be sufficient to account for the differences in the development of Canada and the United States, on the one hand, and the rest of the Western Hemisphere, on the other. Inertia, tradition, superstition, religious conviction, and even economic interest itself may either stay the hand of the inventor or prevent his works from being put to use. The ancient Chinese invented both printing and gunpowder—powerful forces in the development of modern Europe—without the far-reaching effects they had in the West. Moreover, modes of organization, for economic endeavor as well as for other purposes, are also powerful factors in controlling and directing change. The development of the joint stock corporation, for example, was hardly a matter of technology, but its effects were tremendous.

Conclusion

The dichotomy of economic domination over politics and political domination over economics is inadequate and unrealistic. The determining forces of history are more radically pluralistic than that. Any attempt to understand them must take into account a great variety of cultural, ideological, traditional, political, and economic factors; yet, as Montesquieu argued, for any particular society at a given period of time some one or another of these factors may exceed all others in importance. We may gain a richer sense of these interrelations and especially of the interactions between the political and the economic if we examine certain specific periods or situations.

TWO SCHEMATIC MODELS

The Traditional Agrarian Society

Throughout most of history and until quite recently, in fact, society was predominantly agrarian, directly dependent upon nature for its subsistence. It is still true that over half of the people on earth make their living from agriculture. Aside from the primitive agriculture of some African and Asian peoples, most agrarian societies are mixtures of the agrarian, commercial, and industrial; they occur in different stages of development toward a modern economy and technology. Even the specifically agrarian elements show great variations. Certain techniques for organizing production, particular social attitudes, and certain relations between government and the people that are more or less *typical,* though not universally prevalent, in the agrarian or peasant society. Normally, technological innovation and the mobility of land and capital are closely restricted; work is not related to an integrated career or vocation except for a few persons; and governing is largely the occupation of a restricted class that does not have to labor directly on the land.[10] Not only the governing class, but the techniques and organization of politics and government differ sharply from the sort of society we know today, or even from that described by Adam Smith in England or Alexis de Tocqueville in America. The latter, too, were still largely agrarian societies, but ones in which the attitudes toward government and economic enterprise had already radically changed. The difference between modern government and government in a "traditional" or "underdeveloped" country is not simply the contrast between a modern and an agrarian economy. But many of the typical features of the agrarian economy go a long way in explaining, by contrast, what modern government is and how it is related differently to society and the economy from its historic predecessors.

PRIMARY ECONOMIC CHARACTERISTICS

The most important fact of a pure traditional agrarian culture is the universal dependence upon nature and husbandry. Life rests upon the maintenance of a precarious balance of nature. Except for salt and spices, iron and cloth often imported from without, consumption is limited mainly to the harvest of field, vine, and forest. Wood, leather, water, wind, and muscle-power are the foundations of the agrarian technology. The economy is largely "natural" in character: rents and wages are commonly measured by hours or days of work, or by truck and produce that can be easily reckoned as labor; accumulation tends to be limited by the natural fact of organic decomposition, and exploitation by the dependence of all classes upon the economic viability of the household or estate. Life and personality and attitude are largely shaped by daily contact with nature, the rhythm of the seasons, the opportunities and the enjoyments afforded by the land.

For reasons inherent in the situation, property, duties and rights, and cultural institutions tend in varying degrees to be "communalized" or "socialized" in traditional societies. For one thing, agrarian economies, especially those whose technology is but slightly developed, are often soil-exploitive. They lack sufficient manure or adequate knowledge of crop rotation. The basic household units have to draw upon raw nature for their needs—wood for fuel; water and pasture for cattle; mud, wood, and thatch for housing. Each household depends for its continued existence upon a bundle of rights and usages permitting it to appropriate from or use the surrounding material environment for its economic maintenance. In turn, the health of the agrarian economy as a whole depends vitally upon techniques to insure that forests are not exhausted, that some land is allowed to lie fallow while other fields

---

[10] In developing this schematic "model" of the traditional agrarian society, we have relied primarily on historical, sociological, and economic literature. Some useful works, representing these different approaches are: Herbert Heaton, *Economic History of Europe*, rev. ed. (New York: Harper & Row, 1948); Max Weber, *The Theory of Social and Economic Organization*, trans. A. M. Henderson and Talcott Parsons, ed. by Talcott Parsons (New York: Oxford U. P., 1947); and Ragnar Nurkse, *Problems of Capital Formation in Underdeveloped Countries* (New York: Oxford U. P., 1953).

Traditional society: Indonesian farmers

Pix

are planted, that grazing livestock did not threaten agriculture. Some form of cooperative organization has been almost universal, whether it be the clan, the Balkan *Zadruga,* the Russian *Mir,* the Chinese, Indian, or European commune. The husbandmen, usually under the guidance of a headman or an elder, join together in order to pool their efforts for cooperative labor, to control individual enterprise in the interests of a healthy ecological balance, and to insure that no one went without the necessities of existence.[11]

Property in the agrarian society tends to be a much less clear-cut category than it is in the advanced commercial and industrial milieu, and much more linked to personal need, custom, and locale than the abstract property rights of the nonagrarian society. Property includes an ill-assorted collection of easements, customary privileges, limited local jurisdictions, and rights to share and to use along with rights to things, absorbing many things we do not usually regard as objects for ownership.[12] Also, the outlines of property

[11] On the collective or corporate character of control in such a culture, see Albert O. Hirschman, *The Strategy of Economic Development* (New Haven: Yale U. P., 1958), Ch. 1.

[12] Cf. Richard Slatter, *Private Property—The History of an Idea* (New Brunswick, N.J.: Rutgers U. P., 1951).

are vague and usually subject to arbitrary redefinition to the detriment of the inferior classes.

As the corporation is the representative unit of our economy, so the family or the household is the nuclear unit of the agrarian economy.[13] The clan or the stem family is an economic unit, with tasks parcelled out according to a familial division of labor. Important to the general health of the economy, the family in agrarian society is conserved and guarded. Within it, each finds a function and a needed role. The aged are the conservators of custom, folklore and wisdom. Women, whether honored or exploited, find more than enough to occupy their energies. Because there is no choice of occupation and because privileges and immunities are often locally restricted, sons and daughters remain nearby and join in the enterprises of the extended family. Such a family system discourages initiative, by pervasive cooperative controls, by the lack of opportunity, and because the industrious are continually preyed upon by their many shiftless and unscrupulous cousins.

Usually, the agrarian society is resistant to technological innovation. Change must be slow and measured, since the capacities for adjustment are meager. The single-industry economy does not afford new opportunity for surplus labor. Nor does it provide an elastic market for products. Markets tend to be predominantly neighborhood affairs, subjected to customary regulation, and parcelled out among many local monopolies, guilds, and cooperatives, dependent for their continued existence upon an assured sale of their products. Handicraft production is often restricted by regulations of apprenticeship and standards of quality and composition designed as much to exclude competitors and competing methods of production as they are to protect a consuming public. Limitations upon innovation and monopolistic control of the market assure the continued production of a very limited total economic product and a passably equitable distribution to those who cooperate in creating it.[14]

Practically all agrarian economies are marked by poverty. They tend to remain at a bare level of subsistence agriculture because of lack of technical means to increase the yield of their labor. A change in the legal status of the agricultural household may increase production. The enclosures in England and the individual farming household of America, for example, were more efficient economic units than the peasant commune. New crops, such as rice, the potato, and barley may achieve the same result for a time. Sustained prosperity and rapidly increasing wealth require a more extensive division of labor and a greater application of technology than are possible in most agrarian societies. Agriculture wastes labor. The children of peasants stay on the land, half-employed on tiny plots of ground. Their patrimony is too

[13] Max Weber, *General Economic History*, trans. Frank H. Knight (New York: Greenberg, 1927), Chs. 2, 3.

[14] Cf. Wilbert E. Moore, *Industry and Labor—Some Aspects of Economic Development* (Ithaca, N.Y.: Cornell U. P., 1951), Part 1.

small to utilize their energies fully, to yield more than a bare subsistence, or to encourage the investment of capital. Economy demands that large numbers of the peasantry should move from the land to the cities or become middle-men. But either of these alternatives requires new techniques of marketing and production, roads and efficient means of transport, and the accumulation of capital. In Western Europe and elsewhere, a money economy and the development of more extended markets, along with the deliberate intervention of the state, did create these prerequisites for the transition to a modern commercial and industrial economy. All too frequently in agrarian societies, however, poverty reinforces poverty, in a vicious cycle. People cannot save because they are so poor. Yet they are poor in large measure because of inefficiencies caused by lack of capital.[15]

CONSEQUENCES FOR GOVERNMENT

Two factors primarily determine the nature of the state in the agrarian society. One is the lack of liquid wealth. More of this presently. Another great factor is the isolated and attention-absorptive quality of the agricultural occupation. Land-tillage and the care of livestock tie the peasant or serf to his fields, demand continuous if not regular attention, and discourage the regular pursuit of other occupations. He can ill afford to quit the land for extended periods to engage in politics or other public concerns. Public purposes must be attended to and political duties rendered by other classes, freed from the immediate necessity of laboring on the land.

Money tends to be scarce in the agrarian economy, and as a consequence, bureaucracies and governing classes are compensated by other means of payment. Two great expedients have most commonly served to repair this deficiency in liquid wealth. One is to grant and protect a franchise or monopoly to conduct private business. New land is cleared and brought under cultivation by grants of charters and privileges. Roads are built by permitting the exaction of tolls. Handicraft is protected and fostered by guild monopolies and regulated markets. At various times, salt was extracted, iron mined, and gunpowder made by ensuring a profitable monopolistic price to those who conducted these serviceable enterprises.

The second important device to stimulate service in this money-poor society is the decentralization or privatization of some functions of state. In effect, public functions are converted into or allowed to remain private property or privilege, on the theory that the beneficiary would be sufficiently interested in his own income to perform adequately an essentially governmental task. The tax-collecting practices of the agrarian society, for example, may allow a large amount of public revenue to be diverted to the personal uses of the collecting officer. Local legal jurisdiction is sometimes virtually a piece of private property. In most traditional agrarian societies the head-

---

[15] On the "vicious cycle" of agrarian poverty, see Ragnar Nurkse, *op. cit.*

men, and bailiffs that govern locally and regulate agrarian production and distribution live in part upon privileges conferred to exact goods or compel services.[16]

Though government tends to be restricted, and much of it delegated to part-time servants of the state, those who do administer public affairs can exact a high price for their services. They also rule locally with few formal or effective restraints on their activity. In the traditional agrarian society, few are educated, and the common occupation is singularly ill-adapted either for collective organization or for developing public leaders.[17]

At the local level, agrarian governments usually involve much physical or legal compulsion, especially because of the absence of alternate techniques of indirect control. Consequently, the grant of monopoly, franchise, or office often includes supplementary powers to make it effective, exclusive and compulsory jurisdiction, the authority to require or to exclude from participation, the power to regulate and to dispense with respect to the internal government of guild, corporation, or village, and the right to force compliance or service, often with beatings and torture.

The agrarian system for distributing the product of society and compensating nonagricultural pursuits strongly militates against honest, devoted public service. Because the governmental and the private are mixed, private gain is often sought by usurpation of a public function or diversion of state revenues. Both the incentive and the opportunity to convert administrative office or political influence into a personal or family business are inherent in the system.[18]

As a further result of the manner of life imposed by the typical man's mode of earning his living, the shortage of liquid funds, and the difficulty of saving and of achieving technological advances, rulers and ruled in the traditional society tend to be sharply separated. The high price that rulers can exact for the services they perform tends to maintain the poverty of the masses and to perpetuate the class division between ruler and ruled.

In large measure, what we have been saying is that the lack of effective choices that is entailed by the existence of only one occupation and by the subsistence level at which most of the population is maintained in the agrarian society means that economic factors tend to play a rather dominant

[16] Thus extortion for government service—or what would be to us corruption, pure and simple—is often governed by a schedule of customary payments, observed scrupulously by all the parties involved. In countries that have experienced various forms of "neofeudalism," especially during the latter half of the nineteenth century and the twentieth century, this principle of "privatization" of the state was carried far.

[17] As the Marxists were first to realize, the peasantry has seldom been able to organize effectively for political action. See, generally, David Mitrany, *Marx versus the Peasant* (Chapel Hill: North Carolina U. P., 1951), and F. H. Jacoby, *Agrarian Unrest in Southeast Asia* (New York: Columbia U. P., 1949).

[18] Max Weber, "Presuppositions and Causes of Bureaucracy," in *From Max Weber: Essays in Sociology*, Hans H. Gerth and C. Wright Mills, eds. (New York: Oxford U. P., 1946), pp. 204-214.

role. The governors, finding little threat to their position from the masses, are relatively free to use their political power to exploit their position for personal benefit and to perpetuate the system. On the other hand, the possibilities for much coordinated or collective public activity are slight. Sooner or later, also, the balance of the agrarian policy is upset, whether by wars, pestilences, new discoveries and opportunities for trade, technological developments, contacts with alien cultures, or some combination of these and other factors. The new element need not be "economic." If the resulting changes lead, as frequently happens, to greater variety of occupation and a measure of prosperity, noneconomic factors gain in significance, and the room for interplay among a variety of causal factors, both economic and noneconomic, is increased. It is to the consideration of such a society that we now turn.

Laissez Faire

INTRODUCTION

Another model useful for examining the relation of politics to economics is that commercial and industrial order known variously as the "market economy," "economic liberalism," or "laissez-faire" capitalism. This model, as described and defended by its advocates in England and on the continent of Europe, reflected a "strategy of freedom" in economic endeavor and a program to achieve a "liberal state" in politics. The most articulate and systematic theories in defense of these objectives were developed by the classical economists and the Utilitarians of England during the period that opened in 1776 with Adam Smith's *Wealth of Nations* and closed with the publication of David Ricardo's *Principles of Political Economy and of Taxation* (1817). Both the liberal state and the ideals of market freedom had, of course, a much longer history.[19] In fact, they were advocated even at the time when enlightened despotism and mercantilist policies were being most vigorously employed and defended. Thomas Hobbes, for example, combined both of these broad policies by making the aim and rationale of despotism and mercantilist politics a minimal state and expanded market freedom. Both John Locke and Adam Smith, and especially the English Utilitarians, recognized that the state must intervene for freedom to come into being, for it to exist, or for it to last. These men, however, had a revolutionary conception of the relation between the state and the economic system, for they were arguing that whatever may be the role of law, administrative intervention, and state-run enterprises in getting things started, the job of the state was to "wither away": to delegate an increasing number of decisions to the

---

[19] For a discussion of early proponents of liberalism in economic affairs, see Erich Roll, *A History of Economic Thought* (Englewood Cliffs, N.J.: Prentice-Hall, 1940), Chs. 2, 3; and Alexander Grey, *The Development of Economic Doctrine* (London: Longmans, Green, 1951), Chs. 3, 4.

market mechanism and to individual firms operating under the discipline of the market. In this respect, the "market economy" stands in the sharpest contrast to the agrarian economy. In the latter case a continual and central aim, often meeting with only limited success, is that of assembling and concentrating political power. For the "market economy," a major objective is to disperse political power and transform it into the spontaneous adjustments of a "neutral" and impersonal mechanism.

The pure "market economy" is an unusual case of productive and distributive organization. Today, it is extinct except as a subject of occasional advocacy or denunciation. All modern states are "welfare states"; and none of the "underdeveloped" countries regard the laissez-faire "strategy of freedom" as recipes that can be followed faithfully or even primarily. As a coherent articulation of principles and practices, however, this model is useful both to suggest many of the conditions of economic development and also to evaluate the "strategy of freedom" in relation to competing alternatives such as regulation of the economy through law or more direct initiative and control in economic affairs by the state itself.

HISTORICAL CONTEXT

The ideal of the "market economy" grew out of a specific historical context and in response to a set of particular problems. It was advocated as an alternative to mercantilism.[20] In the eighteenth century the two systems co-existed and were fought over as competing ideals. Advocates of the market economy defended the principle that each should be free to use his stock of land, labor, or capital to its most advantageous or rational employment. The first part of their task was to urge the superiority of this solution over that of mercantilism which had been tried and found wanting.[21] More than this,

---

[20] Mercantilism cannot be precisely defined since it was never a definitely formulated program in England or elsewhere. States pursued a series of aims under mercantilism rather than a coherent policy. One aim was wealth. In France, Germany, and England, governments stimulated industry and trade through promotion and by increasing the money supply. They also enhanced the power of government itself by the use of fiscal and colonial privileges and public monopolies to swell the contents of the public treasury. Another central aim of policy was the establishment of the authority of central government. This was the period of council legislation in England, of the Prussian commissars, and the *intendants* of France. It was also the era of enlightened despots who became strong and popular by "nationalizing" or "bureaucratizing" countless formerly dispersed public functions performed by the church, by individual lords of manors, by towns and guilds. A third aim of mercantilist policy was the promotion of unity. Older monopolies, privileges, and franchises were abrogated; local custom was broken; personal dues and feudal encumbrances were destroyed in the interest of administrative unity, legal equality, and a free flow of trade. Mercantilism was a national system, devoted not only to prosperity and power, but to social unity. The job of government was to balance class against class, curb faction and estate, and harness the resources, public and private, for prosperity, unity and national strength. Eli F. Heckscher, *Mercantilism*, 2 vols., trans. Mendel Shapiro (London: Allen & Unwin, 1935).

[21] The success of mercantilist policies is a debatable issue, especially since it was successful in some respects and less so in others. Mercantilism probably fostered economic

they undertook to show in absolute terms that the consistent pursuit of economic liberalism and the political corollaries of this principle promoted in theory and in practice the greatest good of the greatest number. This was not a modest undertaking. It called for a new corrective for the problem of the poor, a substitute for the restraining influence of government and public corporations, a radically new political formula to replace the traditional one, and new forces and new myths to bind society together.

BASIC PRINCIPLES

Adam Smith called his solution a "simple and obvious" system of natural harmony. In fact, many of its conceptions and premises seemed paradoxical in the extreme. His program involved a far-reaching departure from the assumptions and practices both of the "natural" agrarian economy and of mercantilism as well. Indeed, in most categories of thought and action, the philosophers of the market economy proposed to put the economy on its feet by standing things upside down. For the regulated and custom-bound local market they proposed the substitution of the general market economy, the consistent and remorseless transformation of land, labor, and capital in all their forms into commodities in the most universal and abstract sense; objects without country or history, known only as presented for sale. Investment and trade were not to be the instruments of public policy as in a mercantilist system. They proposed instead, to subordinate government as far as possible to the needs of industry and trade and to assimilate law and politics to the principles and categories of economic activity. Instead of looking for the sustenance of the community and its practical and spiritual welfare to the forces of cooperation, customary restriction, and carefully regulated privilege and monopoly, they urged that the most crassly particularistic and socially disruptive of man's dispositions—rationalistic materialism, egoistic individualism, and his longing for progress, change, and novelty —not only could be safely unleashed but also so cunningly harnessed that the public good would automatically ensue. Above all they taught that the economic man was not the sinful man but the natural man and the useful citizen.

In ethical theory the first principle of the "worldly philosophers" of the "market economy" is hedonism. "Nature," said Jeremy Bentham, "has placed mankind under the guidance of two sovereign masters, pain and pleasure. It is for them alone to point out what we ought to do as well as to determine what we shall do."[22] Nature has not made man a kinsman of the

---

progress in varying degrees depending upon the state of local political and economic affairs, the wisdom of individual monarchs, the degree of national unity, and the success of the nation's foreign policies. A corollary of this statement, however, is that everywhere mercantilist policies tended to subordinate economic to political objectives and to become in time a hindrance to healthy commercial and industrial development.

[22] Jeremy Bentham, *The Principles of Morals and Legislation* (New York: Hafner, 1948), p. 1.

angels, nor yet a "social animal": she has made him a calculating, egocentric seeker after utilities. These statements are, of course, simply not true. They are true, even partially, only of a special realm of conduct, and not of "nature" nor of man at all times or in all places. Furthermore, for the kind of rational conduct of which Bentham speaks, to regulate the behavior of men generally, even in commercial and industrial activity, an enormous change in men's attitudes—depending in turn on a whole cultural and social revolution—must have taken place. For present purposes, the important thing about this first principle, hedonism, lies less in its truth or its falsity, than in its applications and its consequences.

The second great principle of economics, the "dogmatics of egoism," is the universal common lot of pain: the shortage of utilities, and the necessity of labor and deprivation in order to gain or create these utilities. By the sweat of his brow shall man eat bread. The mark of the value men place on things is the labor they will expend to get them, directly or in the form of money. A purchase, a contract for hire, a decision to save, all represent equations of pain with pain, an individual choice to exchange or to forego one utility for another. Freedom to follow their own plans and options in economic activity is therefore not only justice in its most essential terms but *the* right closest to the workaday lives of ordinary men and women. To sacrifice this right to the supposed interests of public revenue or "reason of state" is to show contempt for individual man's reason, his free efforts to improve his lot, and the plans and efforts he has made for his own happiness.

Impelled to labor by scarcity, men are driven to calculate the optimum use of their energies and resources. The division of labor facilitates productivity and improves the products of labor. But most fundamentally, it links men together in a form of cooperation that requires each to work for the interest of the whole. Every man must sell in order to buy; produce in order to consume. Self-interest guides each to work in those callings and for so long only as society is willing to pay for their services or to buy their products. Assuming that entrance to the market is free, that people are cognizant of their economic interests, and that the majority of the class of producers are prudent, self-interest and the rational pursuit of it best serve the interest of the whole by working to increase the common stock of utilities and by encouraging the most rational distribution of that common stock. As Adam Smith puts it: "Without any intervention of the law, therefore, the private interests and passions of men naturally lead them to divide and distribute the stock of every society, among all the different employments carried on in it in the proportion which is most agreeable to the interest of the whole of society."[23]

The revolutionary *tour de force* of this social philosophy lay in the seemingly impious attempt to devise a system of natural harmony in which

[23] Adam Smith, *The Wealth of Nations*, (New York: Random House, 1937), pp. 594-595.

individual love of pleasure and gain would constitute the prime force for good. For Adam Smith, the answer was "simple and obvious": an essentially unrestrained market economy is the greatest and most efficacious instrument available for the widespread inculcation of social morality and for the augmentation of economic values. It sets to work human egoism and interest, but under a discipline that evokes self-mastery and rational foresight and releases the energies of millions of hands and individual intelligences. In so doing, through the division of labor and the free market, this economic system frees men from the painful regulations of an older form of cooperation presupposing a constant disposition to sacrifice, and unburdens them of the moral strain of continual conflict between their private good and the public weal.

How is the lone individual to find protection against the subtle conspiracy of large interests or the sinister influence of cheats who prey upon public weakness or ignorance? Law may restrain the open thief or clumsy knave; but the great sovereign remedy lies again in the device of pitting greed against greed and thereby serving the common interest. Any man, if he can, is prone to take that which is not his own. He will adulterate, forestall, engross, screw his prices up above those of the market—but for the scourge of competition. The protection of the individual does not lie in his power, but in his ability to choose wisely. If the product is poor in quality or high in price, the demand for it will drop, or new capital will flow in to make a better use of an opportunity poorly honored. Competition simultaneously regulates price, protects against extortion, brings the optimum quantity of goods to market, and assigns to each—capital, land, and labor —the income due to it. The laws of the market are a great "hidden hand" forcing each man to work for the common good. The great governor or controller of that hidden hand is the force of competition.

Despite their emphasis on "harmony," the advocates of the "market economy" were not unaware of conflict. In fact, with the widespread suffering, riots, and class struggle that attended the early growth of capitalism in Europe only the most purblind optimist could have ignored the clashes of interest between *rentier* and capitalist, possessor and dispossessed. On the other hand, what the advocates of the free market economy were insisting upon was the revolutionary implications of the concept of abundance. If abundance is a practicable aim, then all have a common interest in productivity and progress. If opportunity and material prosperity are rapidly growing, temporary privation or economic inequity are less painful than they would be in the static agrarian economy. Furthermore, only when there is more to bargain over can better bargains be made for all. Neither justice nor wealth will result if men fall to redressing the inequities and distresses of the present by robbing each other. The best hope, as Adam Smith argued, lies in an expanding and progressive future which will afford greater scope for mending the present deficiencies in mutuality of interest. For him, "The progressive state is in reality the cheerful and hearty state to all the different orders of society. The stationary is dull; the declining, melancholy."[24] The agrarian society typically looks to the recovery of the past to restore to each what is his due according to a settled and static pattern of rights and functions; the industrial society can hope to endow with new interests and build a richer future because it is creating more opportunities and goods to bestow.

Laissez faire; laissez passer—was the battle standard of the champions of market freedom. In essence, two theses were being asserted. One was that the decisions made through the market regulated the society, directed its work, and distributed its resources and products more rationally and with less compulsion than could have been done through the agency of centralized bureaucracy or governmental regulation. The second point was that the "market economy" had its own "logic" or principles of operation. The state might establish conditions that would enable these principles to work more effectively; but if it sought to thwart them the economy would suffer. The laws of the "market economy" were a model laid up in heaven. Men might by their policies of state work toward this ideal; they could not improve on it.

POLITICAL IMPLICATIONS

Both in the agrarian economy and under mercantilism, the ideal tended to be that of a strong and active state. The "public interest" of society was generally pursued not as an adjunct of economic behavior but in spite of it or contrary to it. The central point of the advocates of the market economy with respect to politics was that a "hidden hand" effectively protected the "public interest" (to the extent that this concept itself was not merely the posturing of despots or the "sinister interests" allied with them). For most of them, consequently, the state was a "sterile" institution; it could consume wealth and inflict penalties, but it had no creative role. The state's only separate functions were the maintenance of peace internally and abroad, the enforcement of contracts, and the provision of a few collective goods, such as roads.

At this juncture the theory of the market economy and that of the liberal state join. Nowhere was this union more brilliantly celebrated than in the writings of the English Utilitarians, particularly Jeremy Bentham.

The aim of politics, said Bentham, ought not to be national glory, or the "well-balancing of classes", nor even the active promotion of public and private benefit. The first principle of politics is that "government should lie low and practice quietism." It ought to leave the greatest possible amount of decision to the free choice of rational and informed agents seeking their own best advantage. The closest approximation to such a condition is that of economic choice within a free market economy. The same principle of free contract should apply in marriage and for political allegiance—in choice

---

[24] Adam Smith, *op. cit.*, page 81.

of a mate or of a state. The same rule of free competition should apply in the choice of ideas or of a religion.

Secondly, in the interests both of justice and of the augmentation of material wealth, government should provide security for, and protect, all rights of property and person, once acquired, so long as they are not used to invade a legally cognizable right of another person. Of all the rights respecting property, secure protection is most important. On this protection depends the confidence necessary to permit decisions and pledges. Without this confidence, industry, investment, and progress are impossible.

Since all interests stand on an equal footing, the next principle of governmental action is that of legal equality: rigidly equal treatment of all interests and parties. Government and law should be neither a respecter of persons nor of "legitimate" as opposed to noxious interests, saving the rare case where such discrimination can be *proved* to be conducive to the greatest happiness of the greatest number.

The other great guide to policy is that of promoting the highest productivity. This is an essentially negative function of government. Government can have a slight role in providing the "overhead capital" needed for the market economy: roads, lighthouses, and certain other public works. Government can contribute to the knowledge universally profitable to all and useful especially for an industrial society through education and by fostering ingenuity with prizes and patent laws. Beyond these minimal functions, government should restrain itself, taking care to remove artificial impediments to the working of economic law. Fundamentally, the art of politics is to know how to do next to nothing.

Above all, government should not seek to redress the plight of the poor by arbitrary equalizations. To do so is to risk the precarious stock of capital that is the source of progress for all. The remedy for the poor lies in education and opportunity. If aid for them is sought by tampering with the rights to property and freedom, the poor may gain a short-run advantage; but in the long course of history it is invariably the poor and the weak that stand to suffer most from the abandonment of honest justice and scrupulous enforcement, since from the nature of the case they are the least able to help themselves in a society in which power is unrestrained by law.

LAISSEZ FAIRE, CONSTITUTIONALISM, AND DEMOCRACY

The early laissez-faire creed was narrow and harsh; but it was also based upon powerful insights into the relation of politics and economics. For one thing, these theorists understood the significance of a dynamic and expanding economy. In a static agrarian economy, government intervenes directly to protect customary rights and traditional status. The transformation of an agrarian or feudal society into one fitted for the expansion of commerce and industry calls for even more vigorous governmental activity. Once this objective has been accomplished, the facilitation of change and maintenance of an open future comprise the first objectives of policy for an expanding economy. Dynamism has a compulsion of its own. Freedom to apply intelligently and prospectively the private resources of a market economy is a vital condition of prosperity and of industrial expansion. Prosperity and expansion in turn represent a kind of compensating progress to offset the problems that an industrial economy itself generates—such as technological unemployment or forced obsolescence. The desire for an exact social justice is less compelling if the total social product is rapidly increasing. Thus, on all these accounts, government must be less the manager of a household economy and more the agency that equalizes, channels, and expands individual opportunity and freedom. Bentham summarized this view of government by saying that the state could not honor prescription, but it ought not to disappoint expectation. Its guiding stars are the future and progress.

The philosophy of the market economy also provided a significant restatement of the problem of freedom, and gave rise to laws and institutions that expanded the scope for the exercise of freedom. It is not simply that liberty within a commercial and industrial society presupposes stable expectations and the possibility of rational calculation, or that prosperity demands scope for personal initiative. Nor is it simply that liberty is sought in economic and social realms as well as in other protections against arbitrary and oppressive government. Basically, the whole concept of freedom tends to be altered: from one in which liberties, charters, and franchises were part and parcel of a system of status and public responsibilities distributed according to class, it shifts to one in which there is a common interest in an equal freedom for all, because capitalist and worker, farmer and urban employee, desire and need for their purposeful economic activity substantially the same bundle of economic, social, and civil liberties with respect to free movement and untrammeled choice in applying their energies. To a large extent, rights and duties that had been functions of status come to be settled by bargaining, resulting in contrasts. Even Karl Marx, while deploring the suffering attendant upon the liberation of the serfs, recognized that the market economy, replacing the fetters that had been imposed upon industrial and commercial activity by guilds and monopolies, constituted a revolutionary force for freedom and progress.

Just as the market economy entailed new dimensions of freedom, so it was also, in two respects, vitally related to democracy. In the first place, the market economy does not presuppose a "public service" class, as an agrarian economy generally, and a mercantilist society always does. Not only do the citizens "do for themselves," but a market economy also, putatively, schools its citizens by placing a premium upon literacy, self-restraint, prudence, and activism. Furthermore, the public interest and the private interests of groups and individuals are presumed to be so nearly identical that a government responding to the pressure of public opinion and voluntary political organization appeared to offer no threat to stability and efficiency. In its most

Laissez faire, laissez passer. . . . *Pittsburgh at the turn of the century*
Philadelphia Museum of Art

sweeping outlines the theory of the market economy constituted a great
program for creating a modern citizenship, for its implications were these:
that people would enrich themselves through private economic enterprise
and not through the pursuit of military aggrandizement or political power;
that the governors of society would be restrained by the economic interests

of an alert productive class whose attention would be regularly engaged by the relation of their work to the policies of the state; and that the policies pursued by the state itself would be closely assimilated in content and in theoretical principle to the knowledge and the practical wisdom of the average person. Nation-wide democracy and the nation-wide market economy appeared to be natural and hospitable allies.

In fact, however, as so often happens, the new political forms and spirit evoked and facilitated in such large measure by the market economy acquired independent force that often turned directly against the principles of the market economy and enabled groups and classes to use the mechanism of the state to secure both wealth and power which they had not been vouchsafed by the operations of the market.

POLITICS AS THE ARCHITECTONIC SCIENCE

We have examined the relations of politics and economics from the point of view of causation, and we have watched the interplay of political and economic forces in two schematic models or ideal-types of society. The subject may be viewed from yet another perspective, perhaps the most important of all: that of politics as the architectonic science, in Aristotle's pregnant phrase. By definition, politics, and its mechanism, government, provide the means by which a society is shaped and directed, in so far as it is shaped and directed at all by any inclusive and authoritative system of action. Politics is the arena in which the decisions are made as to the collective activities of the society in question. It is here that choices are made between guns and butter, between more or less equality, or between urban sprawl and center-city rot, on the one hand, and planned metropolitan development on the other. Such decisions involve economic calculations, but they involve far more than economics; they entail value judgments, the ordering of priorities among the great ends of life and of the state. These ends and their mutual relations comprise the subject of a later chapter. We need not anticipate that discussion here; we make only the simple but fundamental point that, viewed from this aspect, politics is basic and all-inclusive, subsuming economics within its purview. One example should make the point clear: the very decision to permit and protect the institution of private property, so fundamental to a market economy, is a political decision, and calls for political implementation through the agency of law and government.

"Overhead Capital" and Collective Economic Goods

The first task of government with respect to the economy, or one of the first, is to determine what kinds of decisions will be made politically, through the agencies of government, and what kinds are to be delegated (perhaps simply by taking no action) to the family, the church, or the economy. Under the theory of the market economy, as described above, the deliberate determination is made to leave a maximum of decisions to the market. Even under such a system, however, a great deal is left for government to do—much more than many of the devotees of laissez faire were willing to admit. It was not merely a matter of defending the country against attack, of maintaining internal order and justice, and of protecting property and enforcing contracts. In principle at least, laissez-faire theorists admitted two categories of rightful government functions that were capable of almost indefinite expansion: (1) promoting industry and (2) intervening in the operation of the market in those instances where cooperative endeavor was required that went beyond market incentives and private subscription or purchase. David Hume's description of the typical occasion for intervention is classic:

> Two neighbours may agree to drain a meadow, which they possess in common: because it is easy for them to know each other's mind; and each must perceive, that the immediate consequence of his failing in his part, is the abandoning of the whole project. But it is very difficult, and indeed impossible, that a thousand persons should agree in any such action; it being difficult for them to concert so complicated a design, and still more difficult for them to execute it; while each seeks a pretext to free himself of the trouble and expense, and would lay the whole burden on others. Political society easily remedies both of these inconveniences. . . . Thus bridges are built, harbors opened, ramparts raised, canals formed, fleets equipped, and armies disciplined, everywhere, by the care of government, which, though composed of men subject to all human informities, is by one of the finest and most subtle inventions imaginable, a composition which is in some measure exempt from all those infirmities.[25]

It is doubtful whether Hume realized how much might be covered by his formula for what a state ought to provide. He mentioned bridges, harbors, ramparts, and canals. The American Constitution added "post offices and post roads." Other governments have included in this list factories, dams, and dikes, lighthouses, railroads, public schools, and a host of other works and edifices by no means obviously the province of government. Whatever the technological and economic organization of a society, it needs "overhead capital"—the public works that are the condition for fruitful individual economic activity. The Chinese agrarian economy required the maintenance of irrigation works and great systems of water control. In the more individualistic economic system of eighteenth-century England, serviceable roads and canals, a postal service, a national monetary system, honest standards of weights and measures, to name but a few items, also had to be provided by the government. Much of this foundation for a modern economy had been provided in England and Europe through the policies of mercantilism. As Marx pointed out, when European business and industry assumed these

25 David Hume, *A Treatise of Human Nature* (London: Dent, 1911), Vol. 2, p. 239.

assets as simply given data of the political and economic environment, they were, in fact, ignoring a concealed subsidy. Today, a similar issue arises for the "underdeveloped" countries. They must decide what the balance shall be between the "strategy of freedom" and greater governmental initiative. They must also decide how much "two neighbours" can do for themselves and how much requires more centralized coordination. "Overhead capital" and the conditions for fruitful individual initiative are not "given"; they must be created and paid for.

Legal and Political Foundations of the Economy

Also, wide and free markets do not simply develop in response to the forces of economic evolution. Increasing division of labor and wider use of money encourage the expansion of markets. But no markets could have expanded very widely without the active intervention of government. Obviously, government provided roads and uniform coinage. But it also established the legal concepts and remedies, relating particularly to personal and group property and contractual arrangements, that made nation-wide markets possible. The law of the "market economy" may have been reasonable by eighteenth- and nineteenth-century lights but it was not "natural"; it was more deliberately contrived than most law. Often the growth of the market involved disencumbering economic activity from customary restraints and antiquated legal and administrative interference. Moreover, "free trade" in commodities is not "natural"; it required constant intervention to break up local monopolies, collusive agreements, guild and territorial restrictions, and all the host of protective devices that people could invent to escape the rigorous discipline of competition. Such activity, in the form of antitrust legislation and administration, is just as important today.

Honest and competent government also is an economic resource of prime magnitude. Personal security and stable property expectations are two of its most valuable contributions. Where these are lacking, individual economic endeavor has always been restricted, and government has tended to assume a greater role in encouraging enterprise or investment. Patronage, local favoritism, and various forms of corruption under most systems of government promote or protect, to some extent, political values such as unity or liberty. On the other hand, the market economy could not conceivably function effectively without a comprehensive legal system, administrative unification, and competent judges and bureaucrats. The English Utilitarians themselves, warm advocates of minimal government, recognized this fact. Thus, despite their attachment to liberty, they also promoted administrative reform, active legislation, and a more powerful state with the aim of securing modern and efficient government. Commonly, in Europe and Asia where governments have taken greater initiative, or sometimes simply interfered more, the resource of government is even more closely tied with the effective pursuit of material abundance.

Custom and Attitude

Private initiative, furthermore, is largely a matter of individual attitude and cultural institutions. The theorists of the market economy largely assumed the resource of favorable attitudes and social institutions. Karl Marx, Max Weber, and Werner Sombart, among others, have shown how much individual and collective attitudes had to be revolutionized before people in Western Europe were capable of responding appropriately to the "technological imperative" and the new economic incentives. An interesting case is the early American farmer and townsman. Although Alexis de Tocqueville alleged that they possessed something approaching genius for individual initiative and cooperative behavior, in fact, there was little "genius" involved in their propensities. The American was a colonist from Europe and benefited from centuries of Western European progress. He also started fresh, without the impeding influences of class and cultural divisions. Not so the peasant or burgher of Southern or Eastern Europe or of many Asiatic countries. Here, people have started from a traditional society and their attitudes have been shaped by established status and entrenched loyalties and hatreds. Individual initiative and the "arts of association" have languished. Correspondingly, to foster joint enterprise or provide public utilities, the state has acted, and often by compulsion or exploitation of particular classes, by forced labor or by taxation which rested the burden of payments on the peasant and the merchant.

Conclusions

In short, the liberal economists of the nineteenth century took for granted the contributions of several centuries of social and economic progress. They took for granted the existence of "overhead capital," adminstrative and legal unification, national independence, political stability, and security of persons and property, all of which were largely the contributions of political endeavors. Even the favorable cultural attitudes necessary to a modern economy were as much affected by political developments as by economic changes.

Given a hundred and fifty years' perspective, most people in Western Europe and America have come to understand that the prescriptions of the market economy were doctrinaire formulations which assumed many things and ignored many others. The curious doctrine that government either should or must be the obedient instrument of economic forces was a short-lived heresy of the nineteenth century. Even when statesmen and governments did profess to act in accordance with this principle, they were not simply responding to "necessary laws of development," as Marx would have it, but were putting into effect programs that were compounded of analysis, prudence, and hope. The plain truth about government and economics is that seldom has economic interest been clearly enough perceived and understood by people or governments for them to do what Marx said they *had* to do or for them to adopt the prescriptions that the laissez-faire economists said they *ought* to follow.

POLITICAL CHOICE AND ECONOMIC CHOICE

The import of what we have been saying, especially as it bears on the relations between economics and politics, may become clearer if we view it from still a slightly different aspect. Many decisions in any society could be made by government (directly or indirectly by voting, if the government was democratic) , or they could be made by the market (i.e., bargaining) subject to various governmentally imposed (legal) regulations. That is to say, market processes and political processes are often alternative or complementary means for achieving the same objectives. It is the task of statesmanship to discover which means, or which combination of means, produces the best results for a given type of decision. For many situations it would seem that decisions arrived at by a process of free bargaining would maximize utility. People would agree to a bargain only if they were satisfied that they would be in some sense better off with the agreement than without it. This case for market determinations is powerful. It has definite advantages over determination by ordinary democratic processes. Perhaps a highly simplified example will make this point clear. Three men are living together on an otherwise unoccupied island. One of them, allergic to the salt air, wishes to build a new hut, farther from the sea. But it takes the cooperative activity of the three men to build a hut, and the other two are not interested in moving. Presumably if this kind of decision is made politically, by voting, no action will be taken and the allergic individual will continue to suffer.[26] On the other hand, if the matter is left to free bargaining, the allergic man may be able to buy the services of the other two by giving up part of his share of the coconut crop. Each of the three individuals will be better satisfied than he was before.[27] The superiority of the "economic" means of bargaining, in this case is clear.

But one can imagine other situations where justice would demand a political solution. Hume points to the difficulties of agreement where the parties are numerous and the interests diverse. Or take the case of several oil-well owners who are all tapping the same oil pool. It will probably be to their advantage not to exhaust the supply as rapidly as possible

[26] In our tiny society it might well be that sympathy would move the others to cooperate. In a large, impersonal society, however, the effect of sympathy is attenuated.

[27] For elaborations of this type of analysis, see James M. Buchanan and Gordon Tullock, *The Calculus of Consent: Logical Foundations of Constitutional Democracy* (Ann Arbor: Univ. Mich. Press, 1962).

but to keep production going at a moderate rate over a long period of time. They *might* even voluntarily agree to this course of action. But perhaps one owner, who had reason to think his days were numbered, would not agree and would exploit his well as rapidly as possible. The others would have to do likewise in self-defense. A democratic political solution would avoid this difficulty and prevent the one from injuring all the others.

In certain other situations most people's sense of justice demands a different solution from that given by the market. For instance, the market gives great power to individuals who happen to be very wealthy. Especially when this wealth was inherited, many feel that some qualification of the results of free competition are in order—qualifications that might take the form of progressive taxation and the use of proceeds to help the poorer members of the community. Finally, in democratic societies, the fact that a majority desires something is a persuasive argument for giving it to them, regardless of whether either market processes or an objective determination of what would give most satisfaction to the majority in the long run would dictate this result.

In practice, political decisions are seldom reached by the same processes or in response to the same considerations that ideals of economic rationality would require. Power and prejudice affect the market also; but they have a legitimacy and an honored standing in politics that they do not have in economics. The envy of the poor and the arrogance of the rich, though they are not commodities for the market, are real and important for politics. The value set upon the political commodity is not determined solely by a mechanism that finely grades utilities; but by one that measures the ability to exhort and persuade, and by strategic advantage. In economic endeavor he who does not learn the rational calculus of utility generally does not survive; in politics, he who does not subordinate this calculus to considerations of power, sentiments of right, and stubborn prejudice is as likely to be the one that perishes. In the political arena, wise and foolish men must find a common ground partly by means of struggles for political power, because the alternative to a regulated competition of power is force and violence, not a rational calculus of utility.

CONCLUSION

We have illustrated our general analysis by examining the relations of economic and political factors in two types of society: in a static, poor, and industrially monolithic society in which there is little scope either for freedom or capacity to develop coordinated political power to act for purposes rationally calculated to promote the common good; and in a society which has cast off the shackles of a custom and culture bound economy and the heavy-handed controls of mercantilism in order to allow maximum scope to the dynamic forces of competitive enterprise and to the adaptive mechanism of freedom of contract—a society which also allows opportunity for response to popular demands for liberty and self-government. Also, we have tried to suggest the ways in which politics goes beyond economics. It does so because the polity is ultimately responsible for the effective functioning of all aspects of the society of which the economy is only one, and because today especially it must respond to popular demands that reflect non-economic values—the demand for leisure, for choice, for greater equality, and, of course, for national security.[28] The political decision, and especially the method of that decision, is thus radically different from the market decision, involving different processes, different values, different ways of allocating the power to control and distribute the goods—collective and individual—that the society as a whole needs.

Always economic motivation, economic power, and technology have been closely and reciprocally related to politics. At times economic limitations or economic "forces" have probably been dominant—for example the limitations imposed by technology and poverty in agrarian society, or the economic "laws" that held sway (or were believed to hold sway) for a time in the expanding market economy. During the periods of mercantilist intervention politics seemed to be in the ascendant. Today, in the welfare-state era, cause and effect become lost in the complexity of interaction and the closeness of interdependence. At any given moment, economic factors always impose limits upon what man can do, individually or collectively. In the longer run, he can change those limits. Today, for the Great Powers at least, strategic (national security) rather than economic considerations are of paramount importance. In the United States today the federal government alone is spending twice as much for scientific and technological research and development as all private sources put together.[29] This situation, largely but not entirely the product of military considerations, constitutes a complete reversal of the relative roles of the public and private sectors in this vital segment of the economy.

The contemporary mixed economy is in large measure an expanding universe of choice. Governments and populations can in considerable measure choose the relation of politics and economics they desire, allocating one part of a particular activity to government (regulatory commission or governmental department), another to the market, still others to various combinations of the two.[30] The problem has become more one of what, within wide limits, it makes the most sense to choose to do and how to organize political and administrative devices to carry through that choice than one of close restriction by the "objective conditions of material existence."

[28] These matters will be discussed more fully in Chapter 6.

[29] Much of this work is carried out on a contract basis, by private corporations and universities.

[30] This point of view is developed particularly in Robert A. Dahl and Charles E. Lindblom, *Politics, Economics, and Welfare* (New York: Harper, 1953).

SELECTED READINGS

BEARD, CHARLES A. *The Economic Basis of Politics*. New York: Knopf, 1945. A discussion of economic influences and their relation to history and politics in America and Europe, past and present.

CLARK, J. M. "America's Changing Capitalism: The Interplay of Politics and Economics," in Morroe Berger, *et al.* (eds.), *Freedom and Control in Modern Society*. New York: D. Van Nostrand, 1954, pp. 192-205. Reflections and conclusions by one of America's great economists.

CROPSEY, JOSEPH. "On the Relation of Political Science and Economics," *American Political Science Review*, 54 (1960), pp. 3-14. A sophisticated discussion written from a political scientist's point of view.

DAHL, ROBERT A. and LINDBLOM, CHARLES E. *Politics, Economics, and Welfare*. New York: Harper, 1953. The authors' description of their own work is, "planning and politico-economic systems resolved into basic social processes." The book is particularly useful for a political scientist attempting to understand relations between the polity and the economy that are important for public policy.

DIESING, PAUL. *Reason in Society: Five Types of Decisions and Their Social Conditions*. Urbana: Univ. of Ill. Press, 1962. The discussions of economic rationality in Chapter 2 and of political rationality in Chapter 5 are pertinent to the subject of this chapter.

FIELD, G. C. *Political Theory*. London: Methuen, 1956. The brief but clear discussion of "politics, economics, ethics" in the concluding chapter of this sensible volume makes important points that are often overlooked.

HEATON, HERBERT. *Economic History of Europe*. Rev. ed., New York: Harper, 1948. A standard text, useful for reference.

MACIVER, ROBERT M. *The Modern State*. London: Oxford U. P., 1926. Chapter 9 of this standard work contains a brilliant discussion of economic and political power.

MARX, KARL and ENGELS, FREDERICK. *Selected Works*. 2 vols. Moscow: Foreign Languages Publishing House, 1955. This is the most accessible and comprehensive selection now in print. The passages most relevant to this particular chapter are to be found in Vol. I, especially pp. 361-366; 453-469.

NURKSE, RAGNAR. *Problems of Capital Formation in Underdeveloped Countries*. New York: Oxford U. P., 1953. This volume has become by now somewhat dated because of the rapid growth of this field of study. The book is useful especially because it presents a brief and clear discussion of essentials.

POLANYI, KARL. *The Great Transformation*. New York: Holt, 1944. An able and provocative discussion of "the great transformation" from *laissez faire* to the "welfare state" in the Western world.

ROLL, ERICH. *A History of Economic Thought*. Englewood Cliffs, N. J.: Prentice-Hall, 1940. Perhaps the most useful one-volume work on this subject.

CHAPTER 5

Polity, Law, and Sovereignty:

Nature and Definition

In the present chapter we move on from the consideration of society and some of its forms and attributes to specifically political societies, and to that most highly organized form of political system, the state. In our consideration of the polity, of the state, and of law and sovereignty we attempt only to explain and define the concepts. We leave to later chapters the history that at one time gave a special point to the controversies over such terms as sovereignty, as well as the institutional framework that gives them context and significance today.

The concepts discussed here are important as such for political science. They also stand for important aspects of what we call specifically governmental as opposed to political or, specifically, public as opposed to private. State, law, and sovereignty refer particularly to the most formal modes of governmental behavior. They have particular relevance and significance when, for instance, one tries to explain why the government corporation and the business corporation are very different things, or what is wrong about allowing public decisions to be dominated by the "power structure" or by "mere politics."[1] These concepts are important as well for the succeeding chapter on "Ends of the State," since state, law, and sovereignty are institutions with definite properties. If we are to consider the ends of the state, those properties set the boundaries of the inquiry.

Generally speaking, three qualities or characteristics will determine how well a polity can perform its function of holding society together and facilitating and encouraging man's use of his reason to satisfy his needs. One of these qualities has to do with force and consent. The government must have the general obedience of members of the society—an obedience

---

[1] One way in which the student may get some grasp of these concepts is by asking himself what are the practical and theoretical implications of the Marxist notion of "the withering away of the state."

that will in practice be partly coerced and partly the product of willing consent. It must also have a legal system that gives precision and clarity both to the organs, forms, and institutions of the political system itself, and to the laws that it enforces. Without such a system, inefficiency and unnecessary strife will result from quarrels over what the law requires, and how it is to be made, and identified. The larger and more complicated the society, the greater the need for this kind of precision in the legal system. Without it, in other words, the first requisite, obedience, will be lacking. The third requisite is a mechanism for creating and applying this law and for doing so in a way that secures the maximum of willing consent and of satisfaction of need. This last requisite will come in for extensive discussion in later chapters, especially those in Part III. The present chapter will deal primarily with the nature of the political system itself and of the legal system that gives it its essential form, definition, and effectiveness.

THE POLITY

The state is the most highly developed form of political society. Law is its typical and characteristic medium of control and one of its determining features. Marking off the state from other political entities is the attribute known as sovereignty. All of these concepts, state, law, and sovereignty, will be defined and discussed in this chapter. We have pointed out previously, however, that a state is but a species of a larger genus, the "political system" or "polity." A political system is an aspect, or a "subset" of society. It includes all the members of a given society but not all of their mutual relations or of the norms that govern their conduct. We shall begin our discussion with this fundamental unit of politics.

Like society, the polity is most accurately conceived as a system of norms governing the conduct of individuals rather than as the individuals themselves, because, unlike people, it is a relatively permanent entity. Generation succeeds generation and people migrate across frontiers, changing their political allegiance, but the polity persists. Polities are usually territorially demarcated, but this feature is not absolutely essential.[2]

We have already described the distinguishing nature of the polity as its possession of the most inclusive and final authority to effectuate the conjoint purposes of the society and to reconcile the differences among its members.[3]

---

[2] For a slightly different definition from the one used here—one that does make a territorial base essential and that treats the polity as the *representative* institution of a territorial society, meaning by that term the institution that is seen by its members as constituting its corporate self, embodying the common values of the corporate group, and implying a commitment to accept the authority of the polity to perform acts for its general welfare, see Francis X. Sutton, "Representation and the Nature of Political Systems," *Comparative Studies in Society and History*, 2 (1959), pp. 1-10.

[3] Above, p. 9. Following the lead of Max Weber, it is common to make the defining characteristic of polities the exclusive control over the legitimate use of force in a territory. Max Weber, "Politics as a Vocation," in H. H. Gerth and C. Wright Mills, *From Max*

Like another subset of society, the economy, it includes all the members of the society. Moreover, it is in a unique sense responsible for the preservation, the security, and the viability of the society as a whole.

The agencies of the state for the performance of its functions are law and government. Perhaps it would be more accurate to say that law is the term applied to the norms that comprise the political system, or rather to one subset of those norms. (Another subset would include accepted rules regarding what is "proper" political conduct in a given state.)

The Political Culture

In the present section we discuss what might be called the substructure of government, sometimes referred to as the "political culture," leaving law and government for later. A political system, like any social system, entails a degree of consensus. Certain values must be widely shared within the society. Most obviously the members of the society, must be loyal to it and desire its survival as an independent entity. This sentiment will be encouraged by the existence of common interests and by widespread awareness of this common ground. A community of belief systems also aids in the achievement of political consensus and the development of a common political myth. Religious beliefs, a set of beliefs about the magical properties of various objects and acts, beliefs in the divine ordainment of a particular line of rulers are all likely to play an important role in relatively undeveloped polities, even as shared beliefs and values are a vital element of the political culture of the fully developed polity, or state. Political systems that are less than states are not necessarily primitive in the usual sense of that word. They may them selves be made up of states, as in the case of international political systems. They, too, will be strong or weak in proportion to the strength of their political culture.

A political culture can have too much consensus rather than too little. A healthy degree of conflict, between classes, groups, political parties, and the like, serves to stimulate ideas and encourage development. On the other hand, sharp cleavages, intransigent groups or classes having little in common with the rest of the society, are negative indications for a successful polity. The success of a political system will depend heavily upon the society's ability to develop an appropriate degree of consensus in general and, more specifically, favorable political attitudes, a readiness to perform the necessary roles and to accept responsibilities, including the responsibility of office. Much more is required of some than of others, as in any organization. In other words the society must contain an elite possessing, among them, an

---

Weber: Essays in Sociology (New York: Oxford U. P., 1946), pp. 82-83. We have avoided this limitation on the definition so as to include emerging polities that have not yet established their authority in this exclusive sense but whose authority is yet more inclusive than that of any other organization.

adequate supply of the skills of leadership, administration, interest aggregation, and so on.[4]

POLITICAL SOCIALIZATION

Political scientists refer to the process by which members of the society develop the requisite values, beliefs, attitudes, and skills for effective political organization as "political socialization," while the next step, that of enlisting the services of sufficient supply of politicians and administrators is spoken of as "recruitment." The process of political socialization may be left entirely to chance, or to the unplanned operation of such social institutions as the family or the clan, and the village. At the opposite extreme, as in ancient Sparta or modern Russia and China, the state itself, through schools run by the government (beginning even at the nursery level), through clubs, youth movements, and similar organizations controlled by the ruling elite (the Party, in modern totalitarian societies) assumes practically the whole responsibility for this task. Any society that is seeking to transform itself rapidly, for instance to hasten the processes of political and economic development, is virtually driven to adopt this method. The examples of Sparta and of Plato's ideal state indicate, however, that centralized state control of the processes of political socialization can be put to other uses, such as maximizing military potential or seeking to preserve intact and unchanged the existing constitution and character of the polity.

POLITICAL CULTURE AND THE POLITICAL SYSTEM

We have referred to the political culture as the substructure of the political system. It would perhaps be more accurate to speak of it as playing a supportive role. It supports the system, but not solely from the base. It feeds into it at all levels—generalized support, political leadership (both central and dispersed), and administrative talent. Some political scientists seek to present all of what we have been discussing for the last few pages in schematic form, in some such fashion as is depicted in the following diagram.

FIGURE 2   *Diagram of a political system**

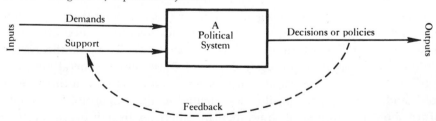

* This diagram is taken from David Easton, "An Approach to the Analysis of Political Systems," *World Politics*, **9** (1956-57), p. 384.

[4] Use of the term "elite," as our previous discussion of the term should indicate, does not necessarily mean that this group is marked off from the rest of society in any obvious fashion, although frequently it is. It means only that persons answering this description do exist.

The society in general supplies the political system with certain "inputs," consisting of both demands (advocacy of particular policies or simply demands for certain goods) and support. The political system, in turn, supplies the goods demanded by adopting general policies and making concrete authoritative decisions. These decisions (the "outputs" of the system) may in turn affect the nature of the inputs, as is indicated by the dotted line labeled "feedback." Expository devices of this kind may be helpful if taken with the appropriate admixture of salt. For instance, the whole schema set forth above might quite properly be thought of as existing or taking place *within* the political system. It might almost be said that it is what the political system is all about, except that this statement does much less than justice to the long and complicated political and governmental processes in accordance with which demands are translated into decisions. Also the demands and support are shaped and encouraged by leadership originating within the system, quite apart from any governmental decisions.

We have noted that the supportive myth that gives unity and power to the polity may be the product of unplanned growth or of collective design, or more commonly of some combination of the two. It remains to point out that in most political societies ethnocentrism—nowadays in the form of nationalism—plays a major role in the political culture. The operation of this force and the problems it creates will be discussed in later chapters.[5] At this point we simply remark that today to form a full-fledged state out of a less developed political system, to bring about the drastic alterations in traditional institutions, is a task that can seldom be accomplished without powerful leaders who whip up the sentiment of nationalism—often a rather synthetic nationalism—to white heat.[6]

THE STATE

In describing the polity and discussing its nature, we have largely covered the subject of the nature of the state; for the state is a polity. It is simply a polity that has reached a certain stage of development. The boundaries between it and other aspects of society have become clearly demarcated and it has achieved legal and substantial independence from other polities. However, the importance of the state for political science is such that some elaboration of these two sentences is in order. Moreover, the state has been defined in so many different ways by highly respectable and indeed eminent writers, that a decent regard for them (not to mention guidance for the student) demands a fuller treatment of the subject.

[5] See Chapters 20-21.
[6] A good brief discussion of this phenomenon is given by Rupert Emerson, in "Nationalism and Political Development," *The Journal of Politics*, 22 (1960), pp. 3-28. An excellent case history of the process is to be found in James S. Coleman, *Nigeria: Background to Nationalism* (Berkeley: Univ. of Calif. Press, 1958).

Defining the State

One reason for the variety among definitions of the state is that they have often been what philosophers call "persuasive definitions," designed rather to support particular purposes or arguments of their authors than to advance the understanding and scientific study of politics. For Karl Marx, the state was an exploitive instrument of the bourgeoisie; for Hegel it was the idea of freedom; for Aristotle it was that most supreme and inclusive association whose purpose was the attainment of the good life; and for Herbert Spencer it was an organization for maintaining order and enforcing contracts, and nothing else—or at least that is what he believed it *should* be. Each of the definitions referred to was devised by its author to stress a certain point, or point of view. We shall do well to avoid them all and many others like them.

TERRITORIALITY AND ALL-INCLUSIVENESS

We have already set boundaries to the definition of the state by defining the political system, of which the state is but the most developed form.[7] It is, in the first place, a political system, or polity, that includes all the people in a given territory. A state is territorially bounded, and anyone who is born within its territorial limits is automatically a member of that state, a fact that distinguishes it from all other organizations.[8]

SUPREMACY

The characteristics of territoriality and of all-inclusiveness or inescapability point to a further and even more basic distinguishing characteristic of the state: its possession of supreme coercive authority and of some mechanism for the effective exercise of this authority. Thus government and law are marks of the state. Many organizations, including all polities, have government and rules, or laws, by which they are governed. States possess the unique element of supremacy within their territory, backed up by the authority to resort to physical violence. To this it should be added that the state possesses a legal monopoly of the use of violence. If others (e.g., parents) are permitted to use violence, they do so on sufferance of the state. Other organizations, when faced by dissident members, have no recourse in the final analysis other than to expel them from membership or to threaten them with divine punishment. If this threat or that of losing the privileges of membership are not sufficient to secure compliance with the rules, laws, or commands of the government of the organization, there is nothing further that the organization can do. The state on the other hand can seize the

---

[7] Of course we do not exclude the possibility that still more developed forms of polity may emerge in the future.

[8] A state may make exceptions to this rule, as in the case of children born to diplomatic representatives from other states, but this is a privilege which it can withdraw at any time.

property of recalcitrants and in the final resort can seize the persons themselves and put them in jail or take their lives. The monopoly of this coercive
power that the state enjoys is something that had to be fought for. In primitive societies each family or clan is likely to enforce the law—frequently by
violence—for itself. Even in feudal society there are powerful and often
successful rivals to the central government's claim of authority. It is precisely
for this reason that we withhold the name of state from such political
systems; the monopoly of the right to use violence or to say who may use
it is part of what the word "state" means.

The power of the state is based upon authority, which has already been
defined as entailing a degree of acceptance or recognition beyond mere
yielding to fear of punishment. Thus, to take an extreme example, there
might be a territorial society, say on a small island, in which a few members
held the others in subjection by sheer force, or threat of force, by monopoliz-
ing the firearms. They might issue orders and even establish general rules, or
"laws," to which they could compel obedience. Nevertheless, unless there
was some degree of recognition among the people generally that these rules
possessed authority, that the organization as a whole served some rightful
purpose (however much wrong it might also be doing), we would not ordinarily call the society or the organization a state.[9]

LEGAL INDEPENDENCE

Finally, a state must be a legally independent unit. This condition does
not mean that the state has no external ties nor that it is not subject to
influence by other states. It may even be subject to legal restraints (if we
recognize international law as true law) and be bound by its treaties. For our
purpose, it is sufficient that the political entity in question should not be
part of another political entity having the characteristics of a state and that
it should not be subject to the supreme coercive authority of a state. There
may be borderline cases between the situation where a state has bound itself
by treaty to submit to the authority of another state in some particular case
and the situation where this process has gone far enough that we would no
longer recognize the independence, and so the statehood of one of the
societies. In general, if one "state" permitted another to exercise power
within its own territory, we should say at least that its statehood was qualified. If each state gives up some of its independence on condition that the
other does likewise, statehood is not lost, unless by their joint action they
have created a third organization that can qualify as a state.

A DEFINITION

The state is both a legal and sociological entity. It is sometimes viewed
purely from the juristic aspect. When we speak of the continuity of the state

---

[9] The statement above is used to assure against misunderstanding. Actually it is redundant, for authoritative rules are recognized as legitimate by definition.

through conquest or revolution, it is primarily legal considerations to which we refer. But it will be apparent from the preceding discussion that the state is more than a system of laws. It comprises all those elements that give it the authority and the ability to act effectively—its political culture, its government, its legal system. Of the latter we shall say more in a moment. Meanwhile, we may summarize by defining the state as *a political system comprising all the people in a defined territory and possessing an organization (government) with the power and authority to enforce its will upon its members, by resort, if necessary, to physical sanctions, and not subject in like manner to the power and authority of another polity.*[10]

When we pledge allegiance to the flag, the state is the entity for which that symbol stands. We are not pledging allegiance to the government, which may be thrown out of office at the next election, nor of course to ourselves, the unorganized people, but to this political entity, the state. It is, as the Germans say, "the bearer" of political authority and of responsibility. The ordinary laws of the state are made, at least enforced by the government. On the other hand, we speak of the *constitution* of the state. It provides for the organization of the government. Moreover, it is the state that deals with other states, through the agency of government. As a final example, we might mention the Congo as it existed in the summer of 1962. Laws and governments there were. Whether there was a single political system with the qualifications we have described as requisite to a state is a question. As long as Moise Tshombe, for instance, behaved as the head of an independent polity (Katanga) and was able to get away with it, it was straining the meaning of words to speak of the Congolese state.

LAW

Fully as fundamental a concept of political science as the state is that of law. We have already discussed it briefly[11] but at this stage further elaboration is in order. In its most general sense, law connotes, more than anything else, the element of regularity. Whether we speak of the laws of God, the laws of the state, or scientific laws such as the law of gravitation or (to take an example from a much less exact science than that of physics), the law of diminishing returns, this statement holds. They may all be expressed as general propositions applying to all members of a given class. In examining different examples of laws, however, one quickly comes upon the distinction

---

[10] In defining a "polity" in Chapter 1 (pages 5-6), we included reference to its primary purpose of maintaining order. It will be noted that here, in defining a fully developed or completed political system, a state, it is no longer necessary to include a reference to its purpose in the definition. In the case of weaker political systems, reference to purpose is essential to distinguish the political system from other subsets of society; but the state is sufficiently distinguished by its possession of power and authority to enforce its commands by physical sanctions.

[11] Chapter 3.

between scientific laws and normative laws. Scientific laws express observed uniformities in natural processes or in human behavior. Prescriptive or normative laws, on the other hand, establish a rule of what *ought* to be rather than of what *is*. To say that men always seek to defend themselves above all else is an assertion (whether or not it is an accurate one), of a scientific law; while to say that man *ought* always to seek his own self-preservation above all else is an assertion of a normative proposition or law. Normative laws may easily be cast in the form of commands and often are. Thus "Thou shalt not kill" is at once a command and an asserted law (of God). It could equally well be stated, "It is wrong to kill" or "It is against the will of God to kill." We deal with normative laws in this section, for political laws clearly belong in this category.

Prescriptive Laws

Wherever we find men in society we find norms, or normative laws, established ways of doing things that people believe ought to be observed. There are generally laws about religious ceremonies; there are certainly laws about family relationships, laws governing who may marry whom, laws against incest, laws against wanton killing within the tribe, and laws regulating property relations and the conduct of economic activities. In civilized societies we can easily distinguish between various kinds of normative laws. The proposition that men ought to be kind to those who are suffering is a statement of ethical law. When we teach children that they should defer to their elders, that is a matter of manners. Private groups, such as clubs and other nonpolitical organizations have their laws, and the rules of a game may also be thought of as a kind of law. In a primitive society, lacking a fully developed state, it is difficult to make all of these distinctions. There is a great mass of custom. Not all customary ways of doing things would properly be called laws. A tribe might follow the custom of taking the evening meal at sundown, or of using a certain path when fetching water from a nearby spring, and yet these customs might not embody any obligation to behave in that fashion. Among the customs that are felt to be obligatory, religious, ethical, and other considerations may be hopelessly confused.

Political Law

The question arises, then, when does law become political law? What marks it as such? Not all the *mores* of a tribe or of any community constitute part of political law. In certain communities, and under certain circumstances, it is bad form for women to wear slacks. Members of the community, will say "women ought not to wear slacks to afternoon tea." Observation will disclose that in fact they do not do so. A woman who did so would probably be faced with raised eyebrows, a definite chilling in the manner of other women in the community towards her, and a lack of further invitations to tea. No other sanctions (means of enforcement) than these would be imposed, but in all likelihood they would be quite sufficient to achieve this purpose.

On the other hand, political law refers to a reality, not to an ideal. It is not to be confused with Natural Law. For present purposes, we need note only that in ordinary usage we clearly distinguish between the law that is and what ought to be. We are constantly criticizing our laws, judging them by some standard apart from the laws themselves saying that this law is bad, that one good, that this one ought to be amended, that one ought to be repealed. At the same time, another should be enacted: "There ought to be a law. . . ."

AUSTIN'S VIEW

Law then is not to be identified either with the *mores* of the community or with any standard of what ought to be enforced. A third possibility, is that law is what the state commands. Such a definition need not deny that the customary practices and the beliefs of the community are powerful influences in determining what the law shall be. It need only assert that these things become law only when they are in some way given the stamp of approval by an agency of the state having the authority to make or declare what is the law. This view has been widely held, especially by lawyers, since the time of the English jurist, John Austin, and has much to commend it. For certain purposes, it is entirely satisfactory. But as a definition for the generic term "law," as that term is used, and needs to be used by political scientists, it is too restrictive.

The Austinian definition would rule out primitive law. Yet primitive tribes that have not yet developed government, or organized sanctions for the enforcement of law, may still have what we would call laws, generally customary laws. They may be distinguished from non-legal custom for they involve obligations, and reciprocal rights and duties. The distinction between law and ethics in a primitive society is more difficult to identify but it clearly exists. Rules that pertain to the practical living and working arrangements of a given community that are recognized as being ethically indifferent, as long as there is agreement on a single rule, clearly cannot be classed as ethical laws. In modern society, the rule that vehicles should keep to the right falls in this class. In a primitive society, furthermore, there may be the added element of enforcement, still without *organized* enforcement. Laws may be enforced by the refusal of other members of the community to cooperate with the offenders, by the withholding of reciprocity where normally the performance of a certain duty by *A* calls for a reciprocal action by *B,* and by individual acts of retribution. Here, then, is an area of legal rules, albeit not sharply defined, that exists in the absence of a state, and yet that would not be included by the definition under consideration.

The Austinian definition departs from general usage also in that it excludes international law. In the absence of a superstate to create and enforce it international "law" cannot be law at all. This conclusion the Austinian boldly accepts. So-called international law, he says, is not law; it is only positive morality. A state, it is held, is under no legal obligation to respect the territory of other states, for example, or to abide by its treaties. Yet surely we speak and think of such international obligations as these as having a legal nature. They are more than custom; they oblige to a certain course of action. People feel that they ought to be obeyed because they are the law. Also, we distinguish between the moral obligation of a state to give assistance, let us say, to displaced persons (especially if it is well able to do so), and its legal obligation to extend reasonable police protection to nationals of other countries whom it has admitted within its borders. International law is analogous to primitive law in many respects.

THE RECOGNIZED NORMS OF A POLITICAL SYSTEM

If then we are to rule out the definition of law as the command of the state, what is the answer to our inquiry?[12] From one point of view it is very simple indeed. The discussion we have just engaged in closely parallels our earlier discussion of states and political systems. We noted there that a state is a kind of political system, but that the latter concept is broader and less definite. So it is with law that is not the command of a state: it is a species of a larger genus than state law. We might possibly define it as simply the system of rules that constitute a political system. It is necessary, however, even within such a system, to distinguish between legal rules and others that might better be denominated "conventions," "understandings," or "rules of the game." With respect to legal rules, in the first place, we must recognize that a high degree of obedience is important. Without this a vital element of the regularity that is of the essence of law is lacking. As we have seen, many forces operate to hold people in line with accepted standards of conduct in any community. Under circumstances like those prevailing in many primitive communities or among sovereign states, informal sanctions like public opinion and the implicit threat of economic sanction may suffice.[13] Under the complicated circumstances and the widely inclusive scope of legal regulation prevailing in civilized states, such vague sanctions are not enough. Here the addition of organized sanctions, relying in the last analysis upon the threat of physical force, is requisite. It is the peculiar function of the state to provide these sanctions. For this reason many students have seized

[12] We may note in passing that there are other, more technical objections, to the definition of law as the command of the state. See H.L.A. Hart, *The Concept of Law* (Oxford: Clarendon, 1961), Chs. 1-4.

[13] As the example of international law reveals, rules may be considered legal even though there is a great deal of noncompliance by a minority of the community.

upon this element of organized sanctions as the critical test of law. Others, noting the importance of some agency to define the law, to give it precision, have pointed to the existence of courts as determinative. It certainly cannot be denied that in almost any society courts are a great improvement in the legal system; but in view of what has been said above they cannot be held absolutely essential. In a complicated and dynamic society the legal system could not survive without them. Even the international society, virtually anarchic though it is, makes use of courts. On the other hand, a society with courts still may not constitute a state as defined above.

We have ruled out various proposed tests but we have not yet said what is the essence of political law. We suggest that *political law consists of rules of conduct pertaining to a given political system that are recognized by the bulk of the members of that society as belonging to it, and as possessing a certain validity or claim upon them for that reason. The fact of their being rules of that political system gives them a 'rightness' or legitimacy they would not otherwise enjoy.*

Here, a further refinement. It is convenient to speak of the defining characteristic of law as relating to a "political system." A few words of elaboration will be useful. The distinguishing characteristic of legal rules, of law, is subjective—it lies in the way the rules are regarded by the bulk of the people to whom they apply. This attitude may be created and fostered by a number of facts, including general obedience, some measure of enforcement, and some belief that the rules are valuable to the collectivity, the political order to whom they apply. In a measure the attitude is produced by obedience and enforcement; perhaps equally obedience is produced and enforcement made possible by the attitude. The relation is one of reciprocity.

HART'S REFINEMENT

Following Professor Hart, the concept of political law may be still further sharpened and refined by remarking that a system of law consists of two kinds of rules: primary and secondary. The primary rules are substantive. They define crimes and their punishment, determine the rights and duties of property owners, regulate business transactions, and so forth. These rules must be generally obeyed. The secondary rules are of three kinds: one group specifies the criteria of legal validity, the tests by which law is distinguished in that society from morals or any other system of norms; two other groups provide respectively for the manner of changing the rules and for the means for settling disputes about the meaning or application of the rules. These secondary rules must, in Hart's words, "be effectively accepted as common public standards of official behavior" by the officials of the government.[14]

[14] *Op. cit.*, p. 113.

SOVEREIGNTY

We have managed to discuss and define the words "state" and "law" without using that controversial term "sovereignty." Yet it is impossible to define these terms without reference to the substance of sovereignty, whether or not the word is used. The "state," we insisted, must have a government with the power and the authority to enforce its will on its members, by resort to physical sanctions if necessary, and must not be in turn subject to any like power. This is the essence of the concept of sovereignty. The difference between law in a state and law in a less well developed political system, to recapitulate, is that in a state there is an agency (government) with final and complete authority to define and enforce the law. The existence of such an agency gives to a state and its legal system the quality of sovereignty. Sovereignty entails legal independence, self-sufficiency, and completeness, and includes machinery for changing the law, for the precise and final determination of what the law is, and what it requires in a particular situation.

A Definition

Sovereignty may be defined as *that quality or characteristic of a state by virtue of which its legal system is unified, self-consistent, self-defining, self-contained, and capable of change.* It provides the distinction between state and prestate, between state law and primitive law. These distinctions, enumerated and discussed in earlier sections of this chapter, are summarily expressed in the word "sovereignty." They comprise its meaning. In a primitive society there may be disagreement over what the law is or about how it should be applied in a particular case; and there may be no clearly defined procedure for resolving this disagreement. It is a mark of the (sovereign) state that for every concrete case such a procedure must exist. It is not essential that the final authority should always reside in the same body. All that is required is that the law should provide some organ with that authority for any given situation and a means for identifying the authority when the need arises. Relatively undeveloped political systems hobble along without sovereignty, though it is frequently an unsatisfactory situation, with deadlock, violent conflict, and even civil war ever threatening. This is the unhappy situation in which the inchoate world political system finds itself. Sovereignty is not simply a theory that is convenient for lawyers of a systematic cast of mind, but a fact of political organization (manifested in its legal system, to which the facts of political life must reasonably correspond) that is of basic importance to the life of a community.[15]

[15] For elaboration of this point, see pages 654-656.

The "Indivisibility" of Sovereignty

One of the attributes of sovereignty that has caused misunderstanding is its indivisibility. Yet, properly understood, the attribution is both unimpeachable and unobjectionable. It has not always been properly understood even by the proponents of sovereignty. Bodin, for example, sought to show, from the indivisibility of sovereignty, that a mixed government, in which rule is shared by king and legislature, is impossible. Clearly this contention is absurd. All that is properly meant by saying that sovereignty is indivisible is that the state's legal system must have ultimate unity. This does not mean that the exercise of authority may not be parcelled out among various organs of government. It means only that there are no legal vacuums, no unresolvable legal contradictions, and no ultimately competing authorities. The constitution of a state may prohibit a law abridging the freedom of speech. But the constitution of a sovereign state will provide a means by which even such a prohibition can be amended. Two laws may seem to be mutually contradictory. Yet, if I, for instance, act to infringe on your interests and I rely on one of these laws and you on the other, in a sovereign state a legal means will be provided for determining which of us is in the right, or what is the legally correct course of action.

The indivisibility of sovereignty is even compatible with a federal system like that of the United States, where various authorities have power that is *final*, within defined jurisdictions. The terminology by which we refer to New York as a "state" is misleading and at variance with the proper signification of that term in political science. Similarly reference to the "states" as possessing "sovereignty" is not in accord with scientific usage. Neither the states nor the federal government, but only the United States as a whole, is sovereign.[16]

Confusion can be avoided only if it is recognized that in popular and semi-popular usage the distinctions and definitions outlined above are not always observed. Just as we speak of "states" of the Union, it is also common to speak of the "sovereignty" of these states, and, sometimes of sovereignty as being divided. In each case it would be more accurate to speak of "power" or "authority" rather than of "sovereignty."

---

[16] Jurists distinguish between sovereignty itself and its exercise. The former is a characteristic of the state as a whole. In any particular case it may be exercised by an organ or branch of government or subdivision of the state. Thus a state of the Union (in the United States) may for certain purposes *exercise* sovereignty. Furthermore, it or its government shares "sovereign immunity" in that it may not be sued without its own consent. See Westel W. Willoughby, *The Fundamental Concepts of Public Law* (New York: Macmillan, 1931), Chs. 13–14. See pp. 249-252 for substantiation of the last sentence in the paragraph above.

Sovereignty and Legal Independence

A sovereign legal system must also be self-contained, legally independent of any other legal system. The reason should be clear. The theory of sovereignty does not place any barriers whatsoever in the way of a given state yielding up its sovereignty to another state or becoming part of a larger political unit which thereby becomes a state. The theory holds only that the subordinate unit itself then ceases to be sovereign. Such a thing occurs, for example, when a group of previously independent states form a federation.

It should also be noted that the theory of sovereignty, when combined with the definition of law advanced above, is not incompatible with the existence of international law. A sovereign state cannot be subject to another state, but it may be subject to certain legal restrictions that emanate from a less well developed political and legal system than that of a state. By the same token, it may bind itself by treaty not to exercise its powers in certain ways. For instance, it might bind itself not to change its tariffs or the value of its currency without the consent of other states.

Furthermore, this theory of sovereignty is entirely consistent with recognition of the facts that there may be legal limitations upon governments and sociological limitations upon states. Let us say a word about each, in turn. Governments in constitutional states are set within legal orders which determine their bounds and may limit their activities. In the United States no government may pass an ex post facto law. Yet this prohibition is not a limitation upon the sovereignty of the state because the Constitution provides a legal procedure for its own amendment by which that limitation could be altered. Even the state, as it operates through the amending power, is subject to limitations. It may strive to enact law that runs so counter to the convictions of large numbers of its people that it fails to be obeyed and to receive the requisite "acceptance." Such was the case with the ill-fated prohibition experiment in the United States, at least in some sections of the country. But this is not a *legal* limitation upon the state; it is a practical limitation.

The theory of sovereignty here defended says nothing about the location of final authority. It is compatible with any location of such authority, including the situation that prevails in the United States, where there is no single point or body in which such authority can be said to reside. Sovereignty is a *quality* of a state. Like the honesty of a man or the beauty of a flower it does not need to be located.

Finally, the moral authority of the state is not in question. The theory of sovereignty is equally compatible with the doctrine that the state's commands are morally absolute and with the contention that they have no a priori validity, or any theory that falls between those extremes.

Political Sovereignty

All that has been said relates to *legal* sovereignty, to sovereignty as a characteristic of the legal aspect of the state. The term is also used in a political sense. Its meaning in this sense closely parallels the meaning of the legal term. A sovereign state,[17] in other words, must not only be legally independent of any other state but it must have a substantial measure of political independence. The point at which a "satellite" loses so much independence as to cease to be a state and to become a part of another state is a matter of degree; but without some measure of independence there is no sovereignty. Likewise, the state must not only have a government with legal authority to defend and elaborate its body of law and to resolve all disputes, but this government must be in practice generally able to enforce its decisions. In short, political sovereignty means merely that there must be a substantial degree of correspondence between the propositions of legal sovereignty and the actual behavioral facts of political life. We have already suggested that a so-called state that is unable to enforce its commands generally is at least verging on the border of ceasing to be a state. One might say, at some point, that it had lost its sovereignty; but by the same token, since sovereignty is a defining characteristic of state it would have lost its statehood as well. To assert that it was still "legally" sovereign even though it had lost effective control (political sovereignty) would simply be to assert that the central government, and perhaps other states, still took the position that it was entitled to the obedience that in fact was denied it. Such a claim would be a tactic designed to win back the support of disaffected elements. The longer it failed the more unrealistic it would be to continue to assert a "legal" sovereignty for which there was no political counterpart.[18]

SELECTED READINGS

AUSTIN, JOHN. Introd. H. L. A. Hart, *The Province of Jurisprudence Determined.* London: Wiedenfeld & Nicolson, 1954. Austin's lectures, first published in 1832, constitute the classic statement of the formalistic theory of law and of sovereignty. See especially Lectures 5, 6.

BARKER, ERNEST. *National Character and the Factors in its Formation.* New York: Harper, 1927. A standard work on national character.

——— trans., introd., notes, apps. *The Politics of Aristotle.* Oxford: Clarendon, 1946. Aristotle's most general discussion of the nature of the state is to be found in Book I of the *Politics*.

[17] Technically, this often used expression is redundant, for a state is sovereign by definition, being thus distinguished from other political systems.

[18] For fuller treatments of the subject of sovereignty, see Willoughby, *op. cit.,* esp. Ch. 8; J. Roland Pennock, "Law and Sovereignty," *American Political Science Review,* 31 (1937), pp. 617-637; and W. J. Rees, "The Theory of Sovereignty Restated," in Peter Laslett (ed.), *Philosophy, Politics and Society* (Oxford: Blackwell, 1956), pp. 56-82.

BENN, S. I., and PETERS, R. S. *Social Principles and the Democratic State*. London: Allen & Unwin, 1959. Ch. 3 of this excellent treatise deals with legal theory; Ch. 12 discusses sovereignty and the state.

BODIN, JEAN, TOOLEY, M. J., abr., trans. *Six Books of the Commonwealth*. Oxford: Blackwell, n.d. Bodin's famous definition of sovereignty, the first to be propounded, appears in Book VIII.

DE JOUVENAL, BERTRAND. *Sovereignty*, trans. J. F. Huntington. Cambridge, Eng.: The University Press, 1957, Part III, "The Sovereign," contains helpful insights.

DE MADARIAGA, SALVADOR. *Englishmen, Frenchmen, Spaniards, an Essay in Comparative Psychology*. London: Oxford U. P., 1925. A stimulating study of national character, especially as manifested in forms of speech.

DIESING, PAUL. *Reason in Society: Five Types of Decisions and Their Social Conditions*. Urbana, Ill.: Univ. Ill. Press, 1962. Chs. 3 and 4, dealing with legal and political rationality respectively, contain valuable insights. Diesing interprets reason broadly, to include much more than calculation.

HART, H. L. A. *The Concept of Law*. Oxford: Clarendon, 1961. The most careful modern statement of the formalistic theory of law.

HOBBES, THOMAS. *Leviathan*. Oxford: Blackwell, 1946. The theory of the virtually unlimited sovereignty of the state receives its most vigorous statement in this political classic.

HYMAN, HERBERT H. *Political Socialization: A Study in the Psychology of Political Behavior*. Glencoe, Ill.: Free Press, 1959. The literature on political socialization is here digested and organized.

LASLETT, PETER (ed.). *Philosophy, Politics and Society*. Oxford: Blackwell, 1956. Ch. 4, by W. J. Rees, "The Theory of Sovereignty Restated," dispells many confusions and obscurities.

LASSWELL, HAROLD D., and KAPLAN, ABRAHAM. *Power and Society, A Framework for Political Inquiry*. New Haven, Conn.: Yale U. P., 1950. A valuable essay supplying political science with a body of precise definitions and significant scientific propositions.

PARSONS, TALCOTT. *The Social System*. Glencoe, Ill.: Free Press, 1951. Perhaps the best treatise on political sociology, especially as it applies to political organization.

WEBER, MAX. *From Max Weber: Essays in Sociology*, trans., ed., introd. by H. H. Gerth and C. Wright Mills. New York: Oxford U. P., 1946. Weber's work impinges on politics at many points. The essay on "Politics as a Vocation," is especially relevant to the present chapter.

CHAPTER 6

Ends of the State

||||||||||||||||||||||||||||||||||||||||||||||||||||||||||||||||||||||||||||||

GENERAL

Security, justice, liberty, and welfare—these are the ends or purposes of political activity, at least in the modern state. They are ends of the state in the sense that they are the human purposes it serves and that justify its existence and the obligation of its members, *certeris paribus,* to obey its commands and render it support.

A critic with an eye for simplicity, or a devotee of laissez-faire policy might argue that the whole of the ends of the state—indeed the unique and comprehensive function of the state—can be summed up in a single word: order. Order provides security; it also sets men free; it not only supplies the foundation of justice but is actually central to it, because orderly as contrasted with arbitrary arrangements comprise a major part of the substance of justice; and finally order is, in society, an absolute prerequisite for welfare. The point is worth making for it brings out sharply an important fact: that order may have value in itself or may be, in some relations, the means to other ends. The modern welfare state also does far more than provide the basis (by establishing order) for the public welfare; it seeks the positive advancement of welfare in ways that go far beyond the provision of order. And while order is prerequisite to liberty, it by no means guarantees it.

"Welfare" might also suggest itself as the inclusive "end" of the state. Other ends, one could argue, are aspects or parts of welfare, but in practice they do not allow themselves to be so easily submerged. The ends of the state, as any governor soon discovers, are frequently at odds with each other. In the welfare state, especially, this problem often becomes acute. The means appropriate for the provision of welfare may conflict with the demands of liberty. Comprehensive medical care could be more easily provided if the freedom of patients to choose their own doctors were drastically curtailed. If farmers are to enjoy both the benefits of high prices for their products and the security of their positions as independent farm owners, their liberty to plant whatever crops they choose may suffer. Regulatory legislation limits liberty at almost every turn. Sometimes it limits one man's liberty to preserve another's; more frequently it curtails freedom for the sake of security, justice, or welfare.

We are, then, making two points. One is that, broadly speaking, the ends we have listed constitute the major purposes toward which governmental activities, in varying degrees, are directed. Time and circumstance, the stage of political development, greatly affect the relative emphasis placed upon each of the ends and the degree to which they may be secured through other social institutions—for instance, the family or the economy—without intervention by the polity. Nevertheless, all states pursue these ends. Our other point is concerned with political science as a discipline. In directing attention to these ends of the state, we are arguing that the most important aim of public policy can be usefully described as that of achieving the best possible ("optimum") combination of these ends. For the political scientist it is important to understand the manner in which these ends conflict and supplement each other, particularly as they are pursued through the institutions of government and the state. Clear thinking also requires that we understand what such terms as liberty, justice, equality, and welfare mean and how they are used.

SECURITY

Since the development of the concept of "the king's peace," the protection of the individual against physical violence has been a major purpose of states. The right to private violence was once the norm; the state's monopoly of violence developed slowly and piecemeal. The duel and the blood feud continued very late in some countries. While the modern state has in most instances prohibited dueling, social approval has often made the law ineffective. Even student dueling experienced a recrudescence in German universities following the Second World War. The persistence of such behavior provides another example of man's ambivalence, indicating that while security is normally a desideratum, it is not under all conditions the most fundamental of human needs. Although in the modern state socially approved violence is highly exceptional, the difficulty of controlling violence during strikes and the common inability of the law-enforcement machinery in such situations to enforce all the legal rights of nonstrikers controvert the easy assumption that law and order prevail in all save the cases of ordinary criminals.

Activities such as we have been describing are directed at the protection of people's property as well as their persons. This aspect of the security function needs no elaboration.

The state is concerned not only with deliberate attacks upon person and property but with accidental injuries as well. Safety regulations for factories, mines, and other places of work or recreation, guard the security of us all. Building codes are designed to prevent the erection of buildings that are unsafe.

Economic Security

At this point security of person and property easily merges into economic security, for the state often provides compensation for the person whose security has been violated. In part, especially in cases where the person held to be responsible for the injury must pay the compensation, the laws may be preventive, designed to prevent injury by making it costly to those who are in a position to secure against it. This is the way with employers' liability laws. By requiring employers to pay compensation for injuries suffered by their employees, such laws make it the interest of employers to take safety precautions. Under workman's compensation legislation, where the payments come out of a general fund, this element of personal liability is minimized or eliminated. The primary objective in the second type of law is to give compensation for injury suffered. Compensation makes the injured person no more secure against injury but it does give him economic security; it prevents the costs of injury using up his savings or reducing him to dependence on charity. Economic or social security will be discussed under welfare, but it is mentioned here to indicate how it grows out of personal security. The modern state, by prevention and inspection, by punishment and damages, endeavors to render persons and their property secure; to impose on others wide duties to prevent injury; and to give injured persons the means, by civil suit or insurance, to offset as far as possible the consequences of injury to person or property when it occurs.

Security Against Abuse of Power by Public Officials

Government itself and its officials may cause great insecurity to many people. In the well-ordered state pains are taken to minimize this danger. In addition to various restraints imposed by constitutional governments upon the acts of their officials, remedies are needed for cases where, inadvertently, agents of the state acting in their official capacity injure or otherwise damage innocent individuals. In common-law countries the doctrine that the state could not be sued without its own consent has in the past worked serious hardship on many individuals. The typical example is that of personal injury or property damage caused by a mail truck. Theoretically, the driver is liable if he was at fault, but in practice he seldom has the means to pay proper compensation. At the present time, tort claims laws grant general consent for damage suits directly against the government in most of these cases.

National Security

In speaking of security against private individuals and public officials, we have thus far neglected the aspect of security that today perforce engages the major attention of many states—national security. The protection of its people against attack and destruction or enslavement by other organized peoples, and the protection of their institutions, have been traditional functions of government. The need for these played a large role in bringing the state into existence. For most states it has always been of major importance. Today war constitutes the most serious threat to personal security to which man is subject. It is also a threat to his way of life and the machinery (independent government) controlling his own destiny.

The continued existence of our present civilization may depend upon war's speedy elimination, but the record to date provides scanty basis for optimism. Just as in the absence of the state men quarrel and resort to violence against each other, so states (lacking a common government) apparently cannot live together in peace. It is significant to note that in the fiscal year 1960 the United States spent approximately 10 per cent of its national income for national security, as contrasted with about one per cent in 1937. Moreover, the fear of war and of cold-war espionage is so great that nations are tempted to take measures that conflict with such ends of the state as justice and liberty, in order to maintain that security upon which all else rests.

The tragedy of this great expenditure of resources and interference with other vital ends of the state is that security from attack is no greater than in the past. In the case of other forms of security provided by the state, we progress. Not so in respect to military security. There have been periods in which the average person could feel fairly safe from the ravages of war, although he generally had to share in its cost, but today virtually no one is safe from direct attack, and undoubtedly fear of annihilation by atomic or other weapons pervades more of the earth's population than ever before. (Even before the ravages of World War II, according to an authoritative estimate, the proportion of the total population whose deaths are directly attributable to war had increased among European countries from about two per cent in the seventeenth century to about three per cent in the twentieth century.)[1] Many states, too, have in the past been relatively secure in their national independence. Of no state in the world can the same be said today.

Reasonable Predictability

Other aspects of the problem of security may safely be left to the reader's imagination. For instance, in the economic realm, a high degree of stability

---

[1] Quincy Wright, *A Study of War*, 2 vols. (Chicago: Univ. of Chicago Press, 1942), Vol. I, pp. 242-248.

or at least of predictability is a *sine qua non* for rapid advance. If individuals cannot be reasonably certain that what they save today will be available tomorrow, the incentive to save will be wanting; and a society that does not save does not advance in productive capacity.[2] Likewise, men will not be inclined to make long-term contracts or to embark upon enterprises requiring long periods before they "pay off" unless they can be reasonably sure that the rules of the game—the laws governing such endeavors—will not be altered to their detriment after they have made their initial investment. If it is a paradox that men insist on a general regime of law and order so as to secure freedom for economic risk-taking, it is one that is easily resolved. Not blind risks, but the opportunity to make *calculated* risks that would enable them to profit by superior shrewdness is what they seek. Whether or not the system of free enterprise, from which our examples are taken, prevails, a state that fails to assure a fair degree of certainty in the area under discussion will not experience economic progress. Such progress depends upon planning, whether by individuals or governments; and useful plans, as distinct from dreams, are impossible without predictability.

The same point can be illustrated in the political field. Here too uncertainty tends to lead to the cessation of constructive action. Take the case of totalitarian regimes. Everyone is aware of the perilous existence led by politicians and bureaucrats in states where purges are substituted for elections; but it is perhaps less generally recognized that one of the great handicaps to initiative and positive action in such regimes is the fear to act. Administrators are fearful because the reaction of higher-ups is unpredictable. They know they may be condemned as saboteurs or traitors merely because it is judged that there must be a change in policy, or because scapegoats are needed. They seek security in inaction, negative action, and "buck-passing." Hardly any characteristic of modern dictatorship is more widely attested to than this.

Other Aspects

Enough has been said to suggest the profound effects of the search for security, of how it is not one thing but many, and of how these various things often conflict with each other and with other ends of the state. It is frequently the demand for greater security that gives rise to a totalitarian regime. Yet the end result of this demand, if it is successful, is to produce a regime of arbitrary rule in which there is very little security indeed. One insecurity is traded for another, greater one.

Similarly, the highest degree of security is to be found in a completely

---

[2] In a fully socialized society, this function may be performed by the state. Even in the Soviet Union, however, individual saving in the form of loans to the state is encouraged.

ordered, static society; yet such a society is by definition incompatible with progress, and is bound to cramp the area of liberty. Man's desires for self-development and for new experience require a dynamic society, one in which men have freedom to choose and to experiment.

LIBERTY[3]

In turning our attention from security to liberty, we move into an area of greater subtlety and difficulty. Liberty is a term of many meanings, or at least it is a concept of many facets. Particular concepts of liberty are important for particular theories or forms of government. Both the theory of the operation of democracy, for instance, and its justification involve conceptions of liberty. Consequently, we shall devote considerable attention to the matter of definitions.

Some states have suppressed liberty for long periods of time. How then can it be said that liberty is a universal political end? The answer lies partly in the fact that sometimes other ends, such as security or welfare, were so threatened that liberty had to be curtailed if the other ends of the state were to be attained, especially in time of war or social revolution.

Of course, states have frequently been governed by minority groups interested only in liberty for themselves. Even in such cases, though, it is liberty for certain people and for certain purposes (political) that is denied. Finally, and this simple point is of prime importance, no state *can* suppress liberty entirely. In fact, it cannot help but greatly increase the extent of effective freedom of action that would exist without the state. This much it does merely by establishing some settled rules and maintaining order.

Definitions

Definitions of liberty can be classified according to general types. A major distinction is between negative concepts, which stress simple lack of restraint, and positive definitions, which emphasize some content or purpose in liberty. The difference is partly a matter of the distinction between definitions that treat the concept as morally neutral and those that define it in such a way as to rule out instances of liberty that may do more harm than good.

From another point of view, definitions may be classified as "objective" or "subjective." Objective definitions stress bodily freedom, absence of specific restraints, and effective legal guarantees of observable freedom; they employ terms that can be readily identified by an outside observer. Subjec-

---

[3] Because liberty is so dependent upon order and security, while welfare is closely linked to justice, we depart in our exposition from the order in which the ends were listed at the beginning of the chapter.

tive definitions, on the other hand, lay primary, if not exclusive emphasis, upon states of mind. They hold that the way to determine whether a man is free is to ask him. If he feels free, he *is* free; even though his body is confined in a jail or is nailed to a cross.

LIBERTY AS FREEDOM TO DO AS ONE PLEASES

Objective definitions of liberty—often called "realistic"—tend to define it as "absence of restraint" or "freedom to do as one pleases." As Hobbes put it, liberty is the absence of "external impediments of motion." In accordance with this most extreme version of the realistic definition, fear and liberty are entirely consistent: if a man points a gun at me and says "Your money or your life," I am perfectly free. I have my choice; I can either give him the money or suffer the consequences. If he takes my money and thereupon binds and gags me, then, and not until then, in Hobbes's view am I deprived of my liberty.

Probably Hobbes himself recognized that his definition was somewhat paradoxical. Of course, the man who hands over his purse to a robber is acting in accordance with his own will, at the moment; but it is stretching matters to say that he is doing as he pleases. The whole situation is probably distinctly displeasing to him! He has a choice, to be sure, but neither choice is a pleasant one. What he faces is not freedom, but a dilemma. The realist generally means by freedom not only a situation in which there is choice but also one where at least one of the possible lines of action may be taken without displeasure. Perhaps even that statement is not completely accurate. It has been suggested that the key is to be found in the *motive* to action. A person is not free, then, if he acts in response to a motive to which he does not *like* to respond, such as fear. On the other hand, making choices in response to positive (liked) or neutral (not disliked) motives is the essence of freedom.

This definition avoids the obvious difficulty of Hobbes's view, which runs counter to ordinary usage in making liberty compatible with coercion. Furthermore, it implies nothing about freedom of the will. It merely recognizes the fact of choice: the fact, that is to say, that there are situations in which neither physical "impediments to motion" nor fear of dire consequences determines our actions. That something does determine our actions and that even our wishes are conditioned by previous training and the society around us, is irrelevant. If I would like to go somewhere but am in jail, I am not free. If I would like to keep my money but hand it over to the hold-up man because of fear of death, I am not free. But, if my early training has conditioned me to want to give my money to charity, I am no less free than if I spent it to gratify more "personal" desires.[4]

----

[4] However, what is sometimes called "psychological freedom" may be limited by psychological compulsions that hamper rational behavior, and a person's "potential freedom" may be interfered with by manipulative practices or institutions of which he is

Suppose, however, that I decline to travel by air because I am fearful of an accident. Surely most of us would not consider this an instance of unfreedom. So we have probably not yet hit upon the exact meaning of those who define freedom as liberty to do as one pleases. Perhaps the key notion, in addition to the basic possibility of choice, is that our actions should not be substantially influenced by the deliberate efforts of others who do so by appealing to our fear or other disliked motives. For example, the normal hazards of air travel, whether or not they fill me with fear, do not interfere with my freedom. On the other hand, if I am prevented from taking a plane by reason of the fact that someone has threatened to wreck the plane if I do so, my freedom is definitely curtailed. Yet again, if someone influences my choice not by threats but by offering me a reward, I would not say that my freedom was in any way diminished. Freedom, then, in the sense which we have been discussing, means the ability to choose—and to act accordingly—without physical impediment or deliberate coercion.

The objections that may be advanced against this definition will be considered in connection with alternative definitions. One important point, however, should be made at this time to forestall misunderstanding. An objection that freedom as just defined sometimes leads to bad results is not strictly relevant. Persons who define liberty as set forth above seldom contend that liberty is always good. What liberty is, is one thing; why, how much, and under what conditions liberty is good is quite another thing—one we shall discuss in due course.

LIBERTY AS FREEDOM OF THE "REAL" OR RATIONAL SELF

At the opposite extreme from the objective or "realistic" definitions are those which insist that true liberty must be used for some good purpose. Such people seem to be confusing the problem of defining liberty with the question of its evaluation. Idealist philosophers, though, have found it possible to bring this notion within the concept of "absence of restraint." The reasoning goes as follows. Surely the root idea of liberty, or freedom, is the absence of restraint; but restraints may be internal as well as external. I may be restrained by my ignorance. Suppose I am trying in vain to escape from the control of a tyrant and someone tells me how it can be done; has he not as truly liberated me as though he had removed the restraints with his own hands? Suppose I wish to get away from my present mode of life, as a common laborer and become a skilled craftsman, and suppose further that a friend or the state provides me with the necessary training, does not that free me? But suppose, then, that as a young man, I am compelled, against my wishes, to undergo such training, with results that I later recognize as having

---

unaware. According to this classification, freedom as discussed above is the area of "social freedom." For a fruitful discussion along these lines, consult Christian Bay, *The Structure of Freedom* (Stanford, Calif.: Stanford U. P., 1958).

freed me from a narrow, shallow, and unsatisfying life; was I forced to be free? It is plain that by this kind of reasoning, each step of which seems logical enough, one may be led from the concept of freedom as absence of restraint to something that is almost the exact opposite.

It may further be argued that not only ignorance but also passion may enslave the real me, my "real" self. We speak of a person as being a slave to his passions. Then surely anything which keeps his passions in control and allows his rational self to prevail makes him free. We all have a concept of our own self as something relatively constant which is not to be identified with the self that acts on a passing whim. The real me is the better, more rational me, the self which more nearly approximates my ideal self. I may say that I yielded to temptation and let my desire for amusement get the better of me—meaning that I let the transient desire prevail over a more settled purpose; but, except as a joke, I would not say that I let my will to study get the better of me—meaning that I let my will prevail over the desire to go to the movies.

If we think of this usage simply in relation to "good" and "bad" desires, it may seem quite arbitrary for us to identify the self with the good, and accordingly to argue that whatever restrains the bad really makes *us* free. If we distinguish, as above, between desires that are relatively constant, on which we have deliberated in connection with other wants, and which form part of an integrated, harmonious pattern of purposes, and other desires that may be transient and that conflict with the attainment of our settled purposes, the matter appears in a different light. The idea of a self connotes the ideas of continuity and integration and is opposed to a congeries of passing and mutually conflicting desires. To put the matter in yet another way, let us suppose two men. One of them allows himself to be tossed hither and yon in purposeless abandon on the tides of circumstance and his own unstable desires. He achieves nothing. He lives from day to day, and such purposes as he does weakly formulate are constantly frustrated by his inability to discipline himself for their accomplishment. Vaguely, he would like to set himself up in business, but instead of saving to accumulate the necessary capital he spends his surplus as fast as he gets it on frivolous pastimes, which he no sooner enjoys than he regrets. The other man knows what he wants in life and gets it. He has learned to curb those of his desires that are most directly incompatible with the attainment of his objective and to modify and redirect others so that he has an integrated personality. He has come to enjoy the things that are necessary for the attainment of his ends so that frustration is minimized, and he experiences a maximum of that "spontaneous activity of the total integrated personality" which is one psychologist's definition of freedom.[5] We do not stretch the common meaning of the term to say that the second man enjoys more freedom than the first.

---

[5] Erich Fromm, *Escape from Freedom* (New York: Rinehart, 1941), p. 258.

If, then, it is the integrated or rational self that must be free, what of external controls on irrational action? Do they increase freedom? Can man be forced to be free, as Rousseau at one point argued? Some would go all the way and say that as long as force is used to advance the development of the "real," "rational," or "good" self it is contributing to freedom. Others, more moderate, would say an action taken as a result of external compulsion could not be free, but that, if the action led to further, uncoerced actions that represented a more integrated purpose than had previously prevailed, then the original compulsion (or restraint) contributed to freedom. As will be discussed, the more moderate conclusion about liberty to be derived from the distinction between more and less "real" selves we believe to be sound, though the extreme view runs too counter to the core of the general understanding of the term, "freedom," to serve as an admissible definition.

A PROPOSED DEFINITION

Definition is in some measure an arbitrary matter. Words, as Humpty-Dumpty said, mean just what we make them mean. A scientist can invent terms and define them as he pleases, simply being careful to adhere consistently to the definitions he has constructed. Theoretically, a social scientist can do the same thing. The social sciences, however, deal with familiar things and ideas for which there are already terms in general usage. Confusion ensues if familiar words are not employed in their ordinary meaning. Unfortunately, common usage, especially in the case of words that stand for very general ideas, like "liberty," is likely to be vague. In fact, the word "liberty" (and "freedom") is used in different senses at different times, by the same people, and doubtless without their being aware of the fact. If we are to speak with precision about the subject, then, we must be somewhat arbitrary in adopting a definition; and it seems to us desirable to define the term at a point somewhere between the extremes of the realistic and idealistic positions outlined above.

We mean by "liberty," or "freedom," the opportunity for deliberate individual self-direction in the formation and accomplishment of one's purposes. The free act must be an act of uncoerced will, involving choice. Moreover, to be free in the fullest sense it must be an act of will, and not of mere impulse. It must relate to the settled purposes (hence the use of the word "deliberate," above) of the doer rather than to a passing whim. We add that the individual who is enabled to accomplish his purpose is to that extent freer than one who is not. An individual may be free even when subject to restrictions (and compulsions), if those restrictions facilitate the achievement of his purposes, and provided he willingly accepts these restrictions in principle. The distinction here is between freedom of the act and freedom of the man. If a student is compelled to attend a given class against his will, it can hardly be said that his act of attendance is a free act. But if he has deliberately decided that he wants to be a physician, and if the class in question is part of a prescribed premedical curriculum, then the restrictions that check his immediate impulse (to cut the class) contribute to his larger freedom. This example illustrates both the point that restrictions can be compatible with freedom and the distinction between whims or relatively fleeting desires and settled purposes. The example also shows the relation between the two; for restrictions may promote liberty precisely by preventing the whims from interfering with the purposes. The two provisos are important; the restrictions must be essential to the accomplishment of the purpose, and they must be willingly accepted in principle even though they are felt as limitations upon liberty in moments of rebellion.

Our definition implies more than has so far been made explicit. An individual who, through education, is able to exercise his powers more effectively than he otherwise could is thereby and to that extent given greater freedom. Also, one who, by learning to observe the rules of good manners, is better able to secure the cooperation of others in the accomplishment of his purposes has also enlarged his freedom. (This statement is not incompatible with the fact that certain people may accomplish their purposes more fully by at least occasional resort to bad manners.) Further, if he has freely adopted purposes that are consonant with those of others about him, and thereby enlisted their cooperation, once more his liberty has been expanded.

Conversely, one who has not the material means with which to gratify his desires is, other things being equal, less free than one who has, though in saying this we are treading on dangerous ground. The means to fulfill one's purposes must not be substituted for freedom to form purposes. He who becomes chiefly concerned with material things as sources of comfort rather than as means to the full development of his powers may find that he has lost that "total, integrated personality" whose spontaneous exercise is the essence of freedom. Hungry men cannot be fully free; but they may be far freer than well-fed men who lack other, more vital elements of freedom. Inequality tends to curtail the freedom of the less privileged; but it is wholly wrong to argue, as some "totalitarian liberals" have argued, that anything that increases equality increases freedom, *regardless of the amount of compulsion involved.*

Finally, one who uses this definition of liberty cannot insist too much that it must not be confused with the view that freedom consists in doing what is right, or rational, without regard for the amount of constraint. The

⁶ For respectively brief, full, and very extensive discussions of liberty, see J. Roland Pennock, *Liberal Democracy: Its Merits and Prospects* (New York: Holt, 1950), pp. 58-63; Dorothy Fosdick, *What Is Liberty?* (New York: Harper, 1939); and Mortimer J. Adler, *The Idea of Freedom, A Dialectical Examination of the Conceptions of Freedom* (Garden City, N. Y.: Doubleday, 1958).

central core remains self-determination. Without that there is no liberty. The permanent rather than the transient "I" chooses; but it is *my* choice, not someone else's, no matter how much better theirs may be.[6]

Liberty for All

Thus far, we have been dealing with liberty entirely from the point of view of the individual. We have said nothing about one person's liberty being limited by that of another. Mr. Justice Holmes once remarked that my liberty to swing my fist ends at the other fellow's nose. But Holmes was there using the term liberty, in accordance with a common elision, to stand for "the right to liberty." What he meant was that I am not *entitled* to use my liberty in such a way as to interfere with the other fellow's liberty or, for that matter, to do him damage in other ways. Or Holmes may have meant that the law, through its threat of sanctions, actually restrains me, and so does limit my liberty. The fact that I am restrained from punching the other fellow's nose is indeed a limitation upon my liberty, although one that ought certainly to be imposed.

The matter may be viewed from another angle: from the point of view of society as a whole rather than from that of a single individual. This coupling does not oppose society to the men who make it up. We are merely broadening the focus to include a large number of individuals instead of only a single one. To take a simple case, suppose we find one man with ten slaves. Let us assume, also, that he has subjected them to slavery by his own superior force and skill. Then let us suppose that some outside force, such as the state, frees the slaves, preventing the master from continuing to exercise his power over them. Surely the master's freedom has been limited. He is not as free as he was before. It would be only confusing to say that since he had no "right" to enslave people, his liberty was not reduced. His opportunity for making choices about how he should exercise his powers has been restricted; he has been thwarted in the accomplishment of his freely formed purpose. On the other hand, of course, the freedom of the slaves has been greatly enlarged. The net result to society, in terms of freedom, is clearly a gain. It is a gain in two respects: because a restraint upon one man has liberated ten, and because the restraint imposed upon that one man deprived him of far less freedom—fewer opportunities for choice—than the previous slavery involved for each of the ten. In some measure, even Holmes's example can be brought within this framework. If most people are restrained from walking abroad for fear of bodily attack, then restraints imposed upon would-be attackers (presumably a minority of the population) are more than compensated for, even in respect to liberty, by the liberating effects on others.

The case of the slaveowner illustrates particularly how tricky it is to define freedom and the extent to which, in the final analysis, any definition of the term must be arbitrary. A man who so denied the fundamental equality of men as to enslave them, one might argue, would in fact be acting contrary to his own inner nature or "real self." Following this line of thought, some philosophers would deny that he could be truly free. We have not chosen to define liberty so as to deny that a slaveowner could be free.

The point we have been making has a double moral. Most obviously, it means that, in speaking of liberty in society, we must consider *all* the people. The other point is that agencies other than government interfere with liberty. One man's liberty may entail another man's slavery. Acts of the state that restrict the liberty of certain individuals may indirectly enlarge the liberty of others by preventing the former from restraining the latter.

Liberty and the State

The exent of liberty varies greatly from time to time and place to place. Conditions may be favorable to it or they may be most unfavorable. The role of the state in providing liberty also varies greatly. Under certain circumstances a self-regulating economy that allows wide range to liberty of contract, for instance, may be entirely compatible with a high degree of economic security, with justice, and with welfare. But the reverse may also be true. These ends, and even liberty itself may require state regulation of the liberty of businessmen to bargain freely. Constitutional states strive to preserve certain essential negative liberties against interference either by the state or by private individuals or groups. (Bills of rights commonly give expression to such guarantees and may provide the means for their effectuation.) Nowadays, however, it is widely felt that negative liberty is not enough —that the state must do more than prevent intrusions upon liberty but that it must also take positive action to enable people to utilize their liberty effectively.

With liberty, as with security, we find the ends of the state tending to merge. Devices that extend liberty or make it effective also come under the head of welfare. For instance, freedom of contract between employers and employees has often in the past led to a one-sided bargain because of the poverty and consequent lack of bargaining power of the employees. Labor long ago discovered that in union there is strength—that by organization in labor unions they could do much to equalize their bargaining power and therefore their effective liberty. At first, however, they found the state opposed to such action, subjecting it to legal penalties as "conspiracies." The theory was that the state was protecting the individual against the group; but the result was to render the individual ineffectual. The first step was to remove this legal obstacle to organization. When, in the United States during the great depression, it was felt that workers were still disadvantaged with respect to employers, the state compelled employers to recognize the right of their employees to unionize and bargain collectively. Employers were coerced, their liberty curtailed, but the effective freedom of countless employees was greatly enlarged. Many employers may even have found that the resulting increase in predictability was liberating.

Considerations such as those urged above help explain why in our age the problem of liberty is more difficult than ever before. The enjoyment of liberty necessitates government with increased functions and also increased powers. As a result, the old problem of restraining authority itself, and of the prevention of arbitrariness and corruption of power becomes more serious than ever. In short, constitutional democratic society must create and utilize public authority with a view to the welfare of all individuals in society, yet it must prevent that authority from becoming a new master which, under the guise of ensuring both security and greater material well-being, destroys the hard-won freedoms of men.

Finally, we must emphasize that, while freedom is many-sided and various, basically it consists of the opportunity to *act* as one wills. We have heard, rightly, much about the "four freedoms": freedom of speech, freedom of religion, freedom from fear, and freedom from want. Yet all of these freedoms may be "enjoyed" in a prison cell. Freedom of speech and of religion are indeed of fundamental importance; but the latter involves only one aspect of life and the former has its greatest value as a means of influencing the conduct of others. Freedom from want and freedom from fear, important though they are, are only specific conditions prerequisite to the effective exercise of freedom of action. It is the latter that is basic—freedom to act, to move about, to choose one's mate and one's occupation and place of abode, and freedom to bargain and make agreements with one's fellows.[7]

JUSTICE

Justice, like liberty, has various meanings. At the outset, however, we make a simple distinction: that between "legal justice" and "philosophical justice." The former means applying and enforcing the law, whatever it may be, in accordance with its own terms. It is for this purpose that the state establishes courts for the adjudication of disputes, for determining when the law has been violated, and for seeing to it that "justice is done." This aspect of justice is almost as basic to the ends of the state as is provision of security. In fact, courts are often the first distinctly political organs to appear in an emerging polity. Here as elsewhere, basic political purposes tend to merge. Even as there can be no justice without a measure of order and security, so also it would be impossible to maintain order for long without at least a minimum of justice.

[7] See further S. I. Benn and R. S. Peters, *Social Principles and the Democratic State* (London: Allen & Unwin, 1959), Ch. 10; Bertrand de Jouvenel, *Sovereignty: An Inquiry into the Political Good* (Cambridge, Eng.: Cambridge U. P., 1957), Part IV; Giovanni Sartori, *Democratic Theory* (Detroit, Mich.: Wayne State U. P., 1962), Ch. 13; and Walter Lippmann, *The Good Society*, (Boston: Little, Brown, 1937), especially Chs. 12, 16.

That legal justice is an end of the state is then beyond dispute. Probably few would question also that justice in a larger sense, "philosophical justice," should be one of the state's basic concerns even though not solely its responsibility. But as to the nature of this broader justice disagreement is widespread. When Pontius Pilate asked the question, "What is justice?" he was voicing a primeval perplexity. Traditionally, aristocrats and democrats have adhered to opposing views of justice. We hear of "revolutionary justice," "Communist justice," "bourgeois justice," "National Socialist justice," and so on. Yet here, even more than in the case of liberty, one finds a common core of meaning. As so frequently happens, the point can be established most readily by asking not what is justice, but what is *in*justice.[8] That I should be taxed at twice the rate of my neighbor for no stated or obvious reason, or simply because I was born on a certain day of the week, would be universally acknowledged to be unjust. Many other examples will readily come to mind.[9]

Equality and Proportion

Central to the most fundamental element of the notion of justice, as the example above suggests, is that of impartiality and its attendant concept of equality. The maxim, "equal treatment for equal (like) situations," is close to the heart of the matter. Even more basic than the ideas of impartiality and equality is the notion of justice as rendering to each his own, or his due, that to which he is rightfully entitled. This was the definition, already traditional in fifth-century Athens, with which Plato opened his inquiry in the *Republic*. This definition immediately encounters the difficulty of determining what is a person's due. It may have been this problem that led to the idea of equality as central. But equality is only a special case of proportionality. Justice, as Aristotle declared, is a kind of proportion. But what kind? If A's income is double that of B and he has the same number of dependents, perhaps he should be taxed at a higher rate. But how much higher? And what factors are relevant to considerations of equality and inequality in a particular situation? If you are more intelligent than I am, better informed with respect to public affairs, and more keenly interested in such matters, should you be given more votes than I have?

Political equality will be discussed more fully in Chapter 11. It should be pointed out here, however, that the appeal to the ideal of justice has played a powerful role in the movement for the universal franchise. While justice is generally understood to entail proportionality, wherever the individual man is valued highly, as in the Judaeo–Christian tradition, the idea

[8] See Edmond Cahn, *The Sense of Injustice* (New York: New York U. P., 1949).

[9] For fuller treatment of this subject as it is relevant to politics, see Benn & Peters, *op. cit.*, Chs. 5, 6, and Richard B. Brandt (ed.), *Social Justice* (Englewood Cliffs, N.J.: Prentice-Hall, 1962).

prevails that in some sense all men are equal—that there is an irreducible minimum of "dignity" to which all sane adults are alike entitled. In democratic countries this equality is symbolized, protected, and given substantive effect by the equality of the franchise.

Applications

After we leave this basic minimum we soon find ourselves embroiled in questions of relevance and degree. Here we find extensive disagreements among men. Many differences of opinion even in this sphere tend to disappear when men of good will examine situations in detail both from the point of view of rational analysis and from that of discovering all the relevant facts. Take the question, the highly inflammatory question, of race relations in the United States. Few people, if any, would deny that Negroes are equally entitled to the protection of the same laws as white men. A Negro should be protected against robbery or assault even as a white man. If accused of crime he should have the same right to counsel and other procedural protections as anyone else. In such matters, however, men frequently seek in practice and often by stealth or anonymously to deny what in public they maintain or at least concede. Negroes are legally entitled to vote on the same basis as white men throughout the country, but ways are found in many places to prevent them from exercising the right. Not only does the conscience of the country at large deplore such activities, but most of those who practice them would not seek to defend them as *just*. Instead, they might contend that the Negroes' ignorance disqualified them from the right to vote or even that the whites, being outnumbered by Negroes in certain areas, must monopolize political power in self-defense.

Nicer questions are raised when the issue is segregation. For a long time, the legal requirement of segregation ("separate *but equal*"), in schools and elsewhere, was not generally condemned as incompatible with equal treatment. The important point is that the concept that Negroes were entitled to equal treatment, that their race was not relevant to their rights and privileges as American citizens, was generally accepted. Gradually the idea of justice, the notion of equal rights and privileges for all, worked out its logic. More and more people were persuaded that in practice segregation implied and contributed to the idea that Negroes were inferior and not entitled to equal treatment with other men. This proposition was eventually incorporated by the Supreme Court into the law of the land.[10] How long it will take to make it fully part of our practice remains to be seen; but the principle has been established.

---

[10] *Brown v. Board of Education of Topeka*, 1954, 347 U.S. 483. For an excellent account of the background of this decision and a discussion of the decision itself, see Robert J. Harris, *The Quest for Equality* (Baton Rouge: Louisiana State U., 1960).

Of course the requirement of justice that all men be treated on a basis of equality does not mean that differences of need or of merit are never relevant to rewards. It means that the presumption is always in favor of equality; that differences must be justified in accordance with principles that are themselves generally accepted and can stand up under rigorous criticism.

Three Aspects of Justice

EQUALITY BEFORE THE LAW

The subject can be made more specific and at the same time more comprehensive by discussing three aspects of justice that are important in politics. We may start with legal justice, or better the slightly broader concept of equality before the law. The state both administers its regulations and decides disputes between individuals and between the state and individuals by machinery and procedures designed to insure that the law is applied impartially. Each side must have an equal opportunity to be heard. Every possible means must be taken, beginning with the independence of the judge, to guard against prejudice, partiality, political influence, or other factors not relevant to a fair decision. The notion of fairness is so elementary that its requirements are generally obvious, although vague at the fringes. The Supreme Court of the United States itself has not been able to articulate all that is entailed by justice or "due process of law," and in seeking to apply it to particular situations constantly recurs to the touchstone of "fundamental fairness."

SUBSTANTIAL EQUALITY

Important as is equality before the law, it by no means exhausts the matter of justice even in the political sphere. The law must be just in substance as well as in application. It is here that we meet some of the more difficult problems. Of course the notions of impartiality, of equality, and of equal treatment of equals remain basic. But now the question of who are "equals" moves to the center of the stage. A law that exempts women from compulsory military service would hardly anywhere be considered unjust, although it does not treat all persons equally. One that drafted the sons of Republicans, or those who had been registered as Republicans on a certain date, and exempted all others would universally be recognized as unjust. Between these extremes there is room for much difference of opinion; yet a surprising amount of agreement can be found by study of the facts and full analysis and discussion. Courts can do something to work out and apply this standard of justice, known to American law as "the equal protection of the laws"; but in the final analysis the greatest protection, in a literate and informed society, is the requirement that all shall have the opportunity to examine and criticize, and to share in the exercise of political power. Not only should all share, but as a symbol and guarantee of their equality of right, democrats believe that justice is best insured when each adult has the same minimum of political power—one vote—and a legally equal opportunity to seek such further power, through the consent of their fellow citizens, as it is within their ability to acquire.

The standard of justice is not merely a *limitation* upon the legislation and other activities of the state. On the contrary, the state positively seeks to promote justice. By its taxing power it seeks to alter the distribution of income in a way more compatible with the requirements of justice. Progressive inheritance taxes, for example, are justified on the theory that the unregulated institution of inheritance contradicts the basic ideal of justice by giving certain individuals a head start in the economic race through no merit of their own. Many regulatory laws, too, have justice as their objective. A law that regulates business practices so as to prevent harsh exploitation of debtors by their creditors is in the interest of justice. Likewise the law of torts, that holds a man financially responsible for damage or suffering caused others by his negligence, is an application of the principles of justice.

CORRECTIVE JUSTICE

Finally, there is another element of political justice—corrective justice. The criminal, the offender against society, must be "subjected to justice" as well as being justly tried. We are dealing here with one of the most primitive functions of the state. Yet just what corrective justice requires is still a matter of dispute. If a man breaks the law he should be punished. On this much there is usually agreement. How much he should be punished is a more difficult question. Other difficult questions are presented when his action may not have been entirely or at all deliberate. Perhaps the act was something he could not help. If someone else forced him at the point of a gun, we would generally not hold him responsible. Suppose he stole to keep from starving? Suppose he stole because he was a kleptomaniac? Suppose he stole because he had been brought up in a community of thieves and felt he had to behave this way to be accepted by his peer group? Such questions as these suggest that various considerations enter into the notion of criminal justice. Society must be protected against further acts of wrongdoing. The criminal, if possible, must be reformed. He must be punished so that others who might be tempted to break the law may be deterred by the knowledge that they too will likely be made to suffer if they misbehave. Finally, many people feel that illegal conduct (and other wrong conduct) ought to be punished just because it is wrong, without regard to the effects on society. This is known as the retributive theory of justice. All legal systems embody it to a certain extent. But today especially there is much disagreement as to whether it is sound.

In general the modern tendency with respect to criminal or corrective justice is toward individuation. Greater attention is given to factors, psychological and environmental, that argue for differential treatment of individual criminals even though objectively the crime they have committed may be the same. Many think this tendency to be a departure from the highest ideals of equal justice for all and argue that it is based upon sentimentality rather than reason. To see the problem in perspective it is useful to consider a wider context. The notion of justice that we associate with the state tends to be cold, harsh, and formalistic. This notion differs from that prevailing in smaller, more intimate units, such as the family, where it is taken for granted that punishment should fit the offender as well as the offense, and where sympathy and affection, and understanding are—rightly, it is felt—brought into play in determining punishments. The extent to which familial justice can ever be appropriate for the necessarily more impersonal state is limited. It is well to recall, however, that our ideas of abstract and impersonal justice for the state grew up when the great need was to prevent arbitrary class discriminations from affecting the administration of justice. As is natural and proper, both the advancing spirit of democracy and our greater understanding of psychology should lead to a system of justice that makes the particular person who happens to be the offender a relevant consideration in determining what his punishment or other treatment shall be.

Justice and Other Ends

Justice, like other ends of the state, sometimes comes into conflict with one or more of those other ends. In one case, the welfare of society may call for punishment (assuming it acts as a deterrent) even though special circumstances seem to make the punishment unjust. In another case the punishment may have no good effect either on the lawbreaker or on society and yet be called for on the retributive theory. Here the ends of justice and utility are at odds. Such a conflict is by no means unusual. In the field of distributive justice, for example, differential incomes beyond the requirements of justice may be necessary in order to call forth the socially useful and desirable degree of productivity. They may also constitute a useful and even necessary device to stimulate the individual to his own fullest development. If we think of justice not only as negative and mechanical but also as positive and dynamic, concerned with treating persons not according to what they may become as well as according to what they now are, we shall realize that justice closely parallels liberty, which also has its negative and its positive aspects, and which also is concerned with individual development.

WELFARE

We come to the final end of the state—welfare. We have confronted it before. Each of the other ends has at some point come in contact with it. Sometimes by almost imperceptible degrees extensions of these aims lead into activities associated with welfare, as when security is extended to social security or personal liberty is extended to "economic" liberty. At other times, the requirements of other ends have conflicted with welfare.

Security, justice, and, in a measure, liberty have always been ends of the state. With welfare it is different. The acceptance by the state of ulti-mate, over-all responsibility for advancing the general welfare is relatively new. In the medieval world, most of the "welfare functions" fell to the church, the guilds, or private charity. Today, the state shoulders much of this burden. Citizens demand it. Welfare is tending to become the new imperative, subject to which governments in all civilized countries operate. Within the limits of what it is possible and feasible for governments to do, the modern state is under great pressure to provide whatever is not other-wise provided.

The reasons for this change are various. To a considerable degree they have been discussed in an earlier chapter (Chapter 4). Popular pressure and criticism arising out of the mass misery that developed under early indus-trialism are in a measure responsible. Pressure came from humanitarians, and from statesmen who perceived the dangers of such misery to the national strength, as well as to the more privileged groups themselves. An increasing number of functions accrued to the state because private enterprise was not interested in, or capable of performing them. The conservation of national resources is an example that comes readily to mind. The development of industry itself often necessitated the provision of means outside the author-ity or the resources at industry's command. To take two quite different examples, both popular education and good roads are essential to an effec-tively functioning industrial society. Yet neither would be adequately pro vided on the basis of individual enterprise and capacity to pay.

The Police Power

In earlier days, in the heyday of laissez faire, the general regulatory power of government for domestic affairs was sometimes referred to as the "police power," further defined as the power to protect the "health, safety, and morals" of the community. These objectives, although less exclusive than they once were, are still recognized as central concerns of government. Statute and ordinance books are crowded with sanitary and other health regulations affecting the processing and sale of food, forbidding the market-ing of poisonous, adulterated, or spoiled products, setting standards of clean-liness for hotels and rooming houses, and so on. Furthermore, the state spends vast sums for free services and educational efforts to check the spread of communicable diseases.

Modern technological developments have led governments to institute a vast number of regulations designed to prevent accidents involving life and limb. Traffic regulations and the requirement of periodic inspection of motor vehicles are familiar examples. Factory laws establish safety standards for most kinds of machinery; buildings and bridges must be constructed and maintained in accordance with established safety standards. Practically anywhere there is a chronic threat to bodily safety governments seek by regulation to limit the hazard.

The class of legislation to protect morals is more vague. It generally includes laws that prohibit or regulate the sale of liquor and habit-forming drugs. The prohibition or regulation of many forms of gambling falls in the same category. Regulations of obscenity, lewdness, and pictures or stories calculated to induce crime or depravity not only come under this heading but they supply examples of particularly difficult problem areas, for here the requirements of welfare often seem to conflict with the area of rightful liberty. How to give authorities power to suppress what may contribute, for instance, to juvenile delinquency, without opening the door to illiberal censorship is a problem that has not yet been solved.

Expanding Concepts of Welfare

Today the conservation of natural resources, the protection of our esthetic sensibilities, and the provision of recreational facilities and of opportunities for enjoyment of music and art all come without question within the legitimate functions of the state. Also, governments now accept a large amount of responsibility for the direct provision of the material goods essential for economic security and for a minimal standard of living. This situation has been brought about partly by changing concepts of state responsibility but even more by the changing facts of industrial life. We no longer accept economic adversity, unemployment, sweatshop wages, and slums as ills which must be silently borne. Regulations and the public treasury are systematically brought to bear on all such problems. Perhaps most characteristic of the welfare state, next to the provision of cradle-to-the-grave security and the provision of adequate housing, is its acceptance of responsibility for the greatest economic hazard of them all, the maintenance of high employment of men and machines and of a high level of productivity. This obligation involves as well the regulation of labor-management relations, in the effort to prevent or settle strikes, and in the gigantic task of alleviating the ups and downs of the business cycle.

Welfare, Planning, and Competing Values

Many of these tasks, and especially the one last mentioned, raise questions regarding the proper extent of governmental planning. Both their practical effectiveness and their consequences for other ends of the state are at issue. Some argue that if the state becomes too paternalistic the wellsprings of individual initiative and responsibility will dry up. Others fear that the power of the Leviathan state required to plan the whole economy will be disastrous to human liberty. For the remainder of this chapter, we shall consider the extent to which the preservation of other values and institutions places limits on what the state should do in the pursuit of welfare.

LIBERTY

First, let us consider liberty. At least since the time of Esau, there have been men who would sell their inheritances for a mess of potage. A law that prohibited the sale or mortgaging of family farms—actually enacted in Nazi Germany—might have definite welfare advantages. Most of us would agree that the loss in terms of liberty, in this example, would be greater than the gain in terms of welfare. When paternalism is justified and when it should be abandoned is, however, a matter of judgment. For a long time the American Indians were treated as special wards of the state and protected in ways similar to the example just given. Recently that policy has been changed in favor of allowing them greater liberty and responsibility, on the theory that they have now, as a group, "come of age." Yet those especially interested in Indian affairs are divided among themselves as to whether or not the time was ripe for this particular act of enfranchisement. If unemployment could be entirely eliminated by substituting state control for freedom of choice of occupation and employer, most Americans would judge that the price was too high—unless, indeed, the alternative was starker than anything we have experienced to date. In addition to the direct threats to liberty, we have the indirect threat of great increase in the apparatus of the state. Perhaps this hazard is the most difficult to appraise, because in each individual case the increase seems so slight.

Restrictions upon individual liberty by the state are often defended on the ground that they merely substitute control by government for some other form of social control, such as control by economic or social pressure. The argument has substance. A man's legal freedom to choose his own occupation and employer, for example, may not be very significant if he dare not give up his present job for fear he will not be able to get another, under any terms. Even freedom of speech may be considerably hedged about by social pressure against non-conformity to community ideals. Nevertheless, it would be wrong to overlook the important differences between governmental and other controls. In the social and economic realm the alternative to submitting to the pressure in question may vary from experiencing mild social disapproval, at one extreme, to the loss of employment at the other. Even in the latter case, in modern society, the price is not starvation. Governmental controls, on the other hand, normally admit of no effective evasion. One must submit or else—the "or else" being loss of liberty by imprisonment. Legal sanctions have an absolute finality and a potential brutality rarely matched by other forms of control.

A healthy society is a pluralistic society largely because numerous associations and organizations provide the most effective means for distributing power. In modern society it is power over economic decisions especially that should be divided. Free trade unions and the institution of private property are, at this stage of our development, the most effective devices for sharing such power with the state.

PROPERTY

Private property, by definition, implies limitations upon the state. The very name, *private* property, suggests opposition to the public realm. It stands for the system under which individuals are permitted to acquire material goods, or anything that has economic value, are protected in their possession, and allowed to do with them and dispose of them much as they will. In civilized society the state creates the law of property. States determine the rules by which property shall be acquired and used and enforce those rules, protecting individuals in the possession of their property and with respect to all the rights that adhere to it. For this reason, to say that property limits the state seems paradoxical. The fact is that, although the state may change the rules, the idea of property contains the implication that the state must abide by the existing rules as long as they are in effect. This in itself is a substantial limitation. The state cannot arbitrarily alter anyone's property rights. It cannot take property from *A* and give it to *B*. There are also limits beyond which the state cannot go in altering the rules and still have a property system left.

Why is property so fundamental? What is the justification for this imperative that may limit the acts of the state even when they are in pursuance of such an acknowledged end as welfare? On examination we discover that property is essential to other ends of the state as well as to the fundamental end of man himself. Since men have great need and desire for all sorts of material goods, the institution of property provides the chief means by which merit can be rewarded. Therefore it is essential to justice, to giving each his due. Not only justice, but initiative and enterprise call for property, again in its role of reward. How men could be generally stimulated to maintain a standard of life above the barest minimum, except through the reward of property, is almost beyond comprehension. In brief, welfare itself requires the institution of property. Then, too, security and liberty, in this context closely related to each other, receive tremendous support from the institution of private property. The man who owns his own home is more secure, other things being equal, than one who does not. Compared, for instance, with one who rents—whether from another individual or from the state—he has far greater assurance of retaining a home even in the event of loss of his job. Compared with the man who is given the use of the house by the state, he is relatively secure from the danger that he might be ousted from his home because of his political views or activities. The man who owns even a small amount of property has a powerful bulwark to his independence, economic, political, and social. He has an area within which he may move freely and without fear.

Property then serves the ends of security, freedom, justice, and welfare. Even more basically, property serves and is essential to the end of life itself, the development, in happy harmony, of human capacities. It is, as Aristotle pointed out, an extension of the personality. All man's wants, all his desires can be better fulfilled with the aid of property. Through it, he develops a sense of responsibility and other aspects of character. The latter fact grows out of the transferability and exchangeability of property. The man who has property can use it for his own present enjoyment (or exchange it for other property that is capable of such use), or he can use it for the benefit of his family or his friends, or for his own care in time of illness or old age. He must make the choice. By exercising self-restraint he can develop character. If he fails to do so, that is the price society must pay. The price must be paid because the only way society can create responsible individuals is to give them power that they can use well or abuse. In the exercise of this choice responsibility is developed. From this point of view property may be seen to be prior even to the state itself.

So far we have been talking about property in general. We have made no reference to the private ownership of the instruments of production. All of the advantages we have been enumerating could be enjoyed, at least in some degree, under a system in which part or possibly even all of the instruments of production were publicly owned. We do not say that such a system would be desirable—or, for that matter, that it would not be desirable—but merely point out the important fact that our justification for property does not itself answer the question as to how extensive that system should be. The greatest problems that arise today between the state and property have to do with the private ownership of the sources of productive power—the natural resources, large industrial enterprises, banks, and the like. Herein lies tremendous power for the comprehensive control of the economy,— power which in sum dwarfs that possessed by most states. Increasingly, the state, either through direct ownership or through regulation (altering the rights of property) is assuming control in this area, to improve the material standard of living of countless thousands whose property is very limited. Necessary though this development is, it harbors a serious threat to liberty. Not only is property in the hands of an individual somewhat of a protection against a potentially arbitrary government, but the division of power among industrial enterprises serves as a protection to all, property owners or not, against totalitarianism. Possibly, there are other ways by which society may be organized pluralistically so as to guard against the evils of monopoly of power. This is not the place to attempt an answer to this problem. All we can do at this point is to emphasize the extent to which property in the instruments of production does, and (in the absence of a suitable substitute) should act as a check to the power of government.

We have taken the economic institution of property as our major example of a social institution that rightly sets limits, flexible though they are, to the welfare activities of governments. Other institutions might also be considered in this context. For instance, the family, the primary social unit, requires for the fulfillment of its proper functions a substantial degree of autonomy. So strongly has the Catholic Church, or at least many Catholic leaders, felt about this matter that they opposed child labor legislation, despite its obvious welfare value, because they feared to give the state an opening wedge into the control of family matters. Totalitarian regimes have regularly sought to impose their authority even within the family unit. It is interesting to note that the Soviet Union, having gone a considerable distance in this direction in its early years, has retreated in numerous respects.

THE CHURCH

Finally, a reference to the church. As the great potential centers for monopoly of power are the political, the economic, the familial, and the ecclesiastical, so each of these provides an appropriate point for the distribution of power in a free society. The church is charged especially with man's spiritual welfare, but it also plays an important role in his social welfare. In both capacities the church needs a certain freedom from interference in order to perform its functions satisfactorily. Freedom of religious belief is a cardinal tenet of liberal democracy. When beliefs call for practices considered by the majority to be injurious to welfare problems arise; and likewise when the state requires behavior that offends the religious beliefs of certain groups. In the United States, such issues have frequently arisen. The Mormons' erstwhile belief in plural marriage was felt by the majority of Americans to run counter to acceptable moral standards. Here the state's power to act for the general welfare prevailed over religious liberty. On the other hand our courts have held that various kinds of state laws and municipal ordinances designed to keep litter off the streets or to protect persons in their homes or on the street from unwanted solicitations may not be applied to limit the activities of religious groups seeking to win adherents to their faith.

In concluding this discussion of the ends and functions of the state, we may remark that the state in its distinctive capacity as the monopolist of force is unfitted for the performance of functions that must depend upon the voluntary actions of individuals. The government can compel a person to do the right thing or prevent him from doing what is wrong (within limits), but it cannot compel him to be good. It cannot force him to be a man of good will. In bearing in mind this important limitation, however, we must not forget that the state can and does do many things simply in its capacity as an agency of cooperative activity. It provides services of all kinds on a purely voluntary basis. Men may avail themselves of them or not as they see fit. Even in providing services, however, the state may be building up a bureaucratic machine that adds to its power, and may also be taking over the functions of, and so weakening, one of the other major institutions of society.

The following chart may be found useful as a recapitulation of some of the main topics of the last three chapters and as a demonstration of the relations among them, of the continuity of the argument.

APPENDIX: MAN, SOCIETY AND STATE—NEEDS, TENDENCIES, ENDS

MAN *Politically Significant* *Needs, Desires, Traits*	SOCIETY *Tendencies* *(toward)*	STATE *Ends*
Desire for security and self- preservation	Political organization	Security
Desire for power		
Sympathy and other "impulses toward unity" (make society possible)	Ethnocentrism	
Norm-creating proclivity	Justice	Justice
Desire for new experience and adventure	Freedom	Liberty
Desire for freedom and self- realization		
Desire for satisfaction of basic needs, and comfort, ease, and leisure	Economic development and social security	Welfare

Note: Certain items are inserted above (e.g., "desire for satisfaction of basic needs") that were not discussed in the appropriate chapter simply because they were too obvious to call for discussion. Also certain psychological traits are related to more than one social tendency and political purpose ("end of state").

SELECTED READINGS

(Asterisk indicates book is available in paperback edition.)

*BARKER, ERNEST. *Principles of Social and Political Theory.* Oxford: Clarendon Press, 1951. A wise and judicious discussion of the state and of the proper relations among society, state, and individual.

BENN, S. I. and R. S. PETERS. *Social Principles and the Democratic State.* London: Allen & Unwin, 1959. Chs. 5 and 10 of this excellent work are particularly pertinent to this chapter.

*BRANDT, RICHARD B. (ed.). *Social Justice.* Englewood Cliffs, N. J.: Prentice-Hall, 1962. While the student will find all of the lectures in this series enlightening, those by Paul A. Freund and Alan Gewirth are especially directed to the concerns of the political scientist.

CARRITT, E. F. *Ethical and Political Thinking.* Oxford: Clarendon, 1947. In Ch. 15 of this volume a leading moral philosopher examines "the rights of man," considered under the headings "liberty," "equality," and "property."

———. Conference on Science, Philosophy and Religion, *Aspects of Human Equality.* New York: Harper, 1956. Chs. 4 (Plamenatz) and 10 (Haller) are particularly useful.

DAHL, ROBERT A. and LINDBLOM, CHARLES E. *Politics, Economics, and Welfare; Planning and Politico-Economic Systems Resolved into Basic Social Processes.* New York: Harper, 1953. This path-breaking volume contains much that is relevant to this chapter. See especially Ch. 2, "Ends and Means," and Ch. 4, Sec. 6, "Freedom, Equality, Rationality, and Control."

DE JOUVENEL, BERTRAND. *Sovereignty, an Inquiry into the Political Good.* Cambridge, Eng.: The University Press, 1957. Both liberty and justice receive discriminating treatment in this volume.

FOSDICK, DOROTHY. *What Is Liberty?* New York: Harper, 1939. A balanced analysis and discussion of the many meanings of "liberty."

FRIEDRICH, CARL J. (ed.) . *Liberty.* New York: Atherton, 1962. This volume of essays touches on many aspects of the subject of liberty.

HAYEK, FRIEDRICH A. *The Constitution of Liberty.* Chicago: Univ. of Chicago Press, 1960. This volume presents a vigorous statement of the case for maximizing individual liberty and minimizing governmental regulation.

HOBBES, THOMAS. *Leviathan.* Oxford, Eng.: Blackwell, 1946. Hobbes's statement of the case for security as *the* great end of the state is unmatched.

MERRIAM, CHARLES E. *Systematic Politics.* Chicago: Univ. of Chicago Press, 1945. Ch. 2 is devoted to the "Ends of Government," enumerated as "External Security," "Order," "Justice," "Welfare," and "Freedom."

MILL, JOHN STUART. "On Liberty," in *Utilitarianism, Liberty, and Representative Government.* New York: Dutton, 1926. Mill's statement of the case for liberty as the chief end of the state is a classic.

OPPENHEIM, FELIX E. *Dimensions of Liberty.* New York: St. Martin's, 1961. A careful elucidation of the meaning of the term "liberty" together with some consideration of the reasons for which it may be valued, by a logical positivist.

Part

A DEVELOPMENTAL VIEW

Two

The first part of this book has been, in the main, discursive or analytical, emphasizing concepts, abstract principles or "laws," and their mutual relations. The emphasis in this section is largely upon a genetic approach: the study of the origins and development of law and political institutions.

The value of a study of origins and development for political science lies partly in two characteristics of that discipline itself. Politics is, for one thing, a probabalistic matter. "Laws" of politics are scarce. Generalizations hold, as Aristotle observed, "always, or for the most part." Thus, a history of origins and development is valuable to judge what things hold "always" and what things are matters of circumstance and occasion. Secondly, political science, like history, is a subject that gets written anew with each passing generation: it is profoundly involved with how we interpret our past and with what we hope for the present and the future. Therefore, a genetic approach has, at least *prima facie*, more relevance to political science than it would, say, for physics or even economics. Political history serves as a critic for present faiths.

Another and still more important point

needs to be made. "Political behavior" is a subject or phenomenon of radically changing boundaries and rapid transformations. The League of Women Voters and the Indian Commune are almost literally worlds and centuries apart. They can both be studied separately and in their own right, just as could a host of other properly political phenomena. The point of a study of political history, especially our own Western political history, is that it is accessible and that it affords a ready introduction to a range of political experience that has considerable relevance to the entire spectrum of political behavior as we find it in the world today. We are not, then, interested in origins and development from the antiquarian point of view. Our concern is still with the fundamentals of politics, and we shall consider political history mainly as a supplement to the analytical approach.

CHAPTER 7

Development of Legal Systems:

General

‖‖

INTRODUCTION

Law is coextensive with all but the most primitive forms of society. The forces that determine the form of political institutions and direct their development make themselves felt through the law and leave their imprint upon it. In the study of the evolution of diverse legal systems we gain a better perspective for judging our own society, its problems and tendencies. The study of private law and the institutions evolved for its application, moreover, yields some of the most instructive insights into the nature of politics. In this and the succeeding chapter we shall attempt to set forth, with a minimum of legal technicalities, some of the contributions of legal history to knowledge about politics and political science.

Our pupose cannot be fulfilled by dealing only with the systems of law now extant and their predecessors in the Greco-Roman civilization to which our own Western civilization is heir. There have been in the history of the world a number of societies that have developed "civilizations." Professor Toynbee, in his *Study of History* enumerates nineteen, most of them now no longer in existence, and known to us only indirectly by way of the science of archeology.[1] Each of these civilizations had its system of law. Fragments of these ancient bodies of law are in many cases available to us. Just as these civilizations often attained levels of cultural development comparable in many respects to our own, or at least to that of Western Europe before the Industrial Revolution, so their legal systems were also similarly advanced. Doubtless in some measure the legal developments themselves fostered the evolution of more complicated stages of society. Generally speaking, however, the behavior preceded the norms. As societies became more complicated, their legal systems followed suit.

Since law is so intimately related to constitutional forms, to political forces, and to major social and economic institutions generally, it is not

---

[1] Arnold J. Toynbee, *The Study of History* (London: Oxford U. P., 1934), Vol. I, Ch. 1.

strange that societies similar in these respects should also have markedly similar legal systems. Thus the laws of contemporary America and those of, say, a primitive African tribe or the Melanesians are strikingly different; while the differences between our law and Roman law at the height of Roman civilization are far less great. Similarly, if we compare the laws of primitive peoples *at the same stages of material civilization and political organization* a marked congruence will be found. With the evidence available, fragmentary but quite extensive, scholars have explored these congruencies in considerable detail. Comparing one group of politically unorganized hunters with another, primitive agriculturalists having rudimentary courts with other tribes at the same stage, more advanced tillers of the soil with their counterparts, and, finally, one vast commercial empire with another, one finds that the likenesses as to law are remarkable. It is not meant to suggest however, that the legal development of all societies follows exactly the same steps—and much less that the timetable is in each case the same. Societies that have only recently begun to emerge from the most primitive forms, for instance, may, by copying the technology and other aspects of "modern cultures," skip many steps that have commonly been taken by earlier societies.

A few societies still remain untouched by the process we today know as "modernization." Whether development in the direction indicated by the latter term is inevitable, we need not here decide. Surely, there have been extended periods, like that following the fall of Rome, when the direction of legal and political change was reversed. Over most of the world, however, small independent political units, like the village or the tribe in most preliterate societies, have tended to give way to larger and more complex polities, with more highly developed technology. Wherever this kind of development has occurred—which is to say over most of the world—certain general lines of legal development, paralleling and serving the social, economic, and political developments, can be charted.[2]

We have spoken of "primitive" law. In addition to this category we shall deal with "archaic" and "mature" legal systems. Primitive law is that vague, indeterminate body of customary law in which there is some distinction between customs that are "binding" and those that are not, but no machinery for marking the dividing line and no organization for enforcement of the law (although there will be unorganized pressures conducing to obedience and socially sanctioned self-help in the form of reprisal or direct action to protect one's person or property.)[3] Archaic law is marked by the correction

[2] Cf. E. Adamson Hoebel, *The Law of Primitive Man, a Study in Comparative Legal Dynamics* (Cambridge, Mass.: Harvard U. P., 1954), pp. 288-293.

[3] Any attempt to draw a line between "stages" of development is bound to be arbitrary. It might be argued for instance that even in the most primitive society there is "family law" which is enforced within the family, with the head of the family acting as judge, constituting himself as a court. However, we are referring to law of a wider scope than that of a single family unit. And at this level, in many primitive societies,

of these deficiencies: that is to say, the existence of courts and of some machinery for law enforcement. Finally, we shall speak of a legal system as "mature" when there is a class of professional lawyers to help apply and develop it.

The following table will help the reader visualize the classification and see how it brings together legal systems far removed from each other in time.

TABLE II

STAGES OF LEGAL DEVELOPMENT, WITH EXAMPLES*

I. *Primitive law*
Has existed in all periods; but, since it is characteristic of preliterate peoples, we have little information about it except for recent times. Common among American Indian tribes until recently, and among many tribes of Asia and Oceania.

II. *Archaic law*
   A. *Early stage*
      Early Anglo-Saxon dooms
      Twelve Tables (Roman)   450 (?) B.C.
      Hebrew Code   375 B.C.
      Lex Salica   (Germanic tribal laws) 450 A.D.
   B. *Middle stages*
      Code of Alfred   c. 890 A.D.
      Anglo-Saxon laws   900-1100 A.D.
      Hittite (Assyrian) Code   c. 1350 B.C.
      Lex Burgundionum   (Germanic tribal laws) 500-900 A.D.
   C. *Late stage*
      Late feudal period   11th and 12th centuries A.D.
      Sumerian fragments   c. 2250 B.C.
      Code of Hammurabi (Babylonian)   1914 B.C.
      Laws of ancient Greek civilization   c. 600-400 B.C.

III. *Mature law*
Roman law from third century B.C. to the fall of Rome
English and European law from about the twelfth or thirteenth century A.D.

---

* Based in part, with modifications, upon A. S. Diamond, *Primitive Law* (New York: Longman's, 1935). Diamond places the Hebrew Code and the Twelve Tables in the late middle stage, largely because of their inclusion of priestly rules. (See Ch. 21, esp. p. 218.) Some modern anthropologists object to Diamond's terminology. They argue that primitive law is the law of small and simple groups; that what Diamond calls "archaic" law is that which characterizes somewhat larger and more complicated societies; and that the so-called "mature" law is the law of large, complex and technologically advanced societies. Somewhere an "archaic" society may still exist, and for it "archaic" law would still be appropriate. These points may be fully conceded; yet it remains a fact that in general political and legal development has taken place in the direction implied by Diamond's classification. In default, then, of better terminology, we adhere to Diamond's terms, without of course implying the existence of a rigid scheme of legal development that all legal systems must recapitulate. It must be recognized too, that the development of a professional class of lawyers is a slow process. In this and other ways English law, for example, might be said to have been maturing from the twelfth to the sixteenth century.

---

courts do not exist, although there may be regularized institutions of mediation, whose function it is to try to bring about appropriate settlement of disputes involving breach of the law. See, for example, Hoebel, *op. cit.*, pp. 114-116.

PRIMITIVE LAW

Subject Matter

In the most primitive societies, "legal" customs are not clearly demarcated from others that are religious, moral, or merely "social" but without any special "validity." Nevertheless, certain customs have legal quality: they are felt to be binding; and their breach is a matter of concern to the kinship group or the village and typically calls forth some kind of "counter-action."[4] Most important among these are the laws regulating marriage, (the law of exogamy, proscribing marriage within a defined kinship group) and the related taboo against incest, and the laws forbidding sorcery (witchcraft). In the latter case, we are distinguishing between religious customs, which may prescribe the practice of certain rituals and the secular (and "legal") prohibitions against the attempt to invoke religious or magical powers against one's enemy (within the family or village). In some cases prohibitions against doing anything that may be thought to endanger the food supply belong in this same category.

These regulations are of outstanding importance in primitive societies because their subject matters constitute threats to the well-being and especially to the unity of the group. The safety and happiness of individuals, in turn, depends upon that of the group to which they belong. To the modern, it may seem surprising that laws regulating crimes of violence do not head the list. A little investigation and thought, however, explains the difference in terms entirely comprehensible to us even with our different value system. In the first place, although the customary laws most relied upon by primitive peoples do not deal directly with crimes of violence, they do deal with matters likely to lead to dispute and so, possibly, to violence. Whether the laws of exogamy are aimed at the avoidance of jealousies, whether they result from a universal abhorrence of incest, or whatever may be their basis, in fact all primitive peoples feel strongly about the importance of adherence to the established norms in this matter, although the content of the norms differs widely from tribe to tribe. At the same time the powerful motive of lust often leads to their violation, thereby placing a great strain on tribal unity.

---

[4] Some anthropologists feel it is misleading to speak of native custom as "law." Among the Tiv (an African tribe), for instance, it has been pointed out that while certain acts (perhaps contrary to custom) will produce "counteraction" and may lead to a dispute that is taken before the *"jir"* (a kind of court), the job of the *"jir"* is to find the right answer. The right answer is firmly believed to have objective existence, but there is no overt reference to rules from which the answer is deduced. The author of this study concludes that law is not universal, but is "a tremendous cultural achievement." Paul Bohannan, *Justice and Judgment Among the Tiv* (New York: Oxford U. P., 1957), pp. 212-214. (The quotation is from p. 214.) This view does not appear to be substantially at odds with the present authors' conception of development from primitive custom, through customary law to mature law.

Hence the importance attached to outlawing this disruptive influence. Similarly with sorcery and with acts endangering the supply of food.

Also primitive law with respect to crimes of violence is generally less well developed because such crimes, especially killing, are not common among primitive peoples. Hobbes's picture of the "state of nature"—a war of all against all—is not borne out by the facts. Disputes, jealousies, and smoldering resentments there are; in some societies they appear to have been rife; but they seldom result in killing. In further explanation of this relatively peaceful situation, it must be remembered that the simple communities of hunters that we are discussing are very small, frequently numbering only a few score individuals.

Other offenses known to modern law either did not occur to any serious degree in the primitive stage (as with theft), or the attitudes toward them and the steps taken when they did occur were so irregular that they could hardly be said to have been the subject of customary law. (Rape seems generally to fall in this category.)

What has just been said about the relative unimportance of crimes of violence and crimes against property owners, however, should not be taken to mean that there was no law on these subjects. On the contrary, in these very areas we find some of the universal principles that appear to characterize the law of all known societies. And it is important to note, especially in the light of much loose talk about cultural relativism, that such universals do exist.[5]

Enforcement

How were the customary laws enforced? By our definition of primitive law, courts and organized sanctions were lacking. However, numerous forces acted as fairly effective deterrents to breach. At one time anthropologists held that primitive people obey custom merely because it is custom; that they are conformists to the nth degree. Later study revealed this theory to be far from the truth. Malinowski goes so far as to claim that no one obeys a custom merely because it is the custom, or merely for the sake of conformity to the rule.[6] It is true, however, that when behavior crystallizes in certain patterns, ideas of "rightness" and even of obligation attach to these patterns. Perhaps this situation is distinct from obedience to custom just because it is custom, but the line is thin and hard to detect in a given case.

[5] For instance, Hoebel lists homicide within the society (variously defined) as legally prohibited everywhere; likewise adultery and theft (although again the definitions vary widely). Hoebel, *op. cit.*, p. 286. It will be noticed that enumeration of the last item, "theft," indicates that property rights in some form appear in all societies. Cf. A. Irving Hallowell, "The Nature and Function of Property as a Social Institution," *Journal of Legal and Political Sociology*, I (April, 1943), pp. 115-138.

[6] Bronislaw Malinowski, *Crime and Custom in Savage Society* (London: Routledge, 1926), Ch. 1.

The desire for the approval of one's friends and neighbors, especially the desire to avoid their disapproval, are powerful influences for conformity. Ridicule is a potent weapon and, when it is almost universal, and perhaps in some fashion organized, it may even drive an individual to suicide.

Sometimes customary law may be violated habitually by a given individual (say, even, the law of incest) without anything being done about it; but if someone calls attention to it publicly, perhaps in accordance with a ceremonial procedure, social sanctions are automatically organized and the offender may even feel that he has to go to the length of suicide. This act apparently accomplishes the double objective of rehabilitating the individual reputation and of turning opinion against the person who has caused the publicity.

Socially approved self-help, retaliatory or compensatory, is heavily relied upon as the appropriate counteractive measure in the case of breach. For example, when acts of violence do occur, especially as between individuals not belonging to the same clan or perhaps even coming from different villages, the remedy is self-help by the band or kinship group, each group acting as a unit and avenging its own members.[7] These acts of vengeance often initiate feuds. But feuds are institutionalized and apparently all societies have some procedure for avoiding them or bringing them to a halt. Barbarous as the whole idea of the feud sounds by modern standards, any system of rules serving to channel and provide a terminus for a feud contributes to order.

Even rules of the feud that seem most irrational, when seen in the total context, are found to have some rationality. To take one of the most bizarre examples, in certain tribes where a high degree of status differentiation has evolved, if a man of high rank kills someone of low rank, a kinsman of the victim may not touch the offender. He may, however, kill a person in the next rank above him. *His* kinsman in turn may then proceed against an individual in a still higher rank, and so on until the original offender is reached. In this way, opinion is mobilized against offenders of high rank in spite of sharp status cleavages.

An interesting device for avoiding feuds is the "expiatory encounter," of which various versions exist. According to one of them, the offender must stand and allow the kin of the person who has been slain to throw spears at him until the blood flows. Elsewhere punishment is even less corporal, the emphasis being upon public humiliation.[8] Soon, however, payments become the standard method of making up for a killing. This device of "composition," as it has come to be called, has a long history in the law. Its beginnings in primitive law as a substitute for the feud were later extended to cover a large array of offenses.

[7] Cf. Paul Bohannan, *op. cit.*, pp. 137 ff.
[8] See Hoebel, *op. cit.*, pp. 93-99, for an account of Eskimo "song duels."

In certain societies a quite complicated system of reciprocity has been developed. Inhabitants of fishing villages make gifts of fish to inhabitants of inland villages with the tacit understanding that they will be repaid with yams at another time. This kind of reciprocity actually is worked out on an individual basis, with each head of a household in one village having a "partner" for the exchange of gifts in the other village. Occasions for the exchange of gifts are numerous, marriages, of course, constituting a prime example. Nor is the exchange always direct. The person to whom a gift is given may not return the equivalent to the giver, but rather to one of his relatives. Apparently, it all works in such a way as to be "fair" and "functional," that is to serve the needs of the society. In such a society, any infraction of customary law may be easily subjected to the sanction of withholding some or all of the "gifts" due under the prevailing system. A person thus frozen out of the economic system would be badly circumstanced indeed.[9]

Throughout, the unity or integrity of the group is the governing principle. Everything possible is done to maintain group unity: acts which threaten it are the chief crimes, and punishment even for such crimes is likely to be limited to expulsion from the group (although the consequences of that may be severe). Furthermore, the kin group itself is held responsible for the acts of any of its members by the village or larger society. This smacks of what we today condemn as "guilt by association;" yet, in the absence of an effective political organization for getting at the individual and holding him responsible for his acts, it serves a rational purpose. In these circumstances, it is the kin group, under the dominance of the head of the family, that can best the individual. Injured parties, then, naturally hold the clan as a whole responsible for the acts of any of its members. In the same way today, in the realm of international law, states are held responsible for the acts of their citizens, at least to the extent of exercising "due diligence" to prevent them from acting contrary to the rights of outsiders. So we hold the German people to be not wholly without responsibility for what their leaders did. The principle of collective responsibility has found and will continue to find application in appropriate situations. As the polity grows stronger, both socially approved self-help and the principle of kinship enforcement yield precedence to sanctions imposed directly by the state upon the individual.

ARCHAIC LAW

Courts and Judicial Procedure

Courts begin to develop as early as the second of the four stages into which Diamond classifies primitive societies (agriculturalists lacking herds of cattle). The development of courts is one aspect of the particularization and

---

[9] See Bronislaw Malinowski, *op. cit.*, especially Ch. 3-5; 8-9.

specialization of institutions that characterizes the emergence of what we call the "state" out of simpler forms of polity. Either the simple fact of larger and more complicated societies or the fact of conquest of one tribe by another with the consequent necessity of holding together groups not knit by kinship bonds would suffice to increase the number of disputes and the need for a recognized authority for their settlement. Modern authorities emphasize the facts of size of unit and complexity of organization as the primary factors.[10]

In the earliest period, courts consisted simply of the chief sitting with the other heads or clans of the village or tribe.[11] The trial took the form of a "judicial duel," with the disputants arguing their case before the court, and perhaps producing witnesses, in the presence of "the public" who may show their sympathy or agreement with one side or the other by audible expressions. When all have been heard, the court renders its judgment. By a series of judgments, since inevitably the court tends to treat like cases similarly, the law gradually becomes more precise and penalties are regularized. Testimony at this stage of development is unsworn and appeals do not exist. Procedural technicalities—special forms that must be complied with if the complainant is to have his suit judged on the merits—are also absent.[11] This lack of procedural technicalities, it may be noted, is quite contrary to widespread beliefs about primitive law.

With the growth of commerce and the consequent multiplication of litigation and proliferation of legal problems, procedural (as distinct from substantive) law came into being. Courts required separate laws to assist them in the trial of cases. Generally speaking, these rules were aimed at the problems arising from lack of evidence. For instance, the Code of Hammurabi provided that there should be no action for a debt if no receipt had been given. Ethically, of course, there is just as much reason why a man should be compelled to repay a loan, for example, if he had not given a receipt for it as if he had. The difficulty of establishing the fact that the loan had actually been made, however, might justify the rule in question. As long as everyone knew of the existence of the rule, no great substantive injustice should result, for all those who made loans would be warned to require receipts. Similarly it was provided that no claim for injury to an ox would be considered unless the injured ox was produced in court.

The problem of lack of evidence was not always so easily disposed of,

[10] Hoebel, after reviewing the law-ways of seven widely scattered primitive tribes, including Eskimos, plains Indians, and South Sea islanders, concludes as follows: "The law of the tribes that have come under purview is obviously not the consequence of conquest, for the social structures that support these legal systems are not conquest states. Law is the inherent product of internal social forces, the creative consequence of people's efforts to achieve and maintain a self-limiting order." *Op. cit.*, p. 326.

[11] At a still simpler stage, near the borderline between "primitive" and "archaic," disputes were settled and consensus achieved by a kind of "town meeting." Hoebel declares that "the legislative halls of civilization have their foundations in the 'town meetings' of the primitive groups." *Op. cit.*, p. 295.

especially in what we would call criminal cases, such as alleged physical injury or homicide. Generally speaking, where evidence other than the unsupported testimony of the parties was lacking, courts would resort to some form of "ordeal." Here men resorted to magic because rational means appeared to be exhausted. Types of ordeal were legion, some particular type frequently prevailing in a given area. One instance of the use of ordeal is the custom of permitting guilt or innocence to be determined by the behavior of some animal. Sometimes the ordeal was to be required to take an oath, generally calling upon some sacred or magical object to do harm to the swearer if he spoke falsely. (Thus even today children challenge each other to "cross their hearts.") With the development of religion, the use of ordeal by oath grew in popularity. Gradually the practice developed of requiring the defendant to get others ("oath helpers") to swear that his oath was "clean." (Character witnesses, we would call them.) Sometimes the requisite number became quite extensive. Even so, it was generally possible for the accused to secure the requisite number of "compurgators" from among his own kin. Among the Germanic tribes at least, the kin group was under obligation either to give such support to any of its members who might need it or else to cast him out of the group, rendering him an outlaw.

During the so-called Dark Age (*circa* A.D. 600 to 750) in Europe, the use of compurgation was greatly extended, including situations other than those where evidence was lacking. Perjury became notoriously common, with the consequence that plaintiffs were dissatisfied with the justice rendered by the courts and increasingly took the law into their own hands. This development, in turn, led courts to provide that the parties might, in some regulated fashion, "fight it out." In this way was born the "ordeal by battle." It appears to have been unique to Europe, and by no means a hangover from more primitive times. Many evidences (as, for instance, the decline of legislation) testify to the growing weakness of both the executive and the courts in the Frankish monarchy following the sixth century. In large measure, it appears to have been this weakness of the courts and their consequent fear to give judgment, especially against strong parties, that led to the great extension of reliance upon the ordeal by oath, and so eventually to the ordeal by battle. As the political organization grew weaker, the Church and the ecclesiastical courts became stronger—a fact of considerable significance in the present context because in Europe (and also among the Hebrews) the ecclesiastical courts had shown themselves particularly fond of the ordeal by oath and had greatly extended its application.

In the last stages of archaic law, even as the condition of maturity is in process of developing, it becomes in other ways more formalistic, with rigidly prescribed procedures and rules of evidence. Indeed, formalism extends into the realm of substantive law itself when its rules become so numerous and complicated that they have to be taught in special schools, and so become the property of a limited number of individuals. As Diamond says, the law at this stage "has ceased to live in the outer, everyday world, to be variable, changed easily by changing circumstances; it lives in a world of its own; it progresses chiefly by logical application of an observed underlying principle to new facts; it is stereotyped and difficult to change except by legislation, which is little resorted to."[12] This stage, too, repeats itself in the development of various legal systems. It was reached, for instance, in the Roman law in the middle of the second century B.C., and about the twelfth century in medieval Europe, subsequent to the rediscovery of the Justinian's Digest.

Legislation

Our discussion of procedural law and, more generally, of the development of legal technicalities has led us ahead of our story. We have gone from the beginnings of the archaic stage to its very end, or beyond. We must now go back to the beginning to pick up certain other threads of the account, in particular, the subject of legislation. Another myth about the history of law is that primitive law is unchanging and that legislation is a comparatively late development, subsequent to the formulation of codes. The facts are to the contrary. It is true that in primitive societies conditions are relatively static for long periods of time and that there is consequently little need for growth in the law. However, conditions do change and at all stages of society of which we have any knowledge, law, even when it was purely "customary law," has been changed to serve new conditions; albeit generally not without considerable delay.

As soon as distinct organs of the state developed, legislation appeared. Frequently, the same council of elders served as both court and legislature. In this connection the so-called "codes," are important. Many of them are extant, in whole or in part, and furnish us with a great deal of our knowledge of early law. Most of them are not in the true sense of the word "codes" at all; that is, they are not systematic organizations of the whole body of law. Rather, they are somewhat random collections of pieces of pre-existing law, largely of previous acts of legislation. Sometimes their purpose seems to have been chiefly, if not solely to make it easier for all to know the law. Where, as in early Rome, knowledge and administration of the law had become the property of a limited group (often, as it was in Rome, the priesthood), this monopoly tended to become a source of abuse. The result, in the case of Rome, was the famous Twelve Tables, which were supposed to have stated the whole of the law in brief, easily understandable, and also authoritative form. In other cases, the main purpose was to bring about reforms in the content of the law itself. In these instances, the codes, while containing much previous legislation, were themselves creative legislative acts. Indeed, in some cases, certain important subjects were not dealt with at all, apparently because no change from the existing law was intended in those areas. Probably,

[12] A. S. Diamond, *Primitive Law* (New York: Longmans, 1935), pp. 344-345.

the development of codes and, more generally, of written legislation is indicative less of a new stage of legal development than of the use of writing. Writing itself (however, as we shall have occasion to point out later) was not without important effects on the history of the law.

Development of Substantive Law

Generally speaking, the alterations in substantive law during the period under consideration are related to two or three principal types of change. First of these is the growth of the political power of the state, which is to say of the king. This trend was sometimes subject to great set-backs, as notably in the history of our own civilization, following the fall of the Roman Empire; and so were the accompanying legal developments. From the broadest point of view, the scope of law widened, both geographically and functionally. As great empires grew, their legal systems expanded with them, and encompassed new relations. Matters that had formerly been handled entirely by the kinship group, or clan, came to be of concern to, and subject to the law of the central government. At the same time the plasticity of primitive law tended to give way to greater fixity, with both the advantages and disadvantages that that involves.

Another significant change was the increasing solidarity of the family, followed by the growing power of the head of the family over the rest of the members. This development, like the preceding one, was at the expense of the old kinship organization, the clan.

The legal device of composition provides an example of these general trends. Long after it had been substituted for the feud, the amount of the payment for a given offense was left to the bargaining of the parties. Gradually, by virtue of the multiplication of cases, or because of a more or less conscious concern of the central government for uniformity, fixed scales of payment for various injuries—physical and otherwise—were evolved, and frequently written down in "codes." Some of these schedules of payments were not unlike the terms of present-day accident insurance policies: so much for loss of life, so much for loss of sight, another sum for the loss of one eye, one arm, and so on.

Civil injuries other than physical violence were dealt with in the same way. In this category fell rape, adultery, and seduction (among which in early law there was little distinction). The laws on these subjects varied widely, although it was closely correlated with the tribal marriage law and sex mores. The husband or father was the injured party and the penalty was generally pecuniary. "As compared with the prices of wounds," says Diamond, "the price of adultery commonly represents something approximately equivalent to that payable for the loss of a toe."[13] Along with this increase in community interest went the development of stronger executive

[13] Diamond, op. cit., p. 325.

authority that made it possible to implement it. Closely related to the last tendency is the growth of a sense of justice. Also, application of the law commonly came strongly under the influence of the religious organization. Indeed, the priests (largely because they were the educated class, and knew how to write) frequently obtained a near monopoly of legal administration. Not unnaturally, the priestly influence tended to be in the direction of modifying the older law with developing concepts of justice, although in some cases their influence was less benign. Also, as societies grew larger, and as the kinship organizations became weaker, acts of violence may have tended to increase, creating a need for more effective means of control.

The shift under discussion involves what in modern terms would be called a transfer from the field of civil law to that of criminal law. In the first case, the action is accusatorial in nature. The court acts only on motion of a private party and then acts in the role of an umpire. The new situation, however, casts the court and its attendant officials in an inquisitorial role. They now have an active interest (on behalf of the state) in seeing that the law is enforced.

How late in the growth of the law the last change occurred is indicated by the fact that among most African tribes classified as in the third agricultural stage, wounds are still the subject of pecuniary sanction only. All of the early codes provide pecuniary sanctions only, while among those classed as "late," such as the Code of Hammurabi (*circa* 1914 B.C.), corporal sanctions account for about 40 per cent of the cases. (The Roman Twelve Tables provide for a nonpecuniary sanction only in what appears to have been a later addition to the original.)

In the early days of the Germanic tribes (around the beginning of the Christian era), the distinction between "civil" and "criminal" acts was established even before the general use of courts. Offenses, such as homicide, that were not recognized as constituting injuries to the tribe were left entirely to the kin organization to handle. The kin of the slain individual could avenge themselves by resorting to feud or by accepting composition, as they chose. But in the case of an offense that was felt to threaten the community, anyone who caught the culprit in the act could slay him, on behalf of the community at large. If the offender escaped, he became an outlaw and could be attacked by anyone who met up with him. Among the earliest recognized "crimes" were treason, arson, and secret slaying. The distinction of "secret" slaying from other cases of homicide represents a forerunner of the modern test of "premeditation" as the mark of murder.

The laws regulating marriage, inheritance, and property (which are closely related to each other) develop along general lines consonant with the principles set forth above. At an early date, the law of inheritance, where no wish to the contrary has been expressed by the deceased, gives all the property to the eldest son. The eldest son receives this property as head of the family, for which he is by the same token responsible. This right of inheritance, once having been recognized and enshrined in law, tended to last even after the responsibility of the head of the family for the other members becomes highly attenuated. In due course, however, following the realities of the situation, other sons come to share equally with the eldest, in rights of inheritance. Eventually, women, too, acquired at least qualified rights in this respect.

We may express the course of developments in even more general terms —by likening the growth of the law to the formation of a path. In a new community, it may be assumed, people needing to go from one village to another might follow different courses. One way may be better fitted to the terrain than the others and here a path would form. Once the path became visible that fact itself would tend to direct steps along it. (Almost any college campus provides illustrations of how difficult it is to *prevent* paths from forming.) So it is with the ways of settling disputes and of punishing offenses, once the occasions for judgment become sufficiently numerous. In addition to the growth in the number of cases, two other factors tend to make the path of the law broaden (or, better) deepen "down from precedent to precedent." One of these is the growing tendency for kings (as they become busier) to delegate judicial functions to specialized officers of justice. It would be only natural that the king should seek to limit the power of these appointees by requiring them to follow already existing precedents. In any case, they, being specialists, would know the precedents and, being agents, would hesitate to innovate, openly. The other factor referred to is the introduction of writing. Once it became possible to write down the law instead of depending upon fallible memory, another powerful force toward standardization was automatically introduced.

Illustrations from Our Own Tradition

The developments we have been discussing have not always pursued an even course. This fact and also the close relation between the development of law and the development of the polity is well illustrated in the early stages of our own civilization. Following the fall of Rome, a highly developed mature system of law was, for centuries, almost completely lost. Men returned to live under legal systems that were archaic at best. Under the strong Frankish monarchy a legal system of considerable maturity was maintained. The law progressed by way of both judicial and legislative organs. Even so, it was far inferior to Roman law. But with the collapse of the Frankish monarchy, political power was parcelled out among virtually autonomous feudal lords. Each was a law unto himself. They neither needed (for their own protection) nor wanted royal justice. Such courts as they established were more interested in favoring the privileged classes than in rendering justice. Ordeal by battle, where the knight in armor could well challenge lesser folk, achieved wide currency.

Gradually, as kings managed to re-establish their sway—first in England, after the Norman Conquest—the community interest in order and justice was successfully reasserted. The story may be told in terms of gradual extensions of "the king's peace." So it had been before the feudal breakup; so it was again. The king's peace often made its way from the peace of the kin (or of the feudal lord) by stages. Special "peaces" were decreed and enforced for special places (such as courts, fairs, and places of worship), and special persons (a freeman's abode, or the vicinity of the king himself). In these areas ordinary misdemeanors were subject to trial in the king's courts and met with especially severe judgments. Also, the king's justice was often first applied to professional criminals, men who could not be dealt with by the kin system.

The advance of the jurisdiction of the royal courts at the expense of those of local feudatories depended upon a combination of force and astuteness. Royal justice was better justice, so plaintiffs—at least meritorious plaintiffs—sought it out; and the force of strong monarchs made it "stick." The royal courts provided better justice in a number of ways. One of the most famous of these was to substitute for the ordeal (which had grown to unprecedented lengths in the feudal courts of this period) the far more rational and reliable instrument of justice, the jury.

With the re-establishment of a statewide system of justice in England, we once more reach a stage in legal development where the law becomes professionalized. At this point, then, we shall move on from our consideration of archaic legal systems to the mature systems of law, especially those of Rome and of the common law.

MATURE LAW

Professionalization of the Law

Maturity of law, as we have defined it, is marked by the emergence of a legal profession, that is of specialists in the law whose main vocation consists in the practice of this specialization. Legal systems usually go through a period when the law is largely a monopoly of religious specialists, or priests, simply because they constitute the literate and otherwise educated class. The development of secular specialists in the law marks the stage now under discussion.

The legal profession at one time or another is called upon to perform four types of work: to give legal advice and expound the law, to draw up legal documents, to act as representatives of litigants for the performance of various legal acts, such as initiating actions, and, finally, to argue cases before courts. For law to be called mature, it is not essential that all of these types of work should be done by professionals. Furthermore, these functions are sometimes performed separately, by different individuals. The trend, however, is toward having all the functions performed by the same individual. England still retains (though the United States does not) the distinction between a "solicitor," who may perform any of the first three types of activity, and a "barrister," who alone may argue cases.

The mark of mature law, specialization, is simply the natural product of advancing complexity of civilization. The same process goes on in countless other fields, although of course not all at the same time. Specialization in the field of law is an answer to felt needs and as such has definitely beneficial results. Among the good effects are a greater systematization of the law, with consequent greater uniformity of treatment of like cases, more analysis and development of theory, with the result that relevant distinctions hitherto disregarded by the law are given legal effect.

On the other hand, not all the results of the professionalization of law are on the credit side of the ledger. Systematization may have its evil consequences. The law tends to become rigid—too rigid. Since no system of classification of events can do justice to the variety of life, cases arise that are substantially different and yet that fall in the same categorical classification of the law and so must be treated alike. In such instances, equality of treatment is defeated by the law's formalization. The law also tends to become highly technical. Especially in the realm of procedure, the lawyers evolve subtle distinctions that easily become traps for the unwary. We have previously observed that the charge of involved procedural ceremonials and technicalities is completely unjustified as applied to primitive law but that something of this sort begins to develop in the later stages of archaic law. In the early stages of mature law it reaches its height. Now we find meticulous and complicated requirements for the forms to be followed in each type of action, with the penalty for mistaking the type of action or deviating in the slightest degree from the prescribed formula or procedure being loss of the suit. Perhaps some sound reason generally existed for the origin of each of these requirements; certainly one was alleged. But two facts seem obvious to us today: one, that in fact the law can be more just with less insistence upon procedural technicalities; and, two, that the more involved the law becomes the more necessary it is for laymen to resort to lawyers for assistance. The suspicion not unnaturally obtrudes itself that, consciously or unconsciously, lawyers were indulging in "make-work" practices of a kind similar to other guilds.

Mature systems of law have had to rid themselves, sometimes on more than one occasion, of these accretions of procedural technicalities, and to combat excessive rigidity of both procedural and substantive provisions. As we shall see, this reform was not always accomplished in the same way. In particular, the Roman- and common-law systems used quite different methods for infusing "equity" into the law. The point is that they both did it. Indeed, a general characteristic of the most advanced stages of legal development, as contrasted with the stages of early maturity is greater flexibility and more responsiveness to the prevailing sense of justice.

Other Factors Influencing the Development of Mature Law

In the history of both Roman law and the common law, as well as in other legal systems, the concept of Natural Law has been influential. Jurists have evolved theories of natural justice, or Natural Law, especially in periods of rapid change in the law, and just before such periods, when there has been a growing consciousness of the law's inadequacy. Although such theories rarely provided a basis for the logical derivation of specific rules of law, they often seemed to do so. That is to say, jurists were able to find a plausible connection between the very general principles of Natural Law (such as that no man should be judged in his own cause), and some more specific rule that the circumstances seemed to render socially desirable or useful (for instance, that an official should not be allowed to have the power to impose fines, the proceeds of which go into his pocket or redound to his advantage).

Just as concepts of Natural Law might well influence legal development even in the absence of professional lawyers, so many factors other than the existence of professional lawyers account for the characteristic features of mature law. Indeed, professionalization of law is but a symptom of the general process of civilization. Of primary significance for the history of the law are the consolidation of political power in the hands of the state, and the tremendous development of commerce, trade, and industry. These major political and economic factors are outstanding among the determining forces in the growth of mature legal systems.

Trend Toward Regularity

The tendency of legal development is to provide for like treatment of like cases. Although we have argued that this trend was fostered by the professionalization of the law, mature law has no monopoly of this characteristic. On the contrary it is the nature of law itself to seek this end. All legal systems tend, moreover, to move in the direction of subjecting the rulers themselves to the very laws they administer and, in varying measures, create. This principle in its fullest measure of development, is the familiar "rule of law." While the history of the modern growth of this principle is intimately associated with English constitutional development, the common law was by no means the first legal system to embody it. The archaic law of ancient Greece, for example, gave it full recognition. Aristotle declared that "the law ought to be supreme over all, and the magistracies and the government should judge only of particulars."[14] And, in fact, the magistrates of Athens were subject to legal penalties if they broke the law. Many centuries earlier than this, the epilogue to Hammurabi's code had declared that "every king that rules in the land shall observe the sentences of justice which are

[14] *Aristotle's Politics,* trans. Benjamin Jowett (Oxford, Eng.: Clarendon, 1923), Bk. IV, Ch. 4, p. 31.

written upon the stele; the laws of the land which he has enacted shall he not alter."[15] Similarly, among the Teutonic tribes of the feudal and pre-feudal period, the doctrine obtained that the law was the property of the tribe and was above the king or chief.

Mature legal systems then had this cardinal principle in their inheritance. Nor did they fail to develop it. It has been said that "the sanctity of the Roman home was respected legally perhaps as much as that of the modern Englishman."[16] Bracton's famous statement that the king, while under no man, was under God and the law was probably based upon a passage from Roman law declaring the same principle. But this particular principle is directly less a function of the maturity of the law than of the stage of political and constitutional development. While these latter are related to the development of law, they by no means march *pari passu* with it. So it happened that in the later periods of the Roman Empire as in certain periods of other mature legal systems, including the totalitarian regimes of our own day, the rule of law largely passed into eclipse, at least in the realm of public law.

In our own legal tradition, and especially in that of modern European countries, the Church has played an important role in fostering the rule of law. The canon law, developed in the Middle Ages for the settlement of purely ecclesiastical controversies, was extended to cover secular matters involving the clergy, and had as well a considerable influence on the development of the secular law. "In the canon law," declares Professor Munroe Smith, "we find . . . in opposition to the later Roman law and to medieval German law, a distinct assertion of the great principle of equality before the law. In the administration of its law the church recognized no distinction between prince and peasant."[17]

Developments in Civil Law

In dealing in slightly greater detail than we yet have with the trend of development of mature legal systems, we must make the broad distinction between criminal law and civil law. The latter term, with which we shall deal first, is ambiguous. Sometimes it is used to stand for the law of countries in the Roman rather than the common law tradition. Here, however, it is used, as commonly, to stand for the body of "private" law—all of the law, in other words, except the law of crimes.

"FROM STATUS TO CONTRACT"

Much of what has come to be criminal law was once a part of what we today would call the law of torts. That is to say, acts which we consider to be of concern to the state were then put in the category of private wrongs, sub-

[15] Stanley A. Cook, *The Law of Moses and the Code of Hammurabi* (London: Black, 1903), p. 12.
[16] William Seagle, *The Quest for Law* (New York: Knopf, 1941), p. 223.
[17] Munroe Smith, *The Development of European Law* (New York: Columbia U. P., 1928), p. 210.

ject to redress only by the injured party or by members of his kin group. Further, the civil law generally, in its immature stages, was dominated by the obligation not to violate laws. In mature legal systems, on the contrary, the dominant obligation becomes not to break contracts—not to violate certain voluntary agreements which individuals enter into with each other. This shift is a natural accompaniment of the change from a simple to a complex industrial society. Again, the statement is little more than another way of expressing Sir Henry Maine's famous generalization to the effect that "the movement of progressive societies has hitherto been a movement *from Status to Contract*."[18] Perhaps it would be more accurate to say that the movement from status to contract made possible the shift in the dominant quality of the legal system.

By "status" Maine meant something very like caste. He had in mind especially the old Roman institution of the family, in which primary rights were almost wholly confined to the *pater familias,* the head of the family, who was in turn responsible for the acts of other members of the family and for their care, and who held property for their benefit. These relations were fixed and unchangeable, save by legislation. By "contract," on the other hand, he meant the modern system under which individuals can make agreements altering their mutual rights and responsibilities. The distinction is perhaps clearest in the case of a serf, who is tied to his land and governed by a whole set of reciprocal rights and obligations over which he has no control, and the free laborer of a later day who can quit his present employment and work for whomever he wishes on whatever terms he can bargain for.

Before this change could come about, the concept of contract had to be evolved. The process was long and tortuous and we need not recount it here. One of the greatest hurdles was the problem of proof. At an early stage, witnesses to the (oral) agreement came to be required. Soon little ceremonies were developed, perhaps to impress the witnesses and give them something by which to remember the occasion. Tokens were often given "to bind the contract." The introduction of writing gave a great impetus to development. A written record was more lasting and reliable than the memories of men. Eventually, but not until long after the use of writing for contracts, the written document came to be thought of itself as the contract, rather than merely evidence of its existence.

The law of contracts achieved considerable elaboration in Roman Law. In fact, Roman Law was more complicated than modern law in this respect. There were four main types of contract, each with its peculiar legal quirks. The Romans did not, however, achieve a general theory of contract. The modern law of the subject is simpler, more flexible, and more readily adapt-

---

[18] Sir Henry Sumner Maine, *Ancient Law,* introd. Sir Frederick Pollock (London: Murray, 1906), p. 174.

able to all sorts of situation, as befits a society in which the movement from status to free contractual relations has gone far beyond that achieved in the most advanced period of Roman civilization.

The development of contract leads to a society in which, at least from the point of view of the law, individuals are free, equally free, to dispose of their labor and their possessions as they choose. Such a society is marked by free men, free ownership, and free markets. Men are no longer slaves, or bound to the soil. They can sell their land and generally buy and sell property of all kinds. They can mortgage or otherwise pledge it as security for debts, making it possible to borrow money with which to embark upon all sorts of productive enterprises. Civil law provided the basis for the system of "free enterprise" under which in large measure we operate in this country today. Gradually the newly developed equality of contracting was also extended to women, who were no longer the mere chattels of their fathers or husbands, but who became fully equal legal entities, with power to inherit and otherwise acquire property, and to exercise all the other rights to which men are entitled.

COMMERCIAL LAW

One part of Civil law, the law of commerce and trade—for example, the law regulating who is responsible for the loss of goods between the time of sale and actual delivery—has always tended toward a far greater universality than has characterized other branches of the law. The reason for this condition is simply that the subject matter of commercial law is highly mobile and often involves linking people who are under different governments. A law of commerce virtually the same throughout the civilized world has been in existence for at least 2500 years. For approximately six centuries it was part of the Roman law, having been borrowed from the Greeks (especially the laws of Rhodes). Rome's empire covered the civilized world and her law (commercial as well as otherwise) was the law for the world. Commercial law that was similar to the later laws from which modern commercial law can be traced was in existence in Babylon as long ago as 2000 B.C. Whether there was any direct line of succession from this law to the Phoenician and thence to the Greek law we do not know. The Roman "law merchant" was kept alive in the trading centers of the Near East after the fall of the West Roman Empire, and was adopted from them and further developed by the trading cities of Europe as they expanded from the tenth century on. In the more recent stages of the growth of the national state, the form of a special law merchant, with its own courts, has been abandoned. Commercial law has been absorbed into the various bodies of national law. In large measure, however, it has remained unchanged, so that the universality of this branch of the law, at least among noncommunist countries, is substantially unimpaired.

CORPORATIONS

A third legal institution, almost as important to the modern economy as free contractualism and common commercial law is that of the corporation. This development marks the later stages of maturity. Roman law provided for corporations in only a limited fashion. It has remained for modern law to fashion this device whereby great aggregations of capital may be accumulated and assigned to "juristic persons" (corporations). In this way it became possible for individuals to invest (risk) specified sums of money in a commercial or manufacturing enterprise without becoming liable beyond this amount even if the enterprise should fail. The enterprise is the person that contracts the debts of the business. It is in principle managed by its stockholders (owners) and the latter enjoy its profits; but its losses are limited to the capital invested in it (rather than to all of the capital of the investors). Without this powerful engine for the accumulation of risk capital (or a device similar to it), the tremendous material advances of our industrial age would have been impossible.

INDIVIDUALIZATION

The great trend in the development of mature law from status to contract, may also be described in terms of individualization. We begin with a situation in which the individual's legal identity and his legal rights and duties are a function of his position in a larger group—the kin group or the family. In large measure, the law deals directly with the group as a unit, or (later) with the *pater familias* as representative of the group. In the course of evolution the law comes to deal directly with the individual. Also, differences in legal status are gradually wiped out, until all are equal in the eyes of the law, and all free of legal restrictions on where they shall live, how they move about, for whom they agree to work, and how they dispose of their property.

SOCIALIZATION OF THE LAW

Within the last century the tendency toward individualization of the law has been reversed; and we nowadays speak of the socialization of the law as its most characteristic trend. The change began in a subtle fashion. Absolute freedom of contract, which would be the epitome of individualism, never prevailed. It has long been tempered, for instance, by the concept of "contracts against public policy." To take an extreme example, a man may not sell himself into slavery. That is to say, he may not contract away his freedom to contract. It has come to be recognized that in other, less obvious ways than this the liberty of the individual may become self-defeating. Far from producing equality of economic condition, equality of legal rights, combined with differences among individuals as to ability, enterprise, luck, and inheritance, leads to great differences in wealth. Under circumstances like these, equality of contractual freedom may lead to greater substantial inequality rather than less. The rich man's (or corporation's) wealth becomes a lever by which he can drive a hard bargain with the man whose circumstances allow him no choice, regardless of his legal rights.

Developments in the field of liability for injuries incurred by workmen while in the employ of someone else provide a nice example of the socialization of the law. Common law was based on the theory of responsibility of the individual for his own acts. If the accident was the result of the negligence or other fault of the employee, his employer could not be held liable. Gradually, in the present century, the doctrine of "liability without fault" has gained acceptance in this and other countries. Accidents came to be considered the inevitable concomitant of modern industry and the doctrine that their cost should be borne by the employer or by industry as a whole achieved acceptance. First, the trend was toward making the employer liable, by way of "employers' liability acts." These were soon largely superseded by "workmen's compensation acts" which either required employers to take out private insurance policies covering accidents to their employees or set up a state insurance fund to which all employers were compelled to make contributions. This development represents a substantial modification not only of the principle of individual responsibility but also of the freedom of contract, for neither employers nor employees are permitted to make contracts of employment waiving the terms of these laws. The rule of liability is fixed by the state and cannot be modified by individual agreement. Here the law not only limits freedom of contract but it also makes positive provision for interests that would have earlier been governed by contractual arrangements.

The example just given is but one of hundreds. The great bulk of modern labor legislation modifies the principle of freedom of contract. Much of it is based on the theory that legal equal freedom to contract does not result in substantially equal freedom for the reason that some individuals (normally employers) are in a far more favorable bargaining position than others (employees). Minimum wage and maximum hours of work legislation, for instance, interfere with freedom of contract on the theory that the "freedom" of the lowest paid workers to refuse to contract on unfavorable terms is no real freedom because their economic circumstances leave them no choice but to accept the terms offered.

This reversal of the individualization of the law can hardly be said to constitute a reversal of the movement from status to contract. The legal freedom of contract is being limited, it is true, but, in the democracies at any rate, there are no indications of a return to status. The modifications of law we have mentioned do not have the effect of making a man's economic welfare depend upon his birth. Indeed the effect of many of them is quite the opposite, insofar as inheritance is concerned. Whether collective (i.e., legislative) attempts to limit the bargaining power of strong parties so as to create real equality of contractual relations can be confined to its original objective, or whether it will tend to transform itself into a movement for establishing equality of condition rather than equality of opportunity remains to be seen. No a priori reason for the last-mentioned shift is apparent. It is worthy of remark that in the fascist regimes just such a course was pursued in certain areas, particularly with regard to land tenure. In Nazi Germany, freedom of disposition of small holdings was drastically curtailed, even eliminated entirely. In this way peasants were tied to their soil in a way quite reminiscent of feudalism.[19] Some have professed to see in this and other characteristics of fascism merely an extension of tendencies inherent in modern industrial civilization; but there is no apparent reason why these tendencies should proceed to their logical conclusion.

Development in Criminal Law

Finally, important developments in the realm of criminal law have attended the maturation process. Although we have arbitrarily delimited the stage of mature law by reference to its professionalization, actually the appearance of professional jurists is only a rough indication of the degree of advancement of a legal system. Except for periods of political as well as legal reversion, the maturation of legal systems is continuous. Many characteristics that authorities quite properly associate with mature legal systems can be found in archaic law, and vice versa.

For Civil law, the causes of legal development from the archaic to the mature were largely economic, at least in the first instance. The development of commerce and industry were dominant factors in the substitution of contract for status. The establishment of a strong state, capable of acting directly on all individuals and not dependent on the family as an auxiliary political unit, was also an important factor. Moreover, the growth of trade and industry was greatly facilitated by the formation of larger and stronger political units, just as the latter was demanded by the interests of commerce. Here, as elsewhere, the economic and the political are inextricably intertwined.

CAUSES OF DEVELOPMENT

In the field of criminal law, the most striking developments resulted from the enlargement and strengthening of the king's peace. As the state became able to assert a monopoly of the use of force, it naturally took over the functions of policing and of prosecuting breaches of the peace.

---

[19] In a quite different situation, Mexico has incorporated a similar provision in her land law as it applies to the peasants who obtained land as a result of the break up of large landed estates. The theory is that these farmers are too weak to retain their land in a free market situation even when it is to their interest to do so. Administrators of the land reform program look forward to an eventual period when this legal limitation, imposed as a protection, will no longer be needed.

Other political factors besides the growth of the state's strength had significant effects on the growth of this branch of the law. The development of humanitarian sentiments of liberalism, and of democracy, for instance, also had important effects on the history of criminal law. Generally speaking, democracy has tended to bring about improvements in criminal law with respect both to fairness in trial procedure and to the humanity of punishments. Economic factors also played a role. They had a great deal to do with determining what should be held a crime. In the days of great landed estates owned by country gentry, poaching became one of the worst of crimes. As movable property achieved greater importance, more attention was given to such crimes as theft and burglary.

PROCEDURAL DEVELOPMENTS

In the development of criminal law one of the major changes, as we have already observed, is that of the transfer of breaches of the peace that had been treated as mere civil injuries, or torts, to crimes. The injured party no longer has the option not to prosecute. The interest of the state has been injured and it takes action against the offender. The shift is not directly from feud or private composition to punishment for crime. At an intermediate stage part of the composition is paid to the court.

In the early stages of procedural development of criminal law, the complaint is still made by a private individual. The trial takes the form of a judicial duel, that is a verbal conflict between accused and accuser, with their witnesses, before a court—a court, incidentally, in which there is normally some element of democratic participation. The accuser need no longer be the injured party or a member of his family or kin group, but may be any individual, conceived as acting on behalf of the state.

During nondemocratic stages of constitutional development, a reversionary modification of this practice is common. By this time, the state has established its own police force and no longer depends upon private individuals to "bring a case" against alleged criminals. This function is performed by the agents of the state itself. The court is also, of course, an agent of the state and sometimes the functions of prosecution and adjudication are not well separated. The judge questions the accused, sometimes badgers him unmercifully. This type of inquisitorial procedure often results in great injustices, especially to members of the poorer classes. At this stage of legal development, an accused criminal normally has no right to have the assistance of counsel at the trial. The ignorant and inarticulate are thus put at a special disadvantage. Gradually, with the emergence of modern democracy, the criminal trial again assumes more of the aspects of a judicial duel in which the parties have equal opportunities. The state remains the prosecutor, but the prosecuting function is performed by a special state's attorney or prosecuting official, while the judge retires more and more into the role of impartial arbiter and is protected from influence by the political branches of the government by a secure tenure of office.[20] The accused is granted right to counsel and the right to have witnesses who might testify in his favor compelled to attend the trial and to testify. Determination of guilt is left to a jury, while the conduct of the trial is subject to appeal to a higher court.

PUNISHMENTS

In punishment as with procedure, an initial reversionary trend was soon succeeded by more humane measures. As tort gives way to crime, corporal punishment is substituted for composition. At later stages the more violent types of corporal punishment yield to imprisonment. This trend appears to be a function both of the strength of the state and of the extent of democracy. A strong state can afford to be lenient and tends to be so, if crimes are being kept at a minimum. Also, democracy tends to check the tendency to inhumanity in otherwise irresponsible governors. In our own legal tradition, the period of the Middle Ages, and also the subsequent period of strong despotisms, were characterized by punishments that seem excessively severe to the modern conscience. In one period the government was weak; during the other it was not democratically accountable. This background gives added meaning to the clauses in many constitutions today, that like our own, prohibit "cruel and unusual" punishments.

Men have generally disputed as to the theory of punishments underlying their laws. In varying degrees, the motives of vengeance, retribution, deterrence, and protection to the community have been mixed. Recently, still another idea has been gaining headway: to consider the criminal a sick person, who, whether because of his environment or as a consequence of hereditary traits, is maladjusted to society. If this concept were fully accepted, there would be no place for punishment. The state should simply treat the criminal for his illness and, until he is cured, prevent him from doing harm to others. Modern penological reform has been considerably influenced by this theory and the effect on our penal law is apparent. One of the most famous cases that served to call attention to the newer mode of thought in this country was the trial of Nathan Leopold, Jr. and Richard Loeb, in 1924. The two boys had admittedly murdered another boy in cold blood. Clarence Darrow, a famous criminal lawyer, defended them. In arguing for a mild sentence, he sought to prove, with elaborate evidence and argument, that the boys, while technically sane, were not fully responsible for their conduct. The whole free will–determinism controversy was given new life and point by this dramatic trial. The outcome is of no importance. (The boys were sentenced to life imprisonment.) The point is that a great criminal lawyer, in a case that focussed the attention of the whole country, attacked the very heart and core of the theory of our criminal law—the responsibility of the individual for his acts.

[20] This statement applies especially to common law countries. In code law countries, the judge plays a more active inquisitorial role, attempting to bring out the relevant facts.

Less spectacular but even more significant evidence of the influence of this approach to the treatment of criminals is the tendency of the law to provide indeterminate sentences. The idea is to allow the length of imprisonment to be determined after, often long after, the conviction, on the theory that it will then be possible to tell whether or not the person is reformed, or cured. Accordingly, the length of imprisonment need bear no relationship to the enormity of the crime. Ideally, this practice is accompanied by provision for care and treatment during the term of imprisonment in accordance with what are believed to be the methods best designed to bring about reform. The decision as to when to release the criminal generally on parole may, and in theory always should be made, by or on the advice of a group of expert penologists.

This last development is comparable to trends we have remarked upon in other aspects of the law. As in the case of the rule of law, the tendency is away from fixity toward giving more discretion to administrative officials. Also, as in the case of much of the Civil law, the trend is away from the theory of individual responsibility toward what may quite properly be called a socialization of the law. The new tendency is to consider that society rather than the individual is responsible for his behavior. (This is especially true in the field of juvenile delinquency.) Modern theory also assumes that the protection of society rather than any idea of retribution should form the rationale for punishment. Since the criminal is considered more as sick than as willfully wrong-doing, protection of society calls for treatment rather than punishment. Indeed, conditions are such in some of our most advanced reformatories, that there are some who feel that the convicted criminal gets "a treat instead of a treatment," to borrow an old advertising slogan.

It will be noted that the developments just discussed reflect not one but two theories. One, that represented by Darrow, minimizes individual responsibility and tends to transfer the blame to society. The other—and perhaps the more influential theory—minimizes the utility and desirability of retributive punishment (regardless of individual responsibility) and emphasizes the importance of treating the criminal in such a way as to maximize the chance of making him once more not only a safe but also a useful member of society. This theory appears to be the one that has chiefly been influential in the development of criminal law and punishment in the United States. It leads to a kind of socialization that does not necessarily deny the individualistic values.[21] As a matter of fact, properly interpreted and applied, it constitutes a further development of individuation in that it

[21] The danger inherent in the theory that denies individual responsibility is that it may lead to denial of the value of the individual as well as to the assertion of the supreme value of society. This theory has found expression in the legislation of totalitarian regimes, especially Nazi Germany. In the latter instance the criminal law was amended to provide for the punishment of crimes against the "healthy sense of right of the community." The opportunities for abuse thus placed in the hands of fallible and often corrupt human beings have been proved far too great to be tolerated.

attempts to deal with the criminal according to his individual needs. Instead of making the punishment fit the crime, according to the formula made famous by Gilbert and Sullivan, it seeks to make the punishment fit the criminal.[22]

CONCLUSION

Our study of law is not yet complete. We have yet to examine the Roman law and common law systems as separate entities and to compare them with each other. At this point, nevertheless, we may note certain conclusions that emerge from our study so far. Specifically, we may observe one constant and one trend.

The constant is the principle of order, of regularity. Law is not always equally successful in attaining this objective. Law may even go through periods of movement away from it. Nevertheless, the essence of law is regularity, an essence that will not be permanently negated even though temporary exigencies force departures from it. This conclusion, for which the material already discussed furnishes evidence, will be further reinforced by the examination of the Roman and common law systems immediately following.

The trend may be described as an increase in individuation. We have noted at least three manifestations of this trend. First, is the tendency to make more and more distinctions, so that the law may fit more exactly the demands of justice in the particular situation. Thus, equity introduced into common law the idea of taking motive into account. Second, is the growing practice of trying to fit the punishment of criminals to their individual needs. Finally, we have that broad development of free contractualism that has pervaded the development of law for centuries. While we noted certain opposing tendencies of recent times in this respect, most if not all of them—barring the extreme reversionary developments in totalitarian regimes—appear to be more apparent than real. They are departures from the movement toward legal freedom of contract, but they are intended to increase real individual freedom by providing an offset for some of the extralegal limitations upon freedom of choice.

(For "Selected Readings," see end of Chapter 8.)

---

[22] For further information on subjects covered in the last few pages, see Seagle, *op. cit.*, Ch. 17 and materials cited there.

Development of Legal Systems:

Roman Law and Common Law

Two great systems of law have been produced by Western civilization; Roman law and the Common law.[1] Together they provide the basis for most of the legal systems in civilized countries today. We shall discuss them separately, as units, instead of moving back and forth from one system to another, as we did in studying the general progress of the law.

A word should be said about the Greeks, for they gave us both the beginning and the early flowering of our civilization. The Greeks did make contributions to law, but in comparison with the quality of the rest of their civilization, these were remarkably slight, particularly with regard to legal organization and procedure. The law of the Greek city-states never reached the stage of maturity as we have (somewhat arbitrarily) defined that term. Many of the substantive rules of law that they developed correspond closely to the later development of Roman or Common law. Furthermore, Roman law undoubtedly borrowed extensively from the Greeks, particularly since many great Roman lawyers were Greeks, while others received a Greek education. But the Greeks did not develop a professional legal class. Consequently their law was not refined and systematized and no group had a professional interest in elaborating and transmitting it to others. An education in Greece or by Greek teachers, therefore, if it involved law at all, would do so only incidentally.

Moreover, in Greece, courts were not developed to a satisfactory stage. This was particularly true in democratic Athens, which in other respects typified the best of Greek civilization. So complete was the power of the popular assembly in judicial as in other matters, that a large degree of ir-

---

[1] See James Bryce, *Studies in History and Jurisprudence*, 2 vols. (New York: Oxford U. P., 1901), Vol. I, Essay II, "The Extension of Roman and English Law Throughout the World."

regularity prevailed in interpretation and application of the law, regardless of the terms of code or custom and in spite of the ideal of the rule of the law.[2]

At the outset of our study of the Roman- and common-law systems, it will be helpful to remind ourselves of the chronology of the comparable stages of development of these two great systems. The following table provides the bare outlines of such a comparison.

TABLE III

STAGES OF DEVELOPMENT: ROMAN AND COMMON LAW

Stages	Roman Law	Common Law
Primitive (no courts of law)	Tribal law prior to 8th or 9th century B.C.	Law of Germanic tribes prior to Christian era
Archaic (courts, but no professional lawyers)	8th or 9th century, B.C., to 250 B.C.	Pre-Norman Conquest Anglo-Saxon law to middle of 12th century, A.D.
Mature (a legal profession)	250 B.C. to 565 A.D.	Middle of 12th century, to date

However, our discussion of these great legal systems will be confined largely to their periods of maturation.

ROMAN LAW

During its archaic period Roman law was formal and rigid. Legal transactions of all kinds had to be validated by the use of fixed and solemn formulas spoken by word of mouth.[3] It was not until the needs of a growing empire and expanding commerce made themselves felt that this stage began to give way to a more flexible system. With the appearance of professional jurists in the third century B.C., however, Roman law was armed for the growth and refinement that enabled it not only to serve the needs of the vast Roman Empire, but also to survive the fall of that Empire and live to become the major foundation of nearly all civilized countries today outside of those where the Anglo-Saxon tradition is dominant. The difference is often ascribed to some peculiar legal genius of the Roman people. Here as elsewhere the attempt to explain history by reference to national characteristics is the last refuge of the puzzled historian. We have already remarked that the bulk of the great jurists of Rome were not Romans at all! The basis for

[2] For a brief account of Greek Law, see John Marcy Zane, *The Story of Law* (New York: Washburn, 1927), Ch. 6.

[3] See J. Declareuil, *Rome the Law-Giver* (New York: Knopf, 1926), pp. 60-92. For a brief general account of Roman law, see Zane, *op. cit.*, Ch. 9.

the growth of Roman law is plain to be seen: it is to be found in the needs of a vast empire, and of the commercial and economic developments that went with it. Mere size is significant in three respects. First, size calls forth the specialist in judicial as in other governmental work. No single body can any longer combine all the functions of government. Whether or not the persons assigned to adjudication are originally professionals, they soon become so. Furthermore, the great number of cases that inevitably come up for trial in a large and populous country insure that the same persons will adjudicate the same or similar points many times. They will have ample opportunity to compare similar, yet different cases and to make nice distinctions between them and the "path" of the law will become more clearly demarcated. Also, a large country naturally leads to geographically distributed courts with a central system of appeals, another fact conducive to the systematization of the law and to the development of legal doctrine for the explanation of decisions and the guidance of courts when new situations arise.

Equally important is the economic factor. The growth of a complicated system of trade and commerce in the last two centuries of the Roman Republic necessitated a refinement of law which only professionals could give it.

Early Stages

A popular doctrine holds that, while the Common law is the product of custom, the Roman law was first set down in the form of the Twelve Tables, elaborated largely by statute, and eventually codified once more in the famous code of Justinian. This picture is far from the truth. Early Roman law was largely customary law. Legislation was not unknown but it was mostly confined to public law. As is usual in the early stages of civilization, the priests (or pontiffs, as they were called in Rome) came to be the king's special advisers in legal as well as religious matters. They soon achieved a practical monopoly of accurate knowledge of the law, and so also of its interpretation, a position which they retained after the coming of the Republic in 509 B.C.

The College of Pontiffs, as they were denominated, comprised a closed, self-perpetuating group, representative of the patrician or aristocratic families. By a series of reforms, however, this situation was amended. The first of these reforms was the publication of the law, for all to see and know, in the form of the famous Twelve Tables. This summary of the customary law, according to legend, was drawn up by a commission in the middle of the fifth century B.C. It was said to have been inscribed on copper tablets placed in the Forum. However, the tablets have been lost and we have only secondary and incomplete accounts of their contents. Some scholars question the authenticity of the whole episode. According to the generally received account, however, they remained almost unchanged by statute for two and a half centuries, although judicial additions and amendments abounded.

Other reforms came later. Notably in 304 B.C., the secretary of one of the pontiffs, with the aid of his master, published the *actiones,* or precedents. At about the same time, a statute was enacted admitting plebeians to the college of pontiffs. In 250 B.C. for the first time a plebeian achieved the office of chief pontiff, Pontifex Maximus. Significantly, it was he who began the practice of expounding legal questions to those who wished to learn the law. During this period also the power of the pontiffs was being modified by the development of private individuals who specialized in the study of the law and gave advice to those who needed it. These men were known as jurists or jurisconsults. The trend of these developments was to inject a democratic element into the law and otherwise to broaden the base of the legal pyramid.

This early stage of Roman law was complicated, ritualistic, and technical—a fact that became a source of chronic discontent. Cases had to be brought according to certain *leges actiones.* If the petitioner did not know the right *actio* for his type of case, or failed to follow the stated ritual in some detail, he lost his whole case. Although this strict ritualism may have served a useful purpose at one time, the abuses to which it was liable led to its early modification. In the last two centuries of the Republic (230-30 B.C.), it gave way to a more flexible "formulary" procedure, described below.

Courts

So far we have said nothing about courts, about the machinery by which justice was administered in concrete cases. Originally, the king himself presided over trials. When the Republic was established in 509 B.C., this task was assigned to the consuls. A century and a half later (367 B.C.), a new elective magistrate, the *praetor,* was created for this purpose. From this time the judicial functions were divided between two officials, neither of whom have an exact analogue in our system. These were the *praetor* and the *judex,* or judge. The *praetor* presided over the trial and stated the law to govern the case. The *judex,* however, not only determined the facts but also delivered the judgment. Curiously enough, neither was necessarily—or even generally—an expert in the law. The *praetor* was like a career politician, and the praetorship was an office to which he was normally elected, for a one year term, toward the middle of his career. The *judex* was a private citizen chosen from a panel, by lot, for a particular case. Both he and the *praetor,* as well as the parties, were likely to seek legal advice from jurists: —self-appointed experts who were the real craftsmen of the Roman law. Furthermore, the parties to a dispute employed trained advocates and frequently got and presented to the court the opinions of jurisconsults, all of which was of assistance to the court. In the later days of the Empire, after the classical period of Roman law, permanent professional judges and court records were established. Probably with this development, but not before, judges began to pay attention to previous decisions in similar cases; but they were not supposed to do so and Justinian, in the sixth century, prohibited the practice. This attempt to prevent courts from being governed by previous decisions, which still is characteristic of countries whose legal system is based upon Roman law, strikes the person brought under the Common-law system as strange. It might even suggest a deliberate encouragement of arbitrariness. The theory, however, is that courts should follow the statute law as they, in their wisdom, and in the light of prevailing circumstances, interpret it, uninfluenced by what may have been the mistakes of their predecessors.

The Praetors' Edicts

An important institution of Roman legal procedure was the *praetor's* edict. Upon their assumption of office, Roman officials were accustomed to issue a pronouncement, known as an edict, that stated the policies they intended to pursue. In the edict of the *praetor* the device of the formula, referred to above, was evolved. By the Lex Aebutia (*circa* 150 B.C.) *praetors* were given the power to modify the *leges actiones* by means of the formulary procedure. (Probably a movement in this direction had already been begun by the *praetor*, without statutory authorization.) Thenceforth, in their edicts, they published the formulas for bringing suits which they would accept for various types of cases. Other modifications of the law were brought about in this way. New situations, not provided for by the Twelve Tables or otherwise, were dealt with in this fashion. Frequently, the *praetor* used the device of the legal "fiction." For example he might announce in his edict that if a prescribed form had not been followed he would nevertheless treat the case *as if* it had been adhered to.

Although a new edict was drawn up each year, by custom the new *praetor* patterned his edict on that of his predecessor, making just such additions and modifications as experience suggested. The law grew by accretion in a way not so different from the method of judge-made law with which we are familiar. Under the Empire, the creative role of the *praetor* was greatly minimized, and the edict of the urban *praetor* was revised and put in statutory form.

Mention of the "urban" *praetor* brings us to one of the most important institutions in the development of Roman law. The old Roman law like all primitive and much archaic law, was personal rather than territorial. It was the law for Romans. The expansion of commerce, however, called for the application of law between Romans and non-Romans. Moreover, as the Republic grew the problem of administering law among the non-Roman subjects called for a solution. The result was the establishment of a separate *praetor* for this purpose. The *praetor* for Roman citizens was the "urban" *praetor;* he administered the *jus civile,* the law of the city (of Rome). The new *praetor* operated in Rome and travelled around the province. He was known as the "peregrine" *praetor (i.e.,* the *praetor* for foreigners). He administered law in all cases involving an alien. He had the great advantage that he was not bound by the *jus civile.* With the advice of jurists, he was to do justice as best he could among men of a great variety of legal backgrounds. It was probably he who initiated the development leading to the formulary procedure and its substitution for the over-formalistic *legis actio.* By the use of reason and his sense of justice, doubtless influenced also by Stoic concepts of Natural Law, he sought to discover the common principles among varying tribal laws, customs, and usages, and to develop them into legal rules. Ironically, this *jus gentium,* or "law of the peoples," as it was called (corresponding to what is today known as private international law), was generally more rational and humane than the *jus civile,* the application of which was reserved as a special privilege of Roman citizenship. It was, in fact, widely borrowed by the urban *praetor,* until it eventually became the dominant element in Roman law. This process of unification was largely completed by the statutory codification of the *praetor's* edict which brought an end to the dual system of law and of courts that had previously prevailed.[4]

Legal systems generally go through recurrent periods of rigidity and of reform, the latter with the objective of making more equitable a system that had ceased to be well fitted to the changed times. In Roman law the peregrine *praetor* was the great instrument for the infusion of principles of equity. More specifically, the rule of good faith and the determination of the legal significance of acts and facts by the intention of the parties, and not by words alone were basic contributions of the *jus gentium,* as they were of equity in the development of English law centuries later.

The Jurists

The role of the jurists as a formative influence in the development of Roman law was enormous. In addition to advising parties, acting as advocates, giving *responsa* (formal legal opinions on difficult points, in answer to requests by either court official or private party), they wrote summaries, commentaries, and extensive treatises on all branches of the law. For a period of some three hundred years the *responsa* of the most famous jurists, officially designated "patented jurisconsults" were given the full force of law. Although this did not officially apply to their other writings, the commentaries of the great jurists, Gaius, Papinian, Paul, Modestinus, and Ulpian (of the second and early third centuries, A.D.) were accepted as almost as authoritative as their actual *responsa.* These commentaries were largely

---

[4] See *Cambridge Ancient History,* Vol. 9, pp. 862-868.

based upon the *praetor's* edicts. The latter themselves became sprawling, disorganized and sometimes inconsistent discourses based on particular cases, greatly in need of harmonization and systematization.[5]

Roman Law in Later Centuries

The later centuries of the Roman Empire added nothing to the development of the grand edifice of Roman law. The tendency was decidedly in the other direction. After the fall of Rome, in the sixth century, Justinian, Emperor of the Eastern Empire, put scholars to work on a great compilation of Roman law. It was made up of four parts: the Code, consisting of a revision and consolidation of the statutory law; the Digest, a great compendium of works of the jurists; the Institutes, which was in fact a textbook of the law; and, finally, the *Novellae,* comprising statutes enacted by Justinian himself after 534.

We shall not tell here of the subsequent history of Roman law. Justinian's compilation, known as the *Corpus Juris Civilis,* soon fell into disuse. We have already seen that the law of Europe in the Dark and Middle Ages was largely the customary law of the Germanic tribes. Naturally, the farther south one goes the greater was the Roman influence. But long before the fall of Rome, the law of the Roman provinces had degenerated. It became quite crude, lacking the refinements of classical Roman law, and was progressively infused with barbarian elements. The decentralized and disorderly political condition of Europe during most of the medieval period prevented the re-development of a great legal system for centuries. For a long period professional lawyers, either as judges or advisers, were lacking, and appellate courts, essential for the growth of the law, were nonexistent. In the twelfth century no such courts were to be found, and in many parts of Europe they did not come into existence until the close of the Middle Ages.

But in the large it was the Roman law, rather than the more primitive tribal customs and manorial usages that was destined to survive. The processes by which it did so are too complicated and various for explanation here. With the rebirth of learning, a body of legal scholars developed in the schools, at Bologna and elsewhere, who studied the Roman law in detail and wrote many treatises on it. Through the influence of these "glossators" and later commentators, there was a gradual interpenetration of local law by Roman law. The canon law of the Church was largely based on Roman law principles and it, in turn, had a great deal of influence on the development of secular law, especially since the latter was widely administered by church-

[5] See *Cambridge Ancient History*, Vol. 11, pp. 816-826. A good brief account of the machinery and procedure for the administration of justice may be found in Edward McChesney Sait, *Political Institutions—a Preface* (New York: Appleton-Century, 1938), pp. 180-190. See also Bryce, *op. cit.*, Vol. 2, Essays 14, 15 for a comparative discussion of Roman and Common Law legal institutions.

men. The birth of the nation state gave great impetus to the extension of the Roman law because Germanic law was local and various, while the new needs demanded bodies of law that were at least nation-wide. Although the local law died hard, and important Germanic elements still characterize European law, European countries generally "received" the old Roman law, as modified by generations of medieval glossators and commentators, as the general body of law to prevail in the absence of clearly established and maintained local custom.[6] Thus, throughout the Continent of Europe, the work of the peregrine *praetor* did not have to be repeated. Across the Channel, in England, however, where the nationalizing process got under way at an early date, following the Conquest, the Roman law was never "received," and the work of the peregrine *praetor* in essence was repeated. This is the story of the Common law.

THE COMMON LAW

The archaic Anglo-Saxon law in effect in England at the time of the Norman Conquest, which remained largely unchanged for some time after that historic event, appears to have reached a stage of considerable formalism and even ritualism. Actions had to be initiated and conducted in accordance with set procedures strongly reminiscent of the early Roman *leges actiones*.[7] Compurgation and ordeal were the accepted methods of proof, trial by battle being introduced by the Normans following the Conquest.

English law of the period under discussion, like early Roman law, was largely customary law. But there was one important difference. England, unlike Rome, did not develop from a city-state. It covered a substantial territory and customs differed from one locality to another, even as they did in Europe.[8]

Consolidation After the Norman Conquest

English development was different from European development in another respect. William the Conqueror established a strong hold in England, not only over the natives but also over his own vassals. Although he followed the prevailing feudal form of organization, he succeeded in re-

[6] See R. W. Lee, *The Elements of Roman Law* (London: Sweet & Maxwell, 1946), pp. 21-24.

[7] At the time of the earliest possible Roman influence on England, when Caesar's legions occupied the land, this Roman procedure had been out of use for centuries in Rome. Consequently there can be no question of influence. Here is one more example of the fact that legal systems tend to develop through the same stages quite independently of one another.

[8] See Sir Frederick Pollock and F. W. Maitland, *History of English Law*, 2 vols. (Oxford, Eng.: Clarendon, 1895), Ch. 2.

taining for himself and his successors a strong overlordship. Within a century after the Conquest, the King's court, (*Curia Regis*) under Henry II, was systematically sending itinerant justices throughout the realm, holding sessions of court. The old manorial courts continued to exist, but the royal courts offered a superior brand of justice. By the purchase of a writ from the king, litigants could buy the privilege of a jury trial in place of the archaic methods of the local jurisdictions. As we have seen, the jury was a peculiarly royal institution. It grew out of the royal inquest, an administrative device for making sure that the king's lands were not being encroached upon and that payments due him were being made. The king took care that his courts alone were given authority to call juries. Moreover the king had and used the power to enforce the judgments of his courts even against the strongest feudal lords. This fact constituted an equally strong attraction for royal justice.

The king's political power enabled him to carry out this transformation in the first instance. It was quite likely his need for revenue that prompted him to do so, for with the jurisdiction went the fines and amercements as well as the price of the writs. The loss of this revenue to the feudal courts further weakened the feudatories and so aided the king in maintaining his ascendancy. Once more we note the interaction of political and economic factors.

Now what law did these royal courts apply? In spite of theory fostered by the courts themselves, it was not "general custom of the realm," for on most points no such general custom existed. Roman law indeed had a better claim to this description, for the Twelve Tables were a codification of general customary law. In fact, it was the judges themselves who made the law. Undoubtedly, they generally selected their rules from among the array of local customs known to them; but it was their selection of a particular custom that made it general and enshrined it in the law of the land. Sometimes they were influenced by Roman and canonical rules in developing their own rules. The fact that the members of the King's court generally spoke no English doubtless encouraged this tendency. In short, if English law was customary law it was as much the custom of the courts as that of the people. As with the Romans, professional students of the law were the primary constructive influences in legal development, but in England these professionals were judges. It has accordingly been said that Roman law was made by the bar and English law by the bench. Generally speaking, the distinction is accurate. So also is the implication that, as far as private law is concerned, statutes (i.e., legislators) played a relatively insignificant role in both cases.

Mention has been made of royal writs. These documents played a very important part in the development of procedural law, comparable to that of the formulas of the *praetors* in Roman law. Just as the edict was of general use in Roman administration, the *praetor's* edict being only a special application, so in English law writs were simply administrative orders addressed to officers of the crown. Writs became the means by which the royal courts were given jurisdiction over civil trials, their powers having been originally confined to criminal cases. Writs were issued by the Chancery, which served as the King's secretariat. They described the method or procedure to be used in settling a particular claim. Sometimes the writ was framed by the Chancery clerks on the basis of a rule that has already been devised or adopted by the judges; sometimes Chancery took the initiative and the judges could either accept or reject it. The writ, while providing the method of suit, also defined the offense which the plaintiff was charging. That is to say it included a substantive rule of law. As more and more "original" writs were framed and used they came, collectively, to be the great embodiment of English law. Many writs naturally became standard forms for certain types of cases and the Chancellor was directed to issue them "as of course," that is, automatically. But new situations were met by the issuance of new original writs.[9]

Originally the jurisdiction of the royal courts was based on the theory of the king's interest in maintaining the peace of the realm. Their jurisdiction, accordingly, extended at first only to criminal actions. The process of extension to civil cases, using the writs described above, was a gradual one. The original pretext was generally that some breach of the peace had been involved. For example, if the ownership of land was involved, as it was in the great majority of cases, it might be that one party had forcibly ejected the other from the land. Such action would constitute a breach of the peace, and so it was provided that the ejected party could sue in the king's court to be restored to possession of the land. Even if the person who did the ejecting was the rightful owner, the writ would run, as the saying goes, because he must establish his claim by proper legal procedure, not by violence. After settlement of this dispute, if the ejector wished further to contest the matter of ownership, he might bring suit to do so, but it would have to be in the king's court. By later extension, force was presumed, even if it had not been used; and by such devices the civil jurisdiction of the king's courts was advanced step-by-step.

The Jury

The jury was one of the improvements in procedure that made royal justice attractive. As noted above, it developed out of the royal inquest which probably had its origin in the latter days of the Roman Empire. *Via* the Franks it came to the Normans, who brought it to England. There it was first used as an instrument of inquisition for compiling the information that went into Domesday Book. The essence of procedure through jury was the calling together of a group of citizens of a locality under royal order and

---

[9] See "writ" in *Encyclopaedia Britannica* (Chicago, Ill.: *Encyclopaedia Britannica*, 1956).

compelling them to give testimony under oath. Almost immediately after the Conquest the jury was used for gaining information about crimes that had been committed in a given neighborhood. This innovation led to the jury system of today. As early as 1075 there is record of the use of a jury of twelve men to make a conclusive statement of facts upon which the judge should make his judgment.

The evolution of the modern jury did not take place that rapidly, however. Not until the reign of Henry II were juries systematically used in criminal cases. At first the jury acted in the role of what we know as the grand jury; it presented suspected criminals for trial. Its presentment constituted a presumption of guilt. The actual trial might still be conducted by ordeal. Church condemnation of the ordeal in the early thirteenth century, however, led to its abandonment and the use of the jury for trial as well. It took some time to hit upon the solution of having an entirely separate jury for the trial. Over a century passed before this distinction was rigorously insisted upon.

Juries in the early stages were used to supply evidence rather than to hear it. They were chosen not, as today, because they were innocent of any knowledge of the crimes in question, but because it was hoped that they would have special knowledge of them. Evolution toward present practice took the course of first bringing in witnesses to give evidence, secretly, to the jurors. The modern system of having all testimony made in open court and subject to cross-examination became established during the sixteenth and seventeenth centuries. Another of the distinctive features of the common-law jury system, the unanimous verdict, did not become established until the middle of the fourteenth century.

Rigidification and the Growth of Equity

Two other important changes took place during the period under review. Originally used in criminal cases only, the jury was soon applied to civil trials as well. Secondly, not long after the provision of itinerant judges, the judicial function of the Curia Regis was committed to specialists. By the middle of the thirteenth century the common law had a professional bench; its maturity was well established.

We have seen before that legal systems, especially under the influence of professional lawyers, tend to rigidify; that times change, and that consequently ways of reforming the law have to be evolved. In England the system of writs accomplished, for a time, the purpose of getting away from earlier formalism in much the same way that the creation of the peregrine *praetor* with his formulas had done for Rome. But something happened. Hardening of the arteries set in. For some reason, not wholly clear, the judges ceased to recognize new writs,—and this in spite of the fact that an increasing number of cases developed for which the old writs were inappropriate.

Partly the cause seems to have been incidental to the struggle to limit royal arbitrariness, while partly it is to be found in the psychology of growing professionalism in the law. As to the first of these points, it must be observed that the power of the king to issue new writs was capable of great abuse. It virtually amounted to unchecked legislative power. Consequently, in 1258, it was set forth in the Provisions of Oxford that the king's Chancellor should frame no new writs without the consent of the king *and his council.* Although some modifications of this drastic provision was instituted by the Statute of Westminster, it remained a severe restriction on the growth of the law.

The other cause is more difficult to pin down but perhaps in the long run even more important. The judges, busily developing new writs for the Chancellor to issue, were in fact creating the common law out of a mass of often conflicting customary law and other elements they saw fit to introduce. The Common law was their creation. They took pride in it. They saw no need to modify it. They cherished it. And certainly they did not want any interference from the king of his Chancellor. They, the judges, were the custodians of the law. Professional pride and professional conservatism almost certainly had a lot to do with the fact that the common law lost its power of growth.

A way of meeting the problem was found. The Chancellor was the head of the King's Council. If he could no longer control the judiciary, he could exercise other aspects of the king's residual powers. In particular, he could dispense grace by the royal prerogative. Petitions to the King's Council praying for relief from conditions which the Common law (either because of its inherent inadequacy or because of the unsettled political conditions of the second half of the fourteenth century) was unable to remedy were quite naturally referred to the king's chief minister, the Chancellor. He granted relief as a matter of "grace" (that is, at his discretion). Originally the action was not a judicial one at all. It had more in common with the act of the chief executive in this country in granting a pardon, although of course the parallel is not a close one. The performance of this function by the Chancellor soon led him to be called the Keeper of the King's Conscience. It was perhaps fitting that at this period and for long afterwards the Chancellor was always an ecclesiastic.

These acts of grace by the Chancellor soon became so common that he had to establish a regular procedure, necessarily somewhat judicial in nature, for their performance. Chancery in fact became a court. Chancellors sought, however, to avoid open conflict with the common-law judges, who were extremely jealous of their jurisdiction. Consequently, especially in the early stages, the pretense was kept up that Chancery did not alter the Common law, but followed it. It merely granted relief in accordance with common-law rights where for some reason it could not be obtained in the regular courts. Equity, as the dispensations of the Chancellor were called, came to deal especially with remedies. Yet it did in effect modify common-law rights, and the conflict between the two jurisdictions could not always be obscured. Particularly was this the case when, as frequently happened, Chancery restrained a litigant from obtaining enforcement of a judgment that had been rendered by a common-law court. Even today our law contains anomalies that are the product of this situation. For example, if *A* persuades *B* by the use of fraud to sign a certain contract, *A* may nonetheless secure enforcement of the contract from a common-law court. Before this judgment is carried out, however, *B* may obtain an injunction from an equity court restraining *A* from seeking execution of his judgment. If in spite of this *B* should proceed he will be subject to imprisonment for "contempt of court." To cap the climax, in many jurisdictions, today, the same judge, acting in different capacities, would pronounce both judgments.

Among the remedies characteristic of equity proceedings, in addition to the all-important writ of injunction, were writs requiring specific performance of contracts (where the common law merely allowed damages for breach of contract), and writs requiring individuals, especially officials, to take specific action (writs of *mandamus*). In addition to providing more suitable remedies, equity was more sensitive to moral considerations than the Common law. The Chancellor took cognizance of motives. He had no patience with petitioners who sought to rely on their technical legal "rights" for unethical ends. The maxim is that "he who seeks equity must do equity." On the other hand, he was anxious to give relief to those who had been taken advantage of unfairly, even though within the letter of the law. A sixteenth century rhyme seeks to sum up the Chancellor's jurisdiction this way:

> These three give place in court of conscience,
> Fraud, accident, and breach of confidence.

Differences in procedure between equity and common law courts were (and are) notable. The judge takes a more active part in the proceedings, engaging in extensive interrogation of the parties. Furthermore, there is no jury. The judge finds his own facts. Finally, his decision, which is known as a "decree," is not confined to a "yes" or "no" judgment. He may not only issue any of the various writs mentioned above but he may decree a long and complicated course of behavior, involving both prohibitions and requirements of positive conduct.

Like the Common law in its early days, equity was highly flexible during its formative period. Although this flexibility made it easier to do justice, it also made it easier to do injustice. Undoubtedly favoritism and arbitrariness were not uncommon under some Chancellors. In two oft-quoted remarks, Seldon declared that "equity is a roguish thing," and added that its measure was "the length of the Chancellor's foot."[10]

---

[10] Quoted by William Seagle, *The Quest for Law* (New York: Knopf, 1941), p. 191.

In due course equity too lost its flexibility. By the end of the seventeenth century it had become as rigid as the Common law. It had its own rules and its own precedents. But it had made a great contribution to the Common law. Not only had it added to the whole body of law its own set of principles and remedies; but also its very existence undoubtedly promoted reforms in the Common law. For instance, the system of original writs which had served to strangle the growth of the Common law and give rise to the development of equity, was eventually modified and then completely abandoned. Partly by judicial and partly by legislative action, the Common law has regained at least some of the power of growth that characterized it in its earlier period.[11]

Precedents

This reference to the part played by precedents in rigidifying equity leads us to a consideration of the role of precedents in the common-law system. In the early days decisions were not published and such a thing as judicial precedents was not known to the law. As the practice of recording and compiling reports of decided cases grew, however, judges began to pay attention to "precedents." Such reports were set forth in the Year Books beginning in 1292. Even before this judges were not only aware of other decisions but cited them in their own opinions. Thus Bracton, writing in the middle of the thirteenth century, was able to cite some five hundred cases. Also, England was a small country; and the judges spent a part of the year together at the Inns of Court and must have become well acquainted with each other's work. It is only natural that they would develop a sense of unity, a professional *esprit de corps,* and that they would seek to develop a consistent body of law. The fact of a fairly uniform body of law, made largely by judges, could not have come about had not the judges tended to follow precedent. It was not until the nineteenth century, however, that English law developed the hard-and-fast rule of *stare decisis.* According to this rule, not only must a lower court be governed absolutely by the rule of a higher court, but the highest court of the land, the House of Lords, is bound by its own previous decisions. In the United States, the latter provision has never been accepted. The state and federal supreme courts feel free to reverse themselves if they are convinced that the original decision was wrong.

Although common-law courts hold that they must follow precedents, just what constitutes a precedent is another matter. No two cases are exactly alike. In theory, it is the *ratio decidendi* of a case that is binding; it is the basis, the logical foundation, the underlying rule of law, which must be

---

[11] On "equity," generally, see Sir Carleton Kemp Allen, *Law in the Making,* 6th ed. (Oxford: Oxford U. P., 1958), Ch. 5.

followed in subsequent cases. Not everything that the court says in the course of its opinion will be necessary to the decision of the case. These unessentials are known as *obiter dicta*. But the distinction between *dictum* and rule is often not a simple matter. It is frequently possible for courts to avoid precedents they do not like by distinguishing the case at hand from the earlier case sometimes by arguing that what appeared to be the rule was only a *dictum*. Such an argument may call for some reinterpretation of the reasoning of the previous opinion but reinterpretation is not beyond either the power or the ingenuity of judges.

Significance of the Growth of Administrative Law

Of great importance in the growth of the law, especially in connection with that basic principle, the rule of law, is the modern development of administrative law. Increasingly, power to interpret the law and to adjudicate disputes is being delegated to administrative agencies rather than to courts. The laws to be interpreted, the standards to be applied, are frequently cast in such broad and unprecise terms that the discretion of the administrator is given wide ambit. We may add that the concepts administrators are called upon to apply—such as "needs" or "public interest"—are unfamiliar to the categories of the Common law. What does all this portend? Does it point to a departure from the principle of the rule of law? It was suggested in the previous chapter that such *might* be the case. Many people, especially many lawyers, fear that it will be.

By this time, however, we have developed sufficient perspective to see that such a consequence is not suggested by the history of law. The law has repeatedly gone through periods when rigid rule gave way to greater flexibility. Often, too, the change was brought about by the development of new judicial organs. When the old *legis actio* became too constrictive, the *praetor* evolved the formula. When even the formulary procedure ceased to be adequate, a new judicial organ, the peregrine *praetor*, became the avenue for the infusion of new principles and greater flexibility into the corpus of Roman law. Similarly, in England, the original writs first modified old customary rules and gradually molded a new Common law. While they gave universality to English law, the immediate effect must have been to create uncertainty, for in creating new rights the king's writs had to destroy old ones. When this system in turn succumbed to old age, it took a new court (Chancery), which at first was not a court at all, to infuse new life into the law. Although the rise of equity, as the word suggests, came from the demand for greater justice, in its early stages it also brought a great deal of arbitrariness into the administration of the law. But new principles and rules were worked out in time; and equity courts were eventually incorporated into the regular judicial system. A transition was made from a body of legal rules and principles that had ceased to be equal to its tasks to a modified and improved system. Constitutionalism was not lost. Finally, the rise and decline of *stare decisis* (although the decline is feared by many) fits into the same pattern.

In the light of these developments, the growth of administrative discretion appears as the latest stage in a series of recurring adjustments in the life of the law. Standards may emerge (as in some measure they have already) for the guidance and control of administrative discretion. The problem of combining judicial impartiality with administrative expertise may also be satisfactorily solved. Legal history does not suggest that the problem is in principle either new or insuperable.

COMMON LAW AND ROMAN LAW

In conclusion, we shall point up some of the similarities and differences between the two great legal systems we have been discussing. The similarities are indeed great. A much more extensive exposition of the contents of the two systems would reveal many further similarities. In ultimate effect the rules of the two systems are often even more alike than they are in form.

One outstanding difference strikes the attention at once and calls for comment. At an early stage in its development, Roman law was codified. Many, if not most, other legal systems that achieved a high stage of development were likewise reduced to writing and some semblance of order. Why did the Common law not follow this course? Three reasons suggest themselves—there are probably others—to explain why no code appeared. In the first place, priestly ascendancy in the law—otherwise almost a universal characteristic of legal systems at some stage of their development—never came to prevail in England. (It was the priests' monopoly of the law and their tendency to keep it secret that led to the popular demands for its publication in Rome.) Probably the fact of the strong secular government established by William the Conqueror and the institution soon after this of professional judges forestalled the more usual development.

A second reason is supplied by the fact that the English, unlike the early Romans, had no single body of custom to codify. Anglo-Saxon England, before the Conquest, was divided among seven kingdoms, and the customary laws were far more localized and disparate than even this fact would indicate. Codification under such circumstances would have required a major, in fact a tremendous, legislative effort. As we have seen, the task of unification—not codification—was performed by judges rather than by legislators.

Finally, some students of the subject attach great significance to the institution of the jury in this connection. The Twelve Tables may have been the result of popular discontent with the law; the jury did in fact provide a popular element in the administration of English law that may well have removed this source of discontent. All of these statements, however, represent no more than plausible speculation.

The fact that the common-law system had no code and that legislation played only a minor role in its formative stages gave it a flexibility that stood it in good stead. Rules were developed in empirical fashion also by the men who had to apply them, in fact in the very course of dealing with concrete cases. Although the rule of *stare decisis* was finally adopted, thanks to the ease of distinguishing precedents, the Common law still enjoys much of the virtue of this down-to-earth, trial-and-error method. The disadvantageous aspect of this same feature is that the Common law is a sprawling growth, less systematic, with more anomalies, and less rich in doctrine than either the ancient Roman law or the modern law of civil law countries. Moreover, today the bulk of reported cases is becoming so vast as to be highly unwieldly. All the ingenuity of countless unofficial digesters and annotators scarcely suffice to reduce the mass to anything like manageable proportions.

The difference between the code system and that of judicial precedents can easily be exaggerated, however. That difference has been expressed by Professor C. K. Allen in the following words: "In one view, the function of the magistrate is to deduce from a formulated general rule of law the principle applicable to the case before him. In the other view, the magistrate is called upon to reason from particular cases to a general principle appropriate to the matter in hand. The former principle is characteristic of codified systems, the latter of English Common law."[12] Two modifying facts are to be noted before this contrast is accepted at its face value.

Regardless of legislative prohibitions of following precedents, civil law judges most certainly do pay attention to the way similar cases have been decided by other, especially superior, courts. The path of least resistance is always to do a thing the way it has been done before. Furthermore, the legal mind naturally and properly attaches a value to regularity. Judges, too, in code or civil law countries are humanly interested in advancement. A judge who has a record of few reversals by superior courts, other things being equal, will be considered a good judge. Who can tell whether this record stems from following sound reason or the known disposition of the higher court? It is significant that Justinian specifically forbade judges to rely on precedents, a fact that suggests that even in the Roman Empire judges were inclined to do just this.

On the other hand, the binding force of precedents in common-law courts is less than is widely believed. We have already pointed out that the rule of *stare decisis* is subject to evasions. There is a marked tendency today, especially in the United States, for the courts openly to modify this nineteenth century rule. Courts increasingly talk about a "course of decisions," that is to say a trend of legal development, rather than a particular decision viewed as in itself laying down a definitive rule of law. Moreover, legislation

[12] Carlton Kemp Allen, *Law in the Making*, 4th ed. (Oxford: Oxford U. P., 1946), pp. 298-299.

has come to play an increasingly important role in common-law countries. Even such branches of the law as commercial law are frequently codified and cast in statute form. The question remains of whether or not, in interpreting the terms of these statutes, courts will consider them as new points of departure or whether they will be governed, in interpreting them, by earlier decisions relating to the law as it stood before codification. Nevertheless, this development represents a significant limitation upon judicial law-making.

Another question has to do with the extent of influence of Roman law on the Common law. The best opinion seems to be that this influence was largely limited to forms and mode of analysis rather than to substance. Was this limitation because of some inherently superior quality of the Common law? Many writers have urged this explanation, but it has little if any foundation. The more reasonable explanation involves the factor of timing. Once more we are taken back to the effects of the Conquest. Nationalization of the law began at an earlier date in England than on the Continent, before the study of the old Roman law had become popular. As McIlwain has stated: "If Irnerius had taught, or Azo had written, a century before he did, or if a Henry III instead of a Henry II had followed Stephen on the throne of England, we might well be using the *Digest* of Justinian as a text today in our American law schools. It was not the merits of English custom, but the uniform writs and the itinerant justices of Henry II that made this custom the 'law of the land.' "[13]

CONCLUSION

A few of the lessons of most general significance for political science that have been garnered from our survey of the development of law and legal systems deserve recapitulation. In the first place, we have noted important evidence for the theory that political institutions that start from unrelated beginning points tend to develop toward similar results. Anthropologists refer to this process as "convergence," as distinguished from "diffusion," which refers to the spread of a given institution from one point. Whether the institution of the state itself was independently invented in more than one place, or whether it had but one point of origin and spread out from there, may be open to dispute, but it seems quite clear that many legal institutions that are found to be similar or identical in different parts of the world and at different points in time had no common origin. To the evidence that has already been set forth on this topic we may add the authority of Diamond and evidence he accumulated. He points out that in the Gold Coast and other West African settlements laws on many different sub-

---

[13] C. H. McIlwain, *Constitutionalism: Ancient and Modern* (Ithaca, N. Y.: Cornell U. P., 1940), p. 61.

jects are strikingly similar to Roman and other laws with which there seems to have been no possibility of contact. He cites as examples such legal practices as the handling over of persons as a sanction for homicide, the talio for adultery, the laws regulating concubinage, and even a technical legal procedure very similar to the Roman *Legis Actio Sacramenti*. It is interesting to observe, too, that certain provisions of a recently discovered Babylonian code, which preceded the famous Code of Hammurabi by 200 years, bear marked similarity to our own law.

We have found too that, despite popular belief in the weird and irrational provisions of early law, a careful study of the culture of which the law is a part generally reveals at least a latent functionality. Laws that appear strange and even unjust to us can generally be found to have served a useful social purpose at one time. A simple example is provided by the institution of the bride price that had to be paid by the husband to the father of the bride. This custom had the socially desirable result of stimulating industry and capital accumulation among the young men. It also brought family pressure upon the wife to remain faithful to her husband for if she left him without cause her father would have to repay the bride price.

Law, we have noted, reflects the prevailing (or the *previously* prevailing) political and economic conditions. At the same time it helps to shape these conditions, especially the latter. It is subject to the same rhythmical oscillation, the same tidelike movement that characterizes the institutions and prevailing ideas of men generally. It goes through periods of rapid growth, periods of hardening and even ossification, followed in turn by periods of reform. These alternations represent the age-old dilemmas of stability and change, of certainty and justice, of liberty and equality, and of emphasis on the individual *versus* emphasis on society. In the law, as in other aspects of society, we note that we are today in the stage of the cycle that lays stress upon change, upon justice as contrasted with absolute certainty, upon equality, and upon social solidarity. In certain respects, the long movement from tribal unity, through familial status to individual rights and contractualisms seems to have taken a new turn. Whether a reversal of the trend impends we know not. Is all history simply a series of cycles? Or does it follow a spiral course? Perhaps we advance like a point on a hoop that is being rolled uphill. Perhaps our law is constantly adjusting to ever-changing conditions, with periods of lag and periods of catching up. Clearly, some elements in the total change do not repeat themselves. The technological facts of this scientific age are not only something new in this world but they have brought with them other conditions that represent both novelty and advance by all commonly accepted standards. The earth now supports more people than ever before in its history. At least in the most advanced regions of the earth, the material standard of living of most people is higher than anything known to previous ages, and a larger proportion of the people in these regions share both in political power and in material prosperity and cultural advantages than ever has been true before. If in meeting these new situations, the law has to follow certain general patterns of previous ages, it by no means signifies that the law has not progressed. The test of progress in the law must be its ability to keep up with advances in technology, in the size of political units, and in the enlargement of the social conscience.

SELECTED READINGS

(Asterisk indicates book is available in paperback edition.)

*ALLEN, CARLETON KEMP. *Law in the Making.* 6th ed. London: Oxford U. P., 1958. This classic work includes excellent treatments of the roles of custom, precedent, equity, and legislation in the development of major legal systems.

BRYCE, JAMES. *Studies in History and Jurisprudence.* 2 vols. New York: Oxford U. P., 1901. Essays 14 and 15, in Vol. II are valuable comparative studies of the Roman and Common Law systems.

BUCKLAND, W. W. and McNAIR, A. D. *Roman Law and Common Law.* Cambridge, Eng.: Clarendon Press, 1936. An excellent comparative treatment.

DECLAREUIL, J. trans. E. A. PARKER. *Rome the Law-Giver.* New York: Knopf, 1926. A standard treatise on the growth and content of Roman Law.

DIAMOND, A. S. *The Evolution of Law and Order.* London: Watts, 1951. The development of legal systems traced through the periods of "Savagery," "Barbarism," and "Early Civilization," with a brief treatment of the modern period.

———. *Primitive Law.* New York: Longmans, 1935. A discussion of the relations of law, morality, and religion in primitive societies, and of the history of primitive law, considered topic by topic.

HARTLAND, E. SIDNEY. *Primitive Law.* London: Methuen, 1924. This relatively short, and very well written book contains a great deal of useful material.

HOEBEL, E. ADAMSON. *The Law of Primitive Man; A Study in Comparative Legal Dynamics.* Cambridge, Mass.: Harvard U. P., 1954. The best general treatment of primitive law, drawing upon specialized studies of numerous primitive societies and relating them all to broad jurisprudential concerns.

JENKS, EDWARD. *A Short History of English Law,* 2nd ed., Boston: Little, Brown, 1922. A useful survey.

LLEWELLYN, K. N. and HOEBEL, E. ADAMSON. *The Cheyenne Way.* Norman, Okla.: Univ. of Oklahoma Press, 1941. In fruitful collaboration, a student of law and an anthropologist have supplied us with a revealing study of the law of the Cheyenne, considered in the light of its implications for jurisprudence.

MAINE, SIR HENRY SUMNER. *Ancient Law.* ed., annot. Sir Frederick Pollock, London: Dent, 1924. A classic study of archaic law, viewed developmentally.

MALINOWSKI, BRONISLAW. *Crime and Custom in Savage Society.* New York: Harcourt, 1932. A path-breaking study, when it was published, based upon field research in Melanesia. Malinowski emphasizes the roles of reciprocity and publicity in the enforcement of primitive law.

PLUCKNETT, THEODORE F. T. *A Concise History of the Common Law.* 2nd ed. Rochester, N.Y.: Lawyers Co-operative Publishing Co., 1936. A standard history of the development of English law.

POUND, ROSCOE. *The Spirit of the Common Law*. Boston: Marshall Jones, 1921. A brilliant interpretive survey, in brief compass, of the growth of the common law.

SEAGLE, WILLIAM. *Men of the Law: From Hammurabi to Holmes*. New York: Macmillan, 1948. This popular account of fourteen great jurists contains much valuable material, both factual and interpretive.

————. *The Quest for Law*. New York: Knopf, 1941. A semipopular history of law from primitive to modern. Some of the author's generalizations have been proved unsound by more recent research. The section on archaic law is perhaps the best part of the book.

ZANE, JOHN MARCY. *The Story of Law*. New York: Washburn, 1927. A readable popular account of legal history.

SCHULZ, FRITZ. *History of Roman Legal Science*. Oxford, Eng.: Clarendon, 1946. A scholarly account of Roman law and of the Roman judicial process.

CHAPTER 9

Development of the National State

‖‖‖

INTRODUCTION

The origin and early development of government and of the state lie hidden in the mists of prehistoric times. If space were available, we might profitably trace the development of early polities to fully formed states. We choose rather to devote our discussion largely to the development of the national state, a development that sheds much light on the nature of the state today. In fact, because of the great setback to political development caused by the destruction of the Roman Empire, much of the earlier story had to be re-capitulated in Europe during the medieval period. Suffice it to say that a study of the primitive origins of government tend to underline and strengthen, rather than to contradict, many of the principles that emerge from an examination of the more modern development. It shows, for instance, that political activity is as fundamental to man as other forms of collective endeavor. As with law, some form of polity is probably as old as human society itself. "Society" or the clan do not stand first; they are woven with the polity.[1] Territories and population increase, technology and wis-

[1] Because of the political importance of the family and other kin organizations, it has often been argued that the kinship tie is the primary social bond. According to this school of thought, it was held that the state, as a territorial organization, was not only a later development, but was built upon an artificial principle of unity, as contrasted with the natural tie of blood relationship. The classic statement of this position is to be found in Lewis H. Morgan, *Ancient Society* (Chicago: Kerr, 1907). Sir Henry Maine's classic work on *Ancient Law* (London: Murray, 1924) also supports the priority of the kinship tie. Marxists have maintained this thesis to support their contention that the state is an unnatural affair that plays no permanently essential role in society and that will "wither away" once the occasioning circumstance of private ownership in the instruments of production is eliminated. Modern anthropological findings indicate that the underlying thesis is without foundation. Important as is the role of kinship in early societies, it appears that the fact of living together within a common territory creates a similarly primordial bond. As just one bit of evidence for this proposition we may note that primitive law regularly

dom, administrative skill and legal instruments cumulate; but otherwise the early growth of government reflects much the same kind of political response to individual and collective needs as that of much later eras.[2]

The state, as we have seen, is not only a *juristic person* but also a *political system,* a way of organizing the relations of persons, corporate bodies, legal jurisdictions, territories, and organs of government. When we speak of "the national state" as a form or organization, we have in mind the contrasts between, say, the states of Western Europe as they existed in a fairly definite and stabilized form after the Peace of Westphalia (1648),[3] and other forms of civic organization, such as the *polis,* leagues of cities, or empires, not to mention less developed polities. The contrasts of civil life, of allegiance, and of legal obligation and political behavior that existed in these different forms of organization are wide and deep. Also the paths that men took, historically, in getting from one to the other provide a record of choices that reveal a great deal of what the modern national state is and of what modern government is about.

A word of caution needs to be spoken at this point. A discussion of the development of the national state is a specialized exercise. We are here concerned with a form or organization that ordered—"harmonized" if you will —many kinds of activity and a host of other organizations. The national state may establish finally, for example, the legal powers of corporations, guilds, towns, and citizens. But it has not *made* the order and the relations that lie underneath. Law, commerce, the arts and technology, government in a hundred forms existed and developed. They were the material that both made sense of the endeavor to found national states and made that endeavor possible.

Also the national state is only one comprehensive form. To look today

---

distinguishes between offenses committed against fellow-villagers and those committed by outsiders (regardless of kinship), the latter being less serious. The evidence against the kinship priority thesis is effectively set forth and discussed in Robert H. Lowie, *The Origin of the State* (New York: Harcourt, 1927), Ch. 4. See also I. Schapera, *Government and Politics in Tribal Societies* (London: Watts, 1956), pp. 11-20.

[2] In our discussion of primitive legal systems, we have already made passing references to the development of organs of government, especially courts and law enforcing agencies. We should add a word about the chiefship. In the first place, we must disabuse ourselves of any notion that leaders generally gain dominion through force. Primitive polities are not normally ruled by absolute rulers; and frequently the emerging form of government is much more nearly democratic, with tribal or community councils where men rise to leadership by persuasion and by establishing a reputation for wisdom. (Hereditary chiefship is a later development.) Agencies of government become stronger and more distinct as the society becomes larger, wealthier, more mobile, and more complex. Perhaps more than any other single factor, at this early stage, warfare and the fear of a common enemy contributes to political development and to the concentration of political authority in the hands of a single individual, be he chief or king. See Ralph Linton, *The Study of Man* (New York: Appleton, 1936), Ch. 14.

[3] Cf. Frederick M. Watkins, *The State as a Concept of Political Science* (New York: Harper, 1934), esp. Ch. 2.

at Jean Bodin's *Six Books of the Republic*[4] or Thomas Hobbes' *Leviathan*[5] will suggest in some measure the degree in which the state was the creation of minds and intellect—that is to say, of choices that people thought about and of expedients they devised. In more modern times, the care with which Sun Yat-sen,[6] the Chinese revolutionist, studied the Western "machine-state" as an engine of social progress and political reform also indicates that such a form of organization is not obvious or even "logical" except in relation to certain social conditions, widely held objectives, and available instrumentalities. It took a lot of persuasion to bring it about. And today the historic national state exists on sufferance as the great subcontinental states and multi-national empires challenge it with even more extensive and effective organizations of political power and as the needs and interests of the people of these states transcend increasingly the political boundaries co-extensive with one sovereign organization. The national state is not, then, an *en telos*, a final object toward which purposive ends directed men's activities and which, once attained, represented an ultimate solution. It is one response to the problem of organizing spatially many other jurisdictions and political techniques to achieve external and internal security and to promote some primary objectives that modern men value according to a schedule of priorities that most would accept.

Principal Aspects of Development

In the developing of modern states out of the political chaos of feudalism, a number of "jobs" or problems seem to have been of particular importance.

The most obvious problem was that of allegiance. This was not only a problem of deciding whom one should follow—whether Emperor or Pope, lord or prince. It was even more a question of what was owing to each, of scheduling loyalties anew and ranking them in a different fashion. How much obedience, from which classes, in respect to what, and in what circumstances? The organizational job was to develop ways of eliciting or assuring this allegiance.

Also a new political behavior, abstract duties toward law and obedience to magistrates, are a condition for the modern state to exist. To obey the will of a "mortal God," a Leviathan, rather than custom, religious percept, or a feudal superior may seem a simple thing. The difficulty, however, was that office, property, and rights and duties were not simple legal objects or com-

---

[4] First published in 1576. An accessible modern text is M. J. Tooley's translation and abridgment, *Six Books of the Commonwealth* (Oxford: Blackwell, 1955).

[5] *Leviathan; or, The matter, form and power of a Commonwealth, ecclesiastical and civil* (1641). A good modern edition is Oxford, Eng.: Blackwell, 1947, Oakeshott Introduction.

[6] See particularly, Paul M. Linebarger, *The Political Doctrines of Sun Yat-sen* (Baltimore: Johns Hopkins Press, 1937).

mands, but mixtures of custom, moral obligation, personal fealty, and the claims of many jurisdictions. Disentangling these many threads was the work of centuries for jurists and administrators. Making effective principles of political organizations and political response out of abstract and impersonal premises of behavior was the job, largely, of monarchs and their allies, building upon the results of economic evolution, the teachings of religion, and the cultural foundations of a thousand years.

Effective tools and methods for boundary maintenance—to mark out and to defend the line between the public and the private, between the state and society—are also essential to the modern state. Malfeasors in public office, encroaching jurisdictions of the lord or the church, nepotism and alienation of office or crown properties are examples of instances where the line between the public and private was most generally transgressed and, in fact, of ways in which many early kingdoms were nibbled to death. To write fully the history of the legal writs and procedures, the bureaucratic organization and practices, and the substantive law devised to curb these activities would be to give the largest part of the story of the modern state.

Continuity of certain principles and organs of government also had to be achieved before the political dynamism displayed by particular reigning houses could have lasting and cumulative effects. Each attempt at state-building left, to be sure, its residue of changed practices and its memory of golden ages and good kings. On the other hand, some innovations in government proved to have greater staying power and to leave more to build upon in future times. Hereditary succession, the legal and fiscal properties of the crown, and the use of salaried officials are examples. It was not that men lacked the wit to dream up such innovations; what they lacked was the power to make them stick. Our interest is in which devices proved useful and why prelates, barons, and princes fought over them.

Lastly, the *national* state is, in two ways, an adjustment of organizational form to political space.[7] Partly political space is a matter of defense or of maintenance of a political system among neighbors. It must be large enough and efficient enough to protect itself from its enemies, and as Machiavelli pointed out, from its friends as well. But also, political space is a problem of collective will within the state, of a size that matches the technology, aspirations, and capacities for effective political organization of the people within that state. Rome expanded and republican virtue languished, not alone because of changes in size, but partly for that reason. Technology and culture changed and Flanders and Holland united. One of the particular achievements in the development of the modern national state, then, was the measure in which it solved, for several centuries at least, the problem of political space.

[7] The concept is taken from Sheldon Wolin, *Politics and Vision* (Boston: Little, Brown, 1960), particularly Ch. 3.

A PRECIS

Between the modern state and the classical world of Greece and Rome lie some important continuities in development and some equally important discontinuities. Europe did not start afresh. On the other hand, the effects of the collapse of Rome, the expansion of Islam, and the invasions of Magyar and Norseman destroyed most of the material and political benefits of Rome's classical heritage.

In Western Europe, Roman patterns of living continued for some time after the "collapse" of the Empire. In the countries of Europe ringing the Mediterranean basin, Roman towns, the *villa* system, Roman law and Latin literature survived for some centuries. Most importantly, Latin Christianity, church organization, and missionary activity continued even despite the ultimate decay of this Mediterranean civilization. Also, Roman law, classical learning, and commercial cities survived in the Eastern Empire and in the Arab world.

For Europe, two events were even more important than the fall of Rome. One was the Moslem conquest of the Mediterranean world. The other was the subsequent invasion of the Norsemen and the Magyars. The first menaced Europe directly. Even more, however, by establishing an empire over the commerce and cities of the south it destroyed the economic foundations of the type of European civilization that was being developed in Spain, Italy, and France. Northmen and Magyars laid waste to the North and much of the rest of Europe—sacking cities, devastating the countryside, and destroying the foundations of stable government. Not until the year 1000 did Europe beat off the last invaders from the outside.

One response to the collapse of political authority was the establishment of feudalism. Also eleventh century Europe saw the beginning of three separate developments that were important for the future. One was the revival and reform of religion and church administration. Another was the founding of relatively stable and efficient feudal states. And a third was the great increase in agricultural productivity that multiplied population, stimulated new settlements, and made possible the growth of cities and commercial and industrial activity.

Nevertheless, Western Europe in the eleventh and twelfth centuries by and large lacked states and governments in the sense in which we ordinarily understand these terms. Neither any one political organization nor any sum of political organizations could regularly secure justice, liberty, and welfare. A congeries of governments existed together. Kings, the Church, the Holy Roman Empire, lords, cities, and many orders and corporations exercised political power, ordered social existence, and competed for allegiance. A vast number of myths and doctrines pulled at men's loyalties in contrary directions. Men lived without a uniform law or a central coordinative government. They had many citizenships; and many groups struggled for a better order of things. No agency and no movement could generate enough legitimate power, however, to organize a satisfactory collective existence.

The universal solution, either under Church or Empire, proved impossible. Nor did European civilization become, as earlier Mediterranean culture had been, an order of cities. The ancestors of the modern states of Europe were the relatively compact territorial kingdoms, based upon feudalism, that began their expansion and development particularly in the twelfth century.

The history of these states was by no means one of unilinear progress. Economic chaos, the Black Death, the revolts of peasants and of lords, and fiscal and administrative incompetence undid the work of many generations. But, increasingly, the foundations of stable and prosperous political orders were laid, both aiding and aided by economic development. Why was this progress possible? Partly, the answer lies in a history of religion and culture: the development of vernacular literature, new religious attitudes, a more rational and humanistic view of the world. Partly, the answer lies in economic and social changes—commerce, social mobility, and the growth of new classes. Kings and their national administrations in Europe, England, and Scandinavia made themselves the agents and the beneficiaries of these changes. But also much of the answer lies in a matter of political space. For compact territorial kingdoms could be administered. They could also elicit men's loyalties and give them a sense of common citizenship real enough to inspire service to the state. In national religions, patriotism, and gospels of equality and democracy, people found, for some centuries at least, myths that could both legitimate secular power and serve as a basis for criticizing and correcting it. On the one hand, these national kingdoms were large enough and powerful enough to afford security and foster abundance. They were not so large that they degenerated into bureaucratic or military despotisms, nor so small that they lacked the checks upon government that diversity brings.

In seeking answers to the question of why one form survived and not another it is important to look briefly at other possible solutions to comprehensive political organization. Cities and empires have, at times in history, provided the basis for enduring and successful political orders. That they did not in Europe is partly a matter of local circumstance and the particular sequence of events. It is also a matter of forms and the potentialities of those forms. In surveying these alternate types, part of the objective is to understand the modern national state more completely by discovering in some measure the problems for which it provided a solution. At the same time, it is important to realize that even today people are citizens under many governments, and the primary focus of loyalties varies over time and from issue to issue.

CITIES

Civic government and the problems that cities have presented have displayed remarkable similarity throughout much of history. According to Aristotle, the greatest philosopher of city-states, men chose the cities for security, for justice, and to live well.[8] These same motives would have been pretty much the operative ones in the Middle Ages.[9] Also, according to Aristotle, the greatest evils of the city were communal warfare *(stasis)*, exclusivism, and the absence of devices to ensure constitutional stability. This list of evils would require some adaptation; but it also would serve fairly well.[10]

Cities grew at a different pace and flourished in different centuries in various parts of Europe. The great revival of cities, generally, did not come until after the economic revival of the eleventh century. Even earlier, however, to meet the needs of sheer physical protection that attended the dissolution of the Carolingian Empire, small agricultural towns were fortified. These could not be called cities. They had no middle-class organization, no communal charters, no separate law. Yet they were often the foundations upon which the later cities grew. Episcopal residences also became the site of cities, not only because they were also fortified, but because they usually had the benefits of enlightened administration. Cities and lords both enjoyed the privilege of fortification. In the case of the cities, this foundation of security and independence acted as a powerful attraction to travelling peddlers, knights, freemen, and all those who had no lord or wished no lord.

By the eleventh and twelfth centuries, the cities, participating in the general economic revival, had not only become prosperous, they had become conscious of their own identity and separateness. They became tremendously active centers of social, economic, and legal innovation—organizing guilds, demanding their own charters, courts, and law, and practicing the arts of urban citizenship.

During the thirteenth century, the cities seemed almost the nucleus of a new civilization, so far had they transformed Europe. No king could hope to prevail without the aid of the cities. Furthermore, the cities were not only centers of a better life, they were spreading their ideals and practices, transforming the countryside and men's conceptions of their place in society. They spread the idea of liberty. They were centers of universities and learning, of new religious ideas and experience. The capitalism and industry of the cities reacted upon the countryside, encouraging commutation, alienation of estates, and the practices of commercialism. Leagues of cities began; and one of them, the famous Hanseatic League of the fourteenth century, became more powerful than most kingdoms.

---

[8] Aristotle, *Politics*, Bk. I, Ch. 2.
[9] Henri Pirenne, *Medieval Cities* (Princeton, N.J.: Princeton U.P., 1925).
[10] *Ibid.*

The creative role of the cities can scarcely be overestimated, especially in supplying the stimulus for innovation and in giving shelter to many institutions and social tendencies that could not have survived under other circumstances. Yet as governments they failed; in fact, they failed so miserably in some instances that many a distraught municipalist could, by the fourteenth and fifteenth centuries, see no way out but a tyrant (hopefully, a good one), or installing an appointed representative of the Emperor. The reasons for their failures are varied and difficult to describe precisely; but several major shortcomings can be noted.

Part of the failure of the cities lay in the conception and practice of municipal citizenship—supposedly their great glory.[11] For the city presupposed more civic virtue than men had. Based upon oaths of citizenship and covenant, civic government was in principle an order of participating equals devoted to the practice of self-government, mutual good, and common defense. In fact, though European cities did not—because of the church and feudal custom—develop the "scourge of debts," they were divided into social orders of rich and poor, of privileged family and guild-master. In addition, their conception of citizenship was narrow. It was, for one thing, monopolistic: the burgher was the member of a privileged order and made his citizenship a monopoly, excluding artisans and peasants living about the town. Municipal citizenship was also narrow because it extended no farther than civic patriotism, lacking either the appeals of the "City of God," or of nationalism. It divided men and foreshortened their horizons at a time when they were already feeling wider unities and deeper meanings in life.[12]

The cities were, by and large, too particularistic and exclusive either to expand or to ally with their urban neighbors. Machiavelli suggested an ingenious adaptation of Rome's "Italian Policy"[13] for the cities of the contemporary Italy. But even he recognized that such a policy could come about only through a public-spirited tyrant. Most cities developed a kind of municipal "socialism" designed primarily to preserve the privileges of those in the town and ensure a supply of goods and services for the city, gained largely from the countryside on terms markedly disadvantageous to the peasant. They fought over trade and territory with their neighbors and could ally with them either for mutual profit or mutual defense only under exceptional circumstances.

If left to their own devices, particular cities could neither defend themselves in times of trouble nor secure their own prosperity in times of economic distress. Consequently, they stood in need of powerful protectors.

[11] See John H. Mundy and Peter N. Reisenberg, *The Medieval Town* (Princeton, N.J.: Van Nostrand, 1958). The appendix contains examples of municipal charters and institutions.

[12] For a good statement of the changing conception of citizenship, see Wolin, *op. cit.*, Chs. 5, 6.

[13] A good discussion is Frederico Chabod, *Machiavelli and the Renaissance*, trans. David Moore (London: Bowes, 1958), especially Ch. 2.

They were, in turn, made the pawns of national, ecclesiastical, and imperial politics, to the point that the natural animosities of family and class that tend to fester within cities in the best of times were increased and repeatedly erupted into communal strife. Only where there was, in effect, another "layer" of government fairly near and reasonably efficacious did cities, in general, manage to avoid these evils.

Internally, cities tended to be too close and too personal to develop the impartial legal structure and administrative offices that would ensure either a stable constitutional order or equitable policy. One result was that much of social and economic relations continued to be regulated by other agencies —the crown, the church, and independent tribunals. Periodic suspensions of self-rule or the election of municipal dictators were other consequences. In any event, the cities were rarely thought to be, and when tried proved themselves not to be viable entities of independent self-government. Rome and Constantinople might serve as great historic examples of municipal success; but both their circumstances and their civic institutions were peculiar to themselves.

EMPIRE

The world has known scores of empires. From the days of the antique state until recent times, in fact, the organization of stable, efficient government over a wide territorial space was possible, barring exceptional circumstances, only through a military-bureaucratic dictatorship, based usually upon one conquering tribe, city, or kingdom, which extended its hold over peoples of other customs, speech, and government. Such a description would not, of course, hold for the sea-empires of history. Land empires, for that matter, have been not of one species, but of many types. But their place in the early history of governance was of enormous importance.[14]

The empire that had great historic significance for Europe was the Roman Empire. Its law and administration, practices and aims were at various times a model, a hope, even in some measure the source of specific practices, especially for the church. It was not only the greatest of empires; in many respects its forms and techniques were extraordinarily suitable for achieving the ends of stable and acceptable government over a wide territory.

Between the fifth and the ninth centuries there were attempts at empire in Europe, none of them notably successful. Some ambitious kinglets tried to copy Roman forms and appropriated Roman titles; but the ends of government that most such horde leaders pursued seldom extended beyond those of looting and slave-hunting and the creation of tribal allies and vassals. Their tactics of expansion and organization, typical of the politics of loosely joined multi-lingual empires, reveal the insubstantiality of the social bases upon

[14] Robert M. MacIver, *The Modern State* (Oxford, Eng.: Clarendon, 1926), Ch. 2, "The Early Empire."

which these warrior-statesmen sought to build. It was a politics of weakness and of the violence and injustice that grows from weakness.[15]

The one important attempt at universal empire was that of the Franks. In 800 Charlemagne was crowned by Pope Leo as "Charles . . . Augustus . . . Emperor of the Romans. . . ." The instruments of his royal will, however, were not the Imperial Council and the Prefects of Roman administration, but counts, marquises, and dukes who ruled by right of a grant of jurisdiction from the king, rendered homage and military service, paid dues and swore him fealty. Indeed, only the great personal talents of Charlemagne made this unwieldy empire function at all. Within seventy-five years the Carolingian Empire collapsed. When the Holy Roman Empire was renewed political development was already shifting to the more compact feudal monarchies, and to an even greater empire, the church.[16]

Unlike the great Roman Empire, the empires of medieval Europe lacked a prime requisite of successful empire—a competent and reasonably trustworthy administrative corps. Charlemagne and other emperors made use of prefects, professional bailiffs, and circuit judges. But in a multinational empire in which the economic base was agricultural and the bases of political loyalty largely personal the tug of localism proved too strong to build a solid hierarchy of professional officers of the crown.

In the absence of effective bureaucracies, even the best of emperors could have done little to consolidate the loyalties of diverse populations. They could not, as the Romans did, enforce local peace and make effective the rights and privileges that might have given some meaning to imperial citizenship. Even the Romans had not been able to create common ties of economic interest throughout the Empire; and on this score the failure of medieval empires was even greater.

By the twelfth century, the great European renaissance was well under way and people were in fact seeking things from life and in their personal and spiritual experience that had little to do with imperial forms. Most empires, the Roman Empire included, have had their greatest success in securing a general peace and administrative stability over a wide territory. They have failed, usually, in securing local order and local justice, in responding to or initiating social or economic change, and in providing a focus for men's more intense loyalties.

[15] *The Cambridge Medieval History*, Vol. II, "Foundations of the Western Empire" (Cambridge, Eng.: Cambridge U. P., 1913), Chs. 4-7.

[16] *Ibid.*, Vol. III, "Germany and the Western Empire," Ch. 3. To say, however, that the Frankish Empire represented the one attempt at universal secular rule is not to say that empires did not remain important and that the way was open for the unchallenged development of independent territorial states. The Hapsburg Empire, for instance, began in the thirteenth century and endured until 1918, a history that testifies to considerable durability and vitality. The Ottoman Turks, beginning about the same time, also showed similar powers of survival as an empire. But empire as a form of government showed little dynamism or capacity for internal growth when compared with the smaller territorial kingdoms.

NATIONAL KINGDOMS

Feudal Beginnings

The dissolution of the Frankish Empire initiated the splitting of Europe into the compact kingdoms of the future. Not for another two centuries were monarchs able to make much headway in establishing their governments firmly and securing law and stable administration within their territories. During this period, however, a political development of great significance took place. The invasions of Norsemen and Magyars destroyed much of the earlier political order, including the Empire. These same invasions encouraged, indeed made well nigh universal many of the general practices of feudalism. It was upon this political base that the European monarchies and the modern European states developed.

Feudalism has been succinctly described as:

> . . . a development pushed to extremes of the elements of personal dependence in society, with a specialized military class occupying the higher levels in the social scale; an extreme subdivision of the rights of real property; a graded system of rights over land created by this subdivision and corresponding in broad outline to the grades of personal dependence just referred to; and a dispersal of political authority amongst a hierarchy of persons who exercise in their own interest powers normally attributed to the State, and which are often, in fact, derived from its break-up.[17]

The bases of feudalism lay in disorder, the weakness or absence of any comprehensive political framework, in the economics of agriculture and landholding, and in the need for a military aristocracy. In one respect it represented a process of conversion of pieces of the Frankish Empire into private property as official counts and their subordinates transformed themselves into local dynasts. But just as fundamentally, feudalism testified to the need for taming raw violence, for protection from wild beast and marauder. Through commendation and swearing of fealty protection was assured and the obligations of military service maintained. Feudalism was also a means of supporting and eliciting public service and keeping order locally without central administration or the bases for bureaucracy. Thus, tenements and benefices were granted to get land cultivated, to support the church, etc. Above all, feudalism was, especially for our purposes, an "economy" of politics in which the categories that are to us distinct and separable were mixed together: private ownership and public jurisdiction were con-

---

[17] F. L. Ganshof, *Feudalism,* trans. Philp Grierson (London: Longmans, 1952), Introduction, p. xv.

founded; public service and hereditary right overlapped; political, military, and economic power merged into one another.[18]

In principle, the essential unit of local government was some lord—lay or ecclesiastical—who ruled over a manor or held under his protection a village, a group of peasants, an abbey, and so forth. Above this lord, in theory, there arose a hierarchy of lesser and greater lords, owing a mutual service and obligation based upon feudal oaths and custom. Each lord received homage, counsel, and military service, and a heterogeneous series of reliefs and extraordinary aides from his vassals. He undertook similar obligations with respect to his overlord. In theory, the public services of military protection, the care for souls, or the extracting of revenue, were rendered in return for confirmation in a grant of land, the building of an abbey, the right to tallage—and above all, the commitment to give protection. Presumably, commendation and solemn oath or written charters, supported by a religion of magic and superstition, stabilized political power through a network of sacred undertakings. At the apex of society, making of the headless body a true political whole, animating the laws, guarding the church and preserving the realm, was the king.

In relation to normal practice, however, the theory of feudalism was primarily a hope or a program rather than a reality. No true hierarchy of power and authority existed, for society was not national, but rather both international and local. Obstructing any compact political community was a whole array of international institutions claiming talents and loyalties: an Empire and a church, a European language, supra-national codes of law and chivalry, and classes of friars, merchants and warriors that were integrated into local society in varying degrees.

From another perspective, medieval society was parochial and almost explosively centrifugal. Protection, subsistence, and government fell to local lords, their armed retainers, and their serfs. Both the grounds for and the opportunity to renounce feudal obligation and convert fief or benefice into private, heritable property were ever-present. Law and political machinery were local, customary, and based on personal relations. The techniques of husbandry, agricultural industry, of taxation, and the exaction of service equally rested upon local controls, either of a community that could function pretty much as one neighborhood, or of a lord that could make his personal might felt.

For centuries the greatest enemies of the feudal "state" were its own officials. Appropriately, the one great common theme of medieval political thought is that of "unity"—an appeal for an organic unity in which each group would find its place in harmony with a great master plan—a program, but not a reality.[19]

[18] Sidney Painter, *A History of the Middle Ages: 284-1500* (New York: Knopf, 1953), Ch. 4, especially.

[19] On this section, generally, see Marc Bloch, *Feudal Society,* trans. L. A. Manyon (Chicago: Univ. of Chicago Press, 1961), Chs. 30-31.

The practical result of disunity and fragmented political power was that enormous disorder prevailed. For this society lived largely without records and charters, without reliable expedients for legal innovation or unification, and with techniques of enforcement that often reduced to self-help, feud, and community lynch-law. The politics of the period was that of struggling to build structures of power stable enough and sizeable enough to afford security; it was a politics of usurpation and aggression, of trying to repress tyrants and to restore ancient rights and the old and customary law. In fact, the operative principles of this polity resembled as much as anything else those of a racketeering empire, with "territories," continual jostlings for power and patronage, alliances of warrior-chieftains based upon comradeship-in-arms or realistic calculations, betrayed allegiance and sanctions, conspiracies against rival lords, the rise and decline of great and lesser feudatories.[20] Even at the end of the Middle Ages, the modern state was only in embryo, and had there been no other forces modifying the political practice of the age, the medieval world would have constituted a system of localism and of near anarchy modified by the practical value of intermittent observance of feudal custom.

The Church

The church served as a great force for regularizing and civilizing the politics of this age. In the period following the Fall of Rome and the Dark Ages the tremendous missionary effort of the church[21] had Christianized virtually the whole of Europe, and had established the most important body of beliefs, common culture, and moral restraints acting upon the uncivilized hordes that had conquered Europe. Throughout the medieval period, the church insisted that it was the function of the secular order to serve by indirect means spiritual ends: it combatted arbitrariness, disorder and lawlessness; it insisted that power was a trust and supported the customary and quasi-contractual relations between ranks and classes in the feudal order and men's duty to their fellow men; the church sanctioned and enforced the submission of people to rightful authority as it enforced proper respect for community needs; it anointed and invested in office lords and kings.

The sources of churchly power were many. One source was the spiritual weapons of a specific and dogmatic religion, and of interdict and excommunication. Another source lay in its power as a great estate. Equally important was the continuity and coordination of effort possible for the greatest and most efficient administrative organization in the world.

One of the greatest reform movements of history, as well as the first great European age of propaganda, began in the Investiture Controversies of

---

[20] Sidney Painter, "The Lords of Lusignan in the 11th and 12th Centuries," *Speculum*, 32 (1957), pp. 27-47.
   [21] A good discussion is Sidney Painter, *A History of the Middle Ages, op. cit.,* Ch. 5.

the eleventh century and Pope Gregory's struggle for a right order in the world.[22] To save the church itself from the vast corruption of medieval politics, nothing less would suffice but that Christendom make itself an efficient, rationally organized, centrally directed movement of reform. Significantly, during this period the church developed the first organization in medieval Europe that embodied the fiscal and legal properties of the modern state. Likewise, it acquired the first pure and uniform legal system (the canon law, a bureucracy that was a "career open to talents," and an attitude toward office based on oath of loyalty not to a feudal overlord, but to an immortal corporation, the holy church.[23]

In two ways, especially, the church broke a path that secular politics later followed. One way was the force of example: from the church, temporal lords and authorities learned the uses of law, techniques of consultation and representation, arts of administration, and concepts of politics. In fact, since church bureaucrats and officers frequently took service under the state, they directly infused secular administration with practices and concepts drawn from the more enlightened and efficient clerical bureaucracy. But, secondly, because secular and ecclesiastical property, jurisdiction, and power were deeply intertwined, the forward advance of the church had the impact of inducing a measure of diffuse competition between various institutions. Church lords were usually less greedy, church law was better, its agents more efficient, its culture of a more enlightened stamp, its bureaucracy a better outlet for talent. The general tendency of the exertion of churchly power was to impel politics in the direction of more rational and equalitarian principles. Many other forces, to be sure, were at work. But the church was for long *the* great force in battling against the principle of hereditary status and kin-right as a basis for organizing society. As kings expanded their power, they moved along parallel lines.

The Crown: Policies and Theory

The path to power and influence for a king of these days had a curious dual aspect. On the one hand, dynasties were made by Machiavellian techniques. Vigorous families, fortunate enough to have many generations of able male heirs, rose in the feudal hierarchy by persistent struggles to accumulate the tangible and intangible ingredients of political power. The methods used were many: usurping vague titles; rendering a weak claim a powerful one; "protecting" and then robbing a ward; imposing heavy demands for extraordinary aides and using liberally the principles of escheat and forfeiture; successively patronizing and then expropriating a clerical lord, or taking

[22] Gerd Tellenbach, *Church, State, and Christian Society at the Time of the Investiture Controversy,* trans. R. F. Bennett (Oxford, Eng.: Blackwell, 1940).

[23] Ernst H. Kantorowicz, *The King's Two Bodies: A Study in Medieval Political Theology* (Princeton, N.J.: Princeton U. P., 1957), Ch. 5.

advantage of the leniency and secure title that vassalage to the church entailed; renouncing fealty to a weak lord and commending oneself to a more powerful one; and, finally, consolidating and stabilizing acquired status through dynastic marriages.

Yet, on the other hand, only by cloaking their private ambitions with a public interest did kings rise to power and establish their power securely. Strong kings made themselves the defenders of the faith and the realm. They also grew stronger by successfully hoarding and accumulating political power that arose from more obscure sources. In its primitive origin the monarchy of the middle ages was largely military in function and private in conception; but in the battles for power and for revenue, kings were forced to move in the direction of new conceptions and practices that strikingly foreshadowed the legal and political elements of the modern state.

To defend the realm, kings had to generate power; and to achieve this latter end they had to expand their own holdings. Not only did they have their own domains, but they strove ceaselessly to expand them by absorbing rival feudatories, by encouraging and acting upon complaints from vassals of other lords, and by dynastic marriage. Within their own domains, kings developed a searching system of police and administration—bailiffs, provosts, and mayors—the distant ancestors of modern bureaucracy, that would tax and govern subjects and administer the domain as officers, not vassals, of the crown.[24] In England, where the whole land was treated, by right of conquest, as a royal domain, kings were also able, following the Frankish practice, to use inquests, juries, and writs to enforce a strict accounting and recover converted properties.

Not only did the crown expand by absorption and by developing professional agents of its will, but its military needs produced a more direct relation between the king and the subject. Thus, kings began to demand both aides and service not only from the lords-in-chief that held from them, but from these same lords' vassals as well, to revive military service and national militia when possible, and to accept "scutage" (or payment in lieu of service), impose "Saladin tithes", or collect "Danegeld." In England, Edward had by the thirteenth century virtually cast aside the feudal army and relied on direct military service of all landholders.[25] In Europe, the expansion of military service moved much more slowly. Yet here, as well, service to lord and service to country were being distinguished. French dynastic loyalty and patriotic pride had so grown by the twelfth century that the whole kingdom rose to resist Henry V of Germany, a significant demon-

---

[24] Joseph Strayer gives a detailed study of the administration of the period. See, Joseph R. Strayer, *The Administration of Normandy Under Saint Louis* (Cambridge, Mass.: Medieval Academy of America, 1932).

[25] For England, Maitland is dated, but for one of the most readable and informative accounts, see, Frederic W. Maitland, *The Constitutional History of England* (Cambridge, Eng.: The University Press, 1920).

stration of the new unity. The Crusades and struggles involving territorial magnates of the church called into being active corps of patriotic propagandists, identifying *"charitas"* or *"pietas"* with service in armies resisting the heathen. By the end of the Crusades, patriotism was acknowledged to be acceptable service to God; and armed contingents of citizens were serving in royal armies.[26]

Kings also found or made themselves the defenders and the creators of law and order. One source of royal power, as well as a basic necessity of political stability, was the extension of the King's Peace—as discussed in Chapter 8. In England, the King's Peace was extended to highways, market places, and linked with the peace of towns. Ultimately the concept was used as well to cover a whole host of offenses from theft to evasion of the jurisdiction of royal courts.

As the power and public purposes of the state expanded, so grew the crown's interest in a law that was definite, actionable, and capable of abrogating and replacing local custom. Both the king and his administrative minions and lawyers looked to Roman law.

By the end of the thirteenth century, various legal and political practices were slowly converging upon the concept of a true political corporation. Jurists and kings, following the church, Roman law, and the needs of radically new practice were insisting that the "fisc" and properties of the crown were inalienable, that "time runneth not against the king". They were also advancing the royal power of eminent domain and arguing the right to break old law in the common interest of public utility.[27] Some entity, not yet a state, had inalienable properties, was immortal, and stood for general purposes transcending all classes or locales. In 1272 when Henry III of England died, Edward was proclaimed king in his absence, and the King's Peace continued to run despite the missing physical presence. On the continent, in 1355 the Golden Bull of Charles IV attempted to make the "constitution" and the electoral mechanisms of the Holy Roman Empire permanent. In conception at least—though only England closely approximated a practical ideal—the polity was independent of time and wider in purpose than any private interest.[28] It was on the way to becoming a state.

Representation

Another enormously important device in crystallizing the state and transforming feudalism was that of representation. From the standpoint of direct lineage, representation derived from the ancient duty of military

[26] Kantorowicz, *op. cit.*, Ch. 5.
[27] Thus, note, the usefulness of Roman Law.
[28] Kantorowicz, *op. cit.*, Ch. 7; also Edward Jenks, *The State and the Nation* (New York: Dutton, 1919), Pt. III.

nobles to render their lord or king aid and counsel.[29] A mature and sophisticated theory and practice of representation was first perfected in the church: international in character, "public" and universal (as opposed to private) in aim and conception, the church needed devices that could link wills and provide "transmission belts" for coordinated purpose. As towns, gilds, municipal leagues, and kingdoms began to develop similar political interests, they readily adopted the techniques and concepts of that supranational state, the church. Practically, however, the kings needed techniques of extending, allocating and securing the performance of duties and rendering aid. On this primitive level, representation is an obvious and sensible technique. The collection of fees levied upon a community, the exaction of duties, or the development of any general purpose, such as a military campaign, proceeds more easily and smoothly and with much greater economy of coercive force if counsel is taken with the headmen or outstanding notables, rather than attempting crudely to enforce a duty against or extort a tax directly from the collectivity. Thus, royal bailiffs would summon the leaders of a village, under threat of direct action, to collect a murder fine or force the rendering up of a guilty party. By treating with the richer and more prominent members of a chartered corporation or city, irregular levies could be converted into regular dues. And, similarly, in setting in motion the cumbersome machinery of military mobilization the king would treat with a representative committee of nobles.

By the twelfth century in Europe, the irregular process of arbitrary "tallages," and of dealing individually with towns and greater lords, was being replaced by the summoning of general councils at which the King-in-Parliament negotiated with estates—the lords temporal and spiritual, the knights and burgesses, or the "third estate." A growing awareness of common interest and corporate consciousness animating baron, clergy, and burgess was matched by royal insistence upon treating his various subjects not as a congeries of individuals but as politically intelligible classes. Often the organization into estates was little recognized. Even when such organization was recognized, delegates frequently continued to vote by estates and refused to conclude business except by unanimous agreement. Generally, government by assemblages of estates and through representation never truly existed or what there was of it speedily broke down, leaving an assortment of political principles honored more in the breach than the observance. On the other hand some governments maintained a more effective practice of representation, marking the path later taken. In cities, in guilds, in cathedral chapters and ecclesiastical synods, systems of weighted voting were widely (and

[29] George L. Haskins, *The Growth of English Representative Government* (Philadelphia: Univ. of Pennsylvania Press, 1948), Chs. 2, 3; also see, Carl Stephenson, *Medieval Institutions: Selected Essays,* ed. Bryce D. Lyon (Ithaca, N.Y.: Cornell U. P., 1954), essays 3, 4.

of necessity) accepted.[30] In England the power of delegates authoritatively to represent their constituents and to bind them was fairly clearly established. Also in England, with the organization of various "model Parliaments", and the division into "houses" rather than estates, Parliaments became national—at least in conception—and no longer feudal. In principal, the extension of territorial representation to politics was of enormous moment. For it implied the notion of a *political* skeleton of the territorial state: a linking of all levels of society with the sovereign through institutions that were distinctively civic and external to the social hierarchy rather than dissolved in private and hereditary relations.

Emergence of a Theory of the Sovereign and the State

In the King's support of communities and interests too weak or as yet not solidly enough established to subsist and thrive under feudalism lay a profoundly important source of royal power. The crown became the curator for all those *persona* considered incompetent to act for themselves: "children, madmen, and cities," as one formula has it. The courts and the legal processes and concepts of the king's jurists supported the principle of general access to the courts, a law of record and writs that were generally available, and a jurisprudence that was generally tending in the direction of the utilitarian, the individualistic, and the equalitarian. (Sir Henry Maine's famous movement of the law "from status to contract" was clearly in progress.) In effect, king's justice encouraged inchoate trends moving in the direction of individualism and equality. From a variety of motives, the kings became patrons of artisans, learning, and commerce. The list grew. The sponsor of widows, Jews, orphans, lunatics, and the university, the king became, more fundamentally, the protector and the ally of the trading townsman, the churchman, and the peasant, against the territorial magnate.

It is a short step from the notion of the king as curator and protector of the weaker *persona* to the idea of a king as trustee for the common good. Thus, as St. Thomas stated it, the king "hath the care of the community." He not only protects and fosters the many "immortal bodies"—the growing list of town, guilds, corporations, and universities—it is his duty to *arrange things* by administrative decree, and arrange them for the common benefit. In this work the king was supported by the church, by paid agents drawn from the towns and from the interstices of the feudal order, and by enlightened men of learning or administrative and legal skill.

The significant tendency was not merely that of selling a better, more efficacious form of "protection" and of justice, but that change—economic, social, and organizational—was generating increasingly the need for per-

---

[30] A good discussion is to be found in Brian Tierney, *Foundations of the Conciliar Theory* (Cambridge, Eng.: Cambridge U. P., 1955).

manent, centralized, administrative activity and for a "sovereign"—for someone who could both regulate and also amend the relations of the subjects.

This trend was enormously accelerated by the economic decay of feudalism, the Black Plague, and a general rising in the level of culture during the fourteenth and fifteenth centuries. Social change demanded a powerful new force to mediate conflict and facilitate adjustment. Increasingly money transactions were replacing payment in kind. Kings, lords, and cities perforce found themselves introducing direct taxation, systems of coinage, and more regular proceedings whereby purchases and sales could take place. As old guilds and guild regulations collapsed, new charters and supplementary economic regulation were needed. Fiefs were being converted into private property and land alienated. Clear titles, reliable charters, actionable contracts, and trustworthy records became a necessity for orderly adjustment. Similarly, some power that could declare (and reform) the "good and lawful customs of the realm" as well as act on the *cahiers* and petitions of parliamentary representatives was urgently needed. Outside of England, Norway and Sweden, governments lacked the political power to meet such demands. But, be that as it may, the feudal, hierarchical state was everywhere moribund, awaiting the final *coup de grace* of the Renaissance and Reformation.

Not until the close of the Middle Ages did a more or less coherent political theory that could give some meaning to these varied tendencies begin to acquire definite form. To be sure, political concepts helped shape immediate practice in the centuries-long process of transforming feudalism into the "premodern" state. For the most part, however, men responded to near and immediate social and political necessities, generally practicing for a long time some specific technique of political action or governance before the challenge of an alien or competing power—the Empire, the church, a local lord, or a monarch—required theoretical justification or defense. Publicists, lawyers, or clerics borrowing by bits and pieces from the literature of the church, from classical philosophy and political theory, and especially from the Roman law and the common heritage of religious ideology, built piecemeal a theory of the state.

Various converging trends of thought were sharpening and completing the outlines of a new conception of polity. No longer a fictive body, the state (which the polity was becoming) was conceived as a *"corpus mysticum"*, later a *"corpus morale et politicum"*—a political corporation, with a constitutional structure, completed in the headship of the crown and dedicated to public ends. Toward it lay duties of loyalty and service, and in it resided prerogative powers to act in the public weal. Against it no prescription could avail; nor did its claims perish with the centuries. In the name of the realm, Kings could act; but they could also be admonished or restrained for alienating the powers and properties which pertained to the crown in its public capacity. As crown, the kingship was identified with all the rights of the realm, the whole public sphere, its duties and its legal properties. The crown, disentangled from the trammels of medieval theory and practice, emerged as a perpetual office, legalized by God and "the people" alone, permanently incorporated with the subjects, and existing even in the absence or infirmity of a mortal king. This theory did not represent a coherent ideology of reform; but in the great upheaval of the Reformation and the religious wars, it came close to being the revolutionary standard of the new national monarchies.[31]

Decline of Medieval Civilizations

By the fifteenth century, the vitality of feudal society and medieval civilization was rapidly diminishing.[32] Forms rather than substance dominated; great courts supported a magnificence that only emphasized their sterile and ornate qualities; chivalry was debased; factionalism and civil war testified to the bankruptcy of the feudal nobility; and opulent court bishops and lazy priests further disgraced a church already moving steadily away from real and vital religious currents into a world of empty symbolism and formality. On the other hand, cumulative forces of social and technological evolution were slowly evolving a civil society underneath this moribund façade that provided the foundations of the modern state. Merchant towns and shrewd capitalist traders grew in number and power, having many a lord in mortgage, even intervening in the election of kings and popes.[33] Gunpowder and artillery challenged the mounted warriors and the feudal castle. Even more fundamentally, the cohesive forces of the culture itself were being slowly transformed. Language and vernacular literature were confirming national cultures and creating the basis of a diffuse public opinion in political and religious matters. In religion, sectaries were searching for more individual forms of religious expression and more direct, mystical communion with God. Skill and money, and new attitudes toward enterprise and adventure encouraged individualism, while vernacular tongues, humanistic letters, and sectional tendencies within Christendom provided a basis for new political unities, both more compact and more pragmatically instrumental than feudal monarchies or the Holy Roman Empire. The Renaissance and Reformation only accelerated and confirmed this transformation by finally dissolving or tearing asunder the attenuated bonds of feudal society.

Consolidation of Modern States

In the final consolidation of the modern state, which took place roughly between Ferdinand's accession to the Spanish throne in 1474 and the Peace of Westphalia in 1648, the first important variable in the equation was the monarch himself. Personal energy, a convenient lack of scruples, capable

---

[31] Cf. Kantorowicz, *op. cit.*, also Sir John Fortescue (1394?-1476?), *The Governance of England* (Oxford, Eng.: Clarendon, 1885).

[32] A classic study is Johan Huizinga, *The Waning of the Middle Ages* (London: St. Martin's, 1924); also, see, Joseph R. Strayer and Dana C. Munro, *The Middle Ages— 395-1500* (New York: Appleton-Century, 1942), Chs. 13, 14.

[33] The famous examples are those of the Fuggers and the de Medici.

heirs, and above all a dominating mission of statecraft were requisite. Generally, the monarchs of this period found their kingdoms near anarchy, revenues reduced, the lands and properties of the realm alienated, and the common folk crying for a protector. Only those monarchs who relentlessly pursued the antifeudal policy of building a nation, enhancing national wealth, and promoting the country's power domestically and internationally succeeded in consolidating a national state. To accomplish these ends, they had ingredients with which to work, rather than true instruments of policy. Revenues, armies, bureaucracies, and institutions for coordinating the general social and political transformation could be expanded and in some instances created anew. But first alien materials had to be bent and adapted to new ends and techniques. And that process required the energy and craft of able monarchies abetted by the skillful officers of royal councils and the few able nobles and officials that associated themselves with the King's revolutionary cause. Machiavelli in considerable measure prophesied rightly: states were made—or more accurately, launched—by men with a cold passion for power and *Machtpolitik*.[34]

RELIGION

In the making of modern states, religion first played the role later filled by nationalism. For religion was a primary basis of social cohesion, and the basic ideological cement of earlier society. On the one hand, cultural evolution was transforming religion from within; on the other, princes were utilizing it as an instrument of *raison d'état*. Both Protestantism and the Counter-Reformation impelled religious notions in the direction of an antifeudal, sovereign monarch, a nation organized to promote the public weal (dimly though that welfare might be perceived), and an equal citizenry united in joint religious participation that transcended the barriers of caste and birth and increasingly identified religious expression with nationalized institutions. But monarchs also directly made religion an instrument of national consolidation. Through concordats with the church they enlisted Jesuits, Dominicans and Protestant preachers as propagandists, and won control of clerical offices and officers, to be used as administrative agencies or for political patronage. By persecuting heretics and destroying the privileges of dissenters they rallied their peoples to a national standard. By becoming the sponsors of religious reform, they became as well the champions of a swelling popular cause and the recognized heads of the church. Simultaneously, they disengaged national states from the vague and unworkable international unity preserved by the Catholic Church and the Holy Roman Empire. The monarchs and the religious statesmen of the age were, for the most part, ruthless, coldly practical, and yet devoted and impassioned men. The

---

[34] Cf. Friedrich Meinecke, *Machiavellism (The Doctrine of Raison d'Etat and Its Place in History)* trans. Douglas Scott (New Haven, Conn.: Yale U. P., 1957); also V. H. Green, *Renaissance and Reformation* (London: Arnold, 1952).

politics of that age required the hammering out of a new equation relating political organization and community with transcendent loyalty and basic human purposes. Thus, it was a period of propaganda, of forcible conversion, of manipulation of belief, in order to create new bases for political cohesion. From it emerged national religions and absolute monarchs.[35]

NEW IDEAS OF AUTHORITY

The kinds of alterations in men's operative beliefs and ideals that appeared in the pamphlets on religion and political obligation in the fifteenth and sixteenth centuries were but one expression of the many ways in which peoples' views were changing, particularly about the way they should be related to each other and to their superiors.[36] Protestant and Jesuit alike preached the notion of covenant and the doctrine of the legitimate power of the people. They were echoing and reinforcing ideals that men in their personal relations—in their contracts with each other and in their establishment of communal and congregational authority—were actively practicing. The patriarchal doctrines that Jean Calvin, the protestant reformer, drew from the Old Testament, were matched by the paternalistic principles of the Catholic, Jean Bodin, and his exalting of the Prince as father of his country. In practical affairs, public magistrates, guild masters, and men generally were applying the doctrine of paternalism as a way of moving from traditional relations of authority to newer and more "modern" ones. Changes in religious belief reflected practice; but also, by settling the issue of religion along territorial and dynastic lines, they helped bring peace. Of almost equal importance was the fact that a settlement of the religious issue enabled men to cooperate, to make some sense of what they were doing, and to move with confidence toward the future.

NEW CLASSES

The new state made itself the ally of active, manipulative classes that were burgeoning rapidly, struggling for expression, and in need of a powerful and autocratic patron. Though kings generally did not think in economic terms, and as managers of prosperity and the economy often proved to be incompetent blunderers, still they enormously speeded, by their pursuit of political power, the emergence of middle-class strength. In one sense, the state was manufactured (or at least the attempt was made) by seeking to make new bases of social control and direction out of "nobilities of the robe", guild-masters, merchant companies, town bourgeoisie, and the yeoman. These classes supplied the bulk of national militia-men that levelled feudal castles, the soldiers that guarded frontiers, and the sailors and adventurers that brought national glory and wealth in war and colonial

---

[35] Green, *op. cit.*, esp. Chs. 3, 12, 16.

[36] The range of theories and of disagreement is suggested by John W. Allen, *A History of Political Theory in the Sixteenth Century*, 3rd ed. (London: Methuen, 1951).

ventures. But, just as vitally, they speeded the transformation of the earlier economy to the new monetary one: they worked, applied skill and capital, ordered the new structure of economic power that was replacing feudalism's military base.

MONEY

As a counterpart of this trend, a vast "monetization" or commercialization of the state took place. In this age of rising prices, steady and ample sources of revenue were the key to power. In the interests of revenue, and in response to economic necessity, kings became the managers of national prosperity: the patrons of fairs, of merchant companies, of gilds, and of sturdy yeomen. They actively intervened in economic matters, to standardize and to secure coinage as their right, to import foreign workers, prohibit exports of gold, skilled workmen, or industrial processes, and to divert and monopolize trade in order to swell the quantity of money and speed its circulation. Allied to the bourgeoisie, the peasantry, and new elites of skill, they wrung taxing powers from the feudal estates with which they built armies, fleets, and a bureaucracy. For revenue, they taxed illegally, plundered churches, bartered franchises and monopolies, and sold offices by the score and the hundred. In effect, the monarchy waxed strong by a new politics of dynastic marriage—this time with the great but undirected power of money.[37]

BUREAUCRACY

Bureaucratization and professionalization of public service was, by all odds, the tendency most immediately connected with the practices and institutions that characterize the modern state.[38] In the main, four great ends were sought in this process. First came the necessity to render the state something other than private property or the mirror of a society of estates and orders. In this task absolutism and national sovereignty were the great levers of policy. *"L'état, c'est moi,"* said Louis XIV: that is, neither is the state hereditable property, nor is it an assemblage of estates. Secondly, bureaucracy gave *permanent* life to the political, administrative, and legal functions of the emerging Leviathan. Also, by giving administrative energy to a sovereign will and by sustaining regular and comparatively much more precise administrative intervention, bureaucracy gave substance to the as yet shadowy principles of social and political organization represented by the modern state. Lastly, professionalization of service opened alternate channels of social mobility—to captains of infantry, to crown lawyers, to tax and customs officers, and to career officials of the state.

[37] One of the classic studies is Eli F. Heckscher, *Mercantilism*, translated by Mendel Shapiro (London: Allen & Unwin, 1935).
[38] Sir Ernest Barker, *The Development of the Public Services in Western Europe, 1660-1930* (London: Oxford U. P., 1945).

IN SUMMARY

The specific techniques employed by particular kings varied widely. Generally, however, the outlines of policy held much in common. On the one hand, national monarchs built an independent state service, relying upon taxation and money revenue, by attempting to professionalize the army and navy, the collection of revenue, and the critical instruments of state policy such as higher administration, justice, and the administration of arsenals and strong-points. On the other, they sought to "bureaucratize" useful orders and classes of the society—by drawing upon church officials, by incorporating chivalric orders, negotiating with and utilizing gild masters and merchant companies, and imposing new duties on towns, rural gentry, and officers of local government. In general, the various sovereigns' attempts met with initial failure; indeed they contributed to future disasters. Parliaments and assemblies of estates withered, effectively killed by the dynanism of centralist, public power. The prematurely rationalized state did not last. Instead, office was again converted into property. Careers, presumably "open to the talents" were still largely the province of family and preferment. And the politics of monarchic favoritism choked the expanding economies in a rank growth of monopolies, privileged companies, and prejudicial concessions. Generally also, such kings eventually ruined the new-born prosperity with their wars and their blundering fiscal policies. On the other hand, the new expansive energies released by their active and encouraging policy built those national institutions, that formed the core of the practices of modern states. Later monarchs used these foundations. Where they were successful, it was largely because they made a wise use of the practices, materials, and principles bequeathed to them by the great age of state-building that was the sixteenth century.

CONCLUSION

The development of the modern national state was a political achievement of the first order of magnitude. In the writing of that period—in the works of such men as Bodin, Hobbes, and the Catholic exponents of the Divine Right of Kings—an awareness of this fact stands out sharply. These men were conscious of the cardinal importance of establishing and securing a new political order, of creating an instrument with which collective well-being could be more effectively pursued.

The possibility of progress in the arrangement of secular affairs was one of the most important of men's interests of this period. Without civil peace and security, this progress was impossible. But the state was not important only for that reason. It could not only protect and preserve the legal frame within which men could calculate, invest, and work productively, a set of legal relations that would enforce a trust or make possible the organization of a corporation. The state enabled people to coordinate their activities for progressive change. It gave an enormous leverage to their efforts; it made sense of what many were seeking in diverse and unrelated areas of activity. Thus, Hobbes' insistence that this work—the secular state —be preserved, however imperfect it might seem to particular sectarians.

Also, as Bodin argued, the territorial state was of not less importance as a political form because it sorted out men's loyalties and the duties they could respond to in a new way that made more sense. The secular state represented a new equation between the two swords of temporal and religious power that both enabled religion to be more personal and immediate and disengaged the state from the administration of religious affairs. It created many forms of civic expression and of political obligation that used directly and indirectly the new relations of subordination and superordination developing in society. The state, as Bodin perceived, was important not only because it released men's economic energies. Possibly this fact about it was not even the most important. The state also stimulated men's civil and administrative enterprise—their desire to sail the seas; to remake the towns; to build roads, dikes and forts; to rise to honor under the crown.

Certainly, if one looks to the techniques by which this achievement was brought about, Machiavelli's injunction that a prince should aim above all else at the accumulation of power shows the deep insight that he had into the politics of the age. On the other hand, of equal importance was the political space within which monarchs sought to build their royal power. For Machiavelli's own prescriptions met with little success applied to the city-states of Italy. The need for a citizenship that was more distant and abstract, as well as a relationship between the Prince and his people that could at the same time join together many loyalties and elements of common interest and profit required a larger territorial theater, more resources of administrative skill and money, and greater distance between ruler and subject.

Only in a wider territorial theatre could monarchs benefit by the symbols that expressed the loyalties and aspirations of that time. For the English or the French, the king was "father of his country", the crown an immortal *dignitas*. Neither cities nor the Empire had that association with a people's first flowering and with their common sacrifice and aspirations over the centuries. Partly, the emergent secular state gave expression to the new relations of commonness, of individuality, and of equality that men were feeling. Just as much, however, monarchs made themselves the agents of change by becoming the personal expression of the new symbols that aided the transition.

As both Bodin and Hobbes were aware, establishing the national state was considerably more than clothing activities in powerful symbols and answering to new interests. It required the tools and procedures, the offices and officers, that could both protect the integrity of the new idea and give it concrete substance. The domain of the public had not only to have a new legitimacy in relation to the private, it was not only a matter of "rightness" and of loyalty; it needed soundness and intelligence in administrative practice and legal form, and sharply drawn, defensible boundaries separating it from the interests of private men, from customary ties of personal loyalty. The state had to be manufactured, in a sense, with loyal bureaucrats and with legal procedures and capacities, with the "passion for objectivity" on the one hand—drawn from new classes and novel cultural tendencies—and with the rich store of legal experience and administrative prudence of able chancellors and officials.

One of the most striking aspects of the emergence of the modern state was the amount of sustained innovation that it required. Customary right had to be replaced, offices rearranged, powers expanded and related to their objects in a new fashion. In this respect, it is well to understand that the process we have been considering is a lengthy revolution, one of the great revolutions in history. One of the prime essentials was a sustained, directed lawlessness, if you will, or a controlled use of procedures to break the law and remake it in a new form by procedures that would both win acceptance and also preserve the foundations of law-observance and of respect for law that would be essential to the new order. To say this much is also to suggest in part why the state can be viewed as a rather remarkable achievement —the expression of law and lawful ways and yet the great instrument for destroying as well as making it.

Also this perspective gives even more point to two other items that have emerged from this discussion. On the one hand, it makes even clearer the importance of those devices that maintain the boundaries between the public and the private, between the legitimate use of the state for public purpose and the use of that state for additional leverage by private persons acting without benefit of public authority. Secondly, this particular aspect of the state explains one of the motives that led political propagandists to sanctify the work of the state and of monarchs—to supply the beliefs, and a confidence in authority that would make the departures from the accepted and the traditional practices legitimate in men's eyes or at least bearable.

Finally, what the builders of the new states aimed at was important. For they did not simply aim at power, or good administration, or even prosperity for their countries. Some rulers were, as Machiavelli's image of Chiron the Centaur suggests, half beast and half man. Most, however, saw a vision of a new age—not an age of equality or of liberty—but one of change and vigorous national activity internally and externally. The image that monarchs of that day chose and that their people often chose for them was a paternalistic one—"father of the country." The image was expressive of several ideas, of sponsorship and patronage on the one hand, but also of creation and birth on the other. The time was one of beginning.

SELECTED READINGS

ALLEN, JOHN W. *A History of Political Theory in the Sixteenth Century.* 3rd ed. London: Methuen, 1951. Contains good discussions of most of the important continental political theorists of the period.

BARKER, SIR ERNEST. *The Development of the Public Services in Western Europe, 1660-1930.* London, Eng.: Oxford U. P., 1945. Shows in brief compass some of the relations between the development of the state and the professionalization of public services.

BODIN, JEAN. trans. and ed. M. J. Tooley. *Six Books of the Commonwealth.* Oxford, Eng.: Blackwell, 1955. Bodin advances the argument for centralized monarchy, for sovereignty, and for the secular state.

GREEN, V. H. *Renaissance and Reformation.* London: Arnold, 1952. A good reference work, useful for the political scientist because of the attention it devotes to political events, institutions, and movements.

HECKSCHER, ELI F., trans. Mendel Shapiro. *Mercantilism.* 2 vols., London: Allen & Unwin, 1931. One of several great classic works on the subject.

HOBBES, THOMAS. Introd. Oakeshott. *Leviathan; or, The matter, form and power of a Commonwealth, ecclesiastical and civil.* A good modern edition is Oxford, Eng.: Blackwell, 1947. Hobbes is one of the first to state with rigor the arguments for the sovereign state or "Leviathan."

MACHIAVELLI, NICCOLÒ. *The Prince and The Discourses.* New York: Random House, 1940. Machiavelli's two works are particularly valuable for the insight they offer into the methods of accumulating power and the techniques and stratagems of power politics which accompanied the building of modern states.

MACIVER, ROBERT M. *The Modern State.* London: Oxford U. P., 1926. A classic work dealing with city-states, early empires, and the development of the modern national states.

MAITLAND, FREDERIC W. *The Constitutional History of England.* Cambridge, Eng.: Cambridge U. P., 1920. Maitland is especially valuable for the political scientist, even though as historical writing his work is dated or superseded by later research.

MUNDY, JOHN H. and RIESENBERG, PETER N. *The Medieval Town.* Princeton, N.J.: Van Nostrand, 1958. See especially the appendix which contains examples of municipal charters and other documents relevant to the civic institutions of this period.

PAINTER, SIDNEY. *A History of the Middle Ages: 284-1500.* New York: Knopf, 1954. A standard and useful text for reference.

———. "The Lords of Lusignan in the 11th and 12th Centuries," *Speculum* 32 (1957), pp. 27-47. An insight into the processes of politics under feudalism.

CHAPTER 10

Constitutionalism

||||||||||||||||||||||||||||||||||||||||||||||||||||||||||||||||||||||||||||||||||||||

It has been said that King James and the Puritans were essentially agreed about ends—but had a falling out over questions of procedure. However that may be, it is true that issues of procedure are often more important than those of substance. Moreover, ends and means, substance and procedure, are extremely difficult to keep separate. Each has a way of influencing, changing, and becoming entangled with the other. An appreciation of these facts is essential for an understanding of constitutionalism, for it presents a special case of means and ends, of procedures and substance.

A constitution must contain the procedures and substantive protections by which most of the political society's other procedures and substantive ends are curbed and channelled. A constitution must be proof, as the *Federalist* papers suggested, against the ambition and avarice of powerful men and the passions of an aroused populace. An effective constitution must encourage and continue a legitimate style of government. Thus, constitutionalism is not simply a matter of procedure and substance, but also the effective control of large blocs of political power, and the intangible and diffuse values of representativeness, symbolism, past tradition, and future aspiration.

The considerations detailed above help to explain why the establishment of effective constitutional regimes has proved difficult. A constitution requires more than political will and opportunity; and more than the rational calculation of means and ends. These elements must be synthesized in a document or set of practices and statutes that somehow also express what is fundamental about the political character of a people and the peculiar "genius" of their institutions. Burke and de Maistre[1] were fond of telling their contemporaries that it was difficult even to understand the

---

[1] Edmund Burke (1729-1797) *Reflections on the French Revolution*, first published 1790.
Joseph de Maistre (1753-1821), especially *Reflections on France* (1796), and *Essay on the Generative Principles of Political Constitutions* (1809).

constitutions one had, worse to try to write different ones, and impossible to install new constitutions and make them work. Since people did manage the impossible, Burke and de Maistre clearly overstated the magnitude of the problem. But many of the difficulties they described were serious both for their contemporary era and more recently for many developing polities.

Constitutionalism is a critical problem for modern societies. France is rich in culture, historic tradition, and the arts of polity. Yet this heritage was not proof against the defects of the Constitution of 1946. In ten years, the Fourth Republic stumbled to a scarce lamented and inglorious end. France labored under a heavy burden from the past and suffered further calamities as well. But the constitution also was faulty: it established a frame of government that encouraged disaster, by renewing bitter memories and ancient vices.

Even in the United States and Great Britain, where the machinery of government generally functions, if not smoothly and noiselessly, at least without critical ruptures or breakdown, issues impinging on constitutionalism are continually arising. The reform of Congress or federal-state relations are constitutional questions. "Ministers powers" over persons and property, or the accountability of the public corporation require a plumbing of the theory of the British Constitution. The commerce clause in America or the British cabinet system are constitutional arrangements that have developed not through crisis, but through political wisdom abetted by a strong constitutional sense among decisive groups, and considerable political virtue throughout the societies.

The examples above are meant to suggest in some measure the pertinence of the major topics considered in this chapter. First, we shall discuss the essentials of contemporary constitutionalism: the functions of a constitution, and the connection between these and its social and political milieu. Secondly, we consider constitutionalism as a genetic phenomenon: how it has developed; and the relation that subsists between various styles or types of constitutionalism.

PART I. ELEMENTS OF CONSTITUTIONALISM

BASIC CONCEPTS

When Aristotle spoke of the *"constitution"* of a state, he referred to its essential make-up.[2] The usage of the term was similar to that in the phrase, "a man's (or the body's) constitution." In this broadest sense of the word, every state has a "constitution", and this usage is occasionally employed. The reference is not to a written document, nor even to a government that

[2] *The Politics of Aristotle,* trans., introd. by Ernest Barker (Oxford: Clarendon, 1946), Bk. III, Ch. 6.

is "constitutional" in the sense that it is limited. The constitution of a state, by this usage, means simply its organization, the laws, rules, customs, or understandings that govern its operation and the more or less permanent social forces that determine its character.

The adjective *"constitutional"* bears a more limited connotation. Following the Aristotelian usage, the Soviet Union or even Hitler's Germany had a "constitution"; but "constitutional" is reserved to describe a government that is subject to limitations and that operates in accordance with general rules rather than arbitrarily. Even Aristotle reserved the word "constitutional" for such a state. "Constitutionalism", similarly, refers to the set of ideas or doctrines describing and supporting a constitution that includes a system of effective restraints upon political power.

The word "constitution" usually suggests to an American a specific document, drafted and ratified at some point in the past. This concept of the constitution as a document is not peculiar to the United States. An eighteenth century Swiss commentator, for example, said of the British constitution that it did not exist because there was in England no document called the Constitution. However, a constitution need not be written. A state may have a system of constitutional restraints none of which have been explicitly set forth or ratified. Even though the restraints are merely traditional or expressed only in the Common Law, as long as they are deeply enough engraved in the minds and habits of the people or of the ruling authorities to be effective checks on government, they can form the basis of a constitutional state.

Since the idea of written constitutions was popularized during the revolutionary struggles in seventeenth century England, it has become customary for civilized countries to have written constitutions. Curiously, England itself remains the only leading country to withstand the trend. Even in England, though no single document embodies the constitution, most of the principles and concepts of the British Constitution are written into ordinary statutes, or in one of the great charters of English liberties like the Magna Carta. For this reason, one writer has suggested that a more useful distinction than written and unwritten constitutions is that of dispersed (like the British) and codified (like the American) constitutions.[3]

A more significant distinction than that between *written and unwritten constitutions* is that between *the formal and the effective constitution*.[4] Normally, states do not have the one or the other: they have both a formal and an effective constitution. The former is the constitution explicitly stated in law, statute, charter, or other authoritative source. The effective constitution is the actual pattern of operation, in matters of constitutional import,

---

[3] Edward McC. Sait, *Political Institutions—A Preface* (New York: Appleton, 1938), p. 325

[4] Cf. Bagehot's distinction between the "dignified" and the "efficient" parts of a constitution. Walter Bagehot, *The English Constitution* (1867) (London: Oxford U. P., 1942), p. 4.

regardless of what the law says. According to its formal constitution, England is a monarchy. Effectively, however, it is a parliamentary democracy. Formally, in the United States, members of the electoral college may elect any eligible person to the presidency. Effectively, the electors pledge themselves in advance and abide by their pledges (subject to rare exceptions). Even here, however, the operation of the effective constitution does not contravene, although it adds to the formal constitution. The Soviet Union provides an example of much more extreme divergence between form and substance. It is ruled, primarily, by the Communist Party. The dictatorship of the Party is limited not by the constitutional distribution of political power as provided in the formal constitution, but by a four-cornered tug-of-war among Party, army, bureaucracy, and industrial managers. In "underdeveloped" countries, the locus of effective power often departs sharply from the theory and mandate of the formal constitution; and political institutions may perform radically different functions from those they serve in modern societies. A parliament can have in theory the full panoply of powers that one sees in Britain, France, or the United States and yet in practice play no significant political role, serving only to rubber-stamp the legislative proposals of the President or ruling group. Such a situation prevails, for example, in Mexico today, and in many other Latin American countries.

The discussion of the relation between the formal constitution and the real powers of government, however, is not intended to imply that formal and effective constitutions never diverge in a healthy constitutional system, or that they should not. Generally they do, and valuable ends are served by the separate existence of the two. Britain's monarchical formal constitution preserves the ancient memories of glory, and also of liberty. It also preserves a valuable tradition of national unity, of continuity in evolution, and of worthy services of many statesmen of past generations. It is a powerful symbolic force and continues like the document of 1787 in the United States to mold and inspire the present. But whatever the symbolic value of the constitution, an effective constitution must also be capable of fixing the basic framework of government. In England charters, bills of rights, statutes, and constitutional "conventions" combine to assure the effective operation of parliamentary democracy, with the powers of the King exercised by Ministers accountable to Parliament.

Constitutions are often classified also according to whether they are "flexible" or "inflexible." This distinction refers to the relative ease or difficulty of changing the terms or provisions of the constitution. The very idea of a constitution implies at least a minimal amount of stability or inflexibility. In a constitutional state, some arrangements must be more fundamental than ordinary law. The American Constitution states that it is "the supreme law of the land," and this provision has been held to mean that, if there is a conflict between the Constitution and an ordinary statute, the former must prevail. But if it were possible to change the Constitution by the same process as is required for passing a law, this clause would have little practical effect. At best, it would depend upon the self-restraint of the legislators, growing out of their respect for the Constitution. Accordingly, most written constitutions set forth a procedure for their own amendment that is more demanding than that provided for ordinary legislation. Sometimes a two-thirds or three-fourths majority is required, instead of simple majority. Sometimes the legislature must pass the amendment twice, at two different sessions. Or it may have to be submitted to the people for popular ratification. The constitutions of federal governments, like our own, may require the concurrence of a prescribed number of their constituent states. And so on.

The distinction between flexible and inflexible constitutions is just as important as ever it was, but today we are aware of the fact that the story cannot be told entirely in terms of the legal provisions for change. In the United States, the individual right of free speech is protected by provisions of a relatively inflexible constitution, while in Britain the same right is at the mercy of a majority of the legislature. In practice, so deeply entrenched is the commitment to freedom of speech in England, that it would appear to be at least as difficult to make a change in this respect in England as it would be in this country. In short, we must distinguish between a flexible formal constitution (referring to the legal provisions for change) and a flexible effective constitution (which refers to the character of the people as well as to their laws).

A constitution is to a state what character is to an individual, a basis an expression of harmony and a foundation for conduct. Both involve the acceptance of discipline, of limitation on the self, and of cooperation with others. Both involve the concept of responsibility for activity and the recognition that well-being both for the individual and others rests on continuously responsible behavior.

Neither constitution nor character, however, operate in a purely rational manner. They are ways of functioning, arising out of experience and acting as directors without continuous recurrence to basic principles of behavior. This statement does not mean that these modes of acting are contrary to or hostile to reason; it does mean that they accept a method and a concept of the society (of the self), as more fundamental than any specific immediate achievement of a particular objective. Under constitutionalism, rights are accepted as absolutes, imposing duties, just as in the individual, recognition of the claims of the self as a whole and continuous person imposes obligations and limitations on vagrant impulses.

THE CONSTITUTION AS AN EMBODIMENT OF ESSENTIAL INSTITUTIONS

Nearly all written constitutions contain a statement of what are to be the major offices and branches of government, what powers they are to possess, and what limitations are to be imposed on them or by them on one

another. Where a country has no written constitution, if it is a constitutional
state, the major governmental institutions will be established historically,
their powers and limitations settled. Written constitutions generally state
what officers or bodies are to perform executive, legislative, and judicial
functions, how they are to come into being, sometimes when and where they
are to meet, and many of their rules of procedures. Normally, constitutions
set forth the *modus operandi* of legal authority, including provision for their
own amendment.

Napoleon's famous dictum that a constitution ought to be "short and
obscure" reflects an age in which constitutions were an assemblage of specific grants and "organic statutes" with little system and much potentiality
of abuse. Many things were best left unsaid and many issues of power left
untouched. Under contemporary conditions, however, one tends to measure
the vitality of a constitution by the extent to which it provides the effective
provisions for such fundamental institutions of government as courts, legislatures, executives, political parties, and bureaucracies.

THE CONSTITUTION AS RESTRAINT

Restraints are the core of constitutionalism; hence some system of
restraints must be central to the constitution of any regime that aspires to
"constitutional" government. Simply by establishing the framework of government, any constitution in a measure acts as a restraint on power. Provision of specific ways and means for governmental action by implication
forbids others. But constitutions usually go further and specifically limit
powers by stating the bounds of governmental authority and by establishing
fixed and fair procedures for governmental action. The ruled are guaranteed
against arbitrary action by governors; men are to be governed only
under law.

RULE OF LAW

The principle of the "rule of law" is probably the deepest and strongest
tradition of constitutionalism. Throughout the long, slow growth of the
modern political order, the rule of law has been the central aim of constitutional reform.[5] Rule of law, today, is nothing more nor less than the principles that public authority in general holds and derives its powers and
exercises those powers on the basis of specific enablement by duly made
laws; that every act of every person filling elective or appointive office is
done under the authority of the law; and that their acts are subject to
judgment and control by appropriate legal authority as to whether they

---

[5] A historical account showing the significance of "rule of law" in English constitutional development is John W. Gough, *Fundamental Law in English Constitutional History*
(Oxford: Clarendon, 1955); for France, see Jean Brissaud, *A History of French Private Law*,
trans. R. Howell, (Boston: Little, Brown, 1912).

were in fact justified by law. Moreover, where the right of life or liberty is involved, that legal authority must be a court of law. It is in this sense that the rule of law is a fundamental restraint on government. As a corollary of this principle, those who act in the name of the government are personally answerable for any illegal acts and are subject to trial or civil action for any wrong they may do. No servant of the state can claim special privilege because of that service.

In a larger sense the rule of law is often taken to mean the process of legal change by duly established means rather than by arbitrary action, on the part either of officials or citizens, to nullify the law or to fail to enforce it. An important prerequisite of constitutionalism (and one frequently lacking) is a willingness to bear with unpopular laws severely detrimental to particular interests until these laws can be changed.

The importance that has been attributed historically to the notion of "contract" and of a "social contract" illustrates this aspect of the rule of law in the development of constitutionalism. Contract and covenant, as expressed especially in Calvinist notions of government[6] and by such political theorists as John Locke were more than a way of expressing symbolically the notion of a common undertaking and a joint and equal responsibility. They were also ways of encouraging a "law sense" in political behavior: a deference to and a regular observance of the *stated agreement,* of the *legal* procedure, the *legal* properties of office, and the precise *legal* mechanisms of constitutional and legislative change. In the absence of such a tradition, the line between constitutional government and various types of authoritarian regimes or "guided democracies" is impossible to maintain, for no procedure or title legitimates the one and condemns the other.

Today it is frequently charged that the rule of law breaks down in the industrial and large-city civilization. Legislative enactments tend to be broad in scope and vague in concept, granting wide discretionary powers to administrative officers. Courts find it difficult to exercise wise control and restraint over administrative actions based on complicated expertise, laborious fact-finding, and very specialized grounds. So the argument runs. Yet this argument misses much of the real purpose lying behind the institution of the rule of law. For one thing, in cases involving life and liberty of the person or the freedoms of speech and assembly, all constitutional governments tend to take a strict view of administrative powers exercised over the citizen. Also the vital purposes of the "rule of law" are served if the administrator is held responsible by clear and effective controls, whether bureaucratic or legal, if actionable remedies are provided for those unjustly injured, and if any general tendency toward arbitrary rule is forestalled. Few figures could be conjured up that would, in one sense, seem a truer incarnation of arbitrary discretion than that provincial viceroy, the French

---

[6] Sheldon Wolin, *Politics and Vision* (Boston: Little, Brown, 1960), Ch. 6.

prefect. Yet, by and large, he is effectively held accountable by the French *Conseil d'Etat;* and the ordinary French citizen probably has a more effective battery of remedies against arbitrary administrative action than his American or British counterpart. In substance, the rule of law survives quite effectively in all modern constitutional regimes.

Rights

Another way in which a constitution acts as an important restraint on power is by singling out certain individual or group freedoms and protecting them as rights of all citizens or individuals within the state—i.e., civil rights or liberties.[7] The place of rights in the tradition of constitutionalism is a disputed issue. In strict theory, the British Constitution recognizes few if any substantive constitutional rights. On the other hand, most Americans probably regard the Bill of Rights as the most important part of their constitution, and the sharp disagreement between Hamilton and Jefferson on this score is famous.

Historically, the struggle for rights was a struggle for individual and group liberties of the person, of religious belief and profession, and of property. These liberties were stated as rights in order to insist on their nature as fundamental moral claims. The struggle to effectuate rights, was initially a struggle to achieve guarantees of acceptance or limitation by an authority which the people did not directly create or control. Later, however, popularly made constitutions embodied these rights as essential claims against the ordinary operations of government and of legislation even when based on majority consent. In the seventeenth and eighteenth centuries these rights were held to be "natural" in the sense that they were the dictates of a rational order of things, the same everywhere and for all times. They were further fundamental in that they were vital to the fulfillment of man and were not to be denied or removed for any cause. Despite Bentham's denunciation of natural rights as "nonsense on stilts," this phase in the evolution of constitutionalism was important in shoring up constitutional limitations with a doctrinal authority that could rationalize resistance to arbitrary

---

[7] The term "a right" is the subject of much confusion and misunderstanding. We define a "right" as a "legitimate claim," moral or legal. Legal rights may be either positive or negative. In the latter case they amount to a claim of immunity, a claim that the person possessing the right should be let alone in a certain respect. My right to free speech means that no one may (legally) interfere with my speaking my mind. A positive right entails action on the part of someone else. If I have a right to a free education, it means that someone, presumably the government, must supply me with an education, or make it available to me. Some rights apply to other private individuals only—for instance, my ordinary property rights. But even the government can not take my property without paying me just compensation. This is a right against the government itself. Finally, rights may be protected by ordinary legislation or they may be enshrined in the Constitution and may be subject to change only by the special process provided for amending the Constitution. Figure 3, may help clarify the subject.

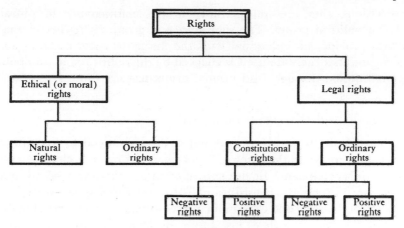

"Civil" rights are generally negative, and
may or may not be constitutional rights.

"Social and economic" rights are generally
positive, and may or may not be constitutional rights.

"Political" rights do not fit neatly into
either of these categories.

FIGURE 3

invasions of private rights and provide a creed that lent a special legitimacy
to the boundary between the state and society.[8] Under the impact of utilitarian and positivistic philosophy, the theory of "natural" rights has been
widely abandoned. Yet the tradition of constitutionalism, taken over and
even further developed by democracy, continues to give effective support
to the ideas of limited government and of a sphere of individual and group
rights.

The concept of equal rights for all has come to constitute one of the
fundamental marks of the constitutional as against the arbitrary or dictatorial regime. It creates an essential bridge between the idea of rule by a
rational principle and its needed corrective of external (pluralistic) checks
upon government by participation in government and the corrective of a
widely shared popular power. Individual rights, such as the right to move
freely or the right to talk openly or espouse some belief or conviction, are
particularly closely related to constitutionalism. In the first place, they are
the assurance that the "marketplace" of ideas is not a rigged market. Also,
when taken together with the rights to associate and participate in commu-

[8] John W. Allen, *English Political Thought, 1603-1643* (London: Methuen, 1938); more
generally, see Leo Strauss, *Natural Right and History* (Chicago: Univ. of Chicago Press,
1953). These works give an account of the struggle for the recognition of particular rights.
Few studies relate informatively the development of both constitutionally protected rights
and constitutional procedure and rule of law. The monumental and compendious work by
William S. Holdsworth, *A History of English Law* (London: Methuen, 1922) does attempt
this job for England.

nity decisions, they are indispensible to the maintenance of pluralistic checks on political power. The significance of group rights lies in the fact that they provide the individual with the means to enforce claims against the state and that the state itself is checked by the political and non-political interests fulfilled through institutional groupings.

Division and Distribution of Power

The rule of law and constitutional rights are crucial to constitutionalism. But how to assure that they will not be defied by men clothed with the authority of government? In the nature of things there can be no final assurance; but historically, constitutionalists have placed great reliance upon the device of dividing the exercise of power among various individuals and organs of the body politic. This simple principle has been applied in a variety of ways. While judges interpret or declare the law, the actual conviction of an individual for a crime may be made to depend upon the cooperation with the judge of a group of lay persons, selected by lot, "peers" of the person being tried. The operations of government may be divided up among separate and independent branches with distinct personnel—the separation of powers; the various branches or organs may be required to collaborate to carry out the business of government, so that any one can block the others; organs themselves may be subdivided, as in bicameralism; and powers may be distributed among various geographical subdivisions of the state, as in federalism.

In more recent times popular participation in political power through the franchise has assumed an ever-increasing role in the constitutional state. Originally, constitutionalism was developed as a protection against the arbitrary power of monarchs. In large measure it was on behalf of a limited number of people, the nobility; and even when the rights of common men came to be respected it was chiefly through the agency of the nobles that they were protected. With the development of representative government and the extension of the franchise, however, the situation was changed. Never were the rights of the common man secure until he had the power, through the vote, to protect them for himself. This immediately raises the question whether in the new situation the other devices, previously mentioned, are any longer necessary, or at least as important as they once were. Without attempting to anticipate discussion that must be reserved for subsequent chapters, two facts may be pointed out. In the first place, although the people in a democracy have no one to fear but themselves, this fact gives little comfort to those who may happen to be in a minority. Masses of people can be as despotic as individuals who wear crowns. Secondly, however, it may still be true that the particular devices of constitutionalism that were developed for a limited representative government are not the best for a fully developed democracy.

Tradition and Social Pluralism

Apart from accountability to the electorate, two other factors variously support or, some would argue, are capable of supplanting many of the devices of constitutionalism. They are tradition and social structure. The importance of a sound *tradition of constitutionalism* can hardly be too much emphasized. Without it, more specific, formal checks against abuse of power are likely to be of little or no effect. It is a commonplace that in many Latin American countries the same constitutional devices that serve integrity, liberty, and justice well in the United States are not sufficient, south of the border, to prevent gross abuses of power by public officials.

For preventing tyranny of the majority over sizable minorities, *social structure* is also a nongovernmental factor of major importance. If the society has a sharply demarcated class structure, especially if two or three classes make up the bulk of the society, power is almost certain to be abused. Whatever class holds power (unless by a very narrow margin) is likely to wield that power rather ruthlessly, and to impede rather than facilitate movement from class to class. It has little sympathy with the other class; it believes its power is politically secure; and it is held together by the self-interest engendered by its monopoly position. Such conditions frequently characterized some of the city states in ancient Greece, and in our own day they have often prevailed in various Latin American countries. In a highly pluralistic and socially mobile society like that of the United States the situation is different. Individuals move more readily from group to group; indeed they often are at the same time members of more than one group, some of which may be in the majority at a given time while others are in the minority. Groups may shift their allegiance from one party to another, converting a present majority into a minority, and *vice versa*. Under such circumstances, self-interest, in the form of a realistically prompted concern for one's welfare in the near future, stimulates a healthy respect for the rules of the game.

For America, many political scientists believe that the combination of electoral accountability and social pluralism would be a sufficient check on the abuse of power by majorities without recourse to other means.[9] (Of course, government officials would still need to be surrounded by judicial and procedural checks, as they are now, to prevent petty arbitrariness.) Others believe these safeguards need to be reinforced with such institutional devices as federalism, the separation of powers, and judicial review. The important point here is not to argue the pros and cons of this disagreement among the specialists, but to point out that such devices for aiding government to approximate its proper objectives, should always be viewed as

[9] See Robert A. Dahl, *A Preface to Democratic Theory* (Chicago: Univ. of Chicago Press, 1956), Ch. 5, esp. p. 135.

supplements to powerful social and individual forces without which they would be ineffective. Their special role in a constitutional system will depend upon the nature of the society.

THE CONSTITUTION AS THE DIRECTOR OF DEVELOPMENT

To be and to remain an effective political force a constitution must achieve two things. It must effectively set the form and boundaries of political struggle. And it must provide a viable plan for future development.

A people's freedom is, as Montesquieu[10] and Acton[11] argued, a parochial or national freedom. They had in mind, among other things, the fact that a constitution far removed from the intellectual and moral standards of the country is a hindrance to the growth of freedom and constitutionalism. Montesquieu, for instance, sought to discover for France the "spirit" that informed the laws so that the constitution could improve mores and the political customs of the people strengthen the constitution in turn. He argued that a constitution that sought too much liberty or prescribed more political virtue than a people can bear would be likely to end in anarchy or despotism. In recent times the history of both Weimar Germany and the French Fourth Republic underscore his arguments.

What Montesquieu and Acton had to say was true; but it was not enough. A constitution must express the national "genius" of a people and the "spirit" of its laws. It must also be a sound strategy for the future: to allow for the expression of nationalism, for instance, or new economic developments, or the access of new groups to political influence. A close reading of the American Constitution suggests the vital role in America's political success played by the brilliant guesses of such men as Hamilton and Madison with respect to the main tendency of future American social and economic evolution.[12] "Commerce among the states," "necessary and próper", "full faith and credit," "no State shall . . ." are phrases that suggest both the wisdom that says when to be vague or silent and that which dictates as well when to be precise and firm.

On the other hand, the disruption of the Union by the two radically different economies of the ante-bellum North and South testifies to the profound difficulties of achieving a successful social and economic plan for the future. For nations just now reconstructing the wreckage of past constitutional orders or setting forth with new and little tried frameworks of government, the problems are magnified by all the forces that have been let loose in the intervening two centuries—dynamic technology, social flux, wholistic ideologies, and mass political movements.

[10] Baron de Montesquieu, *The Spirit of the Laws* (1748), trans. Thomas Nugent (New York: Hafner, 1949), esp. Bk. 19.

[11] John (Lord) Acton, "Nationality," in *History of Freedom and Other Essays* (London: Macmillan, 1907), pp. 270-300.

[12] See especially, *The Federalist*, Nos. 12, 13, 14.

THE CONSTITUTION AS AN ORGANIZER
OF POLITICAL AUTHORITY

A constitution not only sets limits to government and distributes powers horizontally and vertically among the various agencies of government; it also provides a system for ensuring that the acts of government have authority and that the government itself remains legitimate. At this point, the discussion of constitutionalism trenches upon democracy and the institutions of democratic government, but only because today constitutional governments are generally democratic. The two systems are not necessarily one and the same. Any government, democratic or not, must be legitimate government, if it is to last.

A constitution that invests government with authority does so in part because it rests upon, symbolizes, and fosters a consensus about basic issues. The real constitution, said Jean-Jacques Rousseau, is that constitution which is graven in the hearts of the citizens.[13] Thus, a constitution should be a statement of settled fundamentals of government and agreed upon procedures. To take a simple example, the American constitution lays down the principle that our government shall be republican rather than monarchical in form. Similarly, democratic suffrage and majority rule are procedural devices universally accepted today as foundations for the legitimacy of governments. A constitution must, of course, be much more explicit about the actual workings of government than general statements of commonly held principles. At the same time, it must be an effective symbol of the cherished myths and values about government that a particular people hold.

A constitution can destroy consensus by saying or attempting too much. If it is a document subject to a great deal of partisan contention, it cannot serve to invest the government with authority. We all, for example, agree in supporting the principles of free speech, the separation of church and state, and "equal protection of the laws." Not everyone, however, means the same things by these concepts. Many people would rank them differently in order of importance. They would also have different reasons for supporting these principles. Until a dispute about first principles or a concrete issue arises, agreement often seems to be present. But Negro, Catholic, Jew, and White Southerner who appear to agree in constitutional principle will often disagree over issues like integrated schools, birth control, and aid to education. So will most of the rest of us, for that matter. Many issues of this sort, in any constitution, must be left to the political processes of the society and to the needs and virtues of future generations. They cannot be solved merely by inscribing them in a constitutional document.

Although Rousseau said that the real constitution of any society was graven in the hearts of the citizens, he was also wise enough to add that the

[13] Jean Jacques Rousseau, *The Social Contract* (1762), trans. G. D. H. Cole, (London: Dent, 1937), esp. Bk. III, Ch. 12 and Bk. IV, Ch. 1.

constitution must daily take on new powers. It must not only channel and control political controversy; it must gain authority by deepening and strengthening loyalties to certain procedures and substantive provisions about government.

By promoting consensus within the society, a constitution can strengthen the initial agreement upon which the constitution itself rests. American politics provides a good example. On the whole, under the American Constitution, problems are not presented sharply, nor are the solutions to them clear. Over time, the executive, the legislature, and the courts hammer a provisional solution into shape, each conceding some points and winning others, molding an amalgam of policy that contains a plum for everyone and hurts no one badly. We wait upon the society itself to evolve a consensus at the points where hard issues are involved. In effect, our system of government *delegates* a large part of the task of reaching agreement to pressure groups and leaders from private life. The affected parties must, perforce, compromise their interests, pool their resources, and generate the consensus (or manufacture a semblance of its existence) to push their programs further. If all or most of the hard and contentious issues of our society were pushed to a formal and explicit resolution, the authority of the constitution and of the government itself would be less than it is.

However, to generate authority a government must do more than promote agreement over substantive issues. It must also set a style of government that wins loyalty and evokes confidence. It must act so that the connections between its activities and the myths and values embedded in the constitution are clearly and effectively demonstrated in symbolic and practical fashions. Thus, in the United States, liberty and the rule of law are effectively symbolized and their role as an important element of our fundamental convictions strengthened by the continual activity of the Supreme Court. The central principle of the British Constitution—that of responsible leadership—receives renewed strength from the workings of the British cabinet system. Both governments profit, in loyal political support, from the fact that the institutions of government continually reaffirm in their practical operation the deeply held convictions of people about how their governments should operate.

PART II. CONSTITUTIONS: FORMS AND EVOLUTION

To illustrate some of these principles actively at work, we turn now to a genetic and comparative study of constitutions. For this purpose, we have singled out three forms, or styles, of constitutions: the "monarchic," the "oligarchic" (or "oligarchic-pluralistic") and the "democratic." At the outset, we should make two points clearly: that these are types rather than individual cases; and that each represents a typical pattern of practice and of evolution rather than the experience in any one country or under any one constitutional system. Nor are these the only types of constitutionalism that man has known. We are attempting to discuss the *rationale* of constitutional development, employing the history of many constitutions, rather than presenting the history of one country, or a continuous constitutional history of several countries.

Also, our concern is not with monarchy, oligarchy, and democracy as such, but with the particular political ideals and institutional problems peculiar to constitutionalism under Henry VIII or Louis XIV, for example, or to an age of aristocracy prior to the development of wide public opinion, national political parties, and the other accoutrements of democracy. Constitutional ideals of monarchy were stated coherently and articulately by men like Sir John Fortescue and Richard Hooker[14] in England and Jean Bodin in France. With respect to oligarchic constitutionalism, Locke, Burke, and Hume, Montesquieu and de Maistre[15] serve as examples. Bentham and James Mill, or *The Federalist* suggest the rationale of democratic constitutionalism. What these men said is an excellent clue to the historic problems of constitutionalism; but even more we are interested in the practice that lay behind, or was the referent of their political theories about constitutions, rights, the true conception of monarchy or political community, and the like. Professor Herman Finer has described a constitution as "the autobiography of a power relationship,"[16] representing both functioning reality today and the genesis and evolution of many historic techniques for the taming of power or the organization of purposes. By describing constitutionalism in a "biographical" fashion, we are searching for an understanding of the problem of constitutionalism in depth and in perspective. The particular typology employed we have chosen for its usefulness in illuminating and suggesting explanations of the dynamics of constitutionalism.

THE MONARCHIC CONSTITUTION

The Ideals and Practices of the Monarchic Constitution

The essence of the monarchic constitution lies in an attempted reconciliation of two aims or principles. One of these aims is that of preserving traditional liberties and franchises, made familiar in medieval history by the struggles of church and state, town and ruler, baron and king. The other

---

[14] See, for example, Sir John Fortescue, *The Governance of England*, and *De Laudibus Legum Angliae*, written during the War of the Roses. Richard Hooker's *Laws of Ecclesiastical Polity* appeared in 1594; Bodin's *Six Books of the Republic* in 1576.

[15] John Locke, *Second Treatise of Civil Government* (1690); David Hume, *Essays, Moral and Political*, (1742-1752); Baron de Montesquieu, *The Spirit of the Laws* (1748); Edmund Burke, especially *Reform of Representation in the House of Commons* (1782); "Letter to the Bristol Constituency" (1774-5); *Appeal from the New to the Old Whigs* (1791); and *Reflections on the Revolution in France* (1790); Joseph de Maistre, *Essays on the Generative Principles of Political Constitutions* (1809).

[16] Herman Finer, *The Theory and Practice of Modern Government* (New York: Holt, 1949), p. 116.

aim springs from an opposite, or at least frequently opposing, need for a powerful, efficient executive head of state with capacity and disposition to protect the interests of the realm. In other words, monarchic constitutionalism was partly constitutionalism as we have defined that term: that is, it was associated with observance of customary restraints, settled and legitimate procedure, and the "rule of law."

The basic ideal of the monarchic constitution was that of a fruitful compromise, or even better, organic union of these two principles of the preservation of traditional liberties and of an effectively and rationally constituted executive power acting for the public weal. The term "Gothic Constitution"[17] was often employed to give a name to the ideal of the monarchic constitution and the designation is useful for it suggests the antithesis of the modern European experience and that of ancient cities, such as Athens and Rome. The constitution of antiquity was one which sought to preserve equilibrium and shield liberties by a "balanced" constitution that protected one class from another through distribution of offices, collegial checks, and powers of veto. For the monarchic constitution, the ideal—slowly developed and instituted—is King-in-Parliament: a powerful crown, checked by vested interest, but incorporated with the estates and interests of the realm. Against the poverty of initiative, the centrifugal tendencies, the pluralist or "syndicalist" bent of the estates, the monarchy stands for unity, energy, and the permanent interests of the kingdom. The crown "takes counsel" and rules by "consent"—it is King-in-Parliament— but as opposed to mere privilege or the particular power structure of the day it is trustee for the welfare of the whole. To this day, traces of this conception of the monarchy can be seen in the degree to which British cabinet government lodges the responsibility for initiating change and for general leadership in the national interest in a powerful cabinet. Equally in character is the long continuance in Britain of corporative representation and the importance given there to the judge-made common law.

CROWN AND DYNASTY

Among the most fundamental and ancient of the principles of the monarchic constitution is the precept that the monarchy is more than a dynasty or a "house." This distinction of state and family, or dynasty, implied several central norms of political conduct. At the same time, it points to a number of the most primitive and basic problems of constitutionalism.

In three rather obvious ways, the state or the "crown" *was* a dynasty. Early territorial states were often made and even more frequently prominently associated with a successful royal house. Dynastic pride and personal loyalty provided early substitutes for later patriotism or nationalism. More-

[17] Francis D. Wormuth, *The Origins of Modern Constitutionalism* (New York: Harper, 1949), Pt. III.

over, the resources of the kingdom depended upon the successful house management of the crown lands: developing them through wise administration and harvesting their revenues for the private use of the king and his retinue as well as for purposes of state. Also, the politics of early dynasties was in considerable measure familistic—wars were fought over and states cemented by marriage; offices of state and kingdoms were hereditable and often divided, in fact, among sons; and in large measure ties of kinship or blood substituted for more rational bonds of loyalty or principles of organization in bureaucracy, industry, and politics.

One line that constitutional development took was the insistence that the crown or "realm" was not a mere patrimony[18] to be used for the personal profit of the monarchy or at the behest of purely dynastic politics. The demand that the king conduct at least part of his affairs not as a private owner but as the trustee of a public fisc was a central constitutional principle.[19] By implication, the whole realm also, and not merely its revenues, was conceived by constitutionalists as a fiduciary trust for public purposes. Thus, Bodin's *Six Books of the Republic,* insisted that the King could not alienate the kingdom, nor make its offices and essential institutions his own patrimony.[20]

Another form taken by the attempt to constitutionalize the dynastic state was the encouragement of a permanent, competent bureaucracy. Bureaucracy was—and is—in two important ways a constitutional device of the first rank. In the first place, a professionalized public service provides a counterweight to the dynastic politics of personalities, informal authority, and intrigue. Secondly, professionalization of the public service also entails the creation of formal, public institutions, and identifiable agents with definite responsibilities. As a consequence, professionalization opens a path for the enforcement of collegiate and procedural checks upon the executive. The council government and the departments of the Tudors were the predecessors of later ministerial responsibility.[21]

THE INTEREST OF THE WHOLE AND THE PUBLIC

The state or the crown was not a family; neither was it "society": the monarchy stood for and sought to secure a *public* order and political *unity*. Rooted in society, it yet stood above it. This norm was translated into effective constitutional precepts in several ways.

[18] For an account of early applications of this doctrine see Peter N. Riesenberg, *The Inalienability of Sovereignty in Medieval Political Thought* (New York: Columbia U. P., 1955).

[19] A similar controversy is going on today in some of the oil sheikdoms of the Near and Middle East. Cf. also Russia under the Czars and the Balkan kingdoms of the nineteenth century.

[20] Bodin, *op. cit.*

[21] G. R. Elton, *The Tudor Revolution in Government* (Cambridge, Eng.: The University Press, 1953), Ch. 7.

The crown was not a "respecter of persons." That is, monarchy secured an equitable administration of the laws. Crown courts offered justice to the liegeman or the burgher when he could not get it from his lord. And the good monarch saw to it that the path to justice was not blocked by barons. Thus, in his ideal of French monarchy sketched in the sixteenth century, Jean Bodin states as a fundamental constitutional principle that the king cannot close his heart to justice or refuse jurisdiction to appeals. At a later date, Star Chamber proceeding of the Stuart monarchy were defended (speciously, it should be added) because of the need to enforce justice in cases involving notables of the realm who could intimidate or evade the regular common law courts.[22] Modern parallels that suggest somewhat opposing commentaries on this tendency are the administrative courts and boards that have sprouted so vigorously in recent years and the steady expansion of the jurisdiction of central courts in cases involving racial equality, on the other hand.

The slogan, "Better one tyrant than ten thousand," illustrates a second way in which the monarchy was exalted above society. Coordinative power was almost the *raison d'être* for the growth of monarchy. To crush faction and to balance classes were goals dictating the principle that a monarch not meekly allow social power to seek its own level, but that he shape and make political combinations in the public interest.

PROTECTOR OF LIBERTIES

The contrasts of monarchy and dynastic principles on the one hand, and monarchy and the existing power structure, on the other, describe in ideal conception what the monarchy was not. Positively, the aim of a true monarchy was the extension and protection of the liberties and franchises of the kingdom. To that end, the king exercised a general and untrammeled power of police to preserve and to promote the peace and enforce the law. He granted, enfranchised, and constituted. Just as fundamentally, however, the monarch was himself to respect the inheritance of free institutions—that is to say, of an earlier form of constitutionalism.

In giving effect to this conception of the monarchy as keeper of liberties, Roman and medieval jurists, as Professor McIlwain has shown,[23] developed and applied a jurisprudence that contains much of what we later recognize under the categorical headings of "vested right," "rule of law," and constitutional law. The permanent, continuous head of state was the king, together with his officials. As such, he governed; and his administrative acts were beyond question. Assizes, *constitutiones*, and *leges*, which established principles of administrative management, formalized customary practices, and

---

[22] Sir David Lindsay Keir, *The Constitutional History of Modern Britain, 1485-1937*, 3d. ed. (London: Black, 1947), pp. 162-171.

[23] C. H. McIlwain, *Constitutionalism: Ancient and Modern* (Ithaca, N.Y.: Cornell U. P., 1947).

gave effect to royal will through ordinance, were all acknowledged to be matters of prerogative. This general area of authority was *gubernaculum*— government or administration as we would recognize it today. But what were the liberties that the king was to protect? None other than those long since granted, whether in the form of ancient custom, the common law of the realm, or statute law, which partook of the character of a common engagement or contract. Their nature and extent is a matter of *jurisdictio*— the authority to declare the law. And lawyers or courts, not kings, properly should determine the law. Thus, the king was in principle, and in some instances actually, limited by the sum of private-law liberties of his subjects, by the fundamental law of the realm, and by the courts or *parlements* as corporate bodies.

THE CROWN AND THE REALM

It is a short step from the conception of a king as protector of liberties to that of the crown as an immortal unity of King and the Realm—its liberties and constitution, the national heritage, and the permanent welfare of the populus. The conceptions through which and the institutions by which this unity was expressed were, of course, all important. A common symbol in Europe was that of a shepherd, or "father of the country." In Japan, the royal house was conceived as the head of a racial empire. Exalting a racial community or patriarchal authority does not lead readily to the development of precise or effective constitutional devices. But this community of king and realm could be conceived differently—in terms of corporate entities comprehended within a juridical constitution that *was* in fact the commonwealth. Even the despotic Henry VIII acknowledged that "We at no time stand so high in our estate royal as in the time of Parliament; when we as head and you as members are conjoined and knit into one body politic." The next step toward modern constitutionalism from this point is the recognition that not king alone, but only king-in-parliament is sovereign. And this implies the sovereignty of a constitutional frame rather than the sole supremacy of any person or body.

CONCLUSION

One point that should not be missed, however, is the nature of the controls exerted upon monarchy. Although some external limitations upon governmental power were occasionally recognized, by and large the rationale of the monarchical constitution was activity in the general interest. Thus, the effective restraints upon monarchy were for the most part those of the variety termed by Professor Loewenstein "intra-organ controls."[24] That is, governmental power was channelled and regularized rather than limited.

[24] Karl Loewenstein, *Political Power and the Governmental Process* (Chicago: Univ. of Chicago Press, 1957), pp. 164-166.

And the significant constitutional devices were councils, professionalization of service, formalization and rationalization of the structure of the crown itself. Generally, external checks were informal, irregular in operation, and of an extraconstitutional nature.

Deficiencies of the Monarchic Constitution

The most striking deficiency of the monarchic constitution was the lack of effective techniques and sanctions to give practical substance to those very ideals of government that monarchy was presumed to advance. Usually, in the absence of definite sanctions and true constitutional restraints, the material and ideal incentives that energized the monarchy proved too diffuse and too weak to provide effective channels or boundaries, and even directly inclined the politics of monarchy into unconstitutional paths.

A PERSONAL REGIME

Monarchy failed, in practice, to transcend its dynastic foundations; and the nature of dynasty could not in the long run be reconciled with constitutionalism. Ultimately, constitutionalism implies government according to principle and recognition of the authority of the laws. It is in essence rule by legitimate, constituted power and according to formal requisites of action. A dynasty may be legitimate; yet its mode of operation is through personal ties and loyalties rather than by the canons of legal accountability. Within the political "machine" of a monarchy, the closer the ties of personal loyalty and mutual interest, the more solid the government. Note in this respect Meiji Japan in which the concept of personal loyalty and responsibility permeated monarchy, parliament and parties, army and civil service, and the bulk of industry. The Imperial German Army, which swore an oath of personal loyalty to the Emperor and which remained to the last an impassible barrier to constitutionalism, provides a second example. But such personal ties and "family relations" in government are, in the perspectives of early attempts at constitutionalism, the essence of irresponsible government. Powerful monarchs could often break free from close dependence upon particular persons and factions. Rather like a weak President in American politics, however, when the other bases of a monarch's power are weak he, perforce, must give hostages to the notables of the realm and local tyrants. With the growth of alternate foundations of political organization —the national community and skilled, literate elites—monarchical government becomes increasingly anachronistic.

PREROGATIVE AND THE RULE OF LAW

There was, furthermore, an inherent antagonism between *gubernaculum* and *jurisdictio* that proved in practice to be irreconcilable. Monarchy became great by expansion: through extending the king's peace, by fostering enterprise and patronizing new estates, and by increasing the national territory, the nation's power, and its trade. Prerogative and dispensing power were the necessary tools of monarchical policy in searching out and developing new sources of revenue and breaking old custom to make way for the needs of the present. Inevitably, prerogative power and extra-constitutional devices of government encroached heavily upon inherited liberties and a traditional frame of government. Thus, in France the Estates-General were abolished early in the seventeenth century, not to appear again until 1789. Parliament survived in England, though just barely and at times not at all effectively. Even Elizabeth dismissed Parliaments summarily and neglected to summon them. On occasion she resorted to locking the members in until the Parliament could reach a decision she favored. The private law of traditional liberties was directly invaded. The development of a separate administrative law and the use of special prerogative courts to flout the restraints of common lawyers was a standby of royal practice both in England and on the continent from the sixteenth century onward.[25] In England, constitutional evolution returned eventually to its accustomed historic channels. In Europe an age of absolutism left a deep mark.

ABSENCE OF EFFECTIVE AND LEGITIMATE RESTRAINTS

For two immediate reasons, attempts to enforce a constitutional discipline upon the monarch failed. First, and probably most importantly, they failed because at best they interrupted government or seriously impaired its efficiency. At the worst, the struggle for constitutionalism might destroy the central government itself. Impeachment, for example, was a clumsy weapon, equivalent to shooting the staff of an army divisional commander in order to improve his sense of tactics or to relax a galling discipline. The power to refuse supply was, by and large, of small efficacy, except in the context of already firm constitutional principle. A second reason for the failure to develop constitutional restraints was the fact that so commonly the techniques devised stood on no better footing of precedent or constitutional principle than the king's own lawless acts. Revolts of notables and novel claims on the part of parliaments were, as Locke was aware, an "appeal to heaven," since the mode of remedy was as unconstitutional as was the abuse. What was lacking, practically, were effective and *legitimate* techniques for the restraint of governmental power that could serve repeatedly to resolve the successive and often radically new constitutional problems that arose.

NEW IDEOLOGIES

The character of the "mythic" foundations upon which the monarchic constitution rested accounts not only for some of its signal weaknesses but also for many of the bitter ideological disputes that arose under monarchy.

[25] For accounts of such practices see Keir, *op. cit.*, and Brissaud, *op. cit.*

Montesquieu states the principle of monarchy to be that of "honor." He would have been closer to the mark had he also said "awe," "prestige," and "dignity." For monarchy rests upon authority that is necessarily less than fully rational, that is traditional, and that is supported by mystery, distance, and sanctity. Consequently, the "mythic" props of monarchy are all-important.[26] The appearance of both protestant sects and state-dominated Catholic churches often led to an alliance of crown and altar. Even so, more rationalistic and individualistic religions, such as Calvinism, became immediately a challenge to order and monarchic rule as well as defenders, *malgré lui,* of the freedom of worship. But the conflict was one, potentially, of much wider scope, since rival ideologies, or even free opinion, are generally dangerous enemies of the monarchic principle and beget censorship, mystification, and counter-propaganda in turn. The clash of nationalism and legitimacy in Europe of the nineteenth century and the beginning of an "Age of Ideology" inevitably signified the decadence and final collapse of monarchy.

Conclusion

Though monarchy proved itself immeasurably more effective as a technique for developing power on a large scale than the anarchic state of affairs which it succeeded and sought to remedy, in fact kingship was a poor device, in the long run, for engaging the loyalties of awakened nations. Instability and weakness of policy were chronic features. The unpredictable mob and mercurial coalitions of factions made resolute and settled purpose exceedingly difficult to translate into political reality. Lacking strength, monarchic government also tended to surrender to the ten thousand tyrants; for example, to strengthen landlord control in the countryside, to use one nationality to keep another one in captivity, or to support the economic interests of the great magnates of industry. Also the survival power of monarchies was poor in a world of competitive states and awakened nationalism, as the French Revolution and Napoleon showed. From the beginning of the nineteenth century, and even earlier in some countries such as Britain, the choices for monarchs were narrowing to two: to accept weakness and therefore a constitutional monarchy; or to devise some swindle like the policy of "divide and rule" or a form of demagogic monarchy.[27]

However, it would be a mistake to conclude that the *Weltgeist* of democratic constitutionalism has obliterated the past. The monarchic constitution has left its deep mark upon modern states. The centralized government and

[26] The nature and rationale of some of these props is suggested by W. H. Greenleaf, "James I and the Divine Right of Kings," *Political Studies*, Vol. 5 (1957), pp. 36-48.

[27] Cf. Robert A. Kann, *The Multi-National Empire: Nationalism and National Reform in the Hapsburg Monarchy, 1848-1918*, 2 Vols. (New York: Columbia U. P., 1950), Vol. 2, esp. Chs. 15-19.

unified cabinet leadership of Britain is one example. Another is the survival of the stiff backbone of authority and power that is the support of many European polities: code law and administrative courts, ministries of the interior and powerful prefects, bureaucratized judiciaries and educational *corps*.

THE OLIGARCHIC CONSTITUTION

General

In nation-states or territorially extensive polities, as opposed to city-states, the type of constitution that has generally succeeded to the monarchic one or has represented an alternate to it is oligarchic and pluralist in character. The distinctive feature of this constitution is the restraint of the executive and of parliament, both by distribution of power and by setting power to check power. James Harrington, Baron Montesquieu, the Whig Party of eighteenth century England, and James Madison come readily to mind as illustrations of its underlying conceptions and strategies. Absolute legal sovereignty rests in no one body; and political power is widely distributed: hence we call it pluralist. At the same time, the term "oligarchic" is employed to describe such a constitution because, in fact, much that is significant about its operation and essential spirit depends upon the absence of a general political community and the freely adjustive mechanisms of democratic politics, such as political parties, popular devices of representation, and a genuine "marketplace of ideas." In other words, it was a constitution in which government was checked—fairly effectively and regularly checked in this instance, as opposed to monarchic government—by an oligarchic power structure or elite that was not made dependent in turn upon a sovereign public opinion.

Antecedents of the oligarchic constitution are to be found both in the Roman Republic and in medieval Europe. However, the genetic relation between the example of Rome or medieval Europe and more modern developments is a broken one. The rationale of the oligarchic constitution of recent times lies in the constitutional problems that arose under monarchy and in the political issues of the eighteenth and nineteenth centuries. We have noted that the central fault of monarchy from a constitutional point of view was the absence of effective, legitimate restraints upon the king and his governmental "machine." The oligarchic constitution, through separation of powers and similar devices supplied at least a partial remedy for this defect. The monarch's fiscal techniques and his foreign policies, as well as the role that the institution of monarchy itself played in domestic competition of classes would of themselves have been factors providing sufficient incentive for several classes of the population to stimulate attempts at more effective constitutionalizing of power.

The eighteenth and nineteenth centuries were times, also, in which the issue of political liberty was becoming prominent. Inasmuch as political power was not democratically based, one device for protecting political liberty was through distribution of power and external checks upon government. Unable, in Rousseau's language, to obey oneself alone because obeying only the self writ large in a *moi-commun,* one might take an alternate route to freedom (and one that held out much better hopes for some political liberty), to obey government very little, that is to say, to keep the demands of government to a minimum.

Another factor of importance in providing a rationale for the oligarchic constitution was the unsettled question of the locus of decisive power. For the most part, constitutions of the oligarchic type succeeded a constitutional settlement, either tacit or explicit, of important proportions—such as the Settlement of 1689, or the July Revolution of 1830 in France. Commonly, a number of hotly disputed institutions and practices received constitutional sanction: typically such things as regulation of the succession to the throne, the recognition of some civil and political liberties, and the privileges of parliamentary bodies. But the accommodation between monarchy and the nation remained still, in large measure, indeterminate. Consequently, much of the business of government was settled not according to principle, party politics, or constitutional provision, but by a tug-of-war between monarch and notables, the "establishment" and the "country." In summary, the oligarchic constitution, while effective to varying extents in protecting liberty, remained something of a half-way point in the evolution from the monarchic to the democratic constitution.

Techniques and Provisions of the Oligarchic-Pluralist Constitution

How close in spirit the oligarchic constitution was to an antecedent medieval or feudal experience is revealed by the fact that almost invariably the early growth of such constitutions took predominantly the form of attempts to give an explicit and definite cast to ancient liberties, and to secure the autonomy or constitutional status of various branches of government. It was quite usual, for example, to establish the formal structure of representation by simply giving formal constitutional recognition to older estates and granting representation in accordance with estate membership. Such was the case with the Swedish Constitution of 1809 and the Prussian Constitution prior to 1848. At one stage higher up in the evolutionary scale, tax-paying or property qualifications for the exercise of the suffrage translated the principle of caste into a monetary formula, for example, the Prussian three-tiered electorate under the Empire. Without as yet very much articulated theory of government behind them, a series of Petitions, Bills of Right, and sanctions were wrung from or granted by monarchs giving at least a documentary statement and formal recognition to the historic rights of particular provinces, to common law rights such as Habeas Corpus, and to traditional procedures of government like those of petition and redress of grievance. Acts of succession, regulating the hereditary descent of the throne, were common. Some of the constitutions of the nineteenth century would have been scarcely distinguishable in spirit and even in form from the charters of medieval times. For example, the Austrian Pragmatic Sanction of 1711, which was granted as a constitution, recognized the privileges of Hungary, settled the succession, and proclaimed the indivisibility of the Hapsburg realm.[28] Often there was no definite document that could be called a constitution, but only a series of acts establishing certain principles and boundaries of government. Frequently, in theory at least, constitutions were still recognized as acts of royal authority, having no true constitutional status in our modern sense of the concept. Thus, the *Charte Constitutionelle* of Louis XVIII (1814) reads:

> . . . although all authority in France resides in the person of the King, our predecessors have not hesitated to alter the exercise thereof in accordance with the change of times . . . that only the supreme authority can give to institutions which it establishes the strength, permanence, and majesty with which it is itself invested; . . .[29]

However, important differences marked the constitutional efforts from 1689 onward as a new tendency. One such difference was the attempt to settle more definitely a permanent or self-equilibrating frame of government, either through applications of some theory of separation of powers, or by explicitly describing the governmental structure in a constitutional charter. Another point of departure from traditional constitutional notions was the attempt to protect novel freedoms that differed sharply from the older concept of liberties and franchises. In many instances the line between the new and the old was blurred, as in the concept of "property." But grants of and protection for freedom of the press and opinion mark a new era.

SEPARATION OF POWERS

If the central idea of constitutionalism under the older monarchy was that of the King-in-Parliament, the leading notion of the oligarchic constitution was that of Separation of Powers. Americans are accustomed to think of separation of powers as a rather special American institution. But its use was quite common, in fact virtually universal in different forms and varying times and places during the eighteenth and nineteenth centuries in Europe.

[28] A. J. P. Taylor, *The Hapsburg Monarchy 1815-1918* (London: Macmillan, 1942), pp. 7 ff.
[29] Quoted in Carl J. Friedrich, *Constitutional Government and Democracy*, rev. ed. (Boston: Ginn, 1950), p. 180.

Furthermore, the concept has had a lengthy modern history beginning in Tudor days in England, finding expression in a series of revolutionary constitutions both in England and France, and a prominent place in the writings of a host of political theorists in addition to the "celebrated Montesquieu" and John Locke, such as David Hume, Benjamin Constant, Immanual Kant, and liberals of various stamps in Austria, Russia, and South America.

CHECKS AND BALANCES

Separation of powers can be considered both from the standpoint of its techniques and from that of its aim or purposes. As a device of government, the strategy contemplated in separation of powers was that of setting one organ of government to check the others or to restrain their tendencies toward aggrandizement. For separation of powers to have meaning, the activities of government must have first been sorted out into fairly definite departments. The most obvious distinction was that between legislature and executive. Locke further distinguished domestic executive power from the control of foreign affairs, which he called the "federative" power.[30] It was Montesquieu who shifted to what became the standard classification of legislature, executive, and judicial powers and insisted that each should be committed to separate and mutually independent sets of officials.[31] For separation of powers to achieve its objective it must not be complete; the various powers of government must check each other, and the "checks and balances" applied must operate effectively. This necessity entails the employment of instrumentalities with real coercive power, such as impeachment, the veto, or the power of the purse. The confusion of powers and diffusion of responsibility that characterized monarchy together with the great array of powers that the king could potentially use in his various capacities of protector of religion, first civil servant of the realm, disburser of moneys and patronage, and fount of honor and justice, make the significance of separation of powers rather obvious.

The central purpose of separation of powers is that of securing liberty by preventing the concentration of power and by restraining its arbitrary employment. Two primary subsidiary goals or techniques are involved. One of these, which Montesquieu describes as "political liberty"—as opposed to individual liberty ("liberty in relation to the subject")—is secured by devising a self-equilibrating structure of government.[32] To preserve "political liberty," several things are necessary. First, the autonomy of the separate agencies of government must be insured through, for instance, protecting

[30] John Locke, *Two Treatises of Civil Government*, Everyman Ed. (London: Dent, 1937), Bk. II, Ch. 12.

[31] Montesquieu, *Spirit of the Laws, op. cit.*, esp. Bk. XI.

[32] Montesquieu, *op. cit.*, esp. Bk. XI. Strictly speaking, Montesquieu writes of "Political Liberty with Regard to the Constitution," and "Political Liberty in Relation to the Subject."

the independence of the judiciary or the privileges of parliament. Secondly, devices must be found to prevent dominance of one branch by another through covert techniques. The provision in the American constitution prohibiting a representative from accepting any position of profit or honor in the executive stems originally from memories of blandishments used by monarchs to corrupt the membership of legislative bodies. Exclusion of members of the civil service from membership in parliament is a similar device common in European constitutions. Each power of government, moreover, must be given an "independent will," *i.e.*, must be able to enforce its will through either subsidiary powers or its own agents. Legislative powers of investigation or impeachment, the courts' use of marshals or powers of citation for contempt, and civil service immunity from "colonization" by political partisans or the legislature itself are all instances of this constitutional objective. The self-equilibrating constitution is completed by the addition of "checks and balances" as we have already noted.

"MODERATION"

Separation of powers also protected liberty by securing a certain *spirit of government*. Montesquieu has it that such a government is "moderate." For Locke, the corresponding term might have been "reasonable." Moderation is putatively achieved in several ways through the separation of powers. Most directly, separation of powers and "checks and balances," by forcing the various powers to explain themselves and articulate their case to secure cooperation of the other agencies of government, acts as a powerful stimulus to moderation and reasonableness of policy. Furthermore, since functions of policy making are distributed amongst the various powers, any comprehensive undertaking must be in considerable measure a joint product. But above all, only through *facilité*, tact, and endless negotiation could such a constitution work at all. Thus, Burke's insistence upon "circumstances," prudence, and adjustment. So prominent was this aspect of the oligarchic constitution that deMaistre, another worthy advocate of conservatism, insisted that a written constitution of principles and abstract provisions could never work.

"PLURALISTIC" CHECKS

Without more to support it than the principle and practice of separation of powers, the oligarchic constitution would have had no vitality whatsoever. Basically, a vertical and pluralistic distribution of power was needed to supplement the check of one organ of government by another. Monarchs could be deposed and beheaded, but in the regular course of politics, the royal "machine" could always best the other powers of government unless they had firm political support and were also backed up by independent loci of power. One technique used to promote a measure of pluralism was to limit the governments capacities for manufacturing consent. Thus, while such constitutional provisions as separation of church and state, freedom of the press, and jury trial were independently regarded as desirable, they also contributed to curbing the "regimist" tendencies of an administration that included in its entourage judge, bishop, and civil servant.[33] Extensive devolution of power was also a matter of constitutional provision or an accepted accommodation between court and country in the era of oligarchic constitutionalism. Federalism, as proposed by Montesquieu and Rousseau and practiced in Switzerland and the United States, was on the whole regarded as good medicine for the infirmities of republican governments. But under monarchy as well it was commonly recognized that large kingdoms were desirable because they promoted a considerable measure of social pluralism and this in turn encouraged moderate governments. In any event, a truce and even a kind of fairly amicable "agreement to differ" in some instances between the country party in the provinces and gentry control locally and the court party and the Establishment or monarchical "machine" at the center was realized both by the acceptance of the legitimacy of competition for power within representative bodies and by new charters of local and regional government.[34] Furthermore, the constituting of representative bodies or their more explicit recognition and the establishment of electoral systems, corrupt and oligarchic though they frequently were, afforded play to new sources of influence. These same acts were also an acknowledgement that the power of the state was divided and that both executive and parliament must work the government within the constitution.

THE AIM: LIBERTY

This account of the oligarchic constitution, however, has the words that go to describe the structure, without the tune that conveys, finally, why anyone cared about it. The goal of the oligarchic constitution of the eighteenth and nineteenth centuries, in the minds of its apologists certainly, and even from the perspective of many of the more practically minded men that tried to make it work, was to foster liberty. The Revolutionary Assembly of 1789, Abbe Siéyès, the country party of England and many of England's Tories as well, Immanuel Kant and the Frankfurt Assembly of 1848, ex-

---

[33] Cf. David Hume, *Essays, Moral and Political,* particularly "Liberty of the Press," "Independence of Parliament," and "Civil Liberty." Consider also Chateaubriand: [In each province] "a bishop, a commanding officer, a prefect, a public prosecutor, a president of a court of martial law, a commander of police, and a commander of the national guard: let these seven men be for God and the King, and I answer for the rest." Quoted in T. Zeldin, *The Political System of Napoleon III* (New York: Macmillan, 1958), p. 8.

[34] See esp. Sir Lewis B. Namier's two great studies, *England in the Age of the American Revolution* (London: Macmillan, 1933); and *The Structure of Politics at the Accession of George III* (London: Macmillan, 1929).

pressed a mounting desire for free expression, for individual dignity, and a demand that arbitrary and degrading uses of autocratic power be banished from political society. It is true that much of the liberty actually defended was the ancient privileges of landlords and notables. But these were also times in which liberty was coming to mean less and less a franchise or a privilege, more and more a common immunity or general claim for freedom. Freedom of speech and the press, rights of association and free movement proclaimed initially in revolutionary charters survived and were recognized or tolerated, many of them, even under such reactionary documents as the *Charte Constitutionelle* of 1814 and by such arch-conservatives as Metternich.[35]

Defects of the Oligarchic Constitution

On the whole the oligarchic constitution served well and to the benefit of the entire nation only in England. That it did serve England well, despite rampant corruption and the extremely narrow franchise, seems beyond question. Elsewhere, it proved a temporary expedient and, on occasion, produced results directly contrary to what was intended. There were four critical defects, related largely to the growth of democracy, that made the oligarchic constitution ill-fitted to survive, especially in Europe. First, the constitution was called upon to function in the absence of a true political community (the existence of which was tacitly assumed by Montesquieu), with the result that it lacked the sources of vitality and support that democratic politics contributes. Secondly, the oligarchic constitution, depending in its operation upon *finesse,* and the arts of subtle maneuver, lacked the adjustive powers to handle big problems or awkward situations of crisis. Further, for a number of reasons, the oligarchic constitution was anti-progressive and did not respond readily to new imperatives or even to sustained currents of change in society. Lastly, the oligarchic constitution, grounded neither upon ancient heredity nor sprung from democracy, lacked the appeals that would give it legitimacy. Basically, these were the decisive factors that spelled the undoing of this unstable and transitory constitutional type. But this skeletal summary needs illustration from the actual dynamics of the politics of oligarchy.

A DIVIDED COMMUNITY

Though England was, partially, an exception to this generalization, the oligarchic constitution rested upon a divided political community. In the first place, and this was equally true for England despite Edmund Burke's splendid rhetoric, the government depended upon passive acquiescence

[35] Guido de Ruggiero, *A History of European Liberalism,* trans. by R. G. Collingwood, (Boston: Beacon, 1959).

rather than active allegiance.[36] Even Burke tacitly acknowledged this fact when he declared the constitution to be "but a clause in the great primeval contract of eternal society." In effect, he was saying that prejudice, deference, and lack of civil courage—in short, the absence of loyalty to common, rational, constitutional principles—formed the base of contemporary politics. Elsewhere—in France, Germany, Austria and Russia—the absence of a true political community was much more obvious. The "corporative" basis of the constitution was not accepted as legitimate partly because peasant was already at war with landlord or workman with capitalist, but even more because representation by estate or status flew in the face of awakened and expanding notions of a more comprehensive and equalitarian political community: patriotism and citizenship, nationalism, the notions of democracy, or the liberal conceptions of free cultural expression. The critical and disastrous consequence was that the oligarchic constitution lacked defenders: it represented a liberalism too tainted by privilege to win the loyalties of the Paris workingmen of 1848-51, to join with the explosively developing nationalism of the Austro-Hungarian Empire, or to persuade peasant, proletarian, and soldier of the value of constitutionalism in the modern era of social revolution. In fact, the oligarchic constitution was not even proof against reactionary monarchs since many a peasant, worker, or shopkeeper would, like the helots of Sparta, gladly have eaten the gentry and masters alive and rejoiced when they were roughly handled by Czar or Emperor.

CORRUPTION AND NARROW POLITICAL INTERESTS

The oligarchic constitution, though contributing much of the essential mechanisms of constitutionalism to European practice, was not a good technique for imparting lessons in the value of political scruples or constitutional niceties. In some instances, it gravely debauched public morals. True, "politique" and "finesse" were at a premium; but they were put to immoral purposes. The electorate was small, narrowly recruited, and composed of "people who knew what government was," i.e., disposed to do well for themselves by means of their valuable franchise. Seats in parliament went to faithful followers of great notables or political bosses, or to members of crooked rings, interested in schemes of plunder. Governments assiduously "worked the elections" by fraud, intimidation, and corruption. The franchise and political power were capital to be invested and traded and especially to be used for personal gain. Constitutionalism of this sort gave something of an edge to the fear of corruption and "faction" that dominated the thinking of the American Constitutional Convention. Lamentably, it also gave much point to the refusal of European socialists to have their heads broken for liberty, or to take sides, for example, in a war between the

---

[36] Cf. David Hume, op. cit., "On Passive Obedience."

corrupt politics of the French Assembly dominated by Guizot and his manipulators and the more demagogic corruption of Louis Bonaparte.[37]

Extensive corruption was not always the rule, particularly if it was not needed, or if the advocates of particular causes could not be brought off. Where corruption was not widespread, however, the interests pursued were still usually local or narrow and unrelated to broad and practical conceptions of the common political good. The oligarchic constitution represented a "politics of interest," in the main, whether that interest was financial, parochial, confessional, or that of a national or cultural minority. Deputies were frequently enjoined, even by constitutional provision, to remain independent of "politics" and to consider only the "national interest." In practice, they were responsive to narrow interests or to a handful of notables controlling their constituency. One defect of this "politics of interest" is that it may or may not coincide with the needs or objective requirements of constitutionalism.

Benjamin Constant's famous epigram that "To keep one's principles he must change his party frequently" illustrates the problem. Grand principles were seldom backed by real power; and particular interests and factions seldom coincided for long with a particular principle of liberty. Politics of interest could also provide, as in France, one of the strongest incitements to overthrow or transform the constitution in revolutionary fashion, whether in the form of monarchist and Bonapartist assaults upon "Liberalism," or even later radical attempts, such as that of Clemenceau, to re-establish virtue through a "pro-consular" dictatorship. Government that works for clienteles and through "fixers" is a standing invitation for a political conspiracy to seek the realization or the restoration of the nation "one and indivisible."

IMMOBILISM

Politics of interest meant frequently, too, *immobilisme* in policy and lack of political progress. The restricted franchise and particular, often personal, allegiances of the oligarchic constitution do not enforce change or insure that new demands are translated fairly into the currency of politics. Often the oligarchic constitution followed upon some historic struggle for the recognition of venerable liberties or crowned lengthy efforts to curb autocratic abuses. The politically powerful benefactors of such victories usually exploited the newly won ground and did not look to the future, or seek to press more novel claims in the behalf of other classes not yet politically effective. Indeed, had there been a will to extend the benefits of new freedoms widely, it would have been to little good purpose, for such generally was the power of the governmental machine, the official press, and

---

[37] Namier, *op. cit.;* D. W. Brogan, *The French Nation from Napoleon to Petain 1814-1940* (New York: Harper, 1957), esp. Chs. 1, 2. An interesting account of how elections were "worked" can be found in Sherman Kent, *Electoral Procedure under Louis Philippe* (New Haven, Conn.; Yale U. P., 1937).

the police and the prefects that no general election could have had any result but a triumph for a nationalist and monarchical standard. Consequently, maintenance of the balanced equilibrium of government depended upon a compact of mutual forbearance on the part of the Opposition and the Government—the one to refrain from demagogic tactics; the other not to press its heavy superiority in short-run tactical maneuvers. Even with the recognition of limited parliamentary democracy (as in England, France, Germany and Scandinavia during the latter parts of the eighteenth and the early part of the nineteenth centuries) the executive was still obliged to form an administration of all the parties in order to maintain a balance.[38] The parliamentary leaders, from their side, in the interest of the constitution, needed to refrain from partisan colonizing of the administration and to allow the vital administrative business of the state to be continued in large measure free from the menace of factional control of the bureaucracy. Cohesive cabinets united upon partisan principles were, of course, impossible; and ministries were often not parliamentary ministries at all but an "administrative cabinet" chosen from the civil service or from notables or military officers outside the parliament. The relation of this distribution of power to the politics of the day was that of both cause and effect. Since "parties" under the oligarchic constitution were generally either narrowly factional or extremist and grandly principled, "fusion of powers" and political control of the government through a responsible cabinet was hazardous at best, often disastrous. And since real power was excluded from the stakes of the political game, cabinets when they were drawn from parliament occupied themselves largely with skillful log-rolling and political patronage. Parliaments in turn were populated by stalwarts of the government, delegates of the gentry, representatives of the great interests, ideologues, glittering personages and great orators, and usually a small, sometimes saving, leaven of professional politicians. Programs or platforms require common principles and some force to energize politics. In the period before the general franchise and the advent of political parties, these were lacking.

AN UNSTABLE COMPROMISE

The structure of power under the oligarchic constitution was an unstable compromise, likely to revert into some form of monarchic rule at one extreme, factionalism or rule of mobs at the other. Influence ruled; and public opinion though often free was not politically effective, save in rare instances when solidly united. As one result, political unions often had a conspiratorial tinge: note, for example, the long shadow cast by the Carbonari in Italy, or the Masonic Lodge of Grand Orient in France, prior to the twentieth century. Mob appeals were common, often taking the form of Caesarism or distorted nationalism. Among groups excluded from political bargaining, violence and direct action commended themselves: syndical-

[38] Cf. David Hume, *op. cit.*, "The Coalition of Parties."

ism and peasant uprisings, assassination and pogroms. Since the range of politics was arbitrarily circumscribed and because the predominance of patronage and influence tended to favor the party in power, government had a decidedly "regimist" flavor. Majorities were relatively permanent; and it was not uncommon for one party or coalition to stay in power for a generation or more. They exploited the state until some new "cartel" or "union" was goaded into activity, usually posing a serious threat to the continued existence of the constitution itself. With rare exceptions, further-more, bureaucracy and dynasty proved too powerful for fragilely supported parliaments and constitutions. To this day, separation of powers has in Europe a bad name because it has meant executive immunity from parlia-mentary interference, not as is the case in the United States, independence of the representative houses. Communal divisions prevented libertarian groups and their spokesmen from concerting; and threats to the nation enhanced the prestige and power of the executive. The result, for the most part, was that informal cliques presided over by King or Emperor ran the government, named and controlled the cabinet. Parliament was the mouth-piece of a collection of pressure groups that could lobby for concessions from the executive and occasionally win a skirmish over some matter of principle, but could give no real substance or life to constitutional gov-ernment.

TOWARD THE DEMOCRATIC CONSTITUTION

In this relatively brief section we shall not attempt to treat the demo cratic constitution in as comprehensive a fashion as we have the monarchic and oligarchic ones. Rather, we shall restrict the discussion essentially to the relation of democracy and constitutional evolution: the rationale of democratic reforms in relation to the progress of constitutionalism; and the ways in which democracy supplies a corrective, in part at least, for the deficiencies of earlier constitutional attempts.

Common Ideals

The indispensible basis for the development of a democratic constitu-tion is the presence of a community of political ideals and loyalties that are broadly inclusive, egalitarian, and based upon a creed or set of principles sufficiently definite and well enough articulated to provide tough resistance to competing ideologies as well as to enjoin some duties unambiguously. Democratic constitutions may survive, for a time in the absence of such supports, but they are not made or permanently secured without them. At the moment, we shall leave aside some of the qualifications of these state-ments and concentrate on their explication.

Democratic constitutions mostly have been associated with or have come in the wake of great religious movements, profound national awakening, or a revolutionary upheaval that confirmed and legitimated new principles of government. One or more of these forces are usually instrumental in bringing about a sufficient identification of collective and individual interest to make possible a "general will": a structure of loyalties that will permit political decisions to be taken by the inclusive community freely resolving. When these various creeds are highly articulated and identified explicitly or at least strongly with particular institutions, traditions, or observances, they usually prove fairly powerful as constitutional forces and relatively impervious to competing ideologies.

A Contract

Rather naturally, democratic constitutionalism has been associated with the practice of written or formally adopted comprehensive charters of government and with the ideology of contract or covenant. This association is by no means essential. In fact, the need for a written constitution may reveal a diseased political community that must, perforce, disavow its past and make a clean break with familiar institutions. On the other hand, the written constitution and the ideology of covenant and later of contract are related in suggestive ways to problems that commonly occur in the process of evolution toward democratic constitutionalism. Covenant or contract, especially in an age of growing national consciousness and democracy, invests the constitution with a legitimacy that is a needed support in a period when there are competing claims to authority. *"Lex"*, says Bracton, "is a common engagement." That is, the basic law of the commonwealth is that which is consented to and which all undertake to fulfill, not arbitrary power or the decrees of a monarch. Those who covenant *elect:* they bind themselves freely and solemnly to walk in lawful paths. Note, in this respect, the political significance of the ancient Jewish notion of covenant and of this concept, through Puritanism, for constitutionalism in Geneva, Holland, England, and America. On the whole, the covenanters bind themselves only to a good and reasonable discipline. Covenant or contract stresses individualism, voluntarism and reason. Thus, Rainborough, the Leveller spokesman in the Putney Debates of 1647, associates these three values together almost in one breath. ". . . truly sir, I think it's clear, that every man that is to live under a government ought first by his own consent to put himself under that government; and I do think that the poorest man in England is not at all bound in a strict sense to that government that he hath not had a voice to put himself under . . ." And, a moment later: "I do think that the main cause why Almighty God gave men reason, it was that they should make use of that reason . . . and should improve it for that end and purpose that God gave it them."[39]

[39] From the Clarke Manuscripts, in *Puritanism and Liberty*, ed. A. S. P. Woodhouse, (London: Dent, 1938), pp. 53 and 55.

Poor BULL & his Burden — or the Political MURRAION !!!
"And the land stank — so num'rous was the fry"
— What will become of these Vermin, if the Bull should Rise — ? !!!!!!!!!!!!

The "marvelous symmetry" of the Whig constitution

The British Museum

Inclusiveness and General Principle

Since the democratic constitution derives much of its legitimacy from this emphasis on reasonableness and consent it follows that such a constitution also inherently tends toward inclusiveness and general principle. Montesquieu extolls moderation and *finesse*. Rousseau and Kant speak for the *volonté generale,* the "general class" and civil society, the universal moral law. What is at stake, fundamentally, is the consideration that only rational moral principle finally invests the democratic constitution with authority over the citizen.

At the immediate level of practical power struggles, the emphasis of democratic constitutionalism on principle or generality also has a twofold significance: as a technique of politics, and as a strategy of organization. One difficulty with the oligarchic constitution, to consider now the first of these points, was that a "politics of interest" provided no effective counterweight to monarchy. The solution of this difficulty, as Burke saw, required something besides a more ingenious constitution or more skillful electoral gymnastics; it called for rallying to some principle. Monarch *versus* faction was a struggle that could end only in victory for the king. Thus, his solution was that of collective responsibility of the cabinet and a union of factions into a party united on principle. A party, he said in his now famous definition, "is a body of men united for promoting by their joint endeavors the national interest upon some particular principle in which they are all agreed."[40] And despite his adherence to the constitutional ideology of the oligarchic Whig majority, he insisted also that Parliament ought not to be a "congress of ambassadors from different and hostile interests", but representatives guided by "the general good."[41] A politics of principle that can include but that also transcends a politics of interest is one way in which the democratic constitution generates power. Another is by emphasis upon formality of procedure and publicly known, accessible institutions and provisions of government. Thus, again, the emphasis upon *written* constitutions. The oligarchic constitution was a natural haven for aristocrats, notables, seasoned and prudent statesmen. To the middle class, yeomen, and peasants, such a constitution was an instrument of tyranny, both because it was not fixed and definite, and because it could be manipulated only by a narrow, specially skilled class. Obviously, the written constitution can defeat as well as promote accessibility and popularity of governmental institutions; but its tendency is to do the latter.

Electoral Reform

Other important practical tools for transforming oligarchic into democratic constitutions were the reform of electoral systems and the establishment of general suffrage. These tools, to be successfully used, presuppose the existence of a democratic community of ideals and considerable develop-

[40] "Thoughts on the Cause of Present Discontents" (1770), in *The Works of the Rt. Hon. Edmund Burke,* with a preface by F. W. Raffety (London: Oxford U. P., 1906), Vol. II, p. 82.
[41] "Speech to the Electors of Bristol," (1774), *ibid.,* Vol. II, p. 165.

ment in the arts and attitudes of citizenship. Adopted, as universal suffrage by Louis Bonaparte and Bismarck, in a community incapable of using it effectively, it becomes easily a prop to absolutism. But reform of the suffrage was in its theoretical and practical implications contributes those values which most essentially distinguish the democratic constitution from its predecessors. In no place, and at no time was this fact more classically illustrated than in the long struggle for the suffrage in nineteenth century England. No one, moreover, stated more sharply the political values and practices separating the democratic from the oligarchic constitution than the English Utilitarians, especially Jeremy Bentham and James Mill. For their emphasis was upon accountability to majority will rather than the moderation of the oligarchic constitution; upon an equal count instead of the ancient notions of gentry and corporations; upon formality, inclusiveness, and popularity of the institutions of government rather than obscurity and control by the external power structure of the community. For prudence they substituted education; for moderation and liberty, representation and accountability,—the right of the community, "the governed," to have a last say.[42] Bentham's formulations of the rationale of electoral reform were strident and doctrinaire. His emphasis marks though a decisive transition from oligarchic to democratic constitutionalism.

Democratic Liberty

Democratic constitutionalism is completed by a particular approach to the problem of liberty. Under oligarchy, liberty is protected by oligarchic and pluralist checks upon either the people or the monarch. Liberty exists when a balance is secured. But it exists at the price of factionalism and constitutional devices which pervert public policy and provide standing incitements for demagogues or autocrats. In addition, free expression of opinion not secure, even though it may exist, because it is still an accidental result of the rationale of the oligarchic constitution, not an essential principle of its working.

James Madison, in Number Ten of *The Federalist* suggested one direction a solution should take: liberty for factions to form and express themselves, but a liberty that operated within a constitution that could prevent any one faction from becoming too dominant. Thus, he argued that it was safe to entrust the constitution to the competive processes of politics only if the separate interests and factions were rendered "unable to concert." Bentham added another needed element. He argued that the only political force that could finally and decisively defeat the "sinister" faction was the majority. Opinion now rules. Thus, Bentham and James Mill insisted that

---

[42] See esp. James Mill's essay on "Government," in *Essays on Government, Jurisprudence, Liberty of the Press, and the Law of Nations*, ed. Philip Wheelwright (New York: Doubleday, 1935).

open bargaining for factional support and the "free marketplace of ideas," to use a familiar metaphor, were imperative for the new age.

Neither Bentham nor Madison was entirely right or entirely wrong. The age of opinion and of organized faction is upon us. It is also an age of the administrative state, of delegated powers, of many opinions. Free, fair, and inclusive competition of opinion is a serviceable doctrine. The "governed" must have the last say. But devices to make that "last say" a well-considered one, and to prevent the voice of faction from being taken as the voice of the sovereign *populus* are equally essential.

SELECTED READINGS

(Asterisk indicates book is available in paperback edition.)

BARKER, SIR ERNEST. *The Development of Public Services in Western Europe, 1660-1930*. London: Oxford U. P., 1944. This brief and highly readable account of development of "professional" civil and military officials is useful for the understanding that it shows of the relation between bureaucracy and constitutionalism.

BODIN, JEAN. Ed. M. J. Tooley. *Six Books of the Commonwealth*. Oxford, Eng.: Blackwell, 1955. Bodin is usually associated with the concept of sovereignty. He also expounded a mature theory of monarchical constitutionalism. The Tooley edition is a good abridgment.

BRISSAUD, JEAN. Trans. R. Howell. *A History of French Private Law*. Boston: Little, Brown, 1912. The title of this book is misleading—it deals mainly with the evolution of constitutional law. It is one of the few works on this subject readily available in English.

DE RUGGIERO, GUIDO. Trans. R. G. Collingwood. *A History of European Liberalism*. Boston: Beacon, 1959. A classic study of European liberal thought and liberal constitutionalism.

GOUGH, JOHN W. *Fundamental Law in English Constitutional History*. Oxford, Eng.: Clarendon, 1955. Gough shows particularly the importance of the concept of fundamental law and of the rule of law to the development of constitutionalism in England.

HAMILTON, ALEXANDER, JAY, JOHN and MADISON, JAMES. *The Federalist*. New York: Dutton, 1926. Though written largely to secure ratification for the American Constitution in New York, *The Federalist* remains today indispensible to an understanding of American constitutional theory.

*HUME, DAVID. eds. T. H. Green and T. H. Grose, *Essays: Moral, Political and Literary*, 2 vols. London: Longmans, 1875. Hume's essays on politics are particularly valuable for their deep insight into the principles of eighteenth century English constitutionalism.

KEIR, SIR DAVID LINDSAY. *The Constitutional History of Modern Britain, 1485-1937*. 3rd ed. London: Adam and Charles Black, 1947. A useful reference work for much of the period of English history discussed in this chapter, particularly because of numerous succinct and cogent discussions of governmental machinery and its relation to constitutional issues.

*LOCKE, JOHN. *The Second Treatise on Government.* New York: Liberal Arts, 1952, especially Book II. Locke foresaw and also provided one of the best justifications for the constitutional settlement which grew out of the Glorious Revolution of 1688. The work is useful also as an analysis of the constitutional principles that were operative in England during the eighteenth century.

McILWAIN, C. H. *Constitutionalism: Ancient and Modern.* Ithaca, N. Y.: Cornell U. P., 1947. The classic statement of the principles of the monarchical constitution, particularly for England.

MILL, JAMES. Ed. Philip Wheelwright. *Essays on Government, Jurisprudence, Liberty of the Press, and The Law of Nations.* New York: Doubleday, 1935. Mill especially defends the democratic principles of formality, inclusiveness, publicity and accountability. His essays are valuable for the simplicity and rigor with which these principles are stated and justified. A comparison of Mill's writings and *The Federalist* is instructive.

DE MONTESQUIEU, BARON. trans. Thomas Nugent. *The Spirit of the Laws.* New York: Hafner, 1949. The most important European work on "aristocratic" (oligarchic-pluralistic) constitutionalism. The Hafner edition contains an exceptionally good introduction by Franz Neuman.

NAMIER, LEWIS B. *England in the Age of the American Revolution.* London: Macmillan, 1930; and *The Structure of Politics at the Accession of George III,* 2nd ed., London: Macmillan, 1957. These two great classics document for England the movement from aristocratic politics toward a more popular politics. They are among the very few works that give a detailed account of the structure and development of politics at so early a date.

WORMUTH, FRANCIS D. *The Origins of Modern Constitutionalism.* New York: Harper, 1949. An interesting account of the constitutional struggles and political theories of the period of the Puritan Revolution in England. Useful for relating religious and political theories to particular constitutional issues.

CHAPTER 11

Democracy

Most Americans, often without giving the matter much thought, assume not only that they live under a democratic government and in a democratic society, but also that democratic ways are at once morally superior and ultimately destined to gain world-wide acceptance. The purposes of this chapter are to define the nature of democracy, to examine its bases, to assess the conditions for its creation and maintenance, to examine critically the values of democracy, and to make at least a tentative judgment of its course and prospects.

For the sake of perspective, it is desirable at the outset to anticipate one broad conclusion relating to the prospects of democracy. One of the most significant political phenomena of our age is the triumph of democracy as a term and as an aspiration. The Soviet regime and its satellites have described themselves as "People's Democracies." Fascist dictators have spoken sarcastically of the follies and impotence of democracy, yet both Mussolini and Hitler found it vital to stress their popular role and base, and to claim that they themselves embodied the aspirations, and furthered the interests of the whole people. Whatever the actual bases of their support, they emphasized their championship of the broad groups of ordinary men and occupations, and above all of those previously excluded from a functional role and a stake in society. Further, if one looks at the new and aggressive nationalisms of Africa and much of Asia, one observes that aspirations to independence, like much early nineteenth century European nationalism, tend to unite freedom from foreign domination with the democratic aspiration of the native peoples to participate in the control of their own government. The age of the common man is perhaps not yet; and, if this phrase implies cultural as well as economic levelling downward, it is to be hoped it never will be. But the new belief in the common man (to use the name of a book by Professor Carl J. Friedrich) is real enough, if by that is meant a vast spread of awareness of the potentialities of all men, of their needs, and of their dependence upon the state for their fulfillment. Even the leaders of totalitarian regimes are aware of the necessity, for the sake of their own and of national power, to concern themselves with the release of men's energies, and not simply to strive to render them innocuous. At the least they are professedly demophil. They can not publicly ignore, far less malign, the rank and file.

THE NATURE AND MODERNITY OF THE DEMOCRATIC ORDER

Definition

Before going further with our discussion of democracy, we must make our meaning clear, refining the general usage of the term and elucidating the relations among democracy, constitutionalism, and liberalism.[1] Formal definition has its dangers, especially with so broad and fundamental a concept as democracy. Just as twentieth century capitalism differs from that described by Adam Smith and condemned by Karl Marx, so democracy today differs from the theories of Thomas Jefferson or the practices of Andrew Jackson. Yet the general principles and the underlying spirit remain the same. As the Greek derivation of the term indicates, the term democracy was first applied to a form of government and meant "rule by the people." But even among the ancient Greeks it stood for more than a form of government. Political democracy was valued in the age of Pericles because the individual man was valued, because his liberty was cherished and his dignity respected equally with that of other men, and because confidence was felt in his capacity to reach reasonable decisions by means of discussion. Nowhere were these sentiments more simply and eloquently stated than in the famous Funeral Oration of Pericles as recounted by Thucydides. Note this passage:

Our constitution does not copy the laws of neighboring states; we are rather a pattern to others than imitators ourselves. Its administration favors the many instead of the few; this is why it is called a democracy. If we look to the laws, they afford equal justice to all in their private differences; if to social standing, advancement in public life falls to reputation for capacity, class considerations not being allowed to interfere with merit; nor again does poverty bar the way, if a man is able to serve the state, he is not hindered by the obscurity of his condition. The freedom which we enjoy in our government extends also to our ordinary life. There, far from exercising a jealous surveillance over each other, we do not feel called upon to be angry with our neighbor for doing what he likes, or even to indulge in those injurious looks which can not fail to be offensive, although they inflict no positive penalty.

[1] For a brief, lucid discussion of the problem of defining democracy, see Henry B. Mayo, *An Introduction to Democratic Theory* (New York: Oxford U. P., 1960), Ch. 2. For fuller treatment and a wide variety of points of view, see UNESCO (Richard McKeon, ed.), *Democracy in a World of Tensions* (Chicago: Univ. of Chicago Press, 1951).

And again

> We throw open our city to the world, and never by alien acts exclude
> foreigners from any opportunity of learning or observing, although the eyes of
> an enemy may occasionally profit by our liberality; trusting less in system and
> policy than to the native spirit of our citizens.[2]

Democratic government is in some sense government by the people. The
way in which and the extent to which the people can actually govern will
vary tremendously as between rural canton, small city-state, and contemporary America. But in significant degree the government must rest on the
consent of the governed and its policies must be responsive to their desires.
While direct democracy is out of the question in most modern situations, the
principle of democracy calls for more than passive consent. The democratic
ideal includes the individual's liberty and his personal development and to
these ends values his active participation in the political process, at the very
least in the selection of representatives. Finally, the fundament of the citizen's political liberty, his suffrage, must be equally distributed: according to
the rule of "each to count for one and none for more than one."

Use of the term "citizen" calls for further elaboration. The word covers
an unavoidable area of indefiniteness. No one argues that those who have not
yet reached adulthood should be entitled to vote, although opinion and
practice differ as to what the definition of adulthood should be. There are
certain other generally agreed bases for exclusions, such as mental incompetence, confinement in prison, and the fact of past conviction of serious offenses. Also it should be observed that in positing equality of political power
we are dealing only with the legally irreducible minimum, with the basis for
equality of *access* to political power. A man who gets himself elected or appointed to office may enjoy legal political power far in excess of the minimum, while one who achieves some other position of political influence may
in fact exert great political power without legal authority. Insofar as this
influence is not based upon popular consent, however, to that extent the
government departs from the democratic ideal. The equality for which
democracy stands is not "equality of condition" or "absolute equality," by
any means; but it does affirm as its central theme the right of each to equal
opportunity to prove himself, to exert his influence, and to have his interests
considered equally with those of all others.

Corollaries: Democracy and Constitutionalism

Although equality of primary political power, with its implied denial of
the right of any minority to rule, is the root concept of democracy today,

---

[2] Thucydides, *History of the Peloponesian War,* trans. Richard Crawley (New York:
Dutton, 1910), pp. 121-122.

Swiss cantonal meeting

Swiss National Tourist Office

certain corollaries of this objective are so essential to democratic practice that they have in effect become part of the contemporary definition. The general idea that government should operate in accordance with fixed and publicly known procedures, allowing full opportunity for bringing the opinions of the public to bear at appropriate stages is such a corollary. More specifically, democracy implies that the individuals who control policy shall be elected by and accountable to the people at reasonably frequent intervals. The elections must be free, not substantially influenced by intimidation, or administered so as to control the result. A number of more specific requirements follow from this basic corollary. Voters must be allowed to organize themselves into parties for the attainment of legal objectives. Freedom of speech and of the press and of access to information pertinent to public policy are essential. Indoctrination must not be substituted for education. Otherwise the right to vote has no significance. Freedom from arbitrary arrest is likewise indispensable; for without it the party in power may terrorize and weaken the opposition by throwing its leaders in jail on trumped up charges during election campaigns. Among the various means for ensuring this result, a system of politically independent courts is fundamental.

Since equal respect for all individuals is the core of democracy, still other principles and mechanisms of constitutionalism are absorbed into it.[3] Provision for insuring the rule of law and, more broadly, the principle of equal protection of the laws is imperative. Without these guarantees that individuals will not only have equal power to select the lawmakers but also be treated equally by those enforcing the laws and be given equal consideration by the lawmakers themselves, democracy could easily degenerate into a mockery of its pretensions.

The defense of democracy involves limitations upon it. A majority that votes away free speech, for example, is voting away the right of future majorities. A democracy that took such action would cease to be a democracy. Constitutional provision against the power of a majority to change the fundamentals of democracy is not undemocratic. We need not say that a democracy *must* express such limits in its constitution, but one that does so is acting in conformity with its own democratic principles, and indeed in their defense.

Democracy a Matter of Degree

Governments may be more or less democratic. Some states with essentially one-party systems (for example, Mexico) might fairly be called democratic, although in a limited degree, on the ground that (1) political opposition is permitted at least in moderation; (2) that many groups compete for influence, within the single dominant party; and (3) that access to political influence for new groups is permitted and even protected by the regime. To state the matter in another way, democracy would cease to exist were political influence deliberately monopolized by one group or so rigged that the regime could no longer be considered either popularly responsive, accountable, or open to the entry of new political competitors. These conditions do not necessarily require for their fulfillment a model of democracy similar to that of the United States or Western Europe. They do imply either formal constitutional restraints or the observance of some operative constitutional principles such as equal protection of the laws, freedom of expression and association, and respecting "the sovereignty of the rules of the game."

Democracy and Liberalism

Not only does modern democracy tend to absorb the principles of constitutionalism, but it also embraces and actually grows out of the body of

---

[3] Note the importance of chronology, of timing. Where those liberal ideas and constitutional practices that are essential to the maintenance of democracy have already been accepted before the arrival of democracy, the battle for the attainment of a viable democracy is already half won. Conversely where, as is happening in so many countries today, democracy is attempted without a base of well-established constitutionalism, the task is hazardous and the outcome problematic. The various built-in protections enumerated below amount to a listing, by implication, of many of the abuses of democracy that have been so common, for example, throughout much of Latin America.

The French National Assembly

liberal thought.[4] Liberalism stands for an attitude of approval of and confidence in the liberated individual—the individual freed from unquestioning traditionalism, censorship, dogmatic authoritarianism, absolute and irresponsible government, and regimenting controls. Historically liberalism opposed suppression of all kinds. Democracy seeks to implement this attitude, to give assurance that all have equal opportunity to achieve their goals as they come to envisage them, and to provide positive means—especially through political participation itself—for this purpose. Democracy as we know it in the West, often called "liberal democracy," aims to give individuals the right and responsibility of making their own choices wherever that is compatible with other democratic objectives. It sets great store by freedom of action, of movement from place to place, of choice of occupation, of contract, and of the use and disposal of property.

The development of liberal democracy is quite recent. Even in Western Europe and in America, it was not until well after the American and French revolutions that the concept of democracy became respectable. Until then the whole course of Western civilization, in thought, culture, and political prac-

[4] See Theodore Meyer Greene, *Liberalism, its Theory and Practice* (Austin: Univ. of Texas Press, 1957), esp. Ch. 9.

tice, had been dominantly aristocratic, despite the intermittent expression of more generous sentiments and aspirations, and the occasional, but generally short-lived practice of democratic government, most frequently on the scale of cities or provinces. The masses were conceived as subjects rather than citizens—which gives point to the emphasis on "citizen" as a form of address during the French Revolution. (It is likewise significant that modern Communist revolutionaries use a designation, "Comrade," that has the same equalitarian connotations but without the political reference.) The task of governments was to keep their subjects in order, to prevent and put down revolts, and to punish crimes. The welfare of subjects, on a basis appropriate to their station, was a proper concern of good rulers; but the wishes and judgments of the people were almost irrelevant, and their development as full and free persons was not a *desideratum* or even viewed as among the real possibilities of social existence. This fact gave particular significance to American development in the nineteenth century, and made Tocqueville's great work, *Democracy in America,* a prophetic classic. Tocqueville, a Frenchman of aristocratic background, saw the significance of Jacksonian democracy; and, fearful of the dangers of majoritarianism, nevertheless perceived the dynamism, the promise, and the inescapable spread of the theory and practice of democratic equality.

CONDITIONS FOR DEMOCRACY

Why, in the long history of Western civilization, has democracy put in its effective appearance at so late a date? The answer to this question becomes clear when we consider what are the necessary conditions for a democratic regime. For it is only recently that they have come into existence on a large scale.

Democratic Attitudes and Beliefs

A democratic government can not be expected to prosper or even survive in the absence of democratic attitudes and beliefs widely distributed among the people, and strongly held at least by the bulk of the political leaders and activists. (In like manner strongly anti-democratic attitudes held by a coherent minority constitute a serious obstacle to the success of democratic institutions.) The citizens of a democracy must, as J. S. Mill declared, have a strong desire to govern themselves; in Lasswell and Kaplan's terms they must be "politicized"; or, in still other phraseology, they must not be apathetic.

INDIVIDUALISM

To be "politicized" implies not only the desire on the part of a people to govern themselves, but also a considerable amount of the quality of "individualism," and of love of freedom and equality. The cynical shrug of the shoulders is the gesture of traditional society. If the weight of the centuries is so great that it discourages widespread individual initiative and political activism, it is too great for the realization of democracy.[5] Also individualism must be fortified by a strong component of personal dignity and objective estimation of one's own role and the role of others in the society.

The members of a democratic society need not be what we understand by the term "rugged individualists." We are not speaking of economic individualism; nor does democracy depend upon any opposition to cooperation or association. It is important, however, that the individual should be highly valued, and that his claims for a certain autonomy should be respected. This claim for autonomy is based upon respect for men as men and also as rational beings. Reason should lead to harmonious organization, but the rational pattern should be accepted, ideally, by the willing approval of each individual.[6]

MODERATION AND FLEXIBILITY

Inherent in the democratic character though it is, individualism must not be of the strident, anti-social type. Rather, it must be tempered with that third element of the democratic triumvirate of values, fraternity.[7] Not all peoples who love liberty and respect individuality are able to practice democracy successfully. We may point to nations of Latin stock in support of this statement.[8] For some reason they have had great difficulty in making democratic institutions operate successfully; often they have failed completely. Many reasons, in different cases, may explain this phenomenon. Often, as in Spain, Portugal, and most Latin American countries, economic conditions are unfavorable. Often, too, constitutionalism was not well established before democracy was attempted. Perhaps the most pervasive difficulty, however, is the lack of a pragmatic, empirical attitude. In the absence of this softener of political combat, individualism may lead to threatened anarchy and thus to despotism rather than to democracy.

A democratic society must be an open society; it must be ready to accept new ideas and new practices; it must be easily amenable to change; in a word, it must be flexible. A pluralistic society in which of value orderings

[5] It should be said, however, that a dictatorial or quasi-dictatorial regime may frustrate and render apathetic a people that had previously been aroused to political activism. The removal of the smothering hand of dictatorship may, under such circumstances, be the necessary prelude to a revival of political interest.

[6] This subject is well treated in Zevedei Barbu, *Democracy and Dictatorship: Their Psychology and Patterns of Life* (New York: Grove, 1956), esp. Ch. 1.

[7] In parts of Asia apparently the effective operation of democratic institutions is hampered because the strong loyalty to the extended family interferes with loyalty to a wider political community and to democracy as a means to *individual* development. See Werner Levi, "The Fate of Democracy in South and Southeast Asia," *Far Eastern Survey*, Vol. 28 (1959), pp. 25-26.

[8] Possibly—but it is by no means clear—the French are an exception. See John Plamenatz, "Cultural Prerequisites to a Successfully Functioning Democracy: a Symposium," *American Political Science Review*, 50 (1956), p. 116.

vary considerably is likely to be more flexible than one which displays a highly homogeneous scheme of values.

In short, the way of successful democracy is that of moderation. A people who feel intensely about many political matters may be fully as bad as one that is completely apathetic. Political interest and activity was at a feverishly high pitch in Germany shortly before the collapse of the Weimar Republic. Tenseness breeds intolerance. From another point of view what might even be thought of as an anti-political attitude may be favorable to democracy— an attitude of suspicion of authority. It is at least plausible that this kind of an attitude may compel those in positions of authority to make special efforts to gain a broad base of popular support.[9]

PUBLIC SPIRIT AND CONSENSUS

More positively, the successful functioning of democracy depends upon a complex of attitudinal and intellectual conditions including public spirit, willingness to compromise, and commitment to constitutionalism. It is commonly said, and rightly, that democracy can not flourish without public spirit. There must be an underlying sense of unity, a consensus must bind the people together, give them a concern for the welfare of the collectivity, make them willing to accept the decisions of the majority even when they don't like them, and assure their willingness to accept some responsibility for making the democracy work.

Nor can the minority be expected to do all the yielding. Majorities must have respect for strongly held views of minorities, and must hesitate to act on a close vote in matters of great importance. Both sides must show a spirit of moderation and willingness to compromise; they must have a strong commitment to the democratic process itself. Such a tradition takes time to develop, and once developed is not easily dissipated. Constitutional checks designed to promote deliberateness of action and to protect minority rights may be of great assistance, but they can do no more than buttress and encourage an underlying disposition. The better the traditions of the people, in these respects, the less need for reliance upon institutional devices.

One further word about consensus. As with the other "conditions" of democracy, it is not a matter that, once attained, can be dismissed from mind. Democracies may fail because they fail to maintain the conditions for their success. The longer a democracy is in existence, the greater is the sense of legitimacy that is likely to attach to it and, assuming that it solves the problems that create tensions in the society with reasonable success, the greater is the consensus, especially with respect to abiding by the democratic process itself. The qualifying clause, however, must not be neglected. If deep cleavages over policy occur and no acceptable compromises are found, and if this

---

[9] On this point and on the subject of consensus more generally, see V. O. Key, Jr., *Public Opinion and American Democracy* (New York: Knopf, 1961), pp. 44-45.

experience repeats itself in one area of concern after another—economic issues, religious issues, educational issues, and so on—the result may be catastrophic. Reasonableness will give way to bitterness, intolerance, and extremism and the cement of democracy will be rapidly eroded.[10] To be even more specific democratic institutions may facilitate the formation of deep social cleavages. Electoral systems that make it easy for political parties to form along lines of divisive interests, as happened with the extreme system of proportional representation used in Weimar Germany, may have this effect. Any democracy that fails to relieve a serious source of inter-group tension threatens its own foundations. For the whole complex of conditions under discussion here, experience is likely to have a cumulative effect. A government that succeeds in solving the problems that confront it will find it easier to solve the next batch of problems because the process it has just gone through has strengthened the democratic underpinnings. Nothing succeeds like success. The converse also holds.

It is worth emphasizing that public spirit and other democratic attitudes are seldom distributed evenly throughout the population. A leading minority possessed of one or more of these qualities in high degree will do much to overcome a deficiency amongst the rest of the population. It is particularly important to have a body of competent and relatively honest men from whom administrators and politicians can be drawn. Conversely, a powerful minority that is especially lacking in one of these qualities—especially if it is positively anti-democratic or particularistic to the point of being unwilling to make common cause with the rest of the people—may well render democracy unworkable in that society. Particularly the leaders of strong minority parties must accept the rules of the democratic game.[11]

Education

Returning to more specifically political factors, it is clear, if anything is, that democracy demands an electorate with at least moderately high standards of education. That the minimum level is relative to the complexity of the problems faced by the society in question is obvious. That it is not very high even for a society like our own is also evident. Yet even a voter who has little specific knowledge of current events may have good reasons (which he may not be able to articulate without assistance) for feeling that the government is doing a good job, or that it is not. Even this degree of political sensibility was generally out of the question for the average subject before the

---

[10] Cf. Seymour Martin Lipset, *Political Man* (New York: Doubleday, 1960), pp. 89-90.

[11] It is often said that democracy is government by "consent." Without much further clarification this way of putting it is not very illuminating. Probably most of what is sound in the idea is expressed, without resort to the word "consent," in the last few paragraphs. For a clarifying analysis of the idea of "consent" in its application to democracy, see E. W. Cassinelli, *The Politics of Freedom* (Seattle, Wash.: University of Washington Press, 1961), Ch. 6.

days of the popular press and other modes of rapid dispersal of information. These tools for public opinion formation, reasonably free from governmental control, comprise essential conditions for the successful functioning of democracy. Recent studies correlating various factors with democratic stability indicate, however, that education, indeed simple literacy, shows the highest correlation.[12]

Social and Economic Conditions

Important though literacy and education are and basic as are the group of beliefs and attitudes discussed above, still further characteristics may be specified for the social order requisite to a successfully functioning democracy. Not only must citizens possess the leisure as well as the education necessary for effective participation in, and judgment of public affairs; but also social and economic inequalities must not be so great that they interfere with the average citizen's exercise of independent judgment. Likewise, citizens must share in the life and culture of their time. They must not only be able to protect and further their interests; they must also have a broad range of interests and opportunities to protect and further. Democracy thrives best on a realistically held ideal of at once equalizing and broadening the range of choices potentially open to men.

INDUSTRIALISM

While the range of choices could conceivably be equalized in a simple and agrarian society, it could be done only at the price of a stagnant unprogressiveness, material and cultural, wherein none would have the leisure and dignity, or the full means, for the expression of human potentialities; and where men's rich diversities, so frequently suppressed by absolutist governments, would be aborted at the start by the constraints of circumstances. Hence a fully developed democratic order became potential only with the advent of industrialism, of the creation and harnessing of mechanical power. The modern technological order for the first time in history provides the material bases and the amplitude of sheer leisure to permit full citizenship and to give reasonable opportunity for a social order embracing a vast population to be at once democratic and stable.

Industrialism and democracy are closely related. As in the case of education, a priori reasoning is reinforced by statistical evidence. In Europe and Latin America studies show a high correlation between democracy, on the one hand, and certain indices of industrialization and of the closely related items of wealth and urbanization, on the other.[13] A variety of factors, in addition to those that have already been mentioned, account for this correlation.

[12] Seymour M. Lipset, "Some Social Requisites of Democracy: Economic Development and Political Legitimacy," *Amer. Polit. Sci. Rev.*, 53 (1959), pp. 69-105.
[13] See Lipset, *loc. cit.*

We have noted that the complex of attitudes and beliefs that must underlie a democracy are greatly strengthened by its successful functioning. Hence industrialism, in providing the economic bases for education and leisure, in breaking down social and economic rigidities, and in supplying the opportunities for developing and gratifying new wants, supplies that cumulative experience so favorable to democratic attitudes. It also operates in more specific ways. For instance, both reason and experience support the belief that persons engaged in occupations that tend to keep them remote from other men and, especially, remote from those engaged in other occupations and enjoying different experiences, tend to be more extreme and intransigeant in their views, less ready to engage in democratic compromise than those less restricted by geographical and occupational isolation. Such isolation tends to characterize those engaged in agriculture, fishing, mining, the extractive industries generally.[14] The Anti-Masons, Populists, Molly McGuires and "Wobblies" of American history are instances of this phenomenon. In industrial societies, as more and more people are engaged in manufacturing, in distribution, and in service occupations, the percentage of the population who must devote themselves to the extractive industries steadily declines.

The last point merges into a broader one. It is not only that industrialization minimizes a particular source of anti-democratic parochialism; it produces a dynamic and pluralistic society that is positively favorable to democracy. Nothing is so inimical to a class-bound society as the powerful and ever-changing demands of an economy dominated by a rapidly developing technology. More than almost anything else it is the pluralism of an industrial society—the variety of groups and organizations as well as the variety of relations and interests—it is this pluralism that provides checks against the oligarchic tendencies of all organizations, that helps break up the masses of mass democracy into a rich and enlivened society, and that, by providing a variety of interests too great for sharp and simple alignment, keeps partisanship from becoming so intense as to undermine democratic consensus. Finally, it is now almost a commonplace that a relatively large middle class—always produced by industrialization—is almost a *sine qua non* for a stable democracy.[15]

DEMOCRACY APPRAISED

We are all used to hearing democracy eulogized. Short of that, most of us would judge it self-evidently superior to the alternative of totalitarian dictatorship. Yet we are also used to hearing many of its works condemned, and doubtless to condemning them ourselves. We see policies pursued of which we disapprove—policies that may appear obviously to be either in the interest of some special group or in response to ill-informed and shortsighted clamor

[14] See Lipset, *loc. cit.*, p. 96, and references cited there.
[15] For a discerning elaboration of this point, see C. W. Cassinelli, *op. cit.*, pp. 119-133.

on the part of the public. We see irresolution and uncertainty where firm and positive action are needed. From time to time, we also see, blazoned from the headlines and laid bare on the television screen, proof of rampant official corruption. Are these things proof of what John Stuart Mill called "the ideally best form of government"? With much to be said in criticism of democracy, it is well to take stock, to consider its merits carefully and weigh them against its obvious shortcomings.

In performing this evaluation we can do no better than to remind ourselves once more of the great ends of the state and use them as our measuring rod. How does democracy rate as a means for attaining the ends of security, liberty, justice, and welfare? These terms remind us that democracy is more than a form of government. It is the form of government derived from, and based upon the democratic philosophy of life. Even more, it is directed to the advancement of those liberal and humane ends which have (on the whole) been the increasingly accepted values of our civilization for more than two millennia. Carl Becker expressed this point when he wrote:

> To have faith in the dignity and worth of the individual man as an end in himself, to believe that it is better to be governed by persuasion than by coercion, to believe that fraternal good will is more worthy than a selfish and contentious spirit, to believe that in the long run all values are inseparable from the love of truth and the disinterested search for it, to believe that knowledge and the power it confers should be used to promote the welfare and happiness of all men rather than to serve the interests of those individuals and classes whom fortune and intelligence endow with temporary advantage— these are the values which are affirmed by the traditional democratic ideology.[16]

Democracy and Self-Protection

So much for summary statement. Let us examine the matter in greater detail. Most simply and fundamentally, democracy gives to the individual the power of self-protection. In making this point, we by no means adopt the over-rationalistic assumptions of the early Utilitarians who argued that everyone pursues his own interest, that each knows his own interest best, and that universal suffrage will therefore automatically result in the greatest good for the greatest number. But it is one thing to say that many people don't know what is in their best interest and quite another to say that someone else, neither bound to them by family ties nor politically responsible to them, can be trusted to govern in their interest. The operation of modern democracy does not require the individual voter to know whether one or two hundred million dollars should be appropriated for aircraft carriers, whether the federal anti-trust legislation should apply to insurance companies or labor unions, whether merit rating is a sound plan for unemployment compensation, or even whether a scheme to balance the budget is financially

---

[16] Carl L. Becker, "Some Generalities that Still Glitter," *Yale Review,* **29** (1940), p. 666.

feasible. To be sure, the more voters have intelligent opinions on such questions the better will the democracy work. At bottom, however, what the average voter is called on to do is to form an over-all opinion about the operation of his government, to decide if the general direction of its policy is acceptable or not, and to form a shrewd judgment of the competence, integrity, public conscience, and general policy orientation of a few candidates for public office. What he needs, above all, is the power to "throw the rascals out."

If this fundamental power seems to us primitive and insufficient for the role of a citizen, it is only because, on the one hand, we have ourselves advanced to a point where citizens can and do accomplish more than this minimum, and, on the other hand, because we tend to lose sight of where we would be without this shield of our liberties. It is because, in the luxury of security, we tend to underrate one of the political fundamentals—the tendency for power to be abused. The possession of power is an essential guarantee for the equality of consideration that is the heart of justice. Individuals who lack power, the weak and the pusillanimous, are, in the large, viewed with contempt by its possessors. As Bertrand Russell once said, they are harried and ill-treated and subjected to cruelty and accused of all manner of crime.

In the long run, in other words, some form of democracy appears to be the only alternative to autocracy. At least for an industrialized society, it is doubtful whether a middle course can be maintained. The days of aristocracies are gone beyond recall. When society was virtually static and the common man was illiterate and ignorant, government rode relatively easily on the back of tradition. No more than passive consent was required. To control today's literate, demanding, expecting masses is another matter. They must be won, they must be cowed, or they must be manipulated. Unstable systems of "guided democracies" and one-party movements for national rebirth or collective uplift –part democracy, part dictatorship—can exist only so long as the collective aims are highly unified and power and techniques of political opposition are lacking.[17] In the urban, industrial society the choice is *either* democracy *or* autocracy.[18]

Democracy and Self-Development

If self-protection is the foundation of democracy, self-development is its realization. Perhaps it would be better to describe the two as twin pillars of support. Mill pointed out that the effect of a form of government on the

[17] See Ch. 18.

[18] The case of France today is instructive. In the face of the threat of civil war, brought about in the last analysis by the Algerian problem, France adopted a new constitution that was a hybrid of democracy and elective dictatorship. At the present writing, in the wake of the Algerian settlement, the future of this solution is in the balance. If it succeeds it now appears that it will do so by accomplishing a drastic reorganization and "Americanization" of French political parties. If that end is accomplished the new regime might be able to slough off its undemocratic elements and still survive.

citizens as participants may be fully as important as its effect on them as consumers of government services. Quite apart from the fact that the possession of the suffrage is a vital protection to men's liberty, its exercise is itself an important aspect of freedom. We have defined freedom as the opportunity for the deliberate formation and accomplishment of one's purposes. Today, increasingly, individual purposes are accomplished by means of state action, or at the very least in ways that are dependent upon state action. Under such circumstances political liberty—the right to control the policies of the government—becomes a central part of the whole of liberty. Without it, one's area of self-determination is vitally restricted. Power indeed is the condition not only of liberty but of growth.

A man will seldom rise above his own estimation of himself, which in turn will largely reflect the estimates of others. As we have seen, the person who lacks power is not likely to be respected; and while political power is by no means the only form of power it is very important. Moreover, in accordance with what Lasswell and Kaplan call the principle of agglutination, the possession of one kind of power tends to lead to the acquisition of other forms, and vice versa.[19] In the modern world particularly, people deprived of political power find it impossible to be fully self-respecting. Nowhere is this fact more clearly observable than in the struggles by subject peoples for full political independence. It alone can explain what otherwise seems to be the irrational nature of some of their demands. The phenomenon is strictly parallel to the commonly experienced rebellion against authority and demand for independence by adolescents. In both cases the processes of growth, the development of moral responsibility, may give rise to unlovely manifestations.

By giving the citizen a share of control over public affairs, democracy stimulates his interest in them. By making him in a full sense a part of the state it develops his loyalty to it and his care for it. It not only stimulates his interest but also tends to widen his moral horizons. Only when he is forced to give some attention to public problems is the relation between his own well-being and that of others far removed from him brought home to his consciousness. Only when he has some responsibility for the welfare of others is he likely to give it much thought.

DEMOCRACY AND GROUPS

With respect to the last point, it might seem that the result of political power is precisely the contrary—that it stimulates participation in pressure groups whose whole outlook is selfish rather than altruistic. To an important extent this charge is true. However, even an interest group, especially if it is organized on a nation-wide scale, may force its members to broaden their

---

[19] Harold D. Lasswell and Abraham Kaplan, *Power and Society, a Framework for Political Inquiry* (New Haven, Conn.: Yale U. P., 1950), p. 97.

outlook and take into consideration a wider range of interests than they otherwise would. Members of a textile workers union, for instance, may find a pronounced difference between the interests of northern and southern textile workers, and may be forced to modify their own position to achieve unity within the whole group. Also, members of a union that is a political as well as an economic power may be compelled to take account of the interests of other groups. Their leaders will find that only by making certain compromises in the interests of others can they attain their own ends; and soon they will find themselves striving to curb the narrow self-interest of their members and to educate them to a broader view.

Two other points must be born in mind. Group memberships overlap. Most people belong to more than one group having political interests. Many belong to more than one organization possessing political objectives. Thus they find themselves pulled in differing, if not in opposite directions. In this way the disintegrative effect of a pluralistic society is checked. Also, many groups and organizations are not selfishly oriented. Their very excuse for being is to further interests like conservation, the preservation of park areas, development of recreation areas and playgrounds, pursuit of governmental reform, and countless other matters that appeal to the social rather than the selfish man.

COUNTERARGUMENTS CONSIDERED

It may be objected that we are expressing too exalted an opinion of the effects of political participation upon the intellectual and moral development of the individual. When we reflect on how little thought many people give to exercising their political power, how little deliberation goes into their casting of a ballot, if indeed they bother to vote at all, we may well take pause. When we realize that the thought of being one hundred millionth of a sovereign may be actually discouraging and frustrating rather than encouraging, we rightly raise the question as to the validity of our previous argument. These are pertinent points; but replies to them have already been implied in the preceding paragraphs.

Certainly many, possibly most citizens in a modern democracy will experience little of its developmental virtues; but this little may be significant. What is supremely important is that the possibility of this influence should be constantly open to all and that no one should be by law barred from its potential salutary influence.

When we are seeking to measure the effect of the possession of political power on the individual voter, we must not look only at his exercise of the ballot. In most democracies, the great bulk of political activity is not carried on at the polls or in the activities of the political parties. Democracy in America goes on in many ways. In the great organizations such as trade unions and farmers' cooperatives democracy influences the methods and sets limits to the tenure of leaders. Active participation close to the primary duties of citizenship occurs in housing districts, civic leagues, and school boards. In many local communities a close and stable relation of responsiveness and accountability exists between political leaders and the more settled residents. Even publics that often seem unorganized and uninfluential can often move the powers that be by carrying their protests to an influential notable.

A totalitarian regime, some argue, can, and in considerable measure does achieve the same ends (for example, in the U.S.S.R.) by creating a "democracy of participation." To be sure, the element of popular political choice is largely absent. On the other hand, in local soviets, trade unions, and in groups of active citizens who participate in the control of administration there exists much of the same kind of activity that we in America call democratic. But the absence of significant choice is a crucial difference. The quality of experience is not the same in the two situations—participation managed from above less and less satisfies the sensibilities of an increasingly urban, educated population. Moreover, the range and importance of questions open to popular control is minimal in a totalitarian regime, by definition.

It might be contended that the advantages we have been discussing could be obtained without giving equality of political power. In other words, the more educated, intelligent, or otherwise competent citizens might be given more than one vote. In addition to the practical obstacles to such a proposal, certain other points should be noted. In the first place, part of the moral value of political democracy consists in its recognition of the principle of an ultimate equality. Some people are of course more valuable to the community than others. So also, through leadership, election or appointment to office, and the like, some people may have a greater impact on public policy than others. Their possession of a common starting point of equality, in the vote, however, aptly symbolizes the concept that each individual has a worth that is unique and not to be sacrificed for the lesser benefit of any number of others, whoever they may be. Not only does political democracy symbolize this social democratic concept, but it helps to give it support and advancement. Concretely, as far as legal provision can, it guarantees equality of opportunity in the political realm.

Differential voting makes possible minority rule, and minority rule may bring minority tyranny. Of course, a minority may rule in constitutional fashion and a majority is quite capable of being tyrannical. To this argument it might be sufficient to declare that if we must run the risk of tyranny it is better that it should be tyranny over the minority than over the majority. But there is more to be said. If constitutional arrangements single out a particular group or class to enjoy more power than others, these individuals are thereby marked as distinct, and privileged. They tend to unite in self-interest and self-defense,—and ultimately for self-aggrandizement. An invitation to class struggle is created. In this sense, majority rule is not simply the converse of minority rule. Majority rule implies equality of primary political power. No special group—majority or minority—is set apart and given a special interest. The opportunity is open to each to persuade a majority to agree with him. Those who comprise a majority on one issue may not be united on the next question. Alignments and majorities may shift from day to day. Those who are in the majority today are interested in protecting the minority against the arbitrary exercise of power lest they be in the minority tomorrow. For this reason the probabilities are that a majority will abuse its power less frequently than a minority.

Democracy and Cooperation

To the arguments from self-protection and self-development, we have to add a third and last. Not only does democracy provide the individual with the means for his own protection and development, it also tends to make him cooperative and to evoke positive contributions from him, so that society as a whole profits. Of course all social benefit is, in the last analysis, individual benefit. Our point is simply that while the first two factors enable or lead the individual to do things that help himself, we are now dealing with a way in which democracy encourages behavior that is beneficial to others. By the same token, others are led to behave in a fashion that benefits him.

We need hardly argue that a society whose members are cooperative will enjoy more security and be able to afford more liberty than one whose members resist joint activity,—especially in this collectivist age when so much depends upon highly organized group activity. Similarly, a society whose members are anxious to contribute to the common effort and who are alert to discover means of making that effort more effective will enjoy greater welfare, other things being equal, than one whose members are not so minded. The question, then, is simply whether democracy correlates positively with the prevalence of these attitudes. As a matter of fact considerable psychological evidence supports the proposition that democracy tends to encourage cooperation, and even that "a peaceful, cooperative, and non-persecutory society requires that personal and social relations be based on principles of freedom and democracy."[20] A cooperative society necessitates a relatively harmless outlet for the feelings of hostility that are generated in

[20] John Bowlby, "Psychology and Democracy," *Political Quarterly*, 17 (1946), p. 61. Note also Albert H. Rosenthal, "Behavior and Administration," *Public Administration Review*, 19 (1959), pp. 188-193. Mr. Rosenthal asks the following question: "Is it an interesting coincidence, or is it rather the great truth underlying the democratic principle, that the basic concept of psychology, psychiatry, and social work is that each person must be considered as an individual human being with his own values and goals?" *Ibid.*, p. 189.

all of us. The ease with which a protest can be registered or with which the agitated citizen or group can "get in the show" help to supply this condition. Willing cooperation calls for some general understanding of the common aim. Again democratic institutions tend to produce the desideratum. To ask a man's opinion about how something should be done is itself a big step towards gaining both his interest and his assistance. The significance of this common experience for democracy is not hard to see.

The benefits of democracy derive less from the application of political democracy on the top level than from the practice of democratic principles throughout the body politic and in all walks of life. If the fruits of democracy are to be fully enjoyed, we must seek democratic participation at all levels of government, and in the field of administration as well as on the legislative plane. Moreover, to obtain the full benefits of democracy will also require extension of the principle to other phases of society than the political. But only in a society that is democratic politically is this wider diffusion of the democratic spirit possible.[21]

THE PROSPECTS OF DEMOCRACY

Finally, what are the prospects of democracy? It has had rough going in the twentieth century. In the nineteenth century its march was rapid and its peaceful conquest of the world seemed only a matter of time. But during the last two generations it has received a serious setback at the hands of fascism, while totalitarian Communism is today a powerful rival among the emerging peoples of the world and threatens some of the outposts of democracy.

For the long run, we must look to the nature of man himself for the answer to this question. Early optimism was exaggerated and premature. It has been dealt a heavy blow by the discoveries of psychology and the experiences of the last half century. Man's rationality has been found to float on the surface of a deep pool of irrational drives. His humanitarianism has been found capable of being distorted into demonic sadism. The immediate reaction to these discoveries in many quarters has been one of deep disillusionment. But today a reaction to the reaction is clearly observable. Although human nature may develop in many different ways, by no means all of them benign, evidence is accumulating to suggest that there is a norm of human development. The cruelties and the suppressions and the loss of interest in liberty and self-government that characterized even erstwhile democratic peoples under totalitarian rule appear now to have been normal

---

[21] On the justification of democracy, see further H. R. G. Greaves, *The Foundations of Political Theory* (London: Allen & Unwin, 1958), Ch. 11; Henry B. Mayo, "Can We Justify Democracy?" *American Political Science Review*, 56 (1962), pp. 555-566; and J. Roland Pennock, *Democracy, Its Merits and Prospects* (New York: Holt, 1950), Chs. 3-5.

reactions to highly abnormal conditions. Increasingly, psychologists, psychiatrists, and others, are coming to the conclusion that man's basic drives, under favorable circumstances, tend in the direction of producing democratic and humanitarian societies. Students and practitioners of administration, public and private, are discovering that the democrat's belief in the energizing and generally productive effect of collaborative and cooperative rather than authoritarian techniques is soundly based.

The Record

If we turn to the record, it is much better than is frequently realized. In the countries where democracy has once become well established it persists and thrives. This statement is true generally of western Europe and of the English-speaking lands. France perhaps can not be numbered among the countries in which democracy was ever firmly established. It has always led a marginal existence there, and it still does. It is worthy of remark that its most serious difficulties and threats are directly attributable to its most undemocratic aspect—its empire, or what was its empire. In Western Germany and Italy, where young democratic regimes fell under crisis pressure to fascist regimes, democratic governments are once more installed. Democracy has never been established in the Iberian peninsula.[22] Japan is experiencing the precarious period of a new democracy. As for most of the rest of the world, whether currently being governed in democratic or semi-democratic fashion or not, the conditions for stable democratic government have not yet been attained. The material base of widespread industrialization, not to mention other factors, has not yet been achieved. (Even in the Soviet Union nearly 40 percent of the labor force is still engaged in agriculture—as compared with less than 7 percent in the United States—and *per capita* industrial output lags far behind that of the leading democracies.) To be sure, industrialization has advanced farther in some non-democratic countries than it had in England or the United States a century or more ago. What is different, however, is that a century ago we were happily leading the world to standards of living never before known in this world; while today the Soviet Union is trying to "catch up" with us at a pace and with a desperation that creates terrific tensions. To expect the establishment of democratic institutions in a vast continent-state which has never known anything but despotism to make much headway under these conditions would not be realistic. In greater or less degree this is the kind of situation faced by most of the nondemocratic nations today. Often the "catching up" is on the social as well as the economic level. Feudal societies, completely out of step with the modern world, must be socially transformed, "mod-

[22] For an excellent review and analysis of the situation in Europe, see Raymond Aron, "The Situation of Democracy," *Daedalus*, 90 (1961), pp. 350-370.

ernized," before they are capable of organization for modern industrial production. They must indeed be socially democratized before they can develop the economic base for a sound political democracy! Moreover, the drive for social democracy is not entirely because of the necessities for greater productivity, either industrial or agricultural, in a technological society; it is partly because social democracy has come, in these countries as elsewhere, to be valued for its own sake. In brief, it is partly the drive for certain aspects of democracy itself that, momentarily, makes of the attempt to install and operate a democratic government at best a hazardous adventure. From such a picture one may anticipate many vicissitudes for democracy in the future; but it provides no basis for ultimate pessimism—quite the contrary.

Caveats

Lest we seem to be concluding on an unrealistically optimistic note, two cautions should be sounded. We have said nothing about how long the process of modernizing and democratizing the developing nations of the world may take. Perhaps even more seriously, evolution in the democratic direction will depend upon at least a minimal measure of international order and security. What is that minimum? No one can say. Clearly an established democracy can maintain its institutions under conditions of international tension—even under something approaching what Professor Lasswell calls the "garrison state"—when a new or newly modernizing state would not find it possible to move in the democratic direction. The international situation today leaves an ominous question mark over the future of democracy—as it does over the future of the world.

SELECTED READINGS

(Asterisk indicates book is available in paperback edition.)

*BARBU, ZEVEDEI. *Democracy and Dictatorship; Their Psychology and Patterns of Life*. New York: Grove, 1956. A valuable and interesting study of the psychological traits that tend to prevail in democratic societies.

BENN, S. I. and PETERS, R. S. *Social Principles and the Democratic State*. London: Allen & Unwin, 1959. In Ch. 15, on "Democracy," the authors discuss the subject with their usual succinctness, insight, and sureness of touch.

CASSINELLI, C. W. *The Politics of Freedom*. Seattle, Wash.: Washington U. P., 1961. This analysis of the modern democratic state draws widely on the literature of the subject.

*CHAMBERS, WILLIAM N. and SALISBURY, ROBERT H. eds. *Democracy Today*. New York: Collier Books, 1962. Analyses and discussions of critical issues facing democracy today.

DAHL, ROBERT A. *A Preface to Democratic Theory*. Chicago: Univ. of Chicago Press, 1956. A pioneering exploration of problems left unsolved by traditional democratic theory.

FRANKEL, CHARLES. *The Case for Modern Man*. New York: Harper, 1955. In the author's words, "this book is concerned with the contemporary effort . . . to belittle the portion of reason man has." It aims to vindicate the case for liberalism, political and otherwise.

GRIFFITH, ERNEST S., PLAMENATZ, JOHN and PENNOCK, J. ROLAND. "Cultural Prerequisites to a Successfully Functioning Democracy: a Symposium" *American Political Science Review*, **50** (1956), pp. 101-137. Three points of view, differing especially with reference to the role of religious belief.

GREENE, THEODORE MEYER. *Liberalism, Its Theory and Practice*. Austin, Tex.: University of Texas Press, 1957. A broad discussion of liberalism in all its phases and applications. Ch. 9 discusses its application to democracy.

KELSEN, HANS. "Foundations of Democracy," *Ethics*, **66**, No. 1, (1955), Part II. A study of the relation of democracy to philosophy, religion, and economics.

*LINDSAY, A. D. *The Modern Democratic State*. London: Oxford U. P., 1943, Vol. I. An essay relating the development of democratic theory to general economic and constitutional developments.

*MAYO, HENRY B. *An Introduction to Democratic Theory*. New York: Oxford U. P., 1960. Clear, balanced, and enlightening exposition of the theory of popular government.

PENNOCK, J. ROLAND. *Liberal Democracy, Its Merits and Prospects*. New York: Holt, 1950. An evaluation of democratic theory in the light of developments in ethical theory and in political practice.

ROSS, ALF. *Why Democracy?* Cambridge: Harvard U. P., 1952. A compact, semipopular treatment of the political theory of democracy.

*THORSON, THOMAS LANGDON. *The Logic of Democracy*. New York: Holt, 1962. An application of positivistic philosophy to democratic theory and a brave attempt to vindicate the case for democracy.

Part

DEMOCRATIC

INSTITUTIONS

Three

Part II was largely, but by no means solely, genetic in its approach. Here the principal approach will be descriptive and analytical, with two prime objectives: 1) to acquaint the student with the functioning of politics and government in democratic regimes; and 2) to apply to several political systems criteria that will support value judgments with respect to them. We shall be discussing the means by which democratic institutions perform the input and output functions, to use the terms of our earlier analysis (Chapter 5.) Yet for our present analysis, we shall attempt to provide a more "operative" language, suited specifically to the working of governmental and political institutions themselves. We could, for instance, consider how well a given polity accomplished each of the ends of the state. For certain purposes this approach is useful. We could also extend the earlier analysis of basic political functions—the functions of 1) political socialization and recruitment; 2) the articulation of interests; 3) the aggregation of interests; and 4) communication. In fact, however, these basic functions tend to be so pervasive of all political life that, especially for developed states, a discussion that attempted to follow each of them through in turn would do such violence to the structure that it would be confusing to anyone not already familiar with that structure. For present purposes, criteria that refer to the *operation* of the polity rather than to the results are more useful.

The appropriate criteria for evaluating government, and especially democratic government, depend upon time and circumstance. At one time, for instance among the dominant faction in the Federal Convention of 1787, the definition of a good government was its aptness to restrain the tyranny of officials. In England, a generation later, Bentham and his followers stressed the accountability of the government to the people almost to the exclusion of other values. In more recent times, especially with the development of the service or welfare state, prudence and the reasoned exercise of discretion by officials has become important. The older criteria are still relevant, but emphases vary over time. The problem is one of balancing, and of deciding which criteria are important, or more important for a particular instance.

What are the standards by which an impartial observer should judge the conduct of a particular democratic government? Perhaps the most general test is that of *responsibility*.[1] Does the government behave in responsible fashion?

Responsibility itself is a complex notion. In a political context, it has two primary meanings, distinct but related, and each tending to flavor the other. The first is *accountability* or answerability and the second is the rational and moral exercise of discretionary authority. A democratic government must be accountable for its conduct. Governors may or may not have acted in response to public opinion and they may or may not find that the public has a clear opinion about their action after it has been taken. However, these things may be, there must be an opportunity for the accounts to be audited, for the public to pass judgment on what has been done and what has been left undone, and to support its verdict with the political death penalty, dismissal from office, if it so desires. This may be an all-or-nothing affair, the whole policy-making apparatus standing or falling as a unit, as under the cabinet system, or the mechanism may be looser and more dispersed as in the United States, where constitutional arrangements place more power in the hands of particular individuals (Members of Congress) and make them accountable in large measure to their own local constituencies.

What we expect of democratic government goes beyond "accountability", or even "responsibility". The added expectation is best described by the word *"responsiveness."* A democracy should reflect the influence of, *i.e.,*

---

[1] More extended analyses of the concept of responsibility can be found in J. Roland Pennock, "Responsiveness, Responsibility and Majority Rule," *American Political Science Review,* 46 (1952), pp. 790-807; Charles E. Gilbert, "The Framework of Administrative Responsibility," *Journal of Politics,* 21 (1959), pp. 373-407; and Carl J. Friedrich, ed., *Responsibility* (New York: Liberal Arts Press, 1960).

respond to any clear demand of public opinion. What constitutes such a clear demand of the public is another question. Mostly we would recognize a majority opinion as constituting a case in point, although we might hesitate to do so if a large minority opposed a mild majority with intensity. In the great number of cases, in which only a minority of the electorate seems to have an opinion either way (assuming the simple case where there are only two ways) the concept of responsiveness provides no clear standard. It may suggest only that anything of concern to a sizable group should be an active concern of the government. That in itself is considerable.

Pursuit of the notion of "accountability" carried us beyond the strict limits of the concept of "responsibility." Now we must return to the second primary meaning of the latter term; for responding to demands or pressures and acting with due regard for ultimate accountability are only a part of what is expected of democratic government, and only part of what is entailed by "responsibility." When the government acts, whether in response to outside demand or on initiative from within, it must act responsibly; it must make its decisions and otherwise exercise its power rationally and with due regard for its obligations, moral as well as legal. *Rationality* of course is a matter of degree. The test suggested is one of approximation to a standard that is never more than partially attainable and seldom even clearly discernible. Although complete rationality always remains in the realm of the ideal, some of the things it involves can be further spelled out. A completely rational process of making decisions—individual or governmental—must satisfy a number of conditions. Those who make the decisions must possess the relevant information. They must have thoroughly analyzed the problem or situation, having canvassed the possible solutions to the problem and having calculated or estimated the probable consequences of each. This calculation will often include an estimate of the impact of a given course of action on public opinion itself. Often most difficult of all, is the matter of weighing the various values involved and of trying to reach a fair judgment as to whether, for instance, preserving the financial success of peanut growers is worth $50,000,000 to the taxpayers,—or as useful an application of resources as a fifty million dollar expansion of educational facilities. Finally, one decision should not defeat another. That is to say, policy as a whole should be internally consistent.

When it is a question, for instance, of whether or not the President should set in motion the machinery under the Taft-Hartley law for obtaining a "national emergency" injunction against a strike that threatens the national health and safety, he must know the issues involved in the dispute, the significance for the economy as a whole of a long-continued strike, the prospects for early settlement without governmental intervention; and he must weigh the value of settlement by negotiation against the costs of prolonged work stoppage. When Congress enacted this section of the Taft-Hartley law, it had to make even more complicated calculations, calculations so complicated that there could be no one rational decision. A government can only make better or worse provision for maximizing the elements of rationality—information, analysis, calculation (including estimation), and weighing values—that is, estimating net consequences for the general welfare.

A political system must do more than be responsive and act responsibly. It must provide *leadership*. It must, that is to say, not only find solutions to problems—it must see and foresee the problems. It must arouse interest in them and concern for their right solution. It must create a readiness to agree upon a reasonable solution and, frequently, to cooperate in its application. These tasks of leadership, of arousing interest, precipitating fruitful discussion, dramatizing need and public interest, and energizing large numbers of people to take action may be performed at all levels of the political society from the top leadership down to the private citizen who takes an interest in some particular problem, talks to his friends and neighbors about it, and stirs them to take some action. In a democratic society, particularly, this function is widely dispersed; but the ablest leadership is still needed at the center. In an urban and industrialized society, problems of social management (that is of government) are so complicated and all-pervasive that leadership must permeate the whole society.[2] For this reason even a totalitarian regime must have its highly trained, disciplined, and energized party members. We tend to think of the members of the Party in such a state as followers, because they give unquestioning obedience to the Leader, but they are also leaders, performing all the functions just described.[3]

To the criteria of accountability, responsiveness, rationality, and leadership, one might add the general concept of *"effectiveness"*. Responsible government, like any government, should be effective in the achievement of its ends. In particular, this means that it should be vigorous, that it should be able to act positively and quickly; that nothing should prevent it from taking whatever action the needs of the situation demand.

A government that is duly responsive to the popular will, when one exists that is accountable to the majority, that acts responsibly, and that provides effective leadership in the public interest may fairly be said to have measured up to the standard of what a democratic government should be.[4] Yet we should say a special word about *safeguards against misgovernment*. Those who have power are prone to abuse it, and those with the greatest power need the strongest restraints. Significant safeguards against abuse of power are included in matters already discussed. For instance, the greatest of all democratic checks is the ballot itself, and all the mechanisms and

[2] Cf. J. Roland Pennock, "Democracy and Leadership" in William N. Chambers and Robert H. Salisbury, eds., *Democracy in the Mid-Twentieth Century* (St. Louis, Mo.: Washington U. P., 1960), pp. 95-125.

[3] It will be observed that leadership is not precisely parallel to the other criteria we have discussed. It is not an end in itself; it is a means. Particularly it contributes to responsible action in the sense of rational and right action. It is such a vital means, however, that it deserves inclusion in our list of tests.

[4] Note that, in the phrase "effective leadership," we have combined two of our criteria for a good government: "effectiveness," and "leadership."

institutions for insuring the accountability of the government to the electorate. Yet this set of devices is too cumbersome to protect the single individual, the victim of official arbitrariness. A Government or a party will not be voted out of office because its officials have mistreated a few persons. Also, the importance of a sound tradition of constitutionalism can hardly be too much emphasized. Without it, more specific, formal checks against abuse of power are likely to be of little or no effect. It is a commonplace that in many Latin American countries the same constitutional devices that serve integrity, liberty, and justice well in the United States are not sufficient to prevent gross abuses of power by public officials. A constitutional tradition and spirit, on the other hand, however well it may support liberty and due process, does not assure them without the specific techniques and procedures which enable individuals or groups to vindicate their interests or rights.

We are suggesting, then, that the criteria we have enumerated (and which are tabulated in Table IV) are especially valuable for arriving at intelligent and intelligible value judgments with respect to the organization and the activities of government, and the electoral and political processes. Before turning to such matters as electoral accountability, however, we will discuss the nature of the electorate to which accountability is enforced, or, more precisely that intangible but pervasive phenomenon, public opinion.

TABLE IV

CRITERIA FOR A GOOD SET OF DEMOCRATIC POLITICAL AND GOVERNMENTAL INSTITUTIONS

A Tabular Summary

1. *Responsibility.* The political system should
   a. act rationally
      (1) in the light of full information.
      (2) after due deliberation (individual and collective).
      (3) not arbitrarily.
      (4) with reasonable horizontal and vertical (over time) consistency.
   b. act morally
      (1) with probity.
      (2) with primary concern for the public interest.
2. *Responsiveness.* The political system should
   a. be responsive to expressed demand.
   b. be responsive to need (whether or not articulated).
3. *Accountability* —effective institutional machinery for identifying and removing from office persons responsible for unpopular acts or policies.
4. *Leadership.* The system as a whole should encourage and provide opportunities for the exercise of political leadership at all levels.
5. *Effectiveness.* Government should act
   a. energetically.
   b. expeditiously.
   c. efficiently (including the gaining of acceptance and compliance).
6. Protection against oppressive and arbitrary government—safeguards against abuse of power.

These items are not mutually exclusive, nor are they all on the same level of analysis. Perhaps most obviously, leadership runs through most of the others.

CHAPTER 12

Public Opinion

‖‖

INTRODUCTION

Like modern government, earlier governmental systems rested upon opinion. David Hume states this thesis elegantly in one of his *Essays:*

> As force is always on the side of the governed, the governors have nothing to support them but opinion. It is, therefore, on opinion only that government is founded, and this maxim extends to the most despotic and most military govern- ments, as well as to the most free and popular. The Sultan of Egypt, or the Emperor of Rome, might drive his harmless subjects, like brute beasts, against their sentiments and inclination; but he must, at least, have led his mamelukes, or praetorian bands like men, by their opinions.[1]

The opinion of which Hume was speaking, however, was an elite opinion—controlled and circumscribed. It was circumscribed by sharp lines separating the profane and the sacred. It was restricted by ignorance and technically primitive means of communicating opinion. It was controlled by the interests and the loyalties of the "communicators" of the traditional society: churchmen, nobles, trade guilds, and village headmen. In towns, the market or plaza was sometimes a center of free opinion. But popular opinion was seldom mobilized except by secret societies, religious reformers, or agitators of one variety or another. That fact alone would be enough to explain much of the prevalent fear of popular opinion in the past, quite apart from the character of the opinions generally entertained.

By the time Hume wrote, politics and opinion, at least in England, were far advanced beyond this primitive pattern. A free press could on

---

[1] *Essays: Moral, Political and Literary,* T. H. Green and T. H. Grose, eds., 2 vols. (London: Longmans, 1875), Vol. I, p. 110.

occasion mobilize opinion effectively through posters, handbills, and pamphlets. Drama and literature criticized manners, the court, and public policy. The noncomformist chapels and dissenters within the Established Church had their following, as did the universities and political associations of the middle class. Religious conformity was still enforced, the press censored, plays closed, and public assemblies banned as the occasion seemed to demand, which it often did. The social fabric could not have sustained the stresses of popular assembly and sustained direct political appeals. But opinion—diffuse, patchy, and unstable—was capable of deposing cabinets, defeating or imposing policies, and even threatening the crown.[2]

Half a century later when James Mill wrote that "freedom of discussion is the only security which people can have for the prevalence of true opinions,"[3] he was speaking on the eve of modern democracy. Mill wrote for an increasingly urban and literate England in which the middle class was rising to positions of leadership. He was the spokesman for a group—the English Utilitarians—primarily interested in reforming an oligarchic and anachronistic British Constitution rather than in advancing popular democracy for its own sake. Yet, in essence, his thesis was that only free opinion could correct error and only general opinion could restrain sectarian folly. James Mill and his famous son, John Stuart Mill, defended the concept of a nation-wide "marketplace" of ideas: open, competitive, and untrammeled by government.

From the day of the two Mills to the present, in the Anglo-American tradition, the "market" analogy in matters of public opinion has been widely accepted. That analogy was supported and enlarged by several related propositions common to many of the important theorists of liberalism and democracy.

Liberal Assumptions

One of the most important articles of faith of the classical liberals was the proposition that free public debate could go on without seriously undermining public authority and the consensus upon which the polity as a whole rested. John Stuart Mill was confident of the outcome because he believed that public discussion promoted and broadened among the populace a rational conviction of important doctrines.[4] For him, the process and the consequences of public debate were integrative: they fostered and deepened consensus by strengthening reasoned conviction. Later liberals, such as A.

---

[2] W. Ivor Jennings, *Party Politics* (Cambridge, Eng.: Cambridge U. P., 1960), Vol. I, *Appeal to the People*, Chs. 5-8 gives a good historical summary.

[3] James Mill, "Liberty of the Press," in *Selected Writings of Bentham, James Mill, and John Stuart Mill* (New York: Doubleday, 1935), p. 278.

[4] "As mankind improve, the number of doctrines which are no longer disputed or doubted will be constantly on the increase ... " John Stuart Mill, *On Liberty* (London: Longmans, 1913), p. 25.

Lawrence Lowell, pointed out that Mill's optimism depended upon the assumption of a relatively homogeneous community, one not deeply divided by class, racial, or other cleavages. Yet he, too, thought that under reasonably favorable circumstances the process of public discussion could not only preserve but foster consensus and the integration of the political community.[5]

An important reason for the relatively sanguine outlook of the classical liberals was that they, like the laissez-faire economists, believed that freedom in the "marketplace" of ideas and opinion was the best corrective for serious error or bias. Common to most of them was an assumption that the free confrontation of ideas and opinion was "dialectical," that it—like Adam Smith's "higgling of the market"—led to a testing and appropriate determination of the validity of particular opinions.

Note also the assumption implicit in the traditional liberal view of public opinion, closely parallel to contemporary views of the economy, that access to the relevant market is free enough and ready enough to act as an effective restraint upon faction or merely self-interested opinion. People presumably know their interests, act upon them, and are heard with enough attention that their interests (or views) could be effectively represented and act as a check upon opposing opinion.

Changed Conditions

Today, it is important to realize how far our situation and our views of political man have changed from that for which the classical theorists of liberal democracy spoke. Just as economic theory has had to re-examine the assumption of freely operating commodity markets, so modern democratic theory must re-examine parallel assumptions regarding the "marketplace" of opinion. Concern about concentration in ownership of the press is familiar enough. So is popular literature about the "hidden persuaders," public relations experts in politics, and the "manufactured" images of candidates. The opinion-making industries have changed in the last hundred years just as the steel, petroleum, and cotton industries have changed.

Not only have the structure of the public opinion industries and the ways of stimulating public opinion changed, but our view of man has altered considerably since the earlier optimistic versions of liberalism. Psychological and sociological studies of politics, partly led by the changing properties of public opinion itself, have effectively demolished more simplistic views of how people approached the political issues, of how they became engaged themselves, or interacted with leaders. It has become a commonplace to speak of the ignorance and irrationality of the average voter and, correspondingly, of the necessity for the leadership of and even manipulation of popular opinion by the political elites.

[5] A. Lawrence Lowell, *Public Opinion and Popular Government* (London: Longmans, 1913), Chs. 3, 4.

The role of public opinion in the process of government stands in continuing need of appraisal. Today, more than ever before, governments must heed public opinion. The role of opinion in the political process, however, is not an established one, unchanging and unproblematic. Opinion, like parties or interest groups, or legislative bodies, must do its jobs if democracy is to prosper. What public opinion is, how it is formed, and the relation of opinion to government are subjects with which we shall deal in this chapter.

DEFINITION OF PUBLIC OPINION

What is Opinion?

At the outset we must make as clear as we can what we mean by public opinion. We do not include in it all ideas and beliefs that relate to the state. We have spoken in previous chapters of the role of myth and of ideology in supporting, and indeed making possible, the state. The word "opinion" is sometimes used broadly enough to include such beliefs as Hume did in the discussion from which the quotation above was taken. In the present treatment, however, we are distinguishing between opinions, on the one hand, and the belief systems and sentiments which make up the basic myth of the society in question, on the other hand. The latter comprise matters on which agreement is substantially universal in the society. In particular, they include that consensus on which the whole framework of government is based. To all intents and purposes, they are noncontrovertible; that is to say, it occurs to no one in the society to question them; and if anyone did question them he would be greeted with general disapproval. In the United States and other democratic countries, for instance, the belief in the sacredness of the individual forms part of this consensus. It is not a matter of opinion but of fundamental belief. Most people take it for granted without ever giving it any thought. If their belief were challenged by an outsider they might have great difficulty in defending it; but this experience would probably not alter their attachment to it.

The line between what is and what is not debatable in a society is never sharp. This uncertainty is especially characteristic of democracy, for the democratic myth (belief) holds that everything is open to free discussion. Even the example of belief in the sacredness of the individual illustrates the wide middle ground between the areas of consensus and of difference of opinion. All agree on the general proposition. It represents at least a high valuation on the integrity of the person, although by no means an unlimited one. But does it mean that life should never be taken (unless to save other lives)? Today in the United States there is considerable discussion of euthanasia. So far our laws are firmly set against it; but our behavior manifests ambivalence. Juries often refuse to convict in mercy killing cases. Newspapers and popular magazines question the laws. This particular subject has entered into the realm of opinion, although it is part of a broader concept which is, generally speaking, a matter of consensus.

Opinion, then, deals with matters that are debatable or controvertible in the society in question. If I claim that a light is green when everyone else sees a red light, it would be absurd to say that this was a difference of opinion. We have opinions about matters on which normal people can reasonably differ. To be sure not all our differences are reasonable, but they are subject to reasoning. Opinions at least *tend* to have some rational basis. One must be careful in stating this proposition to guard against misunderstanding. Most opinions reflect a great deal of prejudice, of judgment biased by emotion or sentiment, and, of course, of ignorance. Opinion, as we use the term, however, does imply the presence of some element of rational criticism, some thought, or at least some willingness to allow itself to be governed by relevant facts.[6]

What is Public?

By no means all opinion is public opinion, and it remains to consider the meaning of the qualification "public." First, a "public" is not just any group of people.

A mere aggregation of unrelated individuals, no matter how large, would not constitute a public. Members of the group must have settled relations with each other, they must be characterized by a degree of consensus, in short they must constitute a society. Furthermore, public opinion must, naturally, relate to public questions, although this qualification does not restrict public opinion solely to political questions. In a given community, for example, public opinion might condemn drunkenness and yet not favor prohibiting the sale of alcoholic drinks. Public opinion may (or may not) hold that government officials should observe a standard of conduct higher than that which happens to be required by law, and it may adhere to this view even while opposing any change in the law.

Finally, we have the question of the distribution that an opinion must have for it to become "public." Numbers are important; they constitute one dimension of public opinion; intensity constitutes another. Take a specific issue: say, whether automobile owners should be required to carry liability insurance. Suppose 30 percent of the people believe that such a duty should be imposed and that 35 percent believe the contrary, while the remaining 35 percent are uninterested or undecided. Suppose further that the 30 percent who favor the requirement feel strongly about it, while the

---

[6] By the same token, contrary to the practice of some social psychologists, we distinguish between opinion and "attitude." The latter term refers to a disposition to act in accordance with a certain pattern of values, beliefs, or expectations.

slightly larger number who oppose it do so only mildly. Are we to say that there is no public opinion on the subject, or that there are two public opinions, or are we to judge that one of the opinions is dominant and that it therefore represents "public opinion" on this subject. Practice is not uniform in this situation, but the tendency is to equate public opinion with dominant opinion, where that can be determined, regardless of whether it is majority opinion and even if the majority of the people have no opinion at all on the subject. In the present example, however, it would probably be said that opinion was pretty evenly divided, or that opinion had not yet crystallized on the issue.

Probably V. O. Key's proposed "working" definition of public opinion is as good as any. He applies the term to "those opinions held by private persons which governments find it prudent to heed."[7]

MEASUREMENT AND SCIENTIFIC STUDY OF PUBLIC OPINION

In recent years public opinion has become the subject of extensive study by social psychologists and political scientists. Opinion sampling is now a regular and frequent practice not only in the United States but also in Great Britain, France, Germany, and many other countries. The theory behind this practice is that a small but typical cross section of the people will accurately reflect the general state of public opinion. The problem is to get a cross section that is typical. In principle, the method used is simple enough. If x percent of the people live in New England then that same percentage of the sample to be polled should be from New England. If y percent of all the people are trade union members, then y percent of the sample as a whole should be trade union members. Also the New England sample (and of course other regional samples) should contain the proper percentage of trade union members according to the percentage of the New England population who are trade unionists.[8] Although the theory is simple, practically it is a complicated business when one adds to the two classifications suggested above all the group breakdowns that are significant for most particular questions, e.g., sex, age, income, religion, occupation, rural or urban residence, and the like. Many other problems also face the pollster. For instance, there is the matter of phrasing questions in such a way that they will not "lead" the pollee in a given direction. Emotionally loaded

[7] V. O. Key, Jr., *Public Opinion and American Democracy* (New York: Knopf, 1961), p. 14.

[8] The method here described is known as "quota sampling." Other methods are sometimes—though much less often—employed. One is area sampling, otherwise termed probability sampling. In this method a large, but random, sample for several areas is taken and used as a basis for calculation.

words and prejudicial phrasings must be avoided. If people in the United States are asked "Do you believe in socialized medicine?" the great majority answer in the negative, while a question about a federally supported program for medical care is likely to find more support.

Despite the difficulties, great progress has been made in the measurement of opinion. Some agencies now engaged in this business are interested only in finding out what opinions are, to sell the information to newspapers, business concerns, or candidates for public office. On the other hand, much polling is done for scientific purposes in the effort to find out more about the nature of public opinion—what creates opinion? how can it be changed? what opinions tend to cluster together?—and many other questions of this nature.

Another device for the scientific study of public opinion is the selection of a sample, or panel of individuals who are interviewed several times, and at considerable length—say at various stages before, during, and after an election campaign. For the student of political science, some of the most instructive studies of public opinion have used this technique.[9]

The scientific study of public opinion is, however, still in its infancy. It has revealed many interesting and significant facts, some of which are referred to at various points in this book; but it cannot be said that any significant body of laws governing the formation and development of opinion have been discovered.[10]

CHARACTERISTICS OF INDIVIDUAL OPINION

Many important statements could be made about the individual's opinions on public questions, as well as the manner in which he is likely to act upon those opinions he does hold. Here, however, we shall discuss only some of the most general and most important characteristics of individual opinion, which we have grouped under three headings: 1) the importance of stereotypes; 2) the perception of issues; and 3) the structure of opinion.

[9] See Paul Lazarsfeld and others, *The People's Choice* (New York: Duell, 1944) and Angus Campbell, Philip E. Converse, Warren E. Miller, and Donald E. Stokes, *The American Voter* (New York: Wiley, 1960).

[10] One student of the subject has formulated a series of generalizations regarding public opinion in a democracy. See Hadley Cantril and research associates, *Gauging Public Opinion* (Princeton, N.J.: Princeton U. P., 1944), pp. 226-230. The propositions enumerated, however, do not go far beyond common sense. Many are vague and others are of questionable generality. For criticism of Cantril and also for a more modest attempt along the same line, see Leonard W. Doob, *Public Opinion and Propaganda* (New York: Holt, 1948), pp. 61-64. See also Elihu Katz and Paul F. Lazarsfeld, *Personal Influence* (Glencoe, Ill.: Free Press, 1955), esp. Chs. 1, 2, and 12. The Spring, 1957, issue of the *Public Opinion Quarterly* is devoted to a symposium on "Twenty Years of Public Opinion Research."

Stereotypes

Factors of scale and complexity in modern life, combined with natural human tendencies, introduce distortions at the very root of public opinion. Our perceptions of reality, especially of that with which we have not had firsthand experience, tend to be grossly over-simplified. We perceive and think in terms of "stereotypes."[11] Most of our information about the external world is reported information. Much of it is conflicting. In any case, the quantity of different reports is overwhelming. No one has the mental energy or the time to accept each reported item, weigh it, and thoroughly assimilate it. Consequently, reception is selective. The information that is most readily absorbed is that which fits the views we already have. And the views we already have about public events, in particular, contain simplified pictures of a reported reality: stereotypes, for example of the English businessman, the Soviet bureaucrat, or the Indian intellectual.

Stereotypes vary greatly in the extent of inaccuracy they embody. Also many familiar stereotypes are not taken too seriously because we are aware that they are highly distorted versions of reality. Thus, the crude political boss, the frail and burdened taxpayer, Marianne and John Bull are all familiar in political caricature. When the stereotype is one of which we are not aware, and when it also is part of our perception of ourselves or of other groups, then it may have important consequences for politics and government.

People have stereotyped views not only of other individuals and groups but of activities and events as well. Again, these stereotypes may be wide of reality. Many people, for example, have a definite conception of what "lobbying" is: wining and dining the legislator, offering inducements, and threatening him with punishment at the polls. Such a notion helps to perpetuate the view that there is much "sinister influence" in high places. In fact, however, most "lobbyists" would never dream of bribery, either open or covert, seldom threaten, and understand perfectly well that they are likely to be most influential with the legislator if they can present him with facts or put forward a proposal that is useful to him. Nevertheless, the popular stereotype of "lobbying" persists.[12]

Men's opinions tend to be colored by their interests, often because they accept as truth what accords with their interests. This tendency is facilitated by the phenomenon of stereotypes. A trade unionist will see and remember instances where the Taft-Hartley Act has been used to oppose labor's interests. An employer, on the other hand, will overlook such cases but will have a long memory for the occasions on which labor has abused

[11] Walter Lippmann, *Public Opinion* (New York: Harcourt, 1922), Ch. 1.

[12] Another side of this example merits remark. The stereotype as described was at one time a not-too-inaccurate perception of reality. Perhaps its persistence serves a positive function in helping prevent lobbying from returning to the level of conduct from which it has, in general, raised itself.

its power. Whether we are dealing here with the effect of stereotypes or simply with the familiar fact of selective memory is of no consequence for understanding the nature of public opinion. The results are the same: unconsciously biased opinions. Even judgments made with a studied effort at impartiality will be biased.

Such distorting factors tend to make public opinion an unreliable guide for policy. Various biases may cancel each other out; but this effect is not likely to be complete. At the very least bias and distortion make the process of attaining to sound opinions more difficult, because they stand in the way of our seeing our own errors even when they are clearly pointed out to us.

In stressing the distorting effects of stereotypes we must not overlook the favorable side of the picture. Stereotypes, like habits, are not only unavoidable, they are indispensable. They are like theories and generalizations: inevitably inaccurate, but we could not get along without them. The infinite variety of life and circumstances would overwhelm us if we lacked these devices for enabling us to make paths and patterns where otherwise all would be chaos. But, just as "all generalizations are false, including this one," so our stereotypes are inevitably inaccurate—some much more than others.

Perception of Issues

Turning now to the subject of popular understanding of issues regarding public policy, again we find that the real state of affairs is far removed from what it would be if men were well informed, keenly interested, and completely rational. In fact most people's understanding of the issues of any political campaign is, at best, unsophisticated. More typically they are hardly even aware of the issues. Educated people often make a point of being informed about and able to converse on the topics of the day. Political activists are motivated for other reasons to acquaint themselves with the issues and to spread their views. But except for the opinion elites of politics —the political activist, the educated, and the interested—most people have little knowledge about or understanding of the issues.

Polls directed at the man in the street provide countless examples:

Question: Why are you for X?
Answer: He's the best man.
Question: What do you like about the Republican Party?
Answer: They're the friend of the farmer.
Question: Do you approve of foreign aid?
Answer: No. Times are bad. Charity begins at home.

These examples are imaginary. But they follow patterns commonly encountered by interviewers.[13]

[13] For numerous actual examples, see Angus Campbell, *et al.*, *The American Voter* (New York: Wiley, 1960), pp. 218-250.

Explanations for this kind of behavior are not difficult to find. They lie partly in the operation of stereotypes and partly in the fact that to perceive and understand an issue requires considerable effort and the ability to formulate and evaluate abstract propositions. The farmer, the clerk, or the trade-union member may begin the interpretation of his political world with the view that the Republican Party is the party of sound money, or the Democratic Party the friend of the working man. He may also see these parties are aligned with his friends or his enemies. Yet as long as his present concerns are not disturbed, his evaluation of political issues is not likely to be disturbed either. It is not likely to change in response to events. If corn prices are low or "times are bad," then he may think a bit more about the current situation and possibly even reflect upon the issues. But the chances are that even when politics affects him directly he will not link his troubles to specific policy alternatives, but to the "ins" and the "outs." Such questions as whether taxes should be cut (or spending increased) to bring about full employment are complex and technical. Most people do not look at politics in these terms. They may have heard of the issues. They tend to decide or make up their minds by much less sophisticated modes of thought and evaluation.[14]

Let us be a little more specific. In the United States, the Democratic Party launched a major attack upon the Taft-Hartley Act during the 1948 Presidential campaign, while the Republican Party defended it. In spite of these facts, one third of the public, as indicated by polls, indicated in November of 1948 that they had not heard of the Taft-Hartley Act, while another third had no opinion on it.[15] In 1956, on sixteen issues about which a national sample were queried, one fourth were familiar with less than half of them. On the more encouraging side, one third took positions on fourteen of the sixteen issues, but an important qualification must be noted: even among those who have opinions on specific issues, many are not able to relate them to the positions on those issues taken by the political parties.[16]

The Structure of Opinion

In view of what has been said, it will come as no surprise that the political views of Mr. John Q. Public are not marked for their internal consistency. The notion, sometimes defended, that the average voter's ideas all correspond to a common ideology does not stand up well in the light of public opinion studies. However consistency is a tricky concept. Just because a given individual's views do not correspond to the pattern of policy posi-

---

[14] This discussion relies heavily upon Campbell, *et al.*, *op. cit.*, pp. 218-227.

[15] Campbell, *et al.*, *op. cit.*, p. 172.

[16] *Ibid.*, pp. 174-183. The significance of the last fact is difficult to assess. Of course it means that these voters can not express their convictions about issues by their action in the voting booths. However, in so far as elected representatives become aware of these convictions, whether by polls or through the political grapevine, they may respond to and reflect them.

tions held by either major party or the pattern that may be widely identified by students of public affairs as "liberal" or "conservative," he is not therefore inconsistent. A person who believes in extending public support for those in need of medical care is not compelled by logic to believe also in greater public expenditures for foreign aid. If we forget about "liberal" and "conservative" and other ideological concepts and concentrate on a rather primitive view of self-interest as the test of consistency, the views of the public are somewhat more sensible.[17]

HOW PUBLIC OPINION IS MADE

Personal Experience; Informal Discussion; Leadership

How is public opinion made? First of all, by direct, personal experience. This factor is so obvious that we are inclined to overlook it and turn our attention immediately to the so-called opinion-forming agencies; but to do so would be a great mistake. Wherever an individual has had direct experience relating to an issue, that experience is likely to be the most important single factor in determining his opinion about it. A college student who has had even a summer's employment as an interne in a government agency will have opinions about the civil service that will be hard to shake, although it should be noted that his reactions to his experience may also be colored by his preconceptions. A person who has been a school teacher will have firm convictions on many questions of educational policy growing out of his own experience. Send an isolationist Congressman abroad and he may come back more favorably inclined toward foreign aid, although all efforts at persuasion had heretofore fallen on deaf ears.

It is entirely understandable that personal experience should play a large role in determining our opinions. Our own experience normally makes a much more vivid impression on our minds than does the second- or third-hand account of someone else's experience, both because it is directly presented to our senses and also because it pertains to us and so is supported by our self-esteem. Moreover, we are more than a little inclined to discount evidence supplied by others lest it be colored by their prejudice or self-interest.

More than in the past, however, public policy today deals with matters about which most people have had little if any direct experience. The specialization of the modern economy means that the occupational experi-

---

[17] *Ibid.*, Ch. 9. It might seem that voters whose patterns of issue stands do not correspond with those of any major party are faced with a situation in which they can not be politically effective and are destined to be completely frustrated. This conclusion would overlook another important dimension of public opinion: salience. That is to say, a voter, for example, who feels that foreign policy is much more important than domestic issues, at a given election, can express himself effectively even though he has to do so by voting against the party whose domestic program he prefers. Key, *op. cit.*, pp. 172-173.

ence of most people is limited to a small segment of the economy. True, we travel more than did our forefathers and in general our leisure-time activities supplement our work experience so that the effects of specialization in narrowing the range of our experience are somewhat alleviated. In any case, many of the issues with which government deals are complicated, requiring judgments relating a far wider variety of experiences than most people have had. It does not necessarily follow that the individuals concerned will *consider* their experience inadequate; it may mean only that their opinions will be less well grounded. However, most people probably do recognize that their own experience and knowledge is inadequate to judge the desirability of excess profits tax, a restriction on the importation of cheese, or an increase in financial aid to foreign countries.

When we feel our own knowledge (whether from personal experience or otherwise) to be inadequate for the formation of an opinion, we are likely to be strongly influenced by discussion—by the opinions, that is to say, of our friends and neighbors. One of the interesting findings made by Professor Lazarsfeld and his associates was that, for the group studied, personal conversations played a larger role in influencing voting behavior than did party propaganda carried on through public speeches, press, and radio.[18] Of course this explanation of opinion-formation only pushes the problem back another stage. An interpretation that explained all opinions by the influence of other opinions would be strongly reminiscent of that mythical Irish village whose inhabitants supported themselves by taking in one another's washing. Nevertheless this observation is not without significance. Taken together with common experience, it underlines the influence of personal experience on public opinion; this time, however, at one stage removed. When two or more people are discussing a question and one member of the group is able to speak about the subject from firsthand experience his words will carry special weight.

Not only those who speak from experience are influential in this manner. We may be influenced by the opinions of others because they express themselves fluently, because their arguments seem to be cogent, because they are "successful" and have standing in the community, because we have on previous occasions been impressed by the soundness of their judgment, because they speak with conviction and "seem to know what they are talking about," because they have a commanding presence, or for any of many other reasons. Every community has opinion leaders and they make themselves felt not only when they mount the rostrum but continually, even in the course of casual conversations.[19]

[18] Lazarsfeld, *op. cit.*, p. 150.

[19] For more extended discussion, see Elihu Katz, "The Two-Step Flow of Communication: An Up-to-date Report on a Hypothesis," *Public Opinion Quarterly*, 21 (1957), pp. 61-78; also, Elihu Katz and Paul M. Lazarsfeld, *Personal Influence* (Glencoe, Ill.: Free Press, 1955).

LEADERS AND ACTIVISTS

Although leaders are more important than "masses" in public opinion formation, we must remember that leadership permeates all levels of the body politic. "Little," "dispersed" leadership pervades the community, in addition to the "big" leadership at the center. Furthermore, a sharp distinction between leader and masses or leader and follower is a gross over-simplification. A person who is a leader in one context will be a follower in another. Any person who has had direct personal experience pertinent to a question is likely to assume the role of leader in a discussion of that question with individuals who have had no such experience. Also a person who has achieved acceptance as a leader among a certain group may be quite ineffective in another group. And insofar as leadership is a function of general qualities of personality, it is a matter of degree. A person with limited leadership qualities will be effective when he is surrounded only by those who have still less of these qualities, while he will become a "follower" in the presence of more effective leaders.

It is helpful to supplement the concept of "leader" by that of "political activist." Some people are psychologically more involved in politics than others and some are much more politically active. Although the two groups are not identical, they overlap to a large extent and tend, in certain relevant respects, to have similar characteristics. In particular they tend to be better informed about political issues and to hold more consistent positions with regard to various issues.[20] These facts are doubly significant for the present discussion. It follows that the political behavior of the average voter probably tends to be more rational than his response to the questions of pollsters would lead us to believe. He tends to vote as his more politically involved and active leaders—whether they be trade union leaders, party workers, candidates for office, office holders, ministers, columnists, or whatnot—suggest.[21] Moreover, the nonvoters are by all odds disproportionately made up of persons who register low political involvement and are accordingly among the politically least literate. In other words, those whose opinions are least rational or least well founded on fact are most likely to disenfranchise themselves, at least in a situation of political "normalcy" (as contrasted with a crisis atmosphere).[22]

We spoke above of a contrast between "little," "dispersed" leadership and "big" leadership, by which we refer especially to political leaders who have achieved national stature. (Of course there are leaders of all degrees of scope of influence.) We have been dealing largely with the "dispersed" leadership of the political activists throughout the land. We should add a

[20] See Key, *op. cit.*, pp. 179-185, and Campbell, *et al.*, *op. cit.*, p. 111.

[21] Often, too, he may be less stupid and ill-informed than his answers seem to indicate. We often have good reasons that we can not articulate and sound impressions based on information that we have forgotten.

[22] See Key, *op. cit.*, pp. 185, 196-197.

few words about leadership on the larger stage. If the rank-and-file look to the "little" leaders for guidance, the latter in turn receive help from those higher up. At all levels, but especially at the higher levels, good leaders analyze problems into their basic elements, so that they can be understood by people who could not perform the analysis for themselves. They define and clarify the issues and show relevant considerations. Furthermore, they may dramatize issues in such a way as to give a fillip to weak imaginations. By the power of their own personalities they may arouse latent public spiritedness and good will. To be sure not all leaders are "good" leaders. They may be demagogues. They may distort the facts and spread confusion rather than enlightenment; and it is a major problem of democratic government to devise institutions that will favor the selection of the best leaders of opinion.[23] What is important to recognize here is that, while popular government, as Hume said, rests upon opinion, it also *builds* upon it. It is not tied to the quality of information or intellect possessed by the average citizen.

Groups; Associations; Propaganda

Along with personal experience and informal discussion, groups and associations help to form our opinions on public matters in many ways: they make us more conscious of those of our interests that they represent; they provide opportunities for us to meet, talk with, and be influenced by others with like interests; they frequently employ persons whose job it is to explore the implications for public policy of the interests of the group members and then to point out these implications to the members themselves; and they develop among the members sentiments of loyalty to the group as a whole which make them tend to conform in their opinions to the prevailing attitudes of the group.[24]

Modern studies of voting behavior lay great emphasis upon group membership, both formal and informal. If one's aim is to predict how a given individual will vote, information about group memberships (barring knowledge of his party affiliation) is one of the best single guides to success.[25] A man who is a member of the National Manufacturers Association in the United States is very likely to hold opinions favorable to the Republican Party, unless he lives in the South. Labor union members in this country are much more likely than not to be Democrats and in Great Britain the chances are something like three to one that they will favor the Labor Party.

[23] Parts of this paragraph are taken, without benefit of quotation marks, from J. Roland Pennock, *Liberal Democracy, its Merits and Prospects* (New York: Holt, 1950), p. 241.

[24] See Katz and Lazarsfeld, *op. cit.;* also, Dorwin K. Cartwright and Alvin Zander, *Group Dynamics: Research and Theory* (Evanston, Ill.: Row, Peterson, 1953).

[25] For comment, see Campbell, *et al., op. cit.,* esp. Ch. 2; also, Morris Janowitz and Warren E. Miller, "The Index of Political Predisposition in the 1948 Election," *Journal of Politics,* 14 (1952), pp. 710-727.

Similarly American Catholics tend to be Democrats, British Nonconformists tend to be Liberals (especially in certain areas) or Laborites. American Negroes tend today to vote Democratic in about a three to one ratio. These facts in themselves tell us little about the influence of the group on opinions; in some cases, similarity of opinions may create the group; group consciousness may reinforce similarity of opinions. Whether or not it is typical, the case of the American Negro is instructive. From the time of the Civil War until the 1930s the Negroes, where they voted at all, appear to have been predominantly Republicans. This alignment was a response to the fact that the Republican Party had supported the abolition of slavery. The effect remained long after the cause had lost all relevance to their political interests. But during the 1930s the situation changed. The great depression hit this section of the community hardest of all; and the Democratic Party under the leadership of President Roosevelt took many steps to improve their condition. As a result Negro opinion, and political alignment changed. It was group interest, rationally perceived and evaluated, that brought about the change.[26]

PROPAGANDA

Within and among groups and associations, propaganda begins to play a role. Propaganda is nothing new in the world.[27] The word itself comes from the College of Propaganda, instituted by the Catholic Church in the early seventeenth century for the education of priests. The fact is much older than the word; the Church itself has indulged in organized efforts to propagate the faith as long as it has been in existence. Modern societies, however, being generally dynamic and literate are characterized by propaganda activities to a degree unknown to previous ages.

The myriad organizations that in the modern state exist for the protection and advancement of certain interests of their members perform their functions by seeking to influence opinion. They pump a continuous spray of propaganda onto those in influential positions and upon the public at large. To this end they use all the devices of communication available and many or most of the methods of influence and persuasion familiar to propagandists.[28]

[26] See Campbell, *et al., op. cit.,* Ch. 12.

[27] We use the term "propaganda" to refer to organized attempts to influence opinions or attitudes, using argument or persuasion—not violence. We normally use the word, too, to apply to the manipulation of *public* opinion, thus ruling out most advertising. Finally, it operates in controversial fields. Attempts on the part of schools to develop attitudes of fair play, for instance, would not be called propaganda according to our usage. On the other hand, an organized attempt to influence attitudes either for or against health insurance would fall in that category. Other views of propaganda are discussed in Leonard W. Doob, *Public Opinion and Propaganda,* rev. ed. (New York: Holt, 1948), Ch. 11.

[28] The kinds of argumentative techniques have been familiar and pretty well understood from the day of the Athenian Sophists and the Greek study of "rhetoric" to the present: identification with emotionally charged symbols or words; gross exaggeration;

Propagandists and other persuaders (hidden or not) are not confined to the use of words. Symbols play an important role in their art. A flag or banner, a gesture, a picture, and many other signs or things that represent certain ideas and meanings, and that have sentimental associations may be powerful tools for the propagandist. Words themselves are symbols. Take the word "Americanism," for example. It stands for a large and ill-defined body of ideas, of character traits, beliefs, and even institutions. For Americans generally it carries a strong positive connotation. If a propagandist can get his listener or reader to accept the suggestion that what he is defending or advocating somehow comes under the head of Americanism he has to all intents and purposes succeeded in his objective. It follows automatically that it is a good thing and that all right-thinking people should support it.

Propagandists use, or may use all the devices known to the art of persuasion to attain their ends. They may argue, they may state facts that seem to support their position, omitting others, they may lie, they may appeal to prejudice, to bias, to emotions and sentiments. Because all of these devices are used, propaganda tends to have a bad connotation. It should be noted, however, that a propagandist may be perfectly honest and may appeal to reason as well as passion and prejudice. Also he may depart from the purely rational appeal and still behave in a manner which most people would feel was beyond reproach, as for example if he seeks to persuade people to support a policy of giving grain to India on humanitarian grounds. Not all emotions are base nor by the same token are all emotional or sentimental appeals to be condemned.

Since propaganda may be used to subvert the truth and to create or intensify socially harmful attitudes, it is important to know the limits, if any, to what can be accomplished by it. On this subject our information is inadequate. Some students of the subject maintain that propaganda can be effective only when it tends to further a given predisposition.[29] Propaganda that runs counter to existing predispositions, they assert, is bound to fail. So far as is known to the authors, evidence has never been adduced to prove this position and none occurs to them. Possibly Lasswell and Kaplan meant only to assert the more plausible proposition that propaganda can not *reverse* an existing predisposition. In any event, predispositions have to develop or be created in the first instance. It would seem that propaganda can play a role in the *creation* of predispositions. If so, it would seem likely

---

repetition; use of a "red herring" to divert attention from the facts; false statement of the issue, and the like. Simply put, propagandists play upon the weaknesses of man's critical faculties: upon his suggestibility, and of course upon his prejudices and passions. They utilize the modern means of communication especially and exploit properties of contemporary public opinion. But except for the technical means at their disposal and the deliberate and scientific manner in which certain "principles" of propaganda are applied, not much is new about propaganda or propagandizing.

[29] Harold D. Lasswell and Abraham Kaplan, *Power and Society, A Framework for Political Inquiry* (New Haven, Conn.: Yale U. P., 1950), p. 113.

that propaganda may even change an existing predisposition.[30] Undoubtedly, well established predispositions are difficult to change—by propaganda or in any other way. While a predisposition exists furthermore, it is difficult, if not impossible to get the holder to accept an opinion that runs contrary to it. But it does not follow that *any* opinion can be created, given enough propaganda. It may be, for example, that no amount of propaganda or other changes in the objective situation, unsupported by violence, would serve to convince most Americans that they would be better off as slaves. Generally our basic political myths are relatively invulnerable to propaganda. This proposition finds support in experiments with hypnotism, which show that it is usually impossible to persuade a hypnotized person to act contrary to his basic moral convictions. But to say that propaganda has its limits is quite a different thing from saying that it can be effective only in support of existing predispositions.

Many people find the potentialities of modern propaganda methods and organizations frightening. They conjure up visions of a populace at the mercy of Madison Avenue manipulators.[31] The situation is not one that justifies complacency. At the same time, one of the very characteristics of public opinion we sometimes deplore, its lethargy, serves as a protection. Today the instruments of opinion formation are more powerful than ever; but then the size of the politically significant public is likewise greatly increased. Perhaps the balance has not greatly changed. Most important, it is essential not to make direct comparison between what propaganda has accomplished in totalitarian societies, where it is a monopoly of Party and government, and what it can do in a free society, where opposing groups can and do battle for the control of our minds. It is true that in unity there is strength—and, in plurality, protection!

The Mass Media

Personal experience, as we have pointed out, today provides a wholly inadequate basis for people's opinions on most public questions. If public opinion is to have a sound informational basis, it must be obtained through the agencies of news distribution: primarily the press, radio and television. These agencies occupy a strategic position in modern society, especially in democratic society. It would be no harder to run our economy without railroads and trucks than it would be to run government without radio and the press.

[30] On the problem and prospects of "conversion," see Wilbur J. Schramm, ed., *The Process and Effects of Mass Communication* (Urbana, Ill.: Univ. Illinois Press, 1954), Pt. V; also Joseph T. Kalpper, *The Effects of Mass Communication* (Glencoe, Ill.: Free Press, 1960), Ch. 4.

[31] Others see great potentialities for good in the same facts. See the writings of B. F. Skinner, especially his Utopian novel, *Walden Two* (New York: Macmillan, 1948). It should be added that Skinner's Utopia strikes many readers as more of a horror story than a promise of greener pastures.

One can take some comfort in the thought that the great newspaper chains, TV networks, and news-gathering syndicates make mass democracy in the twentieth century viable. On the other hand, it is equally important to realize that the size and huge capital investment of the firms engaged in this industry have brought with them new problems.

Media communication is a corporate product; and the contents of that communication are also in large measure a corporate product. This factor in itself tends to make the news as reported subject to both inaccuracies and distortion. We have spoken of the psychological factors, such as stereotypes, prejudice, and self-interest, that make for faulty observation by the individual; but reporters, re-write men, and editors are subject to these same human shortcomings. Most information about public affairs is (and must be) reported and interpreted information. Under modern conditions, the number of steps and processes between the raw event and the audience has enormously increased. Furthermore, the newsreporter's story must be processed, packaged, and presented in words, some of them highly symbolic. Often, as part of the processing, the original stories are compressed into abbreviated cablegrams and subsequently expanded by someone other than the writer into a full news story. Or the movie and TV shots taken of events are flown quickly back to a laboratory, and a writer there sees the result and writes an appropriate script. The presentation of news entails enormous scope for editing, for selecting the captions or headlines with which the story will be presented. A large measure of distortion and inaccuracy is inevitable. Add to this fact the additional item that the average citizen probably does not spend more than fifteen minutes or, at most, half an hour reading or listening to news, and the wonder is that public opinion is not more ill-informed than it is!

That the news is slanted is easily demonstrated. Misleading reporting is probably less important than other techniques of distortion. Newspaper editors may exclude certain items, dealing, for instance, with political corruption or questionable business activities. Other accounts which they do not wish to emphasize can be buried on a back page. Headlines are used to "editorialize," and are often more effective than editorials in accomplishing this purpose both because they are far more widely read and also because they seem to be simply stating facts rather than expressing opinion. One of the best ways to see the extent to which the news is slanted is simply to compare the accounts given, the methods of presentation and, particularly, the headlines used in several different papers.[32]

[32] The following example of headline commentary on British Government monthly progress reports on its housing program illustrates the point. On December 24, 1946, the London *Times* captioned its story

18,000 More Houses Completed
Increase in Labour Force
November Figures

Under the American system, and also in Britain and Europe, the separation between news reporting and editorializing in radio and TV is much sharper than in newspapers. "Newscasts" are generally factual, while "analyses" and "comments," although varying tremendously in objectivity, are clearly recognizable as expressing an individual point of view. It is, of course, a gain for the individual to be put on notice that comment is comment. On the other hand, radio and TV tend especially to avoid controversy and topics which might shock the listeners or the sponsors. Much comment is colorless and highly edited; and many items of interest are excluded.

Editorial policies of newspapers and the programming policies of the radio-TV stations and networks reflect the economic interests of these industries. A modern metropolitan newspaper, a clear-channel TV station, not to mention chains or networks, represent a huge investment of money. Their owners or important stockholders are wealthy men and usually conservative. To the extent that they set policy they often encourage reporting and editorial policies that reflect their own views.

Actually, the influence of owners is of relatively slight importance compared to the impact of the economics of the industry itself. The strongest single imperative for these industries is to get and keep lucrative advertising accounts. To this end, the journals and the broadcasting programs must have mass audiences: large circulation for the newspapers and a big listenership for broadcast. The mass media tend to be deferential to the interests and prejudices of advertisers. They are even more aware of the need for amusing, exciting, and holding their popular audiences.

The need for a mass audience puts an important limitation upon the extent to which the media can pervert public opinion. Editors and program directors must avoid offending significant portions of a potential market.[33] They must also offer a diversified product that will appeal to various audiences. Therefore, the mass media tend, on the one hand, toward modera-

---

The *Daily Herald* announced, "New Housing Record," while the *Daily Mail* reported, "3,175 Drop in New Houses." On the 9th of August, 1947, the *Times* judiciously remarked

Housing Progress
Large Numbers Awaiting
Completion

The *Daily Telegraph* declared, "Fewer Houses Built in June," and the *Daily Herald* bannered, "Housing is Highest This Year." The November returns, reported on December 31, brought forth the following from the *Times*: "Fewer Houses Built in November"; and from the *Daily Herald* "Another Housing Target Beaten."

This material is taken from the Report of the Royal Commission on the Press, 1947-1949, Cmd. 7700 (London: His Majesty's Stationery Office, 1949), Table 20, opposite p. 310.

[33] Quite apart from the fact that heavy damages can be collected for defamation. People often forget the restraint of the law of torts; but that law is not forgotten by editors or program directors. It bears very heavily upon TV and radio because of the multiple liability that applies here: the performers, the station, the network, and the sponsor may all be sued for defamation.

tion;[34] on the other, they have definite incentives to express more than one point of view.[35]

Next it must be said, however, that the popular press in large measure has ceased to lead public opinion. Generally, at most, it exaggerates existing tendencies. People like their biases reinforced. Moreover, they want to be excited. Long "background" accounts, providing the necessary factual material for sound judgment will not be read. Event, conflict, crises must be featured and magnified. Unfortunately, the events that are most interesting to most of the reading public have nothing to do with public affairs. Crime, private scandals, sports, and comic strips receive far more attention than public affairs. Undoubtedly journalism in the United States and in other countries plays up to these interests and, by its sensationalism, exaggerates them. *A fortiori,* many of these same tendencies are, if anything, more pronounced in the other mass media for their need of large audiences is even greater.

A great many communities are, furthermore, served by only one newspaper. According to an estimate made in 1945, 40 percent of the newspaper circulation in the United States was then noncompetitive for this reason.[36] Many of the newspapers in the remaining 60 per cent are associated in one of the great chains. TV and radio stations are associated predominantly in networks and buy their important programs from the networks themselves. They face, in fact, continuing pressure from the networks to buy increasing amounts of the prepackaged programs and frequently offer themselves little more than local news or sports, weather reports, advertising, and "disk-jockey" programs. These facts do not mean that in such areas only one point of view can be or is expressed. People often both read the newspapers and listen to radio or TV. They take weekly newsmagazines. They may even hold their own meetings (in churches, trade unions, and clubs) and invite speakers to appear. Nevertheless, much of media content is determined largely by the economics of these large-scale industries, and a large part of the population will get substantially only one side of the story in which the

---

[34] Western Germany provides one of the most striking examples. Here, economic considerations have transformed the character of the press considerably. Under the Weimar Republic, no press in Europe was more notorious for vicious tactics and lack of public responsibility. Since World War II, however, the great dailies have become relatively moderate and cautious, in response to their desire for maximum circulation. See Hans Speier and W. Phillips Davison, *West German Leadership and Foreign Policy* (Evanston, Illinois: Row, Peterson, 1957), Ch. 8.

[35] Newspapers whose editorial columns are conservative, for instance, often subscribe to and publish the syndicated columns of writers whose views are distinctly liberal. Networks have commentators of differing views. For years, one of England's most conservative newspaper owners, Lord Beaverbrook, prominently displayed the political cartoons of David Low, although they expressed strong opposition to most of the things that Beaverbrook supported. *The Evening Star,* in Washington, D.C., carries the cartoons of Berryman, even though they are opposed to the paper's editorial policies.

[36] A Commission on Freedom of the Press, *A Free and Responsible Press* (Chicago: Univ. of Chicago Press, 1947), p. 38.

emphasis will be upon a limited range of viewpoints. For these people the cancelling out of competing biases operates imperfectly at best. The most we can say is that the bias to which these members of the public are subjected is not everywhere the same, for chain ownership of the press and the network association of radio and TV have a limited and perhaps even declining influence.[37]

APPRAISAL

It is easy to criticize the mass media. It is far more difficult as both the English and American commissions referred to above discovered to suggest any significant steps by which governments could improve the situation. In the United States radio and TV are, of course, regulated by the Federal Communications Commission, while in Britain and Europe there are varying degrees of public ownership. Under neither system has much progress

[37] In England, for instance, the trend toward concentration of ownership of the press appears to have been reversed; and a royal commission appointed by the postwar Labor Government, concluded that the existing concentration in the ownership of news agencies was not harmful. See *Report, op. cit.,* pp. 175, 176. A similar study in the United States revealed a decline in the extent of chain ownership. See, Commission on Freedom of the Press, *op. cit.,* p. 42. This commission was a private organization.

Politics and opinion: eighteenth-century England

Philadelphia Museum of Art

Italian election posters

Publifoto

been made toward improving the role of the mass media in relation to public opinion. Public ownership may neutralize radio and TV with respect to certain kinds of influence, but it also condemns them in large measure to eschew political views and interpretation. Regulation in the United States has had a limited impact upon media content and upon trends toward concentration and monopoly, but, until recently at least, little influence in relation to public opinion. Perhaps technological developments, such as off-set printing or ultra-high frequency in TV, by changing the economics of the industries will be of some future importance. As for governmental activities, except those of an indirect character,[38] the dangers of political influence over the channels of free public opinion set strict limits to what may be hoped for from government.

In dealing with public opinion it is important, however, to recognize that the impact of the mass media on elections and public policy is limited. Candidate after candidate has been elected despite opposition of the newspapers. The same holds for the passage of new social legislation. The influ-

---

[38] In the United States, for instance, the federal government encouraged both FM radio and the initial steps leading toward the development of UHF channels, both of which represent far-reaching technological revolutions for these industries. In Britain and in Germany independent broadcast channels, in addition to the publicly owned networks, have also been established or will be permitted.

Politics and opinion: twentieth-century America

Wide World Photos

ence of the mass media is limited, not only because these media do not speak with one voice, but also because political opinion is not formed or changed primarily through reading newspapers or listening to broadcasts. The individual's group membership, his family and religious traditions, his perception of his economic and political environment, are all, for most issues, more important than the mass media. Moreover, whether by mass media or otherwise, public opinion is not easily changed. The image of the public as readily stampeded, either by the mass media or by pressure group propaganda campaigns however conducted is less than realistic. People resist new ideas and simply ignore much that does not agree with their existing views or perceptions of reality. As Professor Key has wryly remarked, "it is quite a feat to induce the public to listen, much less to manipulate it."[39]

Also on this matter as on many others it is an aid to perspective to consider alternatives. Were we better off before the coming of mass media? Can we say that the tabloid readers take less interest in political affairs, or are less well informed about them, than their ancestors who had neither radio, nor TV, nor popular press? It seems unlikely.

[39] V. O. Key, Jr., *op. cit.*, p. 270. See also Campbell, *et al.*, *op. cit.*, p. 151.

Government Activities

Mass communication and the expanded role of public opinion in contemporary politics have meant not only that governments must heed public opinion, but that they must make or lead it as well. This proposition may seem disturbing, since it suggests calculated manipulation. Yet a moment's reflection will suggest that such governmental activities are both necessary and desirable under contemporary circumstances.

Today, groups and partisans appeal to the "public," seeking to win a predominant opinion or decisive consensus to their particular view of an issue. Congress has one view of a matter, the President another. Labor wants one outcome, management something else, and the farmer or urban consumer still something else or no action at all. Government, perforce, becomes a business of appealing to the "public"—to the wider public as opposed to a narrower one, to the quiescent public against that already mobilized. This kind of activity is inescapable: motion in the political system and the preservation of a constitutional balance between the branches of government depend upon it.[40]

Frequently, when one speaks of government activities in the field of opinion formation,—especially if it is in a critical vein—one has the administrative branch of the government in mind. President and Congress are supposed to perform political functions, to exert leadership; that is a large part of their function. In the case of administrative agencies, the situation is less clear-cut. However, administrative agencies nowadays are very sensitive to public opinion. They frequently employ public relations experts and make use of scientific polling techniques in the effort to find out public opinions that are relevant to their interests. They may use this information in the actual formation of their policies, insofar as discretionary authority has been delegated to them. The Department of Agriculture, for example, will not wish to institute a crop control program within its authority if it has reason to believe that it will be virtually impossible to obtain adequate compliance. On the other hand, their investigation may not only reveal strong opposition; it may also suggest ways in which the program could be presented so as to overcome much of the opposition. In that event the Department may engage upon a campaign (a "propaganda" campaign) to influence opinion among the group of farmers who are to be regulated so as to gain wider acceptance for their objectives and a greater realization of the relation between those objectives and the means proposed. During the Second World War the United States Treasury Department used opinion sampling techniques to discover what kind of appeals would be most successful in the sale of war bonds.

Congressmen and private citizens often argue that government bureaus should not use "publicity experts" and carry on propaganda campaigns. The

[40] Cf. E. E. Schattschneider, *The Semi-Sovereign People* (New York: Holt, 1960).

administration, it is said, should be neutral. The general issue of administrative neutrality is a separate matter, but a few words must be said about
this specific aspect of it here. In the first place, it is impossible to draw any
sharp line between reporting and propaganda. An agency that did not report on its activities to the general public and also that did not try to
explain what it is doing to the groups most directly affected would be
neglecting its duty. Take, for instance, a Fair Employment Practices
agency. It can hardly hope to achieve any degree of success unless a large
proportion of the individuals it regulates willingly cooperate. Anything the
agency can do by way of propaganda to increase the number of cooperators
will be money well spent and will further the purpose of the agency more
effectively than prosecutions for violation of the law.

Actually, it is chiefly when agencies indulge in propaganda to get their
own statutory powers enlarged or their appropriations increased that they
come in for criticism.[41] In such cases two parts of the government may be in
conflict, and if the legislature wishes to deprive an agency of funds for
carrying on this kind of warfare that is entirely within its province. If the
majority of the legislature is not so minded, that fact in itself would seem
to be a sufficient answer to the objection—sufficient at least to make it unlikely that the situation can be improved by general legislation. Where the
agency is indulging in propaganda to implement the program committed to
it by the legislature it is hard to see reasonable ground for complaint. Government propaganda involves no infringement on the freedom of the press.
Interests other than those that have prevailed in the political-administrative
process are free to indulge in their own propaganda. Presumably, agencies
will report the full facts and will give equal access to the facts to all representatives of the press. Save for security considerations, any departure from
these principles would be grossly improper. Otherwise, however, it would
appear that the criticisms that have been advanced against government
publicity are without foundation.[42]

CONCLUDING REMARKS

Public Opinion and Democratic Theory

Many of the characteristics of public opinion we have discussed do not
fit well with the premises of classical democratic theory. Generally, public
opinion is ill-informed. People have little experience with respect to the

---

[41] See, for example, the discussion of the Army Corps of Engineers, in Arthur Maas,
Muddy Waters (Cambridge, Mass.: Harvard U. P., 1951).

[42] For a full treatment of this subject as regards the United States government, see
James L. McCamy, *Government Publicity* (Chicago: Univ. of Chicago Press, 1939) and
J. A. R. Pimlott, *Public Relations and American Democracy*, (Princeton, N.J.: Prince-
ton U. P., 1951).

issues of which they are, putatively, the judges. Much of the content of public opinion derives from emotion and prejudice. Public opinion is sometimes mobilized and manipulated, often unscrupulously. Important issues are often not decided by a public "dialectic," but simply by stimulating to activity some group of the hitherto quiescent masses. Even in democracies, furthermore, opinion is mediated by instruments such as the press that often have financial and political incentives to conceal or distort the truth. A rather discouraging picture is not hard to sketch. It is time now to view the subject as a whole and weigh these counts against mitigating considerations.

It is true that large portions of the public refuse to become sufficiently interested in many important issues to inform themselves about them. One consequence of this negligence on their part—if that it be—is to permit the relevant decisions to be made by those who are interested and have more information. If, as not infrequently happens, those with a special axe to grind gain a disproportionate influence as a result, there is at least this saving grace: if others suffer as a consequence they may awake, organize, and secure a modification or reversal of the offending decision.

Multiple Modes and Points of Access

We must think not simply in terms of a vast, undifferentiated "public opinion," but of what goes on in various kinds of associations. Organizations of all kinds not only seek to influence opinion by engaging in propaganda activities but also strive to develop the opinions of their own members on important issues. In doing so they normally operate in accordance with rules of procedure designed to promote deliberation and rational criticism and to act as checks upon unthinking reactions. For instance, such an association as the League of Women Voters, in seeking to determine a policy upon a new issue, will first get all the facts it can and then have experts analyze these facts and present recommendations and raise issues to be further discussed by the membership, perhaps over an extended period of time, before the association itself takes a stand.

Even in a democracy, the public governs in an exceedingly indirect way —one that provides opportunities at all levels of government for the kind of process that goes on in the League of Women Voters. Throughout the machinery of government, formal and informal, the process of refining public opinion is carried out. The political parties, the legislature, the executive and administration, all of these instrumentalities are agencies for the refinement of public opinion. They mediate between it and the actual behavior of government. In extreme cases the government, at their behest, may act in ways which public opinion at the time would not approve, and yet may win the public approval, after the fact, by achieving the right results.

Often theories that have enjoyed wide currency in time turn out to be less falsified by events than in need of restatement. So it is with the optimistic theory of public opinion that Mill set forth. The "dialectic" between opposing views of which Mill spoke does occur. But it often occurs outside the public arena, in committees and associations and boards. Furthermore, it occurs between leaders and followers and between sections or divisions of associations more than it does between the great parties and interest groups or among unorganized members of the public. The degree to which mobilized opinion can also be dialectical depends on factors other than the rationality or irrationality of man or groups of men: it depends on education, upon group membership, upon a strong sense of local community. It depends as well upon the collective discipline enforced by the effective constitution of the political society. Even the more irrational aspects of public opinion are important not in themselves but only in a particular political context and when used in certain ways. Irrational sentiments have their use. It is good, for example, to love justice and honor the judge. Public outcry and the aroused populace are also important and valuable in the game of politics. Whether the public debate is to a healthy degree "dialectical," whether in that debate the relevant facts are brought to bear, will depend in part upon political culture but also very largely upon the procedures and the formal instrumentalities of government that guide, focus, and moderate public opinion.

The Communications Industry

Even the alleged evils of modern tendencies in the communications industry are overstated or mistakenly conceived. In spite of concentration in the ownership of the mass media, people in the United States and Western Europe have ready access to competing sources of news and views in the weekly news magazines, over the radio, and from columnists and commentators. Modern society also has the resources that make it easy to cultivate every potential public: farmers, consumers, dentists, high-school teachers, and so on. In view of this fact, the tendency of the mass media to exploit a low common denominator of taste and intelligence should be somewhat discounted, for the development of tabloids and soap-operas is at least partly offset by an opposing development of more sophisticated and reasoned appeals to all sorts of special publics and publics for special purposes even among the "masses." Also, these media, whatever their faults, have enabled democracy to draw national attention to national issues in an age when democracy could otherwise scarcely survive. Finally, we should observe that many—even practitioners of the art of "hidden persuasion"—have argued that radio and television do not make it easier to hoax the public; they make it harder. Television, for example, is a "hard" medium of communication: it presents personalities nakedly and focusses attention in a way that the newspaper seldom does. Spot announcements and flag-waving seldom sell the television or radio campaigner who does not have genuine appeal on other grounds. There remains the question of what does "sell" him; but certainly the evidence is not conclusive nor even persuasive that new media of communications contribute more to the debauchery of the electorate than to its education.[43]

The classic formulation of the doctrine of liberty of opinion, and also the present liberties and franchises of the press, radio, and television, need to be continually re-examined to determine whether present institutions are adequate to the essential ends of that doctrine. Opinion should be free; access to the "marketplace" of ideas should be relatively easy; free controversy is a condition for exposing the unwelcome truth. But do these principles mean that many small radio or TV stations are better than a few large ones; that the greater the air of controversy in the press, the more the public profits; or that in the name of "liberty of the press," even cabinet secrets are the property of the journalists?[44] Today, the media of communications are "big business." Much of that business is licensed by government. Its traditions and organization are affected by the policies of government: by the tax statutes, by regulatory commissions, by postal regulations, by the common law that protects individuals against libel and unwarranted invasions of privacy. On the other hand, the mass media are not simply industries—they are also a "fourth estate," indispenable to democracy and constitutionalism. We could not, if we wished, let the media alone. We can, at least, hope to understand and perhaps thereby to improve—if only marginally—their role in contemporary democratic government.

SELECTED READINGS

CAMPBELL, ANGUS, et al. The American Voter. New York: Wiley, 1960. This book which grew out of the work of the Michigan Survey Research Center is, to date, the most comprehensive and systematic survey of knowledge about the behavior of the voter.

CATER, DOUGLASS. The Fourth Branch of Government. Boston: Houghton, Mifflin, 1959. This book presents some unusual and well-considered arguments about the power of the press, radio, and TV and their relation to government.

Federal Communications Commission. Network Broadcasting, House Report No. 1297, Eighty-Fifth Congress, Second Session. Washington, D. C.: G. P. O., 1958.

[43] Key believes the virtue of TV in revealing personality is overrated. Commenting on the fact that quiz-show operators demonstrated that even amateurs could hoax the general public, he suggests that the effect of TV is simply to give certain types of frauds access to even greater audiences. See, Public Opinion and American Democracy, page 40 on. The least that can be said on the other side is that the extended opportunity is given to the genuine as well as to the spurious.

[44] For an interesting discussion of these questions, see Douglass Cater, The Fourth Branch of Government (Boston: Houghton, Mifflin, 1959).

A comprehensive study of the television industry, this report shows especially the problems of reconciling technology, economic competition, and broadcast standards.

JENNINGS, W. IVOR. *Party Politics.* 3 vols. Cambridge, Eng.: Cambridge U. P., 1960. Vol. I gives a good account of the relation between opinion and politics in eighteenth and nineteenth century England. This account is valuable, particularly, in showing the relation between opinion and democracy.

KALLPER, JOSEPH T. *The Effects of Mass Communication.* Glencoe, Ill.: Free Press, 1960. Contains a survey of current knowledge about the effects of propaganda and mass communication.

KATZ, ELIHU and LAZARSFELD, PAUL. *Personal Influence.* Glencoe, Ill.: Free Press, 1955. A good statement of the importance of groups and opinion leaders in the formation of public opinion.

KEY, JR., V. O. *Public Opinion and American Democracy.* New York: Knopf, 1961. A recent assessment of the character of contemporary public opinion and its relations to democratic government in the United States. The work is valuable particularly not only because it is comprehensive, but also because it relates public opinion theory to democratic theory.

LAZARSFELD, PAUL, *et al. The People's Choice.* New York: Duell, 1944. A pioneering work in the study of voter attitudes. Lazarsfeld's Erie County survey stresses particularly the importance of "overlapping memberships."

LIPPMANN, WALTER. *Public Opinion.* New York: Harcourt, 1922. Now considered a classic, this book was one of the first to register the democratic disillusion that followed the first World War.

MEYER, MARTIN. *Madison Avenue—U.S.A.* New York: Harper, 1958. A popular account of the advertising industry. The author debunks much of the "hidden persuader" thesis, arguing that the threat of Madison Avenue is probably less serious but also more subtle.

MILL, JOHN STUART. *On Liberty.* London: Longmans, 1913. Mill's work is probably the best single statement of the early liberal view with respect to freedom of opinion and the congruence of this doctrine with political liberty and democracy.

CHAPTER 13

Political Parties and

Pressure Groups

PART I. POLITICAL PARTIES
NATURE AND FUNCTION
OF POLITICAL PARTIES

Among the least contrived yet most essential of the institutions of representative government are political parties. Vital instruments for the effective mobilization and organization of opinion and will, they stand between the amorphous body of ideas, demands, and attitudes comprising public opinion and the formal instruments of democratic government.

Definition

Definitions of political parties abound. Essentially, they differ with respect to the emphasis they place upon ideals and principles as the unifying element. Edmund Burke, in a political tract, propounded a famous definition in the following words: "A party is a body of men united, for promoting by their joint endeavors the national interest, upon some particular principle in which they are all agreed."[1] Others, considering this definition too idealistic, stress the desire to gain control of the machinery of government and the *largesse* of office as the chief uniting factors. Ranney and Kendall have supplied a neutral and comprehensive definition that we may well adopt. They define political parties as "autonomous organized groups that make nominations and contest elections in the hope of eventually gaining and exercising control of the personnel and policies of government."[2] This definition is broad enough to cover many types of political parties. In fact, as

[1] Edmund Burke, "Thoughts on the Cause of Present Discontents," in *The Works of Edmund Burke* (London: Bohn, 1861), Vol. 1, p. 530.
[2] Austin Ranney and Willmoore Kendall, *Democracy and the American Party System* (New York: Harcourt, 1956), p. 85.

will appear, parties vary greatly as to whether programs, personalities, or the simple desire to control the organs of government are the *dominant* factors in attracting and uniting their members.

Why Parties are Needed

Why is it that political parties are so essential? (Some people still condemn them as the works of the devil.) The answer to this question lies in terms of size and of diversity of interest. In the organization and government of a club, a union local, or the like, there is enough consensus as to objectives and ways and means, and sufficient knowledge of personalities so that party organization is not needed. Fundamental policy issues are not at stake within the membership because the purposes of the organization are limited and within those limits there is general agreement. So long as no significant division of opinion or of interest exists within the group, officers may be chosen without "party" organization; but, if opposition to the officers or their policies arises, organization becomes essential. The very least that would be required to oust the incumbents—assuming they are unwilling to yield voluntarily—would be for a group of those who are opposed to the existing leadership to get together and draw up a list or "slate" of candidates for office to be nominated at the proper time and to run for office at the ensuing election against the official slate. In this way, all the opposition elements would be able to unite (assuming that the opposition slate was acceptable to them all). While such a movement might not harden into a party, the example shows that where division of interest exists within a group the question of control becomes important; and effective control, in turn, depends upon organization.[3]

Although in most associations divisions of interest are not so great that the problem of organizing the opposition significantly arises, in modern states no such unity of interest exists. The difference is not just a matter of size and number of members; nor is it simply a matter of the scope of the state's power and the number of matters it controls. Perhaps most significant of all the differences between the state and most other organizations is the fact that membership in the state is compulsory while that of other organizations is normally voluntary. Thus with most organizations the very fact of membership provides a certain assurance of unity of will. But with the state, the only alternative to membership is to move to another country. Organization of the electorate becomes essential if the major criteria for the satis-

[3] We do not deny that real divisions of interest may exist within church organizations, trade unions, corporations or agricultural associations. We are arguing only that "private governments" have, usually, much more consensus about goals and less reason for or social bases to support partisan divisions. Often, "one-party" government within such associations is supported by distinct doctrines and myths, such as "labor solidarity" or deprecation of factionalism and "playing politics." Cf. Grant McConnell, "The Spirit of Private Government," *American Political Science Review*, 52, pp. 754-770.

factory functioning of democratic institutions are to be satisfied. Without some such device as political parties, responsiveness to both need and demand is likely to be sluggish, the enforcement of responsibility (accountability) difficult, if not impossible, leadership inadequate, and government ineffective.

Selection of Candidates and Formulation of Issues

In a large body like the state, organized for diverse purposes, and having compulsory jurisdiction, popular control is virtually impossible without political parties. These organizations submit lists of nominations for elective offices, thus reducing the possibilities to manageable proportions, and enabling the individual voter to make himself effective. They also frame questions.[4] Even on a single issue, such as economic aid for foreign countries, ideas as to the appropriate policy will cover a wide range. Some will think we should devote a great deal of our resources to this purpose, some a moderate amount, and some none. Some would emphasize aid for armament while others would stress raising the standard of living. Still others feel that we should not dictate how the funds should be spent. And so on. With so many possibilities, a vote showing the number in favor of each policy would be of little value. In all probability no policy would command anything like a majority. The question then would be, "How would people have voted if they had known that their own favorite proposal would not receive majority support?" To gain this kind of information, in all fields of public policy, by means of successive elections would be manifestly impracticable. The best that can be done is for people to "trade out" their differences to get agreement among sufficient numbers to have a chance of determining action. Political parties provide a mechanism that facilitates trading. Fortunately, it is somewhat less difficult than it sounds, because people, as well as having opinions about matters of public policy, have attitudes. That is to say their opinions tend to cluster in certain patterns, so the process of grouping together the like-minded on matters of politics is less hopeless than it otherwise would be. It would be easy to exaggerate this point. Among the rank-and-file members of a major party there is considerable lack of agreement on specific issues. (The activists, as might be expected, show greater consistency of views.) The degree of organizational and voting unity that is secured in spite of this lack of consensus is facilitated by the fact that different policy-areas assume differing degrees of relative importance ("salience") for different people. Thus a person who feels that the issues in the field of foreign policy dominate all others may be willing to support a party whose domestic program does not accord well with his own preferences; and vice versa.[5]

---

[4] We leave aside for the moment the extent to which the parties or political leaders *alone* perform these functions.

[5] See V. O. Key, Jr., *Public Opinion and American Democracy* (New York: Knopf, 1961), Ch. 7.

Ordinarily the need to get together on candidates as well as issues simplifies rather than complicates the problem. Personalities tend to become associated with certain attitudes. Furthermore, the oppositions of opinion and interest within a party are less apparent in the selection of an individual candidate than in the framing of issues. Candidate Jones may be favorably disposed to the claims of both farmers and organized labor. The fact that he can not yield to all the demands of the one group without opposing the interest of the other group may lie comfortably obscured.

In fact the selection of candidates for office and the expression of views with respect to issues are more closely related even than we have yet indicated. Seldom do a large number of voters have clear opinions on many issues. Particularly where they are large and conglomerate organizations, parties take few clear and sharply demarcated stands. Their platforms tend to be vague and ambiguous, if not actually self-contradictory in certain respects. What happens, however, is that each party tends to assume, in the minds of the voters, an overall coloration or, as we say, an "image."[6] Terms like "liberal" or "conservative" go some way toward suggesting what may be the nature of these images. One party is, putatively, the party of the little man or the poor man, while another may be associated with success in the business world. Images may also include attitudes favorable or unfavorable to the expansion of state intervention and social services, or "internationalism," or "containment" and so on. The words, manner, and appearance of candidates may play a large role in helping shape the image of a party.[7] Thus, too, when a voter votes for a particular candidate (let us say for the Presidency) he is also voting for his image of the candidate's party. Moreover, his image is likely to bear a close resemblance to that envisaged by other voters and also—a fact of primary importance—to the actual attitudes held by the party leaders. It follows, too, that the political party is a powerful force for the creation of a political consensus, at least within a particular party.

Enforcement of Responsibility

Just as parties serve the function of enabling voters to choose candidates and support policies they approve, they also, in two ways, act as instrumen-

[6] V. O. Key, Jr., *op. cit.*, p. 443, and more generally, pp. 432-435; also Angus Campbell, Philip E. Converse, Warren E. Miller, and Donald E. Stokes, *The American Voter* (New York: Wiley, Inc., 1960), pp. 59 ff. We are not, of course, saying that parties do not take stands upon the issues, but only that people also form images of them which for many voters serve as a kind of mental short-cut. This thesis about "images" seems to hold for Britain and Germany, though the case of France is not clear. See D. E. Butler and Richard Rose, *The British General Election of 1959* (London: Macmillan, 1961), Ch. 3; Uwe Kitzinger, *German Electoral Politics* (Oxford: Clarendon, 1960); Martin Harrison and Uwe Kitzinger, "The French General Election, 1958," *Political Studies* 7 (1959), pp. 147-173.

[7] Though as a matter of interest, it appears that people are less affected by candidates' personality, at least over the long run, than might be supposed. Their views of the parties and their choices of party are usually more closely related to significant group and life experiences than to personalities.

talities for the enforcement of responsibility. In the first place, even though a voter opposed a given officeholder, he could not do so effectively unless he had an opportunity to combine with others in support of someone to displace the office holder. In the second place, inasmuch as the principal acts of modern representative government require the concurrence of a number of individuals, without the mutual bond of party it would frequently be difficut to fix the responsibility for governmental policies. With political parties, however, if a given party is in power, that is to say has its nominees in control of the organs of government, the voter does not need to try to apportion credit and blame among particular officials and representatives. He holds the party in power responsible. If he approves, on the whole, of the way things are going, he votes for the candidates of that party. If he disapproves, he supports a rival party. As will appear, this system of responsible party government is only partially effective in the United States. And other means of enforcing responsibility exist and operate. In England party responsibility functions much more effectively. Even in a country like the United States, however, the party is an important part of the mechanism for enforcing responsibility.

Parties as Alternate Governments

We have been considering political parties as instruments for organizing public opinion and bringing it to bear upon government; but another part of their role can best be understood by seeing them from the point of view of government rather than from that of voters. They are in fact unofficial instruments of government. The party—or parties—out of power stand ready to assume the responsibilities of office whenever electoral fate shall bow in their direction. And the party or party or parties in power have played a greater or lesser part in selecting or supporting the men in elective office, in supplying candidates for appointive office, and organizing and stimulating support for the government as well as keeping it in touch with public opinion. What we have said is to some extent true of any democratic government; but the "alternate government" role of party appears most clearly in Britain, where the governing party takes full responsibility for the acts of its leaders and the Opposition is organized literally as another government in "Shadow Cabinet" and opposition Parliamentary Party. In the United States or in the multi-party systems of the Continent, parties cannot be literally conceived as "alternate governments"; but they perform this function in a limited though essential degree.

Political Education

In addition to making nominations, formulating issues, and aiding in the enforcement of responsibility, political parties serve a vitally important function as agencies for political education. Although it is of crucial importance, this function is incidental to the others. In seeking to win support for its candidates and its policies, the party organization must strive to educate its membership and to appeal to those with no firm party allegiance. Such activity is greatest during campaigns but in some measure it is practically continuous. Of course, these educational activities are far from impartial. They come rather under the heading of propaganda. The net effect on the citizen of being subjected to the rival streams of propaganda of the parties is educational, though the value and the impact of the education varies greatly for different party systems.

MULTIPARTY AND TWO-PARTY SYSTEMS

Multiparty Systems

Under democratic governments, the two major types of party system are multiparty systems and two-party systems. In the most common of multiparty systems no one party is able to win a majority in the country. Multiparty systems are found chiefly under the parliamentary or cabinet form of government and result in the conduct of government by coalition cabinets: that is, cabinets composed of members of more than one party.[8] In general, no one party under a multiparty system is sufficiently representative of the nation as a whole to form a government without drawing upon other sections of opinion and influence.

Under a multiparty system, each party represents a clear-cut position on issues of the day. The normal pattern, under a multiparty system, comprises an extreme Right, or reactionary party, an extreme Left party (often Communist today), and other parties representing less extreme positions. Subject to qualifications to be noted, they can usually be arranged along a continuum between the extremes. Customarily, in multiparty parliaments the seats are arranged in semicircular fashion, following the tradition of the French Revolution, with the most conservative or reactionary party seated at the right of the presiding officer, next to it, at its left, the party whose views are closest to it, and so on in this fashion, with the most radical party at the lefthand side of the chamber. The Right-Left alignment, however, based primarily upon views as to economic policy, is a simplification of the real

[8] Occasionally a party such as the German C.D.U. (Christian Democratic Union) wins a majority, even where several sizable parties exist. In France, also, cabinets have been formed primarily or exclusively by one party without a legislative majority, as they have in Belgium and Holland and Scandinavia. But either of these occurrences is unusual in multiparty practice and is often viewed as unhealthy. For example, even though the C.D.U. in Germany won an absolute majority in the 1957 national election, it shared power in the cabinet with both the F.D.P. (Free Democratic Party) and the *Deutsche Partei*. Ministries in the separate states of the Federal Republic were also coalitions of various parties. Leon Blum's all-Socialist cabinet in France, which governed from 1936 to 1938, was possible only by advance agreement of other members of the Popular Front coalition.

situation. Political, religious, national, sectional, and occupational interests that do not readily lend themselves to the Left-Right classification may constitute bases of party alignments under the multiparty system, with Catholic parties, anti-clerical parties, peasant parties, and parties made up primarily of inhabitants of a given region or members of a certain nationality. While such groups generally tend to have characteristic views on economic questions, it is not uncommon for one of them to be to the right of Party X on certain issues and to the left of it on other issues. Frequently, too, parties that could work together on certain issues are so bitterly antagonistic to each other on other questions that cooperation on the concerns they have in common is difficult if not impossible. In Europe, for example, German middle-class parties have been divided over national and religious questions. The center parties in France, which have generally supported moderate progress, have been divided not only over religious and patriotic issues, but also over class differences and revolutionary traditions.

Even though the neighboring parties of a multiparty system seem to differ but slightly in their views, their differences are often insisted upon with a vigor and intransigeance unknown to most countries where the two-party system prevails.

Multiplicity often encourages further fragmentation. To a certain extent, undoubtedly, this tendency is the reflection of a body politic in which political tolerance is low and in which the various shades of opinion are held with uncompromising vigor by their various partisans. Once such a system becomes operative, however, its very acceptance, and the virtual impossibility of any party aspiring to command a majority, encourages its own perpetuation. Dissident elements tend to split off. Sometimes die-hard members remain in full control of party policy. Sometimes the extremists leave to form a new party. In either case, the same groups of people probably manage to sow more discord than formerly.[9]

Two-Party Systems

By a two-party system is meant a regime with two major parties, either of which normally has a chance of capturing a majority of the seats in the legislature, and one of which, at any given time normally has such a majority. No two-party system has literally only two parties. In the United States, many so-called minor parties such as the Communist Party, the Socialist Party, and the Prohibition Party regularly appear on the ballot. Some of these, like the now defunct Progressive Party in Wisconsin, have obtained great strength locally, and even captured several state governments. Great Britain, during the present century, has gone through the experience of

[9] Maurice Duverger, "Public Opinion and Political Parties in France," *American Political Science Review*, 46 (1952), pp. 1069-1078; also, Duverger, *Political Parties*, trans. Barbara and Robert North, (London: Methuen, 1954), pp. 216-228.

having one of its major parties displaced by another, the Liberals having been forced to give way to Labor. While the Liberal Party remains a significant force in British politics, for the most part one party or another has been able to gain a clear majority in Parliament.

Comparison and Evaluation

From the point of view of giving accurate representation to public opinion, the multiparty system is, of course, superior. The wide choice among parties comes much nearer to reflecting the disparity of views among the electorate than is possible with only two parties. (Although the minor parties under a two-party system may, in the long run, have some influence on the major parties, from any short-run point of view they may be dismissed as ineffective. A vote cast for one of them is at best a "protest vote." A sharp increase in such votes will serve as a warning to the major parties.)[10] Also the more sharply defined programs of the parties in a multiparty system give most voters a more satisfactory choice than is possible under the two-party system.

Parties function both as channels of public opinion and as agencies for converting opinion into governmental policy. They also help to mold opinion and to produce consensus. It is especially in the realm of governmental action and of consensus building that the two-party system is superior. The advantage of the multiparty system even in its expressive capacity, moreover, is less than appears at first sight. It may be in the first instance satisfying to the voter to cast his ballot for a party that accurately represents his views; but if the party leader has to trade and compromise with other parties in order to gain even part of the party's objectives, the advantage is more apparent than real. Compromises must be made at some stage or other, in any case. Under the multiparty system they are often made by the party leaders, in forming electoral alliances; under the two-party system they are also made by party leaders, but acting within a party rather than between parties.

More significantly, under the two-party system the compromises made prior to election time are part of the process by which intra-party unity is developed and are likely to be based upon durable mutual advantage. Britain provides the best illustration of this principle. Also in Britain the images of the two parties are distinct and provide reasonably accurate forecasts of their future actions. Multiparty systems often have the disadvantage of setting words and actions in direct opposition to each other by encouraging electoral appeals and promises that effectively mobilize the adherents of the various parties or an alliance of parties only to be forced to betray their promises in practice.

[10] It should be observed, however, that the role of minor parties as a way of registering protest has declined over the last generation.

Often more serious disadvantages of the multiparty system are revealed in the conversion of opinion into action. At best, coalition governments are valuable devices to utilize ministerial talent and to broaden the representative appeal of a regime. They lack, however, the valuable loyalties and informal working consensus that a cabinet based upon a majority party can use with great effect in coordinating government and maintaining a general tendency in legislative and administrative activity. At worst, coalitions are weak and unstable. When they fall apart, government is temporarily brought to a standstill and policy is suspended until a new coalition can be formed or new elections held. Even when weak coalitions manage to hold together, effective action is difficult because agreement upon a positive policy frequently cannot be obtained from all the parties in a coalition. To a limited extent, the parties of a two-party system are subject to the same defect since they are, in effect, federations of factions or local parties. Generally speaking, however, these parties, having a single organizational structure, responding to a single set of symbols, and having committed themselves to partisan unity, have greater strength than party coalitions. If the governmental system discourages the formation of smaller parties by making them ineffective, another element of coherence is added to the two-party system.

Yet we must emphasize that special circumstances may make a multiparty system preferable. Many parties may be preferable to two parties if one of those two parties is, for example, the Communist Party. In Italy, the only major party other than the reigning Christian Democratic Party is the Communist Party. No large, independent, middle group exists.[11] Despite the "logic" of the two-party system, it is not *necessarily* responsive to new popular demands. In Germany, for example, both the C.D.U. and the S.P.D. (German Social-Democratic Party) are to some extent *Sammelpartei*—that is, parties with broad appeal which draw their support from most sections and groups in the country. Nevertheless, both have until recently been somewhat unresponsive to the needs and desires of the youth, the middle-class pensioners, and various sections of the rural populace. A multiparty coalition is often the simplest or even the only practical way to establish a government that rests upon this kind of support. The two-party systems of the United States, Great Britain, and the English-speaking countries depend upon a well-established political consensus and an effective intra-party group diplomacy that is usually lacking in other countries. Long established divisions of class, creed, and section are not magically dissolved by the agency of a political party. They persist; and they frequently make for an organization controlled by a semi-permanent oligarchy drawn from the dominant wing of the party. In Europe, government has been made increasingly responsive and accessible to the masses not through recruitment to the estab-

[11] John Clarke Adams and Paolo Barile, *The Government of Republican Italy* (Boston: Houghton Mifflin, 1961), pp. 150-151.

lished parties and bargaining *within* them but by the organization of separate parties and bargaining among the parties.[12]

What has been true of the past, however, need not necessarily be true of the future. Old divisions are hard to break down and it is not to be expected that any European versions of two-party systems will quickly begin to operate in the long-established pattern of Anglo-American parties. Yet the winds of change are blowing. In Germany the party system has been greatly simplified, and is an improvement on anything known to previous generations. Also in France, de Gaulle may not have succeeded in establishing a new pattern, but the elections of November 1962 eliminated much of the old party leadership and broke down the traditional party alignments.

TYPES OF POLITICAL PARTIES

Political parties, even democratic political parties, with which our discussion is concerned are of various types. In no small measure, as we shall see, this variation in parties is closely related to kinds of party system, whether two-party or multiparty; but there are other important distinguishing factors.

Many typologies have been proposed for describing party variations. Some, like the "missionary-broker" distinction, classify parties by their major purpose and functional relation to the political system as a whole.[13] Other typologies, such as that of Weber and Duverger relate party organization and membership,[14] while still other classifications draw attention to some especially important aspect of party behavior, for example, membership discipline or its lack.[15]

A Suggested Typology

We suggest as a typology useful for this book one that emphasizes mainly the political function of parties, namely, the distinction between missionary and broker parties. If this distinction is considered as representing two ends of a continuum, then most political parties fall somewhere along it, some at

[12] In support of this thesis, see E. Lakeman and J. D. Lambert, *Voting in Democracies* (London: Faber, 1955), esp. Ch. 9; also Dankwart A. Rustow, *The Politics of Compromise* (Princeton, N.J.: Princeton U. P., 1955), Chs. 1, 2.

[13] Sigmund Neumann, "Toward a Comparative Study of Political Parties," in Neumann, ed., *Modern Political Parties,* (Chicago: Univ. of Chicago Press, 1956), pp. 295-321.

[14] Cf., Max Weber, "Politics as a Vocation," reprinted in H. H. Gerth and C. Wright Mills, *From Max Weber: Essays in Sociology* (New York: Oxford U. P., 1946). Maurice Duverger, *Political Parties,* op. cit., Bk. I. Strictly speaking, the Weber distinctions are among "parties of personal following," (factions), "parties of notables," and "mass-parties"; for Duverger, the corresponding (though not precisely identical) distinctions are "parties of notables," "cadre-parties," and "mass-parties."

[15] For example, Philip Williams, *Politics in Post-War France,* (2d. ed., London: Longmans, 1958), makes use of the distinction between disciplined parties and "supple" parties.

the extreme ends, and a few (often not integrated effectively into the political system) beyond either extreme. The scheme is represented graphically below:

Totalitarian	Remnant Parties
Mass Parties	Parties of Personal Following
Missionary - - - - - - *Broker*	
Charismatic	Parties of Notables
Parties	Leagues

MISSIONARY AND BROKER PARTIES

Missionary parties take their principles seriously, often to the point of advocating a "way of life" and not simply political policies in the ordinary sense. Catholic parties and some socialist parties, especially those of a generation ago, might be considered good cases of missionary parties. As parties seek to win votes or to govern they, perforce, must take more interest in brokerage. The British Labor Party, though it takes its principles and ideology seriously, must appeal to many groups. It would accordingly fall somewhat to the right of the pure missionary party on our continuum. The British Conservative Party, along with the major parties of Germany belong still further toward the center.

In contrast to these more dedicated political organizations, we have "broker" parties. Here commitment to program or ideology is minimal and a majority is sought by finding compromises among the differences of many groups that will secure their mutual support. The major parties of the United States are among the purest representatives of this type of party. Obviously, the parties in a two-party system tend, of necessity, to act as brokers in considerable degree, since they must appeal not to a single section or segment of the community but to something approaching a cross-section of the population. But broker parties also abound in multiparty systems, often derived from the more traditional aristocratic or middle-class parties of the past or in some cases representing parties that, for one reason or another, have abandoned much of their earlier ideological commitment. The Radical Socialists of France provide an example of this latter kind of party, while the Liberal parties of Scandinavia and the Low Countries provide instances of the former type.

PARTIES AT THE EXTREMES

Totalitarian mass parties require no comment. The Communist parties in Europe are the best example. These parties are, in general, more interested in ideology than in politics and also more committed to revolutionary methods than to constitutional ones. Some totalitarian mass parties, notably fascist parties, are "charismatic" as well, depending especially upon the charisma, the mystical personal magnetism of a powerful leader. Hitler's National Socialist party is the example that comes first to mind. Charismatic parties need not, however, be totalitarian or revolutionary. In recent times, de Gaulle's U.N.R. (*Union pour la Nouvelle Republique*) provides the leading example of a democratic charismatic party.

At another extreme are some groups that scarcely qualify as political parties in the ordinary sense of the word: remnant parties, descended from nineteenth century middle-class alliances or parties of aristocratic leadership; parties of largely personal following such as Achille Lauro's *Partito Monarchico Popolare;* and leagues that resemble pressure groups more than parties, like the Taxpayers' Defence League in France. "Parties" of this kind have been important historically and are today significant in underdeveloped countries. It is worth while calling attention to this part of the political spectrum since splinter parties, particularly in France and Italy, continue to have collectively considerable importance. The Independents, a powerful alliance in the French Fourth Republic, was primarily a collection of a number of such groups.

OTHER BASES FOR DISTINCTION

A further important distinction is that between disciplined and undisciplined parties. This distinction refers primarily to the behavior of the party's representatives in the legislative chamber, particularly to the extent that they vote in accordance with the orders of the leader or the decisions of the party caucus; but party discipline may also extend to electoral activity, pronouncements by individual members, and so forth. Thus, the parliamentary discipline of the Christian Democratic Party in Germany or of the Conservative Party in England is high though on other matters party discipline is considerably lower; while the British Labor Party or the German Social Democratic Party observe a fairly high level of discipline both within parliament and outside.

For our present purposes, the distinction between disciplined and undisciplined parties is significant because the presence or absence of discipline will affect the way in which the *party itself* facilitates brokerage and the aggregation of interests. Without party discipline, the job of compromising group interests will fall more heavily upon individual office-holders and other extra-party agencies as it does in the United States. With disciplined parties, more decisions will be reached in party councils, and party loyalty creates a matrix of presumptions that relieve the individual office-holder from a number of burdens and risks.

Duverger also notes the difference between "direct" and "indirect" parties: those in which members are affiliated directly and those in which they have intermediate memberships.[16] Thus, in a federal system, state parties may provide a basis for indirect affiliation as they do in Germany. Until 1918, membership in the British Labor Party was virtually impossible except by

[16] Duverger, *op. cit.*, pp. 24-25.

membership in a Trade Union or an associated socialist group. Similarly, Catholic and peasant parties usually have a corporate structure based upon cooperatives or confessional groups.

Duverger's distinction is useful, especially for European parties, since it explains, or helps to explain many sources of intra-party tension and also many party attitudes—for example, toward parliament, or toward other parties, or toward their own leadership.

FACTORS THAT SHAPE PARTY SYSTEMS

We turn now to the operation of political parties, and to their relation to other informal political processes. Here, we are concerned with those factors that have historically shaped party systems and determined the types of parties within them.

In our judgment, three sets of factors deserve special emphasis: institutional factors; influences that have promoted or disrupted inter-group consensus; and timing (the point in constitutional evolution at which effective party systems emerge).

Historic Origins

Often historic accident or the origins of parties at a particular point in constitutional history is mentioned as a particularly important factor in determining the nature of the party system. The initial polarization of parties over issues and the alignments of groups within them tends to persist. In Britain, party struggles began to take a modern form during the period immediately preceding and following the Revolution of 1688. A major issue during this period was the question of parliamentary power *versus* the extension of the royal prerogative. The British parties divided into Court and Country, later Whig and Tory. Substantially the same alignment of forces persisted down to the present century. In the United States, the contest over ratification of the Constitution served the same purpose in polarizing alignments that the issue of parliamentary supremacy did in England.

Writers familiar with the experience of both Europe and America have emphasized the importance of the parliamentary or extraparliamentary origins of parties.[17] Parliamentary parties—in England, particularly—were established early and accepted as part of the constitutional mechanism. One consequence of this fact was that newly vocal segments of the population tended to look to the established parties for political expression. Also, the parties themselves took a lead in recruiting new support and organizing it within the parties. In Europe, where the tradition of constitutional opposi-

---

[17] See Duverger, *op. cit.*, pages xxiv ff.; Carl J. Friedrich, *Constitutional Government and Democracy*, rev. ed. (Boston: Ginn, 1950), Ch. 21.

tion was accepted late and grudgingly, most parties developed outside parliament first—from associations of Freemasons, from philosophical clubs, from student organizations, from trade unions and peasant cooperatives, and even from veterans' leagues. They could not be easily accommodated within the existing parliamentary parties, so they remained separate organizations. Such parties have often displayed a syndicalist or populistic attitude toward parliament while, conversely, parties of parliamentary origin usually have acted as powerful brakes on similar tendencies among their mass followings.

The concept of historic origins has considerable explanatory power, especially because initial party alignments often crystallize deep-lying political sentiments and because political habits are long-lived. Historic origins, however, leave two important aspects of party systems unexplained. One is why certain alignments and party formations become more strongly entrenched than others; the other is why they persist despite issues and political crises that often disrupt or reshape party systems elsewhere.

Social and Cultural Influences

Comparable in importance to historic origins are certain social and cultural influences, forces tending to promote or disrupt intergroup consensus. Both the establishment and the persistence of the national two-party systems in the United States and Britain, for instance, owe much to such influences. Sir Lewis Namier has shown that an electorate in the local constituencies thinking in nation-wide terms was at least as much a condition of the stable British party alignment as its firm roots in constitutional practice.[18] Similarly, in the United States, patriot societies, associations of merchants and manufacturers, the Jacksonian convention system, all testified to groups that transcended both state boundaries and sectional differences.[19] Without these bonds of political community, it is doubtful that modern two-party systems would have emerged or persisted in either country.

In Europe similar ties of political community—between worker, peasant, and the possessing classes, or between Catholic and Protestant—were weaker. These social and cultural divisions fragmented the parties. Even more, crisis and exigent, divisive issues split the political community and the parties. Europe has had no free land, no sustained peace, no breathing spells of relative social harmony. The tasks of government have been hard and the issues of politics bitter. Each great event in modern European history has left behind it a residue of diehard party faithfuls. Each great event has splintered party alignments. Nationalism divided the Liberal parties; while from the battle for the lay state came clerical and anti-clerical parties. Socialist and Marxist

---

[18] L. B. Namier, *The Structure of Politics at the Accession of George III* (London: Macmillan, 1929), Vol. I, pp. 190-191.

[19] Cf. Wilfred E. Binkley, *American Political Parties—Their Natural History* (New York: Knopf, 1954), esp. Ch. 5.

parties derive from the industrial revolution. Fascists and Communists both originated from the First World War. Weak bonds of political community and crisis have divided the European parties, given them shape and purpose.

Institutional Factors

Finally, in accounting for the persistence of particular party alignments and party forms, institutional influences are especially important. Most particularly, we could note their influence in the persistence of the two-party systems of the United States or Britain or the multiparty system of France.

The form of government itself is an important force in determining the nature of party systems. For the United States, and for countries that have followed its model, the power of the Presidency is so important that no political party can hope to obtain its objectives without controlling that office. Such control requires something approaching a majority of the popular votes. The Presidency cannot be put in commission. There is no such thing as a coalition President. It is a matter of all or nothing. No doubt this factor has been of great importance in the United States. Probably nothing else but the desire to elect a President would serve to hold the Democratic Party together or would have prevented the "Solid South" from forming a permanent remnant party.

For Britain, the same kind of argument has some weight. There, the very powerful tradition of cabinet solidarity and effective government provides an important stimulus for party cohesion. To a more limited extent, the same tradition holds in the Dominions.

Both in Britain and the Dominions, another institutional factor has considerable significance. The English-speaking countries all elect representatives to the legislature from single-member districts. In a given district a party must command a plurality of the votes to obtain any power. The minority is entirely unrepresented. To be sure, a party that is in a decided minority in the country as a whole may obtain pluralities in numerous districts. Nevertheless, this situation acts as a damper upon the enthusiasm of minority groups. Many Continental European countries, on the other hand, make provision for minority representation through "proportional representation." They elect several representatives from a given district and apportion them according to the relative strength of the parties. This makes it much easier for a minority group to obtain some power in the legislature and so to gain a foothold.[20]

Electoral machinery may have an influence on the *number of parties;* even more directly it will influence their *electoral strategy and behavior* and thus in a measure their membership, structure, and the location of power

[20] In support of this conclusion, see Duverger, *op. cit.*, pp. 283-299. For an opposing view, consult E. Lakeman and J. D. Lambert, *op. cit.*, pp. 65 ff.

within them. Other things being equal, the single-member district or the direct primary foster independence of candidates and a decentralization of power in the party, while P.R. is likely to encourage a drift of power upward to the officials at party headquarters and those private persons with access at that point.

Conclusions

Since parties are major instruments of government, a knowledge of the forces making for cohesion or fragmentation of the parties is important for the study of government. Modern, popular government has made the role of party even more important, and attempts to regulate the parties and—especially in Europe—deliberately *remake* party systems, give added significance to the study of influences that mold the parties and party systems.

We have described some of these influences, without attempting to say *which* are most important, or *how much* effect deliberate and conscious efforts to improve the functioning of party systems might have. As a corrective to the fatalistic view of parties, however, several things might be said. One is that parties are more the product of deliberate contrivance than is usually thought. The individual effort that goes into shaping them is often not coordinated or scientifically informed, but much of it is conscious and deliberate.[21] Also, most parties are anything but monolithic organs: they are diffuse, led by relatively small elites connected loosely with the party activists and followers. *A priori,* it would seem that forms of government and consciously adopted reforms can have, in time, a major impact upon party systems, especially if there is substantial agreement upon ends, an understanding of social and political forces, and a favorable political climate.

THE VOTERS' CHOICE OF PARTY

The nature of political parties is further illuminated by a consideration of the factors that determine the individual voters choice of a party. Parties are in the first instance organizations seeking votes. Consequently, the regularities of voter choice and behavior set boundaries and channels which the parties heed, usually with considerable accuracy and sensitivity.

Habit and Tradition

A rationalistic approach to the question of the voter's choice of party would suggest, simply, that each individual aligns himself with the party whose program is most favorable to his interests. Most people, however, sup-

---

[21] For a discussion that supports this point of view and cites much of the relevant literature, see William N. Chambers, *Political Parties in a New Nation—The American Experience* (New York: Oxford U. P., 1963), esp. Ch. 5 and Epilogue.

port one party or another for the simple reason that they always have done so and that their forefathers before them did likewise. Anyone at all familiar with the facts of American or British political life cannot fail to realize that the irrational factors of habit and tradition are important determinants of party affiliation in these countries. Ordinary experience suggests that it is the exception when children do not follow the political affiliation of their parents, where both parents belonged to the same political party.[22] Many people take great pride in the fact that their family has always belonged to such-and-such a political party. Or, if they depart from the party of their forebears, they feel that the matter calls at least for an explanation, if not for an apology. Given areas remain from generation to generation predominantly in the hands of the same party.

The most outstanding example of loyalty to a traditional party in the United States is that of the "Solid South." As a consequence of the Civil War and of the subsequent period of "Reconstruction" of the South under the leadership of the Republican Party, Southerners, except for the freed Negroes, aligned themselves almost to a man with the Democratic Party. Whether or not it was generally to their interest to do so at that time, circumstances have changed so decidedly since then that extensive changes in party affiliation would be called for on the interest theory.

Inadequacy of Tradition as an Explanation

Although the importance of the traditional factor is beyond question, the fact remains that tradition cannot explain origins. If some other force creates political alignments in the first instance, presumably it does not cease to be effective. Nor need we confine ourselves to such a priori reasoning. Studies show that switches occur with considerable frequency. During the twentieth century the United States has experienced a gradual increase of independent voting. The case of the Negro vote is particularly interesting. Just as the white South became Democratic following the Civil War, so the Negroes quite generally aligned themselves with the party that had given them their freedom, the Republican Party, wherever they were able to vote. Of recent years, however, the Democratic Party has supported programs favorable to the interests of the lower economic groups, to which most Negroes belong. The evidence is clear that they have responded to this call of interest and have preponderantly switched their allegiance to the Democratic Party.[23]

[22] Investigation in the United States bears out this impression. One study shows that well over seventy percent of the sample investigated followed the political affiliation of their parents (where the parents were members of the same party) and that roughly half of the remainder classified themselves as independents. Campbell, *et al.*, *op. cit.*, p. 147. See also Herbert Hyman, *Political Socialization* (Glencoe, Ill.: Free Press, 1959).

[23] See Campbell, *et al.*, *The American Voter*, *op. cit.*, p. 453.

Where tradition appears to control against economic interest ways are frequently found for accommodating the two. The fact that southern Democratic representatives in Congress often vote with the Republicans was cited above as evidence suggesting that it would be to the interest of their supporters to shift to the Republican Party; but the fact that the representatives do behave in this way makes it less to the interest of these voters to change their allegiance. They can, in some measure, eat their cake and keep it too; support their interests while adhering to their traditional allegiance. This fact does not refute the contention that traditional and sentimental factors play an important part in determining party alignment, but it detracts from its practical significance. In the Presidential vote, where the kind of accommodation cited above is virtually impossible, during the past quarter of a century the Republican Party has been slowly but significantly increasing its share of the vote in the Southern states.

Economic Interest

Abundant evidence shows that economic interest—or believed economic interest—is important in determining party alignment in the United States. The great bulk of the people believe that the Democratic Party has more to offer to the common people than does the Republican Party.[24] One study shows that 64 per cent of the Republicans held this view in 1940. Polls also showed that only 28 per cent of the people receiving fifty dollars a week or more voted for Roosevelt in 1940, while, at the other end of the scale, 80 per cent of those on relief, W.P.A., or old-age assistance cast their ballots for the Democratic candidate. A group of students of the subject have constructed an index of "socioeconomic status," taking into account income and other factors entering into social status. Grouping the population of the county in which their intensive study was made into five groups or levels on this socioeconomic scale they found that 71 per cent of the top group were Republicans and a progressively lower percentage in each group until a low of 35 per cent was struck for the bottom level.[25] On the basis of more recent studies, Clinton Rossiter has estimated that roughly 80 per cent of the upper 20 per cent of American society typically vote Republican, while less than 30 per cent of the lower 15 per cent vote for the G. O. P.[26] In 1956, 84.9 per cent of a representative sample of American voters identified the Republican party as the party that helps big business, the upper class, and the well-to-do.[27]

[24] At least since the beginning of the New Deal.
[25] Paul F. Lazarsfeld and others, *The People's Choice* (New York: Columbia U. P., 1944), p. 19.
[26] Clinton Rossiter, *Parties and Politics in America* (Ithaca, N.Y.: Cornell U. P., 1960), p. 90.
[27] Campbell, *et al., op. cit.*, p. 47.

Other Explanations

The same and similar studies show that other factors also have significant influence. For instance, the following table indicates the extent to which members of certain groups showed a greater tendency to vote Democratic in 1956 than did control groups matched with them for income level and other "life situation" factors.[28]

	Per Cent
Members of union households	+17.1
Union members	+20.4
Catholics	+ 2.9
Negroes:	
Non-South	+11.6
South	+15.4
Jews	+45.4

Clinton Rossiter argues that the Jewish liberalism, so noticeable in this table, is testimony to their relative freedom from economic considerations and their tendency to vote on rational, emotional, or ideological grounds. He adds, quoting Seymour Lipset, that "their sensitivity to ethnic discrimination and their lack of effective social intercourse with the upper-status groups in America" may also have something to do with this phenomenon.[29]

It has been suggested that people can be classified according to whether they tend to be conservative or radical (or liberal), that some people tend to favor change while others would retain the status quo. It is difficult to test the validity of this hypothesis, and what evidence we have suggests that the matter is far less clear and simple than has been widely supposed. For two significant groups, however, the evidence gives some support to the hypothesis in a qualified form: namely, that the broad dichotomy between liberal and conservative attitudes exists and that it bears some relation to party alignment. The groups in question are (1) the political elites, and (2) the party "changers," i.e., those who have switched their support from one party to the other. The finding with reference to the latter group is especially important both because of the role played by "changers" in determining electoral outcomes and because in their case it seems clear that attitudes influenced party commitment rather than party loyalties affecting attitudes.[30]

[28] *Ibid.*, p. 306.

[29] Clinton Rossiter, *Parties and Politics in America, op. cit.*, pp. 98-99. The Lipset quotation is from Seymour Martin Lipset, *Political Man* (New York: Doubleday, 1960), p. 289.

[30] For discussion of findings and of methodological difficulties, see Campbell, *et al., op. cit.*, pp. 209-215; Herbert McCloskey, "Conservatism and Personality," *American Political Science Review*, 52 (1958), pp. 27-45; and Robert E. Lane, "Political Personality

In England and Europe, scientific studies of the problems we have been discussing are such recent developments that generalization is even more hazardous. The studies that have been made, however, tend to show that the voter in these countries behaves rather more like his American counterpart than the usual doctrine on European and English parties and political behavior would suggest. The British voter pays less attention to "principles" and more to the local issues, the party "image," and personalities than traditional texts have held.[31] Similarly, though the Frenchman particularly prides himself on rational analysis of the party's program, research shows that he votes against traditional enemies, for local interests *versus* the outside, and on grounds of sentiment and loyalty perhaps more than either the American or British electors.[32] Yet, the political party in Europe and Britain is a stronger reference group, whatever the party may be. Ideological factors apparently play a greater role relative to other factors, such as interest. But traditional, sentimental, and, indeed, all bases for party identification tend to be stronger in Europe, for parties there substitute to some extent for other group affiliations, such as neighborhood associations, good-citizen leagues, and the like.

Conclusions

Several rather modest conclusions, relevant to our purposes, seem to be warranted by an examination of voter affiliation studies. One is that, barring an unusual polarization of politics or fragmentation of opinion into blocs, no particular factors stand out sharply or separately. In the United States an ill-assorted cluster of attitudes and opinions much less definite than "class" or "economic interest" is likely to be the significant variable for describing individual responses. The mere term, "socio-economic status," widely used in American studies of voting would suggest this conclusion. In Britain and Europe, class loyalties are stronger along with other partisan loyalties. They are probably stronger also *relative* to other loyalties. But they are distorted and cut across by religious, local, and specific symbolic values to the point that "class" by itself does not prove to be a very useful tool for analysis. Nor do any of the bases of affiliation seem to explain a great deal about specific political behavior. People tend to see in the party image what they want to see. One French peasant believes that the Radical Socialists are the party of

---

and Electoral Choice," *loc. cit.*, **49** (1955), pp. 173-190. Note especially the statement by Campbell, *et al.*, that "as we depart from the extreme combinations of involvement, background, and education represented by [political and 'spectator'—journalistic and academic] elites, the significance of familiar ideological frames of reference drops off rapidly.", *op. cit.*, p. 212.

[31] See particularly, M. Benney, *et al.*, *How People Vote*, (London: Routledge, 1956). Also the Nuffield College, Oxford, series on British General Elections.

[32] J. Stoetzel, "Voting Behavior in France," *British Journal of Sociology*, 6 (1955), pp. 104-122; and "The French Election of 1956" in *Political Studies*, 4 (1956), pp. 139-175, 250-282.

the Revolution; another that the Communists are. In the minds of many, both parties in the United States stand for "liberalism." Both in the United States and Europe, a large lump of the population votes, roughly, according to class, religion, section, or tradition. But that "roughly" covers a very important issue for the political scientist. Opinion and given bases of allegiance are raw materials that are malleable within limits. They can be shaped. These considerations suggest that the way in which interest groups and parties define the issues, develop and focus opinion, and educate the voter are highly influential in determining concrete political behavior. This fact is important, for it weighs in the balance against the common demoralizing fatalism according to which the existing divisions and political impotence of a society are "givens" that cannot be transformed by intelligence and leadership.

ORGANIZATION AND ELECTORAL ACTIVITIES OF PARTIES

In the early days of representative government, when the electorate was relatively small, party organization was loose, informal, and simple. With the virtually universal adult suffrage prevailing in the democratic nations of today it is essential for the parties to be highly organized and to maintain a going organization all the time, not merely at election times. In the United States, the large number of units of government arising partly out of the federal system, and the fact that in any given unit more officials are elected than is customary elsewhere, greatly complicates the tasks of the parties. The number of elections and of candidates is greater than in other countries. So, despite the fact that parties as political institutions play a smaller role in the United States than in Europe or in Britain, they are still highly organized. In Britain all, and in Europe most, parties take their "missionary" activities more seriously. Also, campaigning is still done there less by television and radio and more by personal appearance, organizing popular meetings, and party "visitations" or "canvassing" of the individual electors.[33] These activities require large contingents of amateur party workers devoted to the party cause, often referred to as the party "militants."

Party Structure

In general, party organization everywhere follows the electoral constituencies. Communist Parties, which attempt to encourage "cells" (based usually on place of employment) rather than "branches" (based upon electoral constituencies), are exceptions to this rule. But parties that aim pri-

[33] Differences in campaign methods are less than they used to be, and many European political figures and political commentators now refer to campaigns "in the American style," using television and radio appeals and a campaign strategy similar to that employed in the United States.

marily to win elections organize to win voters where they count: in the constituencies. Thus, party organization ordinarily begins at the level of the smallest unit that has elective officials of its own, such as a borough, ward, or parish. The first important unit of political organization is likely to be either one distributing favors locally or one which forms a base for election of prominent candidates, whether by county, Department, or Parliamentary constituency. In England, parliamentary constituencies are banded together into national organizations, maintaining their respective headquarters. Parties in France and Italy are organized in the departments and federated on a departmental basis. In Germany and the United States, state party organizations, intervening between the local and national levels, are powerful units. Primarily, these organizations raise funds, conduct campaigns or at least aid in the conduct of campaigns, and plan party strategy. In England and Europe generally, and in the United States sometimes, they also make nominations.

Since parties in Britain and Europe are more important as channels for political influence and also as institutions for coordinating political endeavor than in the United States, they are usually more elaborately and explicitly organized. The formal constitutions of the parties are often detailed documents, spelling out the composition and powers of party organs. Direct and affiliated membership, dues paying obligations, representative privileges, and party principles are commonly stated formally and fairly precisely in the party constitutions and by-laws. The organization of central party councils and their relations to the parliamentary sections of the parties are basic concerns for almost all parties. Because of this explicit and extensive organization, the term "party government" can have in Europe and Britain a connotation, both good and bad, which it seldom acquires in the United States.

Intraparty Democracy

Party officials are normally elected, either directly or indirectly, by the party membership. These elections may be entirely informal, in accordance with procedures determined by the party, or—as is commonly the case at the local levels in the United States—they may be at regular "primary" elections carried out by the legally provided election machinery of the state. Either way, a party organization, once installed, tends to be in large measure self-perpetuating, partly simply because any opposition elements within the party generally are unorganized; although a major intra-party split may occasion some measure of minority organization. The big check, however, on what otherwise might be intolerably irresponsible party leadership is the simple fact that a party exists to win elections. In seeking to win elections, the party management has to take account of the demands of its own members and adherents just as much as the demands of other groups.

This thesis that party responsibility is maintained by the desire to win elections is subject to some significant qualifications. An entrenched political machine at the local level often enables an oligarchy to persist. The larger the constituency (in a modern political system) the less likely that a narrowly based oligarchy can dominate, especially in a two-party system. In the nation at large the appeal of the party to workers and adherents must be broad and persuasive. Under a multiparty system, where with few exceptions parties do not strike for a majority, the incentive to appeal to many types of members and voters is less strong. These parties are sectoral parties. They tend also to be more intransigeant and militant, for if they cannot win a majority, at least they will strive to hold the faithful. Since the group representation within these parties is more restricted, rivals for leadership or influence tend to be less numerous. Particular sections of the party or particular political symbols and commitments remain dominant for a long time. Thus, oligarchic domination of the European parties is generally a more serious problem than in the United States or Britain, creating frustration among the militants, hostility between the parliamentary and the popular divisions of the party, and distrust of parties themselves among the voters.[34] Significantly, in the two large parties of Germany—the C.D.U. and the S.P.D.—the oligarchic dominance of the party leaders has been effectively challenged only as both parties have begun serious competition for popular majorities in the States and at the national level.[35]

Incentives for Members

Maintenance of these large organizations requires a great deal of work on the part of a great number of people. Of course, much of the work is done on a volunteer basis. It does not follow that the workers in question are motivated solely by their conviction that the policies and leaders of the party in question are more conducive to the national wellbeing than are those of other parties. Many people are attracted by the social fellowship of the party, or by the prestige that party activity brings. Much of the work is done, on a part-time basis, by individuals who have political ambitions. They may be nominated for an elective office, or they may be appointed to office. They may advance in the party organization and enjoy the satisfaction of exercising political power even though they have no governmental office. They may, indeed, obtain benefits of a less estimable nature, involving either actual corruption or legal but unethical practices.

[34] Discussions on oligarchic tendencies within political parties are legion. Some particularly good accounts are Michels, *op. cit.;* McKenzie, *British Political Parties* (London: Heinemann, 1955); Philip Williams, *Politics in Post-War France* (2d ed., London: Longmans, 1958); and Arnold Heidenheimer, *Adenauer and the C.D.U.* (The Hague: Martinus Nijhoff, 1960).

[35] Cf. Heidenheimer, *op. cit.*, Ch. 6, and Uwe Kitzinger, *German Electoral Politics* (Oxford: Clarendon, 1960), esp. Chs. 2, 3.

In countries like Great Britain, where titles of nobility and other "honors" are still in use, the party in power has other inducements at its disposal. Regular party workers are not usually rewarded in this way, but wealthy individuals who contribute liberally to the party treasury are likely to receive consideration when it comes to the distribution of honors. Also, the high prestige of politics in Britain makes party service more attractive.

In Britain and Europe the parties are strong reference-groups for their party workers. They have definite images and they stand for definite principles, or at least are thought to do so by the party activists. Social affiliations are more likely to follow party associations and *vice versa*. Parties maintain their own press and their own social clubs. The symbolic and ideological inducements offered by them are more distinctly emphasized. In all respects, these parties are closer to churches for the party faithful. By the same token, the so-called "flexible" or "cadre-parties" such as the French Radical Socialists or Independents do not draw large contingents of workers. They remain largely federations of parliamentary and party leaders with their own personal followings.

Money

Money is another item in maintaining party organizations, especially today when even European elections are contested increasingly through nation-wide media of communications. However, in Europe several factors tend to minimize the importance of financial contributions. Many parties, like the Socialists, the Communists, and the British Labor Party, assess their members for regular contributions or dues. Also, much more of the party work in Europe is done by "militants" out of loyalty rather than for pay or promise of future reward. Fewer offices are elective, so that the campaigns are smaller in scope. Also radio and television are usually municipally or nationally owned rather than commercially operated. And most European governments foot part of the expenses for the campaigns, including the contribution of free radio and television time. In Britain, campaign expenditures are strictly limited.

According to most students of the subject, money probably does not often determine the outcome of elections.[36] The quest for money, however, can influence the parties and government a great deal, as American experience demonstrates. Office holders at the state and local levels are frequently "assessed" (at least in practical effect) by the party in power, although literal "assessment" is generally outlawed. One effect of this practice has been to perpetuate partisan influence in the civil service at the state and local levels. Also, the level of campaign activity tends to coincide with the

[36] Austin Ranney and Willmoore Kendall, *Democracy and the American Party System*, (New York: Harcourt, 1956), pp. 380-383; V. O. Key, *Politics, Parties, and Pressure Groups*, 3rd ed. (New York: Crowell, 1952), pp. 562-564; Alexander Heard, *The Costs of Democracy* (Chapel Hill: Univ. North Carolina Press, 1960), Ch. 1.

level at which money can be collected and retained. As a consequence, in the United States campaigns are decentralized in conduct and in focus more than might otherwise be the case. It is alleged, though it would be hard to prove, that American parties are overly anxious to have rich candidates and too deferential to large contributors. Several political scientists have speculated that the television revolution in American politics may make the role of the money-raiser more important in party councils than he otherwise would be. These are possibilities; there is some supporting evidence.[37]

Patronage

The support of party organizations especially in the United States often depends in no small measure upon close cooperation between government officials and the party and upon practices that are inimical to the greatest governmental efficiency even where they involve no illegality or dishonesty. The most obvious and common example is the practice of allowing appointments to governmental positions to be influenced or even dictated by party considerations rather than by the interests of the government service. Insofar as appointments of this kind are made on the basis of a merit system that effectively excludes political influence, parties are deprived of this particular form of support. Consequently, some American scholars hold that, desirable though the extension of the merit system is on administrative grounds, we should not extend it so far that it will deprive the parties of the means for holding together their vast, complicated, and politically invaluable organizations.[38] Experience suggests, however, that political parties are not dependent for their continued existence or effectiveness upon any one factor. In England, where patronage is quite limited, the parties are healthy organizations. In the United States, the sprawling, decentralized nature of the country calls, it is true, for a more extensive party organization. Nevertheless, the parties could almost certainly survive a vast diminution of the existing amount of patronage. In fact the combination of declining patronage and diminished power of local political machines (because of the transfer of authority to Washington) has already begun to work a change in the character of grass roots political organization in the United States. The professional politician is giving way to the amateur, in many places, with implications for the whole party system that cannot yet be foreseen in detail.[39]

[37] Note, however, that most of the studies and evidence refer to *national* elections, not to the local or state levels. For state and local elections it is widely believed that money probably has an even greater impact on the outcome of elections. In national elections usually what one party lacks in money it can compensate for in considerable measure by other resources—such as free leg work by trade unionists.

[38] A statement of the main arguments and citation of the relevant literature is given in William Goodman, *The Two-Party System in the United States*, 2d. ed. (Princeton, N.J.: Van Nostrand, 1960), pp. 109-111.

[39] See Frank J. Sorauf, "The Silent Revolution in Patronage," *Public Administration Review*, 20 (1960), pp. 28-34.

Nominations and Elections

The matter of selecting candidates assumes much greater importance in the United States than in most other countries. To a large extent, in other countries, it is performed by party functionaries either by committees in each constituency or by the national party headquarters, or by some combination of the two. Where the multiparty system prevails, the control over the party by the central organization is generally strong and the leaders have a major role in determining who shall be permitted to run for election on the party "ticket." In England also party discipline is strong. Furthermore, the big concern of the voter, at election time, is to secure victory for his party. Who shall represent that party in his constituency is a comparatively secondary matter. Whoever he is, he will follow the party leadership in Parliamentary "divisions" (votes). Strong discipline in Parliament, in other words, goes along with discipline in matters of nomination.

In the United States, on the other hand, the situation is quite different, particularly because of the institution of the "primary" election. In most of the states, all nominations for elective office are determined at a preliminary ("primary") election. At these elections, the adherents of a given party vote to determine who shall be the candidates of that party, and bear its label, at the forthcoming election. Various methods are used for determining eligibility for voting in the primary, but in any case a voter can participate in the primary of only one party for a given election. Any number of people may seek nomination at a primary election by the simple process of having a petition signed by a prescribed number of registered voters. Normally, the party organization draws up its own approved "slate" of candidates and advertises the fact that this list has the official party backing. Normally, too, this slate is victorious. Nevertheless, the direct primary provides a potential weapon for local popular control of the party machine. Party committeemen themselves are elected in the primary. Although the organization candidates generally prevail, primaries encourage the organization to select its candidates with an eye to local party sentiment even more than with regard to the preferences of the national organization or even the party program.

The primary has an important effect in decentralizing party control in the United States. It facilitates the election of "maverick" candidates. Also, as David Truman has suggested, the primary probably encourages the nomination of people with many local group memberships as opposed to the "cosmopolitan" type of candidate.[40]

In practice, then, such institutions as the primaries and a large number of elective offices—especially at the level of state and local government— have an important effect in decentralizing party control and in shaping

[40] David B. Truman, *The Governmental Process* (New York: Knopf, 1951), pp. 293 ff.

electoral and campaign strategies. European parties—most of them—and British parties, also, are more centralized, more programmatic, and more devoted to "educating" the voter and selling him a "way of life." Even though these contrasts are sometimes stated too sharply, and are not so great as they often seem, they are, nevertheless, real and important.[41] They reflect not only differences in political institutions, but a different view of the relation of party to members, to issues and interests, and to government. These different views of the role of party in government as a whole are worthy of attention. Much of what can be said about this subject, however, depends upon an understanding of the activity of other agencies of representation, such as pressure groups, so we reserve the problem of evaluation to a concluding section of this chapter.

PART II. PRESSURE GROUPS

INTRODUCTION

Classical democratic theory had little if anything to say about groups. It spoke in terms of individual and state. The inadequate nature of such an analysis is now generally recognized. The units with which the state has to deal and whose interests it must consider are, in large measure and at least in the first instance, groups rather than individuals. The Congressman in deciding how to vote, for example, thinks not so much of Smith and Jones or of such a vague concept as the "majority"; rather he considers the needs and desires of farmers, organized labor, of the oil interests, the medical association, and so one. On the other hand, the group (speaking particularly here of groups organized to exert political influence) does many of the things that classical theory assigned to the role of the citizen: sorting out and evaluating political issues; watching the activities of government; and acting to advance specific interests.

Of course not all groups have any direct political mission and some even have little indirect political significance. We shall be concerned here with organized groups whose activities are to a considerable extent political.

[41] Real though the differences are, such descriptions should not be over-generalized. Many of the "cadre" parties in France and elsewhere pay little attention to programs, and central executive organs are not strong powerful bodies. In France, even several of the supposedly disciplined parties pay relatively little attention to their programs during the campaign, stress the issues with the greatest local appeal, and usually nominate candidates on the same principle. The C.D.U. central party organization in Germany has run into increasing difficulties in trying to get their slate adopted by the State parties. Even in Britain, campaigning and party propaganda are less matters of principle and sharply defined issue than they seem to Americans. They are devoted largely to creating a favorable party "image," putting forward winning personalities, and stressing local "bread-and-butter" issues. Still, a large part of the electorate in Britain and Europe feel that the party should take stands, and what they *think* the party stands for is important to them.

Such groups are often called "interest groups," but for our purposes we prefer the term "pressure groups." Note also that the "groups" are, strictly speaking, associations.

By way of further introduction to this subject, it remains only to point out that we are here dealing with the second of the two major types of organization that supplement the formal institutions of democracy in mediating between state and individual. The first was the political party. The emphasis of the party, especially where there is a two-party system, is upon achieving organization of opinion on all public issues on a nation-wide scale—on giving expression to a widely held version of the general interest and on the "aggregation of interests." Pressure groups tend to emphasize special areas of interest, giving them sharper and more detailed expression than can be done by political parties: they are specialists rather than generalists in the organization of opinion.[42] They perform the function of interest "articulation." While we have referred to both political parties and pressure groups as informal agencies of government, there is in this respect some difference between the two. Parties are functionally specialized to win elections—to present a slate and a program (or the issues), to mobilize the party workers and the electorate, and to capitalize on their electoral successes. Pressure groups, as the name signifies, are oriented toward affecting policy, especially on the issues that touch them closely.

KINDS OF PRESSURE GROUPS

The organizations that fall under the heading of pressure groups are of many kinds and varieties. Many, probably the great majority, are concerned primarily with the economic well-being of their members. Their concerns are generally vocational. Even so there are great differences among them. Some will represent a specialized and homogeneous occupation, such as the Mushroom Growers Association of America or the beet-root growers of France. Others, like the A.F.L.-C.I.O., the United States Chamber of Commerce, the American Farm Bureau Federation, or the Federation of British Industries include such differences of interest within their own membership that they often have to exert great efforts to come to agreement on a policy and frequently are unable to agree at all on particular questions. Other organizations, like the Izaac Walton League, may cater to a widespread avocational interest. The American Automobile Association is a kind of consumers' group. Still another type of association is represented by the American Legion and the Veterans of Foreign Wars. Reform organizations are numerous, including the American Civil Liberties Union, the

---

[42] This statement is subject to qualification as regards certain pressure groups, such as the League of Women Voters, which concern themselves with a wide variety of issues appealing to no single segment of the population.

Friends' Committee on National Legislation, the National Temperance League, and the Save-the-Redwoods League.

The kinds of activities in which pressure groups engage are much the same in all modern countries. They educate their own membership to an awareness of their mutual interests. They maintain constant contact with government at all levels to supply information useful to legislator and administrator, to represent the desires of their membership, to lobby for favors or concessions, and to cooperate with the friends or enemies of particular programs. They also contribute to the parties, endorse candidates, and support political publicity campaigns. Last, but not least, much of their effort is directed toward influencing public opinion quite apart from election contests, to foster general good will, or to cultivate favorable or negative sentiments toward some particular issue or activity of government.[43]

AMERICAN PRESSURE GROUPS

American pressure groups tend to be "bipartisan," that is, to refuse to associate with or permanently support one party. They prefer to play the parties off against each other. Some pressure groups, such as the National Association of Manufacturers, and the Congress of Industrial Organizations, have tended to violate this rule, at least at times; but most follow Samuel Gompers's famous advice to the infant American Federation of Labor to "reward our friends and punish our enemies," regardless of party. The inducements for pressure group neutrality in the United States are powerful. The parties themselves are not highly disciplined, and the pressure group tactic of keeping a foot in each camp by contributing to both or maintaining a watchful neutrality pays large political dividends. Equally important are the overlapping memberships of many Americans. A businessman may, for example, be a member of the N.A.M., but also engage in the import trade and be descended from a long line of Democrats. A laborer may be a solid trade-unionist, but of Protestant, Yankee stock, and conservative in his attitudes toward government "spenders." Partisan identification by either of these individual's pressure groups risks the loss of their membership. Thus, in the United States pressure groups tend to concentrate on "bread and butter" issues and avoid either "crusading" or partisanship.

Frequently, pressure groups are conservative institutions, concerned to maintain their advantages and their favored access to government, but not to advance any positive program of public welfare. Furthermore, the pressure groups which speak the loudest and are listened to the most carefully, with few exceptions, are the large producer-oriented groups such as labor, agriculture, and industry. Consequently, it is frequently complained that

[43] Truman, *op. cit.;* also Henry W. Ehrmann, *Interest Groups on Four Continents* (Pittsburgh: Univ. of Pittsburgh Press, 1958).

the "interests" are too effectively represented, and the "public interest" not represented enough, especially in the areas of civic improvement and consumer protection. In reply, it is urged that effective pressure group politics is probably, on balance, the most important single political device for assuring reasonably good and effective representation of the interests that people care about most deeply, that is, in giving effect to intensity of interest as well as to numbers.

Table V, made up from the reports required by law to be filed by all Washington lobbyists, may help to give a more concrete idea of the number and nature of lobbying organizations that maintain representatives in the nation's capital and of the extent of their activities. In addition to the list of "top spenders" for the period in question and the summary by categories, we have arbitrarily selected the "Citizens' Groups" from "A" through "L" to give some idea of the variety of organizations in this category.

TABLE V

LOBBYING ORGANIZATIONS AND REPORTED EXPENDITURES

Top Spenders

The top 19 of the 273 organizations filing lobby spending reports during the first half of 1962 are listed below, with comparative figures for 1961. All listed expenses in excess of $25,000.

Organization	First Half 1962	First Half 1961
United Federation of Postal Clerks (AFL-CIO)	$84,005.52	$47,274.35
National Committee for Insurance Taxation	81,203.18	36,424.37
AFL-CIO	70,703.28	67,960.35
American Medical Assn.	67,386.62	142,894.40
United States Savings and Loan League	62,082.21	38,128.74
American Farm Bureau Federation	59,567.00	57,520.00
American Legion	53,858.79	55,376.45
International Brotherhood of Teamsters	52,875.05	26,482.66
National Farmers Union, Farmers' Educational and Cooperative Union of America	48,552.06	45,425.66
National Council of Farmer Cooperatives	45,110.00	17,413.00
Mutual Insurance Committee on Federal Taxation	43,357.75	10,917.16
International Assn. of Machinists, District Lodge No. 44 (AFL-CIO)	40,367.70	35,168.86
AFL-CIO Maritime Committee	36,435.84	—
National Rivers and Harbors Congress	33,659.78	30,072.89
Realty Committee on Taxation	30,775.58	—
American Hospital Assn.	30,525.95	30,493.62
National Assn. of Electric Companies	28,334.98	30,774.92
Committee for Study of Revenue Bond Financing	26,700.20	5,785.08
Citizens Committee on Natural Resources	25,529.19	9,913.23

Breakdown by Category

Here are the number of organizations reporting and the total amount spent in each of the group classifications of lobby interests:

Category	Number Reporting	Amount Reported
Business	149	$ 820,756.08
Citizens	44	262,201.74
Employee and Labor	36	475,542.28
Farm	21	211,036.45
Military and Veterans	6	68,195.94
Professional	17	170,133.38
TOTAL	273	$2,007,865.87

Citizens Groups

American Cancer Society	$16,105.30
American Civil Liberties Union Inc.	2,169.76*
American Israel Public Affairs Committee	5,369.39
American Justice Assn.	1.00
American Parents Committee Inc. and Bipartisan Citizens Committee for Federal Aid for Public Elementary and Secondary Education	10,487.08
Arthritis and Rheumatism Foundation	2,628.95
Canal Authority of the State of Florida	3,214.95
Charitable Contributors Assn.	3,730.16
Christian Amendment Movement	9,795.56
Citizens Committee on Natural Resources	25,529.19
Citizens Foreign Aid Committee	None
Committee for a National Trade Policy, Legislative Committee	8,616.17
Committee for Collective Security	855.38
Committee for Return of Confiscated German and Japanese Property	100.00*
Committee to Support U.S. Congress Bill Creating a Commission on Obscene Matters and Materials	18.02
Family Tax Assn.	4,483.42
Far East Group Inc.	None*
Florida Inland Navigation District	3,031.16
Friends Committee on National Legislation	18,437.78
Home Town Free Television Assn.	None*
International Economic Policy Assn., Legislative Committee	10,613.31†
Japanese American Citizens League	300.00
Liberty Under Law Inc.	92.33
Lobby for Peace	3,928.94*

* First quarter of 1962 only.
† Second quarter of 1962 only.

The material in this table is reprinted, with permission, from the *Congressional Quarterly Weekly Report*, No. 44, for the week ending November 2, 1962.

EUROPEAN PRESSURE GROUPS

In Europe, as contrasted with the United States and Britain, the "art of association," as we understand the term and the activity, is not so well developed. Social and cultural divisions run deeper. In most countries of Western Europe, the agricultural, artisan, and small-business sectors of the population bulk larger in the total census. People are also poorer and, in some countries, less literate. As a result of these various factors, people generally have fewer group memberships and particularly fewer overlapping group memberships. Furthermore, with few exceptions, the intensity of group participation is low: associations have vast numbers of merely "nominal" members and almost all organizations have difficulties in financing their activities on any broad footing.

The consequences for politics of this impoverished group life are direct and significant. "Promotional" groups are not numerous in Europe. Good government leagues, civil liberties unions, and even neighborhood associations are notably absent or poorly organized. Traditionally, in Europe, such matters have been left in large measure to the political parties. Also, the effectiveness with which different groups are organized varies enormously. Usually, business is the most effectively organized, prosperous farmers and laborers come second, and artisans, householders, pensioners or similar groups run a poor third. This ranking is typical of most countries. However, the small farmer, artisan, or small businessman together represent a large part of the population in Europe. Being poorly organized, they are poorly represented.

The absence of overlapping memberships is notable particularly among these groups. The Catholic peasant is likely to belong to a Catholic co-operative and his anti-clerical neighbor to another cooperative or to none at all. Similarly, most European labor movements are split into Communist, Socialist, Catholic, and Independent sections.[44] Group memberships tend to cluster around particular partisan loyalties or ideological commitments more than they do, for instance, in the United States.[45] As one consequence, partisan loyalty is encouraged. But another consequence, not so commonly recognized, is that the parties fragment the interest groups in turn, by dividing their membership along partisan lines.

[44] German and Scandinavian labor movements are an exception to this rule. Interestingly, in these countries the labor unions often tend to dampen partisan activity by requesting particular parties not to force a political issue to the point that it would divide the trade union membership.

[45] A question might be raised about the importance of overlapping memberships even in the United States, and of the consequences of its relative absence in Britain. Our point here is not about the significance of overlapping memberships or their absence, however, but the tendency for the memberships that do exist to cluster about certain loyalties and not to be offset by other influences, one of which might be alternate memberships. See, generally, Stanley Rothman, "Systematic Political Theory," *American Political Science Review*, 54 (1960), pp. 15-33.

Pressure Groups and Government

By contrast with the United States, many of the largest and most important pressure groups both in Britain and on the Continent are intimately associated with government. More functions of government are delegated to them: for example, in setting prices, reorganizing industries according to plan, or enforcing quotas. Direct government support is common, such as joint governmental and private stock-ownership or governmentally sponsored cartels. Both the government and the political parties often take a hand in organizing pressure group activity. Frequently, trade unions and cooperatives have either been initially organized by the parties, or, because of the parlous state of their finances and organization, taken in tow by the parties. Also, since group representation is otherwise likely to be distorted and access to particular branches of government open on more favorable terms to some than to others, the practice of organizing national economic councils representing important interests developed after the First World War and has continued in several countries down to the present.

This practice of associating pressure groups with government or with the parties tends to promote both party loyalty and party discipline. In the most obvious fashion, party discipline is often enforced with respect to pressure group membership because the leaders of the pressure groups are themselves important party officials. Thus, in Italy the Christian Democratic government has been able in the past to keep the Catholic trade unions (C.I.S.L.) firmly in line. The same relation often obtains between Communist Parties and the Communist trade unions.[46] Another factor is the powers that trade associations themselves exercise. Some of these powers are delegated to them by the state. Also, in Europe, exclusion from markets, boycotts, and price discrimination are often used against recalcitrant members. In the United States, such statutes as the Sherman and Clayton Acts outlawing monopolies and regulating trade practices, preclude the use of the more coercive devices for promoting intragroup cohesion. Nor should it be forgotten that close association of pressure groups and government gives these groups a large stake in the policies of particular parties. For example, should the S. P. D. come to power, the loss to German business in favored access and privileges would be enormous.

Pressure Groups and Parties

Both in Britain and Europe, a particular pressure group will tend to support a particular party or sector of parties. In Britain, the major business groups, the Federation of British Industries and the Chambers of Com-

---

[46] Trade unions are beginning to assert more independence, especially as they have found themselves able to bargain collectively with greater effectiveness. On the other hand, party influence is still extensive and oppressive. See Maurice F. Neufeld, *Italy: School for Awakening Nations* (Ithaca, N.Y.: Cornell U. P., 1961), Ch. 10, esp. pp. 478 ff.

merce are closely tied to the Conservative Party.[47] Some of their representatives and staff officials are even Members of Parliament. Conversely, the same relation exists between the Trades Unions Congress and the Labor Party. On the Continent, as a general principle, business leans toward the "supple" parties that lack mass membership or articulate organization. Labor is predominantly Socialist or Communist, although Christian Democratic parties have had limited successes in developing Catholic trade union movements. Landlords, independent farmers, and peasants support different parties; like labor, however, they support them not as autonomous pressure groups bargaining between the parties, but as divided sectors of an occupation, each oriented toward a particular party or bloc of parties. Even the so-called "free professions"—doctors, lawyers, and academicians—concentrate heavily in particular parties, notably center parties with a neutral middle-class ideology or moderately socialist movements with a respectable white-collar leadership.

Lack of Flexibility

The absence of flexibility in the relations of pressure groups in Europe weakens democratic government as a whole. Separate organized interests do not collaborate readily in supporting particular issues and programs as they do in the United States and to a large extent in Britain. As a consequence, a certain number of good causes go amiss for want of popular support.[48] The pressure groups do not themselves do as much to "sell" compromise to their membership as they would in the United States. Even the parties themselves find it difficult to reach out to new sources of electoral support. They cannot "break out" to the right or to the left lest they lost the pressure group support that they have.

BRITISH PRESSURE GROUPS

In Britain, even though parties and pressure groups are often closely associated and the pressure groups are, in any case, seldom bipartisan in orientation, the pattern of pressure group politics is markedly different from European practices. Undoubtedly, national character and political tradition help account for the difference. So does the effective nation-wide confederation of most pressure groups. They include the bulk of the important membership of their particular interest throughout the nation. Even though a

[47] The National Farmers Union, however, nowadays assumes a nonpartisan posture.

[48] Programs such as modernization of industry, promotion of better land use, public housing, and expansion of social services call especially for group cooperation and pooling of interest.

major interest is likely to take a partisan stand on a particular issue, that stand will be moderate, representing the outcome of a great deal of intra-group deliberation and compromise.[49] Furthermore, in Britain, almost every interest is effectively organized, from industry and labor at one extreme to rate-payers, consumers, automobile drivers, and bird-lovers at the other. Many of the "public interest" lobbies and promotional groups are non-partisan. Few good issues go begging for want of popular support. England is both an urban, industrial society and one that can practice the "arts of association" effectively; most elements of the public can join together in far-flung representative groups and collaborate with other interests active in politics. As a consequence, many general interests that cut across or arch over narrow sectoral or occupational concerns get represented in Parliament and effectively pressed upon the cabinet minister and the civil service.

IN CONCLUSION

When the continental and the American political systems are contrasted, pressure group activity in the United States seems much less "sinister" than it otherwise would. In fact, the United States is largely one nation rather than a confederation of sections by virtue of the interests that transcend state and regional boundaries. Significantly, truly national politics emerged late in America,—some would say as late as the close of the nineteenth century, with the appearance of Mark Hanna, a master of group (rather than sectional) diplomacy. Until about the time of Garfield's administration, political coalitions were sectional alliances cemented by patronage. Only by the pooling of interests effected under McKinley's presidency did the United States develop a working alternative to logrolling and patronage that could effectively unite the sprawling American assemblage of local political machines and sectional constituencies. The role of pressure groups in contemporary government is equally vital: to facilitate the bargaining, the representation of interests, and the flexibility in policy upon which contemporary politics depends. Discussions of American politics make continuing complaint that pressure groups usurp the "proper" role of party, that the public interest is obscured by the importunate and clamorous demands of the "interests." Without prejudging the merits of such a view, we suggest that reflection upon the state of politics *without* effective group representation is a valuable corrective to any uncritical acceptance of these laments.

[49] Cf. Samuel E. Finer, "The Federation of British Industries," *Political Studies,* 4 (1956), pp. 61-82; George Allen, "The National Farmers' Union as a Pressure Group" *Contemporary Review,* 195 (1959), pp. 257-268 and 321-329; and Peter Self and Herbert J. Storing, *The State and the Farmer* (London: Allen & Unwin, 1962).

PART III. "RESPONSIBLE PARTIES" OR POLITICAL PLURALISM

Parties and interest groups are the vital agencies in articulating, aggregating, directing, and sustaining public will. The problem of organizing the public will involves much more, however, than the structure of parties or the character of interest groups. Public opinion, political parties, and pressure groups are often competent to do particular jobs and not others. The way in which these components work together is as important as the facts about each of them separately. Consequently, in this section we shall discuss two contrasting systems. One of them is the British system of disciplined and (at least in theory) programmatic parties. It is often called "responsible party government." The other system (of which the American is the leading example) is one in which many and various "forces" or elements cooperate, informally and with shifting alignments but effectively. Perhaps as descriptive a term as any for this system is "political pluralism."

THE BRITISH SYSTEM OF "RESPONSIBLE PARTIES"

In the British system, the theory goes, the parties are cohesive and organized institutions. They propose broad, integrated programs based upon stands of principle. Government is organized to put these programs into effect and the Opposition to criticize them and offer a coherent alternative to them. Party discipline holds the individual member in line. By the same token, it protects him from pressures, since the party label wins elections, not personal appeal or favors done for the local constituency. Thus, the parties can "deliver." Furthermore, a vote is a vote for "something," not just a vote against the party in power or against a prevailing state of affairs for which no one is responsible.

Bases of its Appeal

The appeal of "party responsibility" is strong. It has about it an air of propriety. Politicians speak to a serious purpose and with care, for they know that if they are the Government they should act on what they say and, if they are the Opposition, they may in the future be expected to turn their promises into reality. The parties themselves do the jobs that parties should do. Particularly, they exert a continuous influence upon their supporters—whether individuals or groups—to moderate their claims and to harmonize them with a coherent party program. In Parliament and out, the press, the public, and above all the Opposition watch the parties for signs of unhealed factionalism, for words that do not match deeds, and for any form of patch-work jobbery that would indicate that they were unfit for government. The major concessions and promises must be made in the open, for the nation to view and judge. In effect, party government formalizes and makes public and explicit the process of aggregating opinion and developing a majority will. The competition is close and it is fair. After the people have gone to the polls, even the losers are disposed to say "the people have willed it; let it come to pass."

Its Limitations

Most panegyrics celebrating British government usually stress such items. That the party system has these effects in some degree seems beyond doubt. How marked are these characteristics and how important are their consequences for the whole political system is another question.

To what extent do the British parties take stands of principle and thus give the voters a "real choice"? At times, they certainly do. But the differences of principle between the parties in Britain are not so sharply stated nor so real even in substance as Americans commonly suppose.[50] Usually the voters, except for some rather large issues, are offered a little more of this or a little less of that by each of the parties. In recent party contests, nationalization of industry and intervention in the Suez crisis are about the only issues on which the parties have differed sharply. Even on these issues, the Labor Party was divided over nationalization and both parties were divided over Suez. In 1963, the Common Market was a political issue in Britain, and party divisions have been deep upon this subject as well. Division upon such issues as nationalization, Suez, and the Common Market are real, however, and do give people a chance to express their preferences clearly.[51]

RESPONSIBLE FOR WHAT?

One important question to be asked with respect to party responsibility is: how partisan should government be? In Britain, by constitutional practice many issues are outside the party competition. The partisanship that obtains over most domestic issues is considerably moderated with respect to foreign policy.[52] Election irregularities, parliamentary privilege, legislative investigations, and allegations of corruption are similarly treated as non-

[50] David Butler, "American Myths about British Parties," *Virginia Quarterly Review,* 31 (1955), pp. 46-57.

[51] To be sure, this system has its costs. If I, as a middle-of-the-roader, like neither nationalization (which Labor supported) nor the intervention in Suez (which the Conservatives supported) then the clear choice between the parties does not help much. The same holds for the Common Market. If I dislike the Conservative domestic policy but wish Britain to enter the Common Market, where is my political home? The party alignments on the Common Market are not only an interesting example of the way in which the party lines get twisted but also pose a separate question of whether British politics might not profit from "bipartisanship" on some issues.

[52] M. A. Fitzsimmons, "The Continuity of British Foreign Policy," *Review of Politics* 21, pp. 300-314; L. D. Epstein, *Britain—Uneasy Ally* (Chicago: Univ. of Chicago Press, 1953).

partisan issues. The latter group of issues is particularly interesting since they have been *made* nonpartisan issues precisely because of the temptations for a strong, disciplined majority to protect itself unfairly in these areas. Few political constitutions are so well established that they could restrain a cohesive majority with a popular mandate from abusing its power, as the British constitution does. In Britain, the people have had a long time to learn what the nation could and could not stand.

"RESPONSIBLE" TO WHOM?

In principle, "responsible party government" is democratic because of its accountability. The leadership is held to a rigorous accounting by their followers. The question is: to whom does responsibility lie? Is a Government responsible to the parliamentary party, to the national party, to the majority, or to the whole nation? Actually, the government is wholly responsible to none of these and partly responsible to each of them. Of course, the government stands on a platform and upon its partisan pledges to the nation. However, for the party executive or the Trade Unions of the Labor Party, or the workers and membership of either party to *dictate* to the cabinet or the parliament the particulars or the outlines of policy would be intolerable. A party is a self-selected group of activists, biassed in their views of the nation's welfare, far removed from the active center of decision, and untutored in the arts of government. "Responsible party government," British style, is in fact a finely adjusted accommodation of institutions. The theory of the British Constitution is that parliament must be independent of but supported by the parties in order to govern vigorously for the whole nation.[53] The majority is not important for its own sake. The majority only chooses between two organized, coherent, alternate governments. It takes its choice and that choice may be coerced by the paucity of alternatives.

WEAKNESS OF THE MANDATE THEORY

The greatest weakness of the theory underlying the "responsible party government" model grows directly out of the characteristics of public opinion, as discussed in the preceding chapter. The "responsible party government" model assumes that each party presents a fairly detailed program and that the majority of an informed electorate will find one or the other that meets with its approval. The government so selected will then have a mandate to carry out this program. In some measure all democratic government is based upon this set of assumptions and line of reasoning. It is in those words, "in some measure," however, that the difference between the responsible party government model and the pluralistic model lies. In point of fact, the responsible party government model assumes a degree of educa-

---

[53] As Professor McKenzie has shown, even in the case of the Labor Party where its concept of intra-party democracy diverged from this theory, it was the Labor Party that surrendered and not the constitution. Robert M. McKenzie, *British Political Parties*, op. cit., esp. Ch. 10.

tion, information, and political attentiveness that was more characteristic of British political parties when the suffrage was still restricted to the upper classes than it is under universal suffrage. On many political questions the majority of the voters are either not well enough informed or not sufficiently interested to have an opinion. To that extent the British system makes a false assumption. In favor of making this assumption, it may be argued that at least this system facilitates enforcement of party and governmental responsibility by those who are sufficiently interested and well-informed to take advantage of this situation. On the other side, what is made to appear as the will of the majority under this system frequently is not. Rule by a majority of the majority party may result in minority rule. Take an actual case from British experience. In 1950 a majority of the voters cast their ballots for candidates who were opposed to the nationalization of steel; yet the Labor Party, having gained a majority of seats in Parliament, carried out this aspect of its program. Perhaps more in point, is the fact that the whole nationalization program that was carried out between 1945 and 1950 probably lacked majority support. This statement is based upon the fact that Labor's popular majority in 1945 was a matter at most of only some 65,000 votes out of 25 million, and that nationalization is known to have been the least popular plank in their program—not to mention the fact that many were voting against wartime controls and for a change rather than with an eye to any particular program.[54]

THE AMERICAN SYSTEM
OF POLITICAL PLURALISM

The American political system typifies what we have called "pluralism." Its political parties are notorious for their lack of discipline. They are loose federations of leaders and of state and local machines, held together largely by tradition and by patronage and the favors dispensed through the executive and legislative branches of government, although commitment to the program of a party or a Presidential candidate is also a powerful factor. Decentralized and informal party organization is fostered by American political tradition, by the size and diversity of the electorate, and by the Constitution itself.

As a consequence of this relative lack of discipline, party responsibility does not and cannot function in the United States as it does in Great Britain. A Democratic member of Congress may or may not support the policies of a Democratic President; and the same with a Republican Congressman vis-à-vis a Republican President. It is a rare event when a President can secure legislative approval of his full program, regardless of the political

[54] See J. Roland Pennock, "Responsiveness, Responsibility, and Majority Rule," *American Political Science Review* 46 (1952), pp. 790-807; and also R. B. McCallum and Alison Readman, *The British General Election of 1945* (London: Oxford U. P., 1947), pp. 250-253.

complexion of the Congress. Congressmen are far more responsive to local and sectional interests and to the activities of pressure groups than is the case with members of Parliament. This being the case, the legislative output of Congress is probably less well integrated, more likely to contain inconsistencies, than is the case with Parliament, although it is difficult to provide empirical verification for such statements. Also, one of the major purposes of political parties—focussing responsibility—tends to be defeated. The individual voter can not simply say to himself: "I like the platform of the Democratic Party and the pronouncements of its leaders, therefore I shall vote for the Democratic candidates." If he follows this simple procedure— and it is the procedure that party government is designed to make possible —he may well vote for Congressmen who will do all they can to oppose many parts of the policy he means to affirm.

Lack of Discipline: Appraisal

Are these consequences as bad as they seem? Despite the much touted subservience of the parties to the pressure groups, the fact remains that the parties are themselves the strongest *single* influence on the votes of the legislators. Both parties are "distinct communities of co-believers who diverge sharply on many important issues."[55] They also have distinctive images in the minds of the voters. To be sure, the differences under any healthy two-party system tend to be narrow. After all, each group is seeking to win the support of those voters who are "on the fence." Nevertheless, the elections do offer policy choices and they are real contests.

The most important point to be made in the present context, however, is that weakened party responsibility does not necessarily mean that popular control is lessened. The political party is only one of the devices by which government is kept subservient to the desires of the voters. Indications are that it is becoming less important. Elective and appointive officials alike are today subjected to a constant stream of opinion. The din of the press, the radio, of reports of opinion polls, of letters and telegrams from constituents, and of the facts, arguments, and solicitations of the representatives of pressure groups is so great that none can be deaf to it. To be sure, the very weakness of the political parties encourages these other avenues of public expression. The result is far less orderly and systematic than it would be with a system of two strong political parties. It is, however, far more flexible, far more reflective of the pluralistic and vibrant nature of American life.[56]

---

[55] Herbert McClosky, *et al.*, "Issue Conflict and Consensus Among Party Leaders and Followers," *American Political Science Review*, 54 (1960), p. 426.

[56] A leading American political scientist, Harold D. Lasswell, has put it this way. "In the world of modern industrialism," he writes, "the connections between government and society have been transformed. America is far too diversified, articulate, and swift to abide

Moreover, although American parties are not either highly disciplined or programmatic, they do appear to play a role in making public opinions, and public opinion as a whole, more rational. This result comes about in the following fashion. As was pointed out in the preceding chapter, the opinions of the political activists and party leaders tend to be more consistent, and in this sense rational, than those of the rank-and-file. And the leaders influence the rank and file: that is to say, those who identify with a given party have a tendency to adopt the policy views of its leaders where they are clearly and strongly expressed.[57]

Conclusion

Few impartial observers of the American political scene would say that they were content with the American parties as they stand. They do not draw the leadership from the community that they should. They are not cohesive enough to encourage the concessions and compromises from pressure groups and other constituents that would be desirable. They foster cynicism about politics in the mind of the ordinary citizen since they promise more than they deliver. In addition, they have important jobs to do which they often do not do well or do not do at all. They should more effectively focus and popularize issues to clarify for the individual voter the different sides of an issue and to separate the important and personal problems of government from those that are trivial and momentary. Also, because of their weakness, the parties do not protect the individual legislator or executive officer against those who can threaten him politically in the fashion that hurts the most. In other words, by their weakness, the parties put a great burden upon the courage, the energy, and the initiative of the individual office holder. (By the same token, however, they give him opportunity for the exercise of independent judgment that is lacking in the responsible party government model.)

On the other hand, this evaluation must also be put in its proper perspective. Powerful parties in the United States would themselves present a major problem of control. How to make them responsive to their membership? How to make them moderate and constitutional forces? How to restrain them with respect to the administration? How to insure that they would not alienate people from the political system by their partisanship? Each one of these questions represents a possible abuse of party government.

The important thing at each level of government is not so much the

---

the elephantine routines of party obligation. We act by consensus, a consensus shaped by a million impressions, indulgences, and deprivations. There is no let up on the unremitting pressure to which key policy makers in our mass society are continually exposed." Harold D. Lasswell, *National Security and Individual Liberty* (New York: McGraw-Hill, 1950), pp. 120-121.

[57] Key, *op. cit.*, pp. 449-452.

organization or the role of the parties, though these are important items, as it is a healthy balance of forces. Individual political office holders are important for they are the group most sensitive to the electorate and to the future auditing of accounts in the elections themselves. Public opinion should be active but not continuously and militantly mobilized. If too active, public opinion can hamper compromise and make consensus difficult to achieve.[58] If public opinion is not active enough, the "interests" and the "politicians" can get away with too much. Pressure groups supplement territorial representation in a fashion necessary in modern society by their active and continuous attention to interests that the ordinary citizen does not make articulate or know about. They add centralized intelligence to the process of political bargaining. They give weight to the intensity of need and opinion as well as to its extent. Also they add together the scraps of political power of many people who would otherwise largely have to remain voiceless and without influence, except for political "bosses," aristocratic patrons, or a missionary party. If these three supportive elements—political leaders, interest groups, and public opinion—are present in numbers and effectiveness in a given constituency, the job that the parties have to do is not nearly so important. But parties still must function to simplify and focus issues, to encourage the cooperation of office-holders, and to provide a framework of partisan loyalty strong enough and coherent enough to induce compromise and the evolution of consensus among the interested claimants for political concessions and favors.

SELECTED READINGS

BONE, HUGH A., and RANNEY, AUSTIN. *Politics and Voters*. New York: McGraw-Hill, 1963. A brief, paperback text on voting behavior, pressure politics, political parties, and elections.

BURNS, JAMES McG. *The Deadlock of Democracy*. Englewood Cliffs, N. J.: Prentice-Hall, 1963. A recent study of the American party system which attributes the immobilism of American politics to the structure and functioning of the parties.

BUTLER, DAVID E. and ROSE, RICHARD. *The British General Election of 1959*. London: Macmillan, 1961. The most recent of a continuing series on British general

---

[58] A comparison is of value here. Note that in European political systems, competing influences are weak and partisan ties strong. As one consequence parties often obtrude themselves into public affairs and make much even of the honest and necessary work of government seem to be motivated by considerations of partisan advantage. Their parties also tend to alienate many men from private life who might add their badly needed support to parliament or local government. Probably no factor weighs more heavily in perpetuating the cynicism of the average citizen's views about his government than the political parties themselves. By themselves alone, however, the parties are inadequate as agencies for compromise or political communication. Also, they divide and fragment opinion, so that either cooperation or an effective concentration of effort on many issues is difficult.

elections. The book contains not only a large amount of data on the British election, but also material that is valuable for understanding the organization and functioning of British parties.

CAMPBELL, ANGUS, *et al. The American Voter.* New York: Wiley, 1960. The best summary of existing knowledge about the voter's choice.

DUVERGER, MAURICE. TRANS. NORTH, BARBARA and ROBERT. *Political Parties.* London: Methuen, 1954. This work, which has become a modern classic, is one of the very few books that attempts to set forth a typology of party systems and party organization.

EHRMANN, HENRY W. *Interest Groups on Four Continents.* Pittsburgh: Univ. of Pittsburgh Press, 1958. A comparative study with considerable attention devoted to theories about interest groups and their importance.

EMDEN, CECIL S. *The People and the Constitution.* 2nd ed., London: Oxford U. P., 1959. The best brief introduction to the history of the suffrage and of the political parties in Great Britain.

HARRISON, MARTIN and KITZINGER, UWE. "The French General Election, 1958," *Political Studies,* 7 (1959), pp. 147-173. A study of the first general election under the Fifth Republic.

KEY, JR., V. O. *Politics, Parties, and Pressure Groups.* 4th ed., New York: Crowell, 1958. Probably the best single work on the American party system and politics.

KITZINGER, UWE. *German Electoral Politics.* Oxford, Eng.: Clarendon, 1960. An excellent study of the German party system, of a national election, and of political opinion in Germany.

LEISERSON, AVERY. *Parties and Politics—An Institutional and Behavioral Approach.* New York: Knopf, 1958. The book is what the title says it is: an attempt to combine institutional and behavioral approaches. Professor Leiserson also includes in his book some valuable material on the early history of parties, both in the United States and in other countries.

McKENZIE, ROBERT T. *British Political Parties.* London: Heinemann, 1955. One of the most important books on British political parties written in recent years. Professor McKenzie is particularly interested in the distribution of power within the parties. His work has been the point of departure for many recent articles on British political parties.

MICHELS, ROBERT. Trans. PAUL, EDEN and CEDAR. *Political Parties; A Sociological Study of the Oligarchical Tendency of Modern Democracy.* New York: Hearst's International Library, 1915. An argument that oligarchy is inevitable in modern mass organizations, especially trade unions and political parties. Michels' work is a study which complements the thought of Pareto and Mosca with respect to oligarchy and elites.

NEUMANN, SIGMUND (ed.), *Modern Political Parties.* Chicago: Univ. of Chicago Press, 1956. A comparative analysis of political parties, paying some attention not only to Europe and America but also to non-Western countries and to totalitarian regimes.

OSTROGORSKI, MOISEI. *Democracy and the Party System in the United States—A Study of Extra-Constitutional Government.* New York: Macmillan, 1910. A classic on the American party system at the beginning of the twentieth century.

POTTER, ALLEN M. *Organized Groups in British National Politics.* London: Faber, 1961. One of the more recent general studies of British interest groups.

RANNEY, AUSTIN and KENDALL, WILLMOORE. *Democracy and the American Party System*. New York: Harcourt, 1956. Valuable for the rigorous way in which the authors relate party organization and party politics to the theory of democracy.

TRUMAN, DAVID B. *The Governmental Process*. New York: Knopf, 1951. The most important recent statement of the "group theory" of politics.

WILLIAMS, PHILIP. *Politics in Post-War France*. 2nd ed., London: Longmans, 1958. The most exhaustive and the best single study of French parties and politics under the Fourth Republic.

CHAPTER 14

The Organization of Central

Government

Public opinion and the associations and institutions that channel and organize opinion and the will of the populace involve for the political scientist a distinctive kind of subject matter and an equally distinctive set of methods and problems. It is tempting to continue the discussion of government as though the more formal agencies of government—legislatures, the executive, courts and administration—represented simply additional steps in the process of refining and implementing popular will and opinion. The American political metaphysic of popular sovereignty often lends itself readily to such treatment.

To look at government only or primarily from the perspective of the citizen or the electorate radically falsifies an account of what goes on in the process of government and politics. Sometimes, opinion can be accurately said to start with the populace or some group and to be reflected with greater or lesser accuracy in the decisions of government. Depressed market conditions, for instance, may generate a demand for governmental response that officials can ill afford to ignore. For most situations, however, the relations of government and population are more those of reciprocal influence or of circular patterns of initiative and response. Even this formulation puts the matter too simply. A particular problem for governmental solution is perceived, usually, at many different points and in a variety of ways by elected representatives, administrators, staff agencies, clientele groups, "good government" or other "general welfare" organizations, the political commentator, and particular individuals among the electorate. Through the processes and the procedures of government and politics, people and officials work toward a knowledge, an understanding, a definition, and a final disposition of the particular problem. But the original initiative may come from almost any group, agency, or individual. The organization of government deter-

[379]

mines largely which sources of initiative will receive preference, how the agenda for decision will be set, whose points of view will be consulted and what weight they will receive, what procedures and positive checks are effective in controlling and shaping the whole process.[1]

FORMS OF DEMOCRATIC GOVERNMENT— GENERAL

For the performance of their various activities, modern democratic governments are organized in a variety of ways. All of them, however, have a distinct branch of the government, the legislature, that enacts laws, levies taxes, and makes appropriations. This branch is elected by and representative of the people. The legislature may perform tasks other than those mentioned above. For example, it may conduct investigations and exercise controls over other branches of the government, just as it may be subjected to certain controls with respect to its major functions by other branches of the government.

Other agencies of government carry on from here, performing the various other functions we have enumerated. These agencies or branches of government may be closely united with each other and accountable to the legislature or they may be more dissociated and independent. The process of settling controversies, whether between two or more private individuals or between private individuals on one side and government officials on the other, is, from a theoretical point of view, just one aspect of the executive-administrative complex of activities. In democratic countries, however, this function is largely performed by agencies (courts) that enjoy considerable independence from other branches of government.

Little more can be said about macro-organization (the division of government into major branches) that will hold good for all governments, or even for all modern democratic governments. We should make clear what we have not said. We have not said that there are three distinct governmental "powers," legislative, executive, and judicial, and that these powers either are or ought to be committed exclusively to corresponding branches of government. There is normally a legislative branch, and in democracies this branch plays a key role in the making of major policy. The legislature may, and generally does perform functions that are not properly speaking legislative. Also, legislation, in the sense of laying down general and prospective rules may be performed by other branches of government, both execu-

---

[1] Case studies of decisions are useful to illustrate this point. So also are legislative histories of particular bills. See particular items published by the Inter-University Case Program of the University of Alabama; Stephen K. Bailey *Congress Makes a Law: The Story Behind the Employment Act of 1946* (New York: Columbia U. P., 1950); Daniel M. Berman, *A Bill Becomes a Law: The Civil Rights Act of 1960* (New York: Macmillan, 1962).

tive and even judicial. In like manner, there is no set and final pattern for the allocation of other legislative activities among the other branches of government. The judiciary is more sharply marked off from other parts of the government in some democracies than in others. Whether the remaining agencies are closely integrated in a hierarchical organization under a cabinet or chief executive, or whether many of them sprawl loosely in what in the United States has been called a "headless fourth branch" of government, is another area of difference. A central question is whether or not this executive-administrative complex is wholly or partly accountable to the legislature.

Separation of Powers and Fusion of Powers

The most significant formal classification of democratic governments relates to the distinction between fused and separated powers. The parliamentary or cabinet form of government is characterized by a fusion of powers. Only one body is popularly elected; it is legally supreme and all other organs of government are, in one way or another, accountable to it. The cabinet is responsible to the legislature and the legislature is responsible to the people. On the other hand, where powers are separated, no single path of authority leads from people to governing officials. The chief executive who possesses very substantial powers is not selected by or accountable to the legislature. He may be elected directly by the people or in indirect fashion by an "electoral college." The judiciary in its own right is likely, also to possess substantial powers not subject to control by either of the other two primary sources of authority.

Two-party and Multiparty Cabinet Government

Each category manifests numerous variations in detail; and a few governments may be more accurately described as hybrids. Even more significantly, cabinet governments fall into two subtypes, differing from each other not so much in form as in mode of operation, depending largely on the nature of the party system. We shall refer to them as two-party cabinet government, with Britain as the model, and multiparty cabinet government, with France under the Third and Fourth Republics as the model. We now have three categories differing from each other not only in form but also in spirit, in operative ideas. We shall speak, accordingly, of three different "styles" of government, using this term to stand for a composite of forms, traditions, and underlying theories. We shall discuss the development and present operation of each of these styles of government and make some evaluative remarks.

TWO-PARTY CABINET GOVERNMENT

Origins and Patterns of Development

Cabinet government, as the oldest form of representative government, naturally developed from monarchy. The king's household was gradually expanded to include many officials to help him in the performance of his duties. Gradually, in successive stages, these "ministers of state," as they were called in England where modern cabinet government originated, evolved into the modern minister and member of the government. That is to say, the minister's duties became exclusively public duties. With growing frequency, he was selected from the Parliament, increasingly from the House of Commons rather than the Lords, and gradually he came to be held accountable to Parliament, as the king accepted the principle that he would dismiss ministers who ceased to command the support of a majority of both houses of Parliament. Also the principle was established that all the king's acts must be countersigned by a minister, who thereby accepted responsibility for them. With the further development of the institution of a chief, or "prime" minister, and with the successful assertion on the part of ministries that they would stand or fall together (the principle of collective responsibility), rather than allow Parliament to pick them off individually, the two-party cabinet system assumed substantially its present form.[2]

The organization of British cabinet government reflects a long struggle for legislative supremacy. At one time, notably under the seventeenth- and eighteenth-century constitution, the powers of central government were as much separated and diffused as they were in the early American constitution. The king exercised a veto and special prerogative with respect to the courts, taxes, and foreign affairs. He often chose his ministers outside Parliament and defended them from parliamentary investigation or supervision. His authority over appointments and expenditures, and thus his political influence over the government, were substantial. He was the Commander-in-Chief of the armed forces. Parliament won the battle against the Crown by asserting the authority of the legislature to concentrate control of these matters in its own hands. In particular, Parliament achieved this end by becoming the agent for newly influential groups of the nation. As late as the middle of Queen Victoria's reign, many of these questions of divided authority were still subject to contention. Not until the battle with the House of Lords over the Lloyd George budget, in fact, was the supremacy of the House of Commons over the Lords clearly established (by the Parliament Act of 1911). Most of the great victories won by Parliament, and the

---

[2] A good, brief summary of these developments is George B. Adams, *An Outline Sketch of English Constitutional History* (New Haven: Yale U. P., 1922), Chs. 6-10.

House of Commons in particular, were won by making the legislature an effective instrument to advance or defend group interests. The achievement of this result required leadership and concentrated executive power within the Parliament.[3]

Legislative Supremacy

Basic to the whole operation of the British cabinet system today, is the principle of legislative supremacy. The king (or queen) is a titular or nominal chief executive. He performs ceremonial acts of state, but has few real powers except those of consulting with the government and mediating in the selection of a prime minister. He retains as formal powers all those which ancient kings once had, but all of these powers are exercised at the behest of his (the government's) ministers. The House of Lords, once coordinate with the House of Commons and even in some respects superior to it, now has only a weak "suspensive" veto on matters other than money bills. The Lords can refuse to pass an ordinary bill. If, after a year, the Commons again pass the same bill, it becomes law without the Lords' assent. Money bills automatically become law within one month of their passage by the Commons. Nor do the courts represent a bar to legislative supremacy as they do in the United States. Parliament can make any law whatever. Courts do disallow certain acts of civil servants or of ministers if they transcend, in the judgment of the courts, the powers conferred by the Parliament. In principle, and by well-established rules of judicial construction, however, judicial review of administrative acts completes rather than limits parliamentary sovereignty.

Government and Opposition—Accountability

The government, which includes all the ministers (whether or not they are included in the general policy-making cabinet) and their parliamentary under-secretaries, is a kind of committee of the legislature itself. In fact, the House of Commons can be described as two pyramids of power and authority resting upon the separate rank and file "back-benchers"[4] of each party, one organized by the majority party—and terminating in the government—the other organized by the minority major party and including the shadow cabinet of the opposition. Both pinnacles, the government and the shadow cabinet of the opposition, are less separate clusters of leaders than they are simply the upper portion of an organized hierarchy. The cabinet, which

---

[3] Cf. Cecil S. Emden, *The People and the Constitution*, 2nd ed. (London: Oxford U. P., 1956), Ch. 5.

[4] A "back-bencher" is one who does not sit on the front "ministerial" benches in the House of Commons. Thus, he is not a member of the government or of the shadow cabinet.

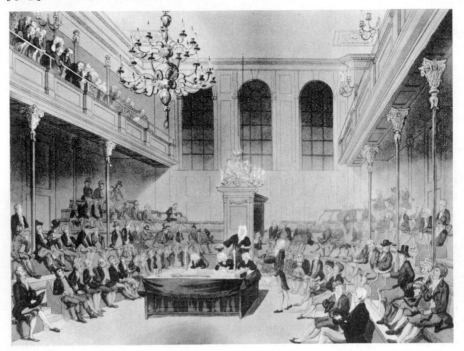

The House of Commons in the nineteenth century prior to electoral reform, cabinet government, and the modern parties

Philadelphia Museum of Art

deliberates collectively and supplies the cohesive and authoritative leadership of government, is surrounded by a wider ring of ministers "not of cabinet rank," who also lead in Parliament, head ministries and assist in the larger ministries. At an even broader and lower level are two-score or more Parliamentary secretaries who act as aids to the ministers themselves. All of them will be close to and involved in the work of the ministry. The government is a large organization, in intimate contact with the Parliament itself, composed of a wide array of senior and junior parliamentary members of talent. Depending upon the size of the majority, from 25 to 35 per cent of the governing parliamentary party are associated with the government. Views are constantly exchanged between this government and the "back-benchers" who also represent the party but are not in the government, the cabinet rallying the members of the parliamentary party, persuading them to accept its views, and the "back-benchers" urging local and particular concern, moderating and tempering the cabinet's stands.[5]

---

[5] A comprehensive and informative account of the organization and functioning of the cabinet is Herman Finer, *Theory and Practice of Modern Government* (New York: Holt, 1949), Ch. 23.

The government remains in office as long as it retains the confidence of the legislature. A lack of confidence can be expressed either by a direct defeat on a "vote of confidence," by passing a "motion of censure," or by defeating some proposition submitted to the legislature by the cabinet. A vote of "no-confidence," however expressed, is normally followed by resignation of the government as a whole. At such a time, either a leader of the opposition may be called upon to form a government, or the House may be dissolved and new elections called. Nowadays, however, party discipline is so strong that it is unheard of for a government to lose power in this way. The normal pattern is for the same government to stay in power throughout the life of a given Parliament, which is limited by statute to five years, and for the House to be dissolved and new elections called sometime during the fifth year in the life of the Parliament. Occasionally a government may "go to the country" somewhat earlier than the last year of its tenure, if it thinks the time is particularly favorable for winning a substantial Parliamentary majority.

The fact that the opposition may, in the not distant future, become the government acts as a powerful force both to temper the critique of the opposition and to induce it to keep its own house in reasonable order. Fiery and intemperate criticism by the opposition of the government may set people to wondering whether the opposition is fit to govern. British government has few brakes except for good sense and careful procedure. Therefore, reckless or speeding drivers are not likely to get the popular mandate to drive. Also, the opposition has another interest in being moderate and sensible. It will be expected to fulfill its pledges and act upon its critique. Just as the government must compose differences and organize itself to govern, so the opposition is under similar, if lesser, pressure to do the same thing, if they are to win approval as an alternate government. Under these circumstances, parties have strong incentives to develop solid and lasting bases of unity and internal harmony—bargains and joint stands of principle and permanent mutual interest that will not be undone by the stress of governing. The rule of British politics is simply: "If you wish to govern, you must first show yourself fit to govern." This rule acts as a powerful and valuable stimulus both to the majority and to the minority.

Collective Responsibility

Occasionally, where a particular minister is under fire for acts within his jurisdiction, a government may allow (or request) him to resign. Normally, however, governments accept collective responsibility for the acts of each of their members and either stand or fall on the joint record. Because collective responsibility has an important place in British cabinet government, any departure from this rule must be justified and is sure to be the subject of criticism. For one thing, accountability may be defeated if the cabinet is held individually rather than collectively responsible. Ministers can be shuffled about endlessly with no real change of policy if the only consequence of bungling is one lopped head. But if all are jointly responsible together, that is another matter. The cabinet will see to it that both the policy and the man charged with primary individual responsibility for that policy can stand the continuous, insistent, and intelligent criticism of the opposition. Collective responsibility also exerts pressure toward consistency of policy. Inconsistency and lack of coordination of policy in Britain creates a strong presumption of bungled management or inept leadership. Thus, the cabinet members, in the development and execution of policy, are driven to try to produce a collective, integrated product—consistent, thought out in all its main principles, defensible as a whole and in detail. The opposition, to compete for the honor of governing, is compelled to match the government's policies with alternatives of its own, equally commendable to the public.[6] Collective responsibility produces an intensive drive within the government to perfect its policy, an equally intensive drive among the opposition to find flaws and offer alternatives.

GOVERNMENT AND ADMINISTRATION

Governments perform a dual role, administrative and political. The members of the government are leaders in Parliament. But in addition, with the exception of two or three leading ministers who may serve "without portfolio" and devote their full time to matters of general policy or party organization, each minister is head of one of the major administrative branches or "ministries". For example, there will be ministries of foreign affairs, military affairs, justice, and finance. These ministers act both as responsible directors of the operations of their departments, and as expert advisors to the cabinet as a whole, whenever their special domains bear on general policy or call for legislative action. They also sit in the legislature and speak on behalf of the government whenever the discussion involves matters pertaining to their Departments.

Cabinet government as practiced in Britain establishes the basic relations of administration to government. Although Britain has quasi-autonomous public corporations, their policies are less free from control by the government than is the case with American regulatory commissions. More-

---

[6] The opposition does not need to differ with the government on *all* points of policy. Moreover, differences where they exist may be incremental, or, as is frequently the case in the United States, they may consist in claims that they can advance the government's policy more effectively or more efficiently.

[7] For the constitutional theory of collective responsibility, see Sir Ivor Jennings, *Cabinet Government* (3rd. ed., Cambridge, Eng.: Cambridge U. P., 1959), pp. 277 ff. For a discussion of the working of the institution in practice, consult Finer, *op. cit.*, also Herbert Morrison, *Government and Parliament* (London: Oxford U. P., 1954); and Ramsey Muir, *How Britain is Governed* (New York: Smith, 1930).

over, excessively large, sprawling and loosely integrated ministries like the American Departments of Agriculture, of the Interior, and of Health, Education, and Welfare, do not exist. Each ministry is supervised by one minister responsible jointly with the cabinet to Parliament. They are, consequently, relatively small and homogeneous, the British preferring more ministries to bigger ministries that are less well integrated.[8]

An elite corps of administrative class civil servants head the ministries on the professional side. They are schooled in the "tradition of civility" and the cult of "playing the game." They direct their departments within the lines of policy set by the minister. They also do a large part of the onerous and knotty task of coordinating administrative policy by mutual consultation between ministries, with the treasury, and among the members of the administrative class. Moreover, top civil servants are likely to have great influence on their ministers in determining actual policy, especially where technical considerations are important. Their function of preparing draft legislation for submission to Parliament provides one opportunity for exerting such influence. With these institutional aids, the responsibility of the cabinet to Parliament for the whole of policy makes sense. The minister can govern his department; the cabinet and minister together can coordinate and direct policy.[9]

Legislative Leadership

The score or more ministers who are also cabinet members make the decisions of high policy. Some of these decisions, such as major matters relating to conduct of foreign affairs, may be carried out by executive action. The government generally has powers to issue decrees or orders which have legally binding effect. This authority may have been delegated by the legislature or it may be a residuum of powers originally possessed by the king. In England, for example, the latter is known as the "prerogative." It is a large and not sharply defined body of powers, compatible with democratic government only because its exercise is by a government which is responsible to Parliament. For the most part, however, this aspect of the functions of the government consists in the formulation of a legislative program and doing what is necessary to secure its enactment by the legislature.

The British cabinet system provides unified legislative leadership of a kind alien to American traditions. The cabinet, consulting with the civil service, with interest groups, and with individual members of Parliament,

[8] D. N. Chester and F. M. G. Wilson, eds., *The Organization of British Central Government* (London: Allen & Unwin, 1957), Ch. 10.

[9] H. E. Dale, "Parliament and the Civil Service," *Parliament—A Survey*, Gilbert Campion, ed. (London: Allen & Unwin, 1952), pp. 121-140. Morrison, *op. cit.*, Ch. 14 gives an account of his experience as a minister that suggests the relations between the civil service and the minister leave much to be desired.

sets the legislative program, the timetable, and the contents of virtually all the important statutes passed by Parliament. Although individual members of the Parliament may introduce legislation, rarely are such bills passed or even acted upon unless the cabinet decides that they are of sufficient importance to warrant the time of the House of Commons. Legislative action is usually confined to debating and saying "yes" or "no" to cabinet proposals. The debate is lively and concessions are often made. Bills are also amended in the committees. In both cases, however, the government may, if it wishes, make the matter a "question of confidence," meaning that unless the Parliament follows the government's wish, the government will resign. Since the British parties are well disciplined and, in any case, are not likely to feel the government should be overturned except upon fundamental issues, such an action by the government is practically always conclusive. Yet it is not uncommon for governments to be forced to make significant concessions at this stage.

The legislative process, like the other aspects of the British cabinet system, features the virtue of coherence. The cabinet is a small body of able and experienced men, accustomed to pulling as a team. They strive to integrate the particular bills into a consistent legislative program. The individual parliamentarians often act more in a representative than in a legislative capacity. They express particular concerns, suggesting the points at which logic and consistency should surrender to circumstance, and supplying the ingredient of local, occupational, and individual opinion. Sometimes, however, it is the member of Parliament who is the doctrinaire advocate of consistent adherence to a program, while the cabinet, sensitive to the politics of marginally held seats in Parliament, strives for compromises. The opposition, organized to criticize coherently and articulately, educates the public in the alternatives to the great policies and programs of the government. They do not greatly affect the legislative product, although significant amendments may be accepted by the government because of their protests or urgings. But the government has the final say, on the theory that the electorate has given them a mandate. The opposition speaks to the future; to a day when the majority will swing to them because the government has lost and the opposition has won the confidence of a predominant part of the nation.

Organization and Procedure in the House of Commons

The organization and procedure of the House of Commons are consistent in all their details with these principles of cabinet leadership. Thus, the parliamentary agenda is entirely at the disposal of the government. Therefore, time is also at their disposal: few matters come before Parliament as a body except general legislation relating to the whole nation or important matters of broad policy. The questions asked of the government, many of which are intended primarily to criticize or influence the cabinet in matters of detail rather than to obstruct or decisively shift government policy, are allotted specific and limited periods.[10] Standing parliamentary committees, which often pretend to leadership under other cabinet systems, are in Britain deliberately kept few in number and unspecialized in subject-matter. Most special committees die with the end of a parliamentary session. Since they cannot busy themselves with governing in detail, the individual parliamentarians are busy with the occupation intended for them by the British Constitution: criticism and debate.[11] The law and custom of parliament supports this same end, both allowing a great part of Parliament's time for debate and placing the primary burden for conducting that debate upon the leadership of the two great parties.[12]

The Essence of British Cabinet Government

The theory of the British cabinet system is that the legislature, at least in indirect fashion, establishes the government, criticizes its work, and holds it accountable. These jobs are done not only in the course of debates on proposed bills and requests for appropriations, which are submitted by the cabinet, but also by means of questions put to members of the government and in the course of debate on the answers given to these questions. They are also done in committees, where bills and issues of policy are examined in detail. But it is the cabinet that governs. So long as it retains the confidence of the House of Commons, it retains also the means to lead and direct. Should it lose that confidence, the government can, on its option, dissolve the Parliament, hold a general election, and carry the issue to the people. The opposition speaks both to the Parliament and to the British nation, criticizing, educating, and seeking to win for itself the title to govern. In the words of Sir Ivor Jennings:

> The Government's majority exists to support the Government. The purpose of the Opposition is to secure a majority against the Government at the next general election and thus to replace the Government. This does not imply that a Government may not be defeated in the House of Commons. Nor does it imply that parliamentary criticism may not persuade the Government to modify, or even to withdraw, its proposals. These qualifications are important;

[10] Question Hour, is allotted about forty-five minutes each day, Monday through Thursday, at the beginning of the sitting. The "Debate on the Motion to Adjourn," a period of about half an hour at the end of the legislative day, offers another opportunity for criticism not related to the business currently before Parliament.

[11] It should be recognized, however, that the typical British back-bencher, unlike his American counterpart, is likely to have a second occupation by which he supplements his rather meager parliamentary salary. Many are journalists, company directors, trade union officials, and the like.

[12] For the procedure and law and custom of Parliament, see Sir Ivor Jennings, *Parliament*, 2nd. ed. (Cambridge, Eng.: Cambridge U. P., 1957).

but they do not destroy the truth of the principle that the Government governs and the Opposition criticizes. Failure to understand this principle is one of the causes of the failure of so many of the progeny of the Mother of Parliaments and of the super-session of parliamentary government by dictatorships.[13]

Evaluation

LEADERSHIP

Organized leadership is the most salient benefit of the two-party cabinet system, and in this respect, Britain stands above all other democratic governments. This is not to say that Britain develops better individual leaders than elsewhere. American presidents, for example, compare favorably in leadership and ability with British prime ministers. In Britain, leadership is better *organized* than elsewhere. In the first place, it is recruited more effectively. Parliament is the center of the nation. It draws many of the best talents Britain can offer. But also, the cabinet, with its wide and deep roots in Parliament and its coordinated handling of government as a whole, is an excellent apprenticeship for future leadership. Once selected, leaders are so circumstanced that they can be effective. Thus, the Leader of the Opposition is in Parliament and at the center of political activity as he should be. As another aspect of the organization of leadership, the cabinet joins together the essential parts of coherent policy-making in one collective leadership. Since the leadership is collective and truly collegial it helps make the burdens of major political leadership bearable, both because the leaders can share these burdens with others jointly responsible with them, and because they have the power to match the responsibility with which they are entrusted.[14] British government also institutionalizes the *functions* of leadership themselves. To fulfill their role, parliamentary leaders must do two things. They must foster compromises that rise above the level of the lowest common denominator. And they must see and foresee both the difficulties that are going to crop up in the future and the problems that are strategic because many lesser adjustments depend upon their solution. Cabinet government in Britain provides effectively for this kind of leadership, both by freeing cabinet leaders of detail and also by placing the responsibility for leadership squarely and unavoidably upon the cabinet.

RATIONALITY AND RESPONSIVENESS

By the test of rationality—as discussed early in this chapter—British government also rates well. The key to rationality as to leadership in British government is again organization, in this instance, organization for two

---

[13] Sir W. Ivor Jennings, *Cabinet Government*, 3rd. ed. (Cambridge, Eng.: Cambridge U. P., 1959), p. 472.

[14] Again, Morrison's comments suggest a gap between theory and practice. He found ministers generally overworked and often unable to cope with the enormous day-to-day responsibility of their office.

purposes: to coordinate policy and to distribute or to keep the influences that go into policy-making to their appropriate level. Coordination of policy in the government and the administration is a way of achieving consistency. Consistency can, of course, be a foolish consistency. But when a government is subjected to the organized criticism of Parliament that will look particularly to the issues of how the government's program coheres as a whole, and whether each part of that program makes as much sense as any part of it does, then consistency becomes a powerful test to insure that each pound spent by Her Majesty's Government, and every sacrifice imposed by the state, is spent or imposed to good purpose and economically. To be wisely consistent, however, a government must also be powerfully organized. It cannot yield to whims and pressures or respond to public desires in an undisciplined fashion. No form of government can meet this ideal, but the position of the cabinet, the organization of the Parliament, and the cohesiveness of the parties, all help British government score high marks from this point of view.[15] In view of what has been said about both leadership and rationality, it is not surprising that the reputation of British government for effectiveness is good.

The emphasis upon discipline often makes the British system seem unresponsive to Americans. Indeed, in Germany, where the cabinet is in an equally commanding position, lack of responsiveness is a continual complaint both from individual parliamentarians and from particular pressure groups.[16] Nor is this complaint unheard in England. In principle, either a particular demand put forward by some group or member of Parliament must fit with the general program or it must be of such wide import that the program itself should be changed. Minor concessions or adjustments, to be sure, are often made by the administration itself in carrying out their programs or in drafting bills. Questions of principle, however, must go to the minister, to the cabinet as a whole, to the assembled Parliament, or possibly even to the nation itself, if they are fundamental enough to warrant a general election. The art lies in considering the issue at the right level for its settlement. There is no guarantee that the cabinet will not settle *in camera* broad issues of policy without a full and fair parliamentary debate, or that it will not yield to pressure from a particular interest without making that concession square with its general policy. The chief protections against these abuses are the threat of public criticism by the opposition and the sense of responsibility of political leaders. On the whole the British

[15] For example, it can be argued that if "bargaining" is important to good political decision, then discipline and the ability to respond coherently to a particular situation on the part of the government makes for better bargains. People and groups are forced to decide much more precisely what political good they are willing to exchange for what other. This line of reasoning would seem to be the rationale of British parliamentary government.

[16] Richard Hiscocks, *Democracy in Western Germany* (London: Oxford U. P., 1959) Ch. 6; and Gerhard Loewenberg, "Parliament in Western Germany: the Functioning of the Bundestag," *American Political Science Review,* 55 (1961), pp. 87-102.

record is good, in these respects. It is difficult to know how much of the credit should go to their form of government and how much to their political tradition. The formal institutions provide a simple and straightforward means for holding the government accountable to majority will. Party discipline, however, may effectively check such responsiveness where partisan alignments and issue alignments fail to coincide, as appears to have been the case with some of the postwar steps in the nationalization of industry.

The values of rationality and of responsiveness may be approached in different ways. It is arguable that the British government might be a better government if it could combine various approaches more effectively. Take rationality, for an instance. Many issues do not lend themselves to broad policies. They cannot even be thought through in any coherent fashion. Writing labor laws is sometimes like that: particular abuses are dealt with, changes made here and there in no very consistent fashion, but each helping to meet a felt need. Administration is sometimes too complex for general directives to control it effectively. Here, a kind of behavior called "incrementalism" may be the most useful.[17] One takes the situation as it is and the problems as they are and pushes for solutions a little bit in this or that direction. Rather than returning to first principles, one deals concretely with limited variations on a familiar set of themes, such as the appropriations for a particular department or the responsibilities and organization of a well-known agency, asking for a satisfactory explanation for each small change in program. To be most effective, incrementalism in politics requires deep knowledge of the particular problem and a good "feel" for the values at stake. British government is certainly not precluded from this kind of activity. The government and committee members engage in it all the time. But it is at least possible that the American system of dispersed policy-making provides a better framework for this important process.

Just as incrementalism has its role in modern government, so also responsiveness that is not effectively subordinated to general programs has its place. How much land under the Town and Country Planning Authority should be foreclosed to industrial and residential development and held for parks and "green belts?" Which is more important: to hold land open for nature lovers and future generations? Or to meet the urgent needs of people now who want to live on this land or build factories and stores on it? The resolution of this kind of issue in Britain shows both the strength and the limitations of British cabinet government. Long years of unplanned industrial and residential growth in Britain had, in many places, made the physical environment ugly. Under the Town and Country Planning Act, county authorities were given the power and the responsibility to plan in collaboration with central and local authorities for more "rational" (and certainly

---

[17] Following the concept of "incrementalism" described in Robert A. Dahl & Charles E. Lindblom, *Politics, Economics and Welfare* (New York: Harper and Row, 1953), p. 82.

more attractive) land use. County planners are backed up by their own statutory authority and the central government. Few interests or groups except those effective either at the level of central government or through large-city governments can have much impact upon the land-use planners of the counties and the central bureaucracy. But what is "rational" land use? Is it rational to pen the factories in the cities, discourage housing projects, and tightly control unsightly "ribbon" development of stores and motels along the highways? The parks and "green belts" are saved in many situations where they would not be in the United States. But these "enclosures" of the county authorities can also pluck down houses and stores and eat up fertile fields just as the enclosures of earlier centuries. Local business-men and residents are often frustrated and angry from dealing with the disdainful county planners who say to them "You do not need a new store or more apartments, or a factory; you need grass and trees." In other words, the interests of the "public" and the future tend to be well protected in Britain; local and particular interests that have little influence with the government because of party discipline and the weakness of individual representatives in Parliament may not fare so happily.[18]

SAFEGUARDS

Turning to safeguards against misgovernment, the above is relevant, for responsiveness is a source of protection as well as a technique for implementing popular wants. Silence is a great problem of modern administration. Administrators have no interest in publicly confessing their mistakes. Nor do the beneficiaries of an administrative policy make a point of explaining that their competitors are harmed by the government's actions. Interests are not protected automatically; they must be brought forcefully to the attention of the level of government at which they will receive effective attention. Largely, this role is performed by groups who can put pressure on individual members of Parliament, committee members, top civil servants, or cabinet ministers.

In Britain, one way that the group clamoring for public attention can get it is through "Question Hour," when the individual parliamentarian of either party can ask the government to give an accounting for particular policies. If that accounting is not satisfactory, if it does not ring true, trouble impends. The question will be repeated. Back-benchers will wait upon the minister and the cabinet. The Opposition and the press will take up the issue to make political capital of it or to redress a wrong.

Particular group claims and minor grievances are aired during committee sessions on the bills, in the twenty-six parliamentary days allotted for debate on Supply, and by complaints made by an M. P. to the cabinet min-

---

[18] See, for example, the running commentary on town and country planning carried on for many years by the London journal, *The Economist*.

ister. Groups are also extensively represented in departmental bill-drafting and day-to-day decisions upon policy. In none of these instances, however, can they press their claims with much force.

In effect, the British system of government depends for the protection of group interests upon the good sense, proper organization, and procedure of the civil service, the conscience of the House of Commons, and the chance to be heard. Several properties of administration and government under the modern welfare state limit the effectiveness of these safeguards. For one thing, issues seldom stand out sharply in the highly technical welfare programs of today. Nor is it necessarily true that in the canvassing of group representatives the most relevant opinion will be consulted or heard. The British system of government puts a premium upon centralized organization of pressure groups. As a consequence, probably fewer distinctive points of view are effectively expressed, and the member of Parliament, who is not schooled by committee service to an expert knowledge of particular subjects, may not perceive real abuses. Also, to get information about administration in Britain is difficult.[19] The civil servant does not appear before committees or the House of Commons to justify his actions. Policy is the business of the minister; and he stands between Parliament and the civil service. Yet information is often precisely what is needed to smell out a real issue. Who and what ought to be protected is always a matter for dispute; but it is perhaps significant that today many reputable English authorities and journals complain that the safeguards against particular administrative abuses are no longer sufficient in twentieth-century Britain. Some look with envy at the powerful and capable American legislative committees and argue that Britain needs less cabinet dominance and less of the tradition of the inviolability of the civil service.[20]

In Britain, accountability to the electorate is the primary constitutional safeguard. Judicial review of legislation does not exist. The committees of Parliament cannot by-pass the minister to get at the civil service. Groups with grievances often have difficulty in getting the ear of a member of Parliament who can press their claims with sufficient vigor. But in the last analysis, if the government botches the job, so the theory runs, it is answerable to the electorate. Accountability is a powerful safeguard, especially with a press and an electorate (or at least, the active elites of that electorate) attentive to constitutional issues and the quality of a government. Accountability through highly disciplined parties, though, has its limitations as a

---

[19] A good account of the role and the plight of the private member in his relation to the cabinet and the administration is Peter G. Richards, *Honorable Members: A Study of the British Backbencher* (London: Faber, 1959), esp., Ch. 14.

[20] Ramsey Muir, *op. cit.*, fired one of the opening salvos. For a recent study that supports this point of view somewhat, see Bernard Crick, *Reform of the Commons* (London: Fabian Society, 1959). Also relevant to this point are Cecil Carr, "Delegated Legislation," in Campion, *op. cit.*, pp. 232-251; and R. Douglas-Brown, *The Battle of Crichel Down* (London: Bodley Head, 1955).

safeguard. In the British setting, it is a splendid device for producing good general management of the whole public enterprise, and also for presenting to the whole people a coherently organized lump of choices. What it cannot do is to make government responsive to highly particularistic and local concerns. In an age when many of the big, constitutional, and programmatic issues of domestic government have been settled, these smaller issues that are less matters of principle than of adjustment may be, in sum, the more important.

Conclusion

Despite the fact that the British cabinet system lacks many of the formal "checks" on the abuse of power with which Americans are familiar, rights are protected in Britain, the government is responsive to wants and injuries, and bungling in the administration of public affairs is kept to a minimum. That so much power is compatible with liberty and constitutionalism, however, is a fact less attributable to the *form* of British government than to its *temper*. It is not so much to the cabinet system and the disciplined parties that Britain owes her liberties. She owes them to her constitutional tradition, to the people that serve her government, and to the responsible and tolerant electorate that supports and watches the system. Given these prerequisites of good government, then it is possible to say also that British cabinet government has a great aptness to encourage further the political temper upon which it depends.

In our times, governments must act with great power and with power that is sure and coordinated. They must search for collective goals and seek to create services and utilities of common benefit as well as arbitrating the group conflict. For these reasons, the British cabinet system is a model worthy of attention. The cabinet system develops unified leadership. It makes possible the political choices that the nation has to take for its welfare. It makes for intelligent government. It makes for honest government and for government that does not shirk the issues or resort to demagogy to get the work done. Not least important, it is government in which the alternatives are made public and articulate so that the electorate chooses with its eyes open. It is government for a mature and relatively homogeneous people.[21]

Some of the greatest virtues of the British system, however, may become serious faults. It is a system of coherent accountability, depending upon

[21] The British form of cabinet government can operate effectively with a considerable spread between classes, especially if there is a large middle class. What is more difficult for it to cope with is a situation like that which prevails in the United States, where regional, occupational, class, and other lines intersect in such a way as to make consistent programs on a two-party basis well nigh unattainable.

party discipline and effective cabinet leadership.[22] Yet both cabinet dominance and party discipline are somewhat oppressive. The cabinet centralizes
intelligence and trains leadership. On the other hand, the cabinet leaves the
back-benches short of talent, and itself shows many of the vices as well as
the virtues of collective thinking and long apprenticeship. Cabinet government in Britain also lacks a measure of flexibility, of pragmatic experimentalism, of novel influences and new faces in politics that enliven the
political scene, make it interesting to the professional of politics and the
amateur alike, and often generate progress and new approaches as well.
Government is stately and sometimes dull. Almost never in modern Britain
does a government resign more than a few months before the expiration of
the legal life (five years) of Parliament, and then only as a result of a general
election in which the party in power loses its Parliamentary majority. Gone
are the days when members of Parliament rather freely crossed the aisle to
vote with the Opposition and governments were brought down as a consequence. Parliamentary debates are somewhat ritualistic. The outcome of
the vote is known in advance. Under these circumstances, some critics wonder how long Parliament will continue to serve the purpose of focusing
public attention upon public issues, if indeed it still does, and whether the
uninteresting life of the back-benchers will continue to attract the best
candidates for leadership posts.[23]

Multiparty Cabinet Government

We have chosen to restrict the discussion of multiparty cabinet government largely to the systems that prevailed in the Third and Fourth French
Republics, with major emphasis upon the latter. For one thing, those systems were classic: they show the problems in their barest, though sometimes
most extreme forms. Also, the minute variations in multiparty cabinet
systems are often both confusing and insignificant. The example of France
will suffice to illustrate the broad principles. The Third and Fourth Republics are chosen rather than de Gaulle's Fifth Republic for several reasons.
De Gaulle's Republic is a "personal" regime, depending largely upon
de Gaulle's role as president; and it is a regime that has yet to develop a
stable pattern of operation.[24] It is also a hybrid regime tending toward a

[22] Most of the virtues we have attributed to this model—its coherency of policy, its
unity of operation, its responsibility, and its strength—would not exist except for the fact
that one party normally holds a majority of the seats in parliament and that party acts
with almost perfect discipline.

[23] See the articles in the London *Economist*, "Premier and Parliament—I: One-Man
Government?" (August 13, 1960), pp. 621-622; and "Premier and Parliament—II: House
in Decline," (August 20, 1960), pp. 705-706.

[24] Probably the best account to date of the Fifth Republic is Philip M. Williams and
Martin Harrison, *De Gaulle's Republic* (London: Longmans, 1960). Stanley H. Hoffmann
gives a succinct summary of the constitutional provisions of the Fifth Republic. See "The
French Constitution of 1958: The Final Text and Its Prospects," *American Political Science
Review*, 53 (1959), pp. 332-357. See also Dorothy Pickles, *The Fifth French Republic* (rev.
ed. London: Methuen, 1962), esp., Ch. 11, "De Gaulle's Republic."

presidential system. At various points, comparisons between it and the Fourth Republic are instructive; but the Fifth Republic cannot serve to illustrate the classical pattern of the multiparty cabinet. Indeed, once de Gaulle departs from the scene, the more traditional pattern may well replace the present system. In any event, the purpose of emphasizing the Fourth Republic is to examine a particular *type* of governmental organization and to use that examination and analysis to enrich an understanding of basic principles. Other governments will be discussed only where they afford especially pertinent illustrations.

Development

Superficially, the growth of cabinet systems on the Continent resembled that in England. A period of absolutism gave way to various patterns of separation of powers during the early nineteenth century. There were reversions toward autocratic government, but during most of the nineteenth century, the prerogative of the king was reduced, his ministers were made increasingly dependent upon parliament, and the power of the more popular branch of the legislature increased. France in 1876, Germany after World War I, and Italy after World War II became republics. France, Italy, and Germany established powerless presidents, while Scandinavia and the Low Countries retained their constitutional monarchs. Generally, in Western Europe significant executive powers are now held by cabinets that are creatures of the parliament, elected and dismissed by a majority of the deputies.[25]

The point at which continental political history differs most profoundly from the British experience is in the relation between the development of cabinet responsibility and the growth of popular democracy. In Britain, cabinet responsibility preceded mass democracy. In Europe, especially in France, Germany, Italy, and Austria-Hungary, mass democratic sentiment preceded responsible cabinet government. Also, on the Continent, the framework of the state was established and ossified prior to the arrival of mass democracy, in contrast to Britain where parliamentary, legal, and bureaucratic reform grew hand in hand. With little chance to make government the instrument of democratic will, individual deputies and their supporters felt that their objective was either to oppose the government or to wring concessions from it. Strong administration—the central bureaucracy,

[25] The French Fifth Republic is, of course, an exception to this statement. The original constitutional provision was for independent election of the president by an electoral college of some 80,000 electors. A referendum in October 1962, approved the direct, popular election of the next president. Since a presidential election will not be due until 1965, the ultimate effect of such a provision remains in doubt. In any event, independent election of the president is established under either provision. Furthermore, ministers must, upon taking office, resign their parliamentary membership, even though the cabinet itself remains accountable to the National Assembly. Thus, "powers" are separated in two ways: by creating an autonomous presidency, and by separating parliamentary and cabinet membership.

a code law and the Ministry of Justice, the army and the police—acted as a supplementary government permitting the parties the luxuries of disagreement. Popular democracy was not, therefore, firmly associated in Europe with the responsibility to govern. In Britain, a Parliament and cabinet bound closely together inherited the full powers of the Crown and became the directing center of the nation. On the continent of Europe, generations of frustrated democracy tended to produce a sharp split in government, leaving the parliament unable to unite, the cabinets without disciplined support, and the administration without a competent and unified political master.[26]

Weak Cabinets

In the Third and Fourth French Republics, cabinets seldom took office as the victorious leaders of a winning electoral coalition. They were made after the elections by parliamentary maneuvering and the search for a majority within the parliament, which often made light of the concept of responsibility to the electorate. On the few occasions that the Assembly did view the elections as a mandate and accept a cabinet organized accordingly, animosities and divisions among the cabinet parties and within parliament usually sprouted so thickly and so soon that the attempt produced little in the way of results and left much bitterness behind. Customarily, the President would negotiate with several leaders who might be able to put together a majority and persuade the Assembly to support their programs. Each of these leaders might try their hand in turn and all fail.[27] When a parliamentary chief did succeed in winning the support of a majority and getting himself and his cabinet installed in office, under the constitution of the Fourth Republic, he faced a second problem of getting that same majority (or another majority, differently composed from that which installed him in office), to support his program.[28]

Under the circumstances, cabinets were put together with bargains and "deals" that mortgaged the future of the government. Many members were "ministers without portfolio," added to win parliamentary support for the

[26] A good account of early French parliamentary democracy is Denis Brogan, *France Under The Republic: The Development of Modern France, 1870-1939* (New York and London: Harper and Row, 1940); for Germany, see Arthur Rosenberg, *The Birth of the German Republic* (London: Oxford U. P., 1931). Lowell is still one of the best and most informative works dealing with the development of parliamentary democracy in Europe. A. Lawrence Lowell, *Government and Parties in Continental Europe*, 2 vols. (Boston: Houghton Mifflin, 1896).

[27] The process and techniques of forming cabinets and coping with crises is well described in Nathan C. Leites, *On the Game of Politics in France* (Palo Alto, Calif.: Stanford U. P., 1959).

[28] In the Fifth Republic, this requirement for a separate approval of the Premier's program has been abolished. The Premier "directs the government", and the Assembly may reject him and his program by overthrowing the government. But they do not have to give positive approval of that program by a separate "second investiture".

cabinet. Occasionally, cabinets were assembled from all the parties, or from individual parliamentary leaders, each with a small personal following. All of these devices enabled cabinets to get the support needed in order to exist; they did not make for active or unified government. As a general rule in France, the larger the cabinet, the weaker the government. French cabinets have sometimes run to thirty-five or thirty-seven members, as contrasted with perhaps a score in Britain. Each member, while he added support, represented one more point of view, one more claimant to be satisfied.

Not only were cabinets weak in France, they were put in a weak position *vis-à-vis* the parliament by the Constitution and the Standing Orders of the Assembly. The agenda of parliamentary proceedings was controlled not by the cabinet but by a committee of party presidents and the President of the Assembly.[29] In debate and legislation, the party chiefs and important committee members were collectively more prominent and often more powerful than the cabinet. The cabinet could be overthrown by a simple majority of the deputies present. Moreover, in France, unlike present-day Germany, the opposition to the government had no responsibility on its part to provide an alternate ministry to replace the one that it overturned. The cabinet could in theory, discipline the individual members with the weapon of dissolution, but only under special circumstances and by an intricate proceeding.[30] Actually, during the whole of the Fourth Republic, dissolution was used only once.[31]

Short Governments

That cabinets have not usually lasted long in France should occasion no great surprise. Both under the Third and the Fourth Republics their average life was about seven to nine months. In some ways, shortness of life was not an evil. Many of the same people continued through successive cabinets, giving a measure of stability and of acceptability to the government. Also cabinets of long duration were not necessarily productive ones: often they lasted only by dint of scrupulously evading any important issue; and frequently the short cabinet was one that acted resolutely, carried through a major piece of legislation or effected a change of front in policy, and then

[29] The President of the Assembly was similar in function and powers to the Speaker of the House of Representatives or the House of Commons. He was partisan as the Speaker in America is, and weaker in powers than either his English or American counterpart.

[30] For parliamentary procedure under the Fourth Republic, see D. W. Lidderdale, *The Parliament of France* (London: Hansard Society, 1951).

[31] That dissolution was not more frequently used is probably just as well. On the one occasion under the Fourth Republic when it was used (1955-56), the act was a surprise to the people, the parties were not ready for it, the campaign was bungled and the outcome was inconclusive. The only striking result was to increase sharply the representation of parties of the extreme Right and Left.

surrendered to a quieter administration.[32] But throughout the Fourth Republic, most activities of government that require coordination, planning, or continuity in policy suffered. Inflation was a continual problem. Ministers worked at cross-purposes in various programs such as housing, wage policy, and planned public investment. The Army in Indo-China and Algeria fought without purpose, resentful of politicians, and enraged by conflicting directives from Paris. Periodically, France was without an agreed-upon foreign policy. For harried ministers who must meet many demands and master a great deal of material, time is precious. In France, many had little time either to master their jobs or to make their influence felt in office. Most of their time was squandered on cabinet politics, negotiating for a government, dickering to hold a government together, bargaining with parliament to continue the support of a policy.

"Replastered" Ministries

In Europe, ministers are by regular practice both collectively and individually responsible to the parliament. In France, the rule has been that ministers are primarily responsible as individuals, not as a cabinet collectively facing the Assembly to defend its policy. Cabinets changed, but usually because they lost support and resigned or were unable to carry a proposal, not because they had been impeached and then dismissed following a general debate. The shifts among cabinet posts and the sacrifice of individual ministers to the Assembly went on weekly and sometimes even daily. This circulation had its valuable uses. Since cabinet policy was less significant than in Britain, personalities were more so. A change in the head of a ministry was a useful way of shifting the emphasis in a particular branch of governmental activity. Also, the practice gave the cabinet flexibility, enabling it to use different talents as they were demanded. When cabinets hung together weakly, moreover, to dispense with one minister and recruit another was often the only way to execute a shift or reversal of cabinet policy.

Individual responsibility of ministers had its dark side as well. Rotation in office was often a substitute for radical surgery. Not infrequently, precisely the ministries that needed a continuous and firm hand were the ones that were sources of popular dissatisfaction and thus used up many ministers in the course of a government. To a harmful extent, individual responsibility did not supplement collective responsibility; it substituted for it. French government lacked the benefit of a cabinet system in which the ministers were compelled to resolve their differences and present to the Assembly one clear program. Parliament and the nation lacked the salutary experience of seeing the issues joined: of having the responsibility for government made clear, and of being able to hold a body of men accountable for their deeds.

---

[32] Philip Williams especially has pointed out some of the valuable uses of cabinet crises and ministerial "reshufflings." Philip Williams, "Compromise and Crisis in French Politics," *Political Science Quarterly*, 72 (1957), pages 321-339.

Constitution of the Fourth Republic: a British view

Cabinet and the Administration

Under the circumstances of weak and divided cabinets, the government was not the master of the administration. Good direction requires both intimate knowledge and the cooperation of administrators. French government often had neither. Ministers ruled by creating within the departments their own "administrative cabinets" of personal proteges loyal to them. In assembling these "administrative cabinets," ministers often drew upon competent career officials. They often, however, promoted upstarts over the heads of seasoned bureaucrats, and found a place in their entourage for cousins and sons-in-law. In the absence of unified and concentrated political power in the cabinet, necessary for major reform or reorganization of the administration, the cabinet ruled by decree. Departments were transferred, responsibilities shuffled about, individuals promoted by decree until the civil service regulations became a jungle of contradictory imperatives and inequitable privileges. Neither of these procedures endeared the ministers to the civil servants. Moreover, the cabinet and the individual ministers often acted in considerable ignorance, asserting their will with respect to a civil service which contains in its elite *corps* some of the ablest and best trained administrators in the world. Naturally, much of the civil service tended to be stubborn and resentful. Employees went on strike. Bureau chiefs and high ranking officers evaded ministerial directives. In times of crisis or ministerial impotence, they took upon themselves the responsibility for preserving a sane regime and fashioned the budget, decrees, and administrative policy according to their own notions of the public welfare. In fact, any chiefs of administration with the welfare of their subordinates and the public in mind would have had little alternative. An administration that is oppressed by ill-considered or conflicting directives can either become demoralized, or it can evolve a sense of purpose and responsibility of its own. Both things happened in France. Much of the administration was disgruntled and cynical. Part of it deliberately usurped power and made itself the trustee of the permanent interests of the state.[33]

Legislative Leadership

Many of the same factors that made for weakness of the multiparty cabinet system in general also tended to make it weak as a device for legislative leadership. The cabinet seldom had the time to mature collectively major legislative proposals. Moreover, it was not, like the British Cabinet, effectively organized and staffed for legislation. In Britain, the cabinet is an elaborate, pyramidal organization, not just twenty-one ministers meeting for two hours together once a week. It has many committees, a secretariat, a legislative counsel, and associated technical experts and planners all grouped coherently about the cabinet to facilitate the work of studying and perfecting policy and legislative proposals. In France there was no such elaborate substructure. A planning commission was attached to the cabinet, but it was in fact an autonomous body. There was a Premier's office and a cabinet secretariat, but these institutions could not substitute for a compre-

---

[33] See Finer, *op. cit.*, Chs. 29, 32; also Alfred Diamant, "The French Civil Service: A Case Study of Administrative Autonomy," *Political Studies*, 6 (1958), pp. 146-166.

hensive system of cabinet committees and planning agencies.[34] The French cabinet was not, by virtue of its organization, an effective device for collective or joint thinking. Its role in leadership suffered.

Part of the cabinet's deficiencies in legislative leadership were remedied, after a fashion, by utilizing the expert knowledge of the civil service. Bills slated for introduction by a minister were shaped and polished by the *Conseil d'Etat*. This same body usually drafted cabinet decrees as well. In practice, the precise content of many bills was in part decided by the professionals of the ministries who lent their expert draftsmen to the parliamentary committees. As a consequence, the legislation was generally consistent with the existing body of laws and decrees. But the impact of the bureaucracy was substantial, for both the cabinet and the committees were dependent upon them. The committees had small staffs of their own as did the cabinet, but they could supply only a part of the skill and knowledge needed in legislation. Much of these came from the bureaucracy, which had its own interests and arrangements to conserve.

Under the Fourth Republic, the standing committees of the legislature also exercised a large share of legislative leadership. Unlike the legislative committees in Britain, the French committees were specialized, and included in their membership men who were expert in particular phases of public policy. Thus, there were committees for agriculture, education, labor, etc. Although the members were selected by proportional representation according to party, the committees were made up largely of men who for one reason or another were particularly interested in a given subject-matter. They tended, therefore, to be "clientele" committees, concerned with the welfare of a particular part of the society and the corresponding ministry, for example, the peasant and the Ministry of Agriculture.[35] The committees developed their particular philosophies, their friends among the civil service, and a "clientele" of pressure groups.[36]

These committees were often centers of legislative activity in which bills received a close scrutiny and in which valuable collaboration between the parties took place. Their power was such that they could and did compete for legislative leadership with the cabinet. The government bills were amended both in detail and in fundamental principle by the committees. Sometimes, these bills were buried in committee, never again to see the light of day. At other times, the titles of government bills were preserved, but a

[34] Roy Macridis, "The Cabinet Secretariat in France," *Journal of Politics*, 13 (1951), pp. 589-603.

[35] P. A. Bromhead, "Notes on the Standing Committees of the French Assembly", *Political Studies*, 5 (1957), pp. 140-158. See also, Lidderdale, *op. cit.*

[36] In the Fifth Republic, the committee system has been copied largely from the British. The committees are general (nonspecialized) committees. Their powers have been reduced. In number, the major standing committees have been reduced from nineteen (Fourth Republic), to six. The first premier, Michel Debré, wanted to reduce the number even further, and to take over the British committee system in its entirety.

new bill was written under the old title by the committee. When bills were reported out of committee, the *rapporteur*[37] and the chairman of the committee took the lead in debate, followed by various party chiefs and ministers. Frequently, the minister or the cabinet scarcely had time to make a coherent defense of its own views or policy.[38] Nor could the cabinet steer the bill effectively in parliamentary debate. Amendments, offered from the floor or by committee members and passed by the Assembly, sometimes left bills in such a state that the government withdrew them or they were sent back to committee for re-drafting. Since the legislative agenda was not at the disposal of the government, the amount of time consumed in passing a controversial bill was likely to be enormous. In their attempt to hasten action or to secure action at all, governments gambled their lives on the fate of particular clauses, making the matter a "Question of Confidence," and trying to force the Assembly to accept the cabinet version of the bill. Often the cabinet itself was overthrown. The alternative was to legislate by special emergency proceedings and by ministerial decree.

Summary

The National Assembly of the Fourth Republic contained four competing groups: the cabinet, the committees, the chiefs of the parties, and the Assembly itself. Each vied for influence in legislation, with respect to the administration, and in the conduct of policy. The cabinet was faced by a circle of party and committee heads, bargaining for concessions and for cabinet posts. It spent much of its time defending itself before the assembly and in interpellations (questions), or attempting to win support for the clauses of a bill. It lacked the power either to control the administration effectively or to push through coherent programs for reform. And the cabinet, if it survived at all, survived weakly, forced to bend this way or that way to satisfy the claims of its own members who were, in turn, importuned and threatened by their party followings.

In actual practice what often emerged was something of a bargaining relation between the various blocs in the Assembly, matched with a weak dual control of the administration that in times of relative normality (of which there were few) worked fairly well. But in times of crisis, the power

[37] A bill, introduced in the Assembly, is then sent to committee. In the committee, each bill is assigned a *"rapporteur,"* who studies the bill in detail and reports on it to the committee. Since he also initiates and, to a considerable extent, leads the debate on the bill when it is reported out to the Assembly, he is in a powerful position to influence its fate.

[38] In the Fifth Republic, a number of devices have been adopted to enable the cabinet to play a stronger role in legislative leadership. The cabinet can now control the parliamentary agenda. It can force the Assembly to consider government business. It can "sever" all committee amendments and Assembly amendments from the bill itself and force the Assembly to vote on the cabinet version. Also, only certain categories of basic statutes require Assembly approval at all. The cabinet, if forced to do so, can govern largely through decree.

of intransigents of the Left and Right, and of stubborn provincial deputies, to break cabinets and stall the processes of politics proved overwhelming. The burden upon the government was too great.

The cabinet systems of the Third and Fourth Republics are extreme examples, and partly illustrative for that reason, since they show the tendency and the "logic" of certain features of the multiparty cabinet system. On the other hand, extreme examples may be misleading since the difference between a tendency and an extreme expression of that tendency is sometimes so great as to create a fundamental difference in the equality of government as a whole. Before turning to an evaluation of the French system, then, it is advisable to say a few words about variations in multiparty cabinet systems.

Other West European Systems

Executive weakness is by no means a necessary feature of such cabinet systems. German government, for example, under Konrad Adenauer, supported by the well organized and disciplined Christian Democratic Party, showed great stability in the executive and vigorous prosecution of policy. Similarly, under the Constitution of the French Fifth Republic, which has created a hybrid of a presidential system with separation of powers and the multiparty cabinet system, stability and forcefulness have been the rule also.[39] The cabinets of Scandinavia and the Low Countries have not been notably weak either.

Nevertheless, in periods of crisis or political dissension, the multiparty cabinet is likely to be more unstable than other forms of government, especially if the system is not reinforced by devices foreign to the original model. By the standard of effectiveness it is inferior to the two-party system. Under the German Weimar Republic, for example, where the government was, furthermore, in a powerful constitutional position, cabinet instability was as grave an evil as in France. Today, in Italy, despite the predominant position of the Christian Democrats, cabinet instability has also been the rule.[40]

Almost nowhere are multiparty cabinets effectively organized teams or real centers of collective initiative in the fashion that they are in Britain. In Germany, the cabinet has been dominant in the past largely because of the enormous power of Adenauer. Power in the Italian parliamentary system is diffused throughout committees and the important leaders of the Christian

[39] Both in the Bonn Republic and the Fifth Republic the position of the cabinet with respect to the parliamentary assembly was strengthened by requiring a positive expression of "no confidence" by an absolute majority to overthrow a cabinet. In Germany, the further provision was added that the Bundestag must not only depose a cabinet by an absolute majority, it must simultaneously elect its successor. In other words, the burden of providing an alternate leadership is put upon the Bundestag itself. Devices of this nature are important, though it seems doubtful that they could much strengthen the executive unless it had other powerful bases of support and stability.

[40] Joseph La Palombara, "Party Systems and Crisis Government—Italy and France," *Midwest Journal of Politics*, 2 (1958), pp. 117-142.

Democratic Party. No multiparty cabinets are organized as extensively and elaborately as the British cabinet. In all of them sectors of policy or particular departmental activities tend also to be the preserves of individual leaders, party fractions, and selected interests rather than part of a unified cabinet policy. Consistency suffers.

Tension between the government and the assembly is also a feature of most multiparty cabinet systems. It results from the cabinet's attempt to represent the general interest while the individual deputies, the committees, and the party organizations largely assume the tasks of representing particular interests, of legislative logrolling, and of close scrutiny of policy. At the same time, these activities often conflict with the objectives of a cabinet. Thus, cabinets and the assemblies tend to be enemies. In Germany, the cabinet and the disciplined parties grind through the agenda, riding roughshod over the committees and the individual members. In France, under the Fifth Republic, the committees have been reduced to near impotence and the Assembly's powers considerably diminished. In both of these cases, the tension has not been abolished. The cabinets dominate, but they do so at the expense of spontaneity in parliamentary proceedings and the equally serious loss of the knowledge and political skills of individual members. These evils are considerably greater for these countries than they are in Britain, for in France and Germany the sense of proportion and fair play are not as effective as political restraints. Also, since the cabinets are less effective teams than is the British Cabinet, the diminished role of the individual member, the parliamentary assemblies, and the committees is a more serious matter.

As in the Third and Fourth Republics, control of the administration also tends to be a major problem under multiparty cabinet systems, and for some of the same reasons. Even in Germany, responsibility for particular departments is allocated largely according to the political preference of particular parties or party fractions within the ruling coalition. In no multiparty cabinet system is the coordination of administrative policy closely meshed with the cabinet itself. Weak connections between cabinet policy and administration is in fact a prominent and important feature of these systems. The reasons are several: ignorance upon the part of ministers; the insulated status and often unresponsive character of the civil service in Europe; the excessive secrecy and silence of administration there; the absence of effective coordination; the constitutional limitations put upon committees to prevent them from stirring up trouble; and the power of special interest groups directly related to particular departments.

Evaluation

SAFEGUARDS

By way of summary comments, we may look first to safeguards. In this respect, most European systems have much in common. They have emphasized three primary techniques or devices: remedies available through administrative courts; the division of ministerial responsibility according to party; and the use of parliamentary investigation through interpellation and the oversight of parliamentary committees. These techniques have worked with varying success in different countries. Again France probably represents the most instructive example, albeit an extreme case.

Divided cabinets are a kind of safeguard against misgovernment. Regular rotation in office at least tends to keep any one reckless minister from remaining too long in the driver's seat. Inactivity, when a country is deeply divided politically is sometimes preferable to misgovernment with a definite and sustained tendency. Also, the practice of dividing ministries according to party is functionally similar to the American device of separation of powers. In France, for instance, Catholic parties will regularly demand and receive the Ministry of Education. Fiscally conservative parties often get the post of Finance. Peasants and Independents control the Ministry of Agriculture. Parties of the Left frequently strike for the Ministry of Defense and the Ministry of Interior. (This practice no longer obtains to the same extent under the Fifth Republic.) Under the Fourth Republic, this party division of ministries served fairly well as a method of protecting the interests that each party held dearest; also, this division of administrative spoils was often the only basis upon which the parties would agree to collaborate. On the other hand, the technique often meant near paralysis of policy, since the parties that demanded, for example, the Ministry of Defense or of Education or of Agriculture were often concerned primarily with protecting the status quo, not driving forward along the path of social progress.[41]

Since divided cabinets could not be in any real sense the master of policy or of the administration, a good part of the defense of promotion of particular interests fell to the committees and to the private members of the Assembly acting through interpellation. What made sense as a matter of form did not work well in practice. The committees and the individual members of the Assembly are the obvious candidates for defenders of group rights and interests. Under the Fourth Republic, they had considerable power to defend the individual or particular groups from the cabinet and sometimes from the administration. Yet they frequently lacked the information to do this job intelligently and rationally. Investigation is potentially an enormous power, both for good and evil. It is the *sine qua non* for effective control of the government or the administration. On the other hand, it may be used to pillory a government or wreck a career. The French system required severe limitations upon this power, for few cabinets could survive the regular inquisitions of the committees or the interpellations of the Assembly. As a consequence, tangled issues were seldom unravelled, and neither the committees nor the Assembly was in a position to lead or command in the

[41] The most notorious instance was the long-continued control of French overseas affairs by the M. R. P.

business of protecting or expanding group rights. They tended to defend rather than expand rights, or to respond to importunities from their constituents without much knowledge of what they were doing or how their actions fitted with established programs.[42]

As a matter of common knowledge and even common consent, much of the defense of group and individual rights and interests depended upon the stability of the administrative establishment and the elaborate set of remedies available to individuals and groups through the administrative courts. In France, administrative law as developed by the *Conseil d'Etat* and a system of subordinate administrative tribunals substituted in considerable measure for morale and responsiveness bred into the civil service, for responsiveness to the citizenry, for legislative oversight of the civil service by the parliament, and for effective direction from the cabinet.

On the whole, as a way of affording negative protection to certain interests, the French system under the Fourth Republic served tolerably well, despite considerable inequities in particular cases. It kept peace among the major interests in the society, protected most of the group interests that people were prepared to fight about, and afforded the individual an actionable set of remedies. In countries less divided by their history and their contemporary problems—Holland and Belgium, for instance—these same techniques have worked well.

RESPONSIVENESS AND ACCOUNTABILITY

Evaluating the French system, or the multiparty cabinet system generally, on the count of responsiveness and accountability is difficult. The great virtue of such a system is flexibility. Not only can and do cabinets often respond ably to the mood of the Assembly and the tasks of the hour; through cabinet transformations they can often make major shifts of front and respond broadly to a need for extensive programmatic changes.[43] Given peace and prosperity, an informed public opinion, and stable moderate parties, such a system is also capable of affording a considerable measure of orderly and effective accountability. Sometimes it is argued that compromises of policy are better reached before elections and within the party caucus or behind closed committee doors. But it is a debatable point. The multiparty cabinet system continues the bargaining process in public and often does considerable violence to the original electoral mandate. At its worst (which was unfortunately often in the case for France), this process appears to be a dirty "game of politics" played by the politicians at the expense of the nation. To the political intransigent, however, any parliamentary regime is likely to seem so. Political bargains and "deals" are the essence of politics

[42] Bromhead, *op. cit.*, Lidderdale, *op. cit.* John E. Howard's, *Parliament and Foreign Policy in France* (London: Cresset, 1948) examines the role of committees in foreign policy under the Third Republic.

[43] Leites, *op. cit.*; and Williams, "Compromise and Crisis in French Politics," *loc. cit.*

and government. The multiparty cabinet system brings some of this process (perhaps too much) into the open. It also continues the process of bargaining, mediation, and negotiation during the life of an assembly and continues it on a somewhat broader basis than is usually the case in Britain, for instance. Rousseau stated once that the citizen in a representative democracy was free only when he acted as an elector. Thereafter, he was a slave to the deputy. The multiparty cabinet system is, for countries such as France and much of Europe, perhaps the best answer that could be provided for Rousseau's complaint. Under reasonably favorable social and economic conditions, it rates as well, with respect to responsiveness and effective accountability, as the British.

LEADERSHIP AND EFFECTIVENESS

Leadership and effectiveness in the face of crisis have always been the weak point of the multiparty cabinet system and proved to be so especially in the Fourth Republic. This is not to say that such a system is incapable of coping with many crises, for it is. Under the circumstances, the French response to several of the great crises of the Third Republic was good. Similarly, the ingenuity and flexibility, even leadership displayed in meeting some of the social, economic, and political problems—domestic and international—after the Second World War were, though not spectacular, at least creditable. For small and intricate crises, and even for great crises when the nation was substantially united, the system has not proven itself to be a bad one. But in the face of both severe crisis and internal dissension, there is no way to rally the nation, to generate forceful executive leadership,[44] or to make the big, and sometimes drastic, step needed for survival. Without the Cold War, the frightful struggle in Algeria, and the sullen threat of the French Communist Party, many of the problems of the French could most probably have been met, and met within a system of liberty and popular democracy. But radical surgery and vigorous leadership to set the stage for "politics as usual" were a prerequisite for success. This, "the system" could not supply.

Without the power to cope with the combination of crisis and division, many features of the French system that might well have been virtues became grave evils. For many situations, such things as ministerial rotation, a bargaining relation between cabinet and assembly, considerable power in the individual deputies and the committees, and various shadings of opinion from right to left facilitate progress, responsiveness, and accountability. In basic design the French system is a sensible one, especially to maximize bargaining and compromise within a narrow consensus. Programs suffer, especially those requiring advance planning, coordination, and effective con-

---

[44] The various emergency proceedings, such as the use of wide decree powers, or the declaration of a "state of siege" will often do for a crisis of short duration. They are of little help in dealing with a prolonged crisis or deeper, underlying, causes of division.

trol of administrative services. But for much of politics, logic and symmetry are not the most important things; and they may destroy even more vital political goods. For many areas of political life, where there was no possibility of agreement or of an amicable disagreement, the French system managed to find compromise solutions. The compromise was achieved noisily, often rancorously, with many an overturned cabinet and enormous waste of the time and talents of able people. Yet within the political consensus that was possible, progress was made.

The misfortune of the French Fourth Republic was that both programmatic progress and "big" leadership were desperately needed in the postwar world. Under these circumstances the "system" proved inadequate. It could not generate enough coordinative power. Lacking were techniques either to stimulate the necessary leadership or to legitimate hard choices. Over twelve years the National Assembly steadily wasted the stock of moral capital with which the new regime began. Under the pressure of crisis and in the absence of effective devices to curb the inherently centrifugal tendencies of the multiparty cabinet system, the Fourth Republic collapsed. *Post hoc* is not *propter hoc*. The system was designed for less pressure—fewer irreconcilables, a speedier recovery, a world of greater international stability. Despite its weaknesses, the basic model of the Fourth Republic has much to commend it. Much of the unpopularity it gained should not be attributed to matters of governmental form but to unlucky circumstance and a burdensome political heritage. Given the circumstances, however, it proved disastrously weak in providing, in renewing, and in making leadership effective. Governments cannot steadily waste their moral capital, as the Fourth Republic surely did.[45]

THE PRESIDENTIAL SYSTEM

General

The major alternative to the cabinet or parliamentary system of government is the presidential system. Although there is considerable variation among presidential systems, their distinguishing features are 1) independent and usually direct election of the chief executive; 2) a separation of powers and personnel between the executive and legislative branches; and 3) the granting of a wide array of executive and administrative powers to the Chief Executive, usually exercised on his initiative, but often subject to some form

[45] Whatever his place in history, de Gaulle's contribution to "setting the stage" for normal politics has been a great one. Whether he should have done more or, like Cincinnatus, have retired once the Republic was saved remains to be seen. Indeed, the Fifth Republic is of interest partly because it can shed so much light upon the relative importance to politics of the several values we have applied to central government. On this subject, see Williams and Harrison, *op. cit.*, Chs. 8, 9, and Conclusion.

of concurring action by the legislature. There are a number of hybrid forms between the cabinet and the presidential systems (of which the French Fifth Republic is one); and for that matter, most cabinet or parliamentary systems usually have a "president of the republic" and most presidential systems a cabinet—so the concept of "presidential system" requires explanation.

Under a presidential system, the powers are "separated" in several senses. One is independent election. The chief executive of a cabinet or parliamentary system is almost invariably a member of the legislative assembly, and is elected to be premier by it or by the majority parliamentary party. Under most modern presidential systems, some form of modified popular election is the rule, and the president is the representative of the people, the whole people, in a sense that no deputy or premier can claim to be. He is usually elected for a fixed term of office, and, although subject to impeachment for grave and flagrant offenses, is not otherwise directly accountable to another body.

Another feature of most presidential systems is the concentration of enormous powers of initiative and direct control in the office of the presidency. Usually, the president conducts foreign policy and is the commander-in-chief of the armed forces. He is invariably the chief executive and administrative officer, carrying out the laws passed by legislatures, but especially also employing his discretion as to the when and how of execution and administration. Most modern presidencies are assigned wide emergency powers. In the American Constitution, these powers were derived wholly by implication from such clauses as "Congress shall provide for . . ." and "The executive power shall be vested in a President. . . ."[46] In some of the more recently established presidencies, this executive prerogative includes the power to dismiss the legislature, to govern by decree, and to .pass emergency budgets.

Presidential systems include also some version not only of separation of powers but of "checks and balances." The device of separate branches possessing independent powers itself springs from the theory of "checks and balances." Legislature and executive (and judiciary, usually) are separated. They also "check" each other, and presumably some sort of balance results. Often the power of judicial review of legislation and of executive acts is a feature of the presidential system, though its effectiveness varies widely. Sometimes, though usually to a lesser extent than in the United States, presidential appointments are subject to legislative approval, as treaties commonly are. Executives in turn usually share in the legislative process. The president can suggest legislation. Outside the United States, most presidents have

---

[46] Under the former clause, Congress is permitted to delegate certain powers to the President, while under the latter the President possesses certain powers in his own right, without Congressional action. On the powers of the Presidency the standard work is Edward S. Corwin, *The President: Office and Powers—1787-1957*, 4th ed. (New York: New York U. P., 1957).

"ministerial privileges"; that is, they can send their administrative representatives to the floor of the legislature. A suspensive or absolute veto over legislation is well-nigh universal.

Most presidential systems have also been associated with federalism and bicameral legislatures. Though this association is not essential, there is a natural harmony about it. Federalism calls for a supreme court and for a bicameral legislature. Federalism also tends to enfeeble a plural executive, and especially an executive constituted within parliament. These factors make separation of powers and thus a presidency rather obvious expedients. On the other hand, dispersed governmental power and sectionalism strengthen external, pluralistic checks on government and provide a counterweight to the enormous executive power in the hands of the presidency.

ORIGINS

One way, especially, in which presidential systems have come about is by a sharp break with a precedent history of monarchical institutions. This kind of genealogy can be traced for the American Constitution and for many Latin American republics as well. Instead of gradually absorbing the powers and prerogatives of the monarch in a cabinet responsible in turn to a parliamentary assembly, they have "republicanized" the institution of monarchy itself, by creating a republican chief of state to exercise popularly and responsibly the powers of the former monarch. Thus, much of the political theory of *The Federalist Papers* echoes earlier English constitutional debates of the period of the Commonwealth and of the Hanoverian rule of George I; while many of the specific institutions of the American presidency are direct derivatives of the earlier British theory of separation of powers under William and Mary or the Hanovers.[47] Latin American republics, especially in the nineteenth century, faced similar problems of a sudden break with monarchical institutions, and looked to the North American experiment as a model.[48] For a rather similar reason (among others) various emerging African and Asian states, particularly those formerly with viceregal and indirect forms of colonial government, have been attracted to presidential models.

The other primary way in which presidential systems have been established is by reaction to weak or ineffective cabinet systems. Sometimes, as in the case of Louis Bonaparte's presidency, parliamentary government was superseded by a semi-revolutionary *coup d'etat* and plebiscite. In other instances, the commanding prestige of one leader or the unforeseen potentialities of an office produced a slow erosion of parliamentary authority and the emergence of a popular president *de facto*, later made president *de jure* by

[47] Cf. the political writings of David Hume or Edmund Burke; also, Sir Lewis B. Namier, *England in the Age of the American Revolution* (London: Macmillan, 1930), and *The Structure of Politics at the Accession of George III*, 2nd. ed. (London: Macmillan, 1957).
[48] R. A. Gomez, *Government and Politics in Latin America* (New York: Random House, 1960), p. 71.

constitutional revision. Such was the case with Turkey and Pakistan, also to some extent in Ghana. The objective of some self-styled "presidents" has been dictatorship, pure and simple. Other presidencies that have emerged from weak parliamentary regimes represented honest and well-considered attempts to improve the management of political affairs by creating a more powerful executive and a more direct, popular relation of the people with him.

STRENGTHS AND WEAKNESSES

The genealogy of the presidential system of government suggests both some of the strengths and some of the weaknesses of the system. On the one hand, presidency associates strong government with constitutional and social, pluralistic checks on the exercise of governmental power. According to an American expression, "The President is more than a prime minister, less than a king." The system seeks to institutionalize in republican form the unity, executive vigor, and symbolic representation that a popular or vigorous monarchy of earlier days might have achieved or aspired to. Associated with this objective are the checks and balances that protect liberty and prevent dictatorship. In principle and at its best, the presidential system allows the luxury of disagreement and fosters compromise, but joins these with great flexibility and a capacity for vigorous and popular leadership.

On the other hand, the presidency institutionalizes a highly personal form of government, subject to many of the frailties, the temptations, and the abuses of personal rule. It stands in peril of constitutional deadlock. Like the older monarchy it puts a premium upon the use of patronage and influence. By imposing upon presidents the necessity continually to augment, capitalize, and invest anew their political resources, such a system also tempts an active or ambitious president to merge the role of political leader with executive chief and to brush aside or reinterpret the constitutional restrictions upon his office. In the worst of circumstances, presidential systems are an incentive and opportunity for dictators.

THE AMERICAN PRESIDENTIAL SYSTEM[49]

A Fortunate Heritage and a Supporting Political Culture

One of the major assets of the American Republic at the time of its founding, and an asset it could have scarcely done without, was the existence of constitutionally minded public elites and especially a large number of

---

[49] On the constitutional development and theory of the American presidency, see Edward S. Corwin, *op. cit.* Two readily accessible treatments of the functioning of the presidency in a contemporary contest are Richard E. Neustadt, *Presidential Power, the Politics of Leadership* (New York: Wiley, 1960) and Clinton L. Rossiter, *The American Presidency* (New York: Harcourt, 1956).

lawyers and other notables with a deep awareness for the importance of constitutional forms and procedures.[50] The American presidential system has tended to reinforce the constitutional morality of the people. But it also depended initially upon a strong "law sense" without which the formally cast separation of powers and the intricate set of checks and balances could scarcely have been effective. The toleration and acceptance by wide masses of people of the leadership of this constitutionally and juridically minded elite was, in turn, equally important.

The United States also enjoyed the good luck of being able to dispense for much of its history with a large military establishment. As a consequence, civilian control of the military has never seriously been challenged. Equally as important, the executive power could be contained more easily, since the opportunity to build up and consolidate a giant administrative machine was missing. Absence of a large standing army or a serious military policy thus removed a major bone of contention between the executive and the legislature that might have put an intolerable strain upon the system of divided powers. It prevented as well the development of the insidious politics of personal and national prestige that has often been an incitement to dictatorship. By the time a large, standing military establishment became a semipermanent need for the United States, civilian instincts were strongly ingrained, even in most professional soldiers.

The specific pattern of development of the American party system has helped make presidential government work in several ways. Frequently it is said that the party system bridged the separation of powers and imparted motion to the constitutional structure—and so it did. But this thesis needs to be stated in more precise form. The fact that the American party system was predominantly one of two national and relatively moderate parties was extremely important. That the presidential system could have worked in this country in a regime of many parties is doubtful. Certainly it could not have worked well. With a multiparty system the President would be perennially a minority president and weak in one or both houses of Congress. Without a national party, he would lack sources of power both in Congress and in the country. Confronted with divided and very likely hostile legislative houses, the alternative would be either deadlock or a personal and irresponsible executive rule, probably approaching dictatorship. Both the moderation and the national character of the parties was important. Sectional parties or an extreme gap between the parties would tend to generate explosive pressures making both constitutional balance and political progress impossible, as it did at the time of the Civil War.[51]

[50] Cf. Carl Brent Swisher, *American Constitutional Development* (2nd. ed., Boston: Houghton Mifflin, 1954), Ch. 3.

[51] See especially, Herbert Agar, *The Price of Union* (Boston: Houghton Mifflin, 1950). At the same time it must be recognized, as was pointed out in the preceding chapter, that the institution of the presidency was probably the most important cause of the two-party system in the United States.

One of the more delicate adjustments upon which the American presidential system depends is that between the professionalization of the administrative services and their political accountability to the Congress and to the President. Patronage and the "spoils system" are natural counterparts of the presidential system. Rampant political control of administration through legislative committees is also an easy response, and one sometimes practiced, for instance, at the level of state and local legislative bodies. Yet the alternative of complete professionalization and insulation of the administration would undo the system of balances and separation as well. The American adjustment involved a response to the needs for civil service reform and a measure of self-denial practiced by both the legislative and executive branches, along with a pragmatic and experimental approach to the problems of a dual system of accountability. That adjustment was not, of course, a work of conscious design. It did, in practice, require a number of successive and well adapted steps.

The last important requisite we call (for want of a better term) "effective social pluralism," a pattern of group attitudes and interests that supports the system of constitutional restraints. In various ways, the United States was exceptionally lucky both in its heritage and in the course of its future economic and social evolution. Although sectionalism existed, it did not combine with racial or class divisions to create an intractable political situation. The country lacked great and historic families or dynastic loyalties. There was no tradition of "classes," nor of ethnic separation, other than the Negro and the Indian. At the same time, there was economic opportunity and great incentives for individual and group self-help. The effect of this latter circumstance was to produce a system of "alternate resources" in which the incentives for capitalizing upon political influence were regularly restrained by people's absorption in their own affairs and their ability to do as well or better by themselves. The effect of the former set of circumstances was to aid greatly the "art of association," which made combined political efforts easy. As a consequence, local political activity could counterbalance centralist tendencies.[52]

When the list is completed, the special circumstances that have attended the development of the American presidential system seem almost as important as the constitutional arrangements themselves, if not more so. Certainly history and culture need to be taken into account here as elsewhere, and especially in attempting to assess generally the principles to be drawn from a study of this particular system. The principles are provisional: they hold "always or for the most part," and subject to the special circumstances. Nevertheless, the model is useful for probing more deeply into some of the problems associated with the organization of central government.

[52] Alexis de Tocqueville still provides one of the most readable and informative accounts of the importance of these factors. See *Democracy in America*, especially Vol. I, Ch. 16.

The Essence of American Presidential Government

POWERS AND SAFEGUARDS

The essence of American presidential government is the balance of monistic and pluralistic institutions. The spirit of cabinet government, in spite of the collegiate form of its executive, is monistic. Authority flows from a single source and through one channel. The pathway of accountability is simplicity itself. In the multiparty form of cabinet government, however, formal simplicity and unity gives way to operative patterns that are more complicated, more pluralistic, and even disintegrated. The presidential system, emphasizing safeguards against the abuse of power and both reflecting and seeking to give expression to a pluralistic society, attempts also to provide the strength it would otherwise lack by providing for a strong executive.

The presidential system, as organized in the United States, combines both strong initiative with deliberation and a system of "concurrent majorities." The bicameral system in the legislature, the operation of the committee system within each chamber, the fact that only one-third of the Senate is elected at any one time and that Senators hold office for six-year periods, the President's veto power, and the power of the courts to invalidate unconstitutional legislation, provide substantial guarantees that legislation will not be rushed through without ample time for all arguments to be heard, for interested and disinterested parties to analyze various proposals and calculate their probable consequences, and, in matters of great importance, for large sections of the public to become sufficiently informed to have intelligent opinions. These safeguards against precipitate action perform more than a negative function: they provide opportunity for deliberation for consensus building, and for action that is more responsible than would otherwise be the case.

MULTIPLE CONSTITUENCIES—RESPONSIVENESS

Two other virtues of the presidential system are so closely related that they will be discussed together. Both unrepresentative action and majority tyranny are checked by certain features of this system, especially multiple constituencies. Under the cabinet system, disregarding the unessential matter of a second chamber, there is only one set of constituencies. Voters cast their ballots for their legislative representatives and for no other national officials. Under the system of separated powers, on the other hand, they vote separately for members of the lower house, the upper house, and the chief executive (or for electors who in turn elect the chief executive). Normally, as in the United States, the electorate is organized in different ways for these different purposes. This is what is meant by speaking of multiple constituencies. With respect to both representation and protection of minorities such a system has its advantages.

In particular, a kind of averaging takes place, as between elections for national representatives in small constituencies and an election for a single office in a national constituency. In the first place, the election for chief executive will focus attention more on national problems, since it is scarcely possible for a multiplicity of local interests and points of view to find expression under such circumstances. On the other hand, elections in local constituencies, even under a two-party system (assuming parties of the American, undisciplined variety), facilitate expression of the particular interests of given sections of the country, and of special economic and functional interests insofar as they coincide with geographical areas. National candidates tend to represent policy differences only in small degree, because each of them must depend for his success in capturing a large portion of the wavering voters, of those who are most middle-of-the-roaders. Small constituencies, by contrast, are often so clearly dominated by people with views considerably to the right or left of center that they will elect representatives who depart to a much greater extent from the median. Never do voters in the United States elect a president who is either as radical or as conservative as some of the members of Congress who are elected at the same time. Moreover the latter, contrary to the case of their British counterparts, will tend to vote in Congress according to their radical or conservative views. Finally, it appears that there is a tendency for a national election to be more easily influenced by certain nationally organized special interest groups than is the case with a nation-wide election by small constituencies. This situation tends to prevail where the interest groups in question are especially strong in the most politically powerful states, as is the case with organized labor. With a truly national constituency this difference would be less marked than it is with the American electoral college system, but even with the former the groups are advantaged. The presidential candidates must pay a great deal of attention to the position of any group capable of swinging enough votes to determine the outcome of an election. Many congressional candidates will come from "safe" districts where the dominance of one party assures them victory without regard to special interest groups. For this reason, the legislature is likely to contain a number of representatives who can be less responsive to such pressures than the chief executive.

On the other hand in the case of certain other groups, those appealing to a special interest that are widely and more or less evenly distributed, where it is the legislature that is most sensitive and the chief executive who can best resist the pressure. David Truman gives an example of the latter situation and at the same time well sums up the whole situation in the following passage:

> The representative, the senator, and the president each must give ear to groups that one or both of the others can ignore. An admirable illustration of this situation is the fact that four successive presidents—Harding, Coolidge, Hoover,

and Franklin Roosevelt—found it possible to veto veterans' bonus legislation passed by the Congress, although on each occasion approximately four fifths of the House of Representatives chose to override the veto.[53]

It is clear why the President is not especially sensitive to special interest pressure where the interest group is evenly distributed; it is less obvious why he should be *less* sensitive than the Congressman. A plausible explanation, however, runs to the effect that, other things being equal, voters are less likely to vote their particularistic interests when voting for a man to fill an office of such power, scope, and dignity as that of the presidency. It seems probable, too, that there is a relevant distinction between special interests, like those of labor or farmer, which it is relatively easy to identify with the general interest, and the special interest of the veteran which, whether or not deserving of recognition, seems a more "private" matter.

Multiple constituencies tend to lead to more representative action, then, both because of the greater richness of representation they provide and because they help check the power of special interest groups even while giving them representation. In similar fashion, the system makes it more difficult for a majority, especially a bare majority, to take action strongly opposed by a sizable minority. Not only may this system give protection to minority rights that the majority might tend to disregard, but also—perhaps more significantly in practical politics, it encourages the majority to seek the concurrence of minority groups by educating and persuading them rather than by riding roughshod over them. One consequence is that greater efforts are made to find compromises and to integrate differences; that is, to find solutions that meet the needs of all concerned.

ACCESSIBILITY

A further advantage to be noted for the presidential system has to do with ease of access to the policy-making machinery of government. American government is dispersed. Power may be wielded at many points and most of these points are accessible to interested parties—perhaps too much so, at times. Partly this is a matter of our traditions. In a country in which, until only a relatively few years ago, any person who would go to Washington and stand in line on the right day of the week could shake the hand of the President, it is not surprising that few officers of government feel they can refuse to see a citizen who is affected by some matter that falls under his jurisdiction. Also in a country in which party discipline is as lax as it is in the United States, individual members of Congress are highly accessible. Finally, and more typical of the presidential system as such, Congress operates largely through powerful committees, and these committees normally act only after having held extensive public hearings at which all interested parties may come and have their say.

[53] David B. Truman, *The Governmental Process* (New York: Knopf, 1951), p. 324.

Drawbacks

DEADLOCK

The presidential system also has its drawbacks. One of the charges often made against it is that it leads to deadlocks, and hence is ineffective, lacking in the ability to produce a prompt, vigorous response to a clear need.[54] For instance, the President and the legislature may be in serious disagreement, with the result that the legislature refuses to enact the President's program and is either incapable of developing a program of its own or does so only to meet with Presidential vetoes. Before saying anything about the extent to which this charge is true, a side remark is in order. Deadlocks may be democratic. A government that takes no action may be reflecting public indecision. Frequently, where there is a great deal of uncertainty or where there are several possible and plausible courses of action, there is no clear majority in favor of any policy. A clear example is that afforded by the last two years of President Hoover's administration. While the people in 1930 expressed discontent with the way things were going, there is no indication that a majority was yet ready for the strong measures later taken under the leadership of President Roosevelt. A big shift both in economic conditions and in ideas as to the proper role of government took place between the era of the Twenties and that of the Thirties. It certainly did not occur all at once. A period of confusion inevitably lay between. The delay of positive governmental reaction to the economic crisis for more than two years may well have accurately mirrored the uncertainty of public opinion during this period.

Inaction does not always characterize periods when legislature and chief executive are controlled by opposing parties. That situation was repeated in 1947-1948 without the same results. This time the fact of divided political leadership did not result in governmental stalemate. Congress enacted a normal amount of legislation. It was not, of course, the legislation the President wanted; but a program was adopted—as consistent a one, it may safely be said, as has characterized most periods when the President and the majority of Congress belonged to the same party. The last six years of President Eisenhower's administration were characterized by the same situation, with much the same results except that, thanks to the alliance between conservative Republicans and Southern Democrats on many issues, the President enjoyed a substantial degree of success in securing the kind of legislative action he favored.

Nevertheless, observers both in the United States and abroad are fearful that the time may come when the American constitutional machinery pre-

[54] Cf. James McG. Burns, *The Deadlock of Democracy, Four-Party Politics in America* (Englewood Cliffs, N.J.: Prentice-Hall, 1963).

Separation of powers: Capitol, White House, and the long mile between
Charles Phelps Cushing

vents the government from reacting to some international emergency with sufficient speed and forcefulness. The nominal President and former military dictator of Pakistan once declared that his countrymen were beginning to think that the governmental machinery of the United States was too "cumbersome," "sluggish," and "clumsy" for the nuclear age.[55]

STAGNATION

Quite apart from the possibility of deadlock, the presidential system as it operates in the United States makes positive action itself difficult. It gives ready access to all groups and is responsive to many demands. The very fact that the concurrence of many centers of power must be secured for action—legislative committees (substantive, rules, and appropriations committees), party leaders in the legislature, the President, and key administrative officials—means that it is easier to prevent action than to take it. Thus we have the phenomenon of "veto groups." A powerful minority group such as agriculture, business, organized labor, or important subdivisions of these groups, are generally able to check legislation to which they are strongly opposed unless there is an overwhelming demand for it. The concurrence of many persons in positions of power compells widespread education, discussion, deliberation, and assent. Especially in a big and varied country, this is no mean virtue. But it has its price; it makes it easier for special interest groups to block legislation or administrative action that would hurt them but that might be in the general interest. An example may give substance to this point. In the United States, the field of labor-management relations is a chronic source of controversy. When major legislation is enacted it is inevitably complicated and the result of many compromises. Partly for this reason, amendments usually seem to be needed, in the general interest, soon after such legislation is passed. Yet, because they often would favor one side at the expense of the other, it usually proves impossible to enact them until a strong enough head of steam is built up to force through a major revision. This feat has been accomplished only twice since the enactment of the Wagner Act in 1935. As another case in point, it is widely believed that the lobbying activities of the American Medical Association have prevented enactment of anything like adequate social insurance against the costs of illness in the United States.

CONFUSION AND COMPLEXITY

The pluralistic nature of the American system has two other significant consequences that are at least partly on the debit side of the ledger. Both grow out of the fact that power centers are dispersed instead of being cen-

[55] *The New York Times*, June 27, 1960, p. 1, col. 5. However, he defended the Presidential system for Pakistan and declared that for them to return to the Parliamentary system would be "the height of stupidity" and "political suicide." *Ibid.*, July 26, 1960, p. 11, col. 2.

tralized in the cabinet as they are under the two-party cabinet system. One consequence is that coordination of policy tends to be weak. Congress enacts laws and appropriations in response to the recommendations of its various committees and subcommittees[56] that are not part of a comprehensive plan and which, accordingly, sometimes are of doubtful compatibility. To be sure the President, through his Director of the Budget, backed up if need be by the veto power, exercises a considerable unifying control over appropriations; but it is by no means always effective. Similarly his own legislative program, as offered by various Department and agency heads, is coordinated through the Legislative Reference Division of the Budget Bureau; but the President's power to coordinate the legislative output of Congress is a function of the balance of political power between the President and the majority of Congress (whether or not of his own political party).

Lack of coordination of policy is not confined to legislation and appropriations but affects administration as well. In fact some students consider this administrative disintegration as more serious than the lack of coordination at the level of the legislature. There are two reasons for it, both flowing from weaknesses in presidential control. In the first place, Congress, and especially its committees, insist on exercising certain direct controls over administration and establishing direct relations with administrative officers. This procedure adds to responsiveness but interferes with coordination. It also makes difficult the lot of the bureau chief or department head, because he must serve two masters—the President and Congress, or perhaps one or more Congressional committee chairmen. A second, perhaps more justifiable and less serious difficulty arises from the fact that numerous governmental functions are entrusted to commissions whose members, though appointed by the President, with the advice and consent of the Senate, he may not dismiss. The idea behind this arrangement is to give stability to certain regulatory policies and to insulate these areas from the immediate pressures of partisan politics. Although the Board of Governors of the Federal Reserve System is hardly typical of these agencies, it illustrates quite well the strength and weakness of the system. Because of the division of power over money matters between the Board and the Treasury it is possible for the President's power over fiscal policy—indeed his power over the economy as a whole, for which he is held responsible by the electorate—to be substantially curtailed and even contravened. On the other hand, it can be argued, as indeed it is argued, that such vital questions as the interest rate and the supply of credit should in large measure be governed by sound banking principles and that a board representative of the central banks and other major interests in the economy, and wholly insulated from presidential power of dismissal, can more safely be trusted with this great power than can the President,

[56] For appropriations there is a single committee in each House, but each contains numerous standing subcommittees which tend to operate as independent entities.

who might be tempted to use it for partisan advantage and in any case tend to be moved by more short-run considerations.

Another debit of the pluralistic system has already been suggested. It had to do with accountability. Where power is so widely dispersed and shared, it is difficult for the average voter to locate responsibility for governmental action or inaction and to vote accordingly. An answer to this criticism depends largely upon the role that the public can and should play in a democracy. If the average voter casts his ballot according to his preferences about numerous specific issues, the presidential system complicates his task and may frustrate him completely, especially in the absence of a strong party system. On the other hand, this view may impute a wholly unrealistic role to public opinion. If, as the authors tend to believe, the role of the public is much more general than this, judging largely in terms of over-all performance, and leaving the care of their interests on specific questions largely up to their various organized interest groups, then this alleged disadvantage is of relatively little importance. Moreover, there is here an advantage, already mentioned in our discussion of disciplined and undisciplined parties, that should be repeated in the present context. The presidential system permits the voter to express discriminating judgments that can not be made effective under the two-party cabinet system, by voting for a President of one party and Congressmen and Senators of another.

The Synthesis of Monism and Pluralism

DIFFERENT WAYS OF BEING "RATIONAL"

Does the lack of central coordination of policy entail lack of rationality? The best answer seems to be, "It depends upon the kind of policy being coordinated." For some policies (planning of investment, a budget) central coordination and an "overview" are at a premium. In other cases (legislation amending the social security provisions), coordination may be best achieved "incrementally," by the maneuvering of interests, by adjustments and accommodations worked out piecemeal in the effort on the part of each group to gain its own ends (which may or may not be selfish ends).[57] In principle the American system scores high marks for its aptness in encouraging pragmatic adjustment of interests and does less well at rational decisions with respect to collective utilities and the amount to be invested in the public

[57] For statements, respectively, of the advantages of incremental adjustment and of the disadvantages of centralized planning, see Charles E. Lindblom, "The Science of Muddling Through," *Public Administration Review*, 19 (1959), pp. 79-88; and Michael Polanyi, *The Logic of Liberty* (Chicago: Univ. of Chicago Press, 1959), Ch. 7. More broadly the issues explored above are discussed from varying points of view in *Democracy in the Mid-Twentieth Century—Problems and Prospects*, by Samuel H. Beer, Leon D. Epstein, Louis Hartz, Charles E. Lindblom, and J. Roland Pennock (St. Louis: Washington U. P., 1960), especially pp. 30-125.

sector. Thus, supposedly, the "public interest" suffers: schools do not get built, highways are put in the wrong place, tariff bills are badly written, and so forth. Case studies of legislative and administrative decisions taken with respect to such policies support this point of view to a limited extent. They also show an awareness on the part of officials of several aspects of programmatic rationality: the interest of the intensely affected versus that of the marginally affected; the short-run interest of the community versus its long-run interest; and the economic consequences of a decision versus its political consequences.

Another subject of considerable importance in weighing and assessing the American legislative-executive balance and the degree of rationality of policy that it produces has to do with the role and nature of the communication of political information. For the rational solution of problems, governments need candid information, they need full information, and they need a reasonable statement of alternatives, whether they are dealing with the problems of agricultural price supports or disarmament negotiations. They must also inform and carry the people along with them. Here is where the role of investigation and the close confrontation of legislative and administrative official in the committee sessions is of great importance. Wholly unjustified, politically motivated attacks upon officials and upon a policy through investigation or under the authority of congressional committees show the price that is paid for this form of control. But too often, especially because this kind of activity is what makes newspaper headlines, only the dark side of the picture is recognized. The example of the French Fourth Republic, on the other hand, shows the price paid for moving in ignorance and for not continually giving the people a fairly sober account of what is going on. It may be doubted also that the "truth will out" unless there are some fairly coercive controls to force people—administrators and group representatives—to come forward with the information.

Partly, the American system of inquisition and investigation is a natural counterpart of the separation of powers; as such, it demands a balance between the prerogatives of the executive and the proper demands of the legislature. But it is also another way of doing things. It puts a heavy burden upon the administrative chief or the expert. It also puts a heavy burden upon the "moving party." It stops in mid-career a good many well-conceived plans. On the other hand, it produces knowledge, a sophisticated appreciation of problems, and a widespread communication of intelligence. These may be of more importance than order and coordinative power. Good ideas and proposals generally find backers, especially in an educated, affluent society. The need today may be more for knowledge communicated and tested than for leadership.[58]

[58] For an interesting commentary on this point of view, as well as a defense of some of the propositions presented here, see Norton E. Long, *"Public Policy and Administration: The Goals of Rationality and Responsibility," Public Administration Review,* 14 (1954), pp. 22-31.

LEADERSHIP

Another way to put the thesis stated above would be to say that more effective leadership can often be achieved by allowing consensus about the facts and values at stake in a particular policy to develop at many points and through many different methods. Leadership is a complex notion; and the situation itself is complicated. One role of leaders is to set the issues —to narrow the number of choices to be made by the rank and file. By this interpretation the presidential system, like the multiparty cabinet system, is far inferior to the two-party cabinet system. On the other hand, a political system can be evaluated also in terms of the leadership that—one way or another—it generates. Here, in some ways, the American system ranks high. It presents opportunities and incentives for individuals to spot and analyze problems and seek support for their proposed solutions, and to do this from positions of some prominence. Leadership is dispersed among the citizenry. Leadership is widely dispersed among officials also: cabinet members and other administrative officials share this opportunity with the President and so do party leaders in Congress, ranking committee members, and every individual Senator. Here is abundant opportunity both for the performance of leadership functions and for the development and display of leadership talents. One is tempted to say, of course, that there are too many self-nominated and self-interested leaders crying for attention. The result seems chaotic. And so it is, if one goes by the volume of noise and the apparent contradictions in policy.

Comparisons are interesting. In Britain, issues are brought to a head and then decided. In the United States, they drag on indefinitely and are blocked at every turn by veto groups. Or so it appears. As·political affairs generally go, however, things move faster in the United States than it might seem. Between the point at which a definite social and political need is widely recognized and the point at which government takes effective cognizance of that need and substantially meets it, the period of time elapsed seems to be about the same both in the United States and in Great Britain. In Britain, the system is centralized, disciplined, and highly organized. It is also slow and stately in its movements, especially in matters of social and economic policy. In the American system, flexibility and ease of access can quickly and effectively register a protest that tends to generate leadership.

The leadership that is developed is not necessarily leadership according to a coherent program of the President or the Congress. It may be leadership from the states and municipalities, from senior Senators and executive officials, or a lead forced upon the President by the imperative need to respond with *something* even though the critics are ill advised and speak with a thousand tongues. The American dispersed leadership is less neat than the British pattern, but it is effective in giving expression to a wide variety of needs and a wealth of ideas for satisfying them. Considering the number and variety of interests to which American government is responsive, the degree to which they are aggregated and integrated is remarkable.

As for presidential leadership itself, much will depend upon the quality of the President and of his immediate entourage. A President who has that magnetic quality and force of personality often spoken of as "charisma" may sometimes so transcend constitutional arrangements as to make even the American government operate in almost monolithic fashion—at least for a little while. Short of this he may be able to secure a reasonable balance between dispersed and centralized leadership. He is aided in achieving this goal by the entourage of personal assistants and advisers with which every President surrounds himself. In selecting these men he has an opportunity to draw on the best political and administrative talent of the country. He can choose cronies and relatives and mortgage the future in a number of ways. Yet the presidency is well "staffed," and has, like the British cabinet, been "institutionalized."[59] It is to some extent proof even against weak men, mediocrities or bunglers—as much as government can be. With an able president, the system can respond well to the need for leadership, assuming that there is an underlying consensus to be integrated.

CONCLUSION

In this chapter, we have dealt primarily with three rather "pure types" of executive-legislative organization: the American presidential system, the British two-party parliamentary regime, and the French multiparty system as it existed and functioned during the Third and Fourth Republic. There are, of course, many hybrid types, from the so-called "two-and-one-half" party system of Germany to the presidential-dominant cabinet system of the Fifth Republic of France and the various mixed types in the Near and Middle East, Africa and Asia. The purpose of choosing these three was not to suggest that any form is "natural" or best, but to illustrate some classic problems of government and some of the approaches that can be taken for their solution.

Several tendencies significant for democratic central government may be observed. For instance, the regulatory and administrative activities of central governments have markedly increased. Certainly in Western Europe and North America this factor has brought about a change in the relations of the organs of central government, and especially in the relative extent of executive power. A revolution in communications—the use of television, radio, and other mass media—has also contributed to executive aggrandize-

[59] For somewhat opposing views as to the effect and value of presidential staff organizations in "institutionalizing" the Presidency, compare Rossiter, *op. cit.*, and Neustadt, *op. cit.*

ment. The Cold War works in the same direction. It heightens the importance of secrecy. It magnifies the role of the executive and of the experts surrounding him. It distorts the traditional relations of the executive and the legislature. The executive is prone to be less than candid. The legislator is often at sea—hesitant to criticize, baffled and irritated. Other representatives see their duty as exposure and demagogy. A new adjustment has not been easy to achieve in any country.

In short, the power of the executive has grown enormously, and parliamentary bodies have not by any means always experienced a commensurate growth in power, in self-confidence, or in public esteem.[60] The ability of oppositional parties and of independent centers of political power to offer effective alternatives or to respond with a valuable critique of government has declined.[61] Measured by traditional theories of the role of the executive and the legislature, these trends in government are unfavorable. They have led some to prophesy a "garrison state." Others foresee the stagnation of popular government. Many say that the prospects for changing the course of events are bad. Some of these expressions of cynicism and disgruntlement may be justified; but the approach through traditional theory probably exaggerates the dangers and tends to overlook countervailing tendencies.

As we have tried to suggest, such concepts as accountability, responsiveness, effective leadership and rationality are more useful analytical tools than the traditional legislative-executive, principal-agent model. Most contemporary governments when examined with these concepts show some of the putatively undemocratic tendencies that are so commonly noted. They show, as well, however, a considerable amount of incremental progress in developing new responses to these tendencies. The theory and the practice of "responsible government" change. A simple theory of the accountability of government to the majority, for instance, is anachronistic; but it does not follow that accountability is lost. Indeed, a system of dispersed controls and accurately conceived delegations of legislative, executive, and judicial powers may enhance effective accountability. By the same token the surrender of some measure of popular accountability can be consistent with the theory of responsible government. Government cannot lead, it cannot behave rationally or fairly without the capacity to exercise a reasoned discretion, without the delegation of powers. The broad objective is responsible democratic government. The means appropriate for its accomplishment vary according to the political culture surrounding the government and the nature of the problems it faces.

[60] See Jean Meynaud, "The Executive in the Modern State," *International Social Science Bulletin*, 10 (1958), pp. 171-198; and "The Parliamentary Profession," *International Social Science Journal*, 13 (1961), pp. 513-640.

[61] Otto Kirchheimer, "The Waning of Opposition in Parliamentary Regimes," *Social Research*, 24 (1957), pp. 127-156.

SELECTED READINGS

(Asterisk indicates book is available in paperback edition.)

The American Political Science Review, 54-56, (1960-1963), has featured a number of articles on Congressional party, committee, and policy organization and behavior. These articles are to be especially recommended, not only because they bring earlier research up to date, but also because they give to the student that sense of intricacy of procedure and of closeness to the details of policy which is essential to an understanding of the American Congress.

CAMPION, LORD *et al. Parliament, A Survey.* London: Allen & Unwin, 1955. This book is somewhat dated, but it covers a good range of topics with essays written by many of Britain's leading authorities on the particular subject.

CRICK, BERNARD. *Reform of the Commons.* London: Fabian Society, 1959. A critique of Parliament with suggested reforms that Americans would find congenial.

DUVERGER, MAURICE. Trans. North, Robert and Barbara. *The French Political System.* Chicago: Univ. of Chicago Press, 1958.

GALLOWAY, GEORGE B. *The Legislative Process in Congress.* New York: Crowell, 1953. An authoritative account of the working of Congress, including suggestions for reform.

*GRIFFITH, ERNEST S. *Congress: Its Contemporary Role.* 3rd ed., New York: New York U. P., 1961. A sympathetic account of the American Congress in action by one who had the opportunity to observe it closely for many years.

HILSMAN, ROGER. "Congressional-Executive Relations and the Foreign Policy Consensus," *American Political Science Review,* 52 (1958), pp. 725-744. This essay shows the way in which diffused leadership in the American system can work to develop a consensus which bridges the division of legislative and executive powers.

JENNINGS, SIR IVOR. *Cabinet Government.* 3rd ed., Cambridge, Eng.: Cambridge U. P., 1959. A comprehensive treatise.

————. *Parliament.* Rev. ed., Cambridge, Eng.: Cambridge U. P., 1959. A standard, authoritative work written by a specialist in constitutional law.

Law and Contemporary Problems, Symposium, "The Presidential Office," 21, (1956). The essay by Steelman and Kreager, "The Executive Office as Administrative Coordinator" is a superb discussion of the role of the President as administrator.

LEITES, NATHAN. *On the Game of Politics in France.* Palo Alto, Calif.: Stanford U. P., 1959. An excellent account of the process of negotiation, compromise, and political response by which parliamentary affairs were conducted under the Fourth Republic.

LIDDERDALE, D. W. S. *The Parliament of France.* London: Hansard, 1951. A meticulous work on parliamentary procedure and organization under the Fourth Republic.

MORRISON, SIR HERBERT. (now Lord of Lambeth). *Government and Parliament: A Survey From Inside.* 2nd ed., London: Oxford U. P., 1959. A discussion and critique of cabinet government written by a former cabinet member. Like many such accounts it is anecdotal and discursive, but has also the merit of dealing systematically with a good many aspects of cabinet government.

NEUSTADT, RICHARD E. "Presidency and Legislation: Planning the President's Program" *American Political Science Review,* 49, 1955, pp. 980-1021. An important article discussing the use of techniques of centralized clearance to integrate and organize the President's legislative program.

TAYLOR, ERIC. *The House of Commons at Work.* 3rd ed., London: Penguin, 1958. An accessible work which also imports vividness and reality into the discussion of parliamentary procedure.

WILLIAMS, PHILIP M. and HARRISON, MARTIN. *De Gaulle's Republic.* New ed., London: Longmans, 1960. An excellent account, critical of de Gaulle, which also predicted many of the problems which have arisen since it was written.

CHAPTER 15

Administration

‖‖‖

THE ROLE OF ADMINISTRATION IN THE MODERN STATE

Administration has usually been central to government, though more at some times than at others. In the making of national states, for instance, the recruitment, professionalization, and centralization of administration was a primary if not the major task of monarchs.[1] In nineteenth-century Britain and America, the prevalence of laissez-faire left only a limited role for administration; but their experience was exceptional. In the twentieth century, such influences as war, modern technology and living conditions, and the demand for new services and the expansion and improvement of older services, have produced spectacular increases in the size and importance of the administrative arm in all modern nations.

Today public administration is the largest single source of employment. In the United States, over six million individuals out of a working population of seventy-one million are employees of one or another of the various levels of government. The federal government alone has over two million civilian employees. In Great Britain, the comparable figure is over a million, representing a much higher *per capita* total than the American. For France or Italy, the proportions would run about the same as in Great Britain.

The size of the administrative establishment and the scope of its activities are important in themselves. Administration touches almost all activities of society, governmental and private, in one way or another. Thus, administrative activity is itself one of the main sources from which new problems for government are brought to the fore.

[1] See, for example, Sir Ernest Barker, *The Development of Public Services in Western Europe, 1660-1930* (London: Oxford U. P., 1944).

In all modern states, administrative agencies have vast discretionary authority: they are powerful. They determine public policy within limits that are frequently broad and sometimes quite indeterminate. As much and sometimes even more than the legislative branch, therefore, these agencies are the subjects of pressure-group activity. As they must consider public opinion, so they are driven to seek to influence it. In short, administrative agencies do not merely administer; they initiate policy; they shape and encourage particular policy decisions by elected officials; and they interpret policy under their statutory authority. For these reasons, administrative agencies are in the thick of politics itself.

Administration is also in considerable measure the source of information and of ideas for government. Administration has the long memory, the knowledge of detail and of general pattern, the involvement with immediate decision and the "overview" as well that elected officials or other representative leadership may lack. The bureaus will assemble information, write the "position papers" or the memoranda, project plans for the future, propose and draft orders and legislation that are often the point from which serious and detailed discussion begins among the formally constituted decision-makers.

In the preceding chapter we noted that the relations between the electorate and the legislature is complex and by no means a one-way affair. The legislative-executive complex must do far more than represent and respond to public opinion. It must create and lead it and act in its absence. Much the same thing might be said about the administrative branch and its relations to legislature and chief executive. Not only its size but also its role in the initiation and shaping of policies, its discretionary authority in the implementation of policy, all give substance to this designation.

Criteria for Administration

It will be clear from this introduction that, in the case of administration, as with the legislative-executive complex, we shall be concerned about responsiveness, responsibility, accountability, leadership and effectiveness; and also with safeguards against abuse. In the case of responsiveness, it is proper for the emphasis to be more on response to need and less on response to demand than in the case of the legislature. The reason for this distinction springs from the function of the legislature as the representative body. Perhaps more than any other organ of government, and certainly more than administration, the legislature is the body in a democracy whose function it is to give due weight to what the public wishes whenever that can be determined. For the administration, on the other hand, the major outlines of policy—and often much more—has been laid down by the legislature or the chief executive (where the two are independent) or the two acting together. Such discretion as is left to administration is presumably intended to be exercised on the basis of its own expertise. And its expertise, unlike that of the legislature, is not presumed to be in the direction of knowing what is desired, but rather in the direction of knowing what is needed, what will best fulfill the policy objectives the legislature was seeking to attain. We are not suggesting that this distinction is or even should be sharply maintained. But it does represent a significant differentiation of function.

Accountability, in the case of administration, is especially complicated under the separation of powers, where it must be divided among legislature, chief executive, and judiciary. Although the President himself is not accountable to Congress, the administrative agencies may be made so in large degree by means of Congressional control over appropriations, and in other ways.

The rationality aspect of responsibility, entailing action on the basis of full information, careful, intelligent, and conscientious deliberation, attention to the criterion of over-all consistency, and the avoidance of arbitrariness, is perhaps especially applicable to the administrative stage because administration is carried on continuously and presumably with adequate technical or professional assistance.

Finally, effectiveness will depend, *inter alia,* upon vigorous and imaginative leadership, unhindered by the binding effect of bureaucracy in the bad sense. In the case of administration, effectiveness implies also efficiency. Administration, like a business enterprise, has a "product," "customers," and roughly similar problems of management. Of course public and private administration differ in some major particulars: checks against arbitrary action are more important for public than for private administration, because public decisions are usually backed up by the sanctions of law; also, the "customers" of public activities are generally not able to turn to another "supplier."[2] Nevertheless, efficiency—maximizing the ratio of output to input—is a desirable goal for public administration just as profit shown in the annual statements is for the corporation. We shall refer to these four tests at appropriate points throughout the chapter as we discuss the nature of administrative activities and problems of personnel, organization, and control; but frequently the student may safely be left to apply them for himself. It is worth noting here, however, that the problem is constantly one of seeking the best balance, for means designed to promote one objective often tend to defeat another. A bureaucracy that is made too responsive to group demands, whether through instruments of formal accountability or otherwise, may act arbitrarily, irresponsibly; or its top officials may seek security by avoiding initiative or preferring the popular to the sound. Likewise devices designed to check irresponsible subservience to partisanship and to encourage independent deliberation may lead to bureaucratic hardening of the arteries.

[2] For a discussion of the contrast, see John M. Pfiffner and R. Vance Presthus, *Public Administration,* 3rd. ed. (New York: Ronald, 1953), p. 154.

Administrative Activities

Any classification of administrative activities is bound to be somewhat arbitrary and not to be equally applicable to all levels of government or all national administrative systems. For present purposes, however, the administrative activities of government may be divided among nine broad categories: (1) fiscal functions; (2) enforcement and implementation of law; (3) investigation; (4) policy recommendations; (5) supplying services; (6) planning and coordinating public and private activities; (7) managing enterprises; (8) scientific research and development; and (9) housekeeping functions. We shall discuss them, briefly, in that order.

COLLECTING THE REVENUES OF GOVERNMENT

Governments must have sustenance. One of the earliest and most basic functions of any government is provision of public revenues to sustain it and its activities. Although in early times much or all of the public revenue could be derived from lands or other property held in the king's name, modern governments depend primarily upon taxation, and thus upon assessors, collectors of taxes (by that or any other name, such as "duty" or "impost"), and accountants. Important though the fiscal branch of public administration is, it is relatively routinized, policy questions being largely determined at the legislative level.[3]

IMPLEMENTING AND ENFORCING THE LAWS

Revenues apart, the enforcement and implementation of laws is perhaps the most obvious function of any governmental administration. The kinds of activity and especially the amount of discretion entailed by this simple phrase runs the gamut from simplicity to complexity, from minimal to maximal discretion. A law that is not observed belies its name; and, save in the rarest instances, one that is not enforced is not observed. At the very least, in addition to courts, law enforcement requires officials to detect and report violations and to take the necessary steps to insure that the violations cease. At the opposite extreme, legislation may direct the administrative branch to implement a long and complicated law providing for the regulation of, let us say, the radio and television industries, stating policies, standards, objectives, but leaving a mammoth job of fact-finding, analysis, rule-making, and application of the law to a myriad of concrete situations. Or again, like the British Agriculture Act of 1947 it may direct the Government to "maintain a stable and efficient agricultural industry capable of producing such part of the nation's food and other agricultural produce as in the national

---

[3] This statement should not be allowed to obscure the fact that in many countries—especially, but not solely "modernizing" countries—enforcement of revenue laws is highly ineffective. When this situation prevails it both creates serious difficulties for the government and is indicative of a bad state of public morale.

interest it is desirable to produce in the United Kingdom" by means of "guaranteed prices and assured markets," using to this end "such devices as appear to [the appropriate Minister] expedient" for this purpose, all the while keeping prices as low as is consistent with "proper remuneration and living conditions for farmers and workers in agriculture and an adequate return on capital invested in the industry."[4]

In short, ordinary criminal legislation, for example, may be enforced largely by policemen acting with the courts. Even more simply, a law making a contract for a gambling debt invalid is self-enforcing: the courts will not entertain a claim based on such a contract. On the other hand, as in the examples cited above, most modern regulatory legislation requires a large, trained, and highly differentiated administrative organization to give it effect. Take, for instance, a type of regulation especially common in the United States, the maintenance of business competition. The theory behind this type of regulation is that it is often easier to prevent the development of monopolies than to check their abuse of power once they are formed. The means used include prohibition of trade practices deemed "unfair," the prevention of mergers tending to reduce competition, and banning certain interlocking directorates. Other regulatory statutes, increasingly important in the modern state, are aimed at keeping the economy running at full blast, maintaining both employment and productivity at high levels. Activities under these statutes take many forms. Some seek to keep the economy on an even keel by manipulation of interest rates, control of bank reserve requirements, and similar devices. Others may involve increasing public expenditures for public works, or, more simply, cutting taxes.

INVESTIGATION

As with law implementation, so with investigation, the range of activities is wide and diverse. Inspection is an indispensable ancillary activity to much governmental regulation. The standards for building construction and maintenance, for instance, would be completely ineffective without building inspectors and procedures for enforcement. Pure food and drug acts would be relatively ineffective without similar administrative adjuncts. And so on. "Investigation" is itself, however, an important independent activity of government. Numerous agencies of government conduct research and other investigatory activities not related to discovering violations of the law. In the United States the Departments of Labor and of Commerce are largely engaged in gathering, compiling, analyzing, and publishing statistical and other material of interest to the particular groups they serve. While the Department of Agriculture nowadays performs extensive regulatory functions, its vast research activities still constitute a major part of its

---

[4] Agriculture Act, 1947, 10 and 11 Geo. 6, Ch. 48. The quoted passages are from Sections 1 and 4 of the Act.

work. The manifold activities of the Bureau of the Census also belong in this category.[5] Investigation is not something that government does alone and unaided, of course, for much of its work depends upon the quality of reports and data submitted by businesses, farmers, and trade associations, as well as other units of government. In France and Italy, for example, where the kind of research and statistical records common in American and British commerce and industry are not so widespread, governmental records and statistics are neither so good nor so generally available for use by either officials or groups within the society. In an era of the welfare state, when the decisions of government and of private enterprise are often closely related and affect each other in many ways, the ability to get and to utilize such information is a primary resource both for government and for the economy.

It will be noted that some of the data produced by investigation are largely for use by business and private individuals. Others are primarily for employment by administration itself. And one of the great uses made by administration of the information it gathers is for the purpose, after extensive study and analysis, of making policy recommendations. These recommendations may relate to how the present laws should be administered, how discretionary authority should be exercised, whether, for instance, the airlines should be permitted to raise their fares; or they may relate to legislative activity, calling on the President to request Congress (or the Government to request the Parliament) to enact new legislation or to amend the old. In the latter instance, the recommendations are likely to go into considerable detail, including the drafting of proposed bills.

PUBLIC SERVICES

The supply of services is again a heading under which many different kinds of activity fall. Perhaps the most important, by almost any test, is that of education. The public school system, extending in the United States and in most modern nations from kindergarten through the university level, usually performs the bulk of the task of formal education, and incidentally accounts for a major proportion of the employees of the state. Construction and maintenance of highways may also be classified under this heading, as can subsidies to public housing, irrigation and pest control, employment exchanges, and the like.

An important type of service activities that are often singled out for separate consideration are welfare programs, such as compulsory schemes of insurance against the hazards of unemployment, industrial accidents, ill health, and old age. These programs employ vast administrative hierarchies in all industrialized countries. A great deal of "welfare" work is also conducted by governments outside of the insurance systems, for example, family

[5] A glance at the *Statistical Abstract of the United States* will give the student a slight idea of how vital as well as how extensive are some of the activities of the federal government in this field.

services, public health, and vocational rehabilitation. The welfare activities of government are worthy of separate consideration for two reasons. They are, for one thing, usually activities that government shares with private groups, for instance, in health insurance or family care. Also, welfare activities often require individuated services that involve the exercise of more than usual discretion and judgment on the part of the civil servant—in deciding, for example, what to do in cases involving mentally disturbed children. In these and other ways the kinds of services being provided involve more "sophisticated" programs.

This general area of services is one in which the changing nature of administration in the twentieth century can be distinctly marked. One tendency has been that of providing more "sophisticated" services: from the "dole" or "relief" to coordinated diagnosis and treatment of family problems. Another tendency has been that of moving from simple "services" into complicated problems like "community development" or mental health, where the services not only involve mixtures of private and public activities, but several forms of governmental activity at once, such as regulation, planning, and public enterprise.

PLANNED DEVELOPMENT

"Planning," or what we have called "planning and coordinating public and private activities" and which we may more briefly designate as "planned development," merits a separate category, so important has it become. The emphasis in this type of administration is upon the joining together or coordination of many activities both in government and private life to achieve certain broad public objectives. Familiar examples are urban redevelopment in the United States and town and country planning in Britain. Planned development also includes such activities as the development or control of regional water resources, the encouragement of industries, or attempting to alleviate the distress of depressed areas. Sometimes the emphasis is upon economic planning as with the British economic plan or the French Monnet Plan. Sometimes the emphasis is upon "social" planning, as with the Tennessee Valley Authority or the Puerto Rican "Operation Bootstraps." Planned development differs from most other activities of government largely in degree. It usually involves the collaboration of more different kinds of agencies, governmental authorities, and private parties and the use at once of a wider variety of tools of government. Also, more than most government programs, planned development is aimed at a progressive transformation of the economic or social environment, or both.

GOVERNMENT ENTERPRISE

The management of business enterprises constitutes still another type of administrative activity. In this category we have the post office, the railroads and telephone and telegraph companies in many countries, electric, gas, and other public utilities, often including street railways, dams, toll-roads, and so forth. The central banking system is also a public enterprise in some countries, as in Great Britain.

Like other forms of governmental activity, public enterprise also appears in many guises in the modern welfare state. The traditional pattern was for government to hold a governmental monopoly or provide a public utility. Monopolies such as salt, tobacco, or gunpowder were established largely because government wanted either the product or the revenues from the sale of the product. Early governmental enterprises—like transportation —were often established either because private capital did not provide it, or because a private monopoly seemed obnoxious. Public enterprise in the twentieth century includes examples of the older type (such as the French tobacco monopoly, the "package-store" for the sale of liquor in many American states, and some of urban public transportation). Public enterprise especially since the Great Depression has moved in many new directions, and particularly toward various kinds of mixed enterprises in which government will underwrite or insure private activities, contribute some essential service, or participate in part of an activity through a government corporation or agency. Government lends money on agricultural commodities or residential mortgages, for instance. Both governments and private enterprise both acquire bonds and stock in enterprises of common concern, like aviation, railroads, or shipping. They both participate in such joint enterprises as the development of atomic energy.

RESEARCH AND DEVELOPMENT

Reference to atomic energy suggests a category of government activity that has become especially significant during and since World War II— scientific research and development. In this type of activity, government undertakes to secure and to provide scientific information, the technological "know-how," and the resources and matériel needed to develop new processes and products, especially in such fields as atomic energy, communications, rockets, and weapons systems. Research and development is by no means a new activity of government. The monarchs of the past who stimulated new enterprises by importing artisans and protecting their guilds were engaged in research and development. Agricultural experiment stations were a modern form of research and development. But the contemporary importance of research and development is new, brought about especially by the revolution in military technology. The amount of research and technological innovation demanded by modern weapons systems and the imperatives of the cold-war environment create a need for coordinated efforts and for expensive prototypes that no private firm could meet. Government must either provide this need directly or bring together and subsidize private firms through various techniques such as government corporations, mixed enterprises, or a variety of contractual devices.

HOUSEKEEPING

Finally, we shall do little more than call attention to the final category of "housekeeping functions." These are matters for internal consumption, to keep the machine going, and going efficiently. They include facilities for securing the best available personnel for all positions, and for organizing them for the most effective operation. They also include accounting and auditing, and central purchasing. Perhaps as important as any of the other things we have mentioned is provision of means for keeping each part of the vast administrative network informed not only about the policies it is supposed to pursue but also about what other parts of the network are doing that affects its own program and operations.

Salient Features of Contemporary Administration

This brief survey of contemporary governmental activities suggests not only the range and scope of public administration today; it also points to some of the newer aspects, the "growing edges" of public administration in the modern state. For instance, one characteristic of contemporary administration is the supplying of relatively "sophisticated services," calling for the effective joining together of many kinds of administrative activity and demanding the exercise of a large measure of discretion, technical skill, and prudence. The prototypes of administration a generation ago—the postal clerk or the fire inspector—might be incompetent and bungling also, and it was a misfortune if they were; but the need for quality in administrative service and for professional attitudes has increased so enormously that the change can be regarded as the emergence of a need different in kind.

Again, modern administrative programs, and especially welfare programs, are increasingly carried out at many levels of government, or at least through territorial subdivisions or regions of administrative activity. In agriculture or in the administration of old age assistance or public health, regional, state, county and sometimes even smaller regional organizations bring administration to the people affected and decentralize decision-making to the operating level. One effect has been to "democratize" administration by increasing the number of voices that will be heard in the administrative process. Another consequence has been radically to change the administrative process by making it almost as much a political process as that which goes on in the parties or legislatures.

A mixture of public and private endeavor is also part of the contemporary scene, and not only in such obvious areas as research and development and semipublic business enterprises. Welfare is itself an area especially where the public and the private mix: where the churches and the public-spirited citizens seek to supplement the programs of government and in turn ask the government to carry certain burdens for them. But the same could

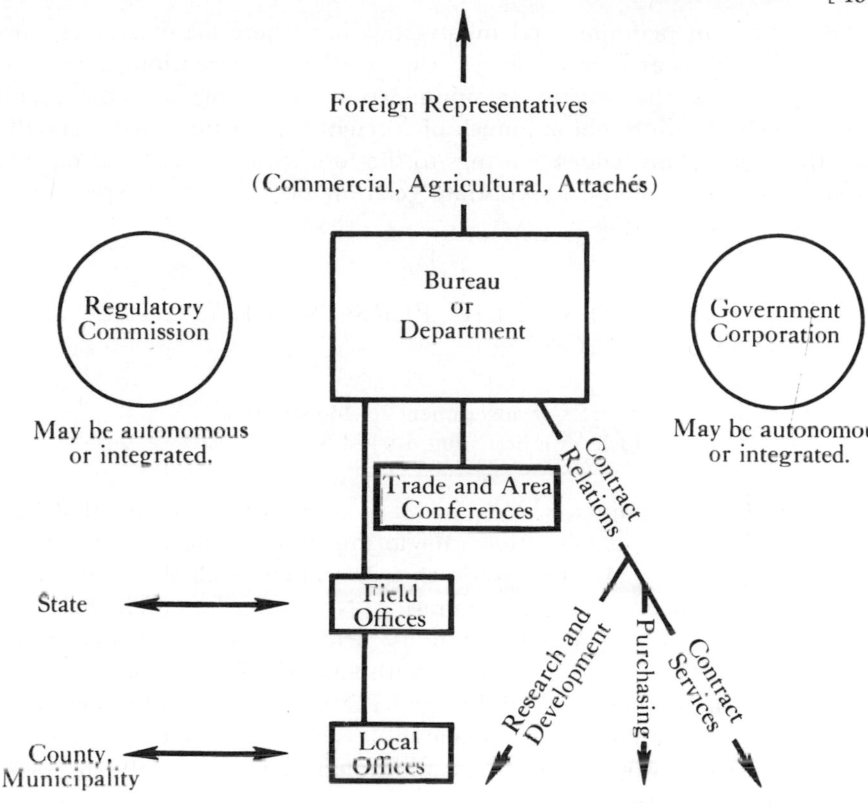

Foreign Representatives

(Commercial, Agricultural, Attachés)

Regulatory
Commission

Bureau
or
Department

Government
Corporation

May be autonomous
or integrated.

May be autonomous
or integrated.

Contract Relations

Trade and Area
Conferences

State

Field
Offices

Research and Development

Purchasing

Contract Services

County,
Municipality

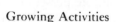

Local
Offices

Growing Activities
1. Research and Information
2. Inspection and "Enforcement"
3. Rule-making and Administrative Adjudication
4. Direct Services
5. Management
6. Contract Relations
7. Cooperation with Private Groups,
   States and Localities
   a) Lending
   b) Advising
   c) Cooperation and Coordination

FIGURE 4 *Administration: schematic representation of the relation between activities and organizations*

be said for many programs, from running the schools and promoting tidier neighborhoods to the development of water resources and putting men on the moon.

Finally, a new and more intimate relation between science and government is much in evidence. Modern government not only needs knowledge of the complicated activities of public administration itself; it is engaged in forecasting, in planning, and in investigation where many sources, governmental as well as private, supply the required information. The need for data and for the effective communication, processing and use of all kinds of technical information, much of it scientific, has increased markedly since the 1930's. This tendency brings to the fore with renewed urgency the perennial question of the appropriate relation between the "expert" and the government.

STAFFING AND PUBLIC PERSONNEL ADMINISTRATION

"For forms of government let fools contest,
Whiche'er is best administered is best."

Pope's famous couplet is never better than a half truth; but that half is important. A good organization can do much to enable and encourage the individuals who make it up to do their best, to give all that is in them. But what is "in them" remains a limitation. No matter how well the materials in a house are organized, the house will not be satisfactory if the materials themselves are shoddy. So it is with an administrative organization. On the other hand, men with ability and the will to accomplish the tasks assigned to them often attain a remarkable degree of success even when they are forced to work through organizational forms that defy the principles of administration.

Broadly speaking, the task of public personnel administration involves most of the problems of personnel administration in private business, in colleges and universities or elsewhere. Pay and tenure, promotion, discipline, and morale, systems for handling grievances and employee representation in various forms, characterize both public and others forms of personnel administration.[6] The public service, however, has special characteristics that much of private employment does not have. In particular, the public service is largely a career service: which means that compensation is closely tied to the holding of a particular office or position, that tenure is relatively secure, and that the sanctions and incentives that can be employed to encourage more apt official behavior are strictly limited.[7] (Dismissals for incompetence are rare.) Consequently, much of government personnel administration has centered around the problems of staffing, conditions of tenure, employee morale, and administrative ethics. Because of their par-

[6] For a good, comprehensive treatment, see O. Glenn Stahl, *Public Personnel Administration*, 4th ed. (New York: Harper & Row, 1956).

[7] Cf. Max Weber's classic description of bureaucracy in *The Theory of Social and Economic Organization*, trans. A. M. Henderson and Talcott Parsons; ed., Talcott Parsons (New York: Oxford U. P., 1947), pp. 329-340.

ticular importance for the public service, we shall concentrate in this section on staffing and upon internal administrative devices to promote ideals of responsible service among government employees.

Staffing

The task of staffing the public service involves selecting, recruiting, and training men and women of ability and diligence.[8] The approach toward the problems of staffing the civil service for particular countries has depended upon the origins of the civil service, the educational system, governmental structure, and constitutional practices.[9] In countries, such as Germany, where administrative hierarchies were highly developed before the coming of democracy, the public career was an honored calling. Germany has experienced a long history of only moderately successful attempts to "democratize" the service—to make it more responsive and accountable and more representative of the whole of the society and not only the upper middle classes and the aristocracy. The United States, where the public service has traditionally enjoyed low prestige, and where factors like federalism and the separation of powers have discouraged a career service, has experienced an equally inconclusive struggle—at least until fairly recently—to establish a "merit system" and to curb patronage and political influence in the civil service. Sometimes, as in the case of France, there have been competing tendencies: attempts to insulate the civil service from political pressures and partisan staffing, to make it more responsive to popular demands by "changing the guard," and to introduce a more democratic curriculum into the prescribed course of training for civil servants.

Recruitment

Selection involves not only getting the right people in but also keeping the wrong people out. Until recently, the latter approach, the war against appointments for partisan reasons, has been to the fore in the United States. True, patronage and spoils have had their valuable uses, in consolidating the power of a regime, in facilitating change and adjustment, and in allowing new political groups to achieve effective access to government. In some

---

[8] It will be observed that we are dealing here with one aspect of one of the major "input" functions of the polity, as set forth in Chapter 5. Note also the element of "feedback," there mentioned. As a consequence of the process of political socialization the political culture supplies government with personnel for filling its offices. But government itself, through its educational system and its recruitment mechanisms, does much both to stimulate and to mold the character of the flow of recruits. Here is a practical example of what is meant in this context by "feedback."

[9] For an exceptionally good discussion of this subject, dealing with Britain, France, Germany, and the United States, see Herman Finer, *Theory and Practice of Modern Government* (New York: Holt, 1949), Chs. 27-34.

transitional and underdeveloped societies today, patronage and even corruption in the civil service are not only widespread but may be necessary aspects of the governing process. Elsewhere, however, even at the level of local or state governments, the practices associated with patronage or the American "spoils system" have steadily lost favor, both because they lead to the appointment of incompetents and because spoils appointees are likely to use their time and even their office to seek support for the party in power by fair means or foul.

One way to improve the quality of recruits is to train them. Long and arduous courses of pre-entry training for would-be civil servants are the usual practice in Europe though not in Britain or America. The pre-entry training and the schools that were established to give it reflect generally a view that administration is a distinctive career; they also grow out of a political history in which the skills of administration had to be taught separately. Thus, in France many of the specialized administrative schools date from the era of the Napoleonic reforms. In Europe there are commonly a series of specialized schools—for example, for the foreign service, for administrative law, and for a variety of technical services—as well as academies for general political and administrative science for the higher careers in the civil service. Pre-entry training is normally the condition for admission to the service and such a system is often referred to as "closed" career recruitment in contrast to the "open" system of the United States where a civil servant may enter the service at various stages of his personal career by taking an examination for a particular job. In all countries, the way in which the educational system is related to career recruitment for the civil service is an important variable, especially in determining the social and economic background of recruits and the kinds of attitudes they are likely to bring to the service.

One important effect of pre-entry training is to imbue the civil servants with a common outlook and morale. For instance, in Germany, where the civil service was considered to be properly judicial in character,[10] a long period of legal training served to imbue the candidates with attitudes of impartiality, objectivity, and precision. In France, the many specialized schools (for instance, for engineers, colonial administrators, archivists, and accountants, as well as judges and general administrators), reflected a technocratic view of the public service. The corporate traditions, the career expectations, and the external relations of the civil service on the one hand, as well as the public attitudes toward the civil service and the prestige of

[10] That is to say, the judicial temper of mind was desired. The statement must be qualified since it applies only to those periods of German history when middle-class values were influential and the ideal of the *Rechtsstaat* was in the ascendant. In more autocratic periods, the policy was one of cameralist management and intervention in the economy and in the affairs of local authorities. The *Polizeistaat* was, for most of modern German history, more nearly the operative ideal.

the service itself on the other, will all be importantly influenced by the pre-entry training programs prescribed for a state's civil service.[11] In Britain, to take an opposing example, specialized training is eschewed, partly because of a conviction that it tends to produce narrow specialists, while in the United States the same tendency is resisted because of a dislike for a strongly ingrained corporate sentiment in the civil service.[12]

Merit Systems

The development of the modern civil service is closely associated with that of recruitment through a "merit system," that is to say, by means of set examinations for particular positions that will establish a list of qualified candidates from which appointments can be made. In the narrowest sense, "merit system" may mean only selection on the basis of objective tests rather than according to personal or political favoritism. Thus, the reforms of the British civil service in the middle of the nineteenth century prescribed a test only for generalized aptitude. By extension, the concept of a "merit system" has grown to include many other practices as well. Most countries, for example, test the candidate's specific preparation in a subject-matter as well as his aptitude or "fitness" for the public service. Not only entry, but subsequent promotion as well may be conditioned, as is frequently the case in the United States, upon a series of examinations and certifications. More and more countries, especially since the Second World War, have adopted such practices as systematic job classification and the centralized administration of the examination process by an independent agency.[13] In Great Britain the supervision of the personnel system is lodged in the Treasury Department, which traditionally has powers of supervision over the other Departments.

The struggle to achieve and protect a merit system in recruiting and promotion of the public official has bulked large in the history of civil services. Important as the principle of the merit system is, however, as a standard for reform it belongs largely to the past, except perhaps at the level of state and local government in the United States. The "merit service" is an essentially negative conception, directed largely toward insulating civil servants from political pressures and the abuses of favoritism in recruiting and in promotion. Such insulation may be purchased at the price of effectiveness—especially initiative, imagination, and energy. In France, and to a considerable extent in the United States, tenure and promotion are so

[11] On this subject generally, see Herman Finer, *op. cit.*, Part VI; and Brian Chapman, *The Profession of Government, op. cit.*, Chs. 2, 3.

[12] For an interesting commentary, see the exchange between Leonard D. White, "The Case for the Senior Civil Service," and Herman M. Somers, "Some Reservations about the Senior Civil Service," in *Personnel Administration,* 19 (1956), pp. 4-18.

[13] For a summary of developments, see Chapman, *op. cit.,* Chs. 2, 3, and 8.

carefully protected that discipline or the rewarding of distinguished service are difficult. If the civil servant has nothing to hope for and little to fear he is not likely to put forward his best efforts or do much beyond carrying out the routine and the safe activities directly enjoined upon him, nor are energetic and imaginative individuals likely to be attracted to the service. In the United States until the 1920's it was still possible to speak as though the "merit system" was *the* objective in American administration. With today's welfare services and complicated economic regulation it becomes ever clearer that while the old principles may constitute a necessary condition for an effective civil service, they are by no means sufficient. "Insulation" of the civil servant is not enough. The modern society needs his best efforts.

Postentry: What Norms are Desirable?

The problem of creating an effective civil service, and one that is responsive both to the policies laid down from above and, within those policies, to the needs of the situation must be understood against the background of some of the evils of large-scale, formal organization.

"BUREAUCRACY"

These disorders are often referred to as "bureaucracy,"[14] and we shall follow that usage here. In the concept "bureaucracy," many evils are rolled up together under one heading. It includes, on the part of individuals, lack of imagination and enterprise, callousness to the feelings and interests of clients, and a tendency to avoid decision-making by means of "passing the buck" and slavish adherence to custom or precedent. Institutionally, it appears as the development of complicated procedure and "paper work," "red tape," and consequent delays and injustices. "Bureaucracy" also is often used to refer to intraorganizational tensions or maladjustments such as lack of candor between colleagues or dissension between subordinate and superior. Most people have been the victims of "bureaucracy" in some of its more familiar manifestations: simple inquiries answered, after long delays, by form letters that do not fit the case; insistence upon supplying detailed information not pertinent to the matter at hand; conflicting injunctions or responses from the same agency at different times; incomprehensible refusals to comply with apparently sensible requests, and so forth.

BIG GOVERNMENT

Just as bureaucracy includes many things, so its causes are various. Frequently it is rooted in the requirements of a properly functioning formal organization. Bureaucracy is by no means confined to government. This fact

---

[14] See, for example, the treatment in James G. March and Herbert A. Simon, *Organizations* (New York: Wiley, 1958), pp. 36-47.

of common experience is often overlooked when the conversation turns to the sins of government. Wherever there is a large organization many of the ills of bureaucracy are likely to put in an appearance. Big business is sadly beset by it. So are the educational institutions and charitable foundations. Partly it is simply a matter of the difficulty of communication within a large organization. Partly it is the psychological problem of making each member of a large organization feel the same sharing in the objectives of the entity as a whole, the same sense of responsibility, as is common in small organizations. Partly it is because the larger the organization the more complicated, necessarily, become the procedures for checking on the efficiency and the plain honesty of the members of the staff. While these reasons apply to private as well as to public agencies, the government is the largest organization of all, and many of its individual functions involve organizations on a vaster scale than any private businesses. For this reason, alone, the problem of bureaucracy besets government with special force.

THE IMPORTANCE OF PROCEDURE

The government has also to take extraordinary precautions against partiality of any kind on the part of its agents. Persons in positions of public authority may attempt to use their power either for unauthorized political ends or to promote their own private objectives. The normal means to guard against such abuses is to insist upon rigorous adherence to detailed procedures, alike for all, and always involving a written record. Out of this situation red tape inevitably develops. In an important measure it is unavoidable. With it goes delay, and the multiplication of personnel whose contribution to the purposes of the organization is only indirect.

An organizational determination of the product of public administration assumes a special importance for government. For one thing, there is generally no market test of the governmental product. The product itself ("Britain's prestige abroad") is intangible; notions of efficiency (the benefits of public education) are diffuse or ambiguous; and competitive yardsticks (public and private electric power) usually mean little, if anything. Government, then, can be analogized to a monopoly, and often it is a monopoly. As a consequence, techniques to insure that all relevant interests are consulted, that each responsible authority has acted, and that the decision has been reached only after observance of all the appropriate procedures are especially important for government.

The monopoly position of the government is significant in another respect. It makes it more important for the client or customer to be treated fairly. If I am dissatisfied with the service I get from a department store I can cease to patronize it; but if my government treats me unfairly I have no place else to turn. Again, the pressure is to insist on equality of treatment by adherence to rigid procedures.

Internal formal procedures[15] comprise a way in which administration seeks to check upon itself. Properly, they are supplemented by a variety of external formal checks upon administrative acts such as the courts, budget and accounting review, and legislative investigations ("Question Hour" in Britain), which impose varying degrees of individual or collective responsibility upon the civil service. These devices are necessary to control and check the administration, to hold it accountable to the representative bodies, and to establish confidence in its procedures. Yet they also contribute to "bureaucracy."

A "RESPONSIBLE" CIVIL SERVICE

Under the negative state, the problem of developing "responsible" administration hardly existed. When government consisted largely of enforcing prohibitions, administrators did not have to be given much discretion, nor did the spirit and temper with which administration was conducted matter a great deal, except at the top levels.[16] Aside from attempts to establish a merit system, efforts at nineteenth century administrative reform, in France and Germany for instance, were concentrated primarily upon the ideal of the legal accountability of the civil servant. "The state," as the French maxim ran, "is an honest man,"—at least it ought to be. In the United States well into the twentieth century, much of the study of personnel administration was aimed at the goal of "efficiency."[17] The requirements of contemporary administration that we have already discussed—such as the demand for sophisticated services—have tended to produce the new emphasis upon securing "responsible" public officials. As a matter of public personnel administration, this objective comes down largely to ways and means by which individual civil servants can be taught or constrained to follow desirable organizational goals. In somewhat the same way that the modern corporation has its problems of developing an "organization man," so the goals of personnel administration in government today have shifted increasingly from those of mere honesty and impartiality, or even "efficiency," to that complex of values comprised in the term "responsibility." Without attempting to discuss all that is entailed in such an objective, we can at least point out some of the approaches toward it and some of the guiding principles and major problems that these approaches involve.

[15] Here we follow the distinction between formal and informal, internal and external procedures made by Simon, Smithburg and Thompson. See Herbert A. Simon, *et al.*, *Public Administration* (New York: Knopf, 1950); Chs. 24, 25; also Charles E. Gilbert, "The Framework of Administrative Responsibility," *Journal of Politics*, **21** (1959), pp. 373-407.

[16] For some studies that are interesting historically, see Henry Taylor, *The Statesman* (Cambridge, Eng.: Heffer, 1957; first published in 1836); also, Honoré de Balzac, *The Civil Servants*, in *La Comédie Humaine* (trans. Wormeley), Vol. 16 (Boston: Little, Brown, 1885-99); In a more contemporary vein, see Morroe Berger, *Bureaucracy and Society in Modern Egypt* (Princeton, N.J.: Princeton U. P., 1957).

[17] Dwight Waldo, *The Administrative State: A Study of the Political Theory of American Public Administration* (New York: Ronald Press, 1948).

Personnel Administration

Most particular systems of personnel administration in different countries or at different levels of government (such as the national, state, and municipal civil-service systems in the United States) have a great deal in common, especially so far as concerns organizational devices. Usually, a code or series of codes defines the rights and duties of the civil servant. Efficiency ratings and other incentives such as honors and promotions are used to stimulate good work. Similarly, there are disciplinary procedures and civil service boards that pass upon disciplinary sanctions as well as promotions. So, too, most contemporary civil-service systems have adopted techniques of employee representation to handle disputes over hours and conditions of service as well as individual grievances. The major differences appear to be with respect to underlying philosophy rather than specific institutions.

EUROPE AND BRITAIN

In general, European systems of personnel administration have depended, especially in the past, upon the leadership of the higher civil service, and the ideals that they could imprint upon the service. They have historically been characterized by long periods of pre-entry and post-entry training, usually accompanied—especially for the higher civil service—by various stages of apprenticeship during which the fledgling civil servant moves toward the first step of his real career. Moreover, under the leadership of the higher civil servants, European and British civil service systems have enjoyed a great deal of independence in the administration of their own internal affairs—for instance in the establishment of boards within particular departments and bureaus for such matters as discipline, tenure, and promotion. More recently, equal and joint representation of subordinate employees and administrative superiors on these boards has become widespread, but the substantive provisions of the codes of civil service behavior that these boards enforce still remain largely those shaped by and consistent with the ideals of a career service. Also, the dominant tenor or spirit of the civil service is set by the close fellowship of the higher civil service. The boards bargain and discuss with them. They are the "employers" in much of the meaning of that term, even though they do not independently hire and fire. They largely express the corporate ideals of the service and take the responsibility for transmitting them throughout the rest of the administration and especially to new recruits.

THE UNITED STATES

In the United States, traditionally, the view has prevailed that government service need not and ought not to be a special career or vocation. Pre-entry training is unusual, except for the technical training that one gets in the ordinary educational process—say, as a chemist, economist, or lawyer—although increasingly graduates of schools of public administration are manning important administrative posts. Postentry training has existed, though usually as a way of mastering specific technical skills; but lengthy periods of apprenticeship or "probation" are unusual. The "ethos" of the public service and the career ideals that should inform the average civil servant have been promoted and implemented largely through "staff" agencies and staff officers within departments rather than by the "senior civil service" as in Britain or Europe. The Bureau of the Budget, the budget officer, and personnel agencies, have done much to spread and implement the career point of view by the way they have exercised their controls. Thus, although in large measure the United States still retains its "open" system of recruitment, it has moved toward some of the ideals and practices of a career service.

Comparison and Evaluation

Comparisons and evaluations are hazardous, especially because it is easy to overstate the contrasts. Since the end of the Second World War, European civil service systems have been modified in some ways so that they are more similar to the American. For instance, staff agencies for planning, for organization and management, and for personnel administration have grown. The closed pattern of career recruitment has broken down in some areas. On the other hand, steady pressure has been exerted, with limited success, to expand the concept of a career service in the United States through interneships, in-service middle-management training, and the creation of distinctively professional administrative careers.

Despite the similarities of problems in most contemporary civil services and the tendencies toward a convergence in theory and practice, many important contrasts persist. The European civil service still remains largely a career service, drawn in the main from particular strata of the population. Compared with that of the United States, the European civil service preserves a strong sense of corporate identity. Its prestige is high. The presence of a relatively similar philosophy and outlook among a large body of civil servants aids greatly in arriving at a common view of policy matters. The European system also has its evils. It tends to be oligarchic. Employment and management policies are traditional; and though checked and restrained by civil service statutes and schemes of employee representation, they still excessively reflect differences in social status between the higher civil servant and his subordinates and older administrative doctrines of official position and hierarchy. The "democratic theory of organization" prevalent among American students of administration is not widely admired by European senior civil servants. Also, since the concept of corporate self rule is strongly entrenched, continual complaints are heard that the civil service is unresponsive, that it is impervious to new influences either from within or from without.

In the United States, the emphasis continues to be upon relatively democratic personnel administration and open access to the service. The benefits for the American system of government are important. For one thing, the American civil service has been on the whole fairly responsive to popular demands. New personnel from the outside continually enliven the civil service agencies. At the same time, the prestige of most of the service is low; and there is continual complaint that "good men in government" are hard to get. Aside from a few elite bureaus, service-wide loyalties are weak and relations with clientele and outside interests often stronger than loyalties to the governmental service. By and large, these criticisms apply even more strongly to state and local administration than they do to the federal service.

Conclusion

Where is public personnel administration heading? Ought the American system to be primarily a career service? Or is it European practice that is out of touch with the new developments? It would be rash to attempt any comprehensive or general answer. However, the convergence in contemporary civil service practices is a distinctive trend; and perhaps we can suggest something of the rationale of this tendency.

The internal "democratization" of the service in Europe has been slowly growing. It will probably continue to do so for some time, for the older pattern of a tight career service and control of the service by an informal oligarchy of senior civil servants who dominate the procedures of discipline, promotion, and employee representation is increasingly anachronistic in the contemporary welfare state. The intelligent administration of welfare and regulatory programs depends upon the representation of many points of view, upon the communication and assimilation of much technical data and information from the field or from direct experience, and upon considerable harmony and candor among superior and subordinate officials. In other words, for these circumstances, democratic principles of personnel administration can be useful.[18] Recognition of this fact long overdue in the business and administrative practices of most European countries, is now unquestionably under way.

In the United States, a different problem obtains. If anything, the need

[18] For an American statement of the argument, see Robert T. Golembiewski, "Organization as a Moral Problem," *Public Administration Review*, **22** (1962), pp. 51-58. For Britain and Western Europe, see Chapman, *op. cit.*, Chs. 4, 5, and 15. Significantly, one contemporary student of French administration sees the major hope for a new and better approach toward the internal formal administrative controls exercised over the French service in a frank recognition of the "group basis" of administrative politics. See Pierre Lalumiere, *L'Inspection des Finances* (Paris: *Presses Universitaires de France*, 1959), pp. 217-222.

of a leaven of career servants has grown. The many views, the technical expertise, and the scientific information now so essential to government always present the danger that the scientist or expert or group representative will actually manage to get his proposition adopted, without benefit of translation or discounting by the administrative point of view that protects other interests and hedges against some of the risks.

More broadly one finds reflected in the field of administration in European and American government the same characteristics, differences, and trends noted earlier in our discussion of the central organs of government. In Europe, features reflecting a monarchical and aristocratic background persist. Responsibility, hierarchy, and overview are stressed, as is elite leadership. In the United States, the emphasis is rather on responsiveness, flexibility, and reflection of the pluralistic nature of the polity. Generally democratic trends combine with more specific demands in modern dynamic economies to compel European modifications in the American direction. The needs for efficiency, energy, and rational coordination in the positive state require improvements in the American administrative system that in some cases look in the direction of European practices.

ORGANIZATION

The basic and most common form of administrative organization is that of a hierarchy or pyramid. The organization may have various kinds of jurisdiction or responsibility. For instance, the enabling statute may direct it to provide a particular service, or to regulate an industry, or to care for the interests of a particular clientele. Within this guiding authority, responsibility is allocated following a principle of hierarchy; and jobs are divided according to a complementary scheme of division of labor. At the top, in principle, one man is charged with responsibility for the whole. He in turn may subdivide his responsibility, commiting each of several parts of it to as many other individuals, who become his immediate subordinates. Each of these may go through a like process, and so on down the line until Departments are divided (for instance) into Offices, Offices into Bureaus, Bureaus into Divisions, Divisions into Sections, Sections into Units, and so on. The head of each such subdivision is responsible directly and solely to the head of the unit above him, in accordance with the principle of "unity of command." Each officer also exercises, in theory, a close and personal supervision over the officials immediately responsible to him—a number of officials presumably within his effective "span of control."

In any sizable organization, some of the subordinate units will not be directly concerned with the main work of the agency. Rather their function will be of a service or facilitating nature.[19] For instance, a Division of

---

[19] Here, we follow the distinction of line, staff, and auxiliary functions made by Simon, *et al., op. cit.,* p. 282.

Personnel and Training will have charge of staffing the organization and providing it with in-service training. Another subdivision will perform accounting functions, another the centralized purchasing for the agency, and so on.

Furthermore, in large units, the administrative heads will need the services of various assistants. Individuals in this capacity are generally known as "staff" members, as contrasted with "line" personnel, who are in the direct line of command. Some staff members are concerned primarily with aiding and advising the chief. They read and digest memoranda for him, perform specific research assignments, write speeches, and do all manner of other special tasks at his request. Many are bright young men of generalized capabilities. Others, in the upper echelons, may be selected because of experience or training that qualifies them to give advice on particular types of problems.

Whole units often also exist to serve in a specialized staff capacity. They may deal directly with other branches of the organization, rather than through the chief, but their functions will be advisory rather than directive. For instance, a staff unit may specialize in the development of improved administrative procedures, with no authority to require their adoption. Similarly, economists in the State Department may make suggestions to economists on the staffs of our embassies abroad—suggestions, however, that must in principle be cleared with direct superiors before being acted upon if they involve matters of policy.

Governmental Organization is Different

Up to this point, our discussion of the normal or hierarchical forms of organization, including line, staff, and auxiliary activities and arrangements, applies equally to private or public administration. On the governmental side, however, the need for making administration responsive to the public introduces a new note. A business organization must also be kept responsive to the demands of the stockholders; but in this case similarity of interest among the constituents makes the problem far simpler, or at least of a different kind, than in the case of public administration. Through the political party, the ministry or chief executive, the Department head, and so on down the line of command, the avenue for the enforcement of the public will directly parallel corporate structure (although the party constitutes an added element). But the two kinds of organization are not comparable. One differentiating factor is the great diversity of interests and issues with which public administration must deal—never adequately reflected through the parties and the legislative representatives alone, and certainly impossible to deal with fairly and justly through one, simple, unambiguous command to a departmental head. Another important difference is the vast size of most administrative establishments. Large-scale organization lengthens the chain of command, diminishing responsiveness and flexibility and increasing the difficulties of communication. In the United States direct contacts between elected representatives and administrators provide a supplementing avenue of influence. In both Great Britain and the United States, however, and in democratic countries generally, one of the most effective means of bringing to bear upon administration the opinions and desires of concerned groups of the public is through the activities of pressure groups, and specifically through the agencies of the paid officers of these groups.[20]

One might discuss the pros and cons of direct contacts between pressure groups and administrations; but we may be sure that it is with us to stay. Frequently—and this is where the subject of administrative organization comes in—it is thought desirable to make formal provision for these contacts, in the form of consultative councils or advisory committees attached to the relevant points in the administrative structure. Composed of repre-entatives of the chief organized interests concerned with the program or agency in question, these committees can be of service in many ways. They can make suggestions for basic legislation itself, or for amendments in existing statutes. They can render valuable technical as well as policy advice regarding procedural and substantive regulations. Typically, proposed regulations are submitted to them for advice and criticism before they are drawn up in final form. The result is often both to improve the regulations and to gain the support of the groups to whom they apply.[21]

The "Principles of Administration"

Along with formal, hierarchical organization are usually associated various other principles of administration. Max Weber, father of the so-called "pure theory of bureaucracy," set out a list of the properties of the official relation, including (in addition to hierarchy) impersonality, legally defined competence, and technical qualifications for the administrative career.[22] In the United States, a somewhat parallel school of theory grew up around the "principles of administration," emphasizing such conceptions as unity of command, a span of control adapted to the needs of strict and systematic supervision, and functional rather than social grouping of employees.[23]

[20] Such contrasts between public and private administration hold for most cases. However, even in business administration customers and suppliers may be represented through councils, for example, in the automobile industry.

[21] The growth in the extent and the importance of group representation has been most marked of recent years in countries such as France or Great Britain in which a marked increase in the welfare and regulatory activities of the state has taken place. See, for example, K. C. Wheare, *Government by Committee* (Oxford, Eng.: Clarendon, 1955); and Henry W. Ehrmann, "French Bureaucracy and Organized Interests," *Administrative Science Quarterly,* 5 (1961), pp. 534-555.

[22] Max Weber, *op. cit.,* pp. 329-340.

[23] See Leonard D. White, *Introduction to the Study of Public Administration,* 4th. ed. (New York: Macmillan, 1955), especially Ch. 3.

Although these principles may seem simplistic, it has not always been so. They developed throughout centuries of experiment with various alternatives such as collegial responsibility, territorial jurisdiction rather than functional authority, and so forth.[24] The hierarchical organization of the public service was, in other words, a response to particular historical and technical circumstances. Many contemporary developments have made this pattern less applicable, generally, than it might have been, say, for the public service of Britain, France, or the United States some generations back.

New Tendencies in Organization

One way of looking at the traditional hierarchical organization of the government bureau or agency is as a system for enforcing accountability, operating through a strict and minute system of reporting and supervision of all decisions. By the same token, this kind of organization is applicable primarily where the red-tape, the delays, and the rigidities associated with bureaucracy can be tolerated. The postal service, for instance, is organized in strict accordance with these principles. Few businesses could survive if so organized and conducted.

The era of the service or welfare state has, in fact, considerably undermined the traditional theory and practice of administrative organization.[25] We have already mentioned the enormous growth in the scale of administrative organizations, the development of elaborate staff activities, and of interest representation, to which may be added the increasing significance of field organization.[26] Such tendencies have led to a reformulation of basic concepts of administrative activity, of what officials actually do, and of the relations between chiefs and subordinates. The idea of "command" plays a much less significant role than it traditionally did. Probably, it is more accurate to describe administration, even within most traditionally organized bureaus, as a special case of the policy-making process, characterized still by hierarchical relations, but also and increasingly by the bargaining, discussion, and negotiation of more informal kinds of organizational behavior, such as political or legislative activity.

Boards and Commissions

The last statement applies with even greater force to the board or commission, in which a group acting collegially is given joint responsibility for administering a particular program. Usually, the board or commission has been associated with the regulatory activities of government, such as licens-

---

[24] Carl J. Friedrich, *Constitutional Government and Democracy, op. cit.,* Ch. 2.

[25] A now famous harbinger of new tendencies is Herbert A. Simon, "The Proverbs of Administration," *Public Administration Review,* 6 (1946), pp. 53-67.

[26] See, for example, James W. Fesler, "Field Organization," in Fritz Morstein Marx, ed., *Elements of Public Administration,* 2nd ed. (Englewood Cliffs, N.J.: Prentice-Hall, 1959).

ing of doctors, granting corporate charters, or establishing and enforcing administrative rules to govern labor relations. Boards and commissions were used in ancient Greece and Rome. They sprouted in great profusion during the age of mercantilist policy. Indeed, they have been so ubiquitous in administration at almost any time in history, including the present, that it seems odd that administrative theory in the past failed to say more about them.

One reason for the use of boards is to give various interests a direct role in determining the regulations that will be applied to them—much more of a role than would be provided by the advisory committee technique. Boards for licensing or setting rules of occupational practice are frequently staffed not with ordinary civil servants but by representatives of the affected occupations or industries. Sometimes, these boards are balanced by a "public" representative or governmental official as, for instance, in the regulation of wages and hours under the Fair Labor Standards Act and in formulating milk orders and commodity agreements for agriculture in the United States. In Europe the principles of direct interest representation on boards and of industry or vocational self-regulation through "domestic tribunals" (as they are called in Great Britain) is carried further than in the United States, where constitutional prohibitions against the "delegation of legislative power" tend to restrain such guild-like arrangements and impose the use of more distinctively public or governmental boards.

Another reason for the use of boards or commissions is to develop a separate body of regulatory jurisprudence—that is to say, different from ordinary administrative orders and decrees or from the decisions of the courts in being adapted particularly to the needs of a given industry or to the particular problems of regulation and enforcement. Again, this is an old practice, found, for instance, in the nineteenth century in the use of boards of zoning appeals in the cities, in the special labor courts under the German Empire, or the French commercial tribunals. European and American practice have been much alike in this respect, though France and Germany especially recognized much earlier the value of a special approach to the problems of regulation.

The Independent Regulatory Commissions

American practice has differed from the European especially in the use of the "independent" regulatory commissions (or boards). At the federal level, the Interstate Commerce Commission is the prototype. The Federal Trade Commission, the Securities and Exchange Commission, the Federal Communications Commission, and the National Labor Relations Board provide other examples. At the state level, there are often counterparts, "little S.E.C.'s," and state labor-relations boards. Such commissions are called "independent" not only because they are outside of the usual administrative department, but also because they are not under the authority of the chief executive either.

"Independent regulatory commissions" have been attacked on a number of scores, some more justifiable than others. They have been called a "headless fourth branch of government," because they are not in the direct line of political responsibility. Because they are engaged in rule-making and enforcement, they have been charged with a tyrannical combination of the roles of law-maker, prosecutor, and judge. They have been frequently accused of falling captive to the interests they regulate. And, lastly, it is often alleged that their independence from the chief executive leaves no one in a position to coordinate their policies and activities with those of other administrative agencies.

Comparisons

Sometimes the European and especially the British approach toward the problem of regulation is contrasted favorably with the American. In Britain, for example, most such boards would be incorporated directly into a department. Similarly, in Germany, the so-called labor courts and cartel courts were responsible to an appropriate ministry. Therefore, the lines of political responsibility are unbroken and presumably clear. One could argue the merits of independence versus those of accountability. It might be pointed out, however, that accountability does not mean a great deal if discretion is essential to the particular activity in question, as it is in regulation. But two other points are of even greater importance. One is that in Britain and Europe the alternative to the independent regulatory commission is often not a board under a ministry, but guild self-regulation of the industry or profession. Orders adopted by the processes of "industry self-government" are given legal sanction by the government. In the United States many such practices have been found both morally and legally obnoxious. Furthermore, there can be little question that the development of a systematic and efficacious jurisprudence to deal with the complex problems of economic regulation has lagged in Europe partly because of the failure to use devices similar to the American regulatory commissions. The alternatives in Europe or in Great Britain have most commonly been corporate self-regulation with limited deference paid to the public interest, or the rather cumbersome expedient of nationalization or socialization. The case is strong for some *via media*. Significantly, some rather halting steps are being made in that direction today in Britain and Germany.[27]

The Governmental Corporation

A third form of administrative organization is that of the corporation. Again, like the board or commission, the governmental corporation has had a long history. Ecclesiastical, governmental, and charitable corporations antedated the business corporation in Europe and America. The modern

[27] For example, in radio broadcasting and restrictive trade practices.

governmental corporation is similar in pattern to the private business corporation, and sometimes there is even joint ownership by public and private interests. It may have a single head, with or without a board of directors, or a collegial head. It is generally used in the case of "business-type" functions, and it is the nature and requirements of these functions that determine its special characteristics.

The governmental corporation is in large measure independent of ordinary administrative controls. For instance, it frequently has its own personnel regulations and its own accounting and auditing system, relieving it of most of the kind of staff controls to which other agencies are subject. Also it can make expenditures from the income received for the sale of goods or services, instead of having to pay all such income over to the Treasury. In making contracts and in the conduct of business activities generally it is exempt from many of the restrictions imposed upon other agencies.

One result of its independence is to give the corporation a degree of flexibility essential to the efficient conduct of business enterprises. Also, it is quite common to provide for extensive participation by private interests in the decision-making process of the governmental corporation. In France, much use is made of the "mixed corporation"—owned jointly by the government and by private investors. In most countries, interest representation on the corporate board or through councils of workers, consumer representatives, or municipal delegates is established to enhance the responsiveness of the management to the various groups that it serves.

The most spectacular development in the use of governmental corporations has been the programs of nationalization since the end of the Second World War in Britain, France, and Italy. But the number and importance of the public corporations has been growing steadily for many years in municipal administration and at the level of national government. These multiplying organizations administer such programs as the generation of electricity, the building and operating of turnpikes, lending on crops and home mortgages, the subsidy of shipbuilding and navigation, and the acquisition of minerals and other raw materials for government stockpiles.

Little more need be said about the growth of the governmental corporation except to observe that this kind of organization is also at variance with traditional views of administrative practice. A corporation can be held accountable only in the most general terms, for its organization and procedures are separated from the hierarchically organized departments.[28] A good many of the employees of such a corporation are not civil servants in any usual sense of the term and they feel little identity with the traditions

[28] A good study of the problems of holding some of the governmental corporations administering the nationalized enterprises in Britain accountable to Parliament or the relevant ministries is given in R. Kelf-Cohen, *Nationalization in Britain* (London: Macmillan, 1958), especially Chs. 8-10, 14.

or practices of public service. Moreover, the governmental corporation is intended and often enjoined to be responsive not only to ordinary administrative considerations but to informal external controls such as group representation and market fluctuations. Complaints are often heard, particularly in Great Britain, that these bodies are "irresponsible" and accountable to no one. A good many proposals have been made to remedy the situation, such as putting many of the corporations under departmental administration or subjecting them to the continuous oversight of a parliamentary committee. Whatever the value of such remedies, modern administrative establishments will probably perforce remain vast, sprawling enterprises; well suited, perhaps, to get the various jobs of government done, but not nicely designed for harmonious and symmetrical organization or coordination.

Contract Administration

A fourth form of administrative organization is often designated, in the United States, as governmental contract administration. We do not refer to ordinary contracts for purchase of supplies or construction of public works, which are almost as old as public administration, but to a relatively recent development. Especially during and since the Second World War great need for highly specialized goods and services has developed: complicated weapons systems built to specifications that are unpredictable and change in the course of development; and consulting, research, and training services from private business and the universities that require continual adjustments in the program and in private and governmental joint endeavor. Here is the field of contract administration. It is in a sense neither administration nor contract. Few of the ordinary principles of administration obtain; and the contract is not negotiated once for all, but continually bargained over and readjusted, with bonuses and penalty clauses waived and renegotiated, new specifications interjected, and final settlements still to be reached.

Contract administration in the United States has been criticized on occasion[29] because it has allegedly given windfall profits to a good many people and also because it tends (so the argument runs) to favor the big firm or university with facilities already in existence. Much of the criticism seems intemperate, given the circumstances and the comparative effectiveness of attempts to mitigate abuses. Procurement statutes are drawn with elaborate provisions to protect the position of small businesses and assure that the prime contractors do not simply favor their own subsidiaries. Small business committees in the House of Representatives and the Senate are not only vigilant, but very jealous for the interests of the smaller firms. Also there are stringent provisions for renegotiation and recapture designed to squeeze out

[29] A critical view is Victor K. Heyman, "Government by Contract: Boon or Boner?", *Public Administration Review,* 21 (1961), pp. 59-64.

undue profits. Of course, abuses occur; but they seem trifling when the magnitude of such programs and the various potentialities for abuse are considered.

Contract administration presents an interesting problem of government: namely, how to establish a fruitful collaboration between governmental and private agencies in an unstable situation with enormous temptations for corruption. By and large, programs conducted under this form of administrative activity have been efficient, fairly honest, and successful. Probably in no other way can a free country, in the contemporary Cold War situation, so quickly and economically mobilize vast technical and material resources.

The Staff Agencies

Finally, hovering above the ordinary agencies and departments are various organizations for control and coordination, designed to check upon the whole administrative system and help pull the joint administrative product into some kind of tolerable harmony. Some of these agencies are concerned solely with narrow functions of control, like the American General Accounting Office, which passes upon the authorization of expenditures and audits the final accounts. Others, like the Civil Service Commission or the Organization and Management section in the Bureau of the Budget, combine checking upon internal procedures with an additional objective of evaluation of future intentions. Again, various organizations are intended mainly for purposes of coordination, like the interdepartmental committees which sprout perennially in Washington. Often an especially strategic agency combines wide authority both to coordinate and control under one head. The Bureau of the Budget in the United States, the Treasury in England, the *Conseil d'Etat* and the *Inspection general des Finances* in France, all answer to this description.

The Problem of Coordination

We spoke above of "coordination and control." Actually, we shall deal here only with the subject of coordination, leaving control for treatment later.

Coordination is a vexatious topic to discuss and even more vexatious to anyone who has ever had to try to coordinate some complicated administrative activity.

Even a rather ordinary administrative decision, such as the final decision on the locating and building of a hospital, involves an enormous amount of coordination. There must be advance planning, decisions about the allocation of funds, agreements upon location, condemnation proceedings, specifications for building and design, negotiations with medical societies and welfare agencies about the clientele served, and the establishment of a master contractual pattern. Each of these decisions entails consultation and negotiation with the "relevant parties"; in other words, with a number of agencies and private organizations. And each of these decisions requires coordination, or some kind of amalgam of policy that does justice to the various claims and integrates the particular decision with the whole programmatic scheme. Coordination is really a term for one major aspect of the administrative process itself.

Coordinating Activities and Policies

IN-BOXES AND OUT-BOXES

Much coordination is accomplished simply by the ordinary routing of papers "through normal channels"; that is, to the appropriate superiors and interested administrative parties. This routing of papers, or "minuting" as it is called in Britain, is a way of focussing all the relevant facts and administrative opinion on the point at issue. As the document travels on its way, it picks up, like a rolling snowball, other memoranda, opinions, exceptions, research findings, and so forth. Much future trouble can be forestalled if this paper work is well done. In the central offices of the German administration, for example, this part of the administrative process has been so carefully designed that few misunderstandings occur and a good many concessions are made as a matter of course. Officials, naturally, also use the telephone and talk to each other outside of normal channels. Thus it is important that the informal organization of an administrative unit support and facilitate its formal procedures. In fact, it can safely be said that the "normal channels" procedure will work no more successfully than its supplementary informal supporting network of personal exchanges of views and understandings.[30]

LIAISON

Subordinate units within a department or separate departments use liaison of varying degrees of formality as a second method of coordination. Officials chat informally over the telephone. They lunch together or drop in for tea. Or, as is the practice in the United States, departments maintain formally designated liaison officers within other departments. The practice is growing of deliberately trading officials to imbue each with the point of view of the other. One benefit, of course, of the European system of higher civil service is that the relative harmony in outlook among these officials greatly facilitates liaison.

---

[30] Chester Barnard, for many years head of the Bell Telephone Company of New Jersey, once asked himself, "What would happen to this company if, overnight, all of its executives were replaced by people of equal competence and experience but no previous working association?" His reply was that he believed the company would cease to function in about twenty-four hours. His remark amounts to an emphatic statement of the point in the text.

COMMITTEES

A third form of coordination is the use of departmental and inter-departmental committees, at various levels of administrative decision. Sometimes units with conflicting or competing interests attempt to coordinate "from below"; at other times, they negotiate at the summit. Affected private interests are sometimes represented in this process. Also, for any important issue it is customary to have present a representative of some of the more important overall agencies of coordination and control, such as a member of the Treasury in Britain, or of one of the various presidential staff agencies in the United States. Since the purpose of these committees is not merely to conciliate and compromise, but also to serve a representative function, they often become too large, diverse, and unwieldy to reach well-integrated decisions. Thus, the process of interdepartmental consultation through committee usually goes on repeatedly and at a good many points. In fact, many such committees have been put on a standing basis and meet regularly with planned agendas and formal procedures, for instance the National Security Council, in the United States.

ARBITRATION BY STAFF AGENCIES

If governments had little occasion to worry about the future, the techniques of coordination we have discussed would do most of the necessary job. But change is the law of contemporary administrative life. Change and the programmatic orientation of administration, along with sheer size, have led to the hypertrophy of specialized instruments of coordination and control in modern government. Departments plan for the future; and they are engaged in the continual implementation of existing programs that have to be interpreted and adjusted over the course of years. Thus, departments staff according to future plans. They negotiate contracts with future objectives in mind. They request funds with an eye to implementing their assigned objectives, and the ancillary objectives that every good administrator feels deeply are essential to make sense of the program that the legislature has entrusted to him. Above all, departments collide with each other in their objectives and their activities, creating a need for special agencies to reconcile and integrate budgetary requests, to harmonize decrees, to examine expenditure and staffing programs, and in a variety of ways to eliminate potential and actual duplication and waste or developing conflicts of policy. As far as concerns coordination, the purposes of such agencies can be described in terms attributed to one high Treasury official: 1) to get the maximum value from the expenditure of each one of Her Majesty's pounds; and 2) to prevent the Government's present convenience from becoming its future embarrassment.[31]

---

[31] Some relatively brief and valuable studies of the role of such agencies are, Samuel Beer, "Treasury Control: The Coordination of Financial Policy in Great Britain," *Amer-*

One final method of coordination deserves brief mention: administrative reorganization. Sometimes reorganization takes the form of relatively minute and marginal adjustments of jurisdictional boundaries; for instance, in the arbitration by the Bureau of the Budget, the Treasury, or the *Conseil d'Etat* of disputes over which agency shall be responsible for hauling the garbage away from public buildings or for providing weed and pest eradication services to the farmers. Reorganization may involve changes in the lines of authority within a department—usually also subject to some agency with a final veto over matters of organization and management. Then there are the large-scale reorganization proceedings involving the transfer and consolidation or creation and abolition of whole units. In Britain, large-scale redefinitions of authority of this sort go on rather continuously and quite efficiently.[32] In the United States, the Brownlow Commission of 1936 (President's Committee on Administrative Management) and the Hoover Commission established in 1948, have been the most famous examples of this latter kind of activity. Administrative reorganization is important not only as a way of periodically "streamlining" government, but also as a way of minimizing conflict and removing some of the fundamental structural and procedural sources of disorganization.

Conclusion

An examination of coordination brings the discussion once again to the topic of administrative organization as a whole. The tendencies that are the most striking can now be clearly discerned. The whole administrative enterprise has grown enormously in scale, and has also changed its mode of organization and operation over the years. Devices like the regulatory commission or the governmental corporation now challenge or compete with the older, more traditional departmental civil service. At the same time, the public and the private are increasingly mixed together, as we saw especially in our discussions of "planned development" and of "contract administration." In rather the same way that students of intergovernmental relations are fond of pointing to the analogy of the "marble cake" (rather than a layer cake) to express the contemporary relations of federal, state, and local governments, we might observe that much of the same sort of evolution has taken place in the development of governmental and private relations. *By traditional standards* the present-day administrative establish-

ican Political Science Review, **49** (1955), pp. 144-160; Alfred Diamant, "The French Civil Service: A Case Study of Administrative Autonomy," *Political Studies*, **6** (1958), pp. 146-166; Georges Langrod, "The French Council of State: Its Role in the Formulation and Implementation of Administrative Law," *American Political Science Review*, **49** (1955), pp. 673-692; and Edward H. Hobbs, *Behind the President: A Study of Executive Office Agencies* (Washington, D.C.: Public Affairs Press, 1954).

[32] See especially, D. N. Chester and F. M. G. Wilson, eds., *The Organization of British Central Government* (London: Allen & Unwin, 1957), Ch. 10.

ment appears ill-coordinated, imperfectly accountable, and prey to group pressures and an erosion of administrative standards.

Proposals for reform are legion. In the United States for over a generation the persistent refrain has been to "uphold the President" by giving him more powerful staff agencies. Some advocate the ideal of a career public service, though European governments that have such a service, lament the same tendencies observed in the United States. Still another proposal is the decentralization of many administrative activities to the state or local level. An expedient often suggested in Europe and popular in American municipal administration is more extensive resort to contracting out governmental services to private firms, especially when there is nothing distinctively governmental about the enterprise.[33]

There are no panaceas. Any one of the expedients proposed above would yield some marginal benefits if applied intelligently. But most of the characteristics of administrative organization we have noted seem destined to be with us for some time, and most of them are likely to increase in significance. Insofar as the discussion seems to lead to any one conclusion of importance, it is that contemporary administration has developed beyond the point where it can be handled effectively by ever more centralized intelligence and centralized collective thinking; and that we must look rather to better ways of bringing intelligence to bear directly at many points in the administrative process. If this is so, then a recognition of it might point toward the corollary that "staffing the Presidency," or "preserving the traditional ideals of the Service" may not be the most important standards for the future. Centralized coordination is not everything. Collaboration between public and private agencies is also important. So, too, is the accommodation reached between the courts and the agencies and between administration and legislative committees. It is important to look to the way in which a governmental system as a whole articulates both among its various branches and also in relation to the efforts and interests of the many groups within the society.

CONTROL

The subject of the control of administration brings into particularly sharp focus four of the objectives or criteria that we mentioned earlier: responsiveness, responsibility, accountability, and effectiveness. Much of the preceding discussion is also relevant here, since the personnel policies and the organization of the civil service will affect the quality of the administrative product even more than controls in the usual sense.

The basic approaches toward the control of administration differ markedly from country to country in the relative importance given to the

[33] For a discussion of this latter point see Brian Chapman, *op. cit.*, Ch. 16.

role of courts (or administrative courts), to legislatures and their committees, to the internal processes of administration itself, or to various devices for facilitating consultation and representation. In general and rather crude terms, Britain and Germany have tended to rely heavily upon internal controls, both formal and informal; France has made particular use of specialized agencies such as the *Conseil d'Etat* and the *Cour de Compte;* and the United States has relied particularly upon external controls of both the formal and the informal variety, including supervision by the courts and by Congress, and the representation of group interests. In all countries, of course, the legislature, the courts, the executive, and internal checks and procedures within the administration are part of the process of control. The differences are a matter of degree, but distinctive and important.

Britain and Germany: Professional Pride and Administrative Self-Rule

One of the most powerful informal internal controls, and one that is particularly characteristic of Germany and Great Britain is the corporate professional sense of the higher civil servants themselves: their loyalty to tradition and to their profession, and the presumably impartial and responsible temper of mind that is developed by lengthy association in the practice of their craft.[34] Well developed and effective techniques of administrative coordination also act as internal controls. For instance, in Great Britain all of the coordinative devices we have discussed above are employed so effectively that coordination by itself becomes a method of insuring administrative "due process" in the implementation of policy. Both in Britain and Germany little formal provision is made by statute for interest representation. The civil servants are expected to consult all the "relevant parties"; but the practice is one of considerable flexibility. To be sure, other checks exist: boards of administrative appeal and the right to review by the courts; moreover, in theory the administration is fully accountable through the minister to Parliament or *Bundestag*. Yet the scope and extent of either review by the courts in England or by the administrative tribunals in Germany is slight. And by tradition the administration is largely immune to legislative attack on anything like the scale practiced in the United States.

This system of extensive administrative self-rule of the administration has produced considerable benefits. In Britain and Germany, high traditions of public service, disinterestedness, fairness, and probity have been the general rule, transmitted and enforced by the higher civil servants. The British civil service, and in some respects the German as well, have often been considered models for imitation by much of the rest of the world. The

---

[34] The term "fellowship of science" is sometimes used. See Carl J. Friedrich, *Constitutional Government and Democracy*, rev. ed. (Boston: Ginn, 1950), p. 409.

prestige of the service and the position of the higher officials attracts able men. These men are skilled in their craft of administration and, for the most part, without the petty narrowness and jealousy that specialization often produces amongst colleagues. Common professional outlook and an acceptance of corporate traditions produces a propriety and sureness of conduct that make also for a "spirit of administration" generally acceptable by parliament and the public. The German civil service has been criticized for its antidemocratic traditions; but not so in the case of Britain, where the civil service gave to the Labor Government the same able and willing service that it has traditionally rendered to Conservative or Liberal regimes.

Critique

Contemporary developments under the modern service state, however, raise the question whether the corporate *esprit* and loyalties of the administrative profession are as efficacious as guides and controls for administration today and in the future. The "tradition of civility" in the civil service of Britain and the "fellowship of science" in Germany depended upon closeness, personal association, and the easy acceptance of a common professional outlook and mutual discipline, especially in the higher civil service. Today, a much larger proportion of the civil service works in regional offices or in various forms of detached service, such as public corporations. Also, the underlying theory of corporate self-regulation of the civil service depends largely upon an assumption that reasonable civil servants will not only agree upon a rational and prudent policy but will have canvassed all the relevant points of view. To put the matter in another way, a contrary view would be that deliberate attempts to secure the representation not only of various interests but also of differing philosophies of public policy are absolute requisites for democratic and responsible administration today. Just as the "spirit of administration" has become increasingly important, so under conditions that require the administration of many services and regulations for a wide variety of clientele groups, the representation of several articulate philosophies of regulation and public service gains in importance. German attempts to broaden recruitment and enrich the curriculum of prospective civil servants show some concern with the latter type of problem. In Britain, significantly, much recent discontent with the civil service appears to stem from a growing awareness that internal informal administrative controls leave something to be desired in view of recent administrative trends toward decentralization of services and delegation and subdelegation of legislative powers. Among the remedies frequently proposed are some that would be familiar to Americans: a greater scope and extent of judicial review; more investigation and oversight by parliamentary committees, and strengthened staff controls; and one that would represent a novel experiment for West European countries, the

Scandinavian *Ombudsman*, an officer who hears, investigates, and reports to parliament individual complaints of maladministration.[35]

France: Staff Controls

The French system of administration depends especially upon the use of elaborate, formal staff controls exercised by such agencies as the *Conseil d'Etat*, the *Inspection générale des Finances*, the Ministry of Finance, and specialized courts of account including one for the nationalized enterprises as well.[36] In part, these controls are implemented through particular quasi-legal penalties applicable to the individual officers.[37] They may be punished in a series of ways ranging from dismissal to temporary reduction in pay for being unresponsive to superiors. The public officer's personal financial responsibility for improper administrative dispositions goes much farther than it would, for instance, in the United States or Great Britain. Also, he may be held accountable for a whole series of "administrative torts," including not merely malfeasance in office, but a variety of forms of misfeasance and nonfeasance. Remedies are available generally both for private and public bodies, through simple and inexpensive proceedings.

The same staff agencies in France are responsible for much of the co-ordination and direction of the departments as corporate bodies. The *Conseil d'Etat*, the *Inspection générale des Finances*, and the Ministry of Finance police the plans and programs of the departments and their relations with each other. The system of control depends partly upon the close personal ties of the higher civil service, especially those that are in the so-called *corps d'état* (meaning primarily these same three agencies). But especially it depends upon the minute and continuing prior examination of decrees and expenditures and the close system of supervision and enforcement that back up the word of these elite agencies. In sum and substance, to the kind of control that would be exercised in Britain by the Treasury, the French have added a system of quasi-judicial review not too different in doctrine and in import from the American practice. And in contrast to the American system, the French have also established a system of unified control over rule-making and administrative orders.

Evaluation

The quality of administrative jurisprudence and of the elite *corps* of administration in France is superb. With these prime administrative resources, the French have been able successfully to carry formal administra-

[35] See, for example, William A. Robson, *Justice and Administrative Law*, rev. ed., (London: Stevens, 1947), Chs. 7, 8; Richard Davies, "The Select Committee on Nationalized Industries," *Political Quarterly*, 29 (1958), pp. 378-388; Chapman, *op. cit.*, Pt. III.

[36] A brief and readable discussion of the *Conseil d'Etat* is C. A. Freedeman, *The Conseil d'Etat in Modern France* (New York: Columbia U. P., 1961); for the system of financial control, see particularly, Lalumiere, *op. cit.*

[37] Cf. Arthur T. von Mehren, *The Civil Law System* (Boston: Little, Brown, 1957).

tive controls over the behavior of individual civil servants farther than in any other country. This approach has the merit of encouraging honesty and circumspection among administrators in a country not otherwise noted for its high standards of public morality or constitutional scruples. With these agencies of specific accountability, the citizen is given a definite and efficient remedy. In dealing with the relations of the public and the private sector the French have at least made notable progress under difficult circumstances. Public enterprise in France has been more successfully integrated into the general administrative pattern than in Great Britain. Also, for a system of government in which sectionalism, the party system, and the parliamentary organization make for fragmentation and particularism, the French higher civil service manages to bring a considerable measure of order and coherence into administrative organization and procedure. It is perhaps worth mentioning, too, that the French civil service has been able to deal rather easily with the problem of technical expertise in government. The members of the elite *corps* are themselves *savants* and technocrats, while the civil service as a whole is well staffed with career servants highly trained in *grande écoles* that offer a technical training the equal of any combination of training and experience to be found elsewhere. As a consequence, the "administrative point of view" is never in danger of being submerged by the scientific or the technical.

The French system of controls is, however, a case of external, formal *administrative* controls and not of controls designed to ensure accountability to political representatives or responsiveness to group constituencies. Parliamentary commissions watch the particular ministries, and deputies importune the civil service for concessions on behalf of their constituents. Syndical representation and group self-regulation under administrative authority are also carried quite far in France; but the tendency has been to concentrate great countervailing power in specialized administrative instruments of control to overcome the particularistic tendencies of group politics. One consequence has been popular frustration and political discontent with the limited measure in which the great French administrative machine has been responsive to political and group demands. Another result has been inequity—for the recognition of group claims has been haphazard, and implemented by a host of separate decrees developed in an *ad hoc* fashion.[38] Furthermore, such a system of control has a great tendency to conservatism, since it is built upon precedent and a semijudicial form of review. The *Conseil d'Etat* has for many years resisted manifestations of what it chose to dub "municipal socialism." Similarly, the development of a system of regulatory jurisprudence to govern (for example) labor relations or unfair trade practices has lagged. One way of summarizing these tendencies would

---

[38] A discussion of the consequences of this "regime of decrees" for the economy is found in Warren C. Baum, *The French Economy and the State* (Princeton, N.J.: Princeton U. P., 1958).

be to say that the administrative system of controls and the group and economic bases of French politics are at war with each other. Under de Gaulle a new array of decrees has done something to break the impasse. Yet the Gaullist regime also stalled in the area of social and economic regulation. What is missing in France is a way to link the administrative machine and the bargaining processes of politics.

The United States: A Variety of External Controls

STAFF CONTROLS

As in France, the United States makes extensive use of formal staff controls implemented by such agencies as the Bureau of the Budget, the Civil Service Commission, and the General Accounting Office. Their role is important. Because of separation of powers, however, they are nothing like as powerful as analogous organizations in France. Neither Congress nor the courts would entertain with equanimity the doctrine of autonomy and exclusive control that gives the *Conseil d'Etat* such a commanding position in France. Such staff agencies in the United States vary in the degree to which they are "presidential" or "congressional" in approach to their tasks; all of them, however, must be mindful of the separation of powers.

The American system, in keeping with the theory of the separation of powers, features external controls of administration by the legislature, by organized groups, and by the courts. We shall deal with each in turn.

CONGRESS

Congress exercises its control in a variety of ways. In laws that are to be administered it tends to be more specific, placing greater restrictions on administrative discretion, than, for example, does the British Parliament. Statutes regularly determine administrative organization and fix the procedures and standards that administrators must observe in the exercise of their discretionary powers. If the basic statutes are specific, the Appropriation Acts, which supply the life blood of the administrative agencies, are even more so. It is standard practice to itemize appropriations in detail.

The last point calls for elaboration. The legislative appropriations subcommittees exercise great power by means of periodic, intensive review of administrative behavior, in a way that has no counterpart in Europe. Members of these subcommittees go over the detailed budgetary estimates of each agency with great care. They interrogate the administrators at length and sometimes unmercifully. They make known their likes and dislikes; and their power is so great that administrators hesitate to cross them. In this way, their control frequently extends far beyond the specifications of statutes and appropriation acts. Moreover, the chairman and other members of appropriations subcommittees constitute strategic points of access for the representatives of pressure groups.

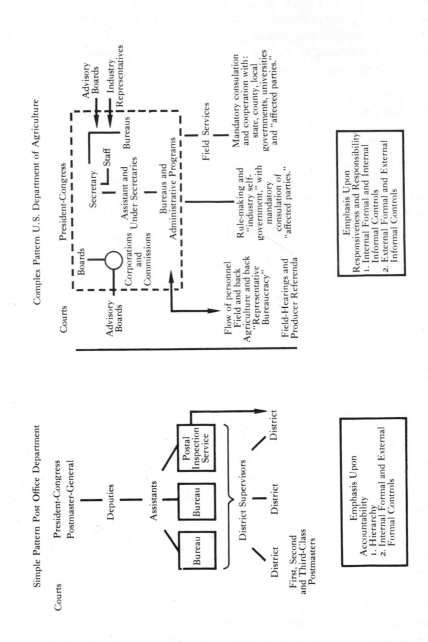

FIGURE 5   *Administrative controls—national government*

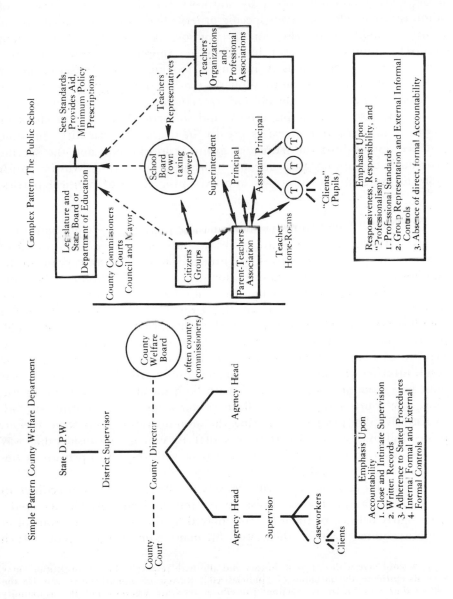

Simple Pattern County Welfare Department

State D.P.W.

District Supervisor

County
Court

County Director

County
Welfare
Board

(often county
commissioners)

Agency Head

Agency Head

Supervisor

Caseworkers

Clients

Emphasis Upon
Accountability
1. Close and Intimate Supervision
2. Written Records
3. Adherence to Stated Procedures
4. Internal Formal and External
Formal Controls

Complex Pattern The Public School

Legislature and
State Board or
Department of Education

Sets Standards,
Provides Aid,
Minimum Policy
Prescriptions

Teachers'
Organizations
and
Professional
Associations

Teachers'
Representatives

County Commissioners
Courts
Council and Mayor

School
Board
(own
taxing
power)

Superintendent

Principal

Assistant Principal

Citizens'
Groups

Parent-Teachers
Association

Teacher
Home-Rooms

T T

T

T

"Clients"
(Pupils)

Emphasis Upon
Responsiveness, Responsibility, and
"Professionalism"
1. Professional Standards
2. Group Representation and External Informal
Controls
3. Absence of direct, formal Accountability

FIGURE 6   *Administrative controls—local government*

GROUP REPRESENTATION

Elaborate provision for group representation and participation in the administrative process is another feature of American public administration. Groups are represented, often by statutory provision, in the making of administrative rules and even specific orders. They are represented on the boards of public enterprises and in advisory boards attached at various points to administrative agencies. They are represented, often, by direct membership on commissions. As in Europe, too, much quasi-legislative power is delegated directly to groups allowing the determination by various procedures of group legislation of trade practices, collective bargaining contracts, agricultural marketing orders, and so forth. This kind of check or control on administration varies greatly in degree of formality—in some instances establishing the nature of group representation and the specific procedures as precisely as for a court hearing; in other cases, trusting much more to representative processes approximating those of political parties.

COURTS

Finally, we have control by the courts, or judicial review of administrative acts. As a matter of constitutional law, judicial review of administrative acts affecting private rights must be ultimately afforded at some point in the administrative process. Any country, for that matter, that upholds the "rule of law" affords opportunities for those affected to question the legal authority of the administration. In the United States, judicial review of administrative acts has, however, a much more important role than it would, for example, in Britain. The fact that the courts pass on legislation itself in the United States implies also that the legislature cannot delegate to the administration the power to act unconstitutionally. Administrative acts must pass a double test: conformity with both the statute and the constitution. The courts have therefore been primary agents in ensuring an "administrative due process": requiring the administration to observe various procedural and substantive restraints that in sum go a considerable way toward ensuring fair administrative behavior with respect to private parties as well as adhering to the law itself.

Another important fact with respect to administrative proceedings in the United States is that administration itself is extensively "judicialized," particularly because of the great role played by the courts in the control of administration.[39] Lawyers themselves fill many administrative posts. Much

[39] A word here with respect to history and also with respect to French institutions may serve to elucidate the meaning of "judicialized." Review of administrative acts by the *Conseil d'Etat* in France is exacting: procedural tests are rigorous and the availability and scope of review are even greater than in the United States. In the United States, courts were for many years extremely hostile to the administration. At one time (1940) adoption of a system of administrative courts similar to the French was seriously considered. Improvement of administrative services, along with other factors, made this

of the procedure is established by law and employs judicial methods as, for example, in administrative "hearings." The consequence is not only to make the administrator continuously aware of the issue of legality, but also to introduce into the administrative process itself the voice of the lawyer. As a result, law and administration in the United States become closely associated.

Some Consequences

One consequence of the American system of controls is the fragmentation of the administrative process. Coordination is weak. Duplication of efforts in the same area and conflicting approaches to the same problem are commonplace. Coherent policy leadership from the top, through the President or the agency head, is difficult if not impossible to achieve. Stagnant back-waters of administrative policy—where programs once established become entrenched and resist for years any effort to review or reorganize them —are not uncommon.

The American system of administration also makes for concessions to group interests that seem to conflict with "the public interest." Whether in fact, in the battle of the pressure groups, that vague entity "the public interest" suffers, or whether the American method achieves an effective practical evaluation of all interests in a rough-and-tumble fashion it is impossible to say. Also whether the American system of relatively overt pressure group activity is better or worse in this respect than the somewhat less exposed operations of groups under the British system remains a matter of controversy among political scientists. Some students of politics point to the British system with envy.[40] Others are more skeptical of its virtues in this regard.[41]

The American system of external controls of administration is, as we have seen, partly a consequence of the separation of powers, partly an offset to the fact that the United States does not have a highly developed career

---

expedient seem unnecessary. Instead, under the Administrative Procedure Act of 1946, a code of behavior was enacted to govern rule-making and adjudication by the Federal agencies. Note, then, that the important difference between the American and the French systems lies not so much in the extent of remedies offered to private parties, nor in the jealousy with which statutory and procedural requisites for administrative action are guarded, but in the introduction of the lawyer and of lawyer-like methods into administration itself. Some political scientists have argued, accordingly, that American administration is hamstrung by legalism and that the influence of the lawyer bulks too large. In the judgment of the authors, both the special training and experience of the American lawyer as well as the distinctive point of view that he can bring to bear partly cancel and definitely outweigh these supposed disadvantages.

[40] See, for an example, Samuel H. Beer, "New Structures of Democracy: Britain and America," in *Democracy in the Mid-Twentieth Century*, ed. William N. Chambers and Robert H. Salisbury (St. Louis, Mo.: Washington U. P., 1960), pp. 30-59.

[41] A statement of this point of view may be found in J. Roland Pennock, " 'Responsible Government,' Separated Powers, and Special Interests: Agricultural Subsidies in Britain and America," *American Political Science Review*, 56 (1962), pp. 621-633.

service, with the effective internal controls that go with that concept, and partly the reflection of a heterogeneous, pluralistic society that is highly suspicious of government. These causal factors point to good reasons for the use of this system of controls. At the same time, they entail a price. They tend to discourage administrative leadership. In the higher civil servant they often produce anxiety and frustration.

One distinguished citizen at the end of a Washington tour of duty during the Korean war was asked whether he would like to return in the event of a future national emergency. He is reported to have said that he would seek a quick and quiet death instead by volunteering for immediate front-line military service. Officials do not like to be blackguarded by congressional committees; nor do they relish the importunate demands of interest group representatives, especially when they feel that the merits of the issue lie on the other side. They hate to see carefully matured plans derailed because some politician has got his back up. They dread the havoc that an adverse budgetary recommendation can produce and the anxiety and internal stresses brought about by a congressional investigation. Administrative leadership is a demanding job in the best of circumstances; the American system of government conspires to make it doubly so.

Evaluation

Some of the faults of the American system are the price of bigness. It is a vast administrative machine, the largest in the free world. It is a decentralized administrative machine, spread across fifty states, and subdivided into hundreds of administrative regions and districts. It is also a complex administrative machine, combining a variety of accommodations between public and private initiative. It is an old saying that "a country can stand a lot of ruining." There has in fact been little evidence of ruin, though a price—perhaps not disproportionate—has been paid for bigness.

More positive defenses of the American administrative establishment can be made. Confusion and conflict are not merely negative quantities. Nor is it only a matter of semantics to say that they often represent experimentalism and the confrontation of desires from which a fresh approach to policy develops. Leadership and innovation often begin at the top. But they also often start at the periphera of events, at the field office, or with the specialist who is absorbed in a particular problem. The American system is sluggish, in the sense that coordinated direction or a major change of policy is difficult to achieve. On the other hand, it is open to new influences and doctrines.

It is true that in the past it was the fashion to point an accusing finger at the courts and at the congressional committees for their role in fragmenting administrative policy and interrupting the flow of presidential or executive influence. They *are* sometimes barriers in the path of progress; but they are also welcome agencies for close and intimate oversight, for the arbitration of small conflicts, and for a microscopic examination of policy.

Confidence that the American system is well suited to domestic problems, however, does not mean that it is equally as suited for the strategy and tactics of Cold War. The system is apt for decentralized "thinking"—for the application of intelligence locally. It affords many remedies and a chance for the intensity of group sentiment to be reflected and communicated upward. It also provides for a fruitful confrontation of views—when the administrator is forced to justify his actions or his policies before the congressional committee or the courts. Whether it can also encourage the clarity of thought at the center of affairs and communicate effectively the right ideas at the right time, and respond to the need for leadership that the contemporary international situation demands is still being tested. Today, perhaps more than at any time in our history, the need for clear and balanced thinking in foreign policy has come to the fore. As is always the case with democratic government, that thinking must be "collective thinking," the joint product of many people and agencies. The premium put upon being right the first time is enormous. So is the importance of getting the best intelligence put forward and accepted. It is a dramatic challenge.

CONCLUSION

In this chapter, we have discussed the importance of administration to contemporary government and some of the ways in which administration can be related to the ends of democracy. The subject of administration is not static. Like the political process itself, administration must be judged by the needs of a swiftly moving contemporary society. Each country has a different schedule of values associated with administration. On the other hand, the institutions of democratic government in all advanced societies contain much that is alike in fundamental spirit and method. We have tried especially to describe some of the present day developments that are important to a sensible theory and practice of administration. It would be fatuous to suggest that Britain has the answer for France, or that the United States should model its system of federal administration on the German. Yet a different experience can and does deepen understanding and enrich the intellectual materials with which the tasks and implements of government are approached.

Often, too, what appear to be movements in opposing directions in different countries represent a convergence from previously contrasting positions. In Britain, for example, where judicial review of administrative action has been minimal, the exigencies of the welfare state have led to demands for more external checks upon arbitrariness. In the United States, on the other hand, where extensive judicial review has frequently impinged upon legitimate areas of administrative discretion, protests that positive governmental action was being hamstrung have led to both legislative and judicial action to redress the balance in favor of the administrators. Converging developments of this sort suggest that common principles are at work and that, as industrialization minimizes the variety of conditions among modern states, their governmental institutions tend also to become less various.

SELECTED READINGS

BARKER, SIR ERNEST. *The Development of Public Services in Western Europe, 1660-1930.* London: Oxford U. P., 1944. A brief account of the history of public administration in Western Europe, relating the public services to constitutionalism and political development.

CHAPMAN, BRIAN. *The Profession of Government.* London: Allen & Unwin, 1959. A topical survey and critique of public administration in Great Britain and the countries of Western and Northern Europe. Clear, interesting, and exceptionally informative.

DIAMANT, ALFRED. "The French Civil Service: A Case Study of Administrative Autonomy," *Political Studies,* 6 (1958), pp. 146-166. A good, brief account of some of the major aspects of French civil service and administration.

FINER, HERMAN. *Theory and Practice of Modern Government.* New York: Holt, 1949. Chapters 27 to 34 give an excellent account of the history of public administration in Great Britain, France, and Germany.

FINER, S. E. *A Primer of Public Administration.* London: Muller, 1950. Although written a number of years ago, this brief work still remains one of the best introductions to the study of the British civil service and administration.

FREEDEMAN, C. A. *The Conseil d'Etat in Modern France.* New York: Columbia U. P., 1961. A brief, elementary study of this institution. The *Conseil d'Etat* is of particular interest because it represents an approach to the problems both of staff controls of administration and of administrative adjudication that is radically different from that in either the United States or Great Britain. The first and second Hoover Commissions in the United States recommended the adoption of a similar institution.

GILBERT, CHARLES E. "The Framework of Administrative Responsibility," *Journal of Politics,* 21 (1959), pp. 373-407. An excellent summary and critique of the literature on administrative responsibility.

MARCH, JAMES G. and SIMON, HERBERT A. *Organizations.* New York: Wiley, 1958. A comprehensive survey of contemporary theory of organization especially (though not exclusively) related to public administration.

PRICE, DON K. *Government and Science—Their Dynamic Relation in American Democracy.* New York: New York U. P., 1954. A series of excellent lectures by one of America's most thoughtful students of public administration and government. He discussed particularly the problem of governmental decision where much of the relevant facts lie beyond the knowledge or understanding of the ordinary layman, politician, or administrator.

SIMON, HERBERT A., SMITHBURG, DONALD W. and THOMPSON, VICTOR A. *Public Administration.* New York: Knopf, 1950. One of the most significant treatments of this subject published during the last twenty years.

SNOW, SIR CHARLES PERCY. *Science and Government*. Cambridge: Harvard U. P., 1961. A series of lectures by a former scientist and public servant (turned novelist) upon the problem of science and government in Great Britain, particularly during the second World War.

STAHL, O. GLENN. *Public Personnel Administration*. 4th ed., New York: Harper, 1956. A representative treatment of the subject.

WALDO, DWIGHT. *The Administrative State: A Study of the Political Theory of American Public Administration*. New York: Ronald, 1948. Schools of thought in early American administrative reform movements. The political philosophy of administrative reform is interesting not only as theory but also because of the sources from which it derives.

CHAPTER 16

The Judiciary

||||||||||||||||||||||||||||||||||||||||||||||||||||||||||||||||||||||||||||||||||||

Law is universal and pervasive in a sense that government is not. Law, the courts, and the judiciary regulate and adjust private affairs in many ways —in the making of contracts or redressing injuries—beyond the point where government normally stops. Law includes many of the concepts and procedural instruments through which collective action or individual purpose is realized.

Today the great extent of the administrative branch and the highly public activities of the executive and legislature have cast the judiciary in what may seem to be a subordinate role. However, looking at the role of the judiciary in the light of newspaper discussion, the quantity of decisions made, or the personnel engaged misses an important point. Courts and the judiciary *preside over the legal process*—they are the authoritative decision-makers that determine much of the doctrine and the procedure by which private parties and public agencies carry out their individual or joint purposes and protect and perpetuate their individual or joint interests. Also, government historically grew, and to a considerable extent today still develops from a background or foundation of law or legal concept.[1] As one consequence, law and the judiciary continue to be especially important both in fashioning the tools of public policy and in controlling their use. Thus, it is important to realize that "the judiciary" is a much wider affair than the activities of the visible officers—the judges. We are dealing with a group of men who stand in a particular and strategic place, both with respect to government and also in relation to the universal institution of law.

[1] In the United States, for instance, until the end of the nineteenth century most legislation was primarily a codification of existing common law. Even today, any given statute will often derive much of its operative language from the existing common law or take the common law as a point of departure.

FUNCTIONS OF THE JUDICIARY

Adjudication

The primary functions of the judiciary may most simply be described as the settlement of controversies arising out of the application of the law, and the determination, within limits established by law, of the consequences that are to attach to a specific instance of violation of law. The controversies may be between private individuals, as when one person sues another for breach of contract, for trespassing on his property, or for carelessly allowing his vicious dog to attack the plaintiff on the public sidewalk; or they may be between the government and an individual, as when the government sues a taxpayer for failure to pay the amount due or when the state prosecutes a man who is accused of having committed murder, theft, or some other crime.

The application of the law, it must be understood, by no means always involves a controversy. The typical situation is for the citizen, knowing the law and the penalty for its infraction, to abide by it. In a sense, then, the law is being applied to me whenever I stop my car at a red light or a "stop" sign, or when I receive a notice that my house has been assessed at so much and that the tax levied on it is a certain amount. If I pay without dispute, the judiciary is not involved. In point of fact, I may even have an opportunity to controvert the assessment before some administrative agency, which may or may not revise it, without resorting to the courts. It is only if I am still dissatisfied or recalcitrant after having exhausted the opportunities for so-called administrative appeal that recourse must be had to the courts.

Resort to the courts occurs, most commonly, because the procedures for resolving disputes have broken down. In the normal course of events, two parties with a legal dispute will generally reach some kind of compromise settlement outside of court, often with the aid of lawyers. Parties may also resort to arbitration. Even with the case docketed for court hearing, they may still compromise the issue, especially if the two attorneys for the opposing parties see, after consultation, that it would be foolish to go to court. The judge may also hold a pre-trial conference and counsel one or both parties to settle rather than proceed. In other words, a good judicial system *keeps people out of court* and minimizes judicial controversy.

When a controversy does reach the judicial stage, it becomes the duty of the court to find out what the facts are, to determine what the relevant law is, and then apply the law to the facts. For instance, suppose John Smith brings suit for damages against me, alleging that he slipped on the ice on my sidewalk and broke his leg, or that I negligently ran my motor car into his, although the light was against me. The court must determine whether the allegation of facts is true. Then it must define the law on the subject, declaring my responsibility under the circumstances. If the law were to state that my only responsibility was—as far as my sidewalk was concerned—to post a warning sign, and if I had done so, then the application of the law to the facts would be so simple as to be practically automatic. If, on the other hand, the law set up a standard of conduct rather than imposing a specific rule—for instance, requiring that measure of care that a "reasonable man" could be expected to exercise—then the third element (the application of the law to the facts) becomes the most difficult of all.

Having determined whether and in what respect the law has been violated, the court then has to determine what is to be done about it. In the case of criminal law, the law itself normally states a range of possible punishments leaving some discretion to the court as to the amount of the fine or the duration of the jail sentence. In a civil case, it is likely to be a matter of determining the extent of damage. Here, again, both facts and law may be in dispute. Generally, the parties must prove their damages to the satisfaction of the court (or jury), but the court will have an important role in determining what may be included in the calculation. Sometimes damages will not afford an appropriate remedy, especially in situations where an injured party does not want money, but the doing or refraining from some specific action.[2] Jones may have taken my ivory-handled umbrella, a "priceless heirloom" given me by my great grandfather. Damages cannot be easily measured, or they will not compensate me. My neighbor periodically pumps sludge out of his swimming pool and dumps it on my land. The damages are trifling and also the act is a recurrent one. In this situation a court may hold that damages are both an inadequate remedy and one that—because of the recurrent nature of the offense—imposes an onerous burden on me, since I must seek a court remedy each time the offense is repeated. In the first instance, specific performance would be the appropriate remedy: an order to Jones requiring him to return the umbrella. In the second instance, the court would issue an injunction, restraining my neighbor temporarily or "in perpetuity" from dumping sludge on my land.

The Creation of New Law

The main business of courts or of the judiciary is to adjudicate: to settle particular controversies as they arise, and to settle them within the established law. But law is relatively static and settled, while human relations are ever changing, presenting novel and unforeseen situations. Consequently, the judiciary must have techniques to create new law that will

---

[2] In common law countries, courts start from the presumption that damages rather than specific performance is the rule, and plaintiffs seeking injunction or specific performance carry a heavy burden of proving that they cannot be compensated by damages. This same presumption does not hold in Europe. Also, in the United States and other common law countries, the availability of injunction or specific performance has been broadened, especially by statute or such codes as the Uniform Sales Act.

meet the altered situations.[3] Consider, for example, the case of a farmer thrown into a ditch because his horse was frightened by a low-flying trainee in a noisy helicopter. Was the Air Force negligent (and therefore liable) for not instructing its pilots not to fly near nervous horses? Most likely, the author of the training manual never thought of the situation, nor did the Secretary of the Air Force, nor did the Congress. Also, it is unrealistic to expect these authorities to provide in detail for all cases that might arise. In this situation, the courts "make law," that is they try to determine from older cases or from other authoritative sources what principle reasonably ought to govern this situation. Law made in this fashion is subject to a later legislative determination, but it is an essential function in the administration of justice on a day-to-day basis, and more frequently than not it is allowed to remain unchanged, as a part of the living and growing body of law. Holmes once remarked that courts legislate "intersticially," that is that they fill in gaps in the law. In performing this function they are acting much as administrators might, or as the legislators would have had they anticipated the situation. But, as the example above suggests, courts also make law at its growing edges, as well as in the interstices. Here again their activity is not sharply differentiated from that of legislator or administrator. But an important distinction exists. It is the function of the courts to discover and apply, as best they can, just solutions for particular controversies, and, at the same time develop rules that will produce just results in the future. Justice, rather than either administrative convenience or popular demand, is the proper goal of the judiciary. It is in this way that their law-making responsibility is most sharply distinguished from that of legislators and administrators.[4]

Supervision

The judiciary acts also in a supervisory capacity. They often supervise the execution of trusts, of corporate reorganizations, of divorce settlements, and the like. They also usually have considerable powers to supervise the acts of government, although the extent of these powers varies considerably in particular systems. In code law systems the latter form of supervision is at a minimum, though even here the ordinary courts usually determine jurisdiction over disputes and decide in most instances what are matters of public law and what are matters of private law. In common law jurisdictions, or where civil law systems are supported by the principle of judicial review of administrative acts, the judiciary becomes in large measure the guardian of the "rule of law."

[3] This statement holds also for the civil law system, although under a code judicial legislation is less important.

[4] Cf. Earl Latham, "The Group Basis of Politics: Notes for a Theory," *American Political Science Review*, 46 (1952), pp. 376-397, at p. 392.

Conclusion

These three activities—adjudication, law-making, and supervision—are in considerable measure common to all judicial systems—at least in constitutional democracies. Consequently, it should not be surprising that the organization and procedure of courts varies less from one form of government to another—even as between democratic and nondemocratic forms —than is the case with some other organs of government. Judicial systems under monarchical forms of government that provided very little in the way of popular participation frequently corresponded closely to those in democratic regimes. Under code-law systems many of the basic problems are analogous, even though the functions of the judiciary or of court-like bodies (such as the *Conseil d'Etat* in France) are divided and allotted differently. The determination of law, the techniques of accommodating new interests, and the vindication of lawful methods of procedure have much in common everywhere.

Common law pleading—early nineteenth century

Philadelphia Museum of Art

ORGANIZATION AND PROCEDURE
OF COMMON-LAW COURTS

In discussing the organization and procedure of courts, we shall be concerned primarily with common-law courts (without going into great detail even with regard to them or with respect to the differences, for instance, between British and American court systems.) We shall, however, have something to say about the French system and the Civil law system generally, which has been more widely copied throughout the world.

The Bench

The key official of a court is the judge; or perhaps we should say that the key position is the Bench, which may be occupied by one or more judges. For all but the most minor positions in the judicial system, training in the law and membership in the bar is a normal prerequisite for judicial office. Unfortunately, other desirable qualifications such as integrity, impartiality, and judicial temperament, are so difficult to measure that little attempt is made, by examination or otherwise, to certify individuals as possessing the requisite minimum amount of these qualities.[5]

With an important exception to be discussed in a moment, the method of selection of judges in common law jurisdictions remains, as it has been from the beginning, appointment by the chief executive for life or until voluntary resignation, barring the possibility of removal by impeachment in the event of corruption or other gross malfeasance in office. This immunity from removal is, of course, the great bastion of judicial independence.

Independence from influence does not assure that the original appointments will be sound. Judicial office may be given as a reward for political service in support of the party in power with the consequence that the qualifications for office are not given proper weight.[6] Moreover, where a particular social and economic class holds power over a long period, it almost inevitably follows that the judiciary will be filled with men whose unconscious bias favors the members of that class. Even though the honesty, the sagacity, and the technical ability, of the British higher judiciary has for a long time been almost beyond reproach, a bias in favor of the propertied classes has been one of its common characteristics.

[5] Bar associations in the United States—both the associations of particular states and the American Bar Association—make some attempt to assess the qualifications of particular nominees and to influence appointments. The consensus of informed persons is that their efforts have not been notably successful. See, for example, Whitney N. Seymour, "The Bar as Lawmaker," in Monrad G. Paulsen, ed., *Legal Institutions Today and Tomorrow* (New York: Columbia U. P., 1959), pp. 174-197.

[6] According to one authority, over the last seventy years, 93 per cent of the federal bench in the United States has been appointed from the political party to which the President and the Attorney General at that time also belonged. Paulsen, *op. cit.*, p. 204.

In the United States, although the general level of federal judicial appointments is one of the aspects of American government to which observers can point with pride, the almost inescapable bias of class and of previous position is frequently noted. A member of the Supreme Court, Justice Miller, once remarked of his experience that judges who had served many years as counsel for railroads, for instance, were likely, after they had reached the bench, to be somewhat partial to railroads when they appeared in court as parties to litigation.

In most American states, unfortunately, the practice of appointing judges gave way before the onslaught of Jacksonian democracy to the election of judges. The fact that American courts, unlike their English counterparts, perform the function of interpreting the Constitutions of the land and of declaring laws void as being contrary to constitutional provisions has often been advanced as both an explanation and a defense of this departure from the common-law pattern. It may be doubted, however, whether it is adequate in either capacity. The change came about along with the same movement that made executive offices (other than that of Governor) elective. The rationale of the movement seems simply to have been that of carrying democracy to what appeared to be its logical conclusion. From this point of view it was successful; but if one wishes judges to bring an independent judgment to their decisions rather than being guided by partisan attitudes and commitments, the results have been unfortunate.[7]

Where election of judges is substituted for appointment, tenure for life or good behavior is also replaced by tenure for a fixed number of years. The term of office is most frequently six years but may run as high as twenty.

Juries

Although judges are the key officials of common-law courts, juries also play a central role. Broadly speaking, the functions of common-law courts are divided between judges, who decide all points of law and regulate the conduct of the trial, and juries which find the facts and, in accordance with instructions given them by the judges, apply the law to the facts. Juries are of two kinds, grand juries and petit juries. The grand jury is used in criminal cases only, and there it plays a preliminary role. A person who is accused of a serious crime is brought before a grand jury for the purpose of establishing whether or not there is sufficient evidence against him to make it worth while to go through with a trial and to justify imposing upon him the expense and ignominy likely to attend standing trial. The grand jury is selected by lot and is normally composed of from thirteen to twenty-three

---

[7] See Stuart S. Nagel, "Political Party Affiliation and Judges' Decisions," *American Political Science Review*, 55 (1961), pp. 843-850. In a number of states, systems combining appointment with election or an opportunity for rejection by popular vote may provide a happy compromise.

men and women. It takes affirmative action on the concurrence of a majority
of its members. The prosecuting official brings before it persons accused of
crimes and details to them the evidence. The proceedings are private and
jurors are bound to secrecy about them. No defense is made at this time and
the jury is called upon simply to determine whether a *prima facie* case for
believing the accused to be guilty had been established. In other words, if
the evidence and sworn testimony is such that, assuming its truth, makes
a good case against the accused, the jury finds a "true bill" and he is held
over for trial in due course. Otherwise, the case is dismissed.

In the days of its origin and for some time after, the grand jury was
useful both for the information that its own members would have about
crimes committed in their neighborhood and because it constituted a protection against frivolous prosecutions which might be pressed for political
purposes. Nowadays, however, it has largely outlived its usefulness. A simple
process of "information," by which the prosecuting official presents sworn
evidence to the court, has largely displaced the grand jury in England and in
many of the American states. In the case of the United States federal government, however, the cumbersome and expensive grand jury procedure is
required by the Constitution for all capital and other "infamous" crimes.
The grand jury does still serve a useful investigatory function when widespread official misconduct is suspected, for it can take the initiative where the
politically appointed or elective prosecuting officials might not choose
to do so.

Far more important than the grand jury, today, is the petit jury which
also traces its origin at least to the early days of Norman rule in England.
Selected in a manner similar to the grand jury, and like the latter also
theoretically comprising a cross-section of the community, the petit jury
consists of twelve individuals. No one is permitted to serve as a juror on a
case if it appears that he is any way prejudiced with respect to it. At Common law the petit jury was used for practically all criminal and most civil
cases. The case is argued by both sides, in accordance with rigid rules of
procedure and evidence. Witnesses testify and are cross-examined. Counsel
argue the causes of the clients. Then the judge "charges" the jury. He summarizes the case, sets forth the law on the subject, and tells them what they
are called upon to do. For example, he may say that if they believe certain
testimony they must find the defendant guilty. Or, in a civil case, such as
the hypothetical case of the man slipping on the ice, he may say that, if they
find that the man did in fact fall because of the icy condition of the walk,
and if further they believe that the owner had been negligent about clean-
ing off the walk, then they should award damages. Juries can convict, or
find for plaintiffs, only if they are unanimous. If their decision is unani-
mously in favor of the accused, that disposes of the case finally. However, if
in a criminal case, the jury is divided, there may be a new trial with a
different jury.

Nowadays the strict common-law requirements as enumerated above are subject to numerous exceptions. In many jurisdictions the jury is not used for some types of civil cases. Even more frequently, it may be dispensed with by the consent of both parties. The latter is also often true even for criminal cases, but never in the case of a capital offense. Also many American states permit jury verdicts by less than a unanimous vote in civil cases.

It should also be pointed out that common-law countries have courts that are not common law courts. Equity courts, for instance, act without a jury. And even where, as in the case of the federal courts of the United States, equity and "legal" jurisdictions have been consolidated, juries are not used for the type of case that was formerly dealt with by equity courts. Thus, the situations in which a jury will *not* be used are numerous. In civil suits parties frequently stipulate for trial without a jury, especially when they want to minimize the hazards involved in the relatively uninformed judgment of the "twelve good men and true." Multiparty litigation involving, for example, a number of claimants for a piece of land or representatives of various classes of stockholders, usually are equity proceedings and do not have a jury. Also, the use of equity may cover a broad range of activities, from the suit for an injunction to the probate of wills and divorce proceedings.

How well the jury system works is much disputed. The gradual diminution of the number of cases for which it is required is itself enough to suggest that there is dissatisfaction with its operation in some quarters. It is frequently contended that juries are too susceptible to irrational appeals and to irrelevancies. The practice of the "general verdict," too, gives the jury wide latitude. The judge may charge the jury that premeditated taking of someone's life is murder, regardless of motive; but if the jury finds the defendant "not guilty" the outsider cannot tell whether they believed the charges had not been proved beyond a reasonable doubt or whether they thought this was a "mercy-killing" and that the law was too harsh. The flexibility thus injected into the common-law system is frequently pointed to as one of its virtues, but it may be a vice as well.[8]

One of the most serious difficulties of the jury system as it operates in most jurisdictions today is that many if not most of the persons best qualified are excused from service. Public employees are generally exempt by statute. Business and professional people are rarely called and excuse from service is relatively easy to obtain. New York State's provision for so-called

---

[8] The example of "mercy-killing" illustrates the point. If the judge narrowly restricted the question of fact ("If you find that X did willfully give a lethal dose, you must find him guilty.") then the probability of a decision adverse to the defendant is increased. Some would argue that flexibility introduced by allowing a general verdict would be desirable in this case. Others say that the court is shirking its lawful responsibility. Also, the general verdict reduces the possibility of successful appeal, because appeals are in principle taken only on points of law.

"blue-ribbon" juries, selected from especially qualified groups and used for very important cases may point the way to at least a partial solution to the problem.

Counsel for the Parties

In a limited sense the legal representatives of the adverse parties—whether the two lawyers in a civil suit, or the prosecuting attorney and the counsel for the accused in a criminal proceeding—are treated as officers of the court. They are expected to observe and uphold the law and the usage and dignity of the court. Though this doctrine is descended historically from the ancient custom of the Inns of Court, it holds also in code-law countries.

The lawyer under the common-law system has three responsibilities—to his client, to his profession (or to the law), and specifically (when in court) to the court itself. With respect to his client he owes a fiduciary obligation—he must treat his client's interests with the utmost probity and disinterestedness. To his profession he owes fidelity to the law and to the ethical canons of the bar. With respect to the court, he must do nothing that would undermine its dignity or corrupt or interfere with its procedures. Penalties may range from damages or fine, through a suspension from practice or disbarment, up to citation for contempt and even jail sentence.

The lawyer's obligations may conflict with each other. In defense of his client, he may resort to unfair tactics, in or out of court, or to deception, corruption of witnesses, and the like. The lawyer who has connived in a violation of the law may be even more tempted to use questionable tactics in court. Partly for this reason, and also to minimize conflicts of interest in his position with respect to his client or clients, the British legal profession is separated into solicitors (who provide legal advice) and barristers (who represent the parties in court). Civil law systems have a similar distinction. In the United States no such formal separation exists, though some American lawyers have recommended it.

Beyond the obligation to observe the rules of the court and to uphold its dignity, the lawyer has a limited and indeterminate duty to behave not simply as a representative of the parties but as an instrument of justice. Application of this principle varies with the forum and with the nature of the case. The adversary method of common-law trial operates to restrict this official responsibility. Nevertheless, attorneys even under the adversary system of advocacy are charged with the duties of candor and fairness. They are expected to cooperate with the court and with the opposing counsel to ensure the effective trial of the issues at stake. Judges will be cool toward attorneys who seek to win cases by mere tactical advantage or by intimidating witnesses. This conception of the counsel as an officer of the court is more important in Britain than in the United States; but it is important in the United States as well. By and large, the enforcement of this role falls largely to the judge, who has great power over the conduct of his own court, and to bar associations that issue hortatory injunctions and canons of good practice having some influence. One instance in which the official role of the counsel has considerable significance is the government attorney who —whether acting in a civil or criminal case—is enjoined to seek a just and fair trial and not merely victory.

Other Methods of Insuring Fairness

Over the centuries, numerous other principles and rules of procedure have been worked out and adopted for adding to the assurance that trials will be fair. We shall enumerate the most important of them. In the first place, either a person accused of a crime or one against whom a civil suit is brought must be informed in detail and in writing of the nature of the charges that are being brought against him. Without such a provision he might be taken by surprise in court and not have sufficient opportunity to prepare his defense, both as to the facts and as to the law. Furthermore, he must be permitted to employ legal counsel both to aid him in the preparation of his defense and to argue his case in court. If the accused is unable to afford counsel, he must be provided with free legal defense, whether by court appointment or otherwise. A few jurisdictions provide an official Public Defender. Defendants and other litigants may of course submit to the court any evidence they wish to, and have witnesses to testify in their favor. Moreover, the court will issue legal process to require the attendance of reluctant witnesses or the production of papers or other evidence if it is convinced that the evidence so obtained may be relevant to the ends of justice. Trials are normally conducted in public. Each side may cross-examine the witnesses presented by the other side—an important privilege, since what is left unsaid is frequently just as important as what is said. The last remark leads naturally to mention of another rule, one that has become the subject of considerable controversy. A relatively late addition to the common law, and one that was generally taken over in the United States, is the rule that no one shall be compelled to testify against himself. This rule is known as the privilege against self-incrimination. It applies in civil as well as criminal cases, both before courts and before investigating agencies. It is by benefit of this provision in the United States Constitution, for example, that a witness before a Congressional investigating committee may refuse to answer whether he is or has been a member of the Communist Party. In criminal proceedings, not only the accused but also witnesses may invoke the privilege. By doing so they may seriously hamper the course of justice. This roadblock may be overcome by guaranteeing the witness immunity from prosecution for any crime on the basis of any testimony he may give; but many critics feel that this price is extortionate.[9]

[9] With such a guarantee, witnesses can take an "immunity bath" simply by testifying to their complicity in or commission of a crime.

Many other rules of evidence, often of a technical nature, are intended to be conducive to a just verdict. Although the common-law rules of procedure and of evidence have been substantially modified in many jurisdictions, the so-called "hearsay" rule may be cited as one that still has general application. Its substance is that witnesses may testify only with respect to facts of which they have direct knowledge. Rumors, gossip, second-hand testimony generally, are banned, on the theory that juries are likely to give them more credence than they deserve. Other rules are designed to exclude from the record, and indeed from the hearing of the jury, all irrelevancies that might prejudice the jury. It is for this reason that court proceedings are frequently interspersed with interjections of "I object," especially from the counsel for the defendant. Sometimes the jury is excluded from the courtroom temporarily while the judge hears from the attorney what he plans to try to show by the line of questions that is being objected to and how it is related to the issues of the case.

As the burden of proof in any argument is always on the affirmative, so in court trials it is the accuser, whether the case be criminal or civil, who must assume this burden. In civil cases, a bare preponderance of the weight of evidence is sufficient for a verdict for the plaintiff; but in criminal cases the common law requires that guilt must be established "beyond a reasonable doubt." The theory underlying this provision is that the injustice of convicting the innocent is so great that it is better to let many criminals go unpunished than to convict one man wrongly.

Finally, an important part of the common law, as of other judicial systems, is provision for appeals from lower to higher courts. It would be inappropriate here to go into detail with regard to the organization of the courts in any particular countries. Suffice it to say that an opportunity to appeal from the verdict of a trial court to a higher court is virtually always provided. Frequently it is possible in common-law countries to carry appeals to still a third level, at which point the highest court of the land or of the jurisdiction in question is generally reached. Appellate courts normally deal only with points of law, treating as final the finding of facts by the court that actually took the testimony and heard the witnesses. Under certain circumstances, however, an appellate court may order the original court to give a new trial, in which case all of the original issues of law and fact are open. Otherwise, the appellate court deals with such questions as whether the original court had jurisdiction of the case, whether it interpreted the substantive law regarding the case properly, and whether or not it made procedural errors in the conduct of the trial. Appellate courts normally have to give opinions, generally in writing, in support of their judgments, thereby submitting their assumptions and reasoning to the criticism of higher courts, their fellow judges, and the fraternity of the bar. Here, again, is a significant deterrent to arbitrary or prejudiced judgments.

Appraisal

On the whole the judicial branch of government in common-law countries probably operates reasonably well. Of course such a general statement must be subject to many exceptions. British justice is traditionally of a high caliber. In the United States, the federal courts are generally superior to the courts of most of the states. Any system will in large measure reflect the moral standard of the political culture within which it operates. At the state and especially local levels in the United States political corruption is not uncommon. Under such circumstances it inevitably penetrates into the judicial system, although it may safely be said that the moral and intellectual level of the courts generally is distinctly above that of the other branches of government in the area in question.

One of the most perennial complaints with respect to common law systems stems from the adversary method of procedure. In principle, a common-law suit is still conducted much as though it were a regulated duel between the two opposing sides, or more accurately, between the counsel for the defendant and the counsel for the plaintiff. The judge considers only evidence presented by the parties. He hears only those arguments brought forward by counsel. The rules of procedure and of evidence are nicely designed to insure that neither side has a forensic advantage. On the other hand, the rules do little to insure full and fair disclosure of the facts, or even to insure that the judge will consider the relevant points of law except as they are presented by counsel. .

The adversary method of legal advocacy is defended primarily on the ground that it ensures fairer treatment of each party. Juries, for instance, are likely to take the judge's statements very seriously. Hence, it is argued, he should say little. Also, a party to a dispute may well feel cheated if judicial intervention cost him the case. The argument that a fuller disclosure of the issues is likely to be assured if the two attorneys know that the court will hear only those arguments that they present may also have merit. Thus, the argument runs, each will do his utmost to acquaint himself with and call to the court's attention all that is relevant to his client's case.

One criticism of the adversary method is that it institutionalizes and encourages the precept: "Win by means fair or foul, but in any case, win." As a consequence, so this argument runs, the adversary method encourages legal trickery and even chicanery. It encourages the abuse of witnesses, emotional appeals to juries, and questionable courtroom strategy. The prosecuting attorney, bent on successful convictions, is a familiar figure of American fiction and folklore, and one that perhaps has considerable basis in fact. In criminal cases, the objective ought not to be conviction, but the fairest trial possible. Similarly, for courtroom proceedings generally, surely the major aim should be a full and fair statement of the relevant facts and points of law. No less an authority than the late Justice Frankfurter has complained that the adversary method does not achieve this goal. He went on to add that he believed it fell short of the goal largely because of the very procedural restraints that are imposed in the interests of insuring a "fair fight."[10]

The adversary system need not lead to such consequences, as the example of Great Britain shows. Courtroom temper in England is justly renowned for its moderation and spirit of fairness. Judges do not permit bullying of witnesses and the prosecutor does not harangue the jury and seek to play upon its emotions and prejudices in an effort to win a conviction. Also, the judge will often intervene in the interests of "fairness", much more than in the United States. Still, the point remains that he intervenes to correct some of the normal tendencies of the adversary system.

Another point of frequent criticism of the common-law system is the expense of trial. For one thing, the common-law method of court procedure invites appeal based upon judicial error, not only because it puts a premium upon careful observance of procedure but also because the ways in which a judge can make a mistake of procedure or of law are numerous. At a more immediate level, any system that leaves it to the attorneys to get everything of relevance into the court record invites lengthy trials, high court costs, heavy lawyers' fees, and extensive printing costs for briefs and depositions.

Common-law justice is widely believed to be good, but expensive. Consequently, formal equality before the law may bear heavily upon the economically less well-to-do. In civil matters the poor man may suffer a wrong rather than go to the expense of bringing suit. If so, he has lost his rights. In criminal cases, too, the poor man is at a disadvantage. The best attorney he can afford—or, in cases of indigency, the one who is assigned to him by the court—may not be the equal of the state prosecutor. He is almost certainly not likely to be on a par with the wealthy defendant, be he gangster or corporate executive.

One way, in principle, that this inequality might be redressed is by awarding the winning party his legal costs. Thus, the poor man—so the argument might run—is not out of pocket for good legal talent, assuming he wins. In England, the losing party usually must pay not only court costs but his opponent's legal fees and expenses as well. In a sense, the principle of full costs to the winner seems fair. If the loser didn't have a good case, why didn't he compromise? Yet in practice, the effect of such a rule is to handicap the less affluent plaintiff or defendant even more. In a situation where costs may run £5,000 or more, the game is too dangerous. One might argue that a big club encourages compromise. But compromise is likely to take place on terms favorable to the one who is least frightened by a big club.

---

[10] Dissenting opinion in *Johnson* v. *United States*, 333 U. S. 46, 53-56 (1948). See also, Jerome Frank, *Courts on Trial—Myth and Reality in American Justice* (Princeton, N.J.: Princeton U. P., 1950).

In the United States a common practice is the "contingent fee." A lawyer often will take a case without promise of definite payment and accept instead a percentage of the judgment should he win. Such a practice tends, no doubt, to put the impecunious plaintiff (the poor widow hit by the automobile) on a footing of equality with the wealthy defendant (the insurance company). On the other hand, it does nothing for the impecunious defendant. Also, it leads to universally condemned practices, such as "ambulance chasing" and manufacturing lawsuits where there is a doubtful or weak cause of action. In Great Britain, Canada, Australia and other common law countries besides the United States such a practice is condemned as "unethical" by the organized bar and may be, furthermore, subject to criminal penalties. It tends to promote equality at the expense of the integrity of the judicial system.

Various attempts have been made to reduce legal costs or the unequal incidence of legal costs. In Great Britain, by Act of Parliament,[11] legal aid is provided for all at a cost that matches their means, the difference between this amount and the actual cost being met by the public treasury. Under this act the indigent pay nothing and those of moderate means pay according to their ability. Legislation of this kind is of some help; yet the man of moderate means may well hesitate before getting involved in any process which can cost him the limit of what he is able to pay. In the United States no such general legislation is on the books. However, privately supported Legal Aid Bureaus, private and state Public Defender's Offices, and governmentally sponsored summary procedures and arbitration arrangements have done something to minimize the problem. The latter category of aids, the governmentally sponsored extra-judicial proceedings, are of considerable help, especially to the person with a modest claim who is also neither wealthy nor indigent. In Pennsylvania, particularly, small-claims courts with informal and inexpensive procedures have been used with great success. The fact remains, however, that common-law justice is, by and large, expensive justice for the litigants, and that it frequently bears unequally upon the less wealthy.

CIVIL LAW COURTS

Organization and Operation

The civil-law system of courts, as exemplified by the French prototype, tends to underline the existence of fundamental principles of political organization and procedure shared by civil and common law alike. The judicial systems of a common-law country and those of a code country do exhibit striking differences, but on examination many of them turn out to be more

---

[11] Legal Aid Act of 1949.

formal than substantial. Similar steps are taken to secure judges of competence and integrity and to protect them from improper influence, and most of the elements of fair judicial procedure that are considered fundamental in common law countries are also recognized in the French system, and in other civil law systems.

Code and common-law countries differ notably with respect to the recruitment of judges. In common-law countries, bar and bench are close kinsmen. Judges are appointed, usually, from the rank of practicing lawyers, although an occasional law school professor is appointed to the bench. In the civil-law system, judges are members of the civil service, must enter it at the beginning ranks, and, normally, make a career of it. While the university training for lawyer or judge is virtually the same, before he takes his examinations, the law student must choose which career he wishes to follow. If he enters the civil service, he may become a judge, after a period of apprenticeship to a court, at what would seem to an American a very early age, say twenty-five. From this position he may be transferred to what is known at the *parquet*. Those who work on the "parquet" are the defenders of the interests of the state; they are the public prosecutors. They are subject indirectly to the Minister of Justice and directly to his representative in their district. Members of the *parquets*, in turn, may be transferred to positions in the ministry, or back to the bench, or from positions in the ministry back to the bench, probably at a higher level than the one from which they got their start.

While the judge has life tenure, barring serious misbehavior, the power that has in the past been exercised by the Minister of Justice in making judicial promotions has constituted a source of considerable political influence over the judiciary. This system has occasioned justifiable criticism. Under the French Fourth Republic, a step was taken to give the courts more independence. A Superior Council of the Judiciary, including both judges and lawyers in its makeup, was made responsible for judicial appointments and promotions. The Superior Council remains under the Fifth Republic, but the Minister of Justice is once more the authority primarily responsible for appointment and promotion.

The extent of baleful political influence that is or can be exerted in this way is difficult to estimate. In most civil-law systems, appointments and promotions are made according to a substantially similar pattern. Yet in Switzerland, in the Netherlands, in Austria, to name but a few cases, political influence has been slight—or at least it has not been a subject for frequent complaint as it has been in France. Even in West Germany, despite the past history of Nazism, little political influence is apparent. It is also debatable whether political influence upon the temper of the judiciary has been any less in the United States. All that it seems safe to say is that the ordinary mode of appointment and promotion under the civil-law system presents a greater opportunity for political influence, and has on occasion facilitated invasions of civil liberty, most notably under the Fascist and Nazi regimes.

Another difference between the French and Anglo-American systems is that in the former, as in most civil-law systems, judges never sit singly. In the regular hierarchy of courts, the bench is always composed of at least three judges, a practice generally confined in the common-law system to appellate courts. In this way, of course, less responsibility falls upon any single judge and the risk of arbitrary action is diminished.[12] Probably this difference is properly looked upon as compensating for the fact that juries are used but seldom under the French system. They are not used in civil cases at all and even in criminal cases they are confined to the most serious crimes.[13]

In the actual conduct of judicial proceedings marked differences may be noted between the code and common-law systems. Civil-law procedure is marked by a much more active role of the judge, by a diminished importance of the attorneys, and by considerably less adherence to technicalities. In broad terms, these differences are the expression of a system of procedure that is inquisitorial rather than adversary in character.[14]

One marked feature of the civil-law system is the extensive participation of the judiciary (usually one magistrate) in the pre-trial phases of a judicial controversy. In civil cases a magistrate will at some point bring the parties together for an informal airing of their differences, with an eye not only to framing the issues but also to securing an out-of-court settlement or compromise. Both in civil and in criminal suits a magistrate participates actively in preparing the *dossier* or record upon which the oral hearing will be based.[15] Witnesses will be interviewed, and even confronted with contradictory testimony at this stage. Expert testimony and depositions will be reduced to writing and included in the *dossier*. As one consequence, a good many cases do not come to court. Criminals confess or parties are reconciled when confronted with the evidence the other side has in hand.

Civil law trials also move more rapidly, are less hampered by adherence to technicalities. The fact that much of the material on which the trial is based is already accepted in evidence and does not need subsequently to be

---

[12] According to a French proverb, *Juge unique; juge inique.*

[13] The jury is also employed differently under most civil-law systems from the way in which it is used in common-law countries. A unanimous decision is not required, though the requirement of a special majority is a common practice. Usually judges and "jury" deliberate and decide together, thus extending the magistrate's influence. Also, the jurors act as assessors as well, participating not only in the determination of guilt or innocence, but in the determination of an appropriate sentence. In the common-law system, the jury has no control—in principle—over sentencing. Cf. Raymond Charles, *La Justice en France* (Paris: Presses Universitaires de France, 1958), p. 104.

[14] The term, "inquisitorial," is not used with pejorative meaning or connotation. It indicates only that the court and judicial administration are thought of as active participants in the discovery process and in the trial.

[15] Charles, *op. cit.*, pp. 62-63.

Civil law pleading —a caricature

introduced by direct testimony helps in this respect, as does the slight use of cross-examination in civil-law courts. Also, the fact that juries play a less significant role in civil-law trials diminishes the need for technical rules of evidence. The court is seeking largely to convince itself, and gets quickly and expeditiously to the main issues.

Justices also actively direct the procedure and the line of questioning in the courtroom hearing itself. Instead of assuming the role of umpire, the judges question defendant, plaintiff, and witnesses at length—in keeping with their inquisitorial role. Procedure can be relatively informal and flexible, especially because technical rules of evidence have less significance.[16] Much of the business of the court is in fact done by consultation between the judges and the lawyers. As a consequence, civil-law trials usually seem tame and prosaic in comparison with the more spectacular and dramatic adversary system. On the other hand, the civil-law trial moves more rapidly and offers less hope of winning through a technicality or mere strategic or forensic advantage.[17]

[16] Hearsay, gossip, and conjecture will, for example, be weighed in evidence in a civil-law trial. This fact often shocks the person accustomed to common-law methods. But the primary reason for excluding such evidence in the common-law courts is because of a belief that they will have too great an effect upon the jury. Where the judges have a more active role in assessing the value of evidence, protections such as the "hearsay rule" lose much of their significance.

[17] Cf. Raymond, *op. cit.*, pp. 74 ff.

Appeals are a less lengthy and cumbersome process under the code law system. Reversible error is less common. Also, judges have less opportunity to make new law or revise the old law upon appeal. At the same time, because no particular sanctity is attributed to oral testimony in the court of first instance, it is an easy matter on appeal to send up the whole record and have a hearing *de novo* on both the facts and the law. Rarely will an appeal be taken beyond one step, since one stage of review gives the appellant all he is likely to get.

Another highly distinctive characteristic of the civil-law system is the role of the judge in relation to the law itself. He is in principle not a creator, but in Montesquieu's language, a "passive mouthpiece of the law." Past decisions are not considered binding precedents,[18] and the judge does not—except in rare circumstances—think of himself as developing new concepts in the law or interpreting statutes in the light of what is reasonable.[19] The authoritative sources of law are the code and statute law amending and supplementing the code. Usages, texts, canons of interpretation, the writings of especially learned judges or professors of law are also influential, but they do not have the force of law, however well entrenched they may be.[20]

It is well not to overemphasize differences, for many of the same basic jobs get done under most judicial systems even though the forms in which activities are carried on differ. In practice, the code is too concise and abstract to guide the courts without some established usages and authoritative sources to supplement judicial reasoning. To a considerable extent, civil-law magistrates rely upon the opinion of their learned brethren in other courts and in the law schools, just as judges do in common-law countries. On the other hand, the differences are real and important. Judicial reasoning starts from the code. Great cases or texts may be cited, but they cannot serve as the basis for decision. Judges, consequently, do not write lengthy and closely reasoned opinions. Lawyers do not study the opinions. No great body of law reports (or complicated system of reporting) summarizes generations of legal experience and wisdom and lays down authoritative guides for the courts. Even the highest courts do not ordinarily state the law when they reverse an appeal, but send the case back for rehearing.

The authoritative role of the code makes the staffing of courts and the recruitment of competent judicial personnel much easier. The future judge, whether of the regular court hierarchy or of one of the specialized tribunals that may handle labor relations, commercial disputes, or family problems,[21]

[18] Administrative courts in France and elsewhere usually do follow precedent.

[19] This is not to say that jurists (the judges, lawyers, and law professors) will not have an important role in amending the code and even in providing authoritative commentary on the code.

[20] A good commentary on sources that influence judicial interpretation under the code is René David and Henry P. de Vries, *The French Legal System, An Introduction to Civil Law Systems* (New York: Oceana, 1958), esp. Pt. II.

[21] Special tribunals supplementing the ordinary court system are the rule in code law countries. In France, beside the administrative courts, specialized courts deal with social

does not need to be learned in the law to the extent that his common-law counterpart must be. Consequently, courts are well staffed, dockets are kept relatively up to date, and judicial proceedings are not ordinarily as lengthy as in common-law countries.

The code is important also because it both frees and constrains the judge. It frees him in the sense that he can often seek to do substantial justice in a particular case without worrying about the wider consequences of a precedent that might unsettle a good many legal relations. He can, for example, award the widows and orphans their due in a close or doubtful case without fear that tomorrow the unscrupulous will profit from such a precedent. Yet the code also constrains the judiciary. They are not sources of law, but only its ministers. They are not, consequently, tempted either to write into the law their own revelations or their own prejudices. There are few "great judges" in the civil law tradition. Judges assume, on the whole, probably a humbler, more practical, and perhaps even more facilitative and helpful role in judicial proceedings than their Common law counterparts.

Evaluation

Any evaluation of the civil-law system, especially an evaluation of this system relative to common-law institutions must begin by acknowledging that few sweeping generalizations can be made. Most differences in the actual performance of the two systems are marginal and so closely related to an offsetting benefit or deficiency that a comparative evaluation is likely to seem an exercise in nit-picking. We cited, for instance, the costs and delay of common-law justice. Attorneys and clients under civil-law jurisdictions complain of costs and delay also, and of the additional hazard of multiple parallel hierarchies of courts. We spoke of the way in which the adversary system encourages irrational appeals to the jury. Attorneys under code law complain of the prejudices of judges and they shape their arguments consciously to meet those prejudices. Precedent or the rule of *stare decisis* in common-law jurisprudence may seem to put an excessive emphasis upon judicial conservatism. Its complementary feature—freedom from the bounds of a rigid code—is seen by some European jurists as an enviable feature of

---

security, farm contracts, children, and commercial and industrial disputes. In Germany, special courts include: administrative, social security, labor, and tax courts. These specialized courts are, of course, in addition to such tribunals as courts-martial, juvenile courts, and divorce courts provided in most modern countries. Because the training of judicial personnel is relatively easy in civil-law countries, such specialized courts can be staffed both with laymen and with trained magistrates, making it possible to afford a wide array of judicial services. On the other hand, deciding which of four or five courts will have jurisdiction over a dispute often creates delay and needless litigation. Cf. Arthur T. von Mehren, *The Civil Law System* (Boston: Little, Brown, 1957), esp. Ch. 3.

the common-law system, because of the opportunity it provides for growth of the law through judicial innovation.[22]

The assimilation of the judiciary to the regular administration is a striking feature of civil-law systems. Yet even in this instance, constitutional temper seems to matter more than governmental form. Political influence over the judiciary has been the subject of comparatively frequent complaint in France; but it has been remarkably rare in other code law countries where constitutional traditions are strong. The separation of administrative law from ordinary civil law is also a notable feature of code law jurisdictions. It flies in the face of Anglo-American assumptions about the rule of law. Yet the jealousy with which administrative courts have guarded the citizen's liberties is a point of considerable pride in code countries. The differences between this system and the common-law principle of the jurisdiction of the regular courts over administrative acts are more a question of *how* and at what personal expense the citizen can vindicate his rights than one of *what* substantive guarantees he will get.[23]

It is frequently charged that civil-law systems afford few procedural protections for the person accused of crime. Neither grand jury nor writ of habeas corpus is provided. Police question friends and neighbors in compiling the *dossier* while the accused is held in detention. Testimony may be compelled and hearsay evidence received. All kinds of rumor, information about previous conduct, and the like, are brought out and submitted as evidence, for whatever they may be worth. During preliminary inquiry and the trial itself, moreover, the magistracy acts as inquisitor and not as umpire. Finally, the jury together with the magistracy often render their decision by majority vote.

Probably it is fair to say that code law jurisprudence shows less solicitude for the rights of the accused and more concern with the protection of public order and the state. The celebrated common-law tradition is "let ten guilty men go free rather than hang one innocent man." The contrast, however, is not so great as it seems. Under the civil-law system more care is devoted to pre-trial investigation with less attention to procedural protections at a later stage. The accused in France—to take the example most frequently deplored—is not entitled to habeas corpus. On the other hand, he may not, according to legal tradition, be detained for more than twenty-four hours[24] without being presented to an examining magistrate. He is

---

[22] The extent of this opportunity depends on how strictly or liberally the judges interpret the rule of *stare decisis*. In England, the practice is to follow a strict interpretation, but in the United States the practice is liberal—some would say "cavalier."

[23] It is perhaps also worth adding that legal protection of the British citizen from arbitrary administrative action is not nearly so efficacious as that afforded by the administrative courts in France or Germany. In this respect the American system of Constitutional rights—especially the "due process of law" clause gives the citizen much better protection than is available in Britain.

[24] A practice that has been widely violated on occasions of crisis or widespread disorder, such as riot or threat of insurrection.

questioned by the authorities with counsel and a judge present. At this preliminary stage a group of at least five judges must be convinced of the probable guilt of the accused or he will not be brought to trial.

The high level of British criminal procedure can be contrasted favorably with France where, on occasions of public crisis or threatened subversion, there has been wholesale violation of civil liberties and the rights of accused persons. On the other hand, the treatment of the accused in West Germany and in several other code law countries is comparable to that of Britain. It is also a nice question whether the United States with its traditional common-law protections for the accused actually protects the innocent man better or even as well as France.

Looking at civil as opposed to criminal suits code law possesses certain distinct advantages especially from the perspective of the litigants. Civil law is less expensive. Not only is the controlling law for most situations more easily discoverable, which reduces lawyer's fees, but court dockets are less crowded, trials briefer, and appeals less expensive. The active role of the magistrate in the pretrial phase of litigation also results in a good many controversies being settled out of court.[25] From the client's perspective, the inquisitorial method has other advantages. The *dossier* or record is in large measure assembled under the supervision of a magistrate. As compared to common-law procedure, it requires less independent search and discovery and less lengthy courtroom testimony, both of which are expensive. In addition, there is only one *dossier,* a practice that reduces stenographic and printing costs. Even on appeal, costs for additional filing and for briefs or printing are minimal.

The merits of the common-law system, by contrast, lie less in the handling of an immediate controversy than in its capacity for sustained legal development. This capacity is largely lacking in the civil-law system. In the treatment of such matters as personal injury, fraud, or overreaching in contractual agreements, civil-law justices develop doctrine and habits of interpretation that enable them to respond to objective needs and to community sentiments of right about as well as their common law brethren. Where, however, a sustained and cumulative evolution of legal doctrine and concept is needed, the code law system has lagged. The most distinctive and the most important area of lag has been industrial and economic relations. In the common-law, concepts such as conspiracy or unfair competition in trade relations or employer's liability for workmen's injuries in industry have had a long history of steady development. This evolution of concept

[25] Pretrial conference is by no means peculiar to the civil-law system. In fact, in some situations under the common law it is universally required whatever the jurisdiction, for instance, in divorce cases. Under the Federal Rules of Civil Procedure a pretrial conference is mandatory in the United States federal courts. Two points are important, however. First, the pretrial conference is far from a universal practice. Second, it may emphasize mainly, and even solely, not compromise but only the formulation of claims and answers to insure a square joining of issues.

and doctrine has aided materially in legislation and in the administration of regulatory and welfare programs. How much benefit this kind of legal evolution may be to the parties in any given suit would be difficult if not impossible to assess. On the other hand, quite apart from its utility for particular cases, the case law of common-law countries is itself a political resource of considerable value, and one that has no equivalent in code law systems.[26]

Code law countries have their own jurisprudence of regulation. Much of it, however, is developed in special courts and does not importantly affect nor is it affected by the ordinary civil law. In our contemporary world of complex interdependence, society suffers some loss by not having legal techniques to insure sustained and systematic growth in the private law as a whole. It is also an interesting commentary on the history of the common law that it should be regarded now as useful for the regulation of industry and the economy, for so often in the past the common law has been condemned especially for being excessively static and individualistic. It has been able to reflect the prevailing temper of the times. The common law contributes both a precision and a capacity for flexibility and development that is valuable in the welfare states of today. The code law tradition of sharp separation of administrative and regulatory jurisprudence from the ordinary civil law, with the objective of insuring the independence of the administration, has had another, less happy result: these polities have been impoverished to the extent of lacking in considerable measure an additional and valuable source of creative innovation.

JUDICIAL REVIEW

Definition

Up to this point, we have discussed the judiciary without any reference to the power of judicial review, as it is exercised in certain countries, and notably in the United States. By this phrase we refer to the power of the courts to interpret the Constitution and to declare acts of the legislature, executive, or administration void, if it finds them in conflict with the supreme law. We have noted previously that courts—either regular or special—normally review the acts of administrative officials with respect to their legality. Where judicial review, as we are using that term, is practiced, however, the acts of administrators are checked not only by reference to ordinary law but also by reference to the Constitution. By far the most striking application of the institution, however, is where courts pass on the

---

[26] Cf. Wolfgang Friedman, *Law and Social Change in Contemporary Britain* (London: Stevens, 1951), pp. 12-13; also von Mehren, *op. cit.*, p. 846.

validity of acts of the legislature.[27] When the British Parliament enacts a law, that is the final word. Courts interpret and apply it in contested cases, to be sure, but the idea that they could declare it void is completely foreign to the modern theory of the British Constitution. In the United States, on the other hand, a whole statutory scheme for the regulation of business may be declared null and void by the Supreme Court if it finds it to be in conflict with some provision of the Constitution, or beyond the powers granted to Congress, as happened, for example, in the case of the NRA, a major part of the National Industrial Recovery Act, in the early days of the New Deal.

Origin in the United States

Although judicial review is not necessarily associated with the separation of powers, it is a not unnatural corollary of that doctrine. It is part and parcel of the same constitutional style. That style includes both the idea that the powers of government ought to be limited and the notion that an effective way of limiting them is to give each independent "power" or branch of the government the ability to check or veto acts of the others.

Just as the doctrine of the separation of powers came to America from England fully as much as it did from Montesquieu, so also the notion of judicial review itself can be traced to an English origin.[28] The idea that the law, at least "fundamental law", was above the king goes back to medieval days, to the distinction between *gubernaculum* and *jurisdictio*. At a much later date, during the struggle with James I, in the early seventeenth century, the courts, especially in the person of the Chief Justice, Sir Edward Coke, sought to assert the doctrine that they had the right to interpret this fundamental law and to apply it even against acts of Parliament. However, the struggle with the crown led to the assertion of the supremacy of Parliament, and the doctrine of judicial review was stillborn.

The Constitution of the United States made no direct provision for judicial review. At most it was provided for by implication, and that is open to argument. What the Framers intended, and even more what those who ratified it intended, has been the subject of much study and considerable difference of opinion. Probably most of those who considered the question, like Alexander Hamilton, who made a forceful argument to this effect in the *Federalist Papers* (No. 78), believed that judicial review was provided for by implication. But probably a majority of the two groups in question

[27] The power of the Chief Executive himself, although it has seldom been judicially contested, is subject to the same check, as was illustrated in a case arising out of President Truman's seizure of the steel mills in 1952. *Youngstown Sheet & Tube Company* v. *Sawyer*, 343 U. S. 579 (1952).

[28] See Benjamin F. Wright, Jr., "The Origins of the Separation of Powers in America," *Economica*, 19 (1933), pp. 169-185; and Francis D. Wormuth, *The Origins of Modern Constitutionalism* (New York: Harper & Row, 1949).

(Framers and ratifiers) had no intention one way or the other, because they had not considered the matter.

Not until 1803, in the famous case of *Marbury v. Madison*,[29] did the Supreme Court find occasion to declare an act of Congress unconstitutional, and, in doing so, to vindicate its authority to take such a step. Speaking for a unanimous Court, the great Chief Justice, John Marshall, decided that in fact the federal judiciary did possess this power. Marshall's reasoning relied heavily on the general idea that ours was a government of limited powers and that the very purpose of a written Constitution was to provide a foundation for the limitations. Moreover, he pointed out, one of the clauses of the Constitution itself states that it shall be the supreme "law" of the land. Surely it is part of the idea of having a written Constitution that it should prevail over ordinary law, where the two conflict. And if it is a question of interpreting the statute and the Constitution, to determine whether or not they conflict, surely it is the function of courts to interpret law; and the Constitution says that it *is* law, and the *supreme* law.

Mode of Operation and its Significance

The fact that judicial review in the United States rests upon the normal role of courts in the performance of judicial functions accounts for some of its important characteristics. Since the right of the courts to declare acts of Congress void arises as an incident to their performance of their regular functions of adjudication, it follows that they possess no general revisory powers. The courts can not take the initiative in reviewing acts of Congress. Nor can they give Congress or the executive advisory opinions as to the validity of actual or proposed legislation. To them is committed only "judicial power" (Art. III), and that means power to settle "cases or controversies" between parties "at adverse interest." When it is essential to the proper decision of a case to pass an act of Congress, then and only then will the courts do so.

Certain consequences of the Court's self-imposed limitations are highly significant. For instance, the fact that it acts only where there are opposing parties, each with his own interest at stake, assures that counsel will make every effort to inform the court of all the relevant facts, arguments, and precedents. The court need not rely upon its own knowledge and research as to the law; the competition of counsel, especially in cases involving important constitutional issues, tends to insure that neither precedent nor argument is overlooked. The fact that decisions are made only after a controversy has arisen ordinarily assures that the act in question has actually been put into effect or at least is on the point of being put into effect in a concrete situation, so that it is possible to make a sound judgment of the

[29] 1 Cranch 137 (1803).

consequences of its application. Although strict legal theory might seem to call for settling questions of constitutionality without reference to consequences, it is characteristic of the empiricism of the common law to avoid abstract judgments. Also, from the point of view of simple self-protection, the courts have been wise to confine their acts of judicial invalidation to the circumstances described. Judicial vetoes are bound to be unpopular with the legislature and perhaps also with the executive. In refusing to take action except where they could argue that it was absolutely necessary to do so in order to protect private rights, they keep the exercise of the judicial veto at a minimum and make it strategically difficult to attack this role of the courts.

Before we comment on the way judicial review has operated in the United States, we should point out that passing upon the validity of acts of Congress or the executive is only part of that institution as it operates here. In the United States, as is normally the practice in federal states, the tasks of delimiting the boundaries between central and local (state) governments falls to the courts, as does the enforcement of limitations imposed on the states by the federal Constitution.

Experience with Judicial Review in the United States— Summary and Evaluation

What have been the consequences of judicial review in the United States? Interestingly enough, the extent of its application to the federal government, which is the most controversial question, has been surprisingly limited. After the decision in *Marbury v. Madison* (which itself invalidated a minor provision of the law setting up the federal courts and establishing their jurisdiction), no further act of Congress was declared unconstitutional for over fifty years. In the decades that followed somewhat more frequent exercises of this type of judicial veto occurred, but the total number is still under 100, and of these the great majority are of relatively minor significance. The great cases can be counted on the fingers of one's two hands. With one or two exceptions, even these decisions were all in the course of time—sometimes as much as twenty years—reversed either by the Supreme Court, constitutional amendment, or the discovery, by Congress, of another, constitutional, way to accomplish the same purpose.[30]

[30] *The Dred Scott Case (Dred Scott v. Sanford*, 1857, 9 How. 393), although it had great political significance in the struggle over slavery, had no Constitutional importance apart from that—and the subject it dealt with—the basis of federal citizenship—was completely overhauled by the adoption of the Fourteenth Amendment, following the Civil War. In 1895, the Supreme Court declared a graduated federal income tax law unconstitutional. (*Pollock v. Farmers I. & T. Co.*, 1895, 157 U.S. 429). The decision divided the Court and the country sharply. It was revised by constitutional amendment in 1913. In 1918 and 1922 the Court struck down two attempts by Congress to regulate the use of child labor, (*Hammer v. Dagenhart*, 1918, 247 U.S. 251 and *Bailey v. Drexel Furniture Co.*, 1922, 259

No major act of Congress has been invalidated since the middle thirties. In 1952, however, President Truman's seizure of the steel mills, in order to prevent a strike, was held by the Supreme Court to be without statutory or Constitutional authority, and therefore void and without effect.[31]

How this record should be appraised depends, in part, upon one's judgment of the acts in question. For our purposes, the cases of the graduated income tax and of child labor legislation are the most significant. In each instance the effect of judicial review was to delay an advancing trend for nearly a generation. The question posed is whether this delaying action constituted an unjustifiable brake on progress and an improper interference with majority rule or whether, on matters of such importance, about which the country was so sharply divided, it was desirable that change should be delayed until the area of popular support had been widened and consolidated.

On at least two occasions, the Supreme Court has enforced important limitations on the powers of the President. In the case of *Ex parte Milligan,* arising out of the Civil War, it was held that his powers as Commander-in-Chief did not permit him to dispense with the Constitutional protection of jury trial in the case of a civilian arrested in territory outside of the fighting theater.[32] The decision has generally been considered one of the landmarks of our Constitutional system. Quite recently, in a decision already twice referred to, the President's peacetime powers as Chief Executive were held not to extend, at least under the particular circumstances of the case in hand, to seizure of the country's steel mills for the purpose of avoiding a strike that threatened defense production.[33] Like the members of the Court itself (the decision was by vote of six to three), commentators have been

---

U.S. 20.) Slightly over twenty years later, however, the Supreme Court reversed the position it had taken in the Dagenhart case and upheld an act of Congress regulating the use of child labor on goods to be handled in interstate commerce. (*United States* v. *Darby Lumber Co.,* 1941, 312 U.S. 100.) The early legislation of the New Deal ran sharply afoul of the Court. The NIRA, the first Agricultural Adjustment Act, a Railroad Pensions Act, and an act providing for a moratorium on farm mortgages were all declared unconstitutional between 1933 and 1936. (*Schechter Poultry Corp.* v. *United States,* 1935, 295 U.S. 495; *United States* v. *Butler,* 1936, 297 U.S. 1; *Railroad Retirement Bd.* v. *Alton R. Co.,* 1936, 295 U.S. 330 (1935); and *Louisville Jt. Stock Land Bank* v. *Radford,* 1936, 295 U.S. 555 (1935) .) In all cases except that of the NIRA Congress promptly modified the original acts in such ways as to come within its powers as interpreted by the Court, while accomplishing the same purposes. (In the case of the mortgage moratorium the revised act was considerably less unfavorable to mortgage holders.) In the case of the NIRA, Congress made no attempt to re-establish the regulatory scheme, for it had become widely discredited by the time it was invalidated. For an account of the history of judicial review in the United States from the point of view of its relation to public opinion, see Dean Alfange, *The Supreme Court and the National Will* (Garden City, N.Y.: Doubleday, 1937). See also Sidney Ulmer, "Judicial Review as Political Behavior: a Temporary Check on Congress," *Administrative Science Quarterly,* 4 (1960), pp. 426-445.

[31] *Youngstown Sheet & Tube Co.* v. *Sawyer,* 1952, 341 U.S. 579.
[32] *Ex parte Milligan,* 1866, 4 Wall. 2.
[33] *Youngstown Sheet & Tube Co.* v. *Sawyer, ibid.*

divided in their appraisal of this judgment. Some hold this "interference" with the power of the Chief Executive in a period of quasi-war anachronistic and dangerous. Others, even among those who supported President Truman's purposes, believe the effect of this decision may someday stand the country in good stead, should a less scrupulously democratic President attain to office.

Although judicial review of acts of the Chief Executive is rare, the courts have frequent occasion to review the acts of administrative officials. This subject has been treated in the chapter on administration, so it will not be treated here. We would be remiss, however, if we did not remind the reader that judicial review of administration is an important aspect of judicial review generally. In the United States, it not only is used to see that administrators stay within their statutory authority, but also to see that they observe the substantive and procedural requirements of the Constitution.

It should also be noted that judicial review in the United States permeates every level of government. Not only does the United States Supreme Court enforce the federal Constitution against the states and local governments, as well as against federal authorities, but also the state and local courts themselves exercise judicial review in the same manner, enforcing, *inter alia*, the restraints of state constitutions. In this way the atmosphere of Constitutionalism—and some would add "excessive legalism"—pervades the entire polity.

However, one may weigh the balance—and the authors feel that the positive values tip the scales—as far as concerns the record to date, it would be easy to exaggerate the influence of judicial review either for good or for ill. When we turn to the record of the court in dealing with the states, the situation is rather different. Here it has had a great deal more to do. It has preserved a balance—though a moving balance—between the powers of the states and of the federal government. It has played an important role in checking state legislation that tended to hamper and restrict the free flow of trade among the states. Above all, on the positive side, it has invalidated a sizable number of state laws and administrative practices that placed limits upon essential freedoms of speech, press, and religion. Nor would a count of such decisions be any measure of their effect. States that had to be prevented by the federal courts from imposing one type of limitation upon essential freedoms might have been inclined to go still further had it not been made evident that they could not get away with it. And other states might have followed suit. Likewise the courts, especially the Supreme Court, has played a major role in recent years in securing equal civil rights for the Negro, whether it be a matter of voting, of securing an education on equal terms with whites, or of being permitted to buy land in spite of restrictive covenants.

On the other side of the ledger, the courts have taken advantage of the vague Constitutional provisions to invalidate much regulatory and social welfare legislation that was not in accord with a majority of the justices' views as to public policy. Especially in the case of vague clauses like that which declares that no state shall deprive any person of his life, liberty, or property without due process of law, judicial review allows ample opportunity for the personal or class bias of judges to influence their judgment. The history of the past seventy-five years or more has been one of gradually advancing ideas of the role of the state in protecting and advancing social welfare even when to do so required modification of existing property rights. Doubtless partly because the training of lawyers in the common law tradition imparts an individualistic and conservative bias, and partly because most Supreme Court justices either came from the propertied classes or had spent much of their time as practicing lawyers defending members of these classes, or both, the justices lagged considerably behind legislators in accommodating themselves to the trend of opinion. The result has been to slow up, but only to slow up, the advance of the kinds of legislation in question in the states. Perhaps the delay, awaiting a consolidation of public opinion, was desirable. Even if it was not, many believe that the positive counts previously discussed outweigh the negative items, a view that the authors are inclined to share.

Before a final evaluation is made, however, another aspect of judicial review requires consideration. We have said that courts inevitably legislate. It follows of course that where they have power to pass on questions of constitutionality they make constitutional law as well as ordinary law. Apart from the kind of judicial lawmaking we referred to above as "intersticial," what are the circumstances under which courts have any special competence for this kind of legislating? We suggest that they have a special competence in situations where change has to be brought about gradually, even incrementally; or where at least the way has to be gradually prepared for a substantial change. These circumstances are likely to prevail where the limits of legislation are set by the prevailing standards of justice, and where the law can move only slowly, sometimes following and sometimes leading but never departing widely from the dominant ethical pattern. The story of the move from the "separate-but-equal" interpretation of the "Equal Protections Clause" through numerous intermediary steps to the final complete reversal of that interpretation in the School Desegregation decision in 1954 is only the most recent and striking example of this process.[34] The history of the concept of freedom of contract in American Constitutional law is equally pertinent.[35] In the first instance, the courts gradually broad-

---

[34] The cases specifically referred to are *Plessy v. Ferguson*, 1896, 163 U.S. 537 and *Brown v. Board of Education of Topeka*, 1954, 347 U.S. 483. For the whole course of development referred to see, Robert J. Harris, *The Quest for Equality; the Congress, the Constitution, and the Supreme Court*. (Baton Rouge: Louisiana State U. P., 1960).

[35] See Walton H. Hamilton, "The Path of Due Process," *Ethics*, 48 (1938), pp. 269-296.

ened their concept of what is relevant to the notion of equality embodied in that clause of the Fourteenth Amendment that says "No state shall deny any person the equal protection of the laws." In its successive interpretations, they took into account ever-expanding circles of interests. In the case of liberty of contract, another clause of the same amendment was in question: that which says "No state shall deprive any person of his life, liberty, or property without due process of law." Specifically, the question was what is "liberty"? In the latter part of the nineteenth century it seemed clear to the courts, as it seemed clear to many if not most Americans, that this "liberty" included the freedom of workers to make such contracts with employers as they might mutually agree to. But over the years the idea gained support that, under many circumstances, enforcement of this liberty, while it protected formal freedom, actually protected the freedom of the employer to exploit the weak bargaining position of employees. Bit-by-bit, the Supreme Court recognized the legitimacy of this argument and permitted legislative infringements on freedom of contract that it had previously banned. The second example is not completely parallel to the first, for in it the court did not take the initiative; it merely validated action taken by state legislatures—action of a kind that an earlier Court had invalidated. But in doing so it gave legitimacy to a step that had been bitterly contested. The move from a laissez-faire philosophy to that of the positive welfare state, of which this line of development was a part, was difficult. It aroused deep feelings on both sides. It called for a shift of values and new and sharpened perceptions of the practical operation both of the laws and of the market place. In facilitating this kind of transformation in the large and pluralistic American society, the Supreme Court plays a vital role.[36]

Adoption of Judicial Review Abroad

While judicial review is often thought of as a distinctively American institution and in fact for a long time was peculiar to the United States' Constitution, it has today been widely adopted throughout the world. Among constitutions adopted during the present century, except for those that have followed the Soviet pattern, most have followed the American tradition. The Marshallian theory that judicial review is called for by the logic inherent in the idea of a written constitution has generally prevailed. Among European nations with new constitutions, France remains true to her original position, which was that a written constitution need not embody

[36] See Robert A. Dahl, "Decision-Making in a Democracy: the Supreme Court as a National Policy-Maker," *Journal of Public Law*, 6 (1957), pp. 279-295.

More generally, by way of evaluation of judicial review in the United States, see Eugene V. Rostow, "The Democratic Character of Judicial Review," *Harvard Law Review*, 66 (1952), pp. 193 ff. Charles L. Black, *The People and the Court, Judicial Review in a Democracy* (New York: Macmillan, 1960).

judicial review.[37] Italy, however, has adopted the institution of judicial review, joining Switzerland, Austria, Ireland, and the West German Republic. Judicial review is also practiced in Australia and Canada and is provided for in the new constitutions of Japan and of India. The overwhelming majority of Latin American states have followed the American example.

An evaluation of the operation of the institution of judicial review among the new postwar governments cannot be definitive since legal evolution is a slow process and even a generation of experience may not tell very much. (Several important observations can be made, however.) Usually, powers of judicial review are committed to special "constitutional" courts (rather than to the regular courts, as in the United States) and exercised in proceedings brought for the sole purpose of testing constitutionality in the abstract. This practice exposes the constitutional courts to greater political pressure than the more indirect American system where rulings on constitutionality are made in the course of ordinary judicial proceedings arising out of the adjudication of private rights. The jurisdiction of the new constitutional courts tends to be restricted to passing on the powers of "organs" and territorial subdivisions of government, the federal system, and some issues of civil liberties. On the other hand, a provision for advisory opinions, which are banned under the American system, is the general rule. Also these courts possess powers unknown to the American practice of judicial review. In Germany, for instance, the constitutional court can outlaw political parties as undemocratic. It has proscribed the Communist Party and one of the neo-Nazi parties.[38] In several countries, important governmental officials can be impeached in a constitutional court. Although these new guardians of constitutionalism are exposed to political attack, without some of the resources for building support enjoyed by the American Supreme Court, they have been generally well received and, after beginning periods of cautious experimentalism, have tended to expand their jurisdiction to include some categories of review familiar to Americans, such as equality before the law, delegation of legislative power, vague legislation, and arbitrary deprivation of property. To this extent, the results have been heartening. In no case, however, have any of these new judicial bodies faced a major constitutional crisis.

THE JUDICIAL PROCESS

Broadly speaking, views on the nature of the judicial process can be classified with reference to two polar extremes. On the one hand, there are the "conceptualists," in earlier generations sometimes referred to as the mechanical school of jurisprudence. According to theorists of this persua-

---

[37] In France there is a constitutional council which reviews legislation and decrees. It has, however, only a weak suspensive veto over new proposals.

[38] The German *Reichspartei*.

sion, the judge is a scientific expounder of the law. He finds and declares the law, but does not create or mould it. Where statutes, constitutions, or precedents are unequivocal, he merely applies the law as he finds it. Where interpretation is called for, he examines the cases to discover the governing rules and principles, and then, by rigorous processes of judicial logic, deduces the proper meaning. At the opposite extreme are "realists" and "functionalists," often spoken of as the same school of thought. The realists contend that judicial opinions are simply rationalizations; that judges decide what results they wish to achieve and then devise arguments in support of them. Contemporary functionalists accept this argument in large part, but they emphasize another point of disagreement with the conceptualist. The functionalist is concerned about the ends of the law, particularly, and argues that its purpose or purposes should be to accommodate interests and to recognize new "social interests" or "social facts." From his point of view, the conceptualist attributes to legal concepts a reality they do not possess (he "reifies" them); he misunderstands the nature and function of legal reasoning (assuming it is logical and that it determines the judges' conclusions); and he applies legal concepts and rules too rigidly in the face of new social realities pressing for recognition.

Much can be said in support of the realist point of view. The logic of judicial opinions, like all logic, must rest on certain premises. But the body of the law is filled with premises that may lead to opposing results. Sometimes it is fairly clear what premise should apply to a given situation. At other times, no one premise obviously commends itself. Holmes had this situation in mind when he said that "general propositions do not decide concrete cases." The critical step of choosing the premise cannot be a mechanical or purely deductive kind of activity.

An example may be helpful. The Constitution gives Congress the power to regulate and to promote commerce among the states. Does this power include the power to prohibit discrimination because of race or color in the hiring and firing of employees engaged in production for interstate commerce? If you begin with the premise that Federal power over commerce includes, by virtue of the "necessary and proper" clause, the power to take all steps that help to carry out that power and make it effective, an affirmative answer to the question can be readily supported. On the other hand, a court could begin with the equally valid premises that the Constitution should be interpreted in accordance with its essential purposes and that among these was the maintenance of a balance of powers between the federal government and the states. The minor premise is: federal prohibition of job discrimination leads logically to the destruction of this balance. Therefore, the conclusion follows, to protect the sovereignty of the states, the question must be answered negatively. Both arguments follow from their premises, and both sets of premises are sound for certain purposes. Choosing the premise is an art, not a matter of pure logic.

The selection of premises apart, concepts like "commerce," provide further problems. Their boundaries and content are not obvious or self-evident, as the functionalists especially have argued. Another example will carry the argument a step farther. A group of newsboys, working for a large metropolitan daily, organize and seek recognition from their employer and certification as a collective bargaining unit by the National Labor Relations Board. Turned down by both employer and Board, they appeal to the courts. The court says: "Though this is an unusual case, not contemplated under the Act, it is perfectly clear to us that newsboys are independent contractors —they are self-employed—and therefore do not fall within the meaning of the 'employees' protected by the Act. Petition denied."

In this case the problem is one of definition: the meaning of the word "employees." It must be interpreted in the light of the "social facts" and "social interests" relevant to the purpose of the Act, as well as in the light of previous interpretations of the term. How then does the judge decide whether newsboys—a case not anticipated by the legislator nor obviously covered in previous acts—are "employees" within the meaning of the law? The judge could argue by analogy. "It seems to me that a newsboy is like a Fuller Brush salesman, who has been held to be an independent contractor, not an employee." In *what* respect, however, are they alike? They both buy their merchandise and retail it. On the other hand, this particular newsboy has definite and compulsory working hours, as an employee does. The argument from analogy depends upon which aspects of the situation are regarded as relevant. In marginal cases, often no analogy is obviously right.

In the case in question, the judge might ask further whether in the custom of the trade, newsboys are treated as employees.[39] He might gather from the broad purpose of the act an intention to extend protection to people who are situated in a particular kind of bargaining relation. Again one judge, in the interest of certainty, might insist that the common law provides the definitive test—the existence or absence of a master and servant relation. Another, more functionally minded judge might feel that the interest of society in helping the presumably underprivileged newsboys should be the governing consideration. In any event the judge must choose and find his way by a process of reasoning, conceptualization, and weighing of interests that has many and often conflicting guiding principles but few absolute imperatives.

With much of this analysis the conceptualist will agree. At two points, however, he may differ in a way that will be determinative. He places a high value on certainty. He believes it is important that businessmen should be able to contract and invest with a maximum of certainty as to how the law

---

[39] If he uses the "business custom" argument, he must also decide at what point a practice becomes the custom of the trade or industry. Does he decide that it is the custom because the trend has been moving toward the adoption of this practice? because 51 per cent follow it? because the dominant firms do?

will treat their actions. By the same token he holds that lawyers should be in a position to advise their clients with precision. Accordingly, he places a high value upon *stare decisis* and upon concepts that can be clearly defined. The concept of the master-servant relation has a long history in the law and has achieved considerable precision. In our example, the conceptualist would lean strongly toward using this concept and the rule of *stare decisis* to settle the matter without further ado. Conversely, he would feel that to take into account the interest of the newsboys would be to trench on the territory of the legislature and to set the judge afloat on a sea of uncertainty, and subject to the winds of politics.

The modern conceptualist, or neo-conceptualist, freely admits that the value of certainty can be exaggerated and that courts must contribute to the growth of the law. But he does wish to impose limits on a vagrant functionalism and to make use of the techniques of judicial craftsmanship to this end. Let us take another hypothetical case.

John Doe alleges that he was discriminated against for union activity when he was discharged by the ABC corporation. The National Labor Relations Board agrees, finding that when Doe was discharged anti-union sentiment was rampant among foremen and that various foremen said they were out to "get" Doe. Can the court then say: "The N.L.R.B. said so and that is good enough for us. After all, glancing at the 'social facts' in this situation we can see that important 'social interests' are pressing for recognition." "No," replies our neo-conceptualist, "the court must ask for a clear demonstration of cause and effect, of substantial discrimination as understood by law, and of calculated plan and exerted influence by the employer or people acting as his agents. The judge must accept the discipline of finding his conclusion fairly within the existing premises of the law and of formulating an opinion that is a fair deduction according to the canons of the judicial craft. It is further his business, when acting upon an appeal, not to let anything get by him that will not meet these tests."

The last statement by our hypothetical neoconceptualist makes an additional point, worth noting. Not only does judicial craftsmanship impose limits upon the discretion of judges; it does the same for administrative agencies whose decisions are subject to judicial review.

Judicial discretion has political as well as legal and administrative overtones. A large element of discretion in the judge's role invites questions regarding his place in a democracy, especially with respect to the institution of judicial review. If the judicial process is one of mere "rationalization" of interests, then judicial review is an invitation to arbitrariness. Why should politically irresponsible (because not removable) judges be entitled to have the last say or even a check upon the democratically elected legislative majorities? Except to say that moving slowly may be a good thing, no especially good reasons appear for arguing that they should. Particularly does this seem to be the case when the courts undertake to give meaning to such broad terms as "due process of law," and "commerce among the states." One cannot conjure away the facts upon which the realist and functionalist bases his arguments. Legal concepts are forever becoming outmoded and inadequate for new social complexities. And the number of relevant premises for any particular case grows as legislators, administrators, and judges identify new interests having a claim to legal recognition. In any dynamic society old legal concepts and rules must give way to new ones, better adapted to the needs of the day. In England, where conceptualism still remains the dominant legal philosophy, the courts limit their contribution to this process and insist that the legislature must assume primary responsibility for performing this task. In the United States, the functionalist philosophy has made great inroads on the doctrine of *stare decisis* and has made judges more willing to embark upon deliberate law-making.[40]

Judicial modification of old precedents is nothing new. What is rather new, however, is the tendency for courts to lay less stress on fashioning new concepts and rules for those they discard, and to be content to seek to apply their own notions of justice in each case as it arises. Of course rules and concepts still play a major if not dominant role in the judicial process. We refer only to a tendency. It is a tendency, however, that takes us back to our earlier discussion of the development of legal systems.[41] It raises once more the question of the future of the rule of law. In the effort to do justice to the individual case, to the infinite and rule-defying variety of circumstances and changing conditions, two risks are run. One is the risk that courts, released from the restraining hand of rule and precedent may become arbitrary. Probably, this risk, in a country like our own, is not so great. Our custom of requiring judges to justify their decisions in written opinions, and the practice of legal scholars of maintaining a constant barrage of criticism of the decisions and opinions of judges, are powerful controls against arbitrariness, at least in the appellate courts. A more serious risk, perhaps, is the decline in certainty of the law. If this tendency proceeds far, appeals are multiplied, the danger of different interpretations of the law for different litigants increases, lawyers are unable to advise clients effectively, and business and other arrangements entered into in good faith may be invalidated, with consequent injustice. We do not wish to overdraw the picture, as has often been done, but simply to call attention to the price that would be exacted if functionalism—within limits, essential to justice and the maintenance of a flexible legal system—were allowed to go too far. Against this danger, legal procedure and tradition, and re-enforced professional criticism is a powerful protection.

The role of the judiciary in contemporary American society has

---

[40] According to the story, it was no brash Californian but an old Vermont judge who, when asked whether judges ever made law, replied: "Yup; sure they do! Made a little myself."

[41] Ch. 7, pp. 188-190.

changed. Obviously, so have the incidence and character of judicial protections. Judges are more hesitant about striking down the substantive propositions advanced by legislator or even administrator. They do not insist so rigorously upon their own judicial formulae. They are less certain about the nature of property or of liberty, and more interested in achieving practical adjustments between competing interests. Yet these statements must be taken in their appropriate context. The new role of the judiciary fits better a society of economic interdependence, of mixed public and private activities, of widely varied governmental activities. In contemporary America the judicial, legislative, and administrative processes articulate well. They function with a considerable awareness of the interests at stake, of the facts and values relevant to their adjustment or reconciliation, and of the procedures and checks that are required for constitutional morality and personal liberty.

SELECTED READINGS

(Asterisk indicates book is available in paperback edition.)

*ABRAHAM, HENRY J. *The Judicial Process.* New York: Oxford U. P., 1962. An easily accessible discussion of courts and the judicial process in Britain, France, and the United States.

BEDFORD, SYBILLE. *The Faces of Justice—A Traveller's Report.* New York: Simon & Schuster, 1961. A narrative of trials in five different West European countries, this book supplies dramatic setting and a personal dimension to the description of judicial procedure.

*CARDOZO, BENJAMIN N. *The Nature of the Judicial Process.* New Haven, Conn.: Yale U. P., 1921. The thoughts of one of America's greatest jurists on judicial decision.

CHARLES, RAYMOND. *La Justice en France.* Paris: Presses Universitaries, 1958. An extraordinarily clear and concise account of judicial machinery in France.

FRANK, JEROME. *Courts on Trial: Myth and Reality in American Justice.* Princeton, N. J.: Princeton U. P., 1950. A lively, though somewhat intemperate critique of the judicial process in the United States, giving many of the views of the judicial realist.

*FREUND, PAUL A., *The Supreme Court of the United States: its Business, Purposes, and Performance.* New York: World, Meridian, 1961. A collection of essays by an eminent student of American constitutional law.

FRIEDMAN, WOLFGANG. *Law and Social Change in Contemporary Britain.* London: Stevens, 1951. A good, brief account of trends in British common law.

HAINES, CHARLES GROVE. *The American Doctrine of Judicial Supremacy.* 2nd ed., Berkeley, Calif.: Univ. of California Press, 1959. The standard work on the subject.

HENSON, ROY D. (ed.). *Landmarks of Law.* New York: Harper, 1960. Part I of this book of selections affords an excellent introduction to jurisprudence for those without previous acquaintance with legal materials.

HURST, J. WILLARD. *The Growth of American Law: The Lawmakers.* Boston: Little, Brown, 1950. An excellent historical account.

JACKSON, RICHARD N. *The Machinery of Justice in England*. London: Macmillan, 1960. A standard work on the organization of courts and the administration of justice in England.

MAYERS, LEWIS. *The American Legal System*. New York: Harper, 1955. A survey of the administration of justice in the United States.

VON MEHREN, ARTHUR T. *The Civil Law System*. Boston: Little, Brown, 1957. A comparative study using cases and materials that deal with the judicial system in France and Germany as well as common law countries.

PAULSON, MONRAD G. (ed.). *Legal Institutions Today and Tomorrow*. New York: Columbia U. P., 1959. A series of essays upon various aspects of the judiciary and the legal system, emphasizing recent or continuing trends of development.

*ROSENBLUM, VICTOR G. *Law as a Political Instrument*. Garden City, N. Y.: Doubleday, 1955. A political scientist looks at courts and the law as instruments of political purpose.

ROSTOW, EUGENE V. "The Democratic Character of Judicial Review," *Harvard Law Review*, **66**, p. 193 ff. An able statement of a perspective of judicial review frequently missed.

CHAPTER 17

The Concentration and Dispersal of

Power—Federal and Unitary States

〜〜〜〜〜〜〜〜〜〜〜〜〜〜〜〜〜〜〜〜〜〜〜〜〜〜〜〜〜

The concentration or dispersal (centralization or decentralization) of power is one of the significant facts to be considered about any polity, and especially about constitutional democracies, for both constitutionalism and democracy are intimately related to the geographical distribution of power.

A territorial dispersal of political power provides levers for enforcing pluralistic checks on governmental authority. The "external checks" on government, mentioned in the chapter on constitutionalism, may in fact require not only pluralistic division of power but also the establishment of territorial political constituencies large and powerful enough and with sufficient autonomy to act as brakes upon centralist tendencies of the national government—especially when the dispersal of power takes the form of federalism. The Allied Occupation Authorities (especially the American) tried to implement this strategy in Germany and Japan after World War II, by insisting upon the creation of elective, territorial governments.[1]

The arrangements by which power is concentrated and dispersed also represent an important datum about any political system, apart from their bearing on constitutionalism. What is practicable and sensible to do in public policy—nationalization through public corporation, regulation of business, or participation in joint international endeavors—is conditioned by the degree to which power is concentrated in a central government or dispersed either to local authorities or separate states.

The issue of distribution of power territorially is closely linked to the concepts and the practice of democracy. We say that people ought to have a voice in deciding what concerns them; that government should generate

[1] John F. Golay, *The Founding of the Federal Republic of Germany* (Chicago: Chicago U. P., 1958), Ch. 2; Harold S. Quigley and John E. Turner, *The New Japan— Government and Politics* (Minneapolis: Univ. of Minnesota Press, 1956), Ch. 23.

responsibility among its citizens by engaging them in political decisions and bringing home to them the consequences of those decisions. But for what purposes is any particular group a community? What concerns it most vitally and what is of greater concern to the nation? When is it reasonable to insist that decision and responsibility for its consequences can or ought to be tied together? The point to be understood here is that the element of territory in political organization is of great importance for understanding much of what we do and think or ought to do and think about democracy.[2]

At the present time, in many governments, the territorial distribution of power is flexible. As governments alter their purposes and the content of their programs changes, the distribution of powers among central, regional, and local governments is altered. Moreover, opponents of the changing policies may call attention to these shifts in power and attack them, using arguments about the proper distribution of power, although their real concern is with substantive policy. For instance some of those who attack federal aid to education on the ground that it threatens to locate control of educational policy in the wrong place may really be attacking high expenditures. Objective criteria for the assignment of functions to one level of government rather than another would help avoid such obfuscation of the issues. The values of efficiency, common rights and citizenship, and democratic control of government meet at the point where decisions are made as to the levels at which various functions are to be performed. Unfortunately, in political discourse, these values often are not well sorted out. We need improved guides to rational choice in this matter of locating various types of decisions.[3]

PART I. CENTRALIZED AND DISPERSED POWER

The issue of centralized or dispersed power may be approached from two perspectives. One, which we shall reserve for subsequent treatment, is the relation of the territorial distribution of power to the values of citizenship. A second problem, which will be our immediate concern, is the effects of centralized or dispersed power upon government and governmental programs.

[2] For discussions of the implications of areas, boundaries, and governmental powers see Herman Finer, *English Local Government*, 4th ed. (London: Methuen, 1950), Chs. 5-7; William Anderson, *et al.*, *Intergovernmental Relations in Review* (Minneapolis: Univ. of Minnesota Press, 1960).

[3] For a sophisticated and interested discussion of the complementary roles played by unification and diversification in decision-making structures, of the necessity for finding an appropriate balance between the two for the attainment of functional rationality in any polity, see Paul Diesing, *Reason in Society, Five Types of Decisions and their Social Conditions* (Urbana, Ill.: Univ. of Illinois Press, 1962), Ch. 5.

ADVANTAGES OF CENTRALIZATION

Uniform Standards and Administration

Normally, greater centralization of political or administrative power leads to greater uniformity of laws, regulations, and standards throughout the country.

Uniformity is not a virtue in itself, and if it is imposed upon highly diverse conditions it may be an absolute blight. Other things being equal, however, uniform laws and administration are a great convenience, to say the least, and ordinary citizens, business corporations and labor unions may join in promoting central and uniform control of certain matters at the same time that they battle tooth and nail to keep other matters reserved to localities or states. It is an advantage to have the same law governing marriage and divorce throughout the land, rather than a situation that enables the couple to be married in one state and divorced in another. It is an advantage to a motorist to know that the traffic regulations with which he is familiar at home will be equally valid elsewhere. It is an advantage also to have only one set of regulations to abide by in doing business: whether issuing corporate stock, bargaining collectively, transporting goods by truck or rail, or merchandising a product.

Today, centralization of power usually means raising the general level of common rights and basic services, and almost always an improvement over the most backward of local conditions. This statement is true because centralization recently has been closely associated with the welfare state. In passing, however, two points are worth noting: that centralization and service or welfare activities have not always been natural allies; and that under contemporary circumstances of mixed public and private activities the common and individual good may not necessarily be best served by a steady advance in the level of universal, minimum rights and benefits.

Economies and Efficiency

In certain instances, centralization in government or administration brings with it economies of scale. Large-scale organization promotes specialization, scientific procedures, and often efficient utilization of resources. Centralized scientific research, specialized medical treatment, consolidated schools, and central depository libraries are all instances of economies that may be realized through centralization. Centralization may offer savings that allow the provision of entirely new services. The British Electricity Authority—a public corporation—by creating a national "grid" that could distribute electricity efficiently throughout Britain, made the use of electricity economical for many additional industrial and domestic purposes.[4]

Quite apart from costs, many functions are less well performed when central authorities are unable to coordinate the activities of the various agencies or governmental authorities dealing with the problem. Enforcement of laws and the regulation of the economy are prime examples. Businesses (for example, common carriers and electric light and power companies) are frequently less effectively regulated because of the diversity of jurisdictions to which they are subject. Jealousies between central and local law enforcement officers often impede activities directed at law enforcement. Where parts of an administrative or regulatory job are interdependent and also require coordination over a wide area, a centralized "authority" (such as the T.V.A. or the Port of New York Authority) may be the only way to get the job done.

Integrity of Procedures

Centralization often—though by no means necessarily—protects the integrity of formal procedures. Centralization is most often made effective through formal internal and external legal and administrative controls, with the consequence that the record, stipulated procedures, and the avoidance of *ex parte* influences are especially important. This proposition holds generally, though not always. For some programs centralization may *defeat* integrity: school districts are usually independent rather than "integrated," the public corporation "autonomous" rather than departmental, and the regulatory commissions "independent," in order at least in part to protect them from political influences. The "home-rule" movement for independent city charters also received some of its impetus from a desire to free municipalities from "state-house politics." Nevertheless, the review of local and state action by the courts, or of local administrative action by central administrative authorities generally has the effect of strengthening the integrity of procedures and sharpening the boundaries between public and private.

ADVANTAGES OF DISPERSED POWER

About some of the advantages of dispersed power, we need say little since they are simply the contraries of those values that attend centralized power. Obviously, dispersed power permits flexibility and variation and more informal methods of procedure. Obviously, too, there can be economies and efficiencies in decentralization. Several other values associated with dispersed power, however, deserve separate discussion.

[4] Ben W. Lewis, *British Planning and Nationalization* (New York: The Twentieth Century Fund, 1952), Ch. 5.

Speedy and Available Remedies

The service and welfare state has brought with it new rights and new remedies and common benefits. It has also produced complexity, pervasive administrative regulation, and lengthy, intricate proceedings. These social costs are defended by appeals to the common interest: in uniform labor laws, or standard public welfare and educational benefits. Beyond doubt these items are important.

For the small employer, the farmer, or the social security recipient, however, lengthy and complex proceedings are often a serious burden. Speed and readily available remedies in such cases are important. Actual decentralization of administrative power to make final dispositions can meet this need. So, too, can local units of government.

Experimentalism

Substantial political or administrative decentralization permits local units of government to experiment with various ways of meeting their problems. States can, for instance, try out the abolition of capital punishment on a small scale or experiment with new methods of unemployment compensation. Municipalities especially develop new forms of cooperation among each other and new techniques of collaboration with private agencies or groups—for dealing with problems of housing, transportation, schools, and youth.

The decline of local governments as "experimental laboratories" is often overestimated because the *field* for experimentation has changed.[5] In the 1920's and earlier, states were experimenting with social security, labor legislation, and such matters. Today, the states and local governments are more likely to be experimenting with new legal instruments, housing, administration of criminal justice, care for the insane, and the like. That experimentalism may be almost as vital today as it was earlier in developing new approaches to issues of public policy.

Unburdening Central Government

Government that makes all important decisions centrally fosters "apoplexy at the center, anemia in the extremities." Decentralization can often, by stimulating local effort and permitting flexible approaches, contribute additional support and talent for particular programs. Equally important, dispersal of power can also distribute the burden of government. *How much* decentralization makes sense will depend upon the way in which economic,

[5] Cf. George C. S. Benson, "Values of Decentralized Government—1961," pp. 1-17, in *Essays in Federalism* (Claremont, Calif.: Institute for Studies in Federalism, 1961).

political, and administrative activities are related to territorial units. In France, for instance, earlier arguments for decentralization were negative ones: a desire to "decentralize discontent" by transferring functions of government from Paris to the provinces. In more modern circumstances, however, the decentralization of public welfare activities—in France and in almost all modern countries—has stimulated local and group cooperation and considerably strengthened the appeal of the programs. Administration of agriculture in the United States or labor relations in France are examples of programs where a transfer of functions to localities have been or could be used to prevent "apoplexy at the center."

GRASS ROOTS AND DEMOCRACY AND LIBERTY

Americans are accustomed to thinking of dispersed power as more democratic and more conducive to liberty than concentrated power. Such homilies as "democracy stops beyond the parish pump" and "charity begins at home" indicate that "grass-roots democracy" holds a special place in American folklore. The traditional image of democratic America was largely established by philosophers of a rustic era—Thomas Jefferson, Alexis de Tocqueville, Henry David Thoreau, and Walt Whitman—to mention a few. Even today, when we picture our democracy, in *The Saturday Evening Post* or in the *Family of Man,* we do so as often as not by showing an assemblage of sturdy sons of toil, many gathered together in overalls, in parish or town meeting.

Reflection upon the images evoked by the concept of "grass-roots" democracy indicates that this notion embodies some dubious propositions.[6] "Grass roots" connotes a rural, not an urban conception of democracy. It suggests that political opinion is formed by inter-personal dialogue rather than by distant report. It presupposes that political action begins from below rather than being stimulated from above. It prefers spontaneous community opinion to the artificial (and often more disciplined) dialectic of large-scale institutions, skilled negotiators and spokesmen, and a wide-flung marketplace of ideas. Surely the merits of these opposing conceptions of democracy are debatable; but it is more important to our purposes to detail the positive contributions of local bases of politics. The subject needs clarification especially because partisans of either cause are prone to ignore the other side. Americans perhaps believe too much that the essence of democracy lies in the *Völkisch,* the spontaneous, and the crudely unsophisticated. The French go to the other extreme, virtually identifying democracy with centralism and uniformity.[7] Some sorting out of these issues is needed.

[6] See, for example, Roscoe C. Martin, *Grass Roots* (University, Ala.: Univ. of Alabama Press, 1957).

[7] Cf. Georges Langrod, "Local Government and Democracy," *Public Administration,* 31 (1953), pp. 25-34.

One way to approach this task is by seeking to discover what decentralization of political power contributes to democracy.

Two of the most distinguished political philosophers who have discussed this issue were Alexis de Tocqueville and John Stuart Mill.[8] Both argued strongly that decentralization of political power was a necessary component of democracy. They also stated a number of theses in support of their contention—theses backed by a wealth of observation and reflection upon the ways of governments and of citizens. Briefly, they believed that 1) local government gave access to government; 2) that it associated the citizens with each other, with the processes of government, and with the rules of government of which they were in part the authors; 3) that local government broadened popular participation and fostered public virtue in the participants and energy in the people; and 4) that decentralization contributed to independence and liberty. Most people would accept a large part of this argument. The important issues turn around two further questions. How should this argument be qualified; and what values do these contributions compete against in the political process? To answer these questions a more concrete exposition of the theses posed by these two men is required

Access to Government

The importance of local government in providing access to administration and politics depends very much upon time, space, and culture. In an agrarian society, especially one that lacks facilities for effective communication and political organization, local administration and government may offer one of the few channels for political expression and for moving from the status of mere citizen to that of active citizen. In the nineteenth century, both in Europe and America, local units of government were important in these respects.[9] Since popular political power could not be effectively exerted at a national level, except by a very few—either notables of the provinces, or political figures of the capital cities—local government was a technique of broadening the basis of political power. In American environs, decentralized power and vital local government enabled the Boston Irish and the East European immigrant to gain a hold on local political power and to move upward in social and economic status as well as to control in some measure his own destiny as a citizen.

In large cities such as New York, Chicago, London, and Hamburg, local government may still provide easier and more effective political access to a wide variety of groups seriously concerned to "get in the show" than other units of government. As a rule, though, the importance of local government

---

[8] Alexis de Tocqueville, *Democracy in America*, Vol. I, Chs. 14, 16; John Stuart Mill, *Considerations on Representative Government*, Ch. 15.

[9] See Sidney Webb's essay, "Social Movements" in the *Cambridge Modern History*, Vol. 12 (New York: Macmillan, 1910), pp. 733-757.

in this respect has declined and other channels have been sought. For one thing, pressure groups, economic associations, and political parties, or the administrative boards and offices of a more centralized government, may be both more accessible and more effective for the average citizen concerned to leave his footprints on the political sands, or to get something from government. A small constituency, or a small city can easily become the political preserve of those people directly and continuously interested (often in a pecuniary way) and so situated that they can and do cooperate as a closed political corporation. "Merchants' row" in a small city, or a restricted group of lawyers and more active farmers in a rural community often convert local politics into the monopoly of a private club. Those outside the charmed circle may more readily gain access to politics through peasants' cooperatives, the trade union, or as a militant of a national political party than by trying to win a voice amongst their social and economic superiors.

For a modern society the argument for local government because of ease of access is weak. Townships and counties offer ease of access to a limited and rather unrepresentative group.

Political Socialization

Tocqueville especially argued that local government was valuable because it associated citizens with each other and with the government. By doing so, he claimed, looking especially at America as contrasted with his native France, healthy local political units could heal communal divisions, diminish the poisonous hatred of the state and of authority (such as affected the French particularly), and foster in the citizen a "sober love of the laws of which he is himself the author."

Tocqueville's thesis has some merit even today, but not a great deal. In the administration or supervision of schools, municipal slaughter-houses and city properties, some businessmen, retired army officers, teachers, and housewives may get to know a few laborers; but relatively few citizens are associated in this fashion. On the whole the people who participate in municipal affairs are neither numerous nor representative of the population as a whole, except where vigorous socialist, trade-union, or racial groups pursue an active program of municipal politics. The "dialectic of classes" is often either limited in extent or bitter in content. After all, local government is the one constituency of government where people can get at each other—with clubs and brick-bats or with direct economic and social sanctions. Also the enemy is often both a personal and a political enemy. Hence, curing or ameliorating social antagonisms by revitalizing the grass roots is a program to be approached cautiously, if at all.[10]

---

[10] Note that in Germany and France the access of socialist and other radical parties to local government did not have the effect of moderating political divisions, but of sharpening and broadening them. The use of proportional representation has often been advocated precisely because it increases the size of the constituency and moderates communal strife.

Citizen Responsibility

Both Mill and Tocqueville argued that local institutions of government promoted virtue in their citizens. The small unit of government, they held, fostered civic morality by linking the exercise of political power fairly closely with the consequences of that exercise. Rate payers taxed themselves. People directly translated their ideas into governmental activity and saw the consequences of their own political choices. They delegated authority to fellow citizens and found them deserving or unworthy of that trust. In juries and on boards they sat in judgment upon their neighbors and learned that government was a serious and sacred thing. Without these lessons of direct democracy, any society would be poorer and meaner. Also many of these lessons of citizenship are best learned here, for only in this situation is the citizen in any important sense a trustee of the public good.

Much of what they said is true and ought to be conceded out of hand. A political shrewdness and a quality of responsibility is acquired at this level of government and in this way that is important in developing political virtues, both locally and for superior ranks of government. Apart from the positive values fostered by direct administration, the passivity and dependent attitudes that can pervade a community in which popular participation is denied are bad both in themselves and for their consequences upon government. France and Italy are poorer in spirit because their local institutions give little scope for popular activity. Communities develop attitudes toward "doing for themselves," as opposed to lobbying a superior government for a concession or a benefit; and a centralized authority in such a context can and does reinforce passivity and a relation toward government that is one of the supplicating client on the one hand and the paternalistic patron on the other.

In contemporary local government, however, actions and responsibility for them are seldom directly linked. Mill wrote for a day in which, locally, only rate-payers voted, and in which it followed that they should tax themselves to pay for what they voted. Direct responsibility for actions is still found in such organizations as school boards (in some measure), or in land-use districts. But to what extent should these agencies be allowed to consider themselves as autonomous units? Should a school board be forced to extend its jurisdiction, for example, to admit children living in low rent and low school-tax areas? Many would say "Yes." Is a land-use district entitled to monopolize water resources for itself? Many would say "No."[11]

For local government, today, it should also be fairly obvious that the link between benefit and responsibility for the voter or the participating citizen is rather intangible. In what sense is the local citizen "author of the

---

[11] This view was steadily and vociferously urged by Bentham. See also Herman Finer, *English Local Government, op. cit.,* esp. Chs. 5-7.

laws" under which a redevelopment authority, subsidized by the federal government, lets contracts to a firm submitting the lowest bid for demolition of a slum and construction of new apartment houses? The citizen is taxed for multiple purposes. The sources of revenue and their actual expenditure are not generally linked either in fact or in theory. And decisions are made by an integration and evaluation of many programs, seldom with an eye to the education of the citizen.

Heavy involvement in local affairs can hinder "virtue" by detracting from national citizenship itself. The good local citizen of nineteenth and twentieth century France or Germany was often the bad national citizen. People are doing different things and pursuing different values in national and local government. The habits and attitudes that suit the one activity often do not suit the other. What is political virtue in the local context becomes parochialism on the national stage.

Liberty

An additional argument usually urged on behalf of dispersed power or "grass roots" democratic government relates to liberty. "In England there has always been more liberty, but worse organization, while in other countries there is better organization but less liberty."[12] With these words, John Stuart Mill defended the tradition of British local government. Tocqueville also argued that local institutions had a special role to play in the preservation of liberty and independence. In principle, multiplication of authorities, and especially federalism, are favorable to liberty. Under a decentralized political system, everyone is at the same time under at least two governments; and since the lines of jurisdiction can never be neatly determined, there is always a certain tension between them. While this condition may make for inefficiency, it allows the citizen a degree of intersticial liberty that may be enhanced by deliberately using each of the governments as a protector against the other. Put it this way: each party—labor, business, agriculture—finds repeatedly that its capacity to protect itself is increased by a system of government that allows it several chances to defend its vital interests and to state its case. If it loses in one forum, it may yet win in the next. Equality and the extension of positive rights, it is true, may lag. But liberty is served in two ways: first, because such a government must often wait while consensus and new ways and means are sought; and second, because overlapping governments offer opportunities for asserting substantive or procedural liberties anew or in a different way. Any sensible child knows that liberty increases when parental authority is divided. The situation with respect to government is not much different.

[12] John Stuart Mill, *On Liberty and Considerations on Representative Government* (Oxford, Eng.: Blackwell, 1948), p. 279.

Yet the libertarian who relies heavily upon local institutions as defenders of freedom is likely to be disappointed. Historically, cities, guilds, churches, and orders defended their corporate independence and privileges, and thereby the privileges of those favored within those organizations. At times these privileges were associated with liberty in a broader sense, but not universally so by any means. In the first place, small governments can more easily become regimes dominated by one clique or one temper of mind. Furthermore, corporate pride can work as easily toward the invasion of liberty as toward its preservation. Nor does local government necessarily foster "constitutional liberty." Cities, like people, can become clients of a powerful patron if their capacity to manage for themselves is limited. Municipal traditions may also have little to do with the spirit of liberty in the nation as a whole. Historically, France lacked municipal independence. Germany had much of it. Yet who would say that the tradition and spirit of liberty has been stronger in Germany than in France? In principle, distribution of power increases freedom and independence, if for no other reason than because corporate units—whether trade unions, churches, or towns— in defending their status often defend rights for all. But in this argument, the distinction between liberties for a corporate body and liberty for an individual must be made clear. As the power of the city grows, the liberty of individuals in the countryside (American suburbanites or Balkan peasants) often diminishes. The liberty that pertains to common citizenship, to the abstract, unassociated individual (for example, for Negroes in relation to whites) presupposes a general structure of rights—usable, generally enforced, and common to all; it cannot be served simply by distribution of power and a multiplicity of concessions. These aspects of legal rights are often lost in making government highly responsive to local power structures. The group basis of society *may* be such that corporate and local liberty promotes individual liberty, but it is not necessarily so.

The Case for the "Grass Roots"

After all these qualifications of the arguments for "grass-roots" democracy, the reader may well wonder where we stand. Is anything left of the case for decentralized power as a means of increasing liberty and "democraticness"? Does "grass-roots" democracy still form a vital element of democracy for the modern state? To be sure, it does. Tocqueville's arguments are not without relevance even today. The case is seen most clearly when one contemplates the situation as it is or would be without dispersed authority. The absence of healthy local political roots is a disaster. Why? Partly because administrative or political action from above is then difficult to legitimate at the local level and is likely to foster hostility and suspicion toward government generally and central authorities particularly. Furthermore, citizens of a democracy must learn to compromise, to adjust wants and needs, and to integrate the pleas of various claimants into an agenda of government that will receive acceptance. Yet this vital activity of deliberately submerging one's individual or group interests to those of a more inclusive entity occurs for many only at the local level. The full implications of citizenship, as the examples of France show, are difficult to teach if, for practical purposes, the whole burden must be carried by "indirect democracy": democracy made effective by pressure groups, parties, and distant political agencies of government. To be sure, few participate even in local government. But that is not the point. The point is that the society requires the continuous leavening of political activists who are not merely party or interest-group members, or claimants for administrative aid. This need is not adequately met by central governments alone, or even by the "multi-group society." Lastly, local democracy gives many people a voice in matters touching them most immediately. Although for a large part of the community this argument has little meaning under modern social and economic conditions, much of any community is not mobile and does live and die largely in one township or even neighborhood. Their fortune and the fortunes of their children are more closely and permanently bound up with the local community. Many of these people know intimately their local political leaders and exert political influence through them. If justice implies that people should have a larger voice in deciding those matters that affect them more deeply and permanently, then local democracy serves this purpose for part—but only part—of the community.

Conclusion

Not only are the arguments for the superior "democraticness" of dispersed power subject to important qualifications; but also powerful arguments suggest that under certain circumstances centralized power may actually be more democratic than dispersed power. Many small groups and also the average citizen can often more readily watch it. For example, if regional political or administrative jobs are handled by many independent "authorities," overlapping in jurisdiction and each administering only a narrow sector of a total administrative program, they tend to be watched and importuned for favors only by those groups that are directly and vitally interested in their activities. Railroads, insurance companies, morticians, trade unions, milk producers, as the case may be, often do well under such a regime; the consumer, the rest of the "public" either has too intangible an interest or too indefinite a sense of what it wants from each authority to be effective in the political or economic scramble. Larger areas with general functions provide opportunity for one special interest group to be checked by another, just because of the diversity of interests represented in such an area. Moreover, many interests that are too small to make organization practicable in a small area can achieve effective organization and hence influence in a larger constituency. This point even applies to political parties: in a small area the chances are great that one party or the other will have so few followers that it is not effectively organized and may even be "captured" by the majority party. Finally, the larger political unit has a net advantage in the matter of formality. While formalism may lead to the ills of bureaucracy it remains one of the major means for insuring that all interests will be fairly heard and their claims treated rationally. Yet small units of government tend almost inevitably to slip into an informality of operation that constitutes a threat to many of the democratic virtues.

This thesis with respect to centralization and wide, general-purpose constituencies holds only for a modern economy, with effective communications and a pluralistic and fluid political process. In a primitive, agrarian economy, large constituencies and centralized power might be just as drastically unrepresentative as would, say, the American political system if members of state legislatures were the only spokesmen for the nation.[13] But, in a modern society with mature political development, centralization of power often tends to promote more balanced representation, greater attention to and publicity of government doings, and more concern with formality of procedure. If, to Americans, it seems curious to say that centralized power may be more democratic than highly decentralized power, the values of inclusiveness, publicity, formality of procedure, and clarity of responsibility go a long way to explain the paradox.[14]

Our discussion does not settle the issue of whether there should be more "grass-roots" democracy or less, or of whether democracy varies in degree proportionally with dispersion of power, nor was it intended to do so. What needs to be gotten straight is what can be fairly claimed for the "grass-roots" and what cannot. Certainly, strong and healthy local government contributes vitally to democracy. But the 1960's are not the days of Thomas Jefferson; and the virtues once promoted through rustic techniques may or may not be more effectively pursued through other means in the modern, pluralistic society. There is no presumption in favor of the lowest level of government. Each piece of government business should be evaluated, in terms of its character and the nature of the program envisaged, to determine the level of government at which it should be located.

PART II. UNITARY AND FEDERAL STATES

Concentration of power is a matter of degree, and regardless of its extent, it may be regulated by ordinary legislative processes. In "federal" states, however, a particular distribution of powers between the central

[13] This point was made by Melancthon Smith in the debate on ratification of the American Constitution at the New York Convention. Earl Latham, ed., *The Declaration of Independence and the Constitution* (Boston: Heath, 1949), pp. 105-111.

[14] Again, one points to Jeremy Bentham. For insight into the importance of these values in problems of centralized and decentralized government the authors are indebted to Professor Charles E. Gilbert of the Swarthmore College Department of Political Science.

government and smaller units is fixed by the Constitution, subject to alteration only by the special machinery for constitutional amendment. In "unitary" states, by contrast, the distribution of authority is subject to change by ordinary legislation. While the precise distribution of powers between central and regional units of government (the latter called "states" in the United States) may vary considerably from one federal state to another, the law-making authority possessed by the regional government must be substantial for the state to qualify as a true federation. Ordinarily too, but not in all cases, the regional governments themselves must participate in the process of constitutional amendment by which the distribution of powers may be altered. In certain states, however, such action merely requires an extraordinary majority in the central legislature, possibly supplemented by a popular referendum.

Still looser types of state organization are called confederations (or confederacies). In these the central government tends definitely to be subordinate. For instance, the regional units may have the right to secede from the union.[15] Also unanimous consent of the regional units, or their representatives may be required for legislative action by the central government. Perhaps the most characteristic difference consists in the fact that in a confederation normally the central government can act directly only on the regional governments (as was the case under the American Articles of Confederation) rather than on individual citizens. Since direct compulsion of another government is politically an awkward and explosive enterprise, such a provision is a means of insuring that the central government will remain weak, and dependent in its actions upon the regional governments.

Most of today's states are federal or unitary. Each of these types, tends to have characteristic problems and to produce a typical style of politics, particular to each and partly determined by the form of state itself. After describing each type of state, we shall explore the second theme of the impact of form upon political content.

UNITARY STATES

France

The degree of centralization of authority in unitary states varies widely. France is typical of the most centralized type and in fact the example of a unitary state that has been most frequently copied by other countries making new constitutions and bent on securing centralized government. French institutions, then, represent an extreme case. Yet they are a good example

---

[15] The formal constitution of the U.S.S.R. is generally classified as "federal" in spite of the fact that it provides for the right of secession. In practical operation in this, as in other respects, the government of the Soviet Union operates without regard for the constitution. According to its effective constitution, it is a unitary state.

for they offer a classic study in the pathology of centralized power, and the characteristic problems raised by it in the context of an actual political regime.

LOCAL GOVERNMENT ORGANIZATION

Even in France, subordinate governments operate at various levels, departmental and local. The distinguishing point, however, is that in each case the inferior governments have certain responsibilities to the more inclusive or more central government along with their responsibilities to the locality, and that the former responsibilities far outweigh the latter. The prefect, for example, who is the most powerful agent of local government—responsible for order and good government in his department and for the supervision of municipal government—is appointed by and directly responsible to the central government, in particular, to the Minister of the Interior. Elected departmental councils and elected local councils as well do exist but the powers confided to them are strictly limited. In large measure, they are advisory. The dominance of the central authorities is further assured by the fact that the sources of revenue and powers of independent expenditure permitted to the local government are so small that they lack the material base for expansion of power.

Under the constitutions of the Fourth and the Fifth Republics, local governments elect their own councils. The councils in turn elect a mayor, may pass on their local budget, and control the local constabulary. They also levy taxes, license, issue ordinances, and have certain powers over local property, administration, and education. Yet over them stands the prefect, the centralized French bureaucracy, the *Conseil d'Etat,* the Ministry of Finance and the Ministry of the Interior. The result in practice is that little scope is left for local initiative. The taxing powers of local governments are strictly limited. Furthermore, about 70 per cent of what they receive in taxes is already earmarked for expenditure. While they may control the local police, serious disorder is a matter for the prefect or the Minister of the Interior, who have at their disposal special police and troops. The prefect will, moreover, intervene to settle strikes, pacify angry peasants, or disband threatening assemblages. Communal administrative orders and dispositions are frequently cancelled or suspended by the prefect who is armed with a general ordinance power to issue administrative decrees with the force of law (subject only to appeal to the *Conseil d'Etat*). If a council or mayor persists in obstreperous behavior, the prefect can dissolve the council and suspend the mayor.[16]

The prefect is himself checked by the *Conseil d'Etat* which ensures the legality of his actions. He is also checked by an elected departmental council; but in practice the initiative is his and he has formidable powers to en-

[16] On the powers of local bodies see Brian Chapman, *Introduction to French Local Government* (London: Allen & Unwin, 1953), esp. Ch. 2.

force his view if the council should prove stubborn. He belongs to a civil service elite *corps,* operating under a special statute. His real loyalties are to himself and his career, to the traditions of his *corps* and that abstraction "the French state." Politically, he is responsible to the Minister of the Interior, which means in practice that he is dismissed if he allows affairs in his department to get out of hand, raise a *scandale,* or prove politically embarrassing. This responsibility also means, as Casimir Perier once put it, that he must show "impartiality" to all, but something more than "indifference" toward the regime in power. Under the Second Empire and the Third Republic, he was often expected to assure a government majority and to harass or suppress the enemies of the regime. Today, he is a more impartial figure. The vast administrative responsibilities that he has acquired, and an increasing observance of ordinary constitutional propriety have considerably altered his role.[17] Still, the prefecture remains, probably, the most important element of administrative power in preserving the solidity of the state.

CONSEQUENCES: FOR LOCAL GOVERNMENT

The approach toward local administration is frankly one of controlling political tendency or expression with a heavy admixture of administrative centralism. As a matter of course, the French assume a considerable measure of irresponsibility in the behavior of local governments. The results are by no means entirely bad. A high degree of uniformity characterizes administrative standards and the provision of services. Civic interest and participation are high, especially because of the almost immediate presence of central government in the person of the prefect and other agents of national administration. Planning, welfare services, highway location and building have all given to the councils a greater role and at the same time restricted the discretion of the prefect. Evaluating the prefectural system and French local government is not so simple a matter as choosing between autocracy and democracy. It is more like asking whether checking and controlling local democracy with a large measure of bureaucratic initiative and power of veto does not yield substantial benefits. In the United States, for instance, local government is closely checked by the courts and—for some functions —by the federal and state bureaucracies as well. In France the same principle holds except that the control is more pervasive and complete, more bureaucratic, and tied especially to a distinctive officer, the prefect.

Much political and administrative initiative are, however, taken from local and departmental government in France. As one consequence, bureaucratic centralization generates its own rationale. Often the quickest and best way to get something done is to approach the prefect, the ministry, or the deputy rather than to seek to do for oneself in a local community or act

[17] *Ibid.,* pp. 225-227. A good discussion of the powers of the prefect is Brian Chapman, *The Prefects and Provincial France* (London: Allen & Unwin, 1955), Ch. 5.

through the communal council. The prefect and the national ministries are also the important figures in coordinating programs and in ensuring compliance with administrative standards. Thus the system tends to set responsiveness and rationality sharply at war with each other. Bureaucracy is substituted for much of local politics. Importuning the civil service or lobbying in the National Assembly for local favors becomes a prime technique for accomplishing something locally. Standing for unified authority and bureaucratic rectitude in the face of factional politics and *clientelisme,* the civil service comes to consider itself the guardian of the national welfare. Many factors have tended to break down the older French pattern of tenacious parochialism matched by autocratic centralism. Urbanism, planning, increased social services, economic development, the growth of regional interests—all of these work in this direction. On the other hand, it by no means follows that what is lost by the prefect has been gained by the local council. Often the response to new problems and to the growing pains of economic, social, and political development has been to restrict the powers both of the prefect and of the local council and to impose still more centralized controls. Probably, the answer in the long run, however, will be considerably greater powers for local, elective bodies. At the present, great tension exists between centralism, uniformity, and bureaucratic rationality and the need for local initiative and responsibility.

CONSEQUENCES: FOR ADMINISTRATION

Distinct evils of administrative practice, limitations upon administrative possibilities, and characteristic elements of bureaucratic pathology are part and parcel of an administrative machine in which centralization is carried to the French extreme. Broadly, centralization of the controls to insure administrative responsibility requires formal rules and elaborate checking by a hierarchy of superiors. Under such conditions, to the clerk or administrator, trouble lies not in the direction of responsiveness to his clientele or the public he is serving, but in deviating from the document, or the administrative law governing his job, and in failing to check all doubtful points with his superior. Memoranda must be initialed, and *dossiers* routed up and down the administrative hierarchies. Furthermore, the letter rather than the spirit tends to rule, for by the nature of the case reliance is placed upon a legal regulation and routine checking of documents, rather than the morale, internalized sense of responsibility, or informal relations with private associations that the bureaucracy might have or generate. Thus both the agents and the administrative decrees of central ministries, the Court of Accounts, and the Council of State proliferate. At the top brains, initiative and, usually, probity are characteristic. At middle and lower levels routine, stagnation, and frustration tend to prevail. From the citizen's perspective, such a civil service may enjoy great prestige; but it also generates hostility. The bureaucracy cannot but appear unfeeling. Furthermore, the time consumed in processing even simple claims or setting in motion ordinary administrative programs can be enormous.[18] In addition, because real initiative often involves scrapping established procedure, the French bureaucracy takes many measures outside the law, frequently cloaks itself in secrecy, and seems generally somewhat sinister.

CONSEQUENCES: FOR POLITICS

In France, the impact of centralization upon politics and the parties also produces untoward effects. For one thing, centralization tends to fuse local and national politics. On the one hand, the national assembly and the national parties are the center in which parochial favors are often won. Hence, localism distorts national politics. But, on the other hand, national divisions in party spirit and loyalties infect localities and make school administration, the wages in municipal power plants, street names, or local holidays the occasions for refighting the issues of the Resistance, the Spanish Civil War, or the Dreyfus Affair. The hostility generated is a direct evil. Even worse, from the standpoint of democratic government, is the impact upon local politics.[19] Local government, particularly if the community is small, depends heavily upon direct association and direct collaboration of the citizens—on municipal boards, in volunteer fire companies, for charity drives, civic improvement ventures, and so forth. With the growth of larger cities and more viable political bases for local government rigid centralism and many of its attendant consequences tends to be less and less the rule in France. But as a general proposition, the French system of local administration and government, while often almost dictated by the character of local communities and past political history, also hampers and constricts normal and healthy political development at the grass roots and to some extent even makes the problem worse.

Party systems tend to parallel the structure of the state, following in their internal structure the boundaries and the hierarchy of the political constituencies. It is too much to say that a federal system necessarily pro-

[18] On the other hand, if this tendency goes to excessive lengths, decentralization of functions to the prefect can offset it. Also, long practice and a high level of administrative competence tend to redress some of the problems normally present with a system of highly centralized administration. Nevertheless, the tendencies are there. Whether the French system is slower and more cumbersome than the American is another question. It is doubtful that it is. For a discussion of centralization and some of the ways in which the French cope with it see Brian Chapman, *Introduction to French Local Government*, op. cit., Ch. 4.

[19] The effects can sometimes be quite marked. In one small village, for instance, the soccer league, the hunting club, and the volunteer fire department were repeatedly disrupted because of political divisions and especially because of the mutual animosities of two local political leaders, one a Radical Socialist and the other a Communist. For a good description of the effect of politics upon voluntary organizations in a French village, see Laurence Wylie, *Village in the Vaucluse* (Cambridge, Mass.: Harvard U. P., 1957), pp. 212-226.

duces highly decentralized parties similar to those in the United States, for Germany offers evidence to the contrary.[20] But the effects on party structure of the centralized unitary state (and especially France) are bad. In France, for example, the parties that pride themselves on democracy (both within the party and in their programs) tend to develop a strong organization and a *mystique* of faithfulness to party principle and to the will of the regular party membership. The parliamentarians in turn are embarrassed in their capacity as legislators and cabinet leaders by solemn party mandates and the noisy clamor of factions within the party. On the other hand, those parties that are "supple" alliances of individual parliamentarians whose stock in trade tends to be local acquaintance or fame and winning concessions for particular interests and the home constituency thrive upon comparative immobility and abhor sweeping changes or "abstract" programs. Too often in parliament and before the eyes of the nation, "supple" politics and the democratic myth are in conflict, producing bitterness, recriminations, and little political gain. To put it another way, the aristocratic constitution and the democratic constitution (that is, the attitudes and loyalties these symbols invoke) meet head on.[21] Intermediary governments with active political constituencies serve in some measure to moderate this collision. For they give incentives to the democratic parties to temper their views in the interests of office holders, workers, and voters with more particularistic loyalties; and they reward the efforts of narrowly based parties to broaden their popular appeal.

A highly centralized unitary government also lacks ways and means to legitimate its decisions or to make its actions *appear* to be in the public interest, even if in fact they are. Much that is normally the province of public political controversy, in the United States for instance, in France is accomplished by winning the prefect's ear or setting the bureaucracy in motion, particularly by bringing pressure to bear on the deputy in distant Paris. This scheme has two flaws. On the one hand, policies are often selected and implemented without a broad and fair public hearing. And, correspondingly, many people with grievances are blocked from giving voice to them. As a result, the myth and the reality of democracy seem too different from each other and too far apart. A federal system, or any government with lively and powerful regional councils may avoid this difficulty by affording many points of access to the governmental process and providing an opportunity for exercised citizens to press a political point.

[20] Even here, though, the federal system has produced marked tendencies toward party decentralization. Cf. Arnold J. Heidenheimer, *Adenauer and the C.D.U.* (The Hague: Martinus Nijhoff, 1960), Ch. 6; Roger W. Wells, *The States in West Germany; A Study of Federal-State Relations, 1949-1960* (New York: Bookman, 1961), Ch. 2.

[21] Maurice Duverger, *Political Parties,* trans. Barbara and Robert North (London: Methuen, 1954), Bk. I, Ch. 3; Philip Williams, *Politics in Post-War France,* 2nd ed. (London: Longmans, 1957), pp. 397-402.

Great Britain and Other Unitary States

We have been describing the situation in France, which is virtually the archetype of unitary states. Many of the problems found here are similar to those that are or have been present in Italy, Eastern Europe before World War II, Japan, and a number of other states at different times. Such political behavior is not characteristic in the unitary states of England and Scandinavia. In Great Britain, for example, a large measure of local self-government exists.[22] There is no centrally appointed regional officer with general powers, like the French prefect. Popularly elected local governments have substantial powers and have the authority to levy taxes ("rates") upon property generally. Furthermore, the popularly elected county councils are important, multipurpose authorities that administer large parts of broad and substantial programs, such as Town and Country Planning, the Health Program, and regional activities of various public enterprises. Legally, to be sure, the kind of decentralization that prevails in Britain constitutes no check on the power of the central government, which could abolish the local authorities completely by a simple act of Parliament. In fact, however, they have generally been considered to be a vital part of the English constitutional system, although even in England the process of centralization may be readily observed and demands for a new reorganization are now being heard.

The English experience (as well as that of Scandinavia) argues that the unitary state is not necessarily subject to abuse. In England, constitutional convention, a great deal of willingness to compromise, and constant attention to the preservation of the values worth saving in the distribution of powers between center and locality are a major part of the explanation. Bills relating to localities are "depoliticized" by sending them to special tribunals in the House of Commons and the House of Lords. In no other country has the distribution of powers received such careful and soul-searching scrutiny as that given by the series of commissions on local government powers. And no place else is more attention devoted to hearing and attempting to compromise all legitimate grievances and claims.[23] The legal restraints protecting local democracy and liberties are relatively few. But the British unitary state works with little abuse because Englishmen are well aware of the possible abuses and are determined to avoid them. Those charged with centralized policy-making, with the avoidance of abuse in the employment of administrative devices (such as the grant-in-aid); with scrupulous consultation of the affected parties and a disciplined responsiveness to their interests have heavy burdens imposed upon them by the unitary state. In

[22] Probably the best single source on British local government is still Herman Finer, *English Local Government*, 4th ed., *op. cit.*

[23] In such matters, for instance, as the administration of grants-in-aid, reorganization of local government units, town and country planning, highways and transport.

short, the English example shows that abuses are avoided by political and administrative self-restraint that would put a severe strain on the governmental virtues of most nations.

FEDERAL STATES

By any reasonable definition, true federal states constitute a minority of all the states of the world today. However, the predominant tendency among large democracies is to adopt the federal form. Federal states are of great interest to political scientists for two other reasons. For one thing, they hold forth the greatest promise for the possibility of consolidating existing states into larger political aggregations, approaching the ultimate goal of a world state. Furthermore, a number of newly emerging states find the federal state more appropriate to their needs. In these states, the citizens often lack experience with a common government and a common sense of political community. For them, the only viable unity is one that permits many territorial units to find their own way according to their separate traditions, loyalties, and political sociology. The fate of these new states will depend in part upon the dynamics of federalism.

How many states are to be classified as federal is a matter of dispute. Amos Peaslee, in his encyclopedic collection and analysis of constitutions, declares that about sixteen of them fall in the federal classification (including West Germany, which he lists as "federal unitary").[24] They are: Argentina, Australia, Brazil, Burma, Canada, India, Mexico, Libya, Switzerland, Union of South Africa, the U.S.S.R., United States of America, Venezuela, Viet Nam, West Germany, and Yugoslavia. On the other hand, the author of a standard work on federalism, using the definition given above, finds only four states that meet the test.[25] They are the United States (the prototype), Australia, Switzerland, and Canada. Many of Peaslee's examples are ruled out either because the deed (practice) does not correspond to the word (Constitution); or because (as is the case of South Africa) their constitutions do not in fact establish regional and central governments of co-ordinate authority.

Prerequisites of Federalism

We may speak of the relative merits of unitary and federal governments, but often it is not a matter of choice. Under many circumstances, only one of these types is possible. It is for this reason that we spoke pre-

[24] Amos J. Peaslee, *Constitutions of Nations*, 3 vols., 2nd ed. (The Hague: Martinus Nijhoff, 1956).

[25] K. C. Wheare, *Federal Government, op. cit.*, p. 21. Wheare recognizes that the distinction is not clear-cut and that classification is therefore somewhat arbitrary at best. Further difficulty is introduced by the fact that the law of the constitution and constitutional practice frequently do not coincide. Canada, he concludes, is only quasi-federal from a strictly legal point of view; but it is predominantly federal in practice.

viously of the "reasons for" centralization or distribution of power. Some of them, like securing the benefits of constitutionalism, are arguments that might be weighed pro and con by the founders of a constitution; but others are factors that leave the constitution framers little choice. It is pertinent then that we should speak of the prerequisites of federalism. Without them, consideration of its merits is academic.

Essentially, the prerequisites of federalism divide into requirements of two kinds: those which relate to political will, and those which relate to political "space." Political will, in this context, means the set of desires and attitudes that sustain the balance of common loyalty and communal cleavage upon which federalism depends. Political space is a convenient term used here to cover those material and social conditions that affect the capacity of a people to organize territorially to sustain these separate governments and the balance between them. Sometimes, when there is a will there is a way. As Charles Beard said of the American Founding Fathers, "the men of Philadelphia could work any constitution." On the other hand, as Tocqueville noted, American capacity for association (and hence for sustaining viable local and regional governments) depended partly on a set of material and social factors, like cheap land, economic opportunity, and the absence of hereditary distinctions. These things affected political space: the size of the constituency that could be an effective unit for popular democracy, the talents that could be drawn to particular governments, and the relation between territory and political power within the system of states.

POLITICAL WILL

Obviously, with respect to political will, the inhabitants must desire to be under a single, independent government for certain purposes; and they must at the same time desire to have independent regional governments for other purposes. As to the first of these, a number of factors tend to produce the desire for unity. Following Wheare,[26] we may enumerate the desire for military security and for independence of foreign powers, anticipation of economic benefits, a history of previous political association, similarity of political institutions, and location in a common geographical neighborhood. No one of these factors is an absolute necessity, but the last two come close. On the other hand, the major stimulants to the desire for local autonomy are a history of separateness, differing local political regimes, geographical considerations (such as natural barriers or vastness of territory), and separate nationalities, races, or confessional groups.

Political will, however, is more than a simple matter of balance of attitudes toward government. A stable federalism demands a considerable capacity to agree in practice upon *what* is a matter for unity and *what* a matter for diversity. This requisite creates a serious stumbling block in

[26] Wheare, *op. cit.*, pp. 37-40.

many federal systems. Regional autonomy is desired—by one province to protect a set of historic privileges, by another to ensure religious freedom, and by yet another for the sake of local trading advantages. But parties and politicians respond to such varied constituencies—a local church hierarchy, a racial community, peasant cooperatives or syndical chambers of business—that they find neither common meeting ground upon national policy nor upon the set of local liberties to be protected.[27] In some federal systems, notably Brazil, Argentina, and Indonesia, regional separation and diversity in political will have been important factors in providing pretexts for various experiments in "guided democracy." From the standpoint of problems of political will, it is essential to establish that the nature of the diversity and of the unity be such that in practice views can be adjusted.

POLITICAL SPACE

Political space can pose difficulties in various ways, but four kinds of problems are likely to be the most important. Size of constituent units, *per se* can be critical: for example, very large units in an agrarian region, or very small ones in a dynamic, industrial economy. Many "democrats" at the time of the founding of the American Republic were convinced that large constituencies were death to popular government.[28] On the other hand, a multitude of small territorial governments in a complicated and modern economy not only seems wasteful, but also probably seriously handicaps local government itself, since separate political units find cooperation difficult. This difficulty is likely to lead either to a move toward consolidation, or else considerable activity on the part of a central government.

Relative size of the different units may also either generate tensions or falsify the legal theory of a federal constitution. The German Empire provided the classic example of this kind of problem, composed of the great state of Prussia, a few moderate sized territories and above a score of tiny principalities. The description of the Empire as the union of a lion, several jackals, and a score of mice points up the difficulty: the system was dominated by Prussia, and increasingly the trappings of federalism seemed wasteful and comical.

Political space also presents the problem of matching the political constituency with an effective and balanced representation. In France, for example, regional decentralization of government has often in the past been considered as an answer to some of the problems of excessive concentration of political and administrative power. One reason such proposals have been

---

[27] Germany and Austria-Hungary in the nineteenth and early twentieth centuries are prime examples. Rudolph Schlesinger, *Federalism in Central and Eastern Europe* (New York: Oxford U. P., 1945), Chs. 1, 2 and *passim*.

[28] Including not merely agrarian radicals but even men like Benjamin Franklin and Gouverneur Morris. See *The Records of the Federal Convention of 1787*, ed. Max Farrand, (New Haven: Yale U. P., 1923), Vol. I, pp. 243, 423, 512, 514. For the Madisonian point of view, see *ibid.*, pp. 84, 476, and Number Ten of *The Federalist*.

scotched early in their history is because of an awareness that the French economy did not give rise to effective regional political constituencies. At the level of regional administration, the active political forces in many a province would have been little more than the regional offices of the parties, inter-departmental organizations of the Chambers of Commerce, an occasional farmers' representative, and possibly a spokesman for the church or a labor syndicate.[29] This kind of representation does not make for sane handling of regional problems, such as dams and water resources, highways, the development and distribution of electric power.

Lastly, the relation between political space and *personnel of government* is important. In one age, a given territorial unit will swarm with competent administrative and political talent. In another, the size and importance of the affairs, for example, of a German or American state may seem so paltry by comparison with the careers of business, the army, law, and the like, that the work of these governments cannot be done well. When political power is so divided and parcelled out that government seems contemptible, regional governments attract neither capacity nor loyalty in the long run, and without these they are not viable. To be sure, all of these difficulties with political space are relative. It is a matter of finding the territorial unit appropriate to a given political culture. In this respect, however, the problem sounds easier than it is. For the territorial constituents of federalism are usually given: they cannot be sliced up or rearranged; or, if they are, they may become political units with no meaning for their inhabitants.

Characteristic Institutions

Though federal states are likely to vary even more widely in their basic constitutional structure than unitary states, their characteristic institutions can be described rather simply. State governments are usually of the same form, generally tending to adopt a pattern that varies only slightly from the central government. The requirement of the United States constitution that all states must have a "republican form of government" indicates the practical importance of such a provision: many states left to themselves might set up a revolutionary dictatorship, a princely regime, or some other form of government equally obnoxious. The central governments invariably control foreign policy, the conduct of war, some aspects of national commerce and transport, and have some exclusive powers over money and financial transactions. Usually the states will control the powers and jurisdiction of local government, laws relating to the family and marriage, education, the

[29] R. K. Gooch, *Regionalism in France* (New York: Century, 1931), Chs. 5-8. In France today, the picture has greatly changed, especially with the development of the economy and the growth of administrative services. On the other hand, the lag in the development of healthy regional constituencies has been and even to some extent continues to be a hindrance to devolution of powers.

status and transfer of real property, and intrastate production and commerce. The powers of the central government may be "enumerated," that is, specifically listed with the assumption that all others powers remain with the states. Or, as in Australia, the states may have the enumerated powers and the central government the "reserved" powers. In any case, certain powers, often termed "concurrent powers," may be shared, as the taxing power invariably is. Some kind of supreme federal court will reconcile conflict of laws and strike down either state or federal laws or actions that overstep constitutional limitations. Federalism is also fortified by dual representation and other political devices: for example, by a second chamber elected from state-wide constituencies, allowing states to pass on the qualifications of electors, and (as in the United States) providing a formula based upon the federal system for the election of the President.

THE POLITICAL ADVANTAGES OF FEDERALISM

Actually, though the matter might seem "as plain as the road from Charing Cross to St. Paul's," the political advantages that can be attributed, with any assurance of accuracy, specifically to federalism are difficult to state.[30] We would all agree that American federalism is a psychological, political, and legal restraint on power; but is it clear that it would be such except for the fact that our political philosophy has made it so?[31] Regionalism in France and South Africa are certainly restraints on power; and yet France is a unitary state and South Africa is a federal state in practice but not in legal form. Does federalism really bring government closer to the people in America than a unitary government does in Britain? To what extent is a distant state capital a focus of "grass-roots" democracy? An affirmative answer to the first of these questions must at least be qualified.[32] Nor is it clear that federalism provides a specific remedy for the problems that arise under unitary systems. Administrative decentralization or some form of regionalism may, under certain circumstances, work as well or better than federalism. And in fact, even decentralization may have little effect in curing the ills normally attributed to centralization, if they are deeply rooted in the social pattern.

PROP FOR CONSTITUTIONALISM

According to Montesquieu, the *Federalist Papers,* and a host of other authorities from Lord Acton to Carl J. Friedrich, one desirable feature of federalism is that it supports constitutionalism. This issue is rather tricky.

[30] It is taken for granted in the present discussion that the arguments both for and against dispersion of power, as discussed above, are all applicable to the special case of federalism.

[31] On this point see Arthur W. MacMahon, ed., *Federalism—Mature and Emergent,* (Garden City, N.Y.: Doubleday, 1955), Chs. 7, 8, 10.

[32] *Ibid.,* especially the essay by Franz L. Neumann, "Federalism and Freedom: A Critique," pp. 44-57.

Federalism provides restraints upon the accumulation of centralized power. Presumably constitutionalism is preserved through dispersing power and through providing many points of leverage for checking a dynamic political process of concentration of authority. Yet fragmentation of power can provide both the incentive and the opportunity for dictatorship. And head-on clashes of political will and legal restraint have usually resulted in victory for will rather than law. In Germany and Austria-Hungary, federalism seemed to promote about an equal balance of dictatorial behavior and constitutional restraint. In France, provincial liberties were a standing justification for policies of enlightened despotism. In the United States, Australia, Canada, and Switzerland, federalism and constitutionalism have worked together. One point seems fairly evident: in a period of rapid social and economic transition, federalism, to be a reliable support for constitutionalism, must provide adequate means for adjusting the distribution of powers to changing needs.

Subject to the proviso just mentioned, federalism, by preventing extreme concentration of power and by forcing upon the attention of central governments a wide array of effectively represented parochial interests, does, on balance, contribute to constitutionalism. Few governments can do a good job of managing highly centralized power without the aid of a complex set of external, pluralistic checks on power. England is a rarity. A pluralistic society might well supply in some countries what federalism does in other contexts. But more often constitutional traditions need reinforcement, and also many groups are not effectively represented by social pluralism.

PROMOTES CONSENSUS

Does federalism promote political consensus? Certainly in some senses of the word "consensus," it does. Multilingual states, federal systems in which the constituent units have widely differing past histories or different forms of government, probably could not exist except as federally organized politics. Apart from such extreme cases, the issue is whether regional, multipurpose, elective governments, enjoying extensive political independence, promote consensus, both within each region and on a national level. These two forms of consensus are to some extent in competition. Fostering consensus among regions may entail various concessions to local pride and the continuance of endemic institutions that diminish rather than increase the sense of common national citizenship.

Other things being equal, however, federalism probably does tend to promote consensus. In particular, federalism makes it easier, usually, for the people of a nation to be united on the things about which they feel united, and separate or even stubbornly particularistic in matters about which they differ.[33]

---

[33] Again note that a federal system begins, almost always, with historically determined units, not ones designed by a constitution maker's art.

The point may be made graphically. Imagine a country with a total electorate of four million, distributed equally among four districts, or "states." For simplicity's sake, let us suppose further that the electorate is divided on just two issues, one a matter of indisputably national concern should be settled on a nation-wide basis and another that could (without loss to the nation) be settled individually by each of the four districts, or "states" (as they might be called under a federal system). Let A stand for the national issue and B stand for the issue that might be decided by the "states" but would be decided uniformly for the whole country under a unitary state.

State 1 1 million pro-*A* 1 million pro-*B*	*State 2* 1 million pro-*A* 1 million pro-*B*
State 3 1 million pro-*A* 1 million pro-*B*	*State 4* 1 million anti-*A* 1 million anti-*B*

In the situation depicted in the chart above, it will be observed that under a unitary state both A and B will prevail and one fourth of the voters will be frustrated with respect to both issues. Under a federal system, however, no one will be thwarted with respect to issue B—everyone will have his way; and only the same number as under a unitary state will be frustrated with respect to issue A. Here is a net "profit", in terms of satisfaction or avoidance of frustration, in favor of the federal system. It can be further demonstrated that under no possible distribution of preferences will a unitary system yield this kind of "profit."[34]

EFFECTS ON POLITICAL ACTIVITIES

Federalism probably tends to encourage pluralistic politics, which may be either good or bad. Federalism more effectively separates national and local politics than do unitary systems. By providing whole separate governments between the levels of local and national governments, often with differing terms of office and separate election dates and with a distinctive set of problems, federalism distorts neat party structures and separates the process of political choice into discrete segments. Federalism also provides a strong incentive for establishing working agreements among central, state, and local politicians not to embarrass each other in their political activities. Usually the effect of such arrangements is in some measure to separate local and national issues. Moreover, the state governments create incentives for parties, pressure groups, and promotional organizations to divert strategic

[34] See J. Roland Pennock, "Federal and Unitary Government—Disharmony and Frustration," *Behavioral Science*, 4 (1959), pp. 147-157. For an argument that federalism, by dividing power, creates disharmony, see William N. Riker and Ronald Schaps, "Disharmony in Federal Government," *Behavioral Science*, 2 (1957), pp. 276-290.

energies in this direction as well. For example, some evidence exists that in Germany federalism has encouraged a tendency toward less monolithic political tactics on the part of business, labor, and agriculture. To the extent, then, that pluralism is considered a good, federalism has had beneficial effects for the political system as a whole.

Federalism can also widen the base for recruitment of political talent. For England or Scandinavia, such a consideration is of little moment. But in the rest of the world, politics is usually a less honorific profession, and popular candidates with governmental experience on a state level enable parties to draw for talent upon elements other than prominent personalities, loyal militants, trade-union secretaries, or party bureaucrats.

In another respect the political effects of federalism may be less favorable. It may obscure the locus of responsibility and thus interfere with the enforcement of accountability. Central and state governments may be able to "pass the buck" to each other. In the United States, for instance, in the general awakening to the evils of organized gambling following a Congressional investigation a few years ago, a public outcry against notorious and chronic violation of the law was in more than one instance hampered if not frustrated by "buck-passing" between law enforcement officials of various layers of government.

LIBERTY

The most weighty advantage claimed for federalism is that it promotes liberty. Does it do so more than decentralized administration or devolution of authority to local governments or regional councils? Probably, the answer is "yes." Liberty is promoted because (1) federalism fragments power more effectively than any unitary system; and (2) because federalism creates two *generally* competent governmental authorities rather than one. Thus in a federal system, the general competence of the states gives almost all groups at one time or another an important defence of their interests that might have been lost under a unitary system. The general competence of the state government gives it flexibility; thus federalism in the United States, through state governments, gives to the small cities alternate channels of influence in an era of direct relations between large cities and .the national government, allows conservation programs that will permit the independent farmer-lumberman to cut his timber according to programs under which he can survive, and favors the farmer in an age when he is becoming a vanishing American. Since state governments are *general* authorities, they are or can at any time become an arena of political struggle to which any champion can carry his cause. Furthermore, they often provide both a definite focus of political will and the means for translating regional political sentiment into concrete results. Usually, therefore, the states of a federal system develop a more balanced and sustained politics than do mere regional administrative authorities or weak elective councils. Consequently, a state's political views on sectional interests are likely to prove important to candidates electioneering in that state for national office. Backed further by the "juridical defence" of specific constitutional guarantees, states are usually fairly successful defenders of local liberties, even in political systems where "states rights" are unpopular.

LEGALISTIC CONTROLS

Sometimes federalism adds specific legal limitations on the distribution of political power, which qualify the advantages that might be served by decentralization. As central power expands, they may force programs into peculiar channels, entailing a loss of efficiency.[35] Thus, in the United States, price supports for agriculture, in the early days, were tied to soil conservation, perhaps helping to create surpluses that tended to defeat the ends of price stabilization. Federalism also tends to convert an issue otherwise political into a legal one. In this respect, it often strains the constitutional virtue of a people, unless they are particularly deferential toward law and the judiciary.

Do the legal forms and restrictions that federalism imposes upon the growth of centralized power have any advantage? The answer will depend upon the circumstances; but the following considerations are especially relevant. For one thing, the "unnatural" channels into which federalism forces programs frequently make them responsive to varied constituencies and less subject to the biasses of any one administrative philosophy—certainly two of the ends sought by federalism. Another advantage of legal settlement may be that of securing acceptance. Rather wide *communities* of political interest meet in issues of centralization and decentralization. Settlement of the issues by power alone without an element of impartial arbitration may not promote general acceptance of the actual disposition of the problem. When, say, the "sinister interests" of centralism in Paris clash directly with the "sinister interests" of "merchants' row" in some French commune or the wine-growers represented in a departmental council, a political decision may dispose of the issue, but leave bitterness and a sense of injury still rankling. In such a situation, the impartial arbitration of the judiciary might serve to moderate the clash of political sentiment and interest. In the United States, in the case of issues arising under the interstate commerce clause the courts add an element of judicial sobriety and impartiality that probably aids in the general acceptance of their disposition. Yet the courts can do only so much. To take another American example, the segregation controversy suggests both the extent and the limitations of their effective power.[36]

[35] For a cogent summary of the ways in which federalism affects programmatic efficiency see the essay by Arthur W. Macmahon, ed., in *Federalism—Mature and Emergent, op. cit.*, pp. 267-277.

[36] On this subject as it applies to the United States, see Paul A. Freund, "Umpiring the Federal System," in Macmahon, *op. cit.*, pp. 159-176.

Courts can also lend clarity and explicitness to the consideration of values involved in the centralization and decentralization of governmental powers. This experience is often salutary especially when the issues are both complicated and "fuzzy." Complexity and "fuzziness" themselves present problems of great magnitude in trying to preserve constitutionalism and insure that rights, apparently protected, are not silently abused. It may not be enough merely to provide for the appeal from "Philip drunk to Philip sober." Even a sober Philip will have trouble sorting out the implications of policy administered through several levels of government. The courts have trouble, also; but their rigorous analytical discipline adds to clarity about rights and powers of citizens and multiple governments.

The Future of Federalism

The values we have associated with federalism are not on the whole political goods that are at a premium today in modern democracies. Federalism may promote a measure of liberty, of pluralism in politics, some additional consensus. But it is not *per se* democratic, for the definition of that community that ought to be allowed to determine its own affairs depends upon the interests of its members, and these are constantly changing. In most federal states, the process of transferring powers from the regional to the central government has been going on at a fairly rapid pace.

CENTRALIZING FORCES

The reasons for this steady shift of powers toward the center are the same political and economic forces that are so dominant in all phases of social life. Largely they stem from the twin factors of war and the industrial revolution. The technological revolution itself has been the direct cause of a great deal of centralization. The speed with which criminals can escape across state borders today—often across several states, in fact—has led to central legislation against certain crimes previously left entirely to the regional unit. In the United States, for instance, kidnapping, automobile stealing and trafficking in narcotics are now federal (i.e., national) crimes where interstate travel is involved. The great enlargement of interstate trade and, particularly, the enlargement of business units attendant upon mass production have been even more potent causes of federal centralization. A large proportion of today's business enterprises are conducted on a multi-state if not nationwide scale, so that effective regulation must be at the national level. Even matters which the regional governments can regulate —for example labor relations—they hesitate to do as vigorously as they might for fear of driving business enterprises out of their jurisdiction, and thereby losing them as sources of tax revenue and of employment.

The geographically unequal distribution of wealth and, especially, of taxing power supplies another incentive for centralization. This factor and the increasing demands upon the state for expenditures for social services means that some regional governments are able to maintain much higher standards than others. Nor can this situation be dismissed as of purely local concern. Bad health conditions in one area may spread disease to other parts of the nation. Poor roads in one district affect the commerce of other sections. Even poor educational standards in one part of the country affect the prosperity of the country as a whole. Hence, increasingly, the central government has to use its taxing resources to aid the regional governments. Here, as elsewhere, "he who pays the piper calls the tune"; subsidies are almost invariably accompanied by the establishment of minimum standards and provision of inspection officers responsible to the central government.

Economic crises, such as the great depression of the 'thirties, or economic reconstruction in post-war Germany accentuate the process. They increase the pressure for financial aid; and they call for the establishment of governmental controls and operations designed to relieve the impact of economic distress. There are many ways of attempting to fight a depression, but none of them is likely to be very effective unless it is practiced on at least a nation-wide scale. Hence we have here another potent centralizing force. The same is true of counter-cyclical programs aimed at avoiding depressions.

Finally, there is war. If anything requires a nation to act as a unit it is warfare. And in modern total war there are few activities of governments, or, for that matter, of private individuals, that may not affect the outcome. In the case of other centralizing pressures, they may be in some degree resisted out of consideration for the advantages of decentralization. But when it is a matter of life or death for the nation, other considerations are swept aside. Prices are set, materials are allocated, consumer goods rationed, labor directed to this or that activity, resources developed, all by, or at the direction of the central government. While many of these changes are for the duration of the war emergency only, the alterations that have been brought about are never completely undone. At the present time, even without actual war, nations are under the necessity of maintaining a large degree of war mobilization at all times; and the effects of mobilization differ only in degree from those of war itself. Today's threat of atomic warfare may call for greater central governmental activity than ever before in peacetime in the effort to decentralize our cities and to spread out the manufacturing potential of the country.

This trend toward centralization in federal governments should occasion no surprise. Historically, federalism has been a device for overcoming the inconveniences, and especially the weakness, of small-scale political organization, especially where diversity of ethos, attitudes, and allegiance made impossible the establishment of a unitary state large enough to supply adequate power for the tasks of government. In general, states already unitary have not adopted the federal technique, despite the alleged advantages discussed above. Federalism has been a means for centralizing power hitherto more completely dispersed rather than for the reverse.[37] So it is not strange that, with growing experience of the national government, with strengthening of national loyalty and broadened ethnocentrism, and with the growth of common problems such as we have detailed above, the powers and functions of the national government have normally increased.

THE PROSPECTS

These developments might seem to warrant the generalization that federalism is an intermediate step (though not a necessary one) in the development towards larger from smaller political units, and that it is by its nature temporary and transitory. In the contemporary world, marked by industrial technology as a foundation for effective power, that generalization seems to gain added confirmation by reason of the needs of economic control and planning, in a mixed not less than in a governmentally directed system. For uniformities on a broad geographic scale are necessary to viability in the effective use of modern techniques of production and distribution. Smaller units of government lack requisite power, geographic span of control, knowledge, and resources to cope with inescapable issues related to economic stability and development, and are unable to assure satisfaction of basic needs and broadening wants, not to be neglected in the age of the common man. The increase in the number of federal states in our time —in Africa and in South and Southeast Asia—may be simply part of the thrust towards broader unities; and its prevalence in underdeveloped areas, hitherto marked by tribal localism, as they strive to catch up, and to gain a place in the modern world, is but testimony to the utility of federalism as a practice of transition, rather than support for it as a principle of good government.

Nevertheless, it is not clear that federal governments must necessarily be transformed into unitary governments in accordance with what a noted political scientist once called the "biological succession of state forms."[38]

Not all the accretion of power to the central government represents a net loss to the regional governments. The latter have also been steadily gaining power, from two sources: from the development of new governmental functions, and by transfer from the localities. The same forces that have made for centralization within the nation have also promoted the transfer of local power to the regional governments.

[37] Herman Finer, *Theory and Practice of Modern Government, op. cit.,* pp. 189-190.
[38] Edward McChesney Sait, *Political Institutions—A Preface,* (New York: Appleton-Century, 1938), p. 374. Sait spoke of unitary government as the higher form and declared that federalism, at best, is a *pis aller,* a concession to human weakness. Perhaps so; but in a sense all government is a concession to human weakness. Human weakness, it may be remarked, shows no sign of disappearing. If federalism lasts as long as human weakness, its future is assured.

Nor is it to be assumed that the sentiment of "states' rights" is dead. No doubt loyalty to the regional units has diminished in many places; but, in Canada, Switzerland, and the United States, at least, regional jealousies of the national government are still so powerful that it is difficult to imagine anything short of a cataclysm that could bring about unification in the forseeable future.

It should also be noted that some of the deficiencies of federalism can be, and are being met in ways other than by transfer of power. States may cooperate with each other in meeting common problems. In the United States they are doing so increasingly. Still more important as an aspect of what is now called "cooperative federalism," is the device of grants-in-aid. While, in federal systems, this method is commonly used to bring pressure on the states to do what the national government desires, to achieve greater uniformity, and to aid in the equalization of tax resources, these are not the only purposes grants-in-aid can be made to serve. They also provide the means for achieving a desirable degree of centralization while leaving to the states not only primary administrative responsibility but also a major degree of policy-making choices.[39]

Finally, without reference to federalism in particular, but regarding the general centralizing movement, it is pertinent to remark that in certain respects the trend is in the opposite direction. In the United States, the federal government has found it wise to decentralize the administration of many of it functions for some of the very reasons recited above as arguments in favor of dispersal of power. To take a single example, the activities of the Bureau of Internal Revenue, which have grown by leaps and bounds in recent years, are subject to much more autonomy in the regional and local offices than was true a generation ago. Many of the newer functions of the federal government, such as the administration of old-age pensions, and the regulation of labor-management relations in interstate commerce are conducted on a regional basis. Business has found that the law of "increasing returns" applies only up to a certain point. After that point is reached, larger units are less rather than more efficient. Accordingly, both business and government recognize that they must avoid excessive centralization if they are to remain efficient.

The last point deserves emphasis and elaboration. Indeed, it suggests what amounts almost to a separate argument for federalism from those we discussed earlier, although more precisely it is a new application of an old argument. Today it is more important than ever that the national government be capable of wielding its powers in the fields of foreign policy, political and economic, with the greatest possible effectiveness. These matters are as important for the maintenance of a healthy viable domestic economy

[39] Many other devices fall within the ambit of cooperative federalism. A good account of the techniques and the advantages as well as some of the limitations of cooperative federalism in the United States can be found in Macmahon, *op. cit.*, Chs. 15-20.

as they are for the conduct of diplomacy. In connection with these and related problems, the burdens piled upon national executive and legislature tend to become overwhelming. Under these circumstances, it is more important than ever to decentralize or keep decentralized whatever tasks either of decision-making or of administration can safely be left to lower levels of government.[40]

IN CONCLUSION

What is most desirable in terms of centralization will vary greatly with conditions of geography and popular sentiment. Sentiment, to be sure, is not a fixed datum. It changes. People can be persuaded that what they have been resisting would in fact be good for them. Under normal conditions, however, popular sentiments change but slowly. At a given time, insofar as a given sentiment is widely and deeply felt, it must be accepted as a datum, and probably as a controlling factor. Of course, where sentiments are evenly divided, there is room for argument.

What is best is also not likely to stay fixed for an indefinite period. Economic and technological changes, wars and depressions render it improbable that any equilibrium will last for long. Sometimes it may be the decentralizing factor of regional national sentiment that gains headway, as was true in Canada for several generations. In any case, changing tensions are to be expected. In a healthy society they will result in changed arrangements.

In general, the balance of trends is toward greater centralization—although certain currents run in the opposite direction. At the same time, federalism constitutes a device for preserving constitutionalism. These two facts, however, do not necessarily add up to a forecast of eventual "consolidation." Techniques for decentralizing authority even within a unitary state, growing awareness of the dangers of over-centralization, and the existence of other bulwarks for constitutionalism provide answers to any harbingers of doom.

Finally, it may be observed that, even though existing federal states were to become unitary—an event not imminent—it would by no means follow that federalism would be at an end. New federal states are being formed. The "integration" of Europe is taking place in various ways. That

---

[40] West German national and state administrative patterns afford an excellent example of this thesis. Here, most direct services of government are performed either by the states or by quasi-autonomous governmental corporations. One consequence is to unburden the central administration of many problems of detail and of coordination. Both the administrator and the legislator are left freer to concentrate on matters of policy since less of their time is taken up with administrative detail and legislative oversight. Partisans of centralization in the United States would find German experience provocative of sober second thoughts about the value of handling matters at the national level when by well-designed expedients they could sometimes be delegated to constituent federal units.

process will most probably involve recourse to the federal principle at some stage of its development, just as in other parts of the world federalism provides for emerging nations a *via media* between fragmentation and impotence on the one hand and centralized dictatorships on the other.

SELECTED READINGS

ANDERSON, WILLIAM. *The Nation and the States, Rivals or Partners.* Minneapolis: Univ. of Minnesota Press, 1955. A succinct and valuable discussion of American Federalism, emphasizing particularly the relations between constitutional form and governmental policy. Chapters 8-11 also offer an exceptionally good discussion of the fiscal problems that arise under federalism.

BENSON, GEORGE C. S. (ed.). *Essays in Federalism.* Claremont, Calif.: Institute for Studies in Federalism, 1961. A collection of essays suggestive of recent trends in federal government.

CHAPMAN, BRIAN. *Introduction to French Local Government.* London: Allen & Unwin, 1953. A clear, readable introduction, enlivened with many interesting anecdotes and shrewd comments.

DIESING, PAUL. *Reason in Society, Five Types of Decisions and their Social Conditions.* Urbana: Univ. of Illinois Press, 1962.

EGGER, ROWLAND. "Nature over Art: No More Local Finance," *The American Political Science Review,* 47, pp. 461-477. An important and classic article discussing some limitations upon tendencies toward centralization and "consolidation."

FINER, HERMAN. *English Local Government.* 4th ed., London: Methuen, 1950. A survey of English local government—its history, its organization, and its operation. A superb treatment of the relations between local government organization and democratic theory.

MACMAHON, ARTHUR W. (ed.). *Federalism—Mature and Emergent.* Garden City, N. Y.: Doubleday, 1955. Probably the best single collection of essays on the general topic of federalism, although the book's emphasis is primarily upon federalism in the United States.

MILL, JOHN STUART. *Considerations on Representative Government.* New York: Dutton, 1910. Ch. 15. In this brief chapter Mill outlines an argument for local self-government that is the counterpart of Tocqueville's argument with respect to the United States.

DE TOCQUEVILLE, ALEXIS. *Democracy in America.* 2 vols. New York: Knopf, 1945. Particularly Vol. I, Chs. 14 and 16. Here, Tocqueville argues the case for local government as an aid and path to good citizenship.

WELLS, ROGER W. *The States in Western Germany: A Study of Federal-State Relations, 1949-1960.* New York: Bookman, 1961. Describes briefly the essential institutions of German federalism. The book is also of interest because it covers a span of twelve years experience with federalism under a new constitution.

WHEARE, K. C. *Federal Government.* London: Oxford U. P., 1946. This book, though dated, gives a clear summary of the federal institutions of Australia, Canada, the Union of South Africa, and the United States.

NONDEMOCRATIC
AND
SEMIDEMOCRATIC
GOVERNMENTS

Four

During most of the period of recorded history the great majority of governments have been monarchical in form and oligarchical in practice, when they have not been outright despotisms. Dictatorship, whether legally provided for, as it was by the Roman Republic (for brief, specified periods), or by seizure of power, has also been a not uncommon phenomenon. Until the present century, however, constitutionalism and democracy have enjoyed a net growth, and have come to dominate the "western" world, despite periods of "reversion" (like the so-called Dark Ages or the period of "Tudor despotism").[1] The first World War disrupted that development. To be sure, the

[1] As these examples may suggest such "reversions" tend to follow conquest, a sudden change in the size of the unit of government, or a crisis in internal affairs caused perhaps by rapid economic and social affairs producing great discontinuities of social structure.

549

Treaty of Versailles created a number of new democratic states. Since 1918, however, autocratic rule, especially in the form of totalitarian dictatorship, has scored great gains. While these gains have not generally been at the expense of constitutional democracy (and where they were they have since been liquidated), they have cast serious doubt in the minds of many upon the ability of democracy to extend its sphere or even to hold its own. In the new regimes the characteristic institutions of democracy have frequently been eliminated or transformed so as to serve quite different purposes from those for which they were designed; and, at least where totalitarianism has prevailed, new political philosophies with their own distinctive political values have been substituted for the philosophy of liberal democracy.

What, more specifically, is a totalitarian dictatorship? It is *"authoritarian"* and *"statist,"*—both in an extreme form. By the first term we mean that the authority of the ruling group or individual is unlimited, despotic, that it is checked neither by accountability to a broad political base nor by any of the checks of constitutionalism. It secures and maintains this powerful position by methods of violence and terror, by full exploitation of the possibilities of propaganda (monopolized by the regime), and by what is today known as brain-washing.[2] By "statist" we mean simply that the state's control is extended to all spheres of life.[3] The economy, the church, all sorts of social organizations, and heretofore private areas of life, the family, and the thoughts of the individual, are subjected to management by the state as far as is humanly possible.[4] Finally, in furtherance of both their authoritarian and their statist objectives, it is usual for totalitarian regimes to adopt and impose upon their people a highly developed *ideology,* tending to cover all aspects of man's existence, and suffused with a romantic mystique.

Totalitarianism is a matter of degree. The same is true of a number of characteristics or dimensions of political societies. One can array polities along continua in terms of these dimensions. In certain cases the lines are more sharply drawn than in others. For instance, we have said that a totalitarian dictator is completely unchecked by accountability to the people. We are here speaking of the degree of consent that characterizes the regime. For a totalitarian dictatorship it is minimal. At the opposite end of this continuum the limiting case would be that of anarchy. The next step, and the first within the range of practicable forms of government, would be extreme or radical democracy—perhaps the direct democracy of a city-state. Next,

[2] See, for example, Eugen Kogan, *The Theory and Practice of Hell* (New York: Berkeley, 1950), and Robert J. Lifton, "Thought Reform of Chinese Intellectuals," *Journal of Asian Studies,* 16 (1956), pp. 75-88.

[3] The word "totalitarian" itself expresses even better than the term "statist" this aspect of totalitarian dictatorship. Since this word is so generally used for the whole complex of ideas and practices we designate as "totalitarian dictatorship," however, we are forced to use another term for that aspect of the whole that relates to its all-inclusiveness.

[4] It should be recognized that here, as in our earlier discussion of democracy, we are describing an "ideal type." Regimes are totalitarian in proportion as they approximate these characteristics or goals.

aristocracy or oligarchy, and then monarchy. But consent varies in kind as well as in amount. It may be the result of deliberation (being in a sense both "rational" and "active") or it may be merely part of a received tradition. It may also be the product of manipulation (with the aid of a monopoly of propaganda tools); and, finally, maximum use may be made of coercion and terror. Polities differ also with respect to the degree of their observance of the rule of law. Here the continuum runs from the *Rechtsstaat,* or completely constitutionalized regime, on the one hand, to the despotism, in which arbitrary action is subject to no restraints, on the other. Finally, with respect to the totalitarian aspect we run the gamut from the minimal controls of a polity in which the sphere of individual autonomy and privacy is maximized and laissez faire prevails in the economic sphere, through intermediate forms that might be called the "liberal service state" and the "welfare state" to totalitarianism at the other extreme. The substance of what we have been saying is displayed graphically in the chart below.[5]

TABLE VI

PATTERNS OF RULE

Bases of classification	Degrees				
Degree of active consent[1]	Anarchy	Democracy	Aristocracy	Monarchy	Dictatorship
Kind of consent[2]	Rational (active)	Traditional (passive)	Manipulated (propaganda monopoly)	Coerced (Maximum use of naked force)	
Rule of law[3]	Rechtsstaat (constitutionalism)				Despotism
Auxiliary functions[4]	Laissez faire State	Liberal State	Service State	Welfare State	Totalitarianism[5]

[1] The continuum runs from the maximum of active, willing (uncoerced) consent to the minimum, stages being indicated by forms of government we associate with various degrees of consent.

[2] Note that, except at the extremes, the chart cannot be read vertically.

[3] Again the line runs from maximum to minimum.

[4] Here the order is reversed, the line running from minimum to maximum.

[5] A totalitarian dictatorship is at the extreme right of each line, except that it may obtain consent by almost any mixture of coercion and manipulation.

Totalitarian dictatorship is defined in terms of approximation to the extreme right-hand end of each of the four axes.[6] It is not meant to imply, however,

[5] This discussion is largely based upon N. S. Timasheff, "Totalitarianism, Despotism, Dictatorship," in Carl J. Friedrich, editor, *Totalitarianism* (Cambridge, Mass.: Harvard U. P., 1954), pp. 39-47, although it departs in certain details from his analysis. Timasheff makes the additional suggestion that totalitarian dictatorships interpret what he calls the "protective function" in a most aggressive manner, as contrasted with pacifist regimes at the other extreme.

[6] The important element of ideology does not lend itself to this kind of graphic portrayal; hence it is omitted.

that other types of rule named along the top line would necessarily fall in corresponding locations on the lower lines, although the tendency is in this direction, especially for the first three axes. But a democracy might be a welfare state and a monarchy might practice laissez-faire.

Totalitarian dictatorship is not alone in presenting the political scientist with relatively new phenomena for analysis and integration into the body of political facts and interpretations that compose political science. Many areas of the world that have until recently been dependencies have now achieved political independence. Something like 30 new states have appeared on the political horizon since 1950. Also other, older states that have been peacefully somnolent in the shadows of tradition have suddenly awakened and are striving to "modernize" in short order. In a belt around the world, corresponding roughly to the tropical and subtropical climes, we find these "emerging" or "developing states." The variety of political situations and problems they display is bewildering. All that can be done in a work of the present order is to deal with this subject in a synoptic fashion, concentrating on the many points of contact between the experience and problems of these states and those to which the major part of this book has been devoted, and also giving some consideration to probable future lines of development.

CHAPTER 18

Totalitarian Dictatorship

||||||||||||||||||||||||||||||||||||||||||||||||||||||||||||||||||||||||||||||||||||||||

The study of totalitarian dictatorship is instructive for the political scientist in several ways. Cold-War conditions make an understanding of totalitarian political systems relevant to the foreign policies of democracies, especially since the behavior of totalitarian regimes in their external relations differs significantly from that of democracies. Also, these systems are relevant for another immediately practical reason: the political, economic, and social institutions of many developing nations closely resemble those of totalitarian systems. Totalitarianism is important, too, for the study of political theory and political institutions generally. Just as historical perspective adds to the understanding of the present, so the extreme case of totalitarian dictatorships shows political principles projected beyond their normal reach, and thus contributes to an understanding of the normal and the usual.

"Totalitarianism," as we have indicated, is a matter of more or less, and few regimes can be accurately described as such without qualification. Whether, for instance, the regimes of Salazar in Portugal and Franco in Spain amount to totalitarian dictatorships, or ever did, is highly debatable. We shall not attempt to decide that point now. Probably Hitler's Germany, Stalin's Russia, and Mao's China provide the purest examples, with Mussolini's Italy, the archetype, not far behind. Our discussion will be confined primarily to Germany and Russia, as leading instances of fascist and Communist totalitarian dictatorships, respectively.

FASCIST TOTALITARIAN DICTATORSHIP

Fascism originated in Italy. It was the name given to the political movement led by Benito Mussolini, the regime he eventually established, and the body of doctrine that was elaborated in justification of the movement and the regime.

Later, in Germany, Hitler's movement, which he called "National Socialism," bore such fundamental similarities to Italian Fascism that "fascism"
has become a generic term, applied to all such movements. Fascism, however,
has no single intellectual progenitor, like Marx; nor does it have, as does
Communism, a single world-wide organization, acknowledging a common
body of doctrine and following the same leadership. The German and
Italian manifestations of fascism, for example, exhibit marked differences.
Generally speaking, the German version was more extreme in all respects;
the mysticism of the doctrine secured a much more profound hold on the
people. Important though they are, we must ignore these differences in the
ensuing brief treatment of the subject.

Fascist Theory

Fascist theory, or ideology, was definitely *post hoc,* although in Germany it was well developed before Hitler came to power. Fascism grew up
in opposition both to democracy and to Communism—a fact that is basic
to an understanding of its doctrines. True, its similarities to Communism
in practice are marked; but it is characteristic of mass movements to be
similar and at the same time to insist in strident terms that they are at
opposite polls.[1]

ANTIMATERIALISM

Even as Communism is materialistic, so fascism asserts that it is anti-
materialistic. Its apologists elaborated a "spiritual" interpretation of history,
in opposition to Communist materialism. They deny that the course of
events is economically determined. They assert that forces of the spirit pre-
dominate and that strong men, great leaders, by their own will, their own
decisions, can shape the course of history. They stress the fact that man does
not live by bread alone; that honor, glory, prestige are potent goals of human behavior. Along with Marxists, they revile the alleged materialism of
bourgeois democracy. Duty, honor, and sacrifice are idealized as against
material welfare, individual "rights," and personal happiness in the form
of pleasure, the alleged goals of the decadent "plutocratic" democracies.
They also glorify strength, hold weakness in contempt, and tend to belittle
or even condemn the whole Christian ethic of humanitarianism. Most of
the rest of their doctrine can be related to this initial orientation.

AUTHORITARIANISM

Fascism is authoritarian. It holds that authority and responsibility
should proceed from the top down, rather than in the reverse order. It
belittles democracy as inefficient and vulgar, as enthroning the ignorant and
the incompetent. The *élite,* the strong of mind, body, and will, should seize

[1] For a perceptive essay on the nature of mass movements, see Eric Hoffer, *The True
Believer* (New York: Harper & Row, 1951).

political power and retain it. They should, in Platonic fashion, select and train their successors. Beyond mere authoritarianism, the doctrine glorifies the institution of a permanent dictator. The leader is inspired. He establishes a mystical relation between himself and the people whereby he is able to represent them, their interests and fundamental needs, far better than could any body of elected representatives—far better, indeed, than they could themselves.

ALL–INCLUSIVENESS—STATISM

Fascism brings all aspects of social life under the control of the state. It proclaims the ideal of complete unity of society and the absolute sovereignty of the state over all the acts of man. It denounces (and, in practice, smashes) independent trade unions, independent cooperatives, and independent political parties. It seeks to control all forms of cultural, social, and economic organization. Everything must be for the state and nothing against the state, as Mussolini proclaimed. All evidence of class struggle must be suppressed. The doctrine of individual rights is explicitly disavowed. The individual owes duties, but is entitled to no rights, except as the state sees fit to grant them. The right of the state is absolute. Liberty is to be found in following the commands of the state. Society is likened to an organism in which the part can have no life except in serving the whole, and in which the whole is greater than the sum of the parts.

EXTREME ETHNOCENTRISM

Fascism is super-nationalistic and (in the case of Germany) race-conscious. Ethnocentrism is carried to the extreme. The apotheosis of the state is justified by a dogma that the national or racial group, as the case may be, is superior to all other such groups, and therefore destined to expand and dominate. Hegel, Treitschke, and Mazzini, to mention no others, are here relied on for support. Might, it is claimed, makes right, for indeed the righteous are mighty. Curiously, although allegedly anti-deterministic, fascist philosophy at this point takes on a deterministic color. Hitler believed that it was the preordained destiny of the Aryan race, with Germany in the lead, to dominate the world.

AGGRESSIVE NATIONALISM OR RACISM

In the case of the leading fascist regimes, their extreme ethnocentrism led, as it naturally does, to expansionist, aggressive foreign policies—which eventually brought them to their destruction—and to the glorification of war. The German Ewald, expressed the spirit of the movement when he declared: "War provides the ground on which the human soul may manifest itself at its fullest height. . . . War is a purifying bath of steel breeding new impulses, and an infallible test of fitness."[2]

---

[2] Quoted by Aurel Kolnai, *The War Against the West* (New York: Viking, 1938), pp. 411-412. The eminent psychologist, Franz Alexander, has argued that a state can enslave its

Fascist aggressive nationalism requires an enemy as a focus of all the frustrations and hostilities that brought it into being and that it, by its acts, creates. This enemy may be within the state as well as without it. Indeed, the "alien within the Homeland" may serve fascist purpose more effectively than an external enemy, who can only be attacked at great cost and perhaps at the cost of the life of the regime itself. In Nazi Germany it was the tragedy of the Jews (and also of the world) that they fulfilled this role.

ROMANTIC ANTI-INTELLECTUALISM

Unlike Marxism, fascism, especially in the Nazi version, is not a rationalistic doctrine. On the contrary, it has many mystical elements, like the leadership principle, the belief in an appointed mission, and the idea of the state or race as an end in itself. Fascism expressly belittles the rational and the intellectual. Its emphasis is placed upon will and upon action. Action is better than inaction even if it is wrong, declared Mussolini.

In its general orientation, fascism attempts to look both backward and forward. It relies heavily upon sentimental attachments to the past. It glorifies the "good old days," and promises their restoration. It talks in terms of return to rural life, to the old-style family life, and to many other lost values. In this respect it is to be contrasted to Communist Utopianism. On the other hand, it promises a better life and a more powerful nation than has ever been experienced before. In this sense, at least, it looks to the future.

ENDS AND MEANS

Finally, fascists hold that the ends of fascism justify any means that may be useful for their purposes. The combination of the legal and the illegal and of violence with propaganda is typical of the methods that enabled both Mussolini and Hitler to accomplish what has been aptly called a "sliding revolution."[3] It is perhaps in the field of propaganda that the fascists, and especially Hitler himself, have made the greatest "advances" over their predecessors in controlled fanaticism. The idea that incessant repetition will gain credence for almost any statement, regardless of its truth or falsehood, has long been well known to advertisers. Hitler grasped its significance for politics and capitalized on it in the political realm to a greater extent than had ever been done before. Moreover, as he set forth in a famous chapter of *Mein Kampf*, far from falsehood being a bar to belief, "the bigger the lie" the more readily will it gain credence.

---

citizens and maintain their support only by giving them some such powerful compensation as actual or promised domination of others. Franz Alexander, *Our Age of Unreason: a Study of the Irrational Forces in Social Life* (Philadelphia: Lippincott, 1942), p. 270.

[3] Cf. Arnold Brecht, *Prelude to Silence* (New York: Oxford U. P., 1944), p. 49.

Institutions

For present purposes we need not tarry long over the institutions of a fascist regime. In general outline they are familiar; in particular they vary from regime to regime. In the Leader, and his immediate, and sometimes shifting, coterie of lieutenants, resides supreme power. The attention of students of the subject is commonly concentrated on the single, monolithic Party as an agency of control. But it must be recognized that that is precisely what it is, especially after the regime has consolidated itself in power—an *agency* of the Leader. He is dominant.[4] Subject to him and his immediate cohorts, the Party, supported by secret police and a subservient army, provide the central engines of control.

SHAM DEMOCRACY

Sham institutions of representative government may be provided. In Italy they were cast in a corporative mold, growing out of Mussolini's early Syndicalist leanings, while in Germany more orthodox forms were retained. But these details are of no great importance. They provide some pageantry, promote the idea of unity (since partisan strife is absent), constitute lip service to the democratic idea, and generally conduce to legitimacy.

So also with popular elections. They are transformed into plebiscites, voters being given no effective alternative to support of the regime. They provide opportunities for educational and propagandist activities. They create the appearance of consensus and doubtless contribute somewhat to its reality.

DESTRUCTION OF VOLUNTARY GROUPS—THE "CORPORATE" SOCIETY

The rulers of all modern totalitarian states recognize the truth pointed out much earlier in this volume[5] that any healthy society comprises a maze of interacting and overlapping groups or voluntary associations and that the individuals within the society must rely overwhelmingly upon this group life for their effective freedom. By choosing the groups to which he shall give his support and by participating in formulating and carrying out the purposes of these groups, the individual develops his potentialities, exercises choice, and organizes powerful centers both for positive action and for resistance against despotic government. Recognizing this fact, advocates of the totalitarian state from Plato to the present have been opposed to the principle of free association. Similarly, today's totalitarians have followed up their seizure of power by declaring relentless war on all manner of associations. Sometimes they have smashed them completely, sometimes they

[4] See C. W. Cassinelli, "The Totalitarian Party," *Journal of Politics*, 24 (1962), pp. 111-141, esp. p. 140.

[5] Above, pages 60-61.

have been content to oust the existing leadership and install faithful followers of the Party in their positions.

In pursuit of its totalitarian aim, the fascist state strives to destroy all
existing organizations and social units, which might constitute centers of
independence and resistance, and to create new, organic structures integrated
into a final, hierarchical unity. The new structures differ from the old not
only in lack of autonomy but also in another significant respect: membership in them is compulsory rather than voluntary. The phenomenon of rival
organizations competing for members from the same categories of individuals is virtually unknown in a fascist state. The various partly competing
and partly complementary leadership elites of pluralistic democracy are
destroyed. In their place, fascists try to build one, integrated dominant elite.
The new elite is not organizationally unified, but is distributed among
party, governmental, military, bureaucratic, industrial, occupational, and
other organizations, including those that have displaced the old voluntary
organizations. Largely for this reason it is vitally important to totalitarian
dictatorships not only to have a single Leader but also to espouse and demand adherence to a common body of doctrine, serving to unite the various
leadership groups.

POLICE STATE

Control is further insured by the all-too-familiar instrumentalities of
the police state. The rule of law is abandoned wherever the interests of the
regime are deemed to require it. Secret police, "blood purges," informers
(even within the family), and all the engines of terrorism are mobilized in
support of those in power.

POSITIVE SUPPORTS FOR THE REGIME

In addition, the regime resorts to a variety of positive devices for evok-
ing support. Party membership is made a matter of prestige and special
organizations for various age groups of youth seek to arouse enthusiasm for
the movement, to instill loyalty to it in the minds of the young, aiding in
the universal process of indoctrination. The communications function is
performed but is perverted in two vital respects. In the first place, it tends
to be much more directed toward passing information from the center to
the periphery than the other way about. Even more fundamentally, *neutral*
institutions for communication (an independent press, for example) are
completely nonexistent, neutrality being incompatible with the nature of
totalitarianism. The communications industries are subjected to complete
government control and propaganda becomes a main activity of the state.

The political party in the totalitarian dictatorship is barely comparable
to the institution that goes by the same name in democracies. It is of course
not an agency for popular control of the government, but rather almost the

reverse, an agency for leadership control of the people. It does, however, play a major role not only in consolidating support for the regime and in creating consensus, but also in the process of political socialization and recruitment. Sometimes it also performs governmental functions, either in its own right or by way of its members in military, administrative or other position of authority. "Boundary maintenance" between government and party and even between polity and society tends to disappear under totalitarianism. But by the same token, the Party (and the same is true of the regime as a whole) is less monolithic than is widely believed. The Party, in particular, at once serves the function of holding together in one organization and subject to one leadership quite disparate groups and interests, and at the same time, by its monopoly of access to posts of leadership, of excluding from the political process those elements that the regime has not been able to integrate.

The fascist regime seeks not merely to generate and channel political support to itself: it aims to combat political alienation, to "politicize" the society. For this purpose, and to dissipate the discontents that both contribute to and grow out of alienation, probably no therapy is more effective than participation. The object of participation matters not. It may be cheering and demonstrating at rallies, marching in uniform on Sundays, or any of a wide variety of kinds of busy-work. In this as in other regards the tactics of the totalitarians are often based upon a sounder appraisal of the psychological needs of the people they are dealing with than that of democratic leaders in similar situations.[6]

ECONOMIC AND SOCIAL POLICY

On the economic side fascism demonstrates its pragmatic nature. It has no specific economic doctrine except that economics must be subordinate to politics. Fascism appeals to all groups, not just a single stratum of society; therefore, its economic doctrine and practices must be flexible. Private property is sometimes extolled, while the abuses of capitalism are condemned. In harmony with their statist doctrine, fascists invade many of the supposed "rights" of private property. Business enterprises are severely regulated, profits strictly limited, and, frequently, owner-managers forced to step aside and yield their places to representatives of the Party.

Finally, while fascists proclaim the ideal of inequality and practice it as far as concerns the distribution of political power, in Germany in particular they did much to establish greater social equality. Many vestiges of feudal privilege were swept aside by the "new order." Also they did much to improve the lot of the working man by increasing his economic security and by other devices intended to inflate his self-esteem.

[6] Cf. Seymour Martin Lipset, *Political Man* (Garden City, N.Y.: Doubleday, 1960), p. 180.

ORIGIN AND NATURE OF FASCISM

Before saying anything about the significance of fascist totalitarianism, we must note the outstanding facts about how it comes into being and the situation that gives rise to it, for here we find some of the most important lessons for the political scientist. When a regime has lost its legitimacy, when the government seems utterly incapable of coping with the problems that confront it, the time is ripe for revolution or *coup d'état*. If the government in power is clearly the organ of a particular class and if the rest of the society or the politically active part of it feels it is oppressed, the result may be a revolution, assuming the class that has been in power is still sufficiently united and willing to fight to make recourse to revolution necessary. Such a condition prevailed in Russia in 1917. Otherwise, however, and especially where the government is not seen as oppressive but simply as inadequate (as in Germany in 1932), a relatively bloodless transfer of power is likely to occur. Moreover, if this condition develops in a country where the class structure is fairly complicated, where important elements of pluralism exist, and where the governmental weakness reflects the inability of numerous strong groups within the polity to compromise their differences, the new regime is likely to be fascistic. A real or putative threat of Communist success adds strength to a fascist movement.

Italy

In Italy where fascism first came into being, several significant facts should be noted. It was a relatively new state, having attained to national unity under the leadership of Cavour and Garibaldi only in 1870. Its experience with democratic institutions was similarly limited. Its parliamentary system was plagued by the difficulties inherent in a multiparty system. In the period following the conclusion of the first World War, severe disappointment with the terms of the peace treaty combined with severe economic distress to dishearten everyone and at the same time to provide socialist parties, with Moscow's support, an opportunity for effective agitation. The strike was almost continuously used as a powerful weapon of economic, social, and political disruption. In the face of this crisis the government was ineffective. Someone has defined fascism as "the forcible reintegration of a disintegrated society." It is hardly surprising that it arose under the circumstances just sketched. In 1919 Benito Mussolini, an erstwhile Socialist agitator, began the organization of a movement, drawing from virtually all elements and levels of society, and committed to attaining power rather than to a specific program. Mussolini's charismatic leadership qualities plus the strategy of gradually infiltrating the government itself and, in various localities, effectively taking over the functions of government where the latter had failed produced a situation in which the actual seizure of power in the famous "march on Rome" was accomplished with hardly a struggle. It is typical of the fascist technique that even after this capture of the machinery of central government, the constitutional mechanism for a while continued with little change, and Mussolini ruled in semi-constitutional fashion, with other political parties continuing to exist. Bit-by-bit over a three year period, between 1922 and 1925, he consolidated his rule until he was able to abolish other political parties and establish himself as a totalitarian dictator.[7]

Germany

We shall discuss the case of Germany in greater detail, partly because in that country fascism achieved its fullest development, and partly because the sources of German fascism and the reasons for its success have been subjected to more extensive analysis. Here too was a country whose national consolidation had but recently been achieved and whose experience with democracy was extremely limited. Germany was not a disappointed victor in war but a frustrated and humiliated loser. Finally, once more economic disaster and an unstable and ineffective parliamentary regime combined with middle and upper class fear of a powerful Communist movement and with widespread frustration and discontent to set the stage for a "man on horseback." Reintegration and rehabilitation of morale were sorely needed. In Germany as in Italy the charismatic leader who won his way, step by step, and largely within the bounds of the constitution to total power relied heavily upon the development of and an appeal to an intensified spirit of nationalism; but in this case racialism became an added element in the drive to attain unity of the in-group.

Although the National Socialist ("Nazi") party, of which Adolf Hitler soon became the "Fuehrer" (Leader), was organized at roughly the same time that Mussolini's movement was begun, it did not become a powerful force until after the financial crisis of 1929 that touched off the Great Depression, and did not attain success until 1933. Also in this case the doctrine, as first set forth in Hitler's *Mein Kampf*[8] preceded the success of the movement.

---

[7] We do not mean by this account to deny that other influences helped shape the crisis of postwar Italian government. The war itself partly brought about and partly accelerated a revolution in political habits and relations. Deep-lying economic tendencies, antedating the war, sharpened disparities of wealth and differences in social station. Also following the war the spectacular successes of two "mass parties," the Socialists and the *Popolari*, or Christian Democrats, unsettled established constitutional relations. For a good, brief summary, see Denis Mack Smith, *Italy, A Modern History* (Ann Arbor: Univ. of Michigan Press, 1959), pp. 320-333.

[8] Adolf Hitler, *Mein Kampf*, trans. Ralph Manheim (Boston: Houghton Mifflin, 1943).

GROUP SUPPORT

What groups composed and supported Hitler's movement, the NSDAP? First of all, *youth*. In disproportionate numbers the young men of Germany flocked to the banners of Adolf Hitler. Unemployed youth, many of whom had been educated for professional work and found no such work to do, were especially susceptible. But not only unemployed youth. Youth with both materialistic and idealistic aims, youth seeking escape or adventure, youth seeking security, and youth seeking reform and the moral elation consequent upon pursuit of high aims in common with others flocked to Hitler's support. Secondly, the *unemployed* generally. Large numbers of those for whom the industrial machine had failed to provide economic security joined the ranks of the brown shirts. A third group, overlapping the others to be sure, was made up of *disillusioned Socialists* and even *Communists*. To these people, when victory for the Left appeared hopeless, union with the radical Right often seemed preferable to any other alternative. Fourth, the *lower middle classes* contributed to the mass base of Hitlerism. Here we find white collar workers, people whose life savings had been wiped out by the ruinous inflation of the post-war years, small businessmen seeking protection against the encroachments of Big Business, and

"First of all, youth"

Wide World Photos

farmers, plagued in Germany as in this country during the 'twenties by agricultural depression. Also, a small minority, but a significant few of Germany's big businessmen contributed heavily to the party coffers of the NSDAP at a time when it was practically bankrupt. These men were seeking protection against the trade unions, against the antimonopoly threats of the Bruening government, and against the possible success of Communism.

It would be a mistake, however, to lay too much stress on any one category, and especially upon any one economic group. Studies of both the NSDAP and of the Italian Fascists indicate that most parts of the population contributed their proportionate share. Earlier interpretations of fascism as primarily a lower middle class movement have been largely discredited. The table below suggests that in Germany, while Nazi party membership was more heavily lower middle class in its composition and less heavily made up of manual workers and peasants than the population as a whole, nonetheless the latter categories were large. In fact, if domestic servants and agricultural family helpers—certainly not middle class elements—be added to these groups, they comprised over half of the Party in 1933. The most important sources of fascist support appear to have been youth, especially newly eligible voters, who had acquired no allegiance to any of the older political parties, and the apathetics.[9] It is a fair hypothesis that both the

TABLE VII

PERCENTAGE OCCUPATIONAL DISTRIBUTION
OF NAZI PARTY MEMBERSHIP*

Occupational Classification	Party Membership		Total Gainfully Employed	
	1933 (1)	1935 (2)	1933 (3)	1935 (4)
Manual Workers	31.5	32.1	46.3	38.5
White-collar Employees	21.1	20.6	12.5	12.5
Independents[1]	17.6	20.2	9.6	9.6
Officials	6.7	13.0	4.6	4.6
Peasants	12.6	10.7	21.1	28.9
Others[2]	10.5	3.4	5.9	5.9

[1] Skilled artisans, professional persons, merchants, etc.
[2] Domestic servants and nonagricultural family helpers.
In Column 3 agricultural workers are included with manual workers. In Column 4 agricultural workers are classified as peasants, so that manual workers are almost all urban.
* From Hans Gerth, "The Nazi Party: Its Leadership & Composition," *American Journal of Sociology*, 45 (1939-40), pp. 517-541, at p. 527. Reprinted by permission of the University of Chicago Press.

[9] See Norman L. Stamps, *Why Democracies Fail* (Notre Dame, Ill.: Notre Dame U. P., 1957), pp. 81-82. This thesis finds further support in a statistical study of German and Austrian Nazis by Walter B. Simon, "Motivation of a Totalitarian Mass Vote," *British Journal of Sociology*, 10 (1959), pp. 338-345. Simon's data suggest that the totalitarian vote was largely a nonideological protest vote cast by previously nonvoters and members of minor parties. The plausibility of the susceptibility of political apathetics to mass movements is supported by American voting studies. See Campbell and others, *The American Voter* (New York: Wiley, 1960), Ch. 15, *passim*. This study shows that American farmers

idealistic aspect of fascist doctrine and the prospect of excitement, adventure, and achievement (which appeals especially to youth) powerfully attracted the latter to fascist movements.

BEHAVIOR

The difficulty of finding any common thread uniting such a variety of interests is manifest. Before trying to interpret these data, let us approach the problem from another angle. Actions speak louder than words. The doings of fascism—and especially of National Socialism—supply us with another important indication of its real nature. First of all, the National Socialists completely abolished democracy and the rule of law. Competition of political parties was superseded by a one-party monopoly. Freedom of expression and of organization was obliterated. All phases of private and social life were "coordinated" under an all-encompassing state control. Jews and Communists were persecuted without mercy or respect for any of the restraints of civilized behavior. Strikes were outlawed, in the name of putting an end to class struggle. Unemployment was eliminated, partly by a large program of public works, but to a greater extent by resort to a gigantic rearmament program. Business was subjected to regulations so extensive that practically no area of what could be called a free economy was left. Price control, credit control, control of foreign trade and of raw materials, taxation, and direct intervention in management—all of these devices were utilized to the fullest. Finally, the Treaty of Versailles was denounced, the Rhineland was occupied by the German army, and German dominance generally was reasserted.

Certain dominant objectives of the Nazis may be readily observed. The maintenance of Hitler and his followers in power at all costs ranks first on the list. Next in order, economic security and national aggrandizement appear to have been the imperatives by which National Socialist policy was governed. It should also be noted, as of more than passing significance, that, in the process, the institutions of capitalism were profoundly modified —almost beyond recognition.

FASCISM AS REACTION TO THREAT OF COMMUNISM

Now, in the light of these facts about the composition and behavior of the National Socialist party, let us consider two or three of the many interpretations that have been offered. A once popular theory holds that

---

tend to be politically apathetic and, in times of crisis, to be relatively easily drawn away from their usual party alignments. A German electoral study also supports the same thesis if it be assumed that German farmers, like American farmers, tend to rate low on the scale of political involvement. The study in question showed that in Schleswig-Holstein the owners of family farms swung to Hitler's support in strikingly disproportionate numbers as compared to other elements of the population. Rudolf Heberle, *From Democracy to Nazism* (Baton Rouge: Louisiana State Univ. Press, 1945), pp. 94-99.

fascism, wherever it appears, is a movement of capitalists to protect themselves from Communism and to reassert their supremacy. In only slightly different forms, this theory has been espoused by both Communists and fascists, the former declaring that fascism is based upon a conspiracy on the part of capitalists to crush all opposition to them, while fascists pose as saviors of Europe from the ravages of Bolshevism. This theory is at least initially plausible. Fascism has generally arisen where Communism was a threat. So in Italy, so in Germany, and so in Spain. Fascist policies lend support to this interpretation. Note, for example, the destruction of the trade unions and the persecution of Communists and Socialists. But, although the theory contains important elements of truth, it fails to account for all of the facts. Fascism, both in Italy and in Germany, was definitely a mass movement. How, under the conspiracy theory, can we account for the predominant support of noncapitalistic elements? This massive fact is in itself enough to indicate the inadequacy of this simple, economic interpretation. It should be noted, too, that in Italy, at least, the danger of Communism had clearly passed before Mussolini came to power.[10]

John Kautsky distinguishes sharply between fascist movements and fascist regimes, contending that the latter always include important elements of the old, landed aristocracy and big business. In other words, he argues that fascist movements can succeed only by allying themselves with these other elements (with their military and bureaucratic strongholds), which then help determine the direction of policy. The cases of the leading examples of fascism lend considerable support to this thesis.[11]

"BLOOD STREAM" AND SIMILAR THEORIES

At the other extreme from theories that would make fascism a necessary stage in the evolution of capitalism, are those that would explain it by conditions peculiar to each of the countries concerned. Something in the blood stream of Germans, or of Prussians, it is said—some special dose of original sin—sets the stage for domestic autocracy and international outlawry. Militancy, expansionism, pan-Germanism, a messianic complex, antisemitism and the idea of the Master Race—none of these is new in Germany. National Socialism is but the modern form of these indelible characteristics of the German people.

Alluring as this theory may be in its simplicity, it will not withstand examination. Fascism presented a well-defined pattern, which manifested itself with only minor variations in many parts of the world. It did not even

[10] For a summary of data supporting the thesis that fascism is, more than anything else, a middle class movement, see Seymour Martin Lipset, *Political Man* (Garden City, N.Y.: Doubleday, 1960), Ch. 5. Lipset also argues in this chapter, entitled " 'Fascism'—Left, Right, and Center," that fascism may, under varying circumstances, assume any of a variety of positions along the political spectrum.

[11] See John H. Kautsky, *Political Change in Underdeveloped Countries, Nationalism and Communism* (New York: Wiley, 1962), pp. 97-106.

originate in Germany. The Italians, who gave birth to it, have not exhibited any recurring strain of expansionism and love of goose-stepping. In many ways the success of Mussolini's movement was in direct defiance of what had seemed to be the national characteristics of Italians. And what about German communities outside of Germany? Far from taking with them their alleged racial characteristics, Germans who have migrated overseas have frequently been leaders in the development of peaceful and democratic societies. The examples of predominantly German and ultra-democratic Milwaukee or Reading are cases in point.

This whole theory commits the common fallacy of reading history backwards. As Peter Drucker says: "If the Germans instead of Nazism had developed a German form of Ghandi pacifism, we would have had many books showing the 'inevitability' of this development in the light of the Reformation, Luther, Kant, Beethoven, or F. W. Foerster. . . . If the English had developed a totalitarian philosophy, the pseudo-historians would have had a field day with Henry VIII, that great totalitarian Cromwell, Hobbes, Bentham, Carlyle, Spencer, and Bosanquet. . . . A century ago it was customary in both England and America to start every history book with a long hymn of praise to those Teutonic qualities which in Arminius, Luther, and Frederick the Great shook off the yoke of Latin tyranny and founded freedom."[12] According to the once-popular Freeman school of historians, many of our most revered Anglo-Saxon institutions, such as trial by jury and even representative government itself, first developed in the forests of Germany, as a product of Teutonic genius. The fact is that the blood-stream theory accepts National Socialism's own fallacies of the uniqueness of the German race and of the dominant importance of race in history.

A study of German election statistics between 1871 and 1933 is both interesting and enlightening.[13] It reveals a remarkable correspondence between prosperity and democratic strength, and, conversely, between economic and political adversity, on the one hand, and the success of the Nazis, on the other. Here is a synopsis of the findings. For the sake of simplicity, the various German political parties may be grouped together into three categories; the nationalistic parties, the nonsocialist republican parties, and the labor parties. (The last group includes both Social Democrats and Communists, of which the former were always the more numerous.) Between 1871 and 1912, the nationalistic parties, which began this period by polling 53 percent of the total vote cast, steadily declined in strength until in the last-named year their supporters comprised only 26 percent of the total

[12] Peter F. Drucker, *The Future of Industrial Man* (New York: John Day, 1942), pp. 13-14. William L. Shirer's best-selling book, *The Rise and Fall of the Third Reich: A History of Nazi Germany* (Simon and Schuster, 1959), is marred by the too easy acceptance of this line of thought.

[13] Sidney L. W. Mellon, "The German People and the Postwar World—a Study Based on Election Statistics, 1871-1933," *American Political Science Review*, 37 (1943), pp. 605-25.

voters. During the same period, the Social Democratic party increased its strength from three to 35 percent. In January, 1919, before the signing of the Treaty of Versailles, the line-up was as follows: nationalistic parties, 15 percent; nonsocialist republicans, 39 percent; labor parties, 45 percent. Five years later in May, 1924, the picture was quite different. The new government had been compelled to sign the Treaty of Versailles, the French had occupied the Ruhr to enforce the blank check included in that treaty, and runaway inflation had wiped out the savings of millions of Germans. Now the nationalistic parties more than doubled their support, obtaining 39 percent of the vote. The nonsocialist republicans declined from 39 to 25 percent and the labor parties from 45 to 34 percent. Just four years later and the trend of events had again taken another turn. The Dawes settlement had eased the burden of reparations, American loans had aided in the reconstruction of Germany, and she was experiencing a considerable degree of general economic recovery. As a result the vote for the nationalistic parties declined to 30 percent, while the other parties showed definite signs of revival, the nonsocialist republicans coming up to 28 percent and the labor parties securing 40 percent of the total vote. Incidentally, the National Socialists never polled a sizable vote or (following 1924) showed signs of growing until after 1929.

In short, the major swings in popular sentiment in Germany during this period can be explained largely in terms of the economic, social, and moral hardships—and recoveries—through which the German people lived. Evidence of an unusually strong predisposition toward dictatorship and aggression is completely lacking. On the other hand, to quote Mellon, "there is plain evidence that when social and economic conditions are tolerable, their political tendencies are preponderantly democratic and reasonable—above all, capable of improving."[14]

AN ECLECTIC EXPLANATION

Only an eclectic theory can do justice to the situation. We may group what seem to be the most significant factors under three heads: (1) the political weakness of the democratic regime, (2) a breakdown of the old nonrational supports of the state, and (3) a revolt against reason, which undermined the rational supports.

As to the political weaknesses, first of all the Weimar Republic lacked a strong democratic tradition. To be sure, every democratic government must sometime get its start, with no democratic tradition to support it. But hard is the way of the democracy that makes its first steps without the support of a strong tradition during a period of adversity. Such was Germany's lot. There had been little real democracy in the imperial institutions of the pre-1914 era. The political parties had been chiefly agencies of criticism

[14] *Ibid.*, p. 623.

and opposition. They had had no real opportunity to be constructive or to assume responsibility. As a result, they were doctrinaire, inflexible.

This heritage was made worse, rather than improved, by the electoral system. The particular form of proportional representation which was provided for the new government was one that encouraged disagreement rather than agreement, the splitting of parties rather than amalgamation, and intransigence rather than compromise. It cannot be doubted that this factor in itself played an important role in preventing the development of a mature party system, without which no democracy is secure.

Uncertainty in the division of power between the legislative and the executive branches of government and between the President and the Chancellor aggravated the difficulties. Especially in the critical period of January and February, 1933, this lack of definition and limitation upon the powers of the President provided the opening whereby the aging Hindenberg admitted the camel's nose under the edge of the tent. The American separation of powers, it may be observed, is in some respects similar to the Weimar system, and provides a like opportunity for weakness in times of crisis. A situation that can be tolerated, however, where there is an underlying consensus among the people, buttressed by a successful political tradition, may be disastrous where that consensus and history are lacking.

The lack of a social basis for democracy constituted still another aspect of Weimar's political weakness. Great numbers of the old aristocracy who still harbored the desire to abolish democracy and all its works were allowed to remain entrenched in their landed estates, in the army, and even in the judiciary and the civil service. They gladly contributed to democracy's collapse.

All of these factors taken together might not be enough, under normal circumstances, to destroy democracy, let alone to produce fascism—but they certainly tempted fate. So much for the political weaknesses of the Weimar regime. We turn to the breakdown of the traditional nonrational supports.

When society is 'settled,' most people accept its institutions without question, even though some of them work pretty badly. But industrial societies in the twentieth century tend not to be 'settled.' Old loyalties have been shattered, people have been uprooted from familiar surroundings and groupings; and they have been deprived of their established expectations. Fathers can no longer assume that their sons will carry on in the traditional family occupation. Sons can not always assume that it will be possible for them to maintain the same manner and standard of living to which they have grown accustomed in the household of their parents. Under these circumstances, the normal calm and acceptance gives way to a restlessness and uneasiness, a craving for excitement and a longing for a return to the security of the old days and ways.

To be more specific, we may mention the decline in religious faith. For thousands of people religion has ceased to provide a soul-satisfying emotional and spiritual experience. This change has left a void, a vacuum, in people's lives, which provides a ready receptacle for a new faith. The uprooting of countless families from their traditional country homes and surroundings, as modern society brings both more frequent changes of habitat and a general movement from country to city, adds to the lack of firmness of society. If country life encourages stability, certainly city life has the opposite effect. Its whole tempo is more exciting and more unstabilizing. Family life is weakened, for example, by the substitution of the movie, the car, and other outside sources of entertainment, for the home as a center of fellowship and recreation. Economic uncertainty attends the occupations commonly accompanying city life. The stakes are higher but the risk is greater. Altogether the loneliness and insecurity of urban life go far to prepare the way for conversion to one of the political religions in times of domestic crisis.[15] These developments make it far more difficult for a society to weather any kind of a storm—and note that these developments characterize all modern industrial societies.

Both of the factors so far discussed, however—the political weakness of Germany and its social instability—are more sources of frailty than positive causes of Hitler's success. We have yet to account for the third and last of our significant factors: the revolt from reason, anti-rationalism, nihilism, or primacy of the will, with its fervent commitment to a Leader despite the fact that his promises could not stand rational criticism. Perhaps this factor is the most complicated of the three. Yet, on the psychological level, the explanation of this revolt from reason is simple enough. It is the product of frustration and despair.

Again, this is not a mood so foreign to the experience of Americans as to be beyond their comprehension. In March, 1933, the United States experienced a milder version of it. Will Rogers felt it, with the true humorist's sensitivity for popular feeling. At the depth of the Great Depression, on the occasion of President Roosevelt's first inauguration, he cried out: "Mr. President, Do Something, if it is only to burn the White House!"

The major causes of frustration and despair in Germany during the period between 1919 and 1933 are easily spotted. First, there was military defeat—a bitter pill for a proud nation to swallow. Added to this were the (believed) injustices of the Treaty of Versailles. And far more important than anything in the treaty were some of the subsequent acts of the Allies, which assured republican Germany's continued status as a second class

---

[15] In less critical periods the same facts may lead to that apathy and conformism about which social critics of the American scene have so much to say today. See David Riesman, *The Lonely Crowd* (New Haven: Yale U. P., 1950). In the text above, we are speaking of the pathology of urban living and of what is particularly likely to happen soon after a period of rapid movement from country to city. In Germany's case, conditions not far removed from feudalism had prevailed long after they had been largely eliminated in other industrialized countries, exaggerating the unstabilizing effects of the rapid transition.

nation: the impossible demands for reparations, the continuance of a system of unilateral disarmament, and the ban on union with Austria.

Of prime significance was the insecurity and often impoverishment of both middle and working classes. Deflated by inflation and oppressed by depression, the middle class felt itself caught between corporate industry and organized labor. On top of this came the staggering mass of unemployment in the early thirties. At the worst one out of every four men of working age was out of a job. Finally thanks to the political weaknesses, already described, at this desperate time when the need for effective governmental action was greatest, the German people were treated to the spectacle of a foundering and pusillanimous government. The constitutional flaws together with the lack of fundamental agreement—social, economic and political—resulted in a general stalemate, exacerbated by the systematic obstructionism of antidemocratic elements from both Left and Right. The resulting specter of governmental pusillanimity and the absence of any inspiring leadership sapped the support of constitutional government and contributed to a mood of despair that welcomed the irrationalism of the Nazis.[16] Fascism came to Germany, as it has come elsewhere, as the product of a lack of power rather than of a concentration of power.

Altogether the sources of psychological instability were too great to be withstood. "In the *Weltanschauung* of the NSDAP," wrote Frederick L. Schuman, "the German people found solace for all its woes, forgiveness for all its sins, justification for all its hatreds, scapegoats for all its misfortunes, and a millennial vision for all its hopes."[17] Dictatorship—a dictatorship based upon an appeal to a unifying principle, such as nationalism—appeared to be the only means of re-integrating a society in which basic agreement was so lacking that political action of any kind had become almost impossible. It was not unnatural that under these circumstances the fascist ideal of unity prevailed over the Communist ideal of class struggle.

The German case lends no support for any theory of a single cause leading inevitably to fascism. Hitler's strength was waning during the months just before he came to power. Had it not been for what must be called either the staggering incompetence or the deliberate treachery of von Hindenberg, he might well have failed completely and ignominiously. He lost two million votes during 1932. It should be noted, too, that his high point, in a free election, was 37 percent of the popular vote.

But National Socialism was not just an accident. It was like a nervous breakdown—not inevitable, but the natural culmination of a series of disorders and the resultant mounting tension. The germs of fascism lurk in every modern, industrial society. They are like the germs of common

---

[16] Cf. Peter F. Drucker, *The End of Economic Man* (New York: John Day, 1939). See also Emil Lederer, *State of the Masses* (New York: Norton, 1940); and Erich Fromm, *Escape From Freedom* (New York: Holt, 1941), Ch. 6.

[17] Frederick L. Schuman, *The Nazi Dictatorship* (New York: Knopf, 1935), p. 109.

diseases that are always around awaiting a favorable opportunity to develop. During any period of lowered vitality they may take advantage of some constitutional weakness and emerge triumphant.

Appraisal

Fascism claimed, of course, to be far more than a haven in time of emergency. It presented itself as an alternative to, and a great improvement on liberal democracy. It will be pertinent to make a few remarks of appraisal of its record in terms of its own major objectives of unity and efficiency. To take the latter first, the supposed advantages of dictatorship in this regard proved to be somewhat chimerical. Mussolini was credited with making the trains run on time. In other respects, too, undoubtedly a measure of efficiency was attained—especially in Italy where previous standards in this respect had not been high. In Germany, however, much evidence that became available after the defeat of Hitler's armies revealed shocking inefficiency. It has been established not only that many serious blunders impaired the efficiency of Germany's production for war but also that in numerous cases the lack of efficiency was directly attributable to the Nazi dictatorship. Rivalries, jealousies, and plain differences of opinion between various Nazi high officials often resulted in costly deadlock. In the United States, similar conditions frequently arose, but in a short time the situation was generally discovered by (or made known to) the press, with the result that the full glare of publicity forced an early settlement of the dispute. In short, one of the very aspects of democracy that is supposed to lead to delays and inefficiency (no matter how otherwise desirable it may be) proved, in certain instances at least, to be an invaluable corrective to the sources of costly delay.

As for the ideal of unity, several points are worthy of attention. The fascists themselves, in the effort to obtain power, did everything they could to create disunity among the elements opposed to them. Like the Communists, on their way to power they pursue a policy of social destructiveness; they thrive on chaos. They do everything in their power to prevent orderly, democratic discussion and to substitute an atmosphere of panic for one of calm deliberation. Nevertheless these tactics are most successful precisely where social unity is already badly marred by class struggle, by group particularism, or by excessive individualism. It is when people feel starved for the psychic satisfactions of healthy group life and frustrated by the inability of their government to take effective action that they are most susceptible to these tactics. Furthermore, the fascists undoubtedly had considerable success in reestablishing unity within the greater part of their national groups. It is the nature of mass movements to have this result. Unfortunately, it is also their nature to rely in part for the achievement of this purpose upon means that are revolting to all humanitarian sentiments, that are destructive of unity in the wider sphere, and that, incidentally, are ultimately self-defeating. Hitler's aggressive and expansionist nationalism led him to plunge the world into the second world war and ultimately brought both Germany and Italy to defeat. Nothing more needs to be said on this subject. The other destructive and antihumanitarian tactic pursued by totalitarian regimes in support of internal unity is that of group persecution. For the Bolsheviks it was bourgeoisie and the kulaks. For Germany, it was the Jews. The record speaks for itself.

Relation to General Principles of Political Science

What principles of political science are illustrated by fascism? In the first place, we see here in bold relief man's eternal need for security. Fascists have succeeded only where insecurity had driven men to despair. Economic insecurity bred of unemployment, loss of savings, inflation, and declining profits was a basic factor, probably a necessary condition of fascist successes. It seems likely too that there were, as probably there are in every industrial society, basic sources of psychological insecurity apart from purely economic matters. A dynamic industrial society, and especially one in which large numbers of people in the cities have but recently been uprooted from rural environments, lacks the sources of stability provided by country or village life. The ties of the family are weakened. The community is often virtually nonexistent. The church frequently ceases to perform its comforting function. The speed of life, the rate of change, means that people are constantly shifting in the social scale. Those who go down are frustrated, while even those who go up are sufficiently conscious of the possibility that the process may soon be reversed to feel insecure. Fascist movements correctly appraised the situation in putting great stress on security in their propaganda and, indeed, in their policies.

Closely related to the need for security is the need for a feeling of "belongingness."[18] Factors discussed in the preceding paragraph and previously indicate that this need tends to be slighted in modern society, especially in times of economic crisis. Fascism thrives on social disruption and on the anomie it creates.

Finally, we need only remark that a dictatorship that seeks to make its principle of legitimacy one of national or racial superiority, consigning other groups to the role of "slave peoples," practically assures its own ultimate defeat by consolidating the opposition.

COMMUNIST TOTALITARIAN DICTATORSHIP

Communist totalitarian dictatorship is the product of Communist theory and practice. The two are not identical but it is hardly feasible to discuss them separately; consequently our ensuing discussion of Communistic

[18] See Ch. 2, pp. 40-42.

totalitarianism, or totalitarian dictatorship, will be cast in the wider setting of Communism generally. Unlike fascism, Communism is first and foremost a body of doctrine as well as a movement designed to put the doctrine in practice by means of social revolution. It had been in existence for over seventy years before it established itself anywhere. Unlike fascism also its goal was not totalitarian dictatorship at all, but a free and democratic society. In fact, a free, equalitarian and cooperative society is still its professed goal. But we run ahead of our story.

Communist Theory

Communism, in its modern form, is a body of doctrine elaborated by Karl Marx and Frederick Engels, beginning about 1845, and their numerous followers since then, most notably by Lenin and Stalin. Since our concern is with present Communist doctrine rather than with its origins, we shall make no attempt to indicate what is Marxian and what is post-Marxian.

PHILOSOPHY OF HISTORY

At the basis of Communist doctrine is a philosophy of history, supplemented by a theory of the state and a body of economic theory. On these foundations are erected a series of propositions in the form of prophesies about the shape of things to come. Finally, the theory has much to say about the means of hastening the inevitable: strategic and tactical theory, and also its own ethics regarding the use of these means.

Communist philosophy of history is variously known as "dialectical materialism," "historical materialism," or the "materialistic conception of history." About the notion of the dialectic, borrowed from Hegel, we shall say little, although its role in giving a pseudo-scientific air to the theory has been great. Briefly, it holds that any given set of ideas and circumstances (referred to, in this connection, as a "thesis"), tends to call forth an opposite or opposing set of ideas and circumstances ("antithesis"), and that out of the clash between these opposing elements arises a third condition ("synthesis") that is different in kind from what went before, although it embodies elements from the previous conditions. This antithesis then becomes the thesis for a new round of triadic progression. Although Marxists have generally claimed that their account of the dialectic contains within it a causal theory of history, outside observers have generally failed to discover such an element, and even some theorists who were otherwise Marxists have disavowed such a claim and have been content to argue that the dialectic provided an insightful frame of reference through which to view history and the social process.

The dialectic came straight from Hegel, but Marx gave it distinctive shape and application by combining it with a form of economic determinism. This theory, which attributed to the mode of production, the relations of production, and the class struggle the leading roles in history, while making forms of government and legal systems only part of society's "superstructure," has been explained and criticized in Chapter IV, above.

The reason Marx fastened upon the mode of production, and especially the system of production as the critical factor is because he believed that systems of production always divided people into classes. A person's class is determined by his relations to the instruments of production. Thus, today, there are those who own these instruments and those who do not. All history, Marx proclaimed, has been a history of class struggle. Under the prevailing capitalist system society tends to be reduced to two classes, as suggested above, known as bourgeoisie and proletariat—the capitalists and the workers, the latter thought of as predominantly unskilled factory workers.

THEORY OF THE STATE

The state, according to this theory, is "superstructure." Its form is determined by the exigencies of the class struggle and the demands of the underlying material situation. Defined as an instrument of coercion, the state is held to be the product and the manifestation of the irreconcilability of class antagonisms. Normally, a single class is predominant, and that class controls the state and uses it to further its exploitation of the subordinate class or classes. Under capitalism, the state is in essence a committee of the bourgeoisie for the oppression and exploitation of the proletariat.

ECONOMIC THEORY

By the further development, and indeed perversion, of the thought of Ricardo and certain other classical economic theorists, Marx evolved the specific economic doctrine of Communism. All true value, he argued, is the product of labor; and the value of anything, therefore, is simply the cost of the labor it took to produce it. This cost, furthermore, is determined by the cost of maintaining the necessary laborers at the subsistence level. On the other hand, manufacturers are able to sell their products, in accordance with the laws of supply and demand, for more than their labor cost. The difference between this market value and labor value, he named "surplus value." It is from surplus value that profits are derived.

The role of the concept of surplus value in Marxian theory is twofold. In the first place, it is used to undermine the ethical position of the capitalist. His gains are ill-gotten; they are the product of exploitation, for they represent, so to speak, an unearned increment, over and above the "true" value of his product. Moreover, the true, or labor value of what is produced is kept down by an "iron law of wages" that holds wages to the subsistence level. This alleged characteristic of the capitalist system further undermines its ethical justification.

Secondly, the argument runs, since labor, as a whole, does not receive in wages a sum equal to the market value of the product, there is a want of purchasing power with which to buy back the product. As a result the capitalist system is subject to recurrent market gluts and consequent depressions or crises. (Incidentally, another result is to force the ruling class to look for foreign markets. Out of this situation arises imperialism, the exploitation of backward peoples, wars among capitalist nations growing out of their competitive struggle to acquire empires, and, finally, wars of liberation when the colonial areas become ready to cast off their shackles.) These crises become progressively worse. Eventually, they drive the suffering proletariat to revolt. Meanwhile, they contribute to another process which is important to the Marxist analysis—the elimination of all classes other than bourgeoisie and proletariat. Under capitalism, the rich get richer and the poor get poorer. Mixed and intermediate classes are gradually squeezed out of existence. Artisans, small shopkeepers, small farmers, are reduced to the status of wage earners. Some others may be promoted to membership in the ruling class; but in any case the bifurcation of society goes on and the stage is set for a final, cataclysmic clash between the small class who own the wealth and the instruments of exploitation and domination with the unpropertied masses.

Technological change is also important. Institutions, including such relations of production as the private ownership of capital itself, become outmoded and cease to contribute to the efficient development of natural resources. Communists do not argue that capitalism was always to be condemned. At a particular stage in the development of the arts and sciences it had a great contribution to make; it was all for the best. But new inventions, perhaps new resources, new economic potentialities call for new forms, new institutions, new property relations. Since these changes will interfere with the privileges of the existing ruling class they will be strenuously resisted. Therefore, only revolution can bring about the needed changes.

THE REVOLUTION AND AFTER

With the last statement we have already moved over into a consideration of Marx's predictions regarding the revolution and after. For reasons advanced above, he believed that the proletariat would ultimately be driven to revolt. And, for reasons less clearly enunciated, he believed that that revolt would be successful.[19]

Following the revolution and the seizure of power by the Communists, the advance guard of the proletariat, Communists postulate a transition period, during which the remains of the previous regime will be liquidated as rapidly as possible. The old state machinery will be smashed and in its

[19] At this point a few parenthetical remarks should be made. Although Marx thought the main prospect for revolution would be a revolt against one of the sham-democratic bourgeois governments of Europe, he acknowledged the possibility that the first revolution might come in a backward country, such as Russia, although this seemed to go counter to his general theory that social evolution must run through the capitalist-democratic phase before the revolution. Later Communists have recognized, too, that capitalist-democratic governments might give way to fascist governments before the coming of the successful Communist revolution.

place a strong "dictatorship of the proletariat" will be established. It will be the task of this government to crush the bourgeoisie and to create a classless society. It will be its task also to socialize the instruments of production, including land, for during this period Socialism, rather than Communism, prevails. The right of inheritance will be abolished. Incomes will not be equalized, but all income will be based on work, on contribution to society. According to the official theory, this "Socialist" stage has now been completed in the Soviet Union, and the transition to Communism has begun.

Finally, when no class but the proletariat remains, and (a recent addition to the theory) when the society is no longer threatened by surrounding capitalist societies (presumably when Communism has triumphed over most of the world), the coercive state will no longer be needed. It will "wither away." According to Communist theory all conflicts of interest arise out of class differences; class differences relate solely to the ownership of property; therefore, once private ownership of the instruments of production is abolished and classes are eliminated, conflicts of interest will cease to exist and, with them, the need for the state. Administrative organization, laws, and much of what we know of as government, today, will still be required; but the distinctive feature of the state, force, will not be needed. Likewise, when this ultimate Communist commonwealth is attained, differential rewards for differences in work will not be necessary. Thanks partly to Communist education and partly to the elimination of the profit motive men will now be altruistic, motivated by the desire to contribute to society, knowing that its institutions are devoted to their welfare. Consequently, the ideal distributive principle of "from each according to his ability, to each according to his needs" can be applied.

THEORY OF MEANS

Communist doctrine has much to say about means as well as ends. As with the fascist, the Communist holds that the end justifies the means. He believes the objectives he is promoting are so important that no moral principles or prohibitions should be allowed to stand in their way. Since he believes the end he is furthering is inevitable, and bound to be accomplished by violent revolution, it would be quixotic to be squeamish about methods. For the Communist to lie, to intrigue, and otherwise flaunt the canons of bourgeois morality is but the fulfillment of his obligation to his class and to mankind.

More specifically, Communists, especially Lenin, have developed the theory of *the* Party as the élite organization working for the proletariat. This party must be rigidly organized and disciplined, bound into a unity of doctrine and action so close that it can carry a weight far greater than that of other organizations larger but less efficient. Not only must the Party be monolithic, but it must contain no doubters, no weak spirits. It is an organization of militants and professional revolutionists ready to do anything at the command from above and to do it with a military discipline and precision.

Communist tactical theory calls for great flexibility. Communists do not hesitate to reverse themselves in midstream or to act inconsistently in different places. Moreover, their belief in the inevitability of revolution leads them, generally, to oppose reforms that might tend to quiet discontent. Rather, the capitalist machine must be made to work as badly as possible, so as to build up opposition to it. Of course, the strategy of the movement at any particular time may dictate a different course. The need to gain supporters for some short-run objective may lead Communists to form "united fronts" or "popular fronts" with reform movements for which they have secret contempt. During the thirties, Communists' fear of rising fascism led them to form united fronts with reform parties throughout most of the world. Now that fascism has been defeated they have generally returned to their more fundamental tactic, but are still ready to work with others in fostering disorder or revolution.

Practice Versus Theory

As we turn from theory to practice, two massive facts in the history of Communism stand out in stark contrast to the body of their doctrine. Marx and Engels believed that history unfolds in accordance with discoverable laws and predictable patterns. They believed that capitalism had played an essential role in historical development, as had feudalism before it, and in fact that in its day it had accomplished wonders in promoting economic development. Only after it had played out its role and a new order had developed within the womb of the old would the time be ripe for revolution and the installation of a Communist regime. How different the event! To date, all industrially advanced countries have successfully resisted the subversive and revolutionary attempts of Communist parties.[20] Communist successes have been in relatively poor and underdeveloped countries, weakened by war and other factors, governed by pre-capitalistic groups striving to protect the vested interests of a minority in an outmoded economic system. So it was in both Russia and China, the great examples of independent Communist successes.[21] Lenin and other modern Communist theoreticians have gone to great lengths to explain this departure from the

[20] The case of Czechoslovakia is not to the contrary. Only the intervention of the neighboring Soviet colossus and their isolation from Western support made possible the Communist takeover of that country.

[21] While most of the smaller nations that have succumbed to Communist regimes fit the same pattern, they also generally adopted Communism—if such a voluntaristic term as "adopted" is appropriate— in the presence and under the duress of Soviet or Chinese military forces. The case of Cuba will be discussed in the following chapter.

timetable of orthodox Marxism.[22] For a non-Marxist, however, the explanation is simple enough. For the reasons just recited the existing governments had lost legitimacy. The situation was ripe for revolution. The Communists above all were organized, disciplined, and trained for revolution; and their ideology, for reasons explained earlier in this volume, was peculiarly attractive to the peoples in question. Also, the requisites for successful democracy were in each case sadly lacking.[23]

The second great discrepancy between Marxian theory and Communist practice is that the "transitional stage" of "proletarian dictatorship" to which Marx and Engels made but passing reference, has proved to be a matter of indefinite duration.[24] Not only has the Soviet dictatorship lasted for over thirty years, but also it is a dictatorship in the true sense of the word; that is to say it is rule by one man or a small group rather than by the working class. Again Communist theoreticians, especially Joseph Stalin, have gone to great lengths to explain this course of events. First the necessity of finally liquidating the bourgeoisie and then the need to protect the regime against a circle of capitalist enemies was used to rationalize the continuing dictatorship (or, in their terms, the continuation of the "state").[25] We reserve comment until the institutions and practices of Communist totalitarianism have been briefly described.

Institutions and Practices

To that description we now turn, using the Soviet Union as our example.[26] It is at this point that the similarities between fascist and communist totalitarianism begin to manifest themselves. They are so great that our description can rely heavily on what has gone before.

CONSTITUTIONAL FORMS

The *forms* of government do not coincide with what has just been said. In accordance with its ultimately democratic ideals, the Soviet Union utilizes constitutional forms that in many respects borrow from Western liberalism.

---

[22] The most striking example is the theory of imperialism. Cf. V. I. Lenin, *Imperialism: the Highest Stage of Capitalism* (New York: International Publishers, 1933). See also David G. Smith, "Lenin's 'Imperialism': a Study in the Unity of Theory and Practice," *Journal of Politics*, 14 (1955), pp. 546-569.

[23] The subject of the relative appeals of Communist and democratic myths for the peoples of underdeveloped areas is discussed above, pp. 67-68 and the prerequisites for democracy are discussed at pp. 284-289.

[24] Except for this fact, which is of controlling significance, we would not be discussing Communism in a chapter on "Totalitarian Dictatorship."

[25] Klaus Mehnert discusses a number of these reinterpretations and amendments of the official ideology. See his *Stalin versus Marx* (London: Allen & Unwin, 1952).

[26] We select the Soviet Union for this description because it has had a longer history than Communist China and more is known about it. The evidence indicates, however, that Mao's China is fully as much a totalitarian dictatorship as is Khrushchev's Russia, or, for that matter, as was Stalin's Russia.

Red Square in Moscow

Sovfoto

Their present Constitution, adopted in 1936, might properly be described as being appropriate for a constitutional democracy. It sets up a federal union, with powers distributed between the central government and the constituent republics. It contains an elaborate bill of rights, setting forth liberties of the individual such as democracies are accustomed to guarantee to their citizens and including an elaborate list of social and economic rights. The legislative bodies, bicameral in form, are elected on the basis of universal suffrage, and what corresponds to the executive is responsible to the legislature. Any realistic description of government in the Soviet Union, however, must point out that this mechanism is a façade behind which the realities of politics are very different from the forms.

DIVERGING PRACTICES—A ONE–PARTY SYSTEM

When we move from formal to informal government, the first great fact that strikes the eye is the absence of competitive political parties. The Communist Party, the successor to the highly selected, trained, and disciplined body of militant revolutionaries that brought the regime into existence, continues to dominate the political scene. Although it is greatly enlarged as compared with its size at the time and the seizure of power, and somewhat watered-down in militancy, it still remains relatively small, comprising less than five percent of the electorate. This organization dominates the political life of the country. In all respects it plays essentially the same role as do fascist parties. Ballots do not provide the voter with alternative names. They confront him with just one name for each office, allowing him to vote "yes" or a futile "no" for that name. Moreover, the Party is able to determine who the nominees shall be, and for important positions they are universally Party members. Thus it is apparent that the real locus of power lies within the Party. More specifically, as under fascism, it lies within the leadership of that party, a small group, normally dominated by a single individual.

DICTATORSHIP

By the device of indirect elections and the use of the principle known as "democratic centralism" this centralized control is maintained within the forms of legality. From the time of the Revolution until his death, Lenin was the dominant figure in this group. After a sharp struggle with Trotsky, Stalin, who as General Secretary of the Party had been in a position to build up a personal machine of supporters, managed to make good his claim to succeed Lenin, a position which he held until his death in 1953.

Stalin's death was followed by a period of collective leadership and by a struggle for supremacy within this ruling group. Out of this struggle, during the next two or three years, by a process in which territorial Party leaders seem to have played a significant and probably determining role, Nikita Khrushchev gradually achieved a position of dominance. How completely dominant an individual must be to be called a "dictator" is not sharply defined, and how closely Khrushchev's power position approximates to that once occupied by Stalin it is impossible to tell. All dictators have to take account of the interests and demands of potential rivals and other leaders of powerful sectors of the polity. Doubtless Khrushchev is in a weaker position in this respect than was Stalin. Before saying more on this topic, however, we shall return to an explanation of the elements and operation of Communist totalitarian dictatorship.

CONTROL OF GROUP LIFE

The elimination of rival political parties is by no means the only device used for the entrenchment of the ruling group. Other associations are controlled and used in similar fashion to that described above in our account of fascism. Even the family is not spared. Communist doctrine reviled the family as a bourgeois institution. In practice the Soviet regime has weakened the family by making both divorce and abortion more easily obtainable, and by compelling mothers to work in industry while even tiny children were taken care of in public nurseries. The Church and all religion were likewise subjected to constant attack by Communist theory and then, in the event, vigorously assailed in practice. By persecution and all manner of harrying practices the number of priests and of churches was cut down by about ninety percent, although it would appear that the percentage of the faithful fell by no such amount. Since the outbreak of the Second World War, the church hierarchy has become obedient to Communist wishes, even as it had at an earlier date lent its support to the Czars; and accordingly the government has altered its policy to one of greater tolerance. All other types of association, cultural, recreational, economic, and the like, if not directly run by the Party, have within their membership well organized groups of Party members whose function it is to guide, as well as to keep an eye on their activities.

VIOLENCE

The policies we have been describing rest upon a firm and hard substructure of violence. Russia is a police state, and the ruling clique is ruthless in weeding out actual or suspected opposition elements, although today, among the higher echelons, it has to proceed with greater circumspection than in Stalin's time. The constitutional guarantees of individual liberties, fair trial, and so forth, are disregarded when it is a matter of suspected disloyalty. In Stalinist Russia the whole paraphernalia of secret police, special courts, concentration camps, and forced labor came into play. The knock on the door at night, the unexplained disappearance of individuals, these things represented the ever-present eye, ear, and hand of the Party.

In the post-Stalin era, the secret police have been at least nominally abolished. No great state trials of alleged traitors have been held in recent years, and it appears that "purging," even when applied to top leadership elements, nowadays usually takes the form of demotion or dismissal from office and Party councils, rather than death or incarceration. Only the course of events will answer the interesting and important question of whether the Soviet Union is undergoing significant change in these respects or whether apparent "liberalization" is characteristic only of a transitional period during which a new dictator consolidates his power.[27]

Today, more is accomplished by indoctrination, agitation, and the distribution of sanctions and indulgences than is done by harsher methods. In every shop, on every cooperative farm, everywhere where men and women work together, the Party has its cells, and that branch of the Party known as "Agitprop" is charged with responsibility for seeing that all are properly indoctrinated with Communist philosophy and with the Party line on current questions as well as stimulating active and enthusiastic support for the regime and its specific policies.[28]

---

[27] At this point it will pay us to take a sidelong glance at Communist China, for it is in that country that the device of "brain-washing" appears to have been most widely used and fully developed. The term and the practice it stands for has become so familiar that little elaboration is needed. Processes of isolation, group pressure, forced (and false) "confessions," and recantations combined with equally forced (using various refined methods of torture as necessary) positive statements of opinion and attitude that accord with the Party line. See Robert J. Lifton, "Thought Reform of Chinese Intellectuals," *Journal of Asian Studies,* 16 (1956), pp. 75-88.

[28] We do not mean to imply that the Agitprop units are always successful or even that they always try very hard. It is clear that the Party has to fight a continuous battle to keep interest in this kind of activity alive.

In Russia the Party is often spoken of as a "transmission belt." This overt recognition of its communications function points not only to its role in propagandizing but also to the fact that the Party provides listening posts as well as loud speakers. The ruling group is well aware of the importance of keeping itself fully informed of what people are thinking, what their criticisms are, and how they are reacting in general to public policies. The Soviet Union is far from democratic; but, in Madison avenue terms, it can be said to be highly public relations conscious. It uses the party to mold opinion; but it also uses it to allow carefully controlled expression of a variety of ideas during the period of maturation of policy and to serve as an agency of critical expression, within a limited framework of settled policy. As with fascism, and perhaps more so, it would be a great mistake to take the term "monolithic" too seriously as applied to either Party or regime.

Along with the crude weapons of the police state and the less violent means of the Party, the government relies for control over the people upon all manner of opinion-making agencies. The Soviet press and radio speaks with one voice. Books, pamphlets, and the like can be published only by state operated publishers. Nor do the people have free access to foreign sources of news and opinion. On the contrary, one of the most significant aspects of the so-called "iron curtain" is precisely the minimization of incoming news. Foreign broadcasts beamed to the Soviet Union are "jammed" by Soviet radio stations so as to make them difficult to receive. Foreign publications are available only in limited supplies. Finally, youth organizations, trade unions, cooperatives, and other forms of association are made the vehicles for the official Party "line" and for whipping up and maintaining enthusiasm for the regime. The school system from the lowest grades to the most advanced educational levels is committed to indoctrination in the principles of Communism. Artistic, literary, and scientific work are similarly bent to the task of molding minds to the Communist pattern, although in this regard recent years have brought partial and spasmodic relaxation of control.

"ORGANIZATIONS"

It can not be said that the Soviet regime is unmindful of the masses. As was indicated above, it makes a great point of maintaining constant and full contact with the people. It loses no opportunity to broaden the base and intensify the strength of its mass support. Today especially, as part of the official program of moving toward the Communist stage of development, it has enlisted the support of a variety of popular "mass organizations" to aid in the administration of the social security program, to settle minor disputes, and to aid in the enforcement of law and order. Within its frame of reference, which is to say the retention of its existing type of economic and political system and the maintenance in power of the present ruling

Trade union local grievance committee in session

Sovfoto

group and the successors they select—within this frame of reference real freedom exists and a real effort is made to give the masses what they want, while seeing to it that as far as possible these wants are what they should be from the point of view of the ruling hierarchy. The regime is despotic in the only way a regime can be despotic in a modern, literate society. Whether and to what extent its despotism is benevolent is an extremely difficult question which it would be foolish to try to answer on the basis of such evidence as can be advanced here. Whether and to what extent it has achieved its professed ideals is one of the matters on which we shall briefly comment in the next few paragraphs.

Goals and Achievements

The ideals of Communism are not dissimilar from those of liberal democracy. Liberty, equality, and material welfare head their scale of values, while security is stressed as a necessary condition. The accent is different. The emphasis is always on the collectivity rather than on the individual— so much so that sometimes they seem to approach the organic view of society, according to which the whole is valued for its own sake; but essentially their doctrine remains one of individual satisfaction.

Mao's "blue ants": afforestation campaign in Chinghai Province

Eastfoto

To what extent have the Russian Communists achieved these goals? Turning first to equality, if one thinks immediately of equality of material rewards, it is doubtful whether much progress has been achieved. It seems to be fairly well established that wage differentials, for example, are about as great in the Soviet Union as in such a capitalist state as the United States.[29] As for political equality, we have already seen that the political

---

[29] See Abram Bergson, *The Structure of Soviet Wages* (Cambridge, Mass.: Harvard U.P., 1944), Chs. 5-8; M. Yanowich, "Trends in Soviet Occupational Wage Differentials," *Industrial and Labor Relations Review,* **13** (1960), pp. 166-191; and Yanowich, "Trends in Differentials Between Salaried Personnel and Wage Workers in Soviet Industry," *Soviet Studies,* **11** (1960), pp. 229-252.

power of the average non-Party member is virtually nil. Here, clearly, inequality is much greater than in a healthy capitalist democracy. Communists lump together their various equalitarian goals in the concept of a "classless society." But the Soviet Union has classes, marked by power, by prestige, by special privileges, by type of work, by income level, indeed by all of the familiar distinguishing marks.[30] The classless society is far from realization.

In one important field tremendous advances have been made: education. The Bolsheviks have transformed the Soviet Union into a society in which illiteracy is rapidly becoming a thing of the past.[31] Nor does general education end at the primary level. Generally speaking, almost anyone in Russia can obtain the education and training for which he is intellectually equipped (with the important exception that political 'slanting' pervades all fields and that political tests are applied). This educational revolution has enormously increased equality of opportunity as compared with Czarist days.

What the Communists have accomplished in terms of material welfare, is far more difficult to say. That they have achieved remarkable progress in industrializing a hitherto predominantly agricultural country is clear. Beyond this point, generalizations become increasingly difficult. Surely, many more Russians have shoes than used to have them. But then factory workers have more need for shoes than do peasants. This kind of factor makes comparison difficult even when reliable statistics are available. Moreover, the Russian economy was expanding rapidly under the Czar, during the prewar period. Therefore, to be fair, one should compare present day Russia with what it would have been like under the old form of government—or, perhaps, under a more liberal regime. Production of many kinds of manufactured material has increased tremendously. Today, however, much of this goes into the war machine. Another big slice is devoted to building up capital equipment. The interpretation of Soviet data is a highly controversial matter, especially when it comes to a question like long-term trends in real incomes. No precise statements can be made with assurance. It does appear that between 1928 and 1948 real incomes suffered a marked decline and that the level in 1952, while considerably above 1948 was still below the 1928 level.[32] It also appears that real incomes rose rather sharply between 1949 and 1958.[33]

[30] See Alex Inkeles and Raymond A. Bauer, *The Soviet Citizen* (Cambridge, Mass.: Harvard U. P., 1959), esp. Ch. 13, for an interesting account of attitudes toward these differences in the Soviet Union.

[31] The census of 1897 showed 78 per cent illiteracy. The figure for 1960 is reported as 1.5 per cent for the age group 9-49.

[32] Robert W. Campbell, *Soviet Economic Power* (Boston: Houghton Mifflin, 1960), p. 142.

[33] United States, Congress, Joint Economic Committee, *Comparisons of the United States and Soviet Economies*, Part II (Washington, D.C.: G. P. O., 1959), p. 399. Whether the rate of economic growth achieved by the Soviet Union during the postwar period is better than might be expected under a different system is another question. At least one authority calculates that it has been no greater than that of Japan. Alec Nove, *The Soviet Economy* (New York: Praeger, 1961), *passim* and p. 305.

When we consider liberty, we are confronted with another difficult question. That liberty, as we in the West understand it, is severely curtailed in the Soviet Union, is obvious. It must be remembered, however, that Russia has never known liberty as we know it. The masses had no significant political power. Moreover, the government ruled with a heavy hand, using secret police and banishment to Siberia as weapons to stamp out radicalism. Whether through inefficiency or leniency, however, political dissidents undoubtedly had a far greater chance of survival then than now. Nor do the records indicate that the institution of Siberian banishment ever operated on a scale that could compare with the ten to fifteen million people said to have populated the slave labor camps of the Soviet Union during much of its history.

Furthermore, the state has as yet shown no signs of withering away in accordance with the Marxist prophecy. The "transition period" continues, although Khrushchev now loudly proclaims that the long-awaited change from Socialism to Communism has begun.

The Russian Revolution and the events in the Soviet Union since that epochal event illustrate vividly many of the principles of political science. In the first place, the very coming of the revolution exemplified much that has been said about political stability and instability. It came in a country in which the normal processes of adjustment to changing conditions had been checked by an unyielding autocratic governing class. It came also in a country that lacked a large middle class. Economic conditions lagged behind the potentialities; political institutions had failed to keep up with the rapid development of constitutionalism and democracy throughout most of Europe. The period of intellectual ferment among the intelligentsia had run its course. Both the foundation and the leadership for an effective mass movement were in existence. Some reforms had been made, following the abortive revolution in 1905-1906, and economic conditions during the years just before the outbreak of The First World War were rapidly improving. Finally, the war itself both revealed the weakness of the old monarchy and, following the defeats administered to the Czarist armies by the Germans, created a condition of crisis favorable to revolution.

Illustration of Principles

The experience of the Soviet Union provides ample illustration of our earlier discussion (Chapter VI) of conflicting goals. Liberty has been the victim both of the attempt to achieve greater equality and of measures taken in the interests of greater productivity, that is to say of greater efficiency. Equality itself has also suffered in the interest of efficiency, as highly differential rewards have been introduced in order to increase production.

If the dynamics of the dictatorship itself have brought little that is new, except for the perfection of the techniques of opinion control, they have certainly once more provided abundant illustration of the old principles.

Those who have obtained absolute power have not relaxed their hold.[34] Turnover within the Politburo notably slowed up during Stalin's regime. Successive purges of leaders who might rival the great chief himself followed the classical tradition. Stalin, like Mussolini and Hitler, grew increasingly suspicious of those around him. The latter, in turn, feared to show any independence of judgment or action; indeed they feared to take any responsibility, lest they be held accountable, perhaps with their lives, if things went wrong. As a consequence of this situation, decisions in the Soviet Union tend to be endlessly delayed. Bureaucracy here appears at its worst, simply because officials believe it is safer to do nothing or to pass the buck to someone else than to take affirmative action.

One of the most commonly noted traits of dictatorship is that of seeking scapegoats for its lack of success, diversions from its mistakes. The kulaks and the *bourgeoisie* served this purpose in the early years of the Soviet regime, but with their rapid elimination from the scene, it has been necessary to find a substitute. During the thirties, the menace of fascism served this purpose. With the destruction of fascism, this ready excuse for the failure to achieve material prosperity—towards which the belt-tightening of successive five-year plans had presumably been directed—suddenly disappeared. Unfortunately for the cause of world peace, a substitute was quickly found: the Western world. We have already noted that the failure of the state to show signs of withering away, the failure for tight political controls to be relaxed, has been laid at the door of capitalism. It is the capitalist democracies that threaten the peace of the world and that therefore require Russia to delay further the attainment of the ultimate cooperative commonwealth. They are the villains. And the United States, as the greatest and most powerful of these and the very heart of capitalism, is the supreme villain. These things are the contemporary illustrations of a political principle that is as old as despotism.

According to Communist theory, the evil in man is entirely a product of the capitalist system, of the private ownership of the instruments of production. The fallacy of this tenet of economic determinism is clearly demonstrated by Communist experience. Capitalism has long since been abolished in the Soviet Union: but crime continues; juvenile delinquency is a problem, even as it is in the Western democracies; and power resides in human hands and is frequently abused.

Soviet criminal law, at first based upon the theory that criminals were ill rather than evil, that society was responsible for their waywardness and that they should be treated rather than punished, has gradually been modified. It now gives recognition to the fact of personal responsibility; and metes out punishment as well as treatment.

---

[34] Russia today shows many evidences of restiveness under strict controls of artistic and other forms of expression. The leadership has vacillated in its response to these symptoms, first giving them encouragement, and then retreating. The difficulty of liberalizing an absolutist regime is apparent. (See below, p. 589.)

Prospects

Now, twisting our analytical tools in another direction, we may ask what of the future of totalitarian dictatorship within Communist regimes and in Russia in particular? Many scholars believe that a liberalizing trend is evident in the Soviet Union, while others believe either that this judgment is in error or that it relates to a passing phenomenon.[35]

Communism faces a dilemma. The doctrine it has preached throughout its existence calls for liberalization. Likewise, the psychological forces and their attendant sociological tendencies discussed in the early chapters of this book would lead us to believe that powerful forces apart from their own propaganda will exert pressure against continuing dictatorship. Certain more directly tangible processes push in the same direction. The Soviet Union is rapidly industrializing. Its standard of living is rising. It is also, and partly for this reason, raising the educational standard of its people. This combination is not favorable to the maintenance of dictatorship. Fénelon's ironic advice to tyrants is à propos. "Render your subjects prosperous," he declared, "and they will speedily refuse to labor; they will become stubborn, proud, unsubmissive to the yoke, and ripe for revolt."[36]

Not only are men who are educated and well fed bound to be unruly subjects of a despotic regime, but a regime committed to maximizing production so as to "catch up" with the industrialized West needs much more than to secure their obedience: it must elicit their most active and effective cooperation and their most energetic work. Can a dictatorship maintain these conditions over the long pull, after the enthusiasm of a revolutionary movement has passed? It seems unlikely. A still further question arises —one as much in the sphere of economics as of politics: can a complex economy be made to operate efficiently under the cumbersome controls characteristic of Communist dictatorship? Both practical experience and general reasoning give strong support for a negative answer to this question.[37]

A further question: can a complex society be governed by a totalitarian dictatorship? It will be recalled that Communism has nowhere come to power in a highly industrialized society. And in the only society remotely meriting that description in which fascist totalitarianism has come to power it was (a) in a move of despair under crisis circumstances, and (b) it can hardly be said to have succeeded even by its own tests. As the society becomes more highly differentiated, as the various groups are increasingly

[35] See Robert Conquest, "Liberalization: a Balance Sheet," *Problems of Communism*, 11 (1962), pp. 1-8; and Jeremy R. Azrael, "Is Coercion Withering Away?" *ibid.*, pp. 9-17.

[36] Quoted in William Godwin, *Political Justice*, 2 vols. (New York: Knopf, 1926), Vol. I, pp. 210-211.

[37] For a brief but persuasive argument to this effect, see Robert W. King, "Communism, a Self-Limiting Order," *Political Science Quarterly*, 77 (1962), pp. 237-247. For the difficulties (if not impossibilities) in the way of economic liberalization while retaining political autocracy, see Alexander Gerschenkron, "The Changeablity of a Dictatorship," *World Politics*, 14 (1962), pp. 576-604.

educated and articulate, and as they grow conscious of the potential power possessed by any large functional group in an industrialized and therefore interdependent society, the ruling group must provide some kind of effective access to more and more of these groups. And to do so is to move in the direction of democracy.

But if it is difficult to attain and maintain either a prosperous, industrialized economy or a viable polity in totalitarian dictatorship, it is also difficult for such a dictatorship to liberalize itself. Not long ago Mao Tsetung experimented with freedom of criticism. The ensuing onslaught forced him to beat a hasty retreat from freedom. In the Soviet Union numerous moves in the direction of encouraging liberty of artistic expression have been followed soon afterward by a return to strict controls. The regime is faced with a dual difficulty when it seeks to liberalize itself. An obvious problem is the threat to the security of the ruling group. And for a man, group, or party to cede power voluntarily is, if not completely unprecedented, at least a rare occurrence. Even if we were to assume the unlikely event of such a voluntary cession of power—or of a willingness to make such a move—the problem of how to accomplish it in such a way that order would be maintained is gigantic. Can a dictator, granted the will, school his people in the ways of democracy sufficiently that he can gradually transfer power to their hands? Or will they, at some mid-point, snatch it from him before they are ready to exercise it responsibly and effectively? Or will he, sensing this danger, reverse himself in midstream?

CONCLUDING REMARKS

As we cast our eyes back over the two types of totalitarian dictatorship we have been discussing, we shall understand both their similarities and their differences better if we bear in mind that Communism began as a highly rationalistic doctrine according to which men desire material welfare and strive for it by rational means, and that its present-day practitioners have become aware of the shortcomings of this view and have modified their program accordingly. Appeals to honor and prestige and also to patriotism and even nationalism now play a large part in the Soviet Union; and familial and religious values have been rehabilitated. Fascism started out with a full recognition of the extent to which man is sentimental and susceptible to all sorts of irrational appeals. It built its doctrine and its tactics on these facts. In some cases it had to modify its practices because they gave too little recognition to the element of rationality. Thus in the economic sphere, while they extolled the virtues of private property and of the small businessman, they were driven by the hard realities of the situation to modify property rights sometimes almost to the point of confiscation and to contribute to the process of economic concentration.

Another basic distinction of great significance in explaining differences between the two movements has to do with the classes of society to which they make their appeal. Communists, of course, are primarily concerned with the proletariat. It is true that in Russia, as in most other countries where they have had any degree of success, the peasants far outnumbered the industrial workers. While according to Communist theory these groups have a common interest, Communists have in fact always made a special bid for peasant support by promising to give them the land—to seize it from the large landholders and distribute it among tenants, sharecroppers, and agricultural laborers. Fascists, on the other hand, have sought to appeal to as many different classes and groups as possible. They have done so partly by demagogic tactics of making incompatible promises to different groups and seeking to conceal or obscure their inconsistency, and partly by appealing to the threat of what the Communists would do to all nonproletarian groups. Partly, too, they have done it by appealing to motives that transcend divergences of economic interest—and it has been part of the strength of their movements that fascists realized the potency of noneconomic motives. They enlist motives that are idealistic—by appeals to duty, to honor, to desire to improve bad conditions—and that are base—by appeals to hatred, jealousy, the desire to vaunt superiority over others, race prejudice, chauvinism, and the like. They appeal to romanticism, to the yearning for the psychological security derived from group membership and complete commitment and subordination, as well as to the desire for the satisfaction, vicariously, of the will to dominate.

The differences between the two types of regime are important, but their similarities are even more striking. Let us look at the matter from the point of view of the basic political function of all political systems. On the input side, it will be recalled that we listed four functions. The first was political socialization and recruitment. In both forms of totalitarian dictatorship, great emphasis is placed upon this function. Both seek to "politicize" their citizens, and to remake them in their own image. Fascism is trying to reintegrate a disintegrated society, and to that end to bring all to submit themselves to the Leader and the state. Communism is attempting to create a "Soviet man," a man who will give according to his means in return for satisfaction of his needs. In both cases, a large share of the resources of the regime are devoted to creating the kind of citizens they desire and recruiting the services of many of them in support of the regime. On the other hand, the functions of articulating and aggregating interests, in dictatorships, are for obvious reasons slighted. Finally, the political communication function is both expanded and distorted. Most significantly, institutions of "neutral" political communication are abolished. Nothing can be neutral in a totalitarian regime. On the output side, little need be said. Rules must be made, applied, and interpreted, and cases adjudicated, as in democratic regimes. But although functions may be divided powers are not. The legislature tends to be no more than a rubber stamp for policy decisions made in secret within the ruling group. Likewise administration is completely subservient to the ruling group. For ordinary cases, the judiciary can be permitted to operate much as in democratic countries. Under Communism, however, the bias of Marxist doctrine has begun against any notion of "neutrality" even here and has stressed the use of courts as agencies of individual reform and of punishment for conduct considered wrong for the "Soviet man."[38] Recently, the Soviet legal code has been modified in the direction of providing greater recognition of the principle of "legality" in nonpolitical cases. To what extent practice follows the revised rules we do not know.[39]

It appears to the authors that both forms of totalitarian dictatorship are political diseases to which healthy societies are not likely to succumb. Further we can even hazard a prediction as to what kind of patient is most likely to fall victim to each disease. A pluralistic society in which consensus has broken down and government is deadlocked or disintegrating is most likely to be the victim of a fascist movement. In the first place, the crying need of such a polity is for a force to reintegrate it, to recreate unity from a variety of contending groups and parties; and it is precisely the objective of a fascist movement to do just this thing. Secondly, a people who have been through the experience of seeing a going concern disintegrate and of experiencing the economic and psychological insecurity that accompanies this process is likely to be in the depths of frustration and despair, psychologically ripe for the kind of irrationalist myth that is characteristic of fascism. Finally, people who have known better conditions will find more attraction in a doctrine, like that of fascism, that lays great stress on the revival of old values than in one that hates the old order.

Communism, on the other hand, is likely to have its greatest appeal in a society that has never been well off and that has never known real political consensus; in a society that, except for a small ruling class, is relatively homogeneous and in which middle class elements have not proliferated; and in a society tortured by an awareness that other people are far better off than it is, but that all efforts at reform (for example, of outmoded systems of land tenure) appear to be stymied by the weakness, ineptness, or self-interest of the existing regime. In this situation a simple apocalyptic vision of Utopia, combined with a doctrine that success is assured is likely to find wide support. Here is where Communism is most likely to gain power.[40]

[38] Likewise the Nazis had a legal provision permitting courts to punish individuals guilty of offending against "healthy popular sentiment."

[39] Such evidence as is known is at best mixed. Moreover, the new popular courts, which operate outside of the formal governmental machinery, introduce a new element of uncertainty. See Leon Lipson, "Soviet Legality: the Mountain Has Labored," *Problems of Communism*, 8 (Jan.-Feb., 1959), pp. 15-19; and also Leonard Shapiro, "Judicial Practice and Legal Reform," *Soviet Survey*, July-Sept., 1959, pp. 54-60.

[40] If one accepts Kautsky's argument (above, page 565) that a fascist movement can succeed only where there is a substantial remnant of the old landed aristocracy with which it may ally itself, it follows that no fully industrialized society will succumb to fascism. However, the evidence that a fascist movement must necessarily secure such an alliance is by no means conclusive. See Lipset, *op. cit.*, Ch. 5. Kautsky also argues that fascism may also succeed in a country that is in the relatively early stages of political and economic development, although he appears to believe this outcome is less likely than a Communist success. Kautsky, pp. 97-106.

SELECTED READINGS

(Asterisk indicates book is available in paperback edition.)

*ARENDT, HANNAH. *The Origins of Totalitarianism.* Cleveland, O.: World, Meridian, 1958. While some of Miss Arendt's interpretations are extreme, she brings both freshness of insight and depth of understanding to the subject.

ARMSTRONG, JOHN A. *The Politics of Totalitarianism, the Communist Party of the Soviet Union from 1934 to the Present.* New York: Random House, 1961. A detailed and comprehensive history of Soviet politics since 1934.

*BARBU, ZEVEDEI. *Democracy and Dictatorship, Their Psychology and Patterns of Life.* New York: Grove, 1956. A psychologist's interpretation. Parts II & III treat the psychology of Nazism and Communism respectively.

BULLOCK, ALAN. *Hitler: a Study in Tyranny.* New York: Harper, 1952. An excellent study of a fascist dictator in action.

*CRANKSHAW, EDWARD. *Khrushchev's Russia.* Baltimore, Md.: Penguin, 1959. Mr. Crankshaw minimizes the role of ideology in current Soviet politics. He even believes that the young Russians want a faith which they no longer have. And he foresees trouble for the regime when today's youth come to maturity.

DJILAS, MILOVAN. *The New Class: An Analysis of the Communist System.* New York: Praeger, 1957. A critical account of the practical operation of Communism by an insider.

EBENSTEIN, WILLIAM. *Fascist Italy.* New York: American Book, 1939. Clear and penetrating description, analysis, and appraisal of Fascism in its homeland.

———. *The Nazi State.* New York: Holt, 1943. The theory and institutions of the National Socialist regime in Germany.

FRIEDRICH, CARL J. and BRZEZINSKI, ZBIGNIEW K. *Totalitarian Dictatorship and Autocracy.* Cambridge, Mass.: Harvard U. P., 1956. A useful study of totalitarian dictatorships on a comparative basis.

FRIEDRICH, CARL J. (ed.). *Totalitarianism.* Cambridge, Mass.: Harvard U. P., 1954. A series of penetrating essays by leading authorities on various aspects of the general phenomenon of totalitarian dictatorship.

FROMM, ERICH. *Escape from Freedom.* New York: Holt, 1941. A psychologist's explanation of the rise of Nazism in terms of the general *malaise* of industrial capitalistic society.

HOFFER, ERIC. *The True Believer, Thoughts on the Nature of Mass Movements.* New York: Harper, 1951. An insightful and original study of the psychology of mass movements.

*MARCUSE, HERBERT. *Soviet Marxism, a Critical Analysis.* New York: Random House, 1961. This account of Soviet political and ethical tenets, while critical, is yet more sympathetic to Marxism and to the Soviet interpretation of that body of doctrine than most Western treatments.

NEUMANN, FRANZ. *Behemoth, The Structure and Practice of National Socialism.* New York: Oxford U. P., 1942. An able and thorough description and analysis.

NEUMANN, SIGMUND. *Permanent Revolution.* New York: Harper, 1942. An analytical study of the phenomenon of totalitarian dictatorship, as exemplified by the cases of Italy, Russia, and Germany.

CHAPTER 19

Developing States

THE PROBLEM

Great wars frequently do not so much initiate completely new historical processes as accelerate those already under way. Certainly the war of 1939-1945 had this effect on the political as well as the economic and social development of vast portions of the world's population. Both political and economic development have been characteristic of all recorded history. The First World War gave a special impetus to the former, numerous new states having been created, for instance, by the Treaty of Versailles. From time to time, people subject to colonial rule have attained political independence, as did the United States in 1776 (or at least by 1783) and the Philippines in 1946 (completing on schedule a process provided for by an Act of Congress in 1934). But never before in history have so many new states won or received their independence in less than a score of years as have done so since 1945. (The number is approximately 50). And never before has the pressure to "modernize" both economies and polities in "traditional" societies been so intense in so many countries as it has been in this same period. When the history of the third quarter of the twentieth century is written, almost certainly, in the sphere of domestic politics, problems of political development will head the list.

Precisely what constitutes political development would be a legitimate subject for a treatise, or at least a monograph, in itself. Fortunately, precision in this matter is not necessary for our purposes. What is meant by the term in a general way is clear enough. A large part of this book has been devoted to it. We have traced the development of the sovereign national state in Western Europe, and we have commented on the growth of constitutionalism and of democratic institutions. We have also sketched the attendant legal developments. In the process, we have touched on many of the problems confronting the new and emerging states of today, but not in a way that is adequate to the perplexities now facing the world. We say "facing the world" because the domestic difficulties of nations, when they threaten the stability of their governments, are the concern of all; not just of the nations in question.

The Developing States—"Modernization"

More specifically, what states and what areas of the world are we discussing? We are talking, for one thing, about that vast continent of Africa, more than four times the size of the United States, the great bulk of which, until quite recently, was made up of dependent territories and most of which now comprises free and independent states or countries on the verge of receiving their independence. We are talking about the Middle East, South Asia, and Southeast Asia. We are, at least indirectly, discussing the Soviet Union, most of its satellites, and China. Last but not least the whole of Latin America falls in this orbit.

The category we have just outlined is extremely broad. The states that compose it vary widely in a number of respects. In size and power they range from tiny Togo to the Soviet Union and Communist China. In standard of living and degree of industrialization the range is equally great. Some like Yemen, Saudi Arabia or Ethiopia, are still in the deep shadows of traditionalism; others are midway in the process of "modernization"; while the Soviet Union has become an industrial power. Many were until recently colonies of one of the Great Powers or were in other forms of dependent status. Of these some, like Algeria, won their freedom by more or less bloody struggles, while others achieved it without strife. Still others, like many Latin American countries, although they won their political independence nearly a century and a half ago, have been slow to develop both economically and politically, and have remained under the political control of relatively small classes, unrepresentative of and unresponsive to the needs of the bulk of the population. They all share, however, not only some degree of political and economic "backwardness" (to use a term no longer popular, but still accurate), but also a response to the "winds of change."

Before proceeding further, we should say a word about the term "modernization," and the related concepts of "traditional," "transitional," and "modern" societies.[1] In an earlier chapter (Chapter 4) we have already described a traditional, agrarian society. (And what we mean by a "traditional" society is, among other things, agrarian.) In societies of this type the people normally live in villages, agriculture is the chief occupation, and technology is primitive and unchanging. Landholding may be on a feudal basis; but in some cases the land is held individually and in common. The gap between the ruling class and the rest of the society is normally wide and the bulk of

[1] The subject is fully discussed in Daniel Lerner, *The Passing of Traditional Society* (Glencoe, Ill.: Free Press, 1958).

the people live in ignorance and poverty. A "modern" society, on the other hand, is characterized by life in large cities, by widespread education, by industrialization and the use of the products of modern technology, by an attitude favorable to change, by political independence of foreign powers, and by democratic aspirations and institutions. By a "transitional" society is meant nothing more than a society that is on the move, modernizing.

Political Development Yesterday and Today

In what ways do the current problems of political development resemble, and in what ways do they differ from the problems attendant upon the political development of the states of Western Europe and North America? The likenesses are extensive. The needs that men seek to satisfy in whole or in part through politics and government are the same. Any improvement in the ways the state fulfills these ends of internal order and security from external attack, of justice, liberty, and welfare constitutes political development. The achievement of these ends, in either period, involves, first of all, the creation of a minimum of consensus and of distinct governmental organs and institutions possessing the essential quality of legitimacy. As the polity develops, this political structure becomes more highly differentiated, the boundaries between the state and society in general are sharpened, and government tends to become more unified and, generally, centralized. A consensus must be developed that will support intervention by the state into areas of the society heretofore left to tradition or private arrangements. Political and governmental institutions are built and refined for performing the basic functions of articulating and aggregating interests, of political communication, and of performing the "output" functions of government—formulating and adopting policies and carrying them out. Means must be found for providing for continuity with changing personnel—the succession problem. And, as education becomes more widespread, as the society becomes more specialized and more dynamic, means have also to be found for allowing an increasing degree of popular participation in the public decision-making process; political power, in other words, has to be shared more and more widely.

These tasks of political development are as old as the process to which they relate. They have already been discussed at appropriate places throughout this book. But we give the subject this separate treatment because political development in our day has distinctive features. It can not be regarded as simply a recapitulation, at faster pace, of Western history, although the pace is immensely significant and involves more than a difference of degree. The states we are now discussing began to modernize only after this process had been going on in most of the so-called Western nations for several centuries and after they had reached a stage of both political and economic development far removed from that of traditional societies. People brought out of a tribal village and given a Western education, perhaps in a Western country, must feel like Rip van Winkle when he awoke from his long sleep. And many who were not given this kind of opportunity were exposed by the armed forces of the Second World War to Western technology and Western ways and saw that life could be entirely different from anything they or their people had ever experienced. Not all believed that this (to them) new way of life was better; but in increasing numbers they did think so. A man who has always tilled the soil with a water buffalo and a wooden stick and who has always threshed grain by hand flailing, and who has previously known of no other way to do these things, may be slow to change his ways even if it becomes possible for him to do so and even if he realizes that the result will be more grain for his family—perhaps also even if he realizes that he could trade the additional grain for something else. But, once he comes to accept the notion that it would be good to have more material things, then the knowledge of how many more material things he and his society might enjoy if they did things like the West is likely to make him impetuous, to say the least. Once the idea of "catching up" is grasped and welcomed, then the notion of doing it by small steps, gradually, so that his grandchildren may be much better off than he, is not likely to satisfy. Similarly, with the ideas of political independence and democracy. Once these ideas are accepted as ideals the question "Eventually, why not now?" becomes exceedingly difficult to answer. In fact, it is this goal that becomes of supreme importance. To attain it emerging peoples frequently take steps that will retard economic development. Knowledge that they were frightening away the only men in their country with technical know-how did not prevent the Congolese from asserting their independence in ways that assured a continuation of the Belgian exodus.

In short, when the Western nations developed economically and politically, they were feeling and finding their way. None was very greatly in advance of the others. And where the lag was considerable, communications were so poor that those who were being left behind did not know what they were missing. Today all that has changed. Even though many leaders in emerging countries are wise enough to see that it would sometimes be well to make haste slowly, the odds are on the side of the demagogue who seeks to arouse masses with visions of riches and power in no time at all. This irresistible demand for speed, "without tarrying for anyone," as applied to the process of modernization creates tremendous problems and makes it a very different affair from anything experienced by today's "advanced" nations.

Another important aspect of this matter of timing relates to the *order* of events. In many Western countries, the traditions and the institutions of constitutionalism had been long in being before democracy was introduced. Autocracy had been curbed; monarchy was constitutionalized. The idea of the rule of law had gained general acceptance. Institutions for dividing and checking power, for channeling, muting, and refining popular demands had been established and had gained legitimacy. Only then did democracy come, and typically by easy stages. Not so, for example, in many of the new African states today. Here full blown democracy is being attempted without a background of constitutional government. History shows that the result of such a move is generally disastrous. Democracy without antecedent constitutionalism tends to be populistic democracy, acting without restraint and without judgment and consequently doing such a poor job that it is soon replaced by some form of autocracy.[2] The history of the West is not without examples of this reversal of the desirable order. French constitutionalism was allowed to die long before the Revolution. And when the makers of the French Revolution tried to establish democracy, the break with the past was too sharp, the traditions of constitutional rule too weak; the result was a reversion to autocracy. A political culture must grow gradually if stable democracy is to be established. The cases of Germany and Italy exemplify the difficulties produced by sharp discontinuities in development.

The fact that democracy is being tried in many of the new states today before constitutionalism has had a chance to develop is only a special case of the broader fact that democratic forms of government are being established while many of the requisites for the successful functioning of democratic institutions are still lacking. The people, in many instances, are divided by both linguistic and religious barriers and lack any but the most superficial bases for consensus. The Congo is an extreme example of a group of native tribes lacking any sense of national unity, thrown together into a single "state" for reasons having little to do with their prospects for a satisfactory independent political life. The masses are illiterate and a trained and educated elite to man the political and administrative posts is generally lacking. Other vital elements, such as a sizable middle class and a viable group life integrated into the polity, are absent. Almost any particular requisite for democratic government may be generated by that government itself, given most of the other "requisites"; but a situation of complete temporal inversion between democratic forms and the requisites for democracy is virtually doomed to failure. Even the less extreme situations pose problems very different from those faced by the Western democracies in their early days.

Apart from the anachronistic features of most of today's rapidly modernizing states, the ex-colonial status of most of them is also important. Not all the consequences are on one side of the ledger. Often the ex-colonial country is better provided with public services than it would be likely to have been otherwise, and sometimes with trained public servants as well. In some cases this statement extends to the educational system, especially at the lower levels. Our present concern, however, is with factors that distinguish

---

[2] See the discussion and analysis of this phenomenon in William Kornhauser, *The Politics of Mass Society* (Glencoe, Ill.: Free Press, 1959).

It should be noted, however, that in non-Western and predemocratic societies, tribal, religious, and other types of traditional social organization often provide a kind of social pluralism that, while it is not democratic, does act as a restraint upon power.

the contemporary problems of development from those that characterized earlier periods, and especially with those that make the situation more difficult. Here two points are of special importance. The erstwhile colonial power was generally forced to govern in large part through the services of natives of the dependent area. Also business organizations owned by the colonial power often employed natives in positions of responsibility. Persons who had served in these capacities tended to adopt the outlook of the dominant power and to be thought of as its instrumentalities by the rank and file as well as by native leaders who had no such ties. Here then was a built-in source of strife and a deep division within the already all-too-small groups capable of assuming leading roles, public or private, in the new state.

The second point may be even more important. Members of political dependencies of other nations have been at best second-class citizens. The affront to their self-esteem was double: they did not share in the government of their own society even to the extent that a privileged elite among them did; and their society as a whole was a pawn of a Great Power in the world of affairs. They were starved for recognition. Probably as long as most of them were ignorant of how the rest of the world lived this "starvation" was no more than latent. But once they became conscious of the alternative, especially after some dependent areas actually obtained their independence and word of this development got around, attitudes rapidly changed. Hence it is that over large parts of the earth's surface today we find people, through their leaders, demanding world recognition. They crave the status symbols of nations that have "arrived," their own airlines and steel mills, and their share of power in the United Nations. They derive special satisfaction from acts of independence that involve assertion of their sovereignty in opposition to erstwhile colonial powers, whether by seizing foreign-owned oil wells or by nationalizing the Suez Canal. These matters are mentioned here not because they cause trouble for the Powers or even because they sometimes endanger the peace of the world, but because they frequently divert the energies and resources of the developing countries from more "rational" endeavors in ways that threaten their own political stability. At the same time—and this fact is too often lost sight of by Western leaders and critics —by helping satisfy the urge for recognition they may do more to foster stability than to unsettle it, especially if the ex-colonial states are sufficiently understanding to turn the other cheek and continue to supply needed capital.

MODERNIZATION AND POLITICAL CULTURE

Modernization, as we have indicated, encompasses several different processes, all of them more or less relevant to politics. Perhaps its most significant features are those of industrialization, urbanization, education, and popular participation in politics.[3] These four elements are closely interre-

[3] For a fuller discussion, see Lerner, *op. cit.*, esp. pp. 50 ff.

lated. From the point of view of the economist, industrialization takes priority. Certainly, too, developing states tend to measure their success by their rate of industrialization, so important is that process to economic development. Also, as we have already implied, industrialization is pursued for non-economic reasons. It has become the hallmark of the "advanced" state. From the political scientist's point of view the installation of democratic institutions is obviously the aspect of modernization that has most relevance, the content of which is most fully political. Equally clearly, however, popular participation in government is not the first stage of modernization. From this point of view we should first of all concentrate our attention upon urbanization (which of course is closely related to industrialization).

In the process of urbanization almost equal political significance attaches to the departure from the old and the creation of the new. The pace of life, and especially of change, in rural environments is slow. Communities are small and highly personal; everybody knows everybody else; one's neighbors watch his every move and criticize any departure from the traditional beliefs, modes of expression, and ways of doing things. In the more anonymous and also more active environment of the big city, tradition loses much of its sanction. At the same time, the stimulus of new and various experiences constantly pushes toward the abandonment of old customs and inherited beliefs. Old loyalties, extended to family, or to tribe, to village, to religious community, to fraternal order or social club are weakened or destroyed. New sources of opinion consequent upon the spread of literacy and the development of newspapers, radio, and television add yeast to the fermenting brew.

The immediate impact both of the new and the loss of the old is unstabilizing. The bonds of community are corroded and revolutionary forces and ideas are created. Whether it is a new state or an old one, changes of this kind, coming about with the rapidity that is characteristic of today's modernizing societies, demand the formation of a new political culture. The process of political socialization never ceases, but in a reasonably stable society it more or less takes care of itself by schools and many other institutions. Even in modern societies during periods of especially rapid change it must be given conscious thought and attention. But in the kind of situation confronted by the transitional societies it is a matter of major importance. A sign posted in the lobby of the Philippine legislative assembly suggests something of the gap between the political culture of a modern state and even such a relatively advanced polity as theirs. Directed to those about to enter the legislative hall, it reads

Firearm is prohibited inside Congress Building
Deposit firearms here[4]

[4] Hadley Cantril, *Human Nature and Political Systems* (New Brunswick, N.J.: Rutgers U. P., 1961), p. 71.

In a society in the early stages of transition to modernity, normally some group, some elite, is already exercising leadership toward modernity. This group must undertake the task of creating a new political culture, of directing the political socialization of the rest of the society. Normally it must deal with at least three groups, each posing quite a different problem. First, come the new urban masses. They are relatively articulate; they are demanding. They are malleable. But they are likely to be impatient, with little sense of what is possible and what is not, easy prey for demagogues. To get them to exert pressure when it is called for, but to be tolerant, patient, and respectful of constitutional procedures and of the rights of minorities, including even those who were yesterday their oppressors, is itself a feat to tax the wisdom of a Solomon. With the rural populace, the task is hardly less difficult or important, and calls for other skills. Here traditionalism still rules. Strange though it sounds to Western ears, peasants must be taught to *want* things— or at least to feel their wants. They must be brought to accept, even to *seek* guidance from the state; their orientation must be at least partly shifted from family and village to the polity as a whole. At the same time, they must not merely shift their dependence from patriarch, tribal leader, or simple tradition to a paternalistic central government. Before they can become effective members of a modern state—certainly of a democracy—they must become *self*-conscious. Until they have a sense of their own individual worth they are not likely either to aspire to improvement, or to be able by their own efforts to contribute to that improvement, nor yet to show respect or concern for the rights and interests of others. Men who think of themselves only as specific parts of a family or similar unit may respect the rights of brothers and even of cousins-in-law, also of fellow-villagers; but the concept of "citizenship," with rights and duties, equally distributed throughout a territory most of which they have never seen will be to them incomprehensible. In some ways the tasks of political socialization of the two groups we have been discussing are at opposite poles: in one case activity must be stimulated, while in the other it must be held in check. But in other respects these tasks are identical—the development of a consensus around the concepts of individualism and constitutionalism and of understanding the institutions and attitudes required to protect and to support human rights.

In addition to the city masses and the peasantry, the traditional elites, the old aristocracy, must somehow and eventually be brought within the newly emerging polity. They—or their ancestors—have led their people; and the new society desperately needs leaders; but rarely are members of this group resilient enough to make the transition from traditional to modern leadership. Even in the Western nations this feat was rarely accomplished. England provided an outstanding exception, while the United States, for the most part, was spared the test, for it never had a feudal aristocracy.[5] In today's modernizing nations the power of this class usually has

---

[5] See Louis Hartz, *The Liberal Tradition in America* (New York: Harcourt, 1955), Ch. 1.

to be destroyed, generally either by revolution or by peaceful "land reform" that destroys the economic base of their political power. It was largely the failure of Latin American countries to take this essential step toward political socialization soon after they obtained their national independence that accounts for the slow progress most of these states have made. Mexico, which did achieve this goal by means of the Revolution of 1910, has proceeded further than any other Latin American country having so large a proportion of indigenous population.

NATIONALISM

These societies require new attachments, new unity, and a nonrational basis for the polity as a whole. A myth must be created. As we said earlier, it is much healthier for myths to grow than to be fabricated. But the societies in question have no choice. Where deep changes both in social structure and in beliefs and attitudes have to be brought about quickly, rational persuasion is obviously inadequate, even when it is a question of dealing with people whom education has made normally responsive to rational appeals. Commonly political integration can be obtained, and social dynamism generated only on the basis of one or the other or (usually) both of two fundamentally emotional and therefore dangerous processes: charismatic leadership and the development of a nationalistic movement.

About charismatic leadership we shall say little. It characteristically emerges where traditional authority is losing its legitimacy, especially in societies where political communication is faulty or weakly developed. Mussolini, Castro, Nkrumah, Nasser—these are among the names that come readily to mind. Such leaders hardly compare with Napoleon, for example, yet they often perform necessary functions; and it is by no means clear that more moderate, less ruthless men could succeed. Few societies, furthermore, have had the luck to possess great leaders with administrative energy and political ability who were also dedicated to humane and liberal ideals.

Seldom does the charismatic leader himself succeed in creating the kind of political culture we have been discussing. Rarely does he succeed in creating a political culture at all. Typically, the society he has been holding together—especially if it had never been a modern or partly modern state before—falls apart and goes through a series of further political upheavals before the basis for a going political concern is finally established. Napoleonic figures generally leave behind some invaluable accomplishments, though it may not seem so at the time and the price for these accomplishments may be high. Their long-run effects are likely to be negative, but none the less essential, as for instance the destruction of a feudal society.[6]

Such a leader usually does not depend entirely upon personal magnetism. In the modern world especially he is more than likely to do all in his power

[6] Cf. Stanley Rothman, "The Future of German Politics: an Analysis," *South Atlantic Quarterly*, **60** (1961), pp. 447-454.

to develop among his people the powerful corporate sentiment of national-ism. Whether or not promoted by a charismatic leader, nationalism today is the virtually inescapable accompaniment of modernization and probably the most effective force in bringing it about.[7] That is to say, something that is called "nationalism" plays that role. In point of fact, we nowadays apply the term to almost any contemporary form of ethnocentrism.[8] It stands for the corporate sentiment that unites a people who either comprise a state or aspire to do so. In the past the term was applied to the political corporate sentiment of a group having a common nationality. And nationality, while it defied precise definition, was the term given to the corporate sentiment of a group that had all or most of the following items in common: homeland, language, religion, history, culture, and tradition.[9] Today, however, we use the term more broadly. The nationalism of Nigeria, to take one example from among many, has nothing to do with common language, for a language map of that country would make central Europe look linguistically homoge-neous. The same is true of the majority of today's modernizing states. More-over, the sentiment precedes the states, although in these cases it does not precede the desire for statehood.[10]

For the most part the essential role that nationalism can and does play in building the foundation for any polity, and especially for one that aspires to democracy will be clear enough. One social psychological point however deserves emphasis. Loyalties and belief systems are not easily changed. And the builders of a new polity never work in a vacuum. They must destroy old sentiments and beliefs in the process of creating new ones. The key fact is that, just as metal becomes malleable at white heat, so beliefs and attitudes are more readily altered under conditions of stress.[11] This crucial point is, perhaps subconsciously, recognized by the great nationalist leaders of our day. They aim to arouse their peoples to peaks of nationalistic frenzy in opposition to this or that domestic or foreign enemy for good reason. Whether the reason is sufficient to justify the damage they frequently do is a judgment that can be made only in the light of the facts of each particular case. Whether the leaders are fully aware of what they are doing may even be open to doubt. The sober truth, however, is that, say, the seizure of foreign-owned property, in a manner and under circumstances that creates the maximum rather than the minimum of conflict and of catharsis, may be

[7] See Rupert Emerson, "Nationalism and Political Development," *Journal of Politics*, 22 (1960), pp. 563-577.

[8] For a discussion of ethnocentrism, see above, pp. 82-84.

[9] See Bernard Joseph, *Nationality—Its Nature and Problems* (New Haven: Yale U. P., 1929).

[10] See John H. Kautsky, *Political Change in Underdeveloped Countries, Nationalism and Communism* (New York: Wiley, 1962), pp. 30-34.

[11] Alexander H. Leighton, *The Governing of Men* (Princeton, N.J.: Princeton U. P., 1945), p. 299.

highly functional. If traditional societies are to be rapidly transformed, if new nations are to be created over night, only such heroic—and sometimes catastrophic—measures as these can do the job.

This need to drain off discontents accounts for a number of policies or activities of transitional societies, ranging from the nationalization of industries to the organization of youth and marching groups and the use of popular organizations outside the government to act as "transmission belts" or to assist the government in various ways, including checking up on compliance and loyalty.[12] For developing nations the impact of such practices upon economic activity may be harmful; but the economic test is by no means the only one and may not even rank first in priority.

THE POLITICAL ELITES

Politicians

Modernization requires the creation and maintenance of an effective, progressive, and reasonably consolidated governing elite. The process cannot even begin without the nucleus of a political elite. Initially, this elite is likely to be pitifully small, and to be made up primarily of agitators, while a newly independent state desperately needs *many* political skills. Beside the agitator, it needs men with imagination to know what policies to agitate for. It needs "politicians" in the usual sense of the word, people with the political skills of mediation and compromise. Even more, probably, than the modern society, developing nations need statesmen with insight and judgment about when to move rapidly and when to consolidate gains already made and about the wise balance between material and psychic satisfactions. A rapidly developing society generates serious discontinuities, testing the skill of the ablest statesmen and political manipulators: gaps between expectations and accomplishments; chasms between the urbanized population (and especially their leaders) and the still tradition-bound inhabitants of the villages; breaches between the group who led a successful revolution and other or later aspirants to power. The transitional society may have many leaders—especially in the cities—who aspire to power, some with political skill; but the number of those who have the wisdom, the restraint, and the finesse required to meet these challenges is bound to be small. Moreover, no easy or sure-fire way to produce them is known.

[12] The Soviet Union today is making increasing use of so-called "popular organizations" to perform numerous activities previously assigned to official channels. Wide use of such devices is by no means confined to the Soviet Union: *vide* Eastern Europe between the wars, Peron's Argentina, Spain, Egypt, Israel, and Ghana, and many other modernizing states.

Administrators

If good politicians are scarce, effective administrators are likely to be in even shorter supply. Their importance in a society trying to build up its essential public services, to produce revenues for development as well as ordinary governmental purposes, and frequently to staff numerous public enterprises is self-evident. Training, at home or abroad, can accomplish much. Yet the transitional society is likely to be faced not only with the problem of immediate need, but also with the dilemma of lack of teachers at home and of training courses abroad unsuited to the needs of their society. Two other dimensions of the problem also pose serious difficulties. One has been alluded to in another context: the problem of creating a working organization out of people—no matter how able and well-trained—who have not previously worked together. Bureaucratic organizations work well largely in proportion to the informal communications systems that have grown up within them, and even the formal relations between superior and inferior are seriously hampered in the absence of easy personal relations based upon long acquaintance. This problem of course is only temporary; but it does impose limits upon the speed with which an efficient administrative organization can be built.

The other problem referred to is that of securing administrators with integrity. A certain amount of graft and of nest-feathering as contrasted with real commitment to and service of the public interest can be tolerated, as demonstrated by the history of most of the Western democracies. It may even be functional, providing avenues of responsiveness to genuine need where other ways are blocked. But the extent of corruption at both the political and the administrative level in many developing states creates a problem of serious proportions. It is not the diversion of resources that matters: it is the down-grading of government and politics in the eyes of the general population and of potential elites; corrosive cynicism replaces the earlier, and essential, idealism of the progressive movement.

Middle Class Elites

No polity, and especially no democratic polity, will be healthy without a variety of elites and a variety of groups and organizations. And, what is little more than another way of saying the same thing, it must have a substantial middle class. This point has been sufficiently supported in earlier chapters to require no elaboration here. It does, however, have a corollary to which we should call attention: industrialization must be fostered for this purpose as well as for economic reasons. A sizable middle class not only acts as a buffer between the very rich and the very poor; with its professionals, other specialists, and vocational groups, it also helps provide the foundations for a healthy pluralism, for institutions within which public opinion may be formed with some degree of rationality and given strength without fanaticism. Together with trade unions and local government institutions, these various voluntary organizations play a key role in building a social and nonpolitical infrastructure for the polity, aiding the latter in its task of structuring the society, channeling the flow of demands or "inputs," decentralizing the making of decisions, training citizens in the acceptance of the authority of democratically organized associations.[13]

Essential though the modernizing elite is to start and continue to stimulate and guide the process of modernization and the development of a political culture to sustain it, this elite may be highly unstabilizing. It is almost inevitably composed, at least in the first instance, of men who have been educated abroad or who through contact with Western administrators or businessmen in their own country have become aware of the outside world and have absorbed many of its ideals and adopted its goals for their own society. Under certain circumstances, especially in the Latin American countries, the educational introduction to modernization may be received in universities in their own countries. It is no accident that the universities in these countries are characteristically centers of revolutionary thought, agitation, and action. Not only do these men acquire for themselves and their countries likes and ambitions that can not be satisfied in a traditional society; but they often find that their own society provides no adequate opportunity to put to work the kind of training they have received, and even that their Western ideas alienate them from the old aristocracy. To make places for themselves and to make their country more like what they have come to admire and covet these "intellectuals" become the vanguard of a modernizing movement. They seek to educate, to urbanize, to industrialize, and to democratize their country. If it is not already politically independent, they try to make it so. And whether or not it is politically independent they will endeavor to free it from dependence on foreign capital and entrepreneurs, impossible of attainment though this goal may be in the short run. All of these objectives naturally bring them into conflict with the traditional ruling class, the old aristocracy. Even if the latter came to share the new national goals, which is most unlikely, they would be unfit by training and experience to play leading roles in their promotion. Hence their opposition

[13] See Edward Shils, "Political Development in the New States," *Comparative Studies in Society and History*, 2 (1960), pp. 265-292; 379-411, esp. pp. 386-387. "By membership in such bodies," writes Shils, "the citizenry, at least that significant section which makes up the 'infrastructure,' becomes trained in the exercise of authority and in making of decisions. Even more important they become jealous of their rights to exercise authority to make decisions and they become attached to the symbols of their autonomy. This not only restricts the power of the state, but it also keeps in check tendencies towards the 'politicization' of life, which are inimical to the regime of civilian rule, representative institutions and public liberties." The whole of the article is an excellent discussion of the problems to which this chapter is devoted.

to change is assured. On the other hand where the old aristocracy is a land-owning class, the peasants are relatively easily aroused to oppose it, and the intellectuals find in the peasants their natural allies.[14]

If anything, the account in the preceding paragraphs underestimates the difficulties of modernizing a political culture. Ignorance, lack of training, heterogeneity, absence of a uniting myth, inadequate functional organizations, the attempt to telescope stages of development, conflict between old elites and new—these liabilities are serious enough. A more subtle perplexity lies in the realm of psychology. Members of transitional societies, plunged into the race for modernization, often lack the personality structure needed for their new roles. This problem is especially severe in the case of societies that have had little contact with the West until recently. As individuals, members of these societies tend to lack the sense of human dignity and individual autonomy that enables them to act responsibly and maturely, supporting their own rights but not losing sight of the rights of others.[15] As leaders and officials they tend to be plagued by a deep sense of inadequacy that exerts a powerful restraint on effective development. Lucian Pye suggests two possible lines of attack upon this problem: a shortcut, which generally fails; and a less flashy, slower acting program, which has some hope of success. The first is that of a charismatic leader with a grand ideological solution. The second is that of assisting individuals, members of both political and administrative elites, to find their sense of identity by the mastery of demanding skills, by professionalization. This line of attack, he argues, has the double function of providing the polity with the skills it needs and of solving the psychological problem of its political elite. But it is not as easy as it sounds. Skills may be taught, but the changing of attitudes comes harder. Many who both accept the ends and understand the means of modernization find it difficult or impossible to bow to the discipline that professionalization entails.[16]

POLITICAL COMMUNICATION

Finally, good, autonomous and neutral agencies for communicating political information and leading public opinion are essential. We refer to all the various media of mass communication. In addition to the obvious way in which these agencies are important, they help too to provide the society with a corps of intelligent and informed men, outside of the government,

[14] This paragraph draws heavily upon Kautsky's discussion. *Ibid.*, pp. 44-49. See also the article by Hugh Seton-Watson, "Twentieth Century Revolutions," *Political Quarterly*, 22 (1951), pp. 251-265.

It should be noted that in many African countries land-holding has traditionally been on a communal basis.

[15] See Shils, *op. cit.*, p. 286.

[16] Lucian W. Pye, *Politics, Personality, and Nation Building, Burma's Search for Identity* (New Haven and London: Yale U. P., 1962), pp. 288 ff.

who can apart from their jobs as well as within them, provide intelligent and temperate criticism of the government and analysis of public issues. Such men also form a pool of talent who can from time to time be called upon to assume important governmental posts.[17]

ADDITIONAL ROAD-BLOCKS TO DEMOCRACY

Underlying what we have been saying is the assumption that the newly developing states would either be democratic or would be aspiring to a democratic form of government. If the emphasis is placed upon the aspiration rather than the realization, this assumption is entirely in accord with the facts. The image of modernization among the elites of the developing states involves democracy just as surely as did the nineteenth century Western idea of progress. And democracy to them means political and civil liberty and representative institutions. Where they depart from this pattern, they do so as a temporary concession to the necessities of the case; and where they admire the regimes of totalitarian dictators they do so because they believe these regimes have had great success in abolishing many of the obstacles to democratization and that they will achieve the institutions of political democracy if they have not already done so.[18]

But a traditional society, even one that is beginning to emerge from the shadows of traditionalism, lacks most or all of the requisites for democracy, as the preceding pages have demonstrated. Today, almost no new states or countries slated for independence have progressed enough to provide a stable foundation for a democratic regime. Some, especially among those few states, like Ethiopia, that were already politically independent, are trying to achieve an economic and cultural base for democracy before modifying their traditional autocratic political institutions. But in the great majority of cases where, because colonial rule prevailed until recently, such autocratic institutions did not exist, democracy was attempted immediately. Many of these experiments have failed.

In addition to lack of requisites (economic, social, and ideological), or absence, that is to say, of a democratic political culture, other factors have contributed to these setbacks. Where dependencies had to fight for their independence, the native population was itself sometimes rift in a way that made any unity, and especially democratic unity difficult to attain. Algeria is the most striking example. Apart from actual civil strife, deep divisions typically exist between the feudal, land-owning aristocracy and the intellectuals, and between urban and rural populations more generally. Also some

---

[17] For a discussion of this point in terms of significant differences among modern, Western states, see Gabriel Almond and James Coleman, eds., *The Politics of the Developing Areas* (Princeton, N.J.: Princeton U. P., 1960), p. 46.

[18] Shils, *op. cit.*, pp. 379 ff.

of the commercial elements among the population who have been closely connected with European business interests find it to their interest to support the existing regime against those who would throw out the foreigners.

Forces that divide the community, like those just mentioned, tend to generate strong, authoritarian governments. So also does the determination on the part of the new, or newly modernizing governments to industrialize with utmost speed. This point will bear elaboration. Today's modern states have proceeded more or less at their own pace. Technological advances themselves set limits to the pace of progress. Today's modernizing states not only have all the sense of urgency created by seeing the gap between themselves and the West, but technologically the possibility of immediate economic development exists—a fact that increases exasperation with the political, sociological, and economic obstacles. Thanks largely to improvements in sanitation and medication that have actually been carried out, the population explosion represents a greater threat than that faced by the Western nations. Productivity must be increased with unheard of speed if living conditions are not actually to deteriorate, as they have been doing in many areas! Nor can governments sit back, as Western governments did, and turn the job over almost entirely to private enterprise. Neither the proper motivation nor the requisite entrepreneurial skills are in sufficient supply or widely enough distributed throughout the population for this system to suffice. So the modernizing governments, with all their initial handicaps, must attempt to increase output with exceeding speed and to make, by Western standards, unwonted use of central planning and direction and public enterprise in doing so, while also providing the amenities of the modern welfare state.

The enormity of the task just described is difficult to exaggerate. That governments attempting it will be forced to use strong arm methods is self-evident. A democratic government, to be sure, is not estopped from taking drastic measures to secure compliance with its decisions. The problem is likely to be in reaching decisions. Leaders of developing nations are prone to waste little time over the often slow and laborious process of obtaining voluntary agreement on priorities and means. Where consensus is lacking, it often can be forced.[19] Much better, then, for the leaders to decide, to act, to compel compliance, and to gain acceptance and even approval after the fact. If the processes of political debate and partisan maneuvering proves to be obstructive, the temptation to interfere with political freedoms is great.

[19] A probably apocryphal but fundamentally sound story is told about Stalin, speaking of the situation in one of the satellite countries shortly after the conclusion of the War. Asked how the Communists would make out in a free vote, he is reported to have replied: "With a completely free vote they would poll about 30 percent of the ballots, but with only a slight amount of coercion they will receive 99 per cent."

THE SPECTRUM OF POLITICAL
AND GOVERNMENTAL TYPES

We have been examining a variety of problems of today's modernizing states all more or less closely related to their political culture. We have said comparatively little about institutions. Yet lack of appropriate and adequate institutions—especially political and governmental institutions—generally constitutes one of the most serious shortcomings of these societies. Irrational and unrealistic behavior is by no means a monopoly of people who are making the transition from traditionalism to modernism. Demagoguery—one of the great banes of the politics of development—is not unknown in Western society. The difference is that in a well established democracy political institutions normally can channel discontent in constructive directions and impose procedural and other restraints on demagogic activities that allow hot heads to cool and provide time for second thoughts, for deliberation, and rational judgment. The building of such institutions, however, is not the work of a day. Their weakness or complete absence has spelled at least temporary failure for more than one aspiring democracy. The development of responsible political parties, of effective legislative bodies that can be more than rubber stamps for a strong executive and yet not be centers of obstructionism and of disintegrative forces, of strong, independent, and wise judiciaries, of competent administrative organs, of effective organs of local government, and of integrity throughout—these tasks are central to the building of viable regimes.

Oligarchies and Dictatorships

Among the developing nations, especially because of the wide variation in past history and present aspiration, forms of government and political organization cover a broad spectrum. Some, only cautiously beginning the modernization process, are still governed by conservative oligarchies (often an old landed aristocracy). Saudi Arabia is one of the few remaining examples of this type. Others, at a further remove from their traditionalist heritage, are dictatorships. More frequently than not these dictators are military men. Their base is in the armed forces. Typically, they have taken over from a democratic regime that was floundering: South Korea, Burma, Pakistan, the Sudan, numerous Latin American countries. In Latin America, especially in the past, they have often been conservative if not reactionary supporters of the old landed aristocracy. Increasingly today military dictators are sympathetic to modernization. They seize power because the existing democratic government is so torn by dissension that nothing is being accomplished, perhaps even essential public services have broken down; or they take over to rout out corruption; or they intervene to prevent seizure of power by Communists or other extremists; or they may even displace a ruling traditional oligarchy. Their intervention is sometimes, by their own choice, only temporary—as has happened in Burma and Turkey. In the past, such dictatorships have often lasted for many years and come to an end only as the result of revolution. In these cases a dictator who began as a "reformer" has often become a tyrant. Cuba under Batista and Mexico under Diaz come readily to mind. In Pakistan today, the military dictator Ayub Khan appears to be making sincere and vigorous attempts to prepare his country for a return to democracy, and the prospects are for an early transfer of power back to elected representatives of the people.

Totalitarian Dictatorships

Some modernizing states have succumbed to a form of totalitarian dictatorship. (The regimes discussed in the preceding chapter fall in the category of modernizing states as well as in that of totalitarian dictatorships.[20] So also do the satellite "people's democracies.") Developing states almost of necessity must adopt some policies and techniques of government that have much in common with the totalitarian dictatorships. The wonder is not that some of the states that are now passionately trying to modernize themselves have become the victims of totalitarian regimes: the wonder is that more have not done so and that even those that have are less thoroughgoing examples of the type than are the states discussed in the preceding chapter.

In point of fact we are hard pressed to find examples of full-fledged totalitarian dictatorships among the states we are discussing. Perhaps the clearest candidate is Cuba, if we do not rule it out as a "satellite." In any case, unlike the other satellite states, Cuba's move toward alignment with one of the Communist powers was entirely voluntary. Castro's regime is a close enough approximation to our definition of totalitarian dictatorship to fall in that category. It is completely authoritarian, Castro is doing his best to create a genuine mass movement in his support, and has—or at least did have—a large nucleus of such a movement in the form of the army with which he gained power. No elections have been held, no legislative assembly functions, no competitive political parties exist, and the courts do the will of the regime, with no regard for the rule of law.

The case of Egypt (technically the United Arab Republic) may also be considered as verging on this category. It began as a simple military dictatorship. But many of the statements just made about Castro's regime apply to Nasser's Egypt. His National Union represents his attempt to shift his power base from the army to that of a mass movement. Although it has no com-

---

[20] Germany's right to be called "modernizing" at the time of Hitler's rise to power might be questioned. She was certainly already industrialized. As we noted, however, much of feudalism remained in her social structure.

petitors, neither can it be said to be very powerful. In this sphere Nasser's battle is against apathy.[21]

In connection with totalitarian dictatorships, the question arises whether they should be considered of the fascist or Communist variety, or whether neither of these designations is appropriate. In Cuba's case, Castro's announcement that he is a "Marxist-Leninist," his reliance on acknowledged Communists for many of the top posts in his government, and his dependence on the Soviet Union for military support, not to mention the permission he gave that country to install missile bases in Cuba, may be considered as answering the question as of the present writing. Nasser presents a different problem. He has been charged, especially at the time of the Suez crisis, with being a fascist, a potential Hitler. He has accepted aid from the Soviet Union but appears to have maintained his effective political independence. He has not proclaimed himself an adherent to the Communist ideology, nor for that matter to a fascist ideology either. His movement is highly nationalistic. In the days of Mussolini extreme nationalism was thought to be a major mark of fascism. Today the situation has altered. Nationalism in the newly developing states, bears a different stamp from the old European nationalism. It aims at the creation of nations without regard for linguistic or other historical bases for nationality. Even more to the point, its central theme is anti-imperialism.[22] Its aim is the full achievement of political and economic independence. This nationalism is not to be taken as a mark of fascism; it is wholly in accord with the present-day Communist strategy. The policies pursued by these states, as well as by many other developing states, are comparable to those of Communism and especially to those advocated by Communists for the new regimes. They feature a drive for industrialization, widespread nationalization of industry, and land-reform. The net result of this analysis is not to argue that these nationalist, totalitarian dictatorships are essentially Communistic. Their situation has driven them to adopt many of the same policies and political devices as those adopted by the Communists. It does not follow that they must ally themselves with Communist regimes, although Cuba seems virtually to have done so. Nor does it follow that they will adopt the same aims for the future as those proclaimed by Communist countries. They seek modernization, independence, power, self-respect. If they can achieve these objectives without alliance with any great Powers, they would undoubtedly prefer to do so.[23] But their situation, as developing countries and often as revolutionary re-

[21] See Alan W. Horton, "A Note on Syria and the United Arab Republic," in *American Universities Field Staff Reports Service*, 9, 1 (1962), pp. 14-15.

[22] More specifically, it is anti-Western imperialism—that is opposed to the kind of imperialism to which the bulk of the developing nations have been subject. Anti-imperialism of this kind is not necessarily incompatible with the development of a native brand of imperialism, of which both Ghana and Egypt have given hints.

[23] See Kautsky, *op. cit.*, pp. 86-89.

gimes, has so much in common with that of modern Communist regimes that both similarities in policy and compatibility of outlook are bound to exist.

Tutelary Democracies

Many developing polities are something short of dictatorships, military or totalitarian, and yet are far short of democracies. The spectrum of intermediate forms and styles of political organization and operation is broad. In many of these states the constitutional forms of democracy exist; legislatures, for instance, go through the motions of performing their normal functions and may actually exert some power, but it is largely window-dressing. Frequently the effective leadership in these countries is consciously making use of democratic forms to build the requisites of democracy to the point where substance may be added to the form of democracy. One student has coined the term "tutelary democracy" for these regimes.[24] In them one party is dominant but other parties are tolerated. Moreover, the dominant party is itself far from monolithic, containing numerous diverging elements. Top personnel of the dominant party tend to occupy the highest posts in government. Charismatic leadership is heavily relied upon; but the rule of law may generally prevail.

Several of today's modernizing states have introduced corporative representation into their legislative bodies. Lacking geographical districts with any homogeneity or corporate sense, they take advantage of existing functional organizations whose primary purpose is nonpolitical to serve as bases for representation. Trade unions, agricultural cooperative associations, employers' groups, even military organizations may be used in this fashion. This device is used for example in Indonesia; it is proposed for the United Arab Republic. In some cases, as in Mexico, the corporate element is introduced in the party structure rather than in the legislature.

The lack of effective party competition in tutelary democracies is a grave weakness, for without it electoral choice and democratic accountability is virtually impossible in a large and complex polity. Furthermore, the role of party competition does not end with elections. The defeated party (or parties) have an important role to play as the opposition. (Incidentally, this means that it should be well represented in the legislature.) From a short run point of view, parties in power may not like opposition. But a good opposition renders invaluable service to democratic government. It provides criticism, information, alternative policies, and new ideas, without which policy might well deteriorate disastrously. It helps keep democratic values to the fore. And it is invaluable in exposing improper practices that might lead to the loss of respect and legitimacy on the part of the government.

---

[24] Shils, *op. cit.*, pp. 389 ff. Shils uses also the category of "modernizing oligarchies."

Electioneering in the Congo

Wide World Photos

Finally, the opposition plays an indispensable role in providing a legitimate and effective outlet for discontent that might otherwise degenerate into apathy, cynicism, or revolutionary activity.[25]

Yet let no one think that it is easy for states of the kind we are discussing to open wide the doors to party competition. Critics who assume the contrary and advocate the immediate formation of a party system on the Western model are being highly unrealistic. A minimum of order and political consensus must first be achieved. Party competition may channel off discontent into constructive paths after a certain degree of legitimacy for the regime has been achieved. But in the earliest stages it can easily be or become an open invitation to factionalism, deadlock, and unrestrained attacks upon the very foundations of the polity. Moreover, in many societies in the early stages of transition from traditionalism, the populace is divided in too many ways and far too deeply to admit of political parties that can work together, compromise, and bargain, in the democratic fashion. Parties in these

[25] See David E. Apter, "Some Reflections on the Role of a Political Opposition in the New Nations," *Comparative Studies in Society and History,* 4 (1962), pp. 154-168, on which the paragraph above leans heavily.

societies tend to be based upon deep ideological splits growing out of religious, racial, and linguistic differences, or reflecting the gulf between traditional peasants and dynamic city people.[26]

India and Mexico—the Approach to Democracy

When we classify developing states according to the degree of democracy they have achieved, or more specifically according to their party systems, we recognize that these political features usually reflect underlying conditions that are not readily changed. With this fact understood, we shall proceed to say something of the types of transitional polity that inhabit the shady area between democracy and dictatorship. The so-called "tutelary democracies," of which we have cited Ghana and Indonesia as examples, stand far from the democratic end of this segment of the political spectrum. Mexico and India, on the other hand, stand close to or at the democratic end. India, particularly, may be entitled to claim that it is a democracy, although its hold on that position is at best precarious. With respect especially to party systems, these two countries have much in common. They both may be described as pluralistic, one-party states. In each we find a dominant political party. In India it is the Indian Congress Party, and in Mexico it is the *Partido Revolucionaria Institucional* (P. R. I.). Yet in both countries political competition is a real force. Other political parties are permitted to exist and to compete at the polls. In India the Congress Party holds 358 seats out of a total of 478 in the national Parliament, but it is less securely in power in some of the states. In one state the Communist Party actually held power for a period of two years. In Mexico a rival party has on occasion polled a large share of the vote for President, but never a majority or a plurality. Whether the incumbent regime would permit another party to win or to take office is untested and unknown, but it is widely questioned in Mexico. For that reason, if for no other, Mexico probably should be classified as less democratic than India. (In the legislature the P. R. I. controls all but a token two or three seats.) Yet, even in Mexico, the element of legitimate party competition is important; it provides the P. R. I. with a strong incentive to make its program popular and to be responsive to local, factional, and corporate demands. In fact, the degree of sensitivity it exhibits is out of all proportion to the share of votes polled by opposition parties. Apart from inter-party competition, it is characteristic of the dominant parties of India and (especially) Mexico that they contain within themselves a variety of interests, hence their designation as pluralistic one-party regimes. They represent a sufficiently significant type of regime and stage in political development that we shall devote some attention to a description.

[26] See Werner Levi, "The Fate of Democracy in South and Southeast Asia," *Far Eastern Survey*, **28** (1959), pp. 25-29, at pp. 27-29.

Both parties espouse a rather diffuse, syncretist nationalism. The Indian Congress Party, long before India achieved independence, became a federation of Westernizers and traditional Hindoos, socialists, agrarian syndicalists, and bourgeoisie.[27] In the same fashion, the P. R. I. at the time of its founding made no attempt to achieve monolithic unity in political doctrine or approach but claimed only to represent the "Revolution," an ideal of democracy, and a rather vague sort of "Mexican creed."[28]

It is significant that neither the P. R. I. nor one of its predecessor parties of the revolution was created until a dozen or more years after the conclusion of the Mexican Revolution and the establishment of their present constitution in 1917. Out of the near-anarchic condition into which Mexico fell after the Revolution and which persisted for a number of years, political parties, if they merited this name, tended to form around the personal leadership of local military leaders ("caudillos"). In the year 1929 no less than 61 political parties were registered. It was this impossible situation that led to the formation of a national revolutionary party.

Time and common endeavor can lend authority to such a movement. So can the personal leadership of great men like Ghandi and Nehru in India or Cárdenas in Mexico. The authority of such a movement tends to become an independent force. In both India and Mexico the parties have proved sufficiently authoritative to facilitate changes in power and to sanction new leaders. At the same time, both the Congress and the P. R. I. have shown a capacity to counterbalance and contain personal leadership and dangerous tendencies toward pro-consular dictatorship.

In India and Mexico the informal intra-party structure has been strengthened and the role of the party broadened by the indirect association of syndicates, cooperatives and regional associations. (In the case of the P. R. I. all membership is indirect, through some member organization.) On the one hand, parties so firmly in possession of many material and ideological incentives as the P. R. I. and the Congress have not found the resulting factionalism threatening. On the other hand, the national aim and the diffuse ideologies of the parties have made the accession of new groups relatively easy. Leaders seeking new sources of support or factions engaged in intra-party competition have welcomed and often openly recruited and organized these elements. Over time, these groups win recognized positions within the parties and establish the right to be heard in particular matters. Through experience, their interests and sense of identity grow more explicit, often leading them to break away from an individual leader or patron and engage in an independent group diplomacy of their own. Alliances made for tactical purposes expand into loyalties built upon substantive issues, bridging divisions of territorial neighborhood and sectoral interests.

[27] Park and Tinker, *op. cit.*, Robert I. Crane, "The Leadership of the Congress Party."
[28] Robert E. Scott, *Mexican Government in Transition* (Urbana: Univ. of Illinois Press, 1959), Ch. 5.

Both the self-image of these two parties and their own political interests in offering programs of greater appeal to groups and sections than those of their near competitors lead them to work hard to interpret the government to the citizen, to mediate between groups and the government, and to attempt to compromise sectional and factional differences within the party. Growing literacy, more effective means of communication, and more active political participation by the villager, the cooperatives, trade unions, and local or ethnic groups have stimulated these tendencies.[29] The result is a slow but perceptible secular trend toward democracy.

Neither the Congress, the P. R. I., nor any other regime in which one party is dominant is distinguished for scrupulous honesty. Nor are they notable for a strong sense of formal constitutionalism. Corruption abounds. The loyalties of many politicians are purchased by presidential patronage. Rights that exist on paper are not always honored by the courts or the administration. These countries are, however, evolving *effective* constitutions, partly from their own political successes, and partly from within the parties. This developing, informal constitution contains factional struggles and protects most major interests. The political systems rest, moreover, upon political authority that is national, stable, and moderate.

Among developing nations, Mexico and India particularly hold great promise for future democracy. They have demonstrated their capacity to develop a healthy political consensus and to draw alienated classes into the nation and into politics. They are increasingly liberating themselves from demagogues and from crude political religions. They are developing a sane and healthy pluralism that could support, in time, free political competition and a change of regime. In Mexico today pressure is growing to abandon the corporative structure of the P. R. I. and establish a fluid interest-group politics.[30] Similarly, in India, a multiparty regime seems to be emerging in which the Congress will no longer be first under all circumstances, but shortly only a dominant party among relatively equal competitors.[31] Meanwhile, both Mexico and India have been able both to maintain a fairly steady forward pace in economic and social development, employing by and large the methods of democracy and constitutionalism.

Although the records of India and Mexico in moving toward competitive party systems and real democracy are encouraging, it would be unwise

[29] Martin C. Needler, "The Political Development of Mexico," *American Political Science Review,* 55 (1961), p. 308; Myron Wiener, "South Asia," in Almond and Coleman, *op. cit.*

[30] Scott, *op. cit.,* Chs. 6 and 15.

[31] See, for example, Myron Weiner, *Party Politics in India—The Development of a Multi-Party System* (Princeton, N.J.: Princeton U. P., 1957). For comparative purposes, the student will find interest in the account of party systems in sub-Saharan Africa in Gabriel A. Almond and James S. Coleman, eds., *The Politics of the Developing Areas* (Princeton, N.J.: Princeton U. P., 1960), pp. 286-313. The discussion of integrative and disintegrative forces, at pp. 296-298, is particularly pertinent to the forces operative in and upon pluralistic dominant political parties.

to assume that success is assured in either case. At the time of this writing it seems clear that Indian politics is more competitive and that government is more democratic also in the sense that the Parliament enjoys far more power than does the Mexican Congress. Power is also less centralized in the national government in India. Some of these virtues India owes to her heritage from British rule. Will they be sufficient to tide her over the rough period ahead: that is the question. It is a serious question because in many ways India is ill prepared for democracy. And Mexico is in these other respects better off. Three statistics will suffice to point up these differences. In India only 28 per cent of the population is literate, while in Mexico the figure is 65 per cent. And in India 22 per cent of the children between five and fourteen years of age are in primary school, while the comparable figure for Mexico is 47 per cent.[32] Finally, *per capita* gross national product amounts to a mere $70 in India, while Mexico enjoys the relatively high figure of $297.[33] Moreover, this figure for Mexico, in recent years, has been growing roughly half again as fast as the comparable figure for India.[34]

Some modernizing states have gone farther than either Mexico or India in developing viable democratic institutions. The Philippines and perhaps Malaya may be cited as examples. Even such states have a long political row to hoe. Only after a considerable history of successfully operating democratic institutions, with developing consensus and a deepening tradition of constitutionalism, with increasingly independent and effective mass media, and with economic progress that keeps well ahead of the birth rate—only then are democratic institutions at all secure.

The Presidential Pattern

Where democratic regimes are established or where at least the forms of democracy are adopted, a choice has to be made as between presidential or cabinet forms of government, or some hybrid form. Previous to the present postwar spurt of political development, the general pattern has been for the presidential pattern to be adopted in the Western Hemisphere and the cabinet form in the Eastern Hemisphere. During the last ten or fifteen years, however, the Presidential pattern has also been attractive to many of the new African and Asian polities.[35] It will be useful to examine the pros and cons for the use of this system in modernizing states.

[32] Almond and Coleman, *op. cit.*, p. 579.

[33] Clair Wilcox, Willis D. Weatherford, Jr., and Holland Hunter, *Economies of the World Today: Their Organization, Development, and Performance* (New York: Harcourt, 1962), pp. 16, 18. (Figures as of 1961.)

[34] United Nations, *Yearbook of National Accounts Statistics*, 1960, p. 267, for India. The data for Mexico are derived from Howard F. Cline, *Mexico—Revolution to Evolution* (New York: Oxford U. P., 1962), pp. 336 and 349.

[35] Of Latin American states, all except Uruguay have a presidential form of government. (Cuba's of course is now in suspense. Brazil recently changed from a presidential

One principal reason, which can be seen from opposing sides, accounts for the trend toward the presidential system outside the Western Hemisphere. Cabinet government tends to be unstable and incapable of strong, decisive action in the absence of a two-party system. It is not always so, as some European countries demonstrate, but it is almost inevitably so unless a strong consensus underlies the multiparty system. A presidential system can provide both strong leadership and, at the same time, allow in some measure the luxuries of disagreement and parochialism. Presidential systems outside the United States are subject to some important difficulties. Opposition is difficult. The presidency is, both as an institution and in the person of the president, sensitive to criticism or political attack. Thus, attacks in the press or by opposition parties are sometimes interpreted as little short of treason. The opposition itself is likely to be ineffectual, partly because it is unable to determine the amount and intensity of criticism that will be tolerated. As for the President, he may think of his mandate not only as an election for a term of years, but also—as one author put it—as a right to govern without annoying opposition.[36]

Military activity in politics and political intriguing over the control of the army is a common tendency of presidential regimes, and especially in Latin America. Generals and colonels intrigue. Politicians seek their support, and strive as well to build a solid core of loyalty among the lower-ranking officers. In some instances the army has been a center for reform movements. Pakistan, South Korea, Thailand, and Turkey can all be cited as examples. Often however, brass-hat politics has resulted in nepotism and government through cronies, attended by governmental disorder and paralysis resulting from the actual or potential intervention of the military in the determination of policy.

Most presidential regimes are characterized by favoritism, patronage, and the "spoils system" in the staffing and management of the administrative agencies and bureaus. Sometimes the courts are as bad or worse. Although patronage—like the "corruption" in eighteenth-century England—has its uses, the consequence in some presidential regimes is not to maintain a constitutional balance, but to upset it. The executive's constitutional powers are already great. With them he can sometimes intimidate the legislature. The power of appointment enables him to blandish and seduce them as well. With a large and politically loyal administrative machine, some presidents have managed to "work the elections" as effectively as Louis Bonaparte's prefects of the nineteenth century.[37] Also, political influence over the courts

---

to a cabinet form, and after a brief period returned to the former.) In Asia and Africa the list of presidential forms of government includes Ghana and several other new states of West Africa, Turkey, the Philippine Republic, and Indonesia.

[36] R. A. Gomez, *Government and Politics in Latin America* (New York: Random House, 1960), p. 80, and, generally, Ch. 5.

[37] See, for example, Robert C. Bone, Jr., "Organization of the Indonesian Elections," *American Political Science Review*, 49 (1955), pp. 1007-1084.

and the administrative machinery is a good way to quiet and tame members of the political opposition.

In most of the modernizing countries pluralistic checks on government power like those that sustain constitutionalism in the United States are notably missing. Political fragmentation is the common situation, and it is often reinforced by a divided cultural tradition, different racial backgrounds, and a history of economic and social diversity. Under these circumstances, presidential government tends to provide unified leadership by encouraging patronage, paternalism, and regimist politics.

Yet for many developing countries the presidential system may represent their best hope for at least semidemocratic rule. Often it amounts to an attempt to institutionalize a moderate elective dictatorship.[38] In the absence of political consensus the logic of this strategy is fairly persuasive. Furthermore, such a system, under favorable conditions, may exercise a slow, long-term pull toward political consensus.

In many presidential regimes, only some of the generally unfavorable circumstances are present. In Turkey, for instance, the army was, for a long period, subject to civilian control; and the prospect of viable two-party system appeared good.[39] Mexico, as a second example, has a small army, a considerable measure of social pluralism, and has managed to "institutionalize" the office of the Presidency.[40] In the Philippine Republic, a small cadre of youthful politicians were able to make considerable headway despite the fact that their country's past tradition and contemporary circumstances were overwhelmingly unfavorable—a large army, internal and external crisis, authoritarianism, and extensive corruption in private and public life.[41] The appearance of effective, democratic leadership, foreign aid well planned and administered, the good fortune of a relatively long period of peace—any number of factors—may swing the balance against the degenerative tendencies, especially if the battle for economic development is being successfully waged.

Federalism

That a government seeking to telescope the normal process of modernization needs a strong central government is not open to dispute. Yet regional, tribal, or religious differences corresponding to geographical areas may compel radical decentralization. In such cases, federalism may provide

[38] In Mexico the one provision of the Constitution that appears to be sacrosanct is that which limits a President's tenure of office to a single six year term. It has not been violated since Obregon was elected to a second (nonconsecutive) term of office in 1928. He was assassinated before his inauguration.

[39] See, Kemal H. Karpat, *Turkey's Politics: The Transition to a Multi-Party System*, *op. cit.*

[40] Robert E. Scott, *Mexican Government in Transition*, *op. cit.*, esp. Ch. 8.

[41] See Harold F. Gosnell, "An Interpretation of the Philippine Election of 1953," *American Political Science Review*, 48 (1954), pp. 1128-1138.

the obvious solution, or at least the only practicable alternative to civil war and complete break-up of the polity. For Nigeria, federalism appears to have been inescapable. It may ultimately enable the problem of the Congo to be solved. India could probably not operate democratically without it. And so on. It seems likely that federalism will experience its most widespread application during the next half century in the modernizing states of the world.

Whether or not the federal form is appropriate or is adopted, however, some form of political organization at the "grass roots" is of crucial importance in a transitional polity. As the authors of a study made for the United States Senate Committee on Foreign Relations put it, "fully as important as plebiscites, representative assemblies, and other instruments of popular participation on the national scale—indeed probably a vital prerequisite for the successful operation of national institutions—are local organizations of many sorts which can engage people actively in matters of immediate concern to them."[42] Institutions of local government constitute an important item in this general classification. So also do community development programs, trade unions, cooperatives, and many other types of voluntary organization. These organizations serve a variety of roles: they help get things done; they defend the interests of groups and of individuals; they contribute to the development of consensus and dissipate alienation; they develop political know-how and self-confidence. They have their failures as well as their successes, their dangers as well as their promises. They may aggravate divisive forces. They may be far less efficient and energetic than a central bureaucracy. At the worst they may cause disenchantment with democratic processes. Nonetheless, they probably are a *sine qua non* for a developing democratic regime. The problem is not whether or not to make use of them but how they can be organized and utilized most successfully.[43]

IN CONCLUSION

In concluding this discussion of the politics of developing states, we should like to stress the necessary cooperation of economic and political forces. Each will condition the other in today's modernizing states just as we observed earlier in our discussion of "Economics and Politics" and in our examination of the development of Western constitutional forms. A democratic polity built upon dire poverty is certainly a house built upon sand.

---

[42] *United States Foreign Policy: Economic, Social and Political Change in Underdeveloped Countries and its Implications for United States Policy.* A report submitted to the United States Senate Committee on Foreign Relations (Study No. 12) by the Center for International Studies, Massachusetts Institute of Technology, Cambridge, Mass. (Washington, D.C.: G. P. O., 1960), p. 48.

[43] The most thoroughgoing attempt at the deliberate development of local agencies of government as democratic training grounds has been carried out by Ayub Khan in his experiment with "basic democracy" in Pakistan. It is ably described, evaluated, and commented upon by K. J. Newman, "Basic Democracy as an Experiment," *Political Studies,* 10 (1962), pp. 46-64. See also Shils, *op. cit.,* pp. 386-387, on the general proposition.

At the same time a society that fails to maintain order, or that tolerates the rule of a tradition-bound, landholding oligarchy, or that fails to enlist the energies of its members in behalf of change and at the same time to satisfy their new aspirations for independence and power as well as for welfare is doomed to failure, both political and economic. In the large, political and economic development tend to go together, although not necessarily step-by-step and at each stage. Tabulations made by James Coleman provide interesting documentation for this statement. He finds, for instance, that among 46 Asian and African non-Communist countries, the seven having competitive political parties all rank among the first 19 on a composite rank order constructed from eleven indices of economic development. Six of the seven are among the first twelve, India being the laggard. Of the 15 countries having authoritarian political parties eleven are in the bottom twenty. One only, the United Arab Republic, is among the top twelve. Countries with semi-competitive party systems tend to a middle ranking.[44] Such a tabulation tells us nothing about cause and effect. (Our own thesis both in this chapter and in Chapter IV is that the relation between economic and political forces is reciprocal.) But it gives positive substantiation to the proposition that the two tend to go together, and it is consistent with the proposition that each helps the other.

It should also be noted that each helps itself. The greater is the progress in either realm, the easier will be the next step. On the political side, it is probably true, as one student urges, that granting universal suffrage, without property or literacy qualifications, "is perhaps the greatest single factor leading to the formation of a political society."[45]

We observed early in this chapter that constitutionalism preceded democracy in the Western world but that the new states are seeking to democratize themselves without awaiting the slow processes by which constitutionalism becomes established. The result may be that political reversions will be more frequent among the modernizing states than they were in the West. Nationalism may often be more intense and more intolerant. But the secular trend of development appears to be the same. The same principles of social dynamics make both Western development and today's "modernization" intelligible. Both sets of states seem to be striving after the same ends.

SELECTED READINGS

(Asterisk indicates book is available in paperback edition.)

ALMOND, GABRIEL A. and COLEMAN, JAMES S. (eds.). *The Politics of the Developing Areas.* Princeton, N.J.: Princeton U. P., 1960. An ambitious and important at-

---

[44] Almond and Coleman, *op. cit.,* p. 542.
[45] Shils, *op. cit.,* p. 287.

tempt at a comparative and functional study of the developing or "transitional" countries of the world.

BRAIBANTI, RALPH, and SPENGLER, JOSEPH J. (eds.). *Tradition, Values, and Socio-Economic Development*. Durham, N. C.: Duke U. P., 1961. Several of the essays in this collection make significant contributions to political aspects of development.

BRZEZINSKI, ZBIGNIEW K. *The Permanent Purge, Politics in Soviet Totalitarianism*. Cambridge, Mass.: Harvard U. P., 1956. Mr. Brzezinski ably supports the thesis that totalitarianism needs, and will continue indefinitely to need the purge in order to relieve its self-generated tensions.

————. *The Soviet Bloc, Unity and Conflict*. Cambridge, Mass.: Harvard U. P., 1960. The author argues that in the long run the unity of the Soviet bloc is likely to dissolve as a result of the erosion of ideology, although serious obstacles confront this line of development.

CANTRIL, HADLEY. *Human Nature and Political Systems*. New Brunswick, N.J.: Rutgers U. P., 1961. Three lectures by a prominent social psychologist, embodying lessons for our time based upon wisdom derived from both academic study and some practical experience in underdeveloped as well as "advanced" countries.

EMERSON, RUPERT. *From Empire to Nation; The Rise to Self-Assertion of Asian and African Peoples*. Cambridge, Mass.: Harvard U. P., 1960. A wise and informed treatment of the concepts of colonialism, nationalism, self-determination, and democracy in developing nations.

*KAUTSKY, JOHN H. (ed.). *Political Change in Underdeveloped Countries, Nationalism and Communism*. New York: Wiley, 1962. A collection of essays by leading authorities. The editor's own substantial introductory essay is an important contribution to the theory of political development.

LERNER, DANIEL. *The Passing of Traditional Society: Modernizing the Middle East*. Glencoe, Ill.: Free Press, 1958. A brilliant study of the conditions and problems of transition from traditionalism to modernism.

PYE, LUCIAN W. *Politics, Personality, and Nation Building, Burma's Search for Identity*. New Haven, Conn.: Yale U. P., 1962. This perceptive study of some of the psychological problems of nation building is of much wider significance than simply an account of a particular country.

*ROSTOW, W. W. *The Stages of Economic Growth, A Non-Communist Manifesto*. Cambridge, Eng.: Cambridge U. P., 1960. This already classic study of the theory of economic development gives more than passing consideration to political matters.

SCOTT, JOHN. *Democracy is Not Enough, a Personal Survey of the Hungry World*. New York: Harcourt, 1960. A popular account by a trained observer, based on personal experience and on-the-spot inquiries.

SCOTT, ROBERT E. *Mexican Government in Transition*. Urbana, Ill.: Univ. of Illinois Press, 1959. A detailed account of the development and structure of Mexico's open, bargaining one-party system.

ULAM, ADAM B. *The Unfinished Revolution, An Essay on the Sources of Influence of Marxism and Communism*. New York: Random House, 1960. Marxism as a revolutionary force, and the conditions under which it is likely to gain widespread support.

WIENER, MYRON. *The Politics of Scarcity, Public Pressure and Political Response in India*. Chicago, Ill.: Univ. of Chicago Press, 1962. A relatively brief and penetrating political study of the largest of the democratic developing nations. A picture of democratic determination against great odds, both political and economic.

Part

INTERNATIONAL
POLITICS AND
GOVERNMENT

Five

We have dealt, in this volume with the principles of politics and with many of their applications; but the vitally important sphere of international relations remains untouched. International relations is a broad subject, usually treated as a discrete subdiscipline of political science. Unfortunately this treatment tends to emphasize the differences between the study of domestic politics and international relations rather than their similarities. International relations, however, like domestic politics is an area of policy choice, of sanction and obedience, of the growth of law and institutions. In some respects the differences between international relations and domestic politics are differences of kind, in other cases of degree only. Differences of kind are numerous and important, because of the absence of a common sovereign. Therefore, we make no pretense of covering the field of international relations either intensively in respect to any particular aspect of that subject or synoptically with respect to the whole. Instead, we have concentrated upon the application to new materials of principles already discussed.

The ensuing discussion falls into four parts: (1) an examination of the ways in which nation states, because of the contemporary pattern of international relations, fail to meet the needs of their citizens; (2) the fundamental principles that must govern steps toward a more effective world order; (3) the primary obstacles that frustrate attempts to move in that direction; and (4) an examination of the progress that has been made. Such a treatment implies the belief that steps toward a "secure and lasting world order" are desirable. The authors avow this belief. On the other hand, we say at this point, to avoid misunderstanding, that it is by no means our view either that progression toward some one form of world order is assured or that such an objective is a sensible aim for the next step. More to the point, immediately, is the fact that we use this particular organization of topics as a device of exposition and analysis. By treating regional and world organization as a possible objective and standard of evaluation, much can then be said about other aspects of international relations.

CHAPTER 20

Bases of International Politics

||||||||||||||||||||||||||||||||||||||||||||||||||||||||||||||||||||||||||||||||

PART I. NEEDS

In internal affairs, the industrialized, democratic states have achieved marked success. In them, domestic tranquility is by and large firmly established, and on this foundation great progress has been made in advancing the other ends of the state. Unfortunately, organization for happiness and abundance on a domestic plane of activity has not been matched in the international sphere. A system of legally independent and politically autonomous states appears to be subject to inherent limitations in the realization of the familiar objectives of security, liberty, justice, and welfare. If these limitations are to be transcended or even mitigated, the effective autonomy of today's sovereign states will have to be reduced, by securing their adherence to a set of limitations or controls operated in some fashion by or for the system as a whole, by creating one world state (carrying the first possibility to its logical conclusion), or by grouping the states into a few, larger political systems, or by some combination of these possibilities.[1]

SECURITY

Security, our most basic need, is the one least adequately fulfilled by the sovereign state, in spite of its internal successes. In the "advanced" states, paradoxically, the insecurity bred by the threat of war is highest. Never has this kind of insecurity been greater than it is today. True, people continue to plan their lives and their activities, subject to the prospect of conscription or destruction or the rigors of a mobilized economy. One might even argue that comparative security exists in the present situation of "no peace, no

---

[1] We are describing abstract possibilities and by no means intend to deny that states today have submitted themselves to certain external limitations.

war." But security is not just a matter of temporarily undisturbed repose—if one *can* "repose" under a Damoclean sword. It is also a function of the state's capacity to cope with change in the environment—that is, to assure continuing order and predictability. At present, the death of a ruler, garbled communications, or misunderstood intentions could almost instantly trigger a set of events which might be uncontrollable by any one state or by the collectivity of states. Viewed in this light, insecurity is probably as great today as at any time in history.

"Cold War" and the diffuse anxiety it induces seriously diminishes the sense of security. We learn to live with this anxiety but its side-effects may be costly. For example, observers have conjectured that one factor that reinforces a careerist mentality today is the feeling of many that the big questions of the era are out of their hands and do not, anyway, bear thinking about. In the United States—not to speak of Europe and Asia—the degree and extent to which stable expectations and personal and economic security are undermined by the "cold war" can easily be underestimated. The case of members of the armed services, potential draftees, reservists, and their dependents is obvious. The government bureaucrat, the school teacher, and the private citizen who suffered from the McCarthy hysteria were also casualties of the "cold war." The impact of this "war" may be diffuse and intangible, or it may be sudden and direct—in any event, it is unpredictable.

The Logic of Conflict Among Independent Political Units

Why a world of mutually independent political units should be unable to avoid conflict, especially in a situation where they are constantly in contact with each other and constantly carrying on relations with each other, is not hard to see. The "inconveniences" that Locke ascribed to the state of nature—an imaginary pre-political condition of man—are equally and even more sharply characteristic of a world of legally independent states. Indeed, when pressed to substantiate his assumption of the existence of a state of nature, Locke pointed to the situation then existing among sovereign monarchs, saying that they were in a state of nature with respect to each other. Sovereign states, like individual men, cannot have continuing and profitable intercourse with each other without established rules of the game to regulate it. Rules will develop in a society of states just as they do in a society of individuals. Frequently, however, their terms will be general enough to allow for conflicting interpretations in a particular situation. Also the application of law to a given case always involves the determination of facts. Here again occasion for difference may arise. States, like men, tend to be partial to their own interests. Hence the need for an impartial judge to give precision to the law and to offset self-interest. Otherwise disputes are inescapable. Moreover, the judge must have at his command an impartial enforcement agency. Conscience can not be relied upon to secure obedience when differences of opinion are wide and strongly held—especially when it is known that others are "getting away" with disregarding the verdict of the court.

To this list of "inconveniences," Thomas Hobbes, the great predecessor of Locke, added other considerations. Gain, safety, and reputation, he declared, are the three great motivating ends of man. Man seeks reputation because he is a prideful as well as a self-interested being. His pride makes him forever jealous lest his associates consider him less worthy than they are. And if a man suspects any of them of such undervaluation, says Hobbes, he will, as far as he dares, attack and subdue them, so that they, and all observers, may pay him greater respect. Thus each man's psychological insecurity contributes to the actual physical insecurity of all.

Nations are even more prone than individuals to behave in such a manner. Hence the importance of "national honor" and of seeing to it that international negotiations are conducted in such a manner that no nation loses "face." For the nation is a creature of opinion, prejudice, and belief. As a people *feel* themselves to be, so in large measure *will* they be. To put the matter differently, collective pride is closely related to morale and dignity.[2] These can inspire a group to become better, in some ways, than the sum of its members would be, taken singly. Thus, the compulsion to maintain place or to gain rank in the councils of nations. In an age of nationalism and mass public opinion, this concern becomes a political imperative. In a second sense, the behavior described by Hobbes is often rational and necessary in foreign policy, for upon prestige rests the confidence of a nation's allies and in considerable measure the calculations of her enemies. Thus, we argue that we fought the Korean war to check aggression. However, the prestige of the United States and of the western democracies was perhaps an even more important stake in the conflict. Prestige is a form of power, and therefore often an alternative to force.

Men often seek power over others, says Hobbes, not for any direct advantage, but merely as a hedge against possible future threats. In a famous passage, he wrote:

> I put for a general inclination of mankind, a perpetual and restless desire of power after power, that ceaseth only in death. And the cause of this, is not always that a man hopes for a more intensive delight, than he has already attained to; or that he cannot be content with a moderate power; but that he cannot assure the power and means to live well, which he hath present, without the acquisition of more.[3]

[2] The more socially undesirable aspects of comparative self-esteem are often suppressed in relations between individuals, only to come out in exaggerated form in the "pooled self-esteem" of collectivities like the state. See the discussion in Arthur O. Lovejoy, *Reflections on Human Nature* (Baltimore, Md.: Johns Hopkins, 1961), pp. 117 ff. Lovejoy borrowed the phrase "pooled self-esteem" from an article by A. Clutton-Brock.

[3] Thomas Hobbes, *Leviathan*, ed. Michael Oakeshott (Oxford, Eng.: Blackwell, 1946), p. 64.

In a world without law and government states behave much as do the individuals that Hobbes described. They seek security through power, by acquiring "natural" frontiers, through an advanced technology of armaments, and by ringing their boundaries with friendly or subservient buffer states and "satellites." As Hobbes perceived, the point about the international competition for power is not that all nations (or even any nations) necessarily lust after power. What is important is that security must be won anew, again and again, for the equations of power between nation and nation are forever changing. Industrial capacity, colonial acquisitions (or losses), democratic or revolutionary myths of government and nuclear capability, depending on the particular decade, weigh differently as components of national power. To be sure, the competition for power, though endless, is not always as urgent or deadly. Since 1789 there have been several periods of "peaceful coexistence," one lasting from 1815 to 1853. Armaments races have not always led to war; and agreements have been for both general and localized disarmament. The real problem, however, lies in the fact that an international competition for power, like destructive competition in the market, can erupt speedily into a deadly race for survival that no one wants and yet no one can terminate.

The teen-age fighting gangs of New York and other modern cities provide a close parallel to the behavior of sovereign states, suggesting that the causes of war are rooted deeply in human nature and in collective behavior. The members of these gangs or "clubs" seek safety and prestige or reputation ("rep" in their lingo). They want "rep" partly for its own sake, for "kicks," partly to enhance their security, and partly—so they have told investigators—because it brings them various good things, such as girls. They claim territory ("turf"); they arm themselves, negotiate alliances, and conduct wars ("rumbles"). Out of fear that someone will cheat, they avoid disarmament pacts. Their wars are over slights to the clubs' "rep," over "turf," over injury to a member, or over threats to their security. Members admit that they are terrified of a "rumble"; yet fear often only accentuates the violence of this state of nature.

The counterpart—or sometimes the cause—of the quest for power is fear. Nations that harbor no imperialistic designs fear the ambitions of their neighbors. Consequently, they seek to make themselves strong, if not through the creation of buffer states then through armament. Others Powers do not see this enhancement of military potential as purely defensive, but rather as potentially offensive.[4] They begin to feel insecure and so increase their own armaments, and, in far less time than it takes to develop an effective international security organization, an armaments race is on. Once started, such a race is difficult to terminate short of the final testing ground

---

[4] Khrushchev may have thought of his Cuban missile bases as defensive: the United States did not.

on the battle field. It is not solely, or even chiefly, out of a cold calculation of self-interest that wars arise, but out of a diabolical combination of pride and fear that appears to be generally characteristic of man.

Man's aggressive tendencies *can* be contained. By the creation of a community and the organization of that community into a state, the use of violence by individuals or groups can be kept to a minimum. It is precisely the lack of a community, politically organized, on a world-wide scale, that leaves mankind prey to the threats and ravages of war and all the insecurity they entail.[5] Whether this solution is attainable is another question.

Imperialism

Before leaving this subject of security, we must add a footnote about imperialism. By this term we refer to the policy on the part of a nation or its rulers of seeking to extend its domain, or at least its control. Various means may be used to this end. The imperialistic Power may seek, by conquest or otherwise, to incorporate new territories within its own boundaries. Or, as is often the case with the buffer states referred to above, it may simply seek to control their policies, perhaps especially in matters of foreign affairs. Again, imperialism may be primarily economic in its objectives. In this case, the imperialistic country may try to control the policies of underdeveloped countries for the sake of providing markets for its products or safe investments for its capitalists. In all cases, imperialism involves an extension of the power of one state at the expense of one or more others. From the point of view of its potential effect on the peace of the world, the important fact is not that certain weak states lose power or independence but that a strong state gains. This gain often upsets the balance of forces between great states and is seen as a threat by other important Powers. In such cases it operates to disturb the existing equilibrium and to set in motion a race or contest for empire that, like an armaments race, is difficult to terminate short of war.

We have defined imperialism in a morally neutral sense. Quite frequently the term is used as an epithet. Historically, in many, probably most cases of imperialism, the power of the strong state has been used to exploit weaker states for its own advantage. Exploitation, however, is a matter of degree. The extension of power in this way is generally accompanied by some advantage to the weaker states. A study of colonialism throughout the world shows that in many cases the "mother" country spent more money on improvements in the colonies than she gained, in any ascertainable fashion.

Imperialism is merely the name given to a major aspect of the struggle for power that is characteristic of a world of independent states. Attempts

[5] For an insightful approach to the problem of war, see Kenneth N. Waltz, *Man, the State, and War* (New York: Columbia U. P., 1959), *passim,* and esp. Chs. 2, 6, and 8.

have been made to explain imperialism on purely economic grounds, both by Marxists and by liberals. Both have argued that the quest for power characteristic of imperialism is stimulated by economic needs—specifically by the need for foreign markets and opportunities for investment.

We have discussed the fallacy of Marxism and, more generally of all attempts to explain all political phenomena in terms of economic causation previously, and we need not repeat the argument here. We may add, however, that history clearly demonstrates the inadequacy of the economic interpretation in this instance. Some instances of imperialism and resulting wars can undoubtedly be explained in this way. But they are outnumbered by the cases in which no such interpretation will hold. Moreover, while the theory calls for big business interests as the warlike, aggressive elements in the population, as Mr. Khrushchev appears still to believe, more frequently than not these interests have been the "appeasers" while the expansionists have been farmers or urban working classes. For all but the most strongly committed economic determinists, the imperialistic policies of Nazi Germany, where the economic was clearly subordinated to the political, put an end to the economic explanation of imperialism. The postwar imperialism of the Soviet Union is almost equally clearly an example of predominantly political motives.[6]

In short, imperialistic policies may be pursued for many reasons, and the motives are generally mixed. They may be instruments for economic advantage; they may reflect fear and insecurity; or they may be expressions of the desire for power and glory for their own sakes. They provide no simple answer to the problem of the causes of war. Imperialism, like armaments, is a symptom, not a cause of the international *malaise*.

Conclusion

It appears from the foregoing analysis that insecurity is inevitable in a world of independent states—independent, that is, in the sense of having neither a common superior nor a comprehensive set of regularly observed rules. Today it is easy to see the great ideological conflict between the democratic West and the autocratic-totalitarian Soviet bloc as the chief source of world tension. So, of course, it is. But to assume that if only this particular conflict could be eliminated all would be well is to fly in the face of history and of the basic reasons for instability that we have just been discussing. The fact of the matter is that there is a tragic logic in the coexistence of independent powers. If anything, it is even more inexorable where those powers are states than where they are individuals. The self-esteem of the individual is magnified in the pride of the nation state.

[6] For a good, brief discussion of this subject, see Hans J. Morgenthau, *Politics Among Nations*, 3rd ed. (New York: Knopf, 1960), Ch. 5.

LIBERTY

Liberty today is as gravely threatened by the international anarchy as is security. Technological developments and the growth of nationalism largely account for this fact. Until the Napoleonic Wars both liberty and property were frequently respected even while wars raged. The French Revolution and its attendant nationalism began the wars of nations in which states sought to mobilize whole peoples. In the American Civil War and the Franco-Prussian War of 1870, technology also began to exert pressure in the direction of making warfare "total," requiring the universal mobilization of manpower and resources. The loss of liberty in time of war is obvious. In the past, however, people used to the ways of democracy have quickly reclaimed their liberty when the need for its suppression has passed. Today, unfortunately, the demands of "cold warfare" tend to perpetuate the need for wartime infringements of liberty indefinitely. Since the bipolar conflict is also one between giant industrial powers that are proponents of rival ideologies, the threat to liberty is extended to many areas and takes many and novel forms.[7]

Freedom of Expression

Consider first the threat to freedom of opinion and expression. The right to believe what we choose and to express our opinions orally or in writing, within certain fairly well defined limits, is basic to democracy, as is the closely related right of free association. Yet these liberties are gravely threatened both by the objective needs of a cold war situation and, perhaps even more, by the attitudes and sentiments it evokes.

First of all, we have the danger of espionage. The enemy is bound to exert every possible effort to get his agents into the government service in places where they may be able to secure and transmit to him secret information of vital military or political importance. The mere passing of information is difficult to detect. Consequently attention turns from the mere outlawing of the act of espionage to examination of the loyalty of government employees.

At this point the nature of the present ideological conflict becomes relevant. The Communist philosophy argues that the liberation of mankind requires the defeat of world-wide capitalist imperialism either through conquest or subversion by the Soviet bloc of "people's democracies." A traitor, then, may be either a man who sells out his countrymen for cash or the high-minded idealist who believes sincerely that a Communist victory

[7] A thorough and systematic analysis of "the threat inherent in the garrison-police state" is set forth in Harold D. Lasswell, *National Security and National Freedom* (New York: McGraw-Hill, 1950), Ch. II. The following paragraphs lean heavily on Lasswell's work.

can benefit humanity. How is the latter type of person to be identified? Obviously, by inquiring into his beliefs.

How does one establish a question about belief? Here one gets into the bog of inference. One inquires about a person's associates and the organizations to which he belongs or has belonged. It can not be denied that such facts may constitute presumptive evidence as to a person's interests and beliefs. However, as is well recognized in law, this kind of inference is extremely liable to abuse. "Guilt by association" is properly condemned in Anglo-American law. But here of course it is not technically a question of guilt. People are not being punished but merely deprived of opportunities. A difference does exist, but it is one of degree only. The danger of substantial injustice remains.

In loyalty investigations at least as they are conducted in the United States, testimony of all kinds is heard by secret agents. It includes hearsay and possibly information or misinformation given from spite. In most investigations of loyalty the person being examined has no opportunity to confront and cross-examine the individuals who testified against him or even the secret agents who gathered the information. Hope of fairness must rest on faith in the competence and integrity of the security organization. The whole procedure runs directly counter to the principles of constitutionalism. It smacks decidedly of the methods of the police state. Democracy must depend upon good will, but it is of its essence not to rely completely on the unchecked good will of its servants.

Under such circumstances, the greatest threat to civil liberty lies in the pall of suspicion and fear that is cast about. It is bad enough that some individuals may be deprived of positions unjustly. In the long run, it is even worse that freedom of opinion and expression, the life-blood of democracy, may be interfered with because of people's fear that through ignorance, misunderstanding, or malice, innocent behavior may be adjudged sufficient evidence to label them as security risks. Even students in the classroom, aware that their professors may later be quizzed as to their ideas, may hesitate to say anything that might be construed as "radical," or that might type them as "controversial."

We have been speaking of loyalty checks for civil servants; but the matter does not end here. Under modern conditions many employees of private companies having government contracts have access to secret information. They may be in positions where, in the event of war, they could do great damage to the war effort by acts of sabotage. Trade union leaders, by instigating strikes, may have similar opportunities. In these ways, the network of loyalty investigations, and so the pall of fear, is spread far beyond the already large area of government employment.

The end is not yet. If beliefs are dangerous, then what of the means of their propagation? Teachers and textbooks that express "controversial" ideas immediately come under suspicion. Again it is easy to say, in answer to the conventional appeal to democratic belief in freedom of opinion, that no one contemplates interfering with the right of individuals to believe and say what they please, within time-honored limits; but that those with certain beliefs should not be allowed to occupy the critical position of teacher, nor should children be exposed to their writings in school. The inadequacy of this distinction, however, becomes greater and greater as the number of positions to which it is applied increases. It must be remembered, too, that the most serious effect is on the children who are deprived of the stimulus of critical ideas, rather than on the teachers.

The same problems present themselves in other agencies of opinion formation: the press, the radio, and television. Thus the net is spread wider and wider.

Access to Information

Liberty is threatened by war—cold or hot—in still other ways. One threat has to do with access to information. Complementary to the role of the press in a democracy in educating the public is its function of obtaining information, of finding the news. During war, censorship, voluntary or imposed, is always resorted to in order to prevent enemy agents from obtaining information that would be of assistance to them. Inevitably under the conditions of modern war this practice results in depriving the citizens of the country of information that in the long run is vital to intelligent citizenship. As in the case of limitations on speech, denial of access to news sources may be tolerated for a limited period, but its indefinite continuance is a serious threat to free government. The danger is enhanced by the fact that the power to deny information for security reasons is so easily abused. Officials often find it hard to distinguish between what is vital to the security of the country and what involves only personal prestige, partisan advantage, or the success of a particular (not crucial) policy.

Civilian Supremacy

Traditionally civilian supremacy has been recognized as a keystone of liberty. Yet a constant and serious military threat inevitably enhances the power and the prestige of the professional soldiers—and also, today, of the atomic scientists.[8] In a democracy, lay personnel, in the United States especially members of the legislature have full authority to grant or deny

[8] Because of the latter clause, we think today less in terms of "civilian" supremacy over the military than of lay and democratic control over the military and scientific specialists. In fact, to the latter group may also be added the top industrialists, whose companies are so deeply involved in the military program. It was General Eisenhower himself who, on his retirement from the Presidency, warned the country against the danger of uncontrolled exercise of power by the military-scientific-industrial complex.

requests for funds for military programs. But how can lay individuals, in dealing with matters so technical and involved, act contrary to the advice of the experts when the very existence of the state, and the lives of millions of its inhabitants, may be at stake? Sometimes, to be sure, they do; but the situation is one to give pause to all democrats. The more serious the military threat, the weaker is the hand of democratic control.

Probably, with respect to liberty most civilized nations in the "cold war" are not really in danger of losing their civil rights completely and becoming like the totalitarian enemies with whom they are struggling. Liberty is a deeply held value and the tradition and practice of freedom is vigorous. But the dangers are serious. Because the issues are complicated and "fuzzy," conscience about matters of liberty is easily blunted; and the ideologies of the cold war corrupt political language and political thought so that people can believe they are defending liberty in silencing dissent. Liberty diminishes by a subtle process of erosion.

A Caveat

Here we must enter a final caveat. Liberty can never be at all fully realized in a world of independent states. We do not assert, however, that a world order collectively more powerful would automatically solve the problem. The fact is that the gravest threats to liberty in modern constitutional states arise from the facts of international anarchy. It does not follow that liberalism and constitutionalism could be institutionalized in regional organizations or in a world state. Such organizations might well be tyrannical. All that we can say with assurance is that this end of the state can be realized only very imperfectly on the present basis of sovereign states.

JUSTICE

As with security and liberty, so with the other ends of the state: their realization is limited by the limited scope of the state's control, by the fact that it is one among many and must respond to the overriding imperatives of external threats.

How matters stand with respect to justice should be obvious from the discussion of invasions of liberty, for it is in considerable measure by violating the regular procedures of justice or the established presumptions with respect to "due process" and fair play that liberty and other rights are invaded. In most contemporary, well-established democracies, probably the matter is not so serious, though the amount of "vigilante" justice dealt out in the United States during the McCarthy Era, for instance, shows that the problem is by no means a trifling one. For countries where democratic traditions are less strong, the cold war is a more important influence in this respect. The effect of the Cold War and the Communist threat in, for instance, Italy and Spain, or several countries of Latin America, the Middle East, or Southeast Asia is to retard and perhaps to stay indefinitely the development of the juristic and procedural underpinnings of constitutional- ism and the growth of secure and predictable legal guarantees. Justice in a wider sense of "social justice" suffers as well, for the Cold War increases the importance of collective goals at the expense of equity between citizens and groups. Responsibilities and benefits tend to fall arbitrarily. From country to country the measure of distortion varies, depending upon eco- nomic and political variables. Even in the United States, however, social justice is affected. The missiles must be built, for example, whether one sector of the economy profits unfairly or not. Students and youth face hard choices and sometimes inequitable sacrifices. In other countries, where the Communist threat is more immediate or the burden of economic and mili- tary mobilization relatively greater social justice suffers even more.

WELFARE

Welfare, like liberty and justice, depends upon security. Accordingly, it follows automatically that if the state system is inherently incapable of realizing security it is by the same token hindered in securing welfare for its citizens. Obviously, armaments budgets are in direct competition with wel- fare expenditures and individual consumers. Armaments investments in the public sector tend to stimulate the economy and thus indirectly to foster a measure of welfare. On the other hand, the burden is so great and so con- stant that few are today prepared to deny that, on balance, welfare suffers. For countries like Britain, France and Germany—not to mention those less fortunately situated—defense expenditures cut deeply into welfare pro- grams, and they do so in circumstances where those welfare expenditures are, relatively speaking, much more necessary than in the United States.

IN CONCLUSION

Our argument goes to this point: that the contemporary nation-state system hinders the realization—in varying degrees—of the ends of the state. The effect of the Cold War is lop-sided or skewed: security is affected most of all; though for some states, liberty, justice, or welfare may be the most important losses. In varying measure, however, all of the objectives that people seek under government are blocked or constrained.

The contemporary nation-state system can be judged not only from the way in which it affects the capacity of each nation to provide for its own benefit, but from the way in which that *system* affects attempts toward securing liberty or justice, welfare and security on an international plane, in the supranational political sphere. The overriding interests and jealousies of states frustrate collective security. They block the growth of private or public international law. They restrict, especially as between power blocs, the free movement of people or of trade and capital. Even an international effort as trifling as UN collaboration on conditions of child labor, uniform social security benefits, health conditions, or the free diffusion of cultural, educational, and scientific information has repeatedly run afoul of national jealousies and the real conflicts of interest that sovereign nations will always have.

PART II. PRINCIPLES

The needs of men that call for political institutions, we have seen, are relevant to the study of international affairs as they are to that of domestic politics; similarly many of the principles that we have encountered in our study of domestic political institutions have application in the international sphere as well. The present section will enumerate and discuss six principles, all of which are the international counterparts of domestic political fundamentals.

These principles relate especially to the conditions for and the impulses toward "political growth," meaning by that term here either the strengthening of existing international political organizations or making them more broadly inclusive. We do not wish to be understood as saying that these principles point toward a given outcome. Nor do we think that they work with constant force. On the other hand, in looking at the growth of political institutions—for instance the American Federal Union or the European Community—certain "principles" of development seem to have been at work. It is in this sense that we use the term; and it is in this context that we think it has value.

THE TREND TOWARD UNIVERSALISM

Our first principle may be cast in the form of the proposition that units of ultimate or independent political organization tend, others things being equal, to grow larger and larger, approaching the limit of universality. Of course, countervailing forces may arise out of one or more of the "obstacles" discussed below, such as nationalism.

We have pointed out that the needs of man, and the ends of the state that derive from these needs can not be fully satisfied short of a more inclusive political organization. To be sure, we have no reason to believe that any political organization can fully satisfy man's needs; but the pressure for political institutions that will make possible fuller satisfaction is always present. In federal states, it appears as a tendency toward centralization of power within the state. In the international realm, this principle has in the past made itself felt chiefly as a drive toward larger states that were still far short of universal (*i.e.* world-wide), but modern technological developments are steadily bringing the last stage of the process closer to the realm of political reality.[9] In the first place, these technological developments greatly increase the need for a geographically all-inclusive political organization. Both economic interdependence and the high price of war point to this conclusion. Secondly, many of the same technological developments that increase the need for central coordination of the governmental activities of the world go part of the way toward making such centralization possible.

The existence of a tendency toward wider and wider political organization seems clear enough even though it is often frustrated by other forces. Specifically, in the modern world, nationalism has frequently contributed to breaking up political units that had once been achieved. Certainly it is an open question whether the requisites for statehood—sufficient consensus and sense of community—could be made to prevail on a worldwide scale. The pressure toward larger units, however, endures. It seems also reasonably certain that unless the traditional sovereign state is increasingly transcended, man's physical security will remain precarious and the other objectives that he seeks through political activity will be measurably frustrated, if in fact he does not completely destroy his civilization.

FOUNDATIONS FOR UNITY: INTEREST AND SENTIMENT; THE INSUFFICIENCY OF FORCE

Our second proposition is that force is not a sufficient foundation for a world order or for lasting supranational states. Any political organization that is to have authority over its members, that is to be able to act in opposition to the will of any of its constituent parts, must have a stronger basis of allegiance than can be produced by force alone. Fear will not permanently constitute a sufficient motive for obedience to the commands of such an organization. Fear plays a relatively small part in securing allegiance to the state. The same psychological principles are applicable regardless of the size of state or government in question. Fear may take care of the marginal case, but the bulk of the population must obey for other reasons. Or, to put the same principle in another way, people must have other reasons than fear for obeying political commands, although fear may be a supplementary factor and may even, in many cases, constitute the difference between obedience and disobedience.

Here again it is useful to consider the example of the teen-age gangs of today's big cities. They behave like men in Hobbes's state of nature. Yet

---

[9] Approaching a similar conclusion from a slightly different point of view, Adolf Berle has argued that a general law of political selection favors political forces that tend to approach universality within their fields of application and that give to individuals a sense of harmony with the universal pattern. Adolf A. Berle, Jr., *Natural Selection of Political Forces* (Lawrence, Kan.: Univ. of Kansas Press, 1950), p. 17 and *passim*.

they are not in a state of nature. Why does not the establishment of civil government and the threat of punishment for law-breakers serve to modify their behavior? Recent investigations, including confidential interviews with gang members engaged in a "rumble," indicate that they *are* afraid. They fear both the rival gangs and the likelihood of apprehension by the police and incarceration. Yet this fear is not sufficient to control their behavior. For a variety of reasons, according to their own stories, they feel rejected by the society in which they live; they find no opportunities for satisfying their desire for status and prestige within lawful channels. In this situation fear is not enough to check their aggressive compulsions.

With states too, force and fear alone cannot permanently check aggression. More specifically, these forces do not provide a sufficient foundation for a supranational government that will endure beyond the amelioration of the immediate threat. Political unity waxes and wanes with the external pressures when fear or force or threatened force provide its sole supports. The United States' frustrating experience with NATO (the North Atlantic Treaty Organization), exemplifies this problem. Time and again NATO has taken on new life in the face of a Soviet threat, only to languish as the diplomatic winds from the East became warmer and gentler.

As Hamilton and other Framers of the American Constitution clearly understood, a government that is to succeed in commanding the support of its citizens must enlist their interest. Interest of course is of many kinds. The primary interests served by government, however, may be classed as political and economic. All the ends of the state we have denominated as security, liberty, and justice may be put under the heading of political. In the avoidance of war and of the threat to all that men love, they have the most powerful single motive for establishing a supranational sovereign, even at considerable cost in respect to corporate pride and independence. Yet, most patently, this motive is not sufficient.

Today it is clear that economic interest is also on the side of more inclusive and stronger international organizations. Time and again it has been demonstrated that all parties lose by war. The costs of war, in preparation, maintenance of armed forces, conduct of war, and payments of pensions and other compensation to the participants afterwards exceed by many fold the possible economic gains for any nation. War, although the greatest, is not the only cost of international anarchy. Interferences with a free market add to this cost in incalculable degree.

What men's interests are and what they realize them to be, however, are often quite different. Men are far less governed by their interests, or even by their interests as they see them, than the rationalistic psychology of an earlier age would have led us to believe. Man is largely a creature of sentiment. The members of any successful political organization must be bound to it by affection and united to each other in corporate unity by sentimental ties. Myths and strongly anchored attitudes must provide a basis at once for rational understanding and appreciation of the organization and for strong emotional attachment to it.

Man is ethnocentric. The task of getting men to develop sentimental bonds of unity and attachment to their group is not difficult. In fact, it is so natural a process that it is misleading to speak of a "task" in this connection. It grows entirely naturally. The problem in the case of international government, however, is to get it attached to the right group. Here we are faced with the fact of strong ethnocentric ties already attached to the existing political units—nationalism. Those who would create a more inclusive political organization, whether on a universal or a regional basis, have the problem of transferring existing ties to the larger unity. (This subject will be discussed more fully in the following section.)

While both interest and sentiment are essential for the development and maintenance of political units, including organs of supranational authority, it is the former, yielding to rational demonstration, that provides the most effective tool for internationally minded statesmen. In recent years, leaders concerned to bring about greater European unity have had marked success in substituting for the traditional politics of nationalism an international interest-group politics revolving about specialized agencies for cooperation in particular sectors. The strategy was bold and simple: if coal and steel, for instance, are made subject to one European authority that is in turn responsive to its constituency of coal and steel producers and consumers, then these interests might behave politically in this limited context not as Germans, Frenchmen, and Italians, but as capitalists, laborers, and consumers. At least in the case of the Coal and Steel Community, it has yielded encouraging results.[10]

THE CONTINUITY OF POLITICAL DEVELOPMENT

Our third principle is that of relative continuity of political development. Political institutions do not suddenly emerge upon the human scene, fully developed. They grow. Gladstone's oft-quoted statement that the American Constitution was the greatest document ever struck off by the mind of man probably was not intended to convey the impression that the institutions it provided for were something wholly new on the face of the earth. Certainly no such idea would be justified. Confederations dot the history of civilized man. The model of the Achaean League, formed in the third century before Christ, was frequently referred to by the Framers of the American Constitution. Our own history before, during, and after the Revolution, shows a step-by-step development from the loosest attempts at cooperative action, through the Articles of Confederation, to the federal government and

[10] Ernst B. Haas, *The Uniting of Europe* (Palo Alto, Calif.: Stanford U. P., 1958), contains one of the most complete and informative accounts of this process. We have relied heavily upon it.

the formation of "a more perfect union" under the Constitution. The latter went further, notably in provision for direct operation of the central government upon individual citizens, than had any of its forebears. Nevertheless, this development was but the next stage in the evolving pattern of institutional arrangements, not a radical departure from it.

Similarly the growth of representative government, of the separation of powers, of judicial review, of constitutionally protected rights, of bicameralism can each be traced in like fashion. In none of these cases did the Framers do more than make relatively slight modifications on familiar institutions.

The development of most "new departures" in politics seem to follow such a pattern. New programs as well as organs of government always have a history. The American "New Deal" or the British Welfare State in a sense "began" about the turn of the century. Politics seems to work that way: the ideal becomes actual by testing the ground ahead, by experimenting and failing, and by slowly cumulating a vision of the future.

Even revolutions, in the upshot, reveal a large measure of continuity with the past. So it was, for instance, with the French Revolution: its executor, Napoleon, carried to conclusion programs that had been the aim of French monarchs for centuries. The Russian and the Chinese Revolutions similarly had deep roots in history. The earliest political institutions, the reader will recall, evolved so gradually out of more primitive social structures that their origins remain obscure. The same is true of the development of these institutions into a state.

When we discuss international organization, we shall find that its development to date has manifested the same characteristic of underlying continuity—even including certain reversions where institutional development had been pushed ahead too rapidly—that we have just been describing.

REGIONALISM

Political organization tends to follow the lines of common interest and common culture. It was more than an historical accident that the English kings lost their Continental domains, while Scotland eventually became part of the British realm, completing the process by which the island of English-speaking inhabitants became a separate state. A casual glance at an ordinary map might raise a question as to why the Iberian peninsula should be politically divided. Reference to a relief map, however, provides the answer: mountain ranges broke the paths of communication so that it was natural for the Portuguese to be politically as well as culturally and economically separated from Spain. Examples of this kind could be multiplied indefinitely.

From a slightly different point of view the history of centralization of power within the United States represents the same underlying principle.

In the earliest days the greatest vitality and power was exhibited by the local governments—the town meetings in small scale New England, the counties in the plantation South. Gradually, as the network of interrelations spread, first the states and eventually the federal government gained in power.

It is reasonable to expect this same process to continue at the next level. National states are likely to transfer sovereign powers to regional units before they give them up to a universal organization. Here, however, we must note a complication. We have referred to both economic and cultural bases for community of interest and sentiment. To these we might add strategic considerations. Political units tend to seek boundary lines that are easily defensible. But the boundaries of the areas marked out by each of these types of consideration are not necessarily coterminous: herein lies a problem that may lead to serious difficulties in determining regional divisions.

The peace settlement following the First World War brought this problem to a head. Then it was a matter of carving up large political units rather than uniting smaller ones, but the principles remain the same. President Wilson, in one of his famous "Fourteen Points," had proclaimed national self-determination as the corner-stone for the Eastern European settlement. This principle took full account of the cultural bases of political organization. Unfortunately it did less than justice to economic and strategic considerations which soon began to work at cross-purposes with each other and with the first. Many of Europe's troubles in the years since 1919 grow directly out of these conflicts. States were established within areas that were strategically and economically weak.

Similarly, one of the great stumbling blocks to European federation today is the fact that Great Britain is pulled in opposing directions by different kinds of ties. Geography tends to place her in a European regional organization. The ties of both economic and political interest pull her strongly in that direction. On the other hand, owing to the fact that in earlier times her people have emigrated to other lands, she now has powerful cultural and economic ties to her dominions overseas, not to mention the United States.

This situation partly accounts for some of the difficulties experienced in the movement toward unity in Western Europe. Six nations formed an organization known as the European Economic Community (more familiarly, the Common Market), while others, the "Outer Seven" were unwilling to join, yet feared the economic effects of exclusion. The hope of the Common Market is that a growing political community will exert a magnetic pull, drawing all of Western Europe together. The others fear the exclusiveness of this tighter community will. Yet two significant facts should be noted. It was the existence of the plan for a common market by the Inner Six that first drew the Outer Seven together to form a plan for a "Free Trade Area."

Moreover, while thus far the two groups remain separate, some members of each group are increasingly uneasy with respect to this division. It may be only a matter of time before the smaller regional grouping is expanded to include most or all of the Seven.

Here indeed we have a principle that could ultimately transcend the concept of regionalism: centers of strength, whether political or economic, exert a certain magnetic attraction. They tend to expand by accretion or to gain in strength by the accumulation of satellites. One can see this principle at work in many places outside of Western Europe: the Soviet Union, the United States, the United Arab Republic, perhaps next China.[11]

THE BALANCING OF POWER AND RESPONSIBILITY

Power and responsibility are in large measure complementary functions. It is axiomatic that a person (or a state) can not be held responsible for acts or conditions over which it has no control. Responsibility therefore can not attach where power is lacking. We are speaking of moral responsibility, but where moral responsibility is absent it would be unjust to create legal responsibility; so it follows that legal responsibility should not be extended beyond the limits of actual power. In accordance with this principle, it would be both futile and wrong to take an extreme case, to hold Finland responsible for checking Soviet aggression.

On the other hand, a person who has power is morally responsible for his actions. Similarly, it is proper to attach legal responsibility for all exercises of power. Accordingly, too, where actual power exists it is appropriate to give legal recognition to it by authorizing its legal exercise and at the same time attaching responsibility for its proper employment.

An example of this principle may be seen in the progress of representative government, which has kept rough pace with the growth in power of the disenfranchised classes. To be sure, actual and legal power exhibit a reciprocal interaction. Legal authority enhances political power. By and large, however, groups succeed in obtaining legal power or authority only when they are in a position to assert considerable actual power without reference to legal authorization. In the international sphere, it follows from this principle that where great inequality of actual power prevails among states, it is fruitless to refuse legal recognition of this fact. Rather, powerful states must be given legal authority in proportions that give some recognition to the actual distribution of force. Any attempt to use the principle of the legal equality of states (to be discussed later) to defeat this proposition is certain to lead to trouble.

---

[11] Other factors, especially ethnocentrism and national pride, may check it or set it back where it has gone too far too fast, as with the United Arab Republic.

The principle of balance between power and responsibility is subject to a final *caveat* that deprives it of some of its exactitude. Power takes various forms; it is not military or physical alone. Stalin is reported to have brushed aside a protest by the Pope with the sneering question, "How many divisions does he have?" If he made such a remark he was overlooking the sage observation of Napoleon that "you can do anything with bayonets but sit on them." Power, as we have insisted, rests upon consent; and beyond a certain point consent can not be forced. Moral power is a great reality. In the progress made by the democratic principle, the battle against entrenched privilege was never won by sheer military force even with the backing of economic power. The moral force that always attends a just cause was an essential ingredient and probably the determining factor.

THE PRINCIPLE OF DEMOCRACY

Finally, we note that the tendency toward democracy—that characterizes the history of political institutions—also extends into the field of international relations. *A priori* this proposition is plausible, for democracy grows directly out of two of the tendencies that are fundamental to human society: the tendency toward freedom and the tendency toward justice or equality. Apart from *a priori* reasoning, however, the proposition is, at first encounter, plausible on other grounds. Democracy has become, probably more than any other single ideal, a universal goal of people everywhere. Also, people are sufficiently infected by it that it is hard to imagine any government (or supranational government) today establishing an enduring political order unless it both professes democracy as an ideal and offers more of it in practice than its predecessor.

The manifestations of the democratic principle in the field of international relations are primarily of two kinds. The first form taken by the democratic spirit then is that of opposition to colonialism and to the enjoyment of special privileges by economically and politically more advanced states. In other words, it takes the form of demands for both political and economic independence. The principle often leads to conflicts of interest within the developing countries. The demand for political independence, for instance, may threaten to leave the country in question inadequately protected against the designs of a predatory neighbor. Nowhere is this situation more clearly exemplified today than in Southeast Asia. On the economic side, until relatively recently, advanced nations had been accustomed to insist on special protections for the capital investments made by their citizens in backward countries. They frequently backed up this insistence by military intervention to protect the property rights of their investors. Such tactics today are ruled out as incompatible with the rights and dignity of the underdeveloped country. The consequence is often that the country remains underdeveloped precisely because foreign capital now considers the risk too great, although both Western powers and the Soviet Union are trying to make good the deficit by direct grants and loans. The extended impasse reached in 1951 between Iran and Great Britain with respect to oil provided a striking example. While ostensibly the dispute between Iran and the Anglo-Iranian Oil Company arose out of the purely economic matter of the amount of the royalty to be paid the Iranian government, it is clear that the situation was exacerbated, if not caused, by Iran's desire for freedom from a long-term lease that limited Iranian independence of action. In this case, the Iranian government and people suffered a tremendous financial loss for the sake of vindicating this application of the democratic principle. Egypt's expropriation of the Suez Canal provides another instance of this quite common problem.

The second type of international application of the democratic principle manifests itself in connection with international organization as the principle of equality of states. As a demand for equality of rights—the demand, that is to say, that the rights of small nations should receive the same protection as those of large nations—this principle is but an elementary application of justice. However, when it takes the form, as it sometimes does, of the demand that each state, regardless of size and strength, should carry the same weight in international councils, it runs counter to the principle of balancing power and responsibility. We shall see later how the success of such a demand constituted one of the weaknesses of the League of Nations. Logic does not compel this application of the democratic principle. It does so only if states be considered the units, without reference to the individuals who make them up. Democracy is a policy applying to men. When international political organization advances to the stage of dealing directly with individuals this particular problem will disappear, or at least take a different form. In the meantime, it constitutes a stumbling block that must be the subject of compromise and invention.

These then are our basic principles. They may be summarized, varying the order slightly and combining certain propositions, by saying that politics is characterized by a drive toward democratic universalism, that this drive advances institutionally by gradual stages, by means of institutions founded on interest and sentiment as well as force, and by virtue of organizations that recognize the need for balance between power and responsibility.

PART III. OBSTACLES TO UNITY

Since the latter part of the nineteenth century ideas of international organization and even of supranational government have taken a more central and important place in men's hopes for a good and abundant life. Movement in this direction is responsive to the "needs" examined above and is in accord with the principles just elaborated. Yet progress toward political universalism has been painfully slow. Why? What are the obstacles? As we turn to this inquiry, we should bear in mind that not all of the obstacles to world unity are unmitigated evils. In the discussion of nationalism, for example, we shall bring out the positive as well as the negative side of this phenomenon. But the fact remains that, whatever else may be true of the factors discussed below, they are obstacles in the path of political universalism.

NATIONALISM

When we speak of "international" politics, "international" law, or "international" relations, strictly speaking we are referring to "interstate" politics, law, or relations. So powerful is the force of nationalism, however, that it has become the general practice to use the terms "nation" and "state" interchangeably. Originally the word "nation" referred to a group possessed of common nationality. It might extend across state borders, as in the case of the Jews, or it might be confined to a part of a state, as in the case of the Welsh. Although the term may still be used in this way, on occasion, both the fact and the ideal of the nation-state, the case where national group and political boundaries coincide, became so dominant in the nineteenth century that "nation" became a synonym for "state."

What is a nation, nationality, or national group? Among other things, it is a particular expression of the general social phenomenon of ethnocentrism.[12] More specifically a group of people having a common nationality is marked both by a certain subjective characteristic and by certain objective attributes. Subjectively, the group, or at least most of its members, must possess a corporate sentiment of a kind that permanently resides in the group and tends to give a sense of distinctive unity to it. The best way, it has been said, to identify a man's nationality is to ask him. This aphorism points to the indefinable and subjective nature of the concept. What has been said so far might be applied to a family or clan, as well as a nation. The sentiment of nationality, however, must pertain to a distinctive kind of group, one having certain collective attributes peculiar to it. Although these attributes may not be exactly the same in each case, generally they include such items as homeland, language, religion, history, culture and traditions.[13]

To this list, we may add one more item: common government. Like each of the other bases of nationality, it is not by itself essential. National groups may exist within "multinational" states, as notably within the old Austro-Hungarian Empire; they may extend across state lines, as do the Basques; and they may be scattered throughout much of the world, as for

[12] See the discussion in Chapter 3, pp. 82-84.
[13] Following Bernard Joseph, *Nationality—its Nature and Problems* (New Haven: Yale U. P., 1929).

centuries were the Jews. It is clear, however, that the existence of a common government for all England and another for France greatly facilitated the growth of national consciousness among these peoples. A common government not only is in itself an added element of community but it also is the instrument by which collective deeds are accomplished, collective aspirations realized. It is the instrumentality, that is to say, through which much of the common historical heritage of a people takes form.

The factor of common government must, Janus-like, face two ways in a discussion of nationality. Not only does it help create a nation, but also a nation tends to demand to be self-governing, that is to say to have its own common government. At this point we reach the concept of "nationalism" itself, which is here our central concern. When a national group either aspires to become self-governing or when, having achieved self-government, this fact becomes part of the complex of national sentiment, we speak of nationalism. In other words, when the sentiment of nationality acquires a political content, then it becomes nationalism. A good example of this relation is that of Judaism and the growth of Zionism that culminated in the founding of the state of Israel. More frequently than not the sentiment of nationality takes on this political form, and it is of course precisely this form that is most significant for us as students of politics. It is nonetheless important for us to note that the inescapable fact of ethnocentrism, in the form of nationality, may manifest itself without nationalism, as we have defined that term. We shall have occasion to refer back to this point.

Nationalism came into its own in the early nineteenth century. Since then it has gradually spread throughout most of the world. Within the last quarter century we have seen it flare up to new heights of militancy in Nazi Germany, we have seen it transform an internationalist movement in Russia into a strongly nationalistic and chauvinistic movement, we have seen it stir passions to fever pitch in the Middle East, leading nations to take actions quite contrary to their economic interest, as in the case of Iran, and probably Egypt, and we have seen it spark powerful drives for self-government in the majority of the colonial areas of the world.

As the last examples indicate, nationalism has outgrown its origin. What we call nationalism in the modernizing states of today is not an outgrowth of nationality. It comes into being where the elements of nationality are almost completely lacking. It is indeed a new form of ethnocentrism, but one so similar in many of its manifestations to that which developed in nineteenth century Europe on the basis of nationality that we use the same term for it.

Nationalism in one or the other of its forms appears today to be virtually inescapable. Moreover, it can be of great positive value. We have pointed out the role played by nationalism in bringing about the transformation from feudal anarchy into the relative efficiency of the modern state. We have also at least hinted that the development of democracy on a large scale would hardly have been possible without the sentiment of nationalism to offset the disintegrative tendencies of a democratic society. Lord Acton put it well when he declared that "the few have not the strength to achieve great changes unaided; the many have not wisdom to be moved by truth unmixed."[14] Political obedience depends upon more than interest and fear; it must have nonrational supports as well. In the past, tradition could be depended upon to supply a large part of the nonrational support, but in our modern, dynamic society, traditional foundations are gravely weakened. Also the power which democracy puts in the hands of the people may easily be divisive rather than unifying. Both of these factors—the passing of traditional bases of allegiance and the growth of democracy—create needs that nationalism is well fitted to fill, and needs that in fact it has come to fill throughout much of the world.

Likewise, as we have seen, the problems of modernizing societies especially call for the sentiment of nationalism for their resolution. It can play a great and positive role in the mobilization of the pre-commercial and pre-industrial peasants of these societies. In those nations it is not likely to diminish in intensity until they have achieved greater social mobility and have otherwise overcome the greatest hurdles to modernism.[15]

Those then who would speak of doing away with nationalism or even of "depoliticizing" it (which, in our terms, would mean abolishing nationalism, while retaining nationality) must take note of two important facts. First nationalism is so consonant with fundamental human nature and so integral to the modern state that to speak of its "abolition" is hardly short of quixotic. Second, even if it were possible to abolish nationalism it would not be desirable to do so unless a substitute for its positive values could be found. In other words, it may safely be asserted that nationalism will neither be abolished nor will it fade away until something else develops to take over its useful functions, but its intensity may be moderated.

In stressing the positive side of nationalism we do not for a moment wish to conceal the negative side. Whatever may have been its relation to democracy and even to liberalism originally, clearly the intense nationalism that frequently develops in those countries where nationalism and even national unity was late in coming (*e.g.* Italy and Germany or present-day developing states) is often antidemocratic and surely antiliberal. Its spirit is too passionate to be compatible with the rational processes of democracy, too narrow and militant to provide the tolerant atmosphere that is basic to liberty and liberalism.

The relation between nationalism and war is too well known to call for more than passing remark. If nations were only content to establish their

[14] John Emerich Edward Dalberg-Acton, *The History of Freedom and Other Essays* (London: Macmillan, 1922), p. 272.

[15] See Karl W. Deutsch, *Nationalism and Social Communication, an Inquiry into the Foundations of Nationality* (New York: Wiley, 1953), pp. 164-167.

independence and to get into occasional squabbles with each other over boundaries or offended dignities or "national honor" it would perhaps be tolerable. However, the combination of the sentiment of nationalism together with the perpetual maneuvering for advantage and vying for power and prestige characteristic of a society of sovereign politics has brought about a great change in interstate relations. Modern wars are life-and-death battles of mobilized populations. Nationalism and sentiments of hatred and vengeance stirred by such struggles encourage both total war and Carthaginian peace, and evoke responses in kind that extend the scope of future war and poison the future peace.

The last and perhaps most important negative count against nationalism is simply that it has crystallized the most powerful of sentiments around a particular set of states, many of which are now outmoded as sovereign units of political organization. That is a great tragedy of our age. As so often happens in the growth of political institutions, a force that was once beneficent has become malignant. It may not prove to be an irresistible force, but in many quarters today it constitutes a discouragingly powerful obstacle to progress.

TOTALITARIANISM

If, from the point of view of world order, world-wide political organization, nationalism has moved from help to hindrance, totalitarianism has demonstrated no such ambivalent history. It is, by definition, an all-or-none doctrine. The degree to which the practice of totalitarianism mirrors its theory will, of course, vary as between (for example) the Soviet Union or China and Mussolini's Italy. But the dictatorial, centralist, and highly mobilized features of totalitarian regimes largely explain the kinds of obstacles they pose to international collaboration and organization.

For one thing, totalitarianism enormously reduces the *scope* for international cooperation. Under a totalitarian regime, everything is subordinated to the central "total" goal of the regime—even the pursuit of peace and international cooperation. Lenin illustrated this point by the significance he attached to General von Clausewitz's maxim: "War is the continuation of politics by other means." The meaning Lenin read into this statement was that all matters of world politics were to be evaluated not from the standpoint of an "abstract" (that is, "bourgeois") interest of nations in peace and cooperation but by reference to their incidence upon the class struggle and the fate of the world revolution. His Russian disciples have apparently acted on a similar conviction in condemning as "bourgeois" or "imperialistic" the Marshall Plan, the European Coal and Steel Community, the Common Market, UNESCO, the International Labor Organization, and even the World Health Organization.

Totalitarian belief systems also constitute a threat to peace because of the way in which these myths distort external reality. Fascism from the start was aggressive and anti-internationalist. Fascist theory held that struggle was a law of life and pronounced this fact to be good. Bourgeois democracies were thought to be corrupt and decadent, fit only to be plundered. Since a world of peace was neither moral, profitable, nor possible, the Fascist policy of aggression was a logical conclusion. For the Soviet bloc, however, the route to this same position is less direct. Communism came to power bearing the standard of internationalism. But Communist mythology prophesies an inevitable world-wide imperialist conspiracy against the revolution and the Soviet Union. To quote Lenin, "As long as capitalism and socialism exist, we cannot live in peace: in the end, one or the other will triumph —a funeral dirge will be sung over the Soviet Republic or over world capitalism."[16] Consequently, any period of "peaceful coexistence" can be viewed only as a tactical expedient, not as a settled accommodation. These beliefs go far to *make* perpetual strife inevitable, since concessions are likely to be interpreted as weakness which must be exploited and a policy of firmness as imperialist aggression requiring counter-measures.

Centralist dictatorship tends to increase the irrationality of totalitarian response to the external world. To be sure, dictatorships often enjoy some superiority in the conduct of foreign policy if maximum advantage is squeezed from their potential strengths of flexibility, unity of command, and expeditiousness in decision and execution. Probably these advantages are over-estimated with respect to totalitarianism, but that is not the central point to be made now. A centralized dictatorship, like absolute monarchy, may act irrationally because it is freed of those constitutional and political restraints upon government that force statesmen to grapple with sharply different opinions and interests, to see the world clearly, and call forth all their resources of persuasion and compromise. In politics, as Edmund Burke once said, "Difficulty is a severe instructor. . . . He that wrestles with us strengthens our nerves and sharpens our skill. Our antagonist is our helper." In the measure that the centralized executive of a totalitarian dictatorship separates itself from politics in the ordinary sense and acts within and upon a world colored by its own guiding myths, foreign policy decisions will be grounded upon nonfactual and distorted premises. The persistent rumor that Stalin, like an ancient Roman emperor, ultimately succumbed to megalomania gives point to our thesis. Hitler is an even better example, for it was plain that so long as Hitler was forced to "play politics"—to bargain and to struggle for power and influence by balancing faction against faction and persuading or cajoling followers—he responded realistically to the political environment. After his overwhelming victories in Poland and Western Europe none dared to oppose him or remonstrate vigorously even though

[16] V. I. Lenin, *Selected Works* (London: Lawrence and Wishart, 1943-46), Vol. 8, p. 296.

many generals and administrators regarded some of his subsequent decisions as sheer lunacy. In foreign policy, the objective bases for decision-making are few. Foreign policy by its nature involves subjective guesses of an opponent's intentions, hunches about the future, decisions based upon a morass of half-facts, inferences, and prejudices. Without the "reality-enforcers" of constitutionalism, parliamentarianism, and an open political system the dangers of reckless gambles or disastrously bad judgment are increased. The threat to amicable relations between nations is obvious. Reasonable men have trouble enough reaching agreement upon questions of sovereign rights, national prestige, and threats to the nation's security. If a political system operates to heighten irrationality the problem is so much the worse.

Tensions within a totalitarian system tend to encourage expansionist and war-like policies. Since the days of the Greek city-state, the coalition among tyranny, internal discontent, and war has been formed repeatedly. The reasons are not difficult to uncover. Obviously, foreign adventures or even war can serve to consolidate a dictatorship in power or to divert attention from internal problems and broken promises of social betterment. Mussolini's sabre-rattling bombast appears to have been used in a fashion almost as crude and direct as this. Possibly, China's entry into the Korean War served for the Communist regime the important goals of strengthening internal unity and entrenching the dictatorship more firmly.

Furthermore, the nature of political victory for a faction within a totalitarian regime is such that changes of policy are applied as ruthlessly internationally as they are domestically. The shift from a "soft" to a "hard" policy, because of the nature of such a regime, would then not only indicate repression at home but very possibly aggression and warlike behavior and declamations abroad. The pressure of totalitarian politics argues for the techniques that Machiavelli commended in the Romans. This Republic, he said, ". . . in their aggrandizement . . . avoided half-way measures and always went to extremes."[17] For Rome such a policy promoted victory, but only at the price of almost continuous warfare.

One other way in which totalitarianism destroys amity among nations, and especially forms of cooperation out of which formal institutions and agencies of international government grow, is by the manner in which totalitarian regimes conduct their foreign policy. Intemperate language, threats, spies, and "fifth columns" both hamper the conduct of normal diplomacy and undermine confidence in it. Khrushchev's shoe-pounding tactics in the United Nations Assembly may be an effective device for influencing opinion in certain areas of the world; but they tend to destroy the possibility of negotiation and agreement.

[17] Niccolò Machiavelli, *The Prince and the Discourses,* The Modern Library (New York: Random House, 1940).

DIVERSITY

The simple fact of diversity provides a fundamental obstacle in the path toward supranational government. The people of this earth comprise a highly heterogeneous collection, and a world state (if one were possible) that took no account of this diversity and of the multifarious demands arising from it would be a tyranny of the first order. But one that is in any measure democratic is faced with a tremendous task. We have not only the problem of whether it would be objectively possible for a single government to satisfy the varied needs of all the people of the world; but also the prior, and more difficult necessity of convincing people that it would be possible and would be done, so that they will be willing to yield up their separate sovereignties.

Quite apart from the existence or nonexistence of a common nationality, a common government, especially for a modern, nontraditional state, requires a high level of common presupposition. Just as successful marriages are rare where the backgrounds of the individuals concerned are highly disparate, so a successful state does not arise unless the citizens have a high level of shared experience, shared ideals, and shared beliefs. Government requires a willingness to differ, an agreement to disagree. But people can differ amicably only against a large backlog of agreement. And this agreement, in turn, must rest upon common ways of looking at things that grow only out of common experience.

Similarly common bonds of sympathy are essential. The people must be united by a large measure of subjective solidarity. Much is said about the objective solidarity, especially in terms of economic interdependence, of the modern world; and it is indeed difficult to exaggerate its extent. Unfortunately, in the absence of understanding and sympathy and good will, dependence upon someone else is an evil rather than a good. Economic interdependence makes international government imperative; it does not make it possible.

The points we have been making can be illustrated by the example of the American Confederation. The case of the union of the American colonies is often used by World Federalists and others to show the possibility of combining hitherto independent political units into a single state. Unfortunately, the example is almost a better illustration of the obstacles to union on a large scale than of its possibility. The thirteen American colonies did unite as they achieved their independence and succeeded, by a rather narrow margin, in establishing a permanent political union. The discouraging aspect of this example is that in spite of the many favorable circumstances the union came perilously close to failure. It is instructive to consider what were some of the favorable circumstances. In the first place, and of immense importance, the great bulk of the people spoke a common language and had a common historical and cultural background. In the majority of cases they are their parents or grandparents had emigrated from the British Isles. Moreover, although their political experience in this country had been characterized by separate and mutually independent governments, these governments were similar in form, and were responsible to a common superior, the British government. Their very internal quarrels between representative assemblies and royal or proprietary governors gave the colonists something in common. More substantially, the trials and vicissitudes of life in frontier communities provided an immense fund of common experience tending to set the level of common presuppositions at a high point. Finally, the colonists, having experienced the same difficulties with the government of the home country, were driven to revolt together. Both the common enemy and the organizational and sentimental ties created by fighting the war were powerful forces in creating a nation and a state. The elements favorable to political organization on a world scale today are indeed weak and scanty by comparison to those enjoyed by the American states.

THE IDEA OF SOVEREIGNTY

Kings achieved their independence of the Holy Roman Empire and their unquestioned ascendancy over their feudal vassals only after a long struggle. Throughout this contest an important ideological weapon in their armory was the concept of sovereignty, as defined and championed by Jean Bodin in the late sixteenth century. This concept held that all political power and authority should be centralized in the state. It took its place alongside the idea of the Divine Right of Kings, with which it was often closely associated, as part of the mythology of the state. When the idea of Divine Right gave way to the notion of Popular Sovereignty, the mystique accruing to the idea of sovereignty was reinforced. In this way the concept of sovereignty, originally allied with absolute monarchy, became equally compatible with the ideal and fact of democracy. On the other hand, it remained as completely opposed as ever to any limitation of the power of the state on behalf of the community of states. The doctrine of the sovereign equality of states became a cornerstone of International Law and an added support and focal point for national pride. Anyone who would urge us to give up any of our national independence of action to an international organization, whether world-wide or regional in character, has to contend with the powerful emotional appeal of the argument that such a step means giving up our sovereignty.[18]

[18] A poll of opinion in the United States in 1947 gave some surprising results. Seventy-five per cent of those polled approved United States membership in an international police force. Only 17 per cent of that same group of 75 per cent said they would be willing to have the U.S. join such an organization if the U.S. were to have fewer troops under

The historical evolution of the doctrine of sovereignty and the sentimental associations with that doctrine could hardly account for the persistently incorrigible assertions of it as an element of independence in the behavior of nations. Sovereignty is not simply a prejudice rooted in national pride. It is a highly practical and valuable concept. It corresponds to and reinforces the decentralized rule of law that prevails in the world today. According to general practice and strongly-held conviction nations are treated as sovereign, independent, and equal. Though, as in Locke's state of nature, the law is vague and lacks an impartial judge, a generally recognized Law of Nations by which nations are usually guided does exist. Sovereignty is at present the most important principle of the informal constitution which governs the relations of states. The settled rules of unfettered jurisdiction over territory, of noninterference in domestic affairs, of equal rights of great and small powers—to mention only a few corollaries to the doctrine of sovereignty—work effectively to remove many subjects for dispute, to provide grounds for appeal to principle rather than to arms, and to give maximum leverage to the limited moral consensus that does exist in the international arena. Restricting the legal and practical usage of the doctrine could, for example, work to the substantive disadvantage of small or weak nations, especially in a world order dominated by several giant powers.

But we must look beyond this point, for it is the big states that insist most strongly on retaining sovereignty. One of the strongest arguments for it is the thesis that it joins together power and responsibility. Sovereignty locates authority in the government so that it can be held accountable by those governed. Sovereignty, moreover, is the counterpart to the protection and powers granted by a government to its citizens and its officers. An illustration will make these points clearer.

Several years ago the Superior Court of California held that California's alien land laws, forbidding land ownership to Japanese, were unconstitutional because of the United States' adherence through treaty to the United Nations' Declaration of Human Rights. Few people would wish to reverse this decision. Yet it poses a real problem: a state government accountable to a lively and effective political constituency, capable of responding sensitively to its citizens' needs, was overruled, ultimately, by the action of a body with considerable independent powers resting upon a crude representative base and popularly accountable only in the clumsiest fashion imaginable. The case can be made that any surrender of sovereignty transfers power from a government that is effectively accountable to one that is not. The problem, as with federalism, is one of "political space." In the absence

---

arms than the total of such a police force. Whatever the respondents may have thought of sovereignty, clearly they highly approved of the concept as a pragmatic instrument of foreign policy. (Cited in Hans Morgenthau, *Politics Among Nations, op. cit.*, p. 330.)

of means for making democracy effective within political units of far greater scale than have yet been managed democratically, sovereignty remains a protection for democratic practices. But by the same token the relations of separate sovereignties, even if they are democratic, remain anarchical, with consequences that are all too well known.

Yet this discussion must not be allowed to obscure the fact that the concept of sovereignty is a rallying point for particularism, parochialism, and chauvinism. Just as it provided a weapon for the Senatorial opponents of the League of Nations in 1919 and for those who would repeal the Connolly Resolution (accepting the compulsory jurisdiction of the World Court) today, so it can be used to fight every proposal for the extension of international authority. As a reminder that legal authority must parallel political power, it serves a useful function; but as a slogan to call forth sentimental attachments to existing power centers and boundaries in opposition to every attempt to extend the scope of commonalty it frequently stands in the path of progress.

CONCLUSION

The nation-state system as presently organized frustrates many of men's political and social objectives. At the least, what is called for is a shift in the units of political organization pointed toward a more effective world order, whatever form that world order might take—whether it be a more effective balance of power system, the emergence of new regional groupings, or even, ultimately, some kind of world government with final authority. Various principles of political organization and behavior indicate that supportive tendencies for such an evolution exist; but the obstacles in the way of a more adequate world order are of frightening proportions. They lie partly in objective facts and partly in the realm of ideas and sentiments. The latter are at least as difficult to change as the former. But they do change. The history of the world is full of examples of great myths that have gone out of existence and given place to others more in accord with the needs of the times. Seldom are these transformations accomplished, however, without periods of turbulence and violence. The clash of arms often constitutes a powerful and successful catalytic agent for the engrossment of a new myth. Unfortunately, it often seems to require a repetition of the ordeal to accomplish its erasure from the minds of men as an effective force.

In the present case, the movement toward international cooperation and organization is well past the stage of mere conception. The present century has seen the emergence of embryonic instruments of international government at regional, functional, and universal levels. At the present time, it is especially the movement toward the formation of stronger regional supranational political entities that is making painful headway.

Between "making headway" and ultimate success lies a wide chasm, even in the growth of regional organizations. Significant progress toward world government, if ever the world reaches that point, will involve a new problem. In the case of regional organization, sentiment and economic interest always find an important ally in fear—fear of the out-group. We have already remarked how NATO, for instance, waxes and wanes with the fortunes of the cold war. So it has been throughout history: federations (like our own), alliances, and other moves toward larger bases of political unity have always been made in the face of—and in some degree in response to—rival centers of power. World organization would itself swallow up this incentive to union. Under these circumstances, can this final step ever be taken? or, if taken, could it maintain its unity without the unifying force of a competing group? The most hopeful view of the matter arises out of contemplating the possibility that fear of war itself, in the nuclear age, might prove a sufficient incentive to unity to play the role of fear of the out-group. At the same time, it is well to note that fear seldom produces unity unless strongly supported by other interests. In the next chapter we shall make an inventory of the progress that has been made and discuss further steps that might be taken.

SELECTED READINGS

(Asterisk indicates book is available in paperback edition.)

BERLE, JR., ADOLF A. *Natural Selection of Political Forces.* Lawrence, Kan.: Univ. of Kansas Press, 1950. A brilliant and original essay seeking to discover general laws of politics applying especially to the relations among states.

*BRENNAN, DONALD G. (ed.). *Arms Control, Disarmament and National Security.* New York: Braziller, 1961. Technical and political problems of arms control approached from a number of points of view.

BRIERLY, J. L. *The Law of Nations: An Introduction to the International Law of Peace.* 6th ed., ed. Sir Humphrey Waldock, New York: Oxford U. P., 1963. The best brief introduction to the subject.

BULL, HEDLEY. *The Control of the Arms Race; Disarmament and Arms Control in the Missile Age.* New York: Praeger, 1961. A rigorous analysis of this central problem.

CARR, EDWARD HALLETT. *The Twenty Years' Crisis, 1919-1939; An Introduction to the Study of International Relations.* New York: St. Martin's, 1956. A classic blending of history and analysis.

CLAUDE, JR., INIS L. *Power and International Relations.* New York: Random House, 1962. Three approaches to world security—balance of power, collective security, and world government—are here analyzed and compared.

DEUTSCH, KARL W. *Nationalism and Social Communication.* New York: Wiley, 1953. A sophisticated study of nationalism and its causes from the perspective of the study of communication.

*ETZIONI, AMITAI. *The Hard Way to Peace, A New Strategy.* New York: Collier Books, 1962. An elucidation and evaluation of alternative military and political strategies for the avoidance of war.

FOX, WILLIAM T. R. (ed.). *Theoretical Aspects of International Relations.* Notre Dame, Ind.: Univ. of Notre Dame Press, 1959. An excellent series of essays on various theoretical aspects of the subject.

GOODRICH, LELAND M. *The United Nations.* New York: Crowell, 1959. An authoritative, historical, descriptive, and analytical account of the United Nations and its work.

HAAS, ERNST B. *The Uniting of Europe.* Palo Alto, Calif.; Stanford U. P., 1958. An excellent treatment of the development, organization, and significance of the European Coal and Steel Community, and other European international organizations.

*HERZ, JOHN H. *International Politics in the Atomic Age.* New York: Columbia U. P., 1959. Less technical than many recent studies emphasizing the implications of modern weaponry for international relations.

HOFFMAN, STANLEY H. (ed.). *Contemporary Theory in International Relations.* Englewood Cliffs, N.J.: Prentice-Hall, 1960. Selections from several of the best theoretical analyses of international relations.

KAPLAN, MORTON A. *System and Process in International Politics.* New York: Wiley, 1957. An elaborate and ambitious application of systems theory and game theory to international politics. For the serious student only.

KISSINGER, HENRY A. *Nuclear Weapons and Foreign Policy.* New York: Harper, 1957. One of the earlier and still valuable attempts to consider foreign and military policy as a unit.

LASSWELL, HAROLD D. *World Politics and Personal Insecurity.* New York: McGraw-Hill, 1935. A study of the implications of psychoanalytic theory for world order.

MITRANY, DAVID. *A Working Peace System.* London: Royal Institute of International Affairs, 1944. A powerful argument to the effect that the road to peace lies through the development of functional international organizations rather than by concentrating on a universal organization the main purpose of which is to maintain order.

MORGENTHAU, HANS J. *Politics Among Nations, The Struggle for Power and Peace.* 3rd ed., New York: Knopf, 1960. A thorough and comprehensive text by one of the leading authorities on international affairs, written from a "realistic" point of view.

NICHOLAS, HERBERT. *The United Nations as a Political Institution.* New York: Oxford U. P., 1959. A splendid, brief introduction.

ROSENAU, JAMES N. (ed.). *International Politics and Foreign Policy; A Reader in Research and Theory.* Glencoe, Ill.: Free Press, 1961. An extensive collection of sophisticated readings on many aspects of the study of international politics.

SHELLING, THOMAS C. *The Strategy of Conflict.* Cambridge, Mass.: Harvard U. P., 1960. A rigorous application of game theory to problems of international political bargaining.

SHELLING, THOMAS C. and HALPERN, MORTON H. *Strategy and Arms Control.* New York: Twentieth Century Fund, 1961. Arms control proposals evaluated in the light of their fundamental theory and of their feasibility.

STONE, JULIUS. *Quest for Survival; The Role of Law and Foreign Policy.* Cambridge, Mass.: Harvard U. P., 1961. These lectures, delivered over the Australian Broadcasting system, provide a brief, simple, clear, and sensible treatment of the subject.

TUCKER, ROBERT W. *The Just War; A Study in Contemporary American Doctrine.* Baltimore, Md.: Johns Hopkins U. P., 1961. A rigorous critical analysis of the doctrine of "just war."

WALTZ, KENNETH N. *Man, the State, and War: A Theoretical Analysis.* New York: Columbia U. P., 1959. Mr. Waltz brings the insights of traditional political theorists to bear upon the problem of international relations. He also examines the causes of war inherent in man himself, in the state, and in the system of independent states.

CHAPTER 21

The Problem of International Order

To promote the international order and security that the world so badly needs we can only seek to strengthen the devices that statesmen and nations understand and will accept by virtue of usage and familiarity: diplomacy and balance of power, international law, and international organization. It would be dangerous folly, today, to aim our endeavors principally at a world state. This species of idealism—by ignoring the present differences in condition, in the senses of the right and the proper, and in political ideals between the nations of the earth—prejudices the cause of peace. Yet lasting peace cannot be won without expanding and deepening the sentiments and interests that support an international political community. So the problem of international order has two aspects: one, that of working for peace with familiar tools; the other, that of striving toward a world community of nations.

Traditionally, such order as has prevailed among nations had depended upon four principal techniques or institutions. The balance of power, supported by a flexible diplomacy, was probably the most effective instrument of peace until the twentieth century. Americans—good disciples of John Locke—have (verbally, at least) favored legality: international law and permanent tribunals of international justice. Functional and regional international organizations have sprouted thickly since the last quarter of the nineteenth century. After the First World War, the founding of the League of Nations initiated a fourth approach: world-wide organization to implement collective security. The United Nations in 1945 took over the same task from the defunct League.

Students and theorists of international relations have disagreed, over the years, about the relative importance each of these four approaches should have in preventing war and fostering amity among nations. Though the cold war, the ever-present possibility of thermonuclear war, and the spectacular post-war growth of regionalism have altered the grounds of the dispute, we can still decide the direction in which we wish to point our efforts for peace only by examining the merits of these various approaches.

THE BALANCE OF POWER

As a consciously pursued system for regulating international relations, the balance of power is almost as old as diplomacy and relations between states. It existed in ancient China and Egypt, among the Greek city-states, and the empires ringing the Mediterranean basin during the Hellenistic era. In Europe the system arose during the latter part of the fifteenth century, first among the Italian city-states, then in the politics of the papacy, the Holy Roman Empire, and the growing kingdoms of Spain, Austria, and France. Between the Treaty of Westphalia (1648), which set the basic pattern of the European state system, and the Peace of Utrecht (1713), which closed the War of the Spanish Succession, the balance of power system was firmly established among the states of Western Europe. Other states and regional systems of states were drawn into the European balance of power. From 1713 until the twentieth century the system was practiced with greater or lesser faithfulness. Excepting periods of revolution or the birth and dissolution of states, the techniques of the balance of power system worked effectively to limit aggrandisement and to prevent total war. Most notably, the policy of balance of power failed in the twentieth century to prevent either the first or the second World Wars. In the period between the wars, though nations professed the doctrine of collective security, they actually pursued a balance of power strategy. The Rome-Berlin "Axis," the overtures by the Axis powers towards Japan, and the Soviet-German nonaggression pact were examples. Today the system, or the technique, still persists. East and West equally vie for the support of uncommitted nations. Many of the latter seek power of their own by concerted action, for instance in the form of an Afro-Asian bloc. Some members of this group have also aspired to Britain's nineteenth century role as "balancer" in the power conflict. The Soviet bloc, as has happened to alliances from time immemorial, now appears to be split —how seriously we do not know—between the Soviet Union and Red China. And the Western alliance, perhaps responding to the Eastern weakness just referred to, has developed its own internal difficulties, most sharply indicated by President de Gaulle's opposition to American influence.

Homeostasis or equilibrium in the system of states is the basic conception underlying the doctrine of balance of power. Equilibrium is achieved by the calculated endeavor of at least some of the participants in the game. If one state aims at aggrandisement through any of several policies such as increased armaments, annexations, or the acquisition of new allies, its moves are countered by other members of the system who seek opposing alliances, compensating territories or other elements of power. Since, in principle, the weak coalition will pay handsomely (in the coin of diplomacy) for the support of uncommitted states, sustained aggrandisement will be met with at least enough countervailing power to induce the aggressors to seek modest goals either through negotiation or limited war. Also, each state in the interests of its future security will seek to prevent any one member of the system from becoming overwhelmingly powerful. Hence, the balance of power system tends to divide the politically active states into two camps and to preserve a roughly equal distribution of power between the rival groups. A single power may even make itself consciously the "arbiter" of the balance of power by throwing its weight behind the weaker coalition to restore equilibrium. Louis XIV aspired to this role of arbiter. Britain successfully pursued such a policy during most of the nineteenth century. At other times the "system" operates more automatically, with no single power acting as "balancer" and without even the participants generally thinking in terms of a "system."

Its Operation in the Eighteenth and Nineteenth Centuries

The classical balance of power "system" worked, after a fashion. During most of the eighteenth and nineteenth centuries, with no other mechanism for preventing conflict, major wars were avoided. The situation fostered a rational pursuit of limited objectives. But it did so under conditions and in accordance with principles that were peculiar to the political environment of the time. In the first place, alliances had to be concluded or abandoned with little regard for sentiment or past loyalties. National hatreds or undue prejudices against particular forms of government tended to polarize the distribution of power and increase the probabilities of war. The "system" worked best when there was an effective "holder of the balance."[1] England filled this need. Her interests lay in peace and in a continental balance of power. She was willing to spend blood and treasure in forestalling massive concentrations of power or any state of affairs that would threaten general war in Europe. Intervention without squeamishness was another principle of the balance of power system. In some instances, intervention signified taking a hand in other nations' quarrels regardless of doctrines of neutrality or past commitments. But the domestic affairs of nations were equally important as objects of diplomacy. Since national or democratic movements could radically upset the balance of power in Europe, the practice of intervention either to aid or suppress revolutionaries was common. In either case, the balance of power system presupposed a coldly rational and amoral use of power to support its workings. Matching the Machiavellian policy of intervention was the cynical doctrine of "compensations." Compensation

---

[1] Hans J. Morgenthau, *Politics Among Nations,* 3rd ed. (New York: Knopf, 1960), pp. 194 ff.

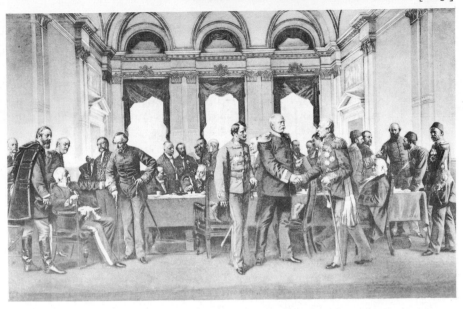

The Congress of Berlin (1878): a monument of traditional diplomacy
Charles Phelps Cushing

permitted elasticity within the balance of power system. If one nation's territorial acquisitions disturbed the balance of power, other powerful states were compensated at the expense of the weak. Thus, the Spanish Empire was divided, Poland was ruthlessly partitioned, and colonies in Africa and the Near and Far East were parcelled out to restore equilibrium in Europe. Lastly, maintaining a balance of power implied general commitment to the "system." Such commitment was in part secured by the similarity of political institutions and the unity of temper and outlook among the ruling governmental elite in Europe. Economic and technical conditions in Europe discouraged extensive armaments or lengthy wars. As with many a political myth, however, the balance of power system was sustained by a belief that it did work. That belief helped make it a reality.

Changed Circumstances

Although balance of power continues to be one of the facts of international life, it seems unlikely that the kind of deliberate balance of power policy sometimes pursued by Europe and Great Britain in the past will play a similar role in the forseeable future.[2] For at least four reasons the old policy is less likely to work under modern conditions. We shall consider each of them briefly.

[2] The possibility that a modified form of balance of power system may achieve some success in the thermonuclear age will be considered below, pp. 687-689.

DEMOCRACY

In the first place, the fact of democratic politics has changed the conduct of international relations, at least by democratic countries. The British balance of power policy depended upon the conduct of diplomacy in a manner no longer possible. Diplomats had to operate like horse traders or poker players. In particular, not only their negotiations but also the agreements arrived at with other nations often had to be kept secret, at least from the general public. The bargains struck might prove too embarrassing to one side or the other if they were made public. Woodrow Wilson's demand for "open covenants, openly arrived at" typified the new era. While it can not be said to have marked the death of secret diplomacy, it certainly did mark its decline.

For the old balance of power game, too, diplomats had to be in a position to act quickly, within a large area of discretion, and with assurance that their governments would back them up. Policy, that is to say, had to be flexible. It could not be rigidly bound, either by a set of rule or principles, or by the necessity of getting popular approval. Formerly, in matters of foreign policy, the British cabinet, if not virtually a law unto itself, at least had great discretion in matters of foreign policy. It could even bind the country to treaty obligations without consulting Parliament. New conditions are today reflected in the fact that, regardless of its legal power, no Government would negotiate a major treaty without submitting it for Parliamentary approval. While such approval presents considerably less of a hurdle than does Senatorial approval in the United States, even in Britain the need for popular consent in matters of foreign policy has placed effective restraints on the conduct of diplomats.

Some argue today that we should go back to the days of old-fashioned diplomacy. It is a mistake, they contend, to treat international politics in terms of high moral principle. Realism demands that states pursue their national interests with cool calculation, being prepared to shift their ground (and their alliances) and modify their policies from time to time as circumstances dictate.

As applied to ordinary diplomacy, this line of reasoning is itself highly unrealistic. It overlooks the practical development of the democratic principle. Today, outside of totalitarian states at least, governments have no choice but to conduct foreign policy, like other policy, with popular approval. But the populace is not generally sufficiently sophisticated, or cynical, to operate along the lines advocated. Of course national interest is a matter of great popular concern. So is national honor. And if, as frequently happens, national interest seems to demand that a position previously taken be suddenly modified or even reversed, such a move is often difficult to square with the popular view of the nation's dignity or honor. The process of finding a method of accommodation that also "saves face" is often slow and difficult—

sometimes impossible. Even dictatorships have to cope with this problem in some measure.

To "sell" the people on a particular policy it is often necessary to relate it to some moral principle. Because the interest of all in a particular foreign policy is likely to be dimly perceived by the man in the street, democracies are especially dependent upon moralizing appeals to arouse the electorate or to secure their approval for a new policy. If, later, statesmen in charge of foreign affairs want to change this policy, perhaps to exploit a bargaining advantage, it is hard to explain this change in such a way as to secure support for it. Or, essentially to put the same thing in a different form, a sensible politician knows perfectly well that he is giving hostages to his political opponents by forsaking the policy and moral principles that he has once defended before the people. Regardless of the merits of the gesture, any American President in the year 1963, for example, would hesitate long before recognizing Communist China precisely because of this kind of consideration.

Whether this limitation imposed by democracy on both flexibility and deviousness in conduct of foreign policy is on balance good or bad is not our concern. It is a fact; and those who ignore it are simply closing their eyes to an important part of reality.

TOTALITARIANISM

A second reason for the change in nature and conduct of international relations arises out of the emergence of totalitarian states. While they themselves may be less affected by the considerations we have just been discussing than are the democracies, their powerful anti-democratic ideologies tend to divide the world into two sharply opposed camps. Under such circumstances, it is difficult for any country to assume the role of "balancer", throwing its weight now with this group and now with that. True, certain countries today aspire to form a "Third Force." India sought to play the role of mediator, if not balancer, as between East and West. But Communist China's invasion of her territory seems to have occasioned a sharp shift in Indian policy. Nor has the Afro-Asian bloc had much success in the pursuit of a balancing policy. Certainly one reason for their failure is the fact that the Communist ideology is made part-and-parcel of the foreign policy of Communist states and it is so dogmatic and so sharply opposed to all that is not Communist that a middle ground is difficult to find, while a series of alternations from one side to the other is virtually impossible.

BIPOLARITY

The third reason is closely related to the second. It is the political condition of bipolarity. The fact that the world is today largely divided into two camps is partly a result of totalitarianism itself. Partly, however, it springs from the fact that two superpowers far exceed all other nations in strength. This situation also makes it difficult, ideological considerations apart, for any state to play the role of balancer. We have already noted that Britain's success in this role owed much to her preponderance of power. Today, at the very least, only a *combination* of weaker nations could hope to pursue the policy with success; and for a group of states to be able to coordinate their foreign policies sufficiently to admit of performing this delicate operation would indeed be a feat. It would have been difficult enough in the days when kings or foreign ministers carried the policies of their countries in their vest pockets.[3]

Still another consideration militates against the success of the nineteenth century "balancer" principle in a bipolar world. In such a world, theoretical analysis indicates, national alignments tend to be related to the long-run interests of states rather than toward their interests in particular situations.[4] This condition runs contrary to a basic requirement of the "balancer" system: namely, that states should be able rather readily to shift their alignments and that one system of alliances is just as likely as another.

WEAKENED MORAL CONSENSUS

Finally, the moral consensus among the nations is less than prevailed a century ago. It is true that democratic regimes are likely to anchor their policies to certain principles of right and justice. However, these same principles are not accepted by all nations—especially not by Communist nations. Hence the lack of moral consensus. Moreover, general agreement on the preservation of the existing order in something like its present form no longer prevails. As during the period between 1789 and 1815, an all-out struggle for the transformation of the world is involved. In the absence of common ground between the parties, the more or less tacit agreements that previously prevailed for the limitation both of the objectives and the methods of war tend to dissolve. Here, then, is one more factor, partly derived from conditions discussed above, that increases the intensity of the struggle for power and tends to harden the alignments beyond the point where a policy of consciously shifting the balance is practicable.

General Weakness of International Equilibria

Before leaving the concept of the balance of power, we can with profit consider another aspect of this subject. Conflicting physical forces tend to reach a point of equilibrium, at which they cancel or balance each other out. Also in economics the schedule of prices of various commodities and services at a particular time reflects the balance of supply and demand. As long as the latter forces remain constant the prices will remain fixed—that is, in a

[3] As will be noted more fully on later pages, bipolarity, thanks to Mao Tse-tung and de Gaulle, is less completely characteristic of the world today than it was throughout the fifties.

[4] Morton A. Kaplan, *System and Process in International Politics* (New York: Wiley, 1957), p. xiv, and Ch. 5, generally. Students interested in the logic of power balances should read the chapter just cited.

state of equilibrium. To a certain extent, but unfortunately only to a limited extent, the same process operates among independent states. (This system, as far as it operates, is that of a balance of power without any particular state playing the role of balancer.) Each state expresses its needs, more or less overtly, in terms of demands. Most if not all of these needs may be classified under one of three heads: security, welfare, and prestige. While a state is not a person and does not act precisely like one, at any given time it is perhaps fair to assume that it has a kind of "demand schedule." It wants prosperity, it wants prestige, and of course it wants security; and in a rough sort of way it tends to know how much of each it is willing to sacrifice to gain a unit of the others. In a process of trial-and-error experimentation it finds out, again only roughly, how much of each it can get and at what cost. If we assume that all nations value security highly, recognizing that it is fundamental to welfare, for instance, and if we further assume that they behave rationally and are fully informed as to the potential consequences of their actions (*i.e.*, how other states will react to their conduct), it might be supposed that an equilibrium would eventually be established and wars would cease. Unfortunately, as we have already seen, not all of the postulated assumptions hold. States and their citizens are often ill-informed in respect to the consequences of their action. When Hitler invaded Poland in September 1939, he may have thought that Britain and France would not fight. Or he may have thought that he could defeat them before the United States came to their aid. Whatever his reasoning, it cannot be presumed that he envisaged the ultimate catastrophe to him and to Germany that resulted. Also, conditions change. The price of a state's needs at a particular time is a function, among other things, of its bargaining power, which is partly a function of its relative military potential. Now, more than ever before, military might depends upon industrial power and technological developments. The perfection of an intercontinental ballistic missile may today completely upset the previous balance while tomorrow the development of an adequate protection against such weapons may once more upset the balance. Under these circumstances an equilibrium, at best, is a most uncertain affair.[5]

INTERNATIONAL LAW

We have spoken thus far about the relations existing among sovereign states as though they occurred in a realm where law had no place. The student may well have asked himself "what of international law?" Early in this book we have seen that no society can exist for long without the devel-

---

[5] For a theoretical analysis of international politics from this point of view, see George Liska, *International Equilibrium—a Theoretical Essay on the Politics and Organization of Security* (Cambridge, Mass.: Harvard U. P., 1957); also Samuel P. Huntington, "Arms Races: Prerequisites and Results," in Carl J. Friedrich and Seymour E. Harris, *Public Policy*, 8 (1958), (Cambridge, Mass.: Graduate School of Public Administration, 1958), pp. 41-86. This subject will be pursued further, in today's context, below, pp. 687-689.

opment of law; and also that a society of states tends to develop rules of conduct that possess legal character. The proposition, "Where there is society there law exists." continues to hold true. However, it takes more than separate units in mutual juxtaposition to make a society. Close ties always exist within certain groups of nations. During the nineteenth century, for instance, most Western civilized countries were closely enough linked that they could be spoken of without hyperbole as "the family of nations." Today, however, that family is so divided that it requires considerable stretching of the term to speak of a society of states, a fact that finds reflection in the present parlous status of International Law.

Nature and Manner of Growth

The beginnings of modern international law date from the emergence of the sovereign state. As Bodin, whose theory of sovereignty was first set forth in print in 1576, set the stamp of achievement on the internal sovereignty of the state, so Hugo Grotius's *Law of War and Peace,* published in 1625, at once marked the fact of sovereignty from an international point of view and attempted to cope with the problems it posed. The Dutch scholar did far more than recognize a fact. In elaborating his treatise on the law of nations, he accomplished three purposes. In the first place, he organized and reduced to a systematic whole existing international practices. Secondly, he filled out this body of law by reference to principles of natural law, some "self-evident", others gathered by reference to the works of earlier writers. Finally, he set down persuasive reasons why states should be bound by the principles and rules contained in his book.

Since that beginning, the body of international law has grown in a similar manner to that of primitive law and early national laws. That is to say, custom or practice is the stuff out of which much international law grows. So it was with the rules governing the acquisition of hitherto unoccupied territory, and the law of diplomatic immunity. What comes to be customary is frequently the practice of a few dominant states. Also, like early domestic law, international law often takes an incident of some proportions to harden a custom into law. If a dispute arises, for example with regard to the question of where the marginal or territorial waters surrounding a state end and the open sea begins, a powerful state may successfully assert that the line is at a certain distance. Thereafter this determination may be generalized and may achieve universal recognition.[6]

---

[6] The example, perhaps, is more apt for illustrating other possibilities than the one hypothesized, for it is believed that the three-mile limit for territorial waters came to prevail because that was, at the time the rule originated, the effective limit of gun-fire from shore batteries. Moreover, this rule has never been universally accepted and is today being widely challenged, especially as it applies to fishing and mineral rights.

Disputes may be settled by negotiation and agreement rather than imposition and yet serve as precedents which go a long way toward determining
a rule. Often, too, disagreements have been submitted to arbitration. The
decisions of arbitral tribunals are likely to carry great weight as precedents
for the determination of future disputes involving the same kind of issue.
The settlement of a dispute by any means will carry more weight as a precedent (and so as the basis for a rule of law) if it is founded on some generally
accepted principle of law or equity or if it is cast in terms of a rule that is
convenient or commends itself to common sense. For instance, the rule that
sovereigns and their diplomatic representatives are immune from the legal
processes of other states is thought to flow logically from the fundamental
principle of the equality of states. Often, too, rules of international law are
based upon analogies from private law. So it is with the law of prescription,
which provides that undisputed possession becomes legal right after a period
of time. The doctrine of the *Thalweg*, according to which the channel of a
navigable river marks the line where the river constitutes the boundary between states, is probably an example of a rule based upon simple convenience.

The incidents among a society of fifty or even a hundred or more states
are few in comparison with those that arise in any normal-sized society of
individuals. Hence precedents are scarce and arbitrators, courts, and others
dealing with the settlement of legal disputes often have to look beyond the
practice of nations and the decisions of tribunals to find a basis for decision.
One important source of the law regularly consulted is the writings of jurists.
Unofficial authorities, from at least the time of Grotius, have thus played a
great role in the development of international law, even as did the Roman
jurists with Roman law. These jurists themselves attempt to evolve a systematic body of law out of practice, precedent, analogy, theories of justice,
and logical deductions from a few fundamental principles, such as the concepts of equality of state persons, the independence of states, the right of
self-preservation, the presumption against acts in derogation of sovereignty,
and the duty of states to keep their promises (*pacta sunt servanda*).

Much international law has been elaborated by national courts, which,
in the absence (until recent times) of international courts have often furnished the only mode of redress for an injured party. Suppose, for instance,
that a crime is committed on board a foreign vessel within the territorial
waters of the United States. An American police officer, boards the vessel
and arrests the offender. He is subsequently brought to trial in an American
court. The first question the court will have to decide is whether, according
to international law, it, or any American court, has jurisdiction over the case.

In the days before warfare had become "total," the law of war and the
law of neutrality constituted large sections of the *corpus* of international law.
Of the latter, much had to do with the rights of neutrals to trade with bellig-
erents. Neutral vessels engaged in such trade were subject to capture and
condemnation as prizes of war by the offended belligerent, if they violated

this law. Captured vessels, however, were never condemned out of hand. Rather they were taken to a convenient port and the case submitted to a prize court for determination of facts and law. The same procedure was followed with regard to unarmed enemy vessels. The coming of the submarine, or "U-boat," during the first World War rendered this procedure obsolete. The resulting disputes with Germany over neutral rights brought the United States into the war.

Ordinary treaties between two states do not constitute international law, although international law commands their observance. In modern times, however, it has become a frequent practice to codify and modify international law by means of multilateral treaties to which a great many nations are parties. It frequently happens that other nations, not parties to the treaty, nonetheless accept them and consider themselves bound by them. During both the First and Second World Wars various states accepted the terms of some of the Geneva conventions (multilateral treaties) regulating the conduct of war even though they had not signed or ratified them. During the Korean fighting, both North Korea and the United States appealed to the Geneva convention regulating the treatment of prisoners of war, although neither was a party to it. In short, to the means of creating and developing international law already discussed it is necessary to add that of the multilateral treaty.

Inadequacies

Although the family of nations is not without its body of law, that law is notoriously weak and inadequate. None of the difficulties to which Locke pointed in the state of nature is adequately met. The law itself often lacks clear definition. Custom and case-by-case adjudication are far more inadequate as means of evolving a body of law for states than for individuals, because states are so much less numerous than individuals have been in any autonomous society in which law developed. Fewer units means few issues and cases, fewer opportunities for precedents to be created. And existing precedents are frequently of such long standing that the relevant conditions have been so greatly changed in the interim as to deprive them of support in general sentiment.

As to interpretation, until recent times international tribunals were non-existent. Even since the creation of such agencies they have lacked general compulsory jurisdiction over all international disputes. Some, but not all members of the court organizations, have bound themselves in advance to accept their jurisdiction in so-called "justiciable" disputes. These commitments have generally been so hedged about by reservations as to limit their applicability to a relatively small area. The basic weakness remains with respect to the subject matters giving rise to the most serious sources of international strife.

An even more critical weakness of international law than the lack of means for interpretation is the absence of enforcement agencies. Law must depend on much more than force to secure acceptance; but without some force to be brought to bear upon recalcitrants the whole of its moral foundation will be seriously eroded. Successful defiance is contagious. The community of states has, in this respect, the additional difficulty that its members vary greatly in size and strength. In some primitive societies law is enforced with a minimum of organization simply because any would-be violator knows he is hopelessly outnumbered by those of his fellows who will be outraged by his act. Among nations, however, the lawbreaker may be so powerful that he has no reason to fear even a coalition of those other states close enough to be much concerned about his actions. Under these circumstances the system of "self-help" (analogous to the right of self-defense among individuals) is pitifully inadequate.

Finally, the classical system of international law is woefully deficient in instrumentalities for change. Even in domestic realms, custom and precedent, the method of the common law, has more and more given way to legislation as the needs of a dynamic society rendered the former method of change inadequate. Although increasingly during the past century the device of an international conference for the negotiation of multilateral treaties has been used in the effort to supply this lack, it has proved inadequate to the task. Its weakness is simple but crucial: its dependence upon unanimous consent. We need only try to imagine the Senate of the United States trying to accomplish its work with a unanimity requirement to understand why the device of the international conference has been a weak reed in the concert of nations.

World Courts

During the last half century or so, important steps have been taken toward the development of organization to offset the weaknesses enumerated above. Just as a sporadic series of international conferences (for example, that preceding the Declaration of Paris in 1856, which codified part of the law of neutrality,) pointed the way toward the creation of international legislatures, so also the practice by quarrelling nations of submitting their disputes to arbitration foreshadowed the development of international courts. During the nineteenth century a great many disputes were settled by this device. The disputants would select arbitrators, perhaps at the urging of third parties who had been seeking to conciliate them. These arbitrators would then be empowered, by agreement of the parties, to arrive at a settlement and make a binding award. While arbitrators examine the law on the questions before them and give weight to precedent, they normally have power to take other than legal considerations into account in arriving at their decision. For this reason, among others, their decisions are less valuable than those of regular courts in the development of legal rules.

Frequently, going beyond arrangements made after a dispute had arisen, the United States, as well as other countries, negotiated bilateral treaties providing for the submission of all of certain types of disputes between the parties to arbitration. Another forward step was taken at the first of two great world peace conferences, the Hague Peace Conference of 1899, which established a Permanent Court of Arbitration at the Hague. Although hardly a court, for it had only a large panel of arbitrators from which individual arbitrators were selected by the parties when a dispute was submitted, this organization marked a definite advance in the growth of international adjudication. Nevertheless, out of over 120 arbitral awards made between 1899 and 1932, only 18 were by the Hague Court, 14 between 1899 and 1916. Attempts to give the Court compulsory jurisdiction were unsuccessful.

After the First World War, in connection with the formation of the League of Nations, the first real international court of anything like world-wide scope was established. This court, known as the Permanent Court of International Justice, had a fixed bench of fifteen members and was to make its judgments on purely legal grounds, unless otherwise agreed by the parties to a particular dispute. In the first instance jurisdiction was not compulsory, but by signing the so-called "optional clause" members could accept compulsory jurisdiction regarding all disputes turning on treaty interpretation or other legal matters, subject to such reservations as they might choose to make. In addition to the power to decide cases, it could be called on by the League to give advisory opinions in cases before the Council or the Assembly. During the period from its creation in 1920 until 1942 it rendered 30 judgments and 27 advisory opinions.

The new International Court of Justice, provided for by the Charter of the United Nations in 1945, substantially continues the old Permanent Court of International Justice, with only minor modifications. Over thirty nations, including all the great Powers save the Soviet Union, have accepted its compulsory jurisdiction, subject to the usual reservations.

Both the number and, for the most part, the importance of the cases that have been submitted to these international courts for decision, or even for advisory opinions, is relatively slight. The reason is obviously not a lack of international tensions and disagreements. Nor is it far to seek. The simple fact is that the law, at least in the absence of an effective legislature, is nearly always on the side of the *status quo*. The great causes of war arise out of situations where some state is dissatisfied with the *status quo* in a fundamental respect. Frequently its existing borders were imposed upon it at the conclusion of a war in which it was defeated. It does not feel morally bound by such a determination. At the same time no legal way exists to secure a change without the consent of other states. These other states normally will have both interest and moral conviction on their own side, so agreement is not likely to be forthcoming, while adjudication holds no hope for the party desiring change.

FUNCTIONAL AND REGIONAL INTERNATIONAL ORGANIZATIONS

Before going on to examine the development of world-wide legislative, and executive (enforcement) agencies, we must examine two other lines of development. Specialized organizations for the performance of certain functions have been created on a universal[7] basis, and other organizations of a political nature have been established on regional bases.

Functional Organizations

The specialized, or functional organizations are of many kinds. Each has its own constitution, its own membership, budget, and operating agencies. First the League of Nations and then the United Nations took most of these organizations under its wing, but they remain essentially autonomous. Others have been formed at the instance of one or the other of these two great universal political bodies; but they also are established as autonomous units. Some of them deal with highly technical and noncontroversial matters, as does the Universal Postal Union, or, to a slightly lesser extent, the International Civil Aviation Organization. The World Health Organization also has an important role to fill in a non-political sphere. Others, dealing with such matters as labor legislation (International Labor Organization), agriculture (Food and Agricultural Organization), regulation of international exchange controls (International Monetary Fund), and loans for development and reconstruction (International Bank for Reconstruction and Development), work in areas where the conflicts of interest are much greater. In some cases, as with the International Labor Organization, their powers are limited to making recommendations to their member governments, while in other cases they are vested with authority to act for themselves, without the concurrence of all member governments. The International Bank and the International Monetary Fund fall in the latter category.

While in each of the instances named and in others like them the sole purpose in forming the organization was to accomplish its highly specialized objective, it is generally thought that they have other, indirect effects particularly pertinent to the subject of this chapter. Insofar, that is to say, as these organizations facilitate international intercourse, insofar as they serve the needs of the potential world community, to that extent they help to bring a world community into being. The value of this kind of development is recognized by all students of international government, while some of them contend that it provides the great and only road to organization for

---

[7] Here as elsewhere, when we use the term "universal" as applied to an international organization, we do not mean that all existing states belong to it but that it aspires to such universality, and that all are eligible for membership on the same terms.

peace.[8] They believe that this is the natural approach for developing community; that by means of it, national lines of demarcation can be gradually rendered insignificant, as a web of international activities and organizations gradually is superimposed on them and tends to supersede them. Others, less optimistic, insist that, important though the work of these organizations is, two facts seriously limit its effectiveness. In the first place, the average citizen is completely unaware of the work, and generally even of the existence, of these organizations. Their dealings are largely with governments. The size of the international civil service employed by them is infinitesimal compared to that of the national governments with which they deal. The second drawback is that national security assumes such an all-important place in the minds of most men that, until it is assured, functional international organization will occupy a decidedly inferior place in the value structure of the average man. If, for example, proposed action by an international trade organization should threaten the economic independence of a state in the event of war the proposal would assuredly be defeated. For this reason the United States would be likely to insist on producing synthetic rubber, even if, in peacetime, it could secure it more cheaply from Indonesia and Malaya. On the other hand, a nation convinced that its "vital interests"— e.g., maintenance of its relative power position—called for action inimical to one of the technical organizations would probably take the action in question without hesitation.

One international organization has been created for the specific purpose of developing a world community, a communal basis for world political organization. This is the United Nations Educational, Scientific, and Cultural Organization, generally known as Unesco, dedicated to fostering an awareness of "the intellectual and moral solidarity of mankind." The indirect effects of the other functional organizations are here the specific objective. Unesco's activities are so varied as to defy brief description. It strives to increase international exchange of students and scholars, to conduct studies of social problems likely to create national and international tensions, and to provide technical assistance for the economic and political development of underdeveloped areas. How great the value of activities of this kind may be it is impossible to say, but presumably their total impact is highly significant. It is as reassuring from one point of view as it is unfortunate from another to learn that states are requesting more technical assistance from Unesco than it has funds to supply. The habit on the part of many countries of turning to an international agency for help can hardly fail to develop international-mindedness in important measure, in spite of the limitations upon this approach pointed out above, and of the obstacles thrown in its way by Communist opposition to its activities.

[8] Cf. the works of David Mitrany, e.g., his *A Working Peace System* (London: Royal Institute of International Affairs, 1944).

Regional Organizations

Many problems that extend beyond state boundaries are still not world-wide in scope. Even where they have a wider scope, it is often possible to get the requisite confidence and understanding for organization among neighboring states where it is not possible on a wider basis. For both of these reasons we have numerous regional international organizations. Some are functional in the sense of being single-purpose agencies, while others are more general in nature. Among the latter, an outstanding example is provided by the Organization of American States. While it maintains a permanent secretariat, this organization functions primarily through its periodic conferences and through the treaty arrangements established at one or another of these conferences. By means of it a system of collective security has gradually been substituted for the self-appointed policing previously exercised by the United States.

Recently, regional organizations, especially organizations that are both regional and specialized, have been growing rapidly in Europe. The story of their growth and of their vicissitudes provides a fruitful case study in many of the problems of international organization and of the principles underlying it. First of all, one is impressed by the magnitude of the pressures required to overcome the obstacles and to get movements of international integration under way. Even though sentiment and interest might encourage governments to surrender their independence and join together in a wider political unity, such a step is almost impossible without some events which break the mold of ordinary politics. In the initial stages, the really powerful domestic economic interests—agriculture, labor, and business—are mobilized behind such moves only with the greatest difficulty, if at all. Lowering tariff walls or surrendering power to a European agency may win a vague and general approval, but these measures in practice often get only a few strong and continuing supporters, since they offer endless opportunities for disagreement about concrete measures, and usually threaten the interests of some groups directly and tangibly. Furthermore, supranational government not only threatens many particular interests, but involves a change in the political structure itself. The ordinary politician resists "upsetting the apple-cart." No politician who is winning at the game wants election districts radically changed or the ground rules for winning friends and influencing people altered in some novel way that he does not understand. In the same manner, interest groups with settled and profitable lines of access to government and a known political environment resist innovation. In settled times, consequently, internationalism tends to be the avocation of a few statesmen and intellectuals, but not the trade of most practical politicians and businessmen.

The Common Market: little summit conference

Wide World Photos

FAVORING FACTORS

For Western Europe, the Second World War destroyed the settled political environment. Much of Europe was occupied territory at some time or other. The economic mobilization of the Continent by the Nazis and the destruction of war itself wrecked factories and disrupted whole economies, leaving the countries of Europe in need of a great collective effort to restore their economic health and prosperity. From the war emerged new leaders, new political movements, and a new found solidarity. The European movement sprang into being before the postwar upsurge of idealism could die and before the channels of political influence and economic interest could become encrusted with the sanctity of usage and prescription. War has been the most revolutionary force of modern times. The growth of a unified Europe from the wreckage of her greatest war is grimly ironical.

Differing pressures from the United States and the Soviet Union are the major external forces that have pushed the European movement ahead. Soviet threats and menacing gestures have repeatedly induced European nations to draw closer together, to surmount petty squabbles, and to bury domestic political differences. The role of the Soviet Union has been an inadvertent one, probably testifying in some measure to the irrationality and inefficiency of totalitarian foreign policy. The part played by the United

States has been enormous, and also occasionally unintentional. America underwrote much of the bill for rearmament and supplied the initial protection that made it possible. In giving Marshall Plan aid, the United States insisted that the European nations cooperate and plan collectively to use it to maximum advantage. Marshall Plan experience supplied much of the impetus and practical experience that helped convert European economic cooperation from a vague goal into a concrete undertaking. In fact, the framework established to plan and cooperate for American aid still exists in the O.E.C.D. (Organization for Economic Cooperation and Development), which functions today as a kind of "tent" or covering organization to coordinate other European endeavors and to cooperate in new collective aims. Consistently, American influence has been used to promote all West European ventures, not excepting the Common Market which may be economically disadvantageous to the United States.

It must be said that other factors have been influential in the remarkable progress made toward the unity of part of Europe during the postwar years. Chief among these is the extraordinary prosperity enjoyed by all of the countries concerned. Nothing could be better calculated to quiet the fears of business and labor groups that might otherwise have blocked the movement. Whether by coincidence or consequence, the first tariff reductions made by the European Economic Community (the "Common Market") were followed by even greater prosperity. This fortunate sequence appears to have won these groups (or dominant sections of them) over to the idea that they have more to gain than to lose by mutual reduction and gradual elimination of trade restrictions.

EUROPEAN ACCOMPLISHMENTS

Considering the obstacles, what has been accomplished within the European Community is truly remarkable. Building on the foundations of an extended Benelux, six nations—Belgium, France, West Germany, Italy, Luxemburg, and The Netherlands—have made the greatest strides. They have organized themselves into three distinct "communities": the European Coal and Steel Community, the European Atomic Energy Community (Euratom), and the European Economic Community (the Common Market). The first of these has been in operation since 1952; the others only since 1958. The E.C.S.C., itself formed to provide a common market for two commodities, steel and coal, is the most advanced and the most interesting as a step toward supranational political organization. It has a High Authority, an Assembly, a Council, a Court of Justice, and an Economic and Social Committee. The High Authority, which is the executive organ, operates within its sphere independently, without instructions from member governments. Its decisions on such important matters as prices for steel and coal are final. The 78 members of the National Assembly are chosen either by the national parliaments or by popular elections within the member countries. It can force the resignation of the High Authority, but only by a two-thirds vote. The Council of Ministers (one from each member state) has power to veto certain of the most far-reaching decisions of the High Authority.

So remarkable is the degree to which ordinary notions of state sovereignty have been modified to permit the formation of the Coal and Steel Community, that the whole process will bear further examination. The politics surrounding the E.C.S.C. shows a steady decline in national or ideological controversies and an increasing preoccupation with pragmatic issues of tangible benefit and loss.[9] Interest group behavior has become steadily more "fluid," groups finding themselves with one national bloc today, another tomorrow, pro-"government" on one issue, anti-"government" on another. Coal and steel users, *regardless* of country, make common cause with the High Authority against coal and steel producers and trade unions. National and international commercial groups join to defend their interests. The Coal and Steel Community began its work in an area of ideological diversity and doctrinal vagueness. The tendency of Coal and Steel politics has not been to create or intensify issues that would lead to divisions along lines of national loyalties, but rather to erode differences of principle and ideology. For the most part, only small business and agriculture invoke patriotic symbols and the shades of national heroes. Leading businessmen and trade union leaders are less prone to resort to these appeals.

The most important fact about the various European international organizations is that they appear to have passed the point of "take-off." That is to say, their development is now self-sustaining. It has gained enough momentum to continue without further stimulation from elements outside of the system itself.[10] Under these circumstances, sectoral "governments" tend to expand. They grow by exerting their authority in response to pressure and exploiting their powers to deal with "spill-over" problems of regulation in specific areas. Thus a manufacturer who is adversely affected by the action of the Coal and Steel Community or the Common Market may turn to his own national government for redress; but he may find that getting his foreign competitors regulated by the same authorities is more profitable. In the same fashion, a trade union whose members are hit by a decision to close a coal mine or to cut off a government subsidy to an industry may—judging a direct attack likely to be unsuccessful—attack on a collateral ground: for example, it may influence the European authority to implement its powers to resettle and retrain workers. In other words, the rational response to constituency pressure tends to be to influence the policy of the supranational

[9] Ernst B. Haas, *The Uniting of Europe* (Palo Alto, Calif.: Stanford U. P., 1958) contains one of the most complete and informative accounts of this process. We have relied heavily on it.

[10] See Amitai Etzioni, "A Paradigm for the Study of Political Unification," *World Politics*, 15 (1962), pp. 44-74. The discussion of the "takeoff" concept will be found on pp. 66-69.

authority rather than to fight for its abolition. Further, civil servants working for these various supranational agencies find that they must coordinate their efforts across agency lines to achieve harmony with other European organizations, such as Euratom or G.A.T.T. (General Agreement of Tariffs and Trade). Administrative officers invoke scrap metal controls or set investment rates, consult and collaborate with their European colleagues in response to the programmatic needs and the whole cluster of European agencies.

Thus, these "governments" grow by exploiting "spill-over," and through the necessity for coordination. Their evolution has also been a consequence of the rapid growth of a new political constituency. European federations of pressure groups—of industry, commerce, labor, and the consumer—were organized quickly and effectively to represent common, Europe-wide, economic interests. These sectoral agencies constitute, furthermore, a new *level* of government; and national parties and interest groups have responded to them in some measure as they would to another level of domestic government. They have delegated difficult decisions to the Coal and Steel Community or to the Common Market, invoking their authority, for example, to restrain price or wage increases. Socialist parties and labor federations have attempted to win at this level of government some of the political goals they have failed to win domestically, such as new forms of worker protection and benefits. To the internal pressures generated by the group struggle and the necessity of administrative coordination, this "sinistration" (or left-wing pressure) upon European agencies adds a salutary driving force to expand the scope of regulation as a whole.

To date, the Coal and Steel Community has shown a convincing pattern of growth to support the "logic of sector integration;"[11] also, progress toward the European Common Market has repeatedly led to demands for acceleration. Whether further experience with other European agencies will fulfill similar expectations remains to be seen. However, the European movement is still young. There seems to be no logical reason why the same strategy could not be successfully implemented for any number of additional fields such as transport, the generation and distribution of hydro-electric energy, European aid to underdeveloped countries, the manufacture of military equipment, and the like.

European experience tends to confirm the proposition that some feasible pattern for the growth of supranational political communities can be found. The example is worth pondering for this reason. Yet several words of caution are in order. The special circumstances pertaining to this European experience are notable. Also, while progress with respect to the Common Market and the Coal and Steel Community justify a moderate optimism, and treaty agreements on agriculture, atomic energy, civil aviation, and aid to underdeveloped countries tend to confirm this optimism, the fact remains

---

[11] The terminology is Professor Haas's. See, *The Uniting of Europe, op. cit.*, Ch. 8.

that much of the program for unification remains in the area of solemn commitment only with few steps taken to implement these commitments. In addition, de Gaulle's demands in 1963 for a sober second look raise a number of fundamental questions that have perennially plagued regional organizations, such as: how exclusive shall the organization be? what collective foreign policy shall it pursue? and who is to be first among equals?

WORLD SECURITY ORGANIZATIONS

While the experts have been arguing whether regional organizations should proceed or follow those of the universal type and whether a functional approach was better than one that was more generalized, the world has gone ahead in its muddling way creating all three types, often without much apparent rhyme or reason. Dreams of world government are at least as old as Dante Alighieri, who proposed a universal empire to bring an end to medieval strife. During the seventeenth and eighteenth centuries projects for the attainment of universal peace by way of world government were numerous. Among the most famous of these is the *Project de paix perpetuelle*, published by the Abbé de Saint-Pierre in 1713.

The League of Nations

It was not until the conclusion of the First World War, however, that the establishment of the League of Nations brought into being the first organization that could lay claim to both generality of purpose and something approaching universality of membership. By 1928 fifty-four states, including all the Great Powers except the United States and the Soviet Union had ratified the League Covenant. In 1934, the Soviet Union joined. The League solved the problem of giving recognition both to the principle of equality of states and to the substantial differences in power among the states in somewhat the same way that was used by the Framers of the American Constitution. That is to say it provided for two representative bodies, in one of which all of the members were represented equally, while in the other equalitarianism did not prevail. The first of these was the Assembly and the second the Council.[12] The Council was a relatively small group within which the Great Powers had permanent seats. The other seats were filled by election by the Assembly for four-year terms. On all important questions, both the Assembly and the Council were governed by the rule of unanimity, except that in the case of the settlement of disputes threatening war the interested parties were not permitted to vote.

[12] Here the parallel to the American and other bicameral legislative bodies ends. As with the present Charter of the United Nations, most actions did not require the concurrence of both bodies. Instead a kind of division of labor prevailed and on many matters one of the bodies could act without the other. On the most important matters the Council had jurisdiction.

While the League performed many functions, and had a sizable Secretariat to administer them, its major purpose and concern was the prevention of war. Peace was to be enforced. All members were under obligation to settle their disputes by peaceful means, and the Covenant was peppered with provisions to facilitate such settlements. However, if a dispute was submitted to the Council and the Council was unable to agree on recommendations within a certain period of time, the disputants were free to go to war. Apart from this exception, members resorting to war would be violating the Covenant and other members were under obligation immediately to break off all economic relations with them, thus subjecting them to an economic boycott. The Covenant also provided for military as well as economic sanctions, but their application was not intended to be automatic.

Although the League settled numerous minor quarrels and accomplished much that was valuable among its auxiliary functions, it notoriously failed in its main objective. In fact it never succeeded in checking aggression by a major power. Military sanctions were never invoked. A half-hearted attempt to use economic sanctions against Italy at the time of her attack upon Ethiopia was ineffective.

Article X of the League Covenant, which guaranteed the territorial integrity of all League members, is often blamed for the League's failure. It supported the *status quo,* including the new boundaries imposed by the Allies at Versailles, permitting change only by unanimous consent—that is to say, in the case of territorial changes, with the consent of the state that would be giving up territory. As we have already remarked, the crucial problem facing any international security organization is that of reconciling demands for change, especially on the part of those who feel that earlier settlements were unjust, with the demands by others for security and self-preservation. Article X was the focal point of this problem. But to suggest that it was the *cause* of the League's failure is to assume that a better solution was available. This suggestion also places the burden of proof on the defender of the *status quo.* One may question whether this way of looking at the matter does it full justice. We must remember that the first great failure of the League arose out of a case where the aggressor (Japan) was attacking a weak state that had gained none of its territory from Japan. The same was true of the second great test case, the Italian attack upon Ethiopia.

Probably, the existence of more effective provisions for peaceful change would not have helped in such key situations as these, where not only law but also generally accepted standards of justice were on the side of the *status quo.* Rather, the blame must be placed on the unreadiness of nations, especially of the Great Powers, to implement the provisions that were in the Covenant. Specifically, had they been willing to act as strongly as the case might require to check the Japanese invasion of Manchuria, Italy might not have risked her attack upon Ethiopia. Had both of these aggressors been checked, it is at least possible that German ambitions and resentments might have been sublimated into less aggressive forms. Indeed, under such circumstances Hitler, with his program of militant expansionism, might never have attained office in Germany. However, we shall shortly review why it was extremely unlikely, in principle, that the "collective security" formula should have worked. Unlike the cases of Italy and Japan, German demands, partially a reaction to the "Versailles *diktat*," had some foundations in justice. The path to world peace, however, cannot lie along the road of redressing all such injustices. It would be a never-ending process, for rightful claims are so intermingled that it is impossible to correct one wrong without doing another. Probably the only final solution for such disputes is to render the grounds of quarrel less important. The original American states had conflicting claims to territories west of the Alleghenies; but where men and goods may move freely across lines and differences in currency are no bar to trade, territorial "ownership" becomes of secondary significance. For the world, the solution is neither easy nor likely to be soon achieved. For that reason it would be a mistake to concentrate all efforts on removing grounds for dispute, when partial solutions may be secured in other ways. At the same time, we are likely to reach the ultimate goal sooner, if we understand why it is, or should be the goal.

The United Nations

Following the conclusion of the Second World War, no attempt was made to rehabilitate the League; but a new world organization, the United Nations, was established in its stead. Again two representative bodies constitute the heart of the organization: a General Assembly, in which each member state is represented and has one vote and a Security Council containing five permanent members (Nationalist China, France, Great Britain, the Soviet Union, and the United States) and six members elected for stated terms. Unlike the Assembly of the League, the General Assembly may act by two-thirds vote. On the other hand, this abandonment of the unanimity rule is offset by the fact that the General Assembly has only powers of recommendation. In the Security Council again the rule of unanimity is modified; substantive questions may be settled by seven out of the eleven votes. The seven votes, however, must include the concurring votes of each of the "Big Five" (the permanent members).[13] In other words each of the Big Five has a veto. Moreover, this veto extends to the question of applying either economic or military sanctions even where the vetoing power is a party to the dispute. A Great Power, that is to say, may veto the applications of sanctions against itself.

[13] Literally construed this provision would mean that an abstention by one of the permanent members would have the same effect as a negative ballot. In practice, on several occasions the Soviet Union has raised no objections to permitting the Security Council to take affirmative action on the basis of a vote from which the Soviet abstained.

Clearly the UN Charter, as contrasted with the League Covenant, and in spite of the statement that "the Organization is based on the principle of the sovereign equality of all its Members" (Art. 2) takes account of the fact that the actual power of states varies in tremendous proportions. The UN is to this extent realistically based. To insist that all states are equally entitled to justice, or that they should all have an equal right to express themselves is one thing; to give them equal voting power is quite another. For, where actual strength is largely in the hands of certain states, they must inevitably carry the major responsibilities; and to deny the need for equating responsibility and legal power, at least in a measure, would violate a fundamental political principle. Within the UN no state has more than one vote; but responsibility and power are crudely equated. States not permanent members of the Council acquire a full vote only when they sit as one of the non-permanent six; otherwise they may obtain some representation of their interest through minor powers who are members. On the other hand, the veto provisions give the Great Powers ample protection against being saddled with duties by those who will have no effective responsibility.

Another way of putting the matter is to say that the Powers recognized that the hope of world peace lay in the willing cooperation of the Big Five. In making no provision for UN sanction against one of these powers, the drafters were only being realistic. The inability of the United Nations to take effective action now to end the "cold war" springs directly from the fact that the Great Powers are not united and that the two greatest of them are sharply at odds with each other.

WEAKNESSES OF THE CONCEPT OF "COLLECTIVE SECURITY"

One further point along the same line. We hear less of "collective security" than once we did. Before the Second World War it was widely believed that the general interest in maintaining peace was so great that all nations could be counted upon, operating through the machinery of the League of Nations, to support joint action against an aggressor. Among various factors that today make such an assumption unrealistic, two call for special mention.

One is the importance, today, of political and social revolution. When many regimes are committed to a policy of subversion of other regimes, the line between domestic questions and matters of proper international concern is far more difficult to define than once it was. Under these circumstances one of the prerequisites for a working system of collective security —that the potential sanctioning states have the same view of the circumstances under which they should agree to put sanctions into effect—is almost sure to be lacking. Secondly, the power of the strongest states today is so great that the application of sanctions to either of them is completely unrealistic.[14] This situation was sharply underlined at the time of the Hungarian uprising. In other words, at the very point where the threat of total war is greatest, the system breaks down.

In spite of this situation, the United Nations did succeed in sanctioning military action to check aggression in Korea. This action was taken within the framework of the Charter when the Soviet Union temporarily vacated her seat prior to the outbreak of hostilities. Now, should the Security Council fail to act in a similar situation, the Assembly may do so, acting under Article 51. Although this clumsy strategem has been used four times, whether it could again be made to work quickly enough to be effective is an open question.

Auxiliary Agencies

With reference to the United Nations, as with the League, we have concentrated our attention upon its machinery for maintaining peace. Both the League and the United Nations had an international "bureaucracy," a Secretariat, and various ancillary specialized agencies. The International Court of Justice is associated with the United Nations. There is also a Trusteeship Council, intended to exercise a limited guardianship over "non-self-governing territories" placed under United Nations trusteeship by colonial powers. Loosely grouped together under the Economic and Social Council (ECOSOC) are the familiar agencies responsible for health, trade, labor, child welfare, and the like. ECOSOC is a representative body, elected by the General Assembly, and dedicated to finding ways and means for the economic and social development of the members of the United Nations. The Council holds conferences, makes studies, recommends action to the General Assembly, and seeks to coordinate the work of the numerous specialized agencies. Under Article 71 of the Charter, the United Nations has made provisions for consultation between these functional organs and non-governmental organizations that have related interests or competences. Thus an interest group constituency for the United Nations' functional administrative programs is in existence, but it is much more fragmentary and much feebler than its counterpart that supports the European agencies for promoting integration.

The suggestion of structural similarities between European and United Nations specialized agencies, however, should not obscure the basic difference between the European movement and the United Nations. The objective of the United Nations is primarily peace; the European movement is directed toward common government. The only significant delegated powers exercised by the United Nations are those that relate to the peaceful settlement of

---

[14] For fuller analysis of the flaws in the logic of collective security, see Hans J. Morgenthau, *Politics Among Nations*, 3rd ed. (New York: Knopf, 1959), Ch. 24.

The UN "presence" in the Congo

Wide World Photos

disputes. On social or economic programs, common undertakings require adherence by separate action of the member states to make them effective. Even the United Nations organs that are directly concerned with the problem of peace are important only as make-weights in the bipolar world conflict or as neutral instrumentalities to be used at propitious junctures. In Western Europe the social and economic community of interest has so far proven stronger than any concrete differences. But within the United Nations, differences of belief, condition, and interest are the most basic sources of conflict, while the desire for peace is the one powerful bond of unity. "To lie low and practice quietism" has been the course of the United Nations specialized agencies. Unfortunately, that practice is wise; for significantly greater powers in their keeping would only sow discord in our divided world.

THE WAY AHEAD

A world state, in our time, is not a sensible aim. We face the discouraging fact that the world as a whole is about as united at present as it is prepared to be. In fact, at the times these lines are being written (February, 1963), regionalism has gained ascendancy over universalism. The two great power blocs have each developed sharp internal divisions. And the struggle over Britain's bid to join the European Economic Community has produced great uncertainty about the future shape of Western alignments.

In the long run, a shift from a bipolar world to one following regional lines might be an improvement. With just two blocs sharply opposed, a common government resting upon an elective political base would be equally as unstable and even more unpredictable than present world politics. What, furthermore, would be the political process through which such a world state could be made responsive and accountable to its constituency? Government growing from a community of divided sentiment and fragmented interests is likely to be either impotent or tyrannical. Possibly world government could begin as a federal association resting on member states that delegated powers to a central authority. A formula for weighting representation might be devised to ensure that power and responsibility, rights and duties, were commensurate. Yet if nations balk at the first hesitating steps in such a direction, it is madness to suppose that they will eagerly make a leap in the dark. Nor is it certain that a common government of the world, established under present conditions, would be a gain. Law and government that do not square with the real conflicts of interest and desire among nations can only fail. The bloodiest and most cruel wars of history have usually been civil wars, fought against common governments or ruling elites. The differences in condition and sentiment prevailing today among the people of the earth are much greater than those same differences within France on the eve of the Revolution or in Russia in 1917. Without for a moment suggesting that human needs would not best be served by an ideal world order, wisdom still bids us seek what we can achieve now.

Nothing of importance can be won for the internationalist cause without a lessening in the ferocity of cold war conflict. At present all gestures are suspect, all agencies of world cooperation are battlefields. Even worthy purposes of bettering the state of impoverished nations are poisoned by the urgency to create allies rather than friends. The race for superiority in armaments and for preponderance of power is so intensive that it leaves no room for maneuver or experimentation. Each coalition looks to its own devices when survival is at stake. Witness Cuba. Whether disarmament must precede political settlement or political settlement disarmament is a dispute we cannot settle. What seems important now is that hope of settlement through negotiation not die, that some progress be made. Patently, the technique must be diplomacy, for a major international settlement is a constituent act, not the work of subordinates or intermediaries for sovereign powers. Once basic bargains are struck, but only then, the United Nations and other international agencies can and should be given a role in ensuring that the bargains are kept, for example, by inspection and adjudication. Operating within a settled framework of agreement, these instruments of common government can augment their authority, but not otherwise. A day may come when we shall see a United Nations police force capable of keeping the peace on a world wide scale. But that step must be taken in order. First things come first. It is possible that a precarious first step has been made in the Congo.

A New Balance of Power?

As at least an interim device, we should give some consideration to the role of balance of power politics under present circumstances. At an earlier point in this chapter, we pointed out various developments that seemed to make the old balance of power system unworkable today. Particularly this conclusion seemed to be justified with respect to the idea of having one power play the role of "balancer", swinging its weight, as occasion demanded, from one coalition to the other. Let us examine the whole situation once more.

Three of the developments unfavorable to balance of power politics seemed to be consequences of democracy: the modern era of "open covenants, openly arrived at," the necessity for governments to secure popular approval for important steps in their international relations, and the commitment of popular electorates to broad and sometimes simplistic beliefs in certain moral principles that are difficult to accommodate to a policy of compromise and shifting alignments. But democracies may be learning to conduct their foreign policies in the manner required by the H-bomb world without giving up their principles. Secret treaties are "out." Complete publicity of negotiations, however, is neither required by democratic theory nor has it ever been practiced. Moreover, the relations between the great Powers of today tends to be conducted by a diplomacy at once more crude and more subtle than that which we associate with the morning coats and striped pants of yesteryear. In these days when the insistent banging of a shoe on a desk has become a symbol for the language of at least some diplomats, noisy language may be used to drown out the silent whispers of implicit agreements. When, some months ago, tension at "the Wall" between West and East Berlin reached the point where American and Russian tank crews were staring at each other's gun muzzles, at short range, one side— ours, that time—withdrew. Within a few hours the other side did likewise. Escalation went into reverse. Probably no agreement was made. But it was clearly understood that a bargain was being proposed and that, if the Russian tanks had not followed suit, the matter would not have been allowed to end there. On a larger scale, the nice balances that entered into the dialogue—still not published—between President Kennedy and Prime Minister Khrushchev over Cuba in late October, 1962 doubtless carried with them overtones of implied agreements.

With respect to the necessity for gaining popular approval for major acts of state, we have already noted—as a problem of democracy—that in matters of highest security in a world in which a nation might be crushed in a matter of an hour or two—popular controls are inevitably weak. While treaty-based alliances are not readily switched—not even by the Communist bloc—the solidarity, and therefore the strength, of a power-bloc (whether Eastern or Western) frequently increases or decreases with great speed and without a popular mandate.

As to the flexibility-inhibiting effect of moral principle in a democracy, again some modification may be observed. Democracies have not become less moral, but they may have become less moralistic. That is to say, they may be less inclined to maintain certain moral principles intransigeantly in the face of other morally relevant considerations. In particular, the obvious importance today, from the moral as well as other points of view, of avoiding nuclear warfare is such that many other moral considerations must be subordinated to this one. While it cannot be said that public opinion in democracies, and in the United States in particular, has fully accepted the corollaries of this fact, the authors believe it is moving in that direction.[15]

Finally, we pointed out that the kind of flexibility of policy and alignments that is demanded by a balance-of-power system is incompatible with an international system in which two great superpowers dominate all the rest, and especially so when the lesser powers are divided by the same ideological split that characterizes the split between the superpowers. We have already referred to developments that are qualifying this picture: the two great power blocs each look much less monolithic than they did a short while back. And the Russians at least are trying to play down the ideological rift, by emphasizing the doctrine of "co-existence." Moreover, the uncommitted nations of the world have become more numerous and some of them at least seem to be becoming increasingly secure in their ability to stand in the middle or to lean this direction or that depending upon what their national interest seems to demand. A continuation of this process—especially if more powers secure nuclear capability—might possibly provide the conditions for a balance of power system to operate. At best, the security that can be obtained by such a system is precarious; but, living as we do in a far from ideal world, even such possibilities are not to be overlooked, especially not for the short and intermediate terms.[16]

Short of an effective balance of power situation of the kind we have

[15] Hard evidence on this kind of question is difficult to obtain. Most issues of foreign policy are so complicated that it is impossible to infer from a person's policy-stand what his governing principles are. Take the question of recognition of Communist China. Many people feel that a realistic foreign policy for the United States would include recognition of Communist China; and persons who hold this view often impute to their opponents an unrealistic, "moralistic" position, based on the proposition that we should not in this way dignify a regime that has so flagrantly violated principles of both law and morality. But the opponents of recognition may be reasoning in quite different fashion. They may believe that for us to recognize this Communist regime would dishearten many of our friends and allies in the areas surrounding China and that the ultimate effect would be both to defeat our own security interests and to subject more millions to Communist mistreatment.

[16] On the characteristics of balance of power systems and of loose and tight bipolar systems, see Morton A. Kaplan, "Balance of Power, Bipolarity and Other Models of International Systems," *American Political Science Review*, 51 (1957), pp. 684-695. The analysis of the multi-bloc model is carried further by Roger D. Masters, "A Multi-Bloc Model of the International System," *American Political Science Review*, 55 (1961), pp. 780-798.

been discussing, it is possible that total war may be at least indefinitely postponed by the existing nuclear stalemate. In the past the idea that the fear of war itself would be enough to prevent nations from resorting to war has always proved fallacious. Dangerous though the assumption is, this time it *may* be different. The diabolical logic of an anarchic society may be checked by the appalling prospect of nuclear warfare. That is to say, it may be checked short of total war. And limited warfare, once thought a thing of the past, may still take place from time to time.[17] The Korean episode serves as an example of what may happen. Had either side pressed ahead for complete victory, total war would almost certainly have occurred. Neither was prepared to do so. Perhaps we had here an example of one of these tacit understandings referred to above. Incomplete though any understanding in this case must have been, it may have been enough to prevent catastrophe. Again the case of Cuba suggests itself as an obvious example where the prospect of nuclear war was enough to halt a course of events moving rapidly in that direction. We are far from saying that we can rely on the fear of nuclear war to prevent it. We are saying that it is at least possible that this factor and the possibility of a new balance of power system, precarious though it may be, may keep the world from self destruction, if not from all warfare, long enough for the sociological foundations for a firmer world order to develop.

Possible Next Steps

It should be noted, too, that if by processes like those we have been examining, the exigencies of the present power struggle were reduced, two further steps would be practicable. Regional blocs, which now often undermine the authority of the United Nations and work at cross-purposes to it, could be more closely integrated with programs and goals acceptable to the United Nations as a whole. Also, technical programs of cooperation and aid could, with profit to the whole world, be increasingly channelled through the United Nations or associated with it. The difficulties along these paths are legion. Many regional blocs are, plainly and frankly, the instruments of power politics or great-nation imperialism. Those who profit by such arrangements would not welcome a change. Nations do not generally give of their resources without retaining some controls over their disposition. In selection of personnel the United Nations is often hampered by the practical necessity of observing national quotas. All of these obstacles are important; but they do not prevent a beginning being made. Motion in this direction would tend to "de-politicize" to some extent both regional security

---

[17] On the possibilities for two or more parties who passionately desire something (like the avoidance of destruction) concerting their actions, *without consultation,* so as to achieve their goal, see Thomas C. Shelling, *The Strategy of Conflict* (Cambridge, Mass.: Harvard U. P., 1960), Ch. 2.

pacts and international aid and development. It would also nourish world community.[18]

Yet it would be foolish not to realize the extent to which the contemporary interbloc conflict is also mirrored within many countries by the threat of civil war. Economic development does not necessarily diminish class conflict in the short run. But it does so over time; and economic development will certainly take place, whether through the sponsorship of the United Nations, a Western bloc, or "neutralist" (and nationalist) dictatorship, or Communist dictatorship. The point that aid to underdeveloped countries is necessary to world peace is obvious. What is less obvious is the equally important point that only a more even social and economic condition of the nations of the earth can make the goal of greater political unity tolerable. Common government has to be approached by making the lines of jurisdiction that separate nation and nation less important, by blurring them through free markets, unhindered mobility of populations, and rights and interests that transcend national borders. Internationalism of this stamp is hard to swallow even in Western Europe where standards of living and cultural attitudes are relatively similar. Where the social and economic status of two populations differs markedly, the difficulties become enormous: witness American grumblings over the influx of an insignificant number of Puerto Ricans, while Jamaicans are producing a similar reaction in Britain. Against the culturally and economically underprivileged alien, the established and prosperous society will always act to assure jobs to its accepted members and to preserve the "integrity" of its schools, its housing, and its local communities. If we can ever hope to see boundaries erased or rendered insignificant in comparison with the world community of sentiment and interest, we can do so only upon the antecedent condition of a world in which material prosperity and social equality have been vastly expanded.

As we have indicated the world is no longer "bipolar" in any final sense. Not only have the uncommitted areas become so extensive that their weight can not be neglected, but a substantial rift within the Eastern power bloc has been publicly disclosed. With the Soviet Union's aid to India in the face of Chinese attack, this split has transcended the ideological realm. And now President de Gaulle's insistence upon independent control of his own nuclear force, and similar actions, casts doubt upon the unity of the West. How much this new turn of events results from the weakening of Communist unity one cannot say, but it certainly adds support to the argument that lasting international unity is difficult to maintain in the absence of a threat from without.

---

[18] For a discussion of the dynamics of "super-systems," see Amitai Etzioni, "The Dialectics of Supranational Unification," *American Political Science Review,* **66** (1962), pp. 927-935.

In the Longer Run

What the distant future may hold we shall not attempt to say. Our argument is that several great preparatory steps must be taken before a world development similar to that in Western Europe becomes even conceivable, let alone practicable or likely. All of the countries of Western Europe substantially conform to a pattern of social pluralism, economic abundance, and constitutional democracy. The state of the world as a whole is more like that of Europe late in the Dark Ages than the progressive, urban, enlightened Europe of today. Sun Yat-sen, one of Asia's greatest modern leaders, once commented that China—his native land—had to create both democracy and common government starting from chaos and anarchy. The task of achieving world government is somewhat analogous: to establish first that bare minimum of security and equality that will permit common government to exist and grow. When, and if, these minimal conditions are met a more direct strategy of creating vigorous and expansive agencies of supranational government will make sense. Until then it behooves people and nations to realize that their common security and prosperity can only be won by "a slow boring of hard boards," to appropriate the metaphor by which Max Weber once described the work of statesmen.

Do men wish to be brothers? We must ask that question and understand when we ask it what we mean. Universal government does not imply necessarily a code of saintly charity. Nor, on the other hand, is mankind plagued chiefly by the vicious choice of evil over good. As Reinhold Niebuhr has observed, our fatal tendency is to choose a lesser good over a greater one, and particularly to persuade ourselves that family, group, neighborhood, or country are the sufficient object of our loyalties and endeavors. One man will devote himself to his native state, another to the oppressed working class, still another to his profession or his corporation. No one resists the lowering of trade barriers or the immigration of impoverished foreigners on the grounds that he is entitled to privilege and others are not. Tariffs and immigration quotas are defended in the name of the working class or of the cultural community of the nation. No one says that United States Steel or the Tenth Regiment are holy and other organizations are reprobate. They say that morale and a "tight ship" are fine things whatever others may do. No one denies that the Negro has a right to education, or to good housing, or to recreation. People only wish to protect their children or their community. We have only to look now at the American trade union movement or at the segregation controversy to understand how subtle and insidious is the lure of collective identity. Certainly, many collective identities could and must find their place in a world order. Yet the history of political morality could be written largely as an account of the transcending of group egoisms. The consolidation of national states probably never had to contend with corporate sentiments so powerful as the nationalisms and group loyalties that are the great stumbling blocks to internationalism today. Nevertheless, much progress has been made from the time of the earliest tribal states and the most primitive legal systems, although drastic setbacks have also been experienced. Progress towards greater unity is being made in various areas today. We find neither grounds for dark despair nor for simple optimism.

Before closing, however, we must advert to a possibility as yet unmentioned. We have been assuming that if a worldwide political organization were ever to be attained it would be accomplished by essentially democratic processes. It is conceivable that conquest rather than consent may yet pave the way to unity, whether the conqueror be a representative of the Communist movement or of some political movement not yet brought into being. In the past, wars and conquests have been powerful instruments of political unification. To the authors, however, it seems unlikely that such means would ever achieve a lasting political unity of the world. We are witnessing today the dismemberment of great empires built up by force, in the face of powerful demands for self-determination. True, the Soviet Union, still holds firm control over many peoples added to their domain by force or threats of force. These successes of strong-arm methods, however, are confined to groups that are weak compared to the Russian nation. And such unity as exists between the two greatest of Communist powers, Russia and China, seems to be precariously based upon their antagonistic rivalry with the West. Although force alone cannot create unity, it may destroy the obstacles to it. Today, however, such an alternative would almost surely involve nuclear warfare on a grand scale. Serious as are the obstacles to universal political order based on consent, the obstacles to a permanent arrangement on any other basis seem even greater.

(For "Selected Readings," see Chapter 20, pp. 657-659.)

Epilogue

IIIIIIIIIIIIIIIIIIIIIIIIIIIIIIIIIIIIIIIIIIIIIIIIIIIIIIIIIIIIIIIIIIIIIIIIIIIIIIIIII/II;

The purpose of an introduction is to start a conversation or a dialogue. The good hostess tells each of her guests, if they have not met before, enough about the others to stimulate their interest and to provide a basis for fruitful interchange, and then moves on, leaving the newly introduced guests to carry on for themselves It is much the same with introducing a person to a subject. If this volume has not raised more questions than it answers, and stimulated a desire to seek those answers, it has failed of two of its major purposes. The authors also hope the reader will have gleaned enough information about the major aspects of Political Science to ask himself and others questions that are intelligent and informed.

It will be apparent to anyone who has read through this volume that those who dispute about whether Political Science is a "behavioral science" or a "humanistic study" miss the point. Such sharp separations and artificial dichotomies are not only wrong, they are harmful. We find out what we need to know partly by inquiring into what we desire and by attempting to get our purposes straight. We discover what it is reasonable to do by looking also to institutions, to law, to administration, and the tools of public policy. Yet how these institutions will themselves "behave" is a matter of their history, of their setting, and also of general laws of human behavior. Recent trends are toward more understanding of how various aspects of the field are related to each other, and toward collaboration among the practitioners.

One of our major concerns has been to demonstrate the unity of Political Science. It is often said to be an eclectic subject; and to a certain extent it is. But the problems of politics, the problems of governing a society, have their own special character. One needs to rely on history, on economic and psychological analysis, on sociology, on organizational theory, and so on, to achieve a full understanding of these problems. As politics is the meeting place of many forces and government the means for fulfilling many needs, so Political Science is the point of convergence of numerous disciplines—as, for example, is medicine. But this focal point of problems not only occupies a critical place in society; it also has its own unity. The same kinds of forces and values must be balanced and weighed whether we are dealing with local government, national government, or the international order; whether the institutions used for the purpose are democratic or autocratic. And, while the institutions relied upon may vary widely as between democratic and autocratic extremes, the demands placed upon them will be similar; the problems whose solutions they must facilitate will combine the same elements, though the proportions of the mixture may vary considerably, and the outputs may be as different from each other as Boston Common and a concentration camp.